About Island Press

Since 1984, the nonprofit organization Island Press has been stimulating, shaping, and communicating ideas that are essential for solving environmental problems worldwide. With more than 800 titles in print and some 40 new releases each year, we are the nation's leading publisher on environmental issues. We identify innovative thinkers and emerging trends in the environmental field. We work with world-renowned experts and authors to develop cross-disciplinary solutions to environmental challenges.

Island Press designs and executes educational campaigns in conjunction with our authors to communicate their critical messages in print, in person, and online using the latest technologies, innovative programs, and the media. Our goal is to reach targeted audiences—scientists, policymakers, environmental advocates, urban planners, the media, and concerned citizens—with information that can be used to create the framework for long-term ecological health and human well-being.

Island Press gratefully acknowledges major support of our work by The Agua Fund, The Andrew W. Mellon Foundation, Betsy & Jesse Fink Foundation, The Bobolink Foundation, The Curtis and Edith Munson Foundation, Forrest C. and Frances H. Lattner Foundation, G.O. Forward Fund of the Saint Paul Foundation, Gordon and Betty Moore Foundation, The Kresge Foundation, The Margaret A. Cargill Foundation, New Mexico Water Initiative, a project of Hanuman Foundation, The Overbrook Foundation, The S.D. Bechtel, Jr. Foundation, The Summit Charitable Foundation, Inc., V. Kann Rasmussen Foundation, The Wallace Alexander Gerbode Foundation, and other generous supporters.

The opinions expressed in this book are those of the author(s) and do not necessarily reflect the views of our supporters.

Site Design for Multifamily Housing

Site Design for Multifamily Housing

Creating Livable, Connected Neighborhoods

By Nico Larco, Kristin Kelsey, and Amanda West

Washington | Covelo | London

Library of Congress Control Number: 2013956121

♲ Printed on recycled, acid-free paper

Manufactured in the United States of America
10 9 8 7 6 5 4 3 2 1

KEYWORDS: bicycle and pedestrian access, bicycle facilities, building massing and orientation, edges, mixed-use development, multifamily site design, open space and landscape design, parking, pedestrian network, street design, street network, suburban commercial development, suburban retrofits

OTREC
OREGON TRANSPORTATION RESEARCH
AND EDUCATION CONSORTIUM

Funding Support Provided By:
Oregon Transportation Research & Education Consortium

Sustainable Cities Initiative
University of Oregon

Acknowledgements

Sustainable Cities Initiative
University of Oregon

We would like to thank the Oregon Transportation Research and Education Consortium (OTREC) for funding the research that led to the development of this book. We would also like to thank the students and staff of the Community Planning Workshop (CPW) that contributed to much of this earlier research. This includes Robert Parker (CPW Director), Bethany Steiner (CPW Associate Director), Barry Gordon, Kevin Belanger, Emma Pachuta, and Becky Rottenstein. We also want to thank the architecture students that helped with the communication and presentation of this material including Joe Holm, Will Krzymowski, and Rebecca Mann.

We are very thankful for the reviews and comments on earlier versions of this book that we received from Doug Bencks, Howard Davis, Ann Delaney, Rebeca Guerra, Susan Handy, Rachel Ferdaszewski, Roger Hawk, Scot Hein, Kent Jennings, Allen Lowe, Shelia Lyons, Lauren McGuire, Steve Oulman, Steve Pesci, John Rowell, Marc Schlossberg, Patricia Thomas, Anne Vernez-Moudon, and Greg Winterowd. We also received extremely helpful comments from a number of individuals who reviewed this manuscript for Island Press. All of this feedback and guidance was tremendously helpful and cannot be overstated. That said, any shortcomings of this book lay firmly on our own shoulders.

This work was part of a research project conducted through the Sustainable Cities Initiative (SCI) at the University of Oregon. We are thankful to the faculty and staff of SCI that help make that organization a leader on issues of sustainability and livability.

Finally, we would like to thank the staff and editors at Island Press, especially Heather Boyer and Courtney Lix whose diligent attention and guidance helped shepherd this project to its completion.

Contents

Acknowledgements   **vii**

Introduction   **1**

Site Design Criteria   **11**

    1. Pedestrian Network   14
    2. Street Network   18
    3. Access Points   22
    4. Edges   26
    5. Parking   30
    6. Street Design   34
    7. Building Massing & Orientation   38
    8. Open Space & Landscape Design   42
    9. Bicycles   46
    10. Relationships   50

Project Profiles   **57**

    Heron Meadows - Eugene, Oregon   58
    Cherry Orchard - Sunnyvale, California   62
    Colonial Grand - Huntersville, North Carolina   66
    Sheldon Village - Eugene, Oregon   70

Project Retrofits   **77**

    Riviera Village - Eugene, Oregon   78
    Villas at Union Hills - Phoenix, Arizona   82

Project Checklist   **87**

Code Guide   **91**

Code Guide Appendix   **119**

    Arlington, Virginia   120
    San Jose, California   128
    Eugene, Oregon   135
    Huntersville, North Carolina   148
    Asheville, North Carolina   152

Image Credits   **157**

Introduction

Connectivity and Livability

Suburban Multifamily Housing

The Latent Potential for Livability in Suburban Multifamily Housing

The Book's Purpose

How to Use This Book

Further Reading

Increasing the livability and vitality of cities and suburbs is within reach and the design and development of urban and suburban multifamily housing is a key component of achieving this goal.

This book provides guidance for planners, developers, designers, and citizens to create more livable, connected, and vibrant multifamily developments and neighborhoods. Livability is a measure of a community's quality of life and includes factors such as access to education, employment, entertainment, and recreation. The last few decades have seen a groundswell of interest in livability and how our built environment can hamper or promote it. Dense and compact development, the design of transportation systems, the design and distribution of open space, and the mixing of uses all contribute to an area's livability.

The typical disconnected and isolated models of development seen throughout the country have been linked to reduced quality of life, health, and social connections. Yet because of codes and the culture—and at times, simply habits—of planning, development, and design professionals, this form of development persists. This book is focused on shedding light on these codes, cultures, and habits and on describing the aspects of multifamily site design that contribute to livability.

A key concern of the current livability movement has been to increase accessibility, safety, and social interaction by reducing the dominance of the automobile— and design is central to this concern. Single-use, low-density, segregated, and disconnected environments that are uninviting or hostile to pedestrians and cyclists strongly favor auto use. The design of these environments typically lacks basic pedestrian amenities such as sidewalks, allows parking to dominate the landscape, provides no direct route to destinations, and frequently leaves pedestrians and cyclists exposed to fast-moving and dangerous traffic.

When faced with these environments, residents make rational choices and elect to travel by car, even when their destination is within walking or biking distance. Changing the design of these areas in a way that balances the needs of pedestrians, cyclists, and transit riders with the needs of motorists is a key step in increasing livability.

Multifamily housing features prominently in livability discussions, as increased density is an important component of compact and walkable development. This is compounded by the fact that multifamily housing is typically located near destinations such as shops, services, and parks. This condition makes multifamily development an ideal candidate for the livability concept of the "twenty-minute neighborhood"—the idea that many of our daily needs should be located within a twenty-minute walk from our homes.

By focusing on local daily trips and not on work commutes, the twenty-minute neighborhood increases the quality of life for residents by making it easier for them to access the activities, goods, and services they regularly desire. Year after year, surveys have shown increasing interest in living in areas that are well connected to shops, services, and schools. While for some people this is merely a preference, for others it is a life-changing characteristic of their neighborhoods as greater accessibility increases independence for the elderly, the young, and the economically disadvantaged.

Focusing on the livability of multifamily housing can truly move the dial on livability. There are currently more than 20 million units of multifamily housing in this country and they are nearly evenly split between urban and suburban locations. Nationally, it is one of the fastest growing housing types and more than half of the new multifamily developments in the next twenty years will be in infill and redevelopment areas. Increasing the livability of these developments and taking advantage of their location near a mix of uses is an important first step in affecting the livability of the country as a whole.

Connectivity and Livability

A key aspect of livability is the accessibility of nearby destinations. An important means of increasing accessibility is increasing connectivity. Connectivity refers to the amount, directness, and type of routes within an area. The connectivity of an area affects the distance people must travel to desired destinations with higher connectivity correlating to less difference between the 'as-the-crow-flies' distance and the actual walking distance between two points.

This is especially significant in suburbia as street patterns are often a fragmented mix of cul-de-sacs as well as curved, looped, and dead end streets. This causes direct paths to destinations to be virtually impossible and instead forces long, convoluted routes. These longer routes discourage walking and biking and reduce the connectivity of an area.

In multifamily housing developments—especially large-lot developments—internal site routes connect residents to the buildings and amenities in their development while access points and external routes connect them to nearby areas such as commercial destinations, parks, and neighboring residential development. The number, length, distribution, and interconnectedness of these routes affect the overall connectivity of an area. This connectivity, along with the aesthetics and design of the path itself, can affect the ease of walking and biking and ultimately the decision residents make to walk, bike, or drive for short trips.

In well-connected areas, distances are shorter and physical barriers to walking and biking are removed, reducing residents' reliance on automobiles and increasing 'active modes' of travel such as walking and biking. This can reduce vehicle miles traveled, which has positive impacts on health, congestion, air quality, and greenhouse gas emissions.

The relationship between connectivity and site design plays out differently in urban and suburban locations. In dense, urban areas, the site design of multifamily housing projects—often smaller than two acres—is more constrained and connectivity is easier to achieve. Urban areas often have tight street networks with street-facing buildings built up to the lot line and parking typically located below or behind buildings. Connectivity in these areas is often dictated by the existing street network and not by the internal site design of multifamily projects. In these developments, it is the distribution and location of building and site entrances and the overall design of the façade that contributes mostly to the connectivity and livability of the area.

In suburban multifamily housing and large-lot urban projects (typically larger than two acres), however, site design is critical to the overall connectivity. These developments are often located in areas that have no legible block structure or, if one does exist, the developments often supersede that structure. Due to the size of these developments, they necessitate their own internal vehicular and pedestrian circulation and structure. With this, the connectivity of these areas is not universally or often even primarily carried by the street system. Instead, the organization of buildings, the form of the internal multifamily site circulation, the design of parking areas, and the distribution of site access points play leading roles in defining area connectivity. The site design of these developments is especially critical in defining an area's livability and this is the primary focus of this book.

Suburban Multifamily Housing

Although urban and suburban multifamily housing are related, suburban multifamily housing is sufficiently different to necessitate an introduction of its own. While multifamily housing may have historically been an urban typology, that is far from the truth today. Multifamily housing is a widespread example of dense residential development in suburbia and it holds great potential for increasing livability and promoting smart growth goals. There are currently over nine million units of suburban multifamily housing in the country and it has been one of the fastest growing housing types in the United States since 1970.

Multifamily housing is home to a wide variety of people and represents some of the most demographically diverse areas of suburbia. Many suburban multifamily residents are drawn to the suburbs due to its amenities or proximity to employment. These residents often choose multifamily housing because of the increased ease of changing places of residence, the lower cost, or the decreased maintenance relative to single-family housing.

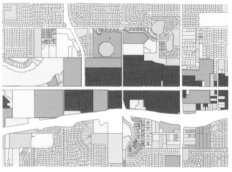

Examples of typical land use patterns with suburban multifamily housing developments (yellow); buffering commercial parcels (red); and single family developments (white) in Annapolis, Maryland (top left); Eugene, Oregon (top right); Phoenix, Arizona (bottom left); and Orlando, Florida (bottom right).

While single-family housing is made up primarily of nuclear families, about two-thirds of households in suburban multifamily housing are what the U.S. Census defines as "non-families." These are individuals living alone or with roommates, divorcees, widows, and unmarried couples. In addition, suburban multifamily housing is significantly more ethnically and racially diverse than suburban single-family housing.

Suburban multifamily housing is built at densities of up to 30 units per acre and is typically located along arterials. Critical to the issue of livability and connectivity, this housing type is often located around commercial development and is often used as a buffer between neighboring commercial and single-family home developments. Because of their design, these developments unfortunately often act as large barriers that impede access of neighboring residents to these areas.

Suburban multifamily housing is different than multifamily housing found in urban areas in that it often occupies large lots, includes multiple buildings within the same site, and typically has its own internal circulation infrastructure. Buildings tend to be two or three stories in height with double-loaded corridors, wood frame construction, exterior vertical circulation, and balconies. Parking is typically exterior to the buildings and often dominates the space around them. Many developments have assigned parking spaces, with one or more spaces per unit.

Examples of typical multifamily housing from Asheville, North Carolina (top left); Salem, Oregon (top right); Phoenix, Arizona (bottom left); and Chelsea, Massachusetts (bottom right).

The Latent Potential for Livability in Suburban Multifamily Housing

Suburban multifamily housing is mid- to high-density and located near commercial development, meaning that there is a significant opportunity for walking and biking as it puts a large population of residents near daily destinations such as grocery stores, drug stores, banks, dry cleaners, restaurants, and cafes. While density and proximity to destinations exists, the primary factor in deciding if a development will capitalize on this potential for walking and biking is in a project's site design.

Recent studies of suburban multifamily development have shown that increasing the connectivity of developments leads to dramatic increases in residents' rates of walking and biking to local commercial destinations. A 2009 study comparing well-connected and less-connected multifamily developments found that the residents of well-connected developments made more than two and a half walking and biking trips per unit per week to their local commercial area.

This equaled nearly half of their total trips to their local commercial area and represented more than a 60 percent increase in walking trips compared to less-connected developments. In addition, almost three quarters of residents of well-connected developments walked or biked to their local commercial area at least once a week. Of these residents, nearly half did most of these trips walking, and more than 20 percent only walked or biked for these trips. For many residents of the well-connected developments, walking or biking was the default mode of travel for local trips—and site design was the critical factor.

Given the number of units in typical suburban multifamily developments, there is potential for a striking number of walking and biking trips occurring in

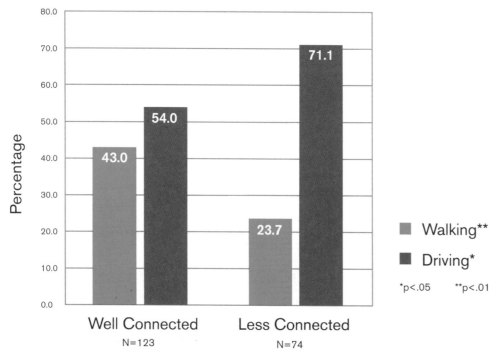

Percent of Trips per Week to Local Commercial Areas

What It Means

The Environment, Health and the American Household

A recent study found that residents of well-connected suburban multifamily developments walked to their local commercial area nearly 60% more than residents of less-connected developments (Larco et al, 2010). This equaled nearly one additional walking trip per week per household with the data suggesting that this walking trip was substituting a driving trip . Changing one vehicle trip into a walking trip for suburban multifamily residents around the country can have a powerful cumulative effect.

If all suburban multifamily units in the country were well-connected and their residents switched only one driving trip per week to walking we could...

Reduce

 1/2 Billion Vehicle Miles Traveled

 22 Million Gallons of Fuel Used

 5.5 Million Pounds of CO$_2$ Emitted

Burn

 21 Billion Calories per Year

Save

 **Households $59.5 Million Yearly**

Larco, N. J. (2010). "Overlooked Density: Re-Thinking Transportation Options in Suburbia." OTREC-RR-10-03, OTREC. Portland, Oregon.

well-connected areas. A single, well-connected multifamily development of 200 units can generate more than 500 walking and biking trips in a single week, drastically reducing dependence on the automobile, increasing residents' independence, and minimizing surrounding traffic and pollution. Multiplying this shift across all of the suburban multifamily developments within a municipality can significantly change the transportation patterns of that city, alleviating congestion in key arterials and intersections and helping attain target automobile travel reductions.

Suburban multifamily housing holds a tremendous latent potential to shift the livability of suburban areas. Many of the changes necessary to do this, both in the retrofits of existing developments and in the typical design approaches in new developments, are not expensive or difficult to layout. Often, the key to implementation is expanding the awareness of planners, developers, and designers to site design and connectivity issues so that more-connected approaches are integral to the design, development, and regulatory process.

This book hopes to be a fundamental step in helping with that implementation.

The Book's Purpose

This book is meant to serve as a desktop reference and guide to planners, developers, and designers involved in multifamily projects. It is part of the larger movement focused on creating more livable, sustainable, and vibrant communities, but it is more narrowly targeted on the multifamily housing typology and on the issue of connectivity.

While larger changes to our built environment may be necessary to fully realize livable communities—especially in suburbia—this book is focused on changes that are doable in the short term, work within existing and accepted development typologies and opportunities, and can be widely applied. This book looks at the incremental changes that can be made within existing development patterns and can have a profound effect on livability.

The book introduces ten key elements of multifamily site design, comparing typical and recommended conditions. Through text, images, and graphics, readers can become familiar with site design elements and learn how these elements affect residents' day-to-day use of multifamily developments and their larger neighborhoods. The book also includes case studies of successful large lot multifamily developments as well as retrofit proposals for existing developments with low internal and external connectivity. A planner checklist, code guide, and code summaries are included to help professionals apply the ideas presented in this book to projects currently in development.

Because of the challenges that exist in large-lot development and the fact that most large-lot multifamily developments are in the suburbs, many of the examples in this book are from suburban multifamily housing projects. While this is case, the principles presented in the book and in the examples shown apply equally well to urban and small lot multifamily developments as well.

How to Use This Book

This book has six components: 10 Site Design Criteria, Project Profiles, Project Retrofits, Project Checklist, Code Guide, and Code Guide Appendix. Each section supports the others and most are organized around the 10 Site Design Criteria framework. At the beginning of each section is a "How-to" page that describes the organization and layout of that section.

Different parts of this book will be helpful to different types of professionals and/or different phases of the design, review, and regulatory process. The 10 Site Design Criteria, Project Profiles, and Project Retrofits give an in-depth understanding of the issues related to suburban multifamily housing site design and are a critical base for professionals as well as interested and involved citizens.

The Project Checklist, Code Guide, and Code Guide Appendix are more technical in nature and are meant to be used by professionals as they are designing or developing multifamily housing projects or the codes that regulate them.

Below is a description of each of the book sections:

Site Design Criteria: The criteria section looks at key issues related to suburban multifamily site design and connectivity and provides descriptions and examples of successful projects. The criteria are organized by scale and complexity, starting at the largest scale first. This section is critical for anyone interested in suburban multifamily site design.

Project Profiles: This section includes suburban multifamily projects from around the country and presents basic background information for each development as well as an analysis of the project's pedestrian networks, access points, parking strategies, and street network design. Each project includes photographs that help illustrate key points.

Project Retrofits: This section shows how existing projects might be modified to incorporate some of the ideas discussed in the Site Design Criteria section.

Project Checklist: The checklist is a reference that can be used during project design and development or permit review. It is meant to be a guide for planners, developers, and designers and can be modified to include local code issues and conditions.

Code Guide: This section looks at codes from five progressive cities across the country that have focused on multifamily housing development. The guide is organized by the 10 Site Design Criteria and includes specific code language from the case study cities.

Code Guide Appendix: While the Code Guide includes edited sections of the codes from the different case study cities, the Code Guide Appendix shows relevant code sections in their entirety. This section, along with the Code Guide, is an excellent reference for planners who are reviewing their current codes.

Further Reading

Cervero, R. and K. Kockelman (1997). "Travel demand and the 3Ds: Density, diversity, and design." Transportation Research Part D-Transport and Environment 2(3): 199-219.

Duany, A., J. Speck, et al. (2010). The smart growth manual. New York, McGraw-Hill.

Dunham-Jones, E. and J. Williamson (2009). Retrofitting Suburbia : Urban Design Solutions for Redesigning Suburbs. Hoboken, N.J., John Wiley & Sons.

Ewing, R., T. Schmid, et al. (2003). "Relationship Between Urban Sprawl and Physical Activity, Obesity, and Morbidity." American Journal of Health Promotion 18(1): 47-57.

Frank, L. D., J. F. Sallis, et al. (2006). "Many Pathways From Land Use to Health - Associations Between Neighborhood Walkability and Active Transportation, Body Mass Index, and Air Quality." Journal of the American Planning Association 72(1): 75-87.

Handy, S. L., M. G. Boarnet, et al. (2002). "How the Built Environment Affects Physical Activity: Views from Urban Planning." American Journal of Preventive Medicine 23(2S): 64-73.

Handy, S., R. G. Paterson, et al. (2003). "Planning for Street Connectivity: Getting from Here to There." Planning Advisory Service Report #515. J. Hecimovisch. Chicago, IL, American Planning Association.

Haughey, R. M. (2005). Higher-Density Development: Myth and Fact. Washington, DC, Urban Land Institute.

Hess, P. M. (2005). "Rediscovering the Logic of Garden Apartments." Places 17(2): 30-35.

Larco, N. (2009). "Untapped Density: Site Design and the Proliferation of Suburban Multifamily Housing." Journal of Urbanism 2(2): 189-208.

Larco, N. (2010). "Suburbia Shifted: Overlooked Trends and Opportunities in Suburban Multifamily Housing." Journal of Architectural and Planning Research 27(1): 69-87.

Larco, N., B. Steiner, et al. (2011). "Pedestrian-Friendly Environments and Active Travel for Residents of Multifamily Housing: The Role of Preferences and Perceptions." Environment and Behavior 44(3): 303-333.

Moudon, A. V. and P. M. Hess (2000). "Suburban Clusters: The Nucleation of Multifamily Housing in Suburban Areas of the Central Puget Sound." Journal of the American Planning Association 66(3): 243-264.

Saelens, B. E. and S. L. Handy (2008). "Built Environment Correlates of Walking: A Review." Medicine and Science in Sports and Exercise 40(7): S550-S566.

Schmitz, A. (2000). Multifamily Housing Development Handbook. Washington DC, ULI-The Urban Land Institute.

Tachieva, G. (2010). Sprawl Repair Manual. Washington, Island Press.

10 points to well-connected
multifamily housing

Site Design Criteria

1. Pedestrian Network
2. Street Network
3. Access Points
4. Edges
5. Parking
6. Street Design
7. Building Massing & Orientation
8. Open Space & Landscape Design
9. Bicycles
10. Relationships

Topic Area   Definition   Topic Headings

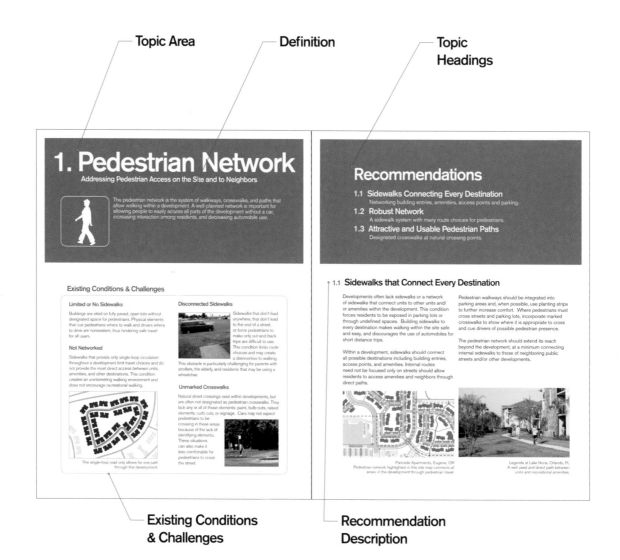

Existing Conditions & Challenges

Recommendation Description

How to Use the Site Design Criteria

Definition — Describes the topic being discussed and its relationship to connectivity

Existing Conditions & Challenges — Gives examples of what currently exists to help orient you to the topic

Recommendations — Describes and gives examples of site design elements needed to increase connectivity and active transportation

Resources — Provides examples of codes that promote connectivity or examples of what others around the country have done in this area

Introduction to Site Design Criteria

This section is divided into 10 different topic areas. Each topic is a part of a collection of characteristics that make up well-connected, livable and vibrant communities. The topics are arranged based on their scale and complexity. The recommendations for each topic area work best as a complete set of design guidelines, but are not mutually exclusive. They can be used together or as individual elements. Each topic area has a direct link to increasing the connectivity in and around a multifamily housing development.

1. Pedestrian Network

Addressing Pedestrian Access on the Site and to Neighbors

The pedestrian network is the system of walkways, crosswalks, and paths that allow walking within a development. A well-planned network is important for allowing people to easily access all parts of the development without a car, increasing interaction among residents, and decreasing automobile use.

Existing Conditions & Challenges

Limited or No Sidewalks

Buildings are sited on fully paved, open lots without designated space for pedestrians. Physical elements that cue pedestrians where to walk and drivers where to drive are nonexistent, thus hindering safe travel for all users.

Not Networked

Sidewalks that provide only single-loop circulation throughout a development limit travel choices and do not provide the most direct access between units, amenities, and other destinations. This condition creates an uninteresting walking environment, longer travel lengths, and does not encourage recreational walking.

This single-loop road only allows for one path through this development.

Disconnected Sidewalks

Sidewalks that don't lead anywhere, that don't lead to the end of a street, or force pedestrians to make only out-and-back trips are difficult to use. This condition limits route choices and may create a disincentive to walking. This obstacle is particularly challenging for parents with strollers, the elderly, and residents that may be using a wheelchair.

Unmarked Crosswalks

Natural street crossings exist within developments, but are often not designated as pedestrian crosswalks. They lack any or all of these elements: paint, bulb-outs, raised elements, curb cuts, or signage. Cars may not expect pedestrians to be crossing in these areas because of the lack of identifying elements. These situations can also make it less comfortable for pedestrians to cross the street.

Recommendations

1.1 Sidewalks Connecting Every Destination
Networking building entries, amenities, access points, and parking.

1.2 Robust Network
A sidewalk system with many route choices for pedestrians.

1.3 Attractive and Usable Pedestrian Paths
Designated crosswalks at natural crossing points.

1.1 Sidewalks Connecting Every Destination

Developments often lack sidewalks or a network of sidewalks that connect units to other units and/or amenities within the development. This condition forces residents to be exposed in parking lots or through undefined spaces. Building sidewalks to every destination makes walking within the site safe and easy, and discourages the use of automobiles for short-distance trips.

Within a development, sidewalks should connect all possible destinations, including building entries, access points, and amenities. Internal routes should not be focused only on streets but should allow residents to access amenities and neighbors through direct paths.

Pedestrian walkways should be integrated into parking areas and, when possible, use planting strips to further increase comfort. Where pedestrians must cross streets and parking lots, incorporate marked crosswalks to show where it is appropriate to cross and cue drivers of possible pedestrian presence.

The pedestrian network should extend its reach beyond the development, at a minimum connecting internal sidewalks to those of neighboring public streets and/or other developments.

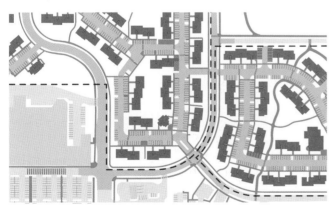

Parkside Apartments, Eugene, OR
Pedestrian network highlighted in this site map connects all areas of the development.

Legends at Lake Nona, Orlando, FL
A well-used and direct path between units and recreational amenities.

1.2 Robust Network

A robust sidewalk network incorporates many route choices to all destinations, not only the path going between cars and units. Creating a robust sidewalk network gives pedestrians options and makes it easier and thus more likely that they will choose to walk to their destinations. The access points, streets, units, and amenities should all be easily accessible on foot. Making this system attractive for walkers can increase activity and social interaction among residents and the community.

Many developments only provide single-loop street and sidewalk circulation. This type of system offers minimal route choices and often increases the distance pedestrians must travel to their destinations.

Legends at Lake Nona, Orlando, FL
The pedestrian network flowing through this site allows access to all areas of the development.

Resources:
Green Buffers

Green buffers are natural dividers between two elements. Commonly, buffers are green strips consisting of grass or other plantings that separate the sidewalk from the street realm. Buffers provide a more comfortable walking environment for pedestrians by adding a perceived distance from traffic. Green buffers also provide for stormwater remediation on site. These areas also provide great places for street trees to grow.

Buffer Recommendations:

1. Plant native vegetation.

2. Opt for low-maintenance vegetation, with paving that is on-grade so that it can be easily mowed.

3. Avoid 90° angles in paving as these are difficult to edge and increase the cost of maintenance.

1.3 Attractive and Usable Pedestrian Paths

Eola Heights, Salem, OR

Areas with unattractive, unusable, disconnected, or nonexistent sidewalks deter residents from walking within the development. Creating attractive and usable pedestrian paths encourages residents to walk and engage with their neighbors both inside and adjoining the development. The goal is to create the 'stroll effect' by making the development a pleasant and easy place to walk.

Paths should be located at appropriate distances from buildings so that pedestrians feel a part of the public realm and building occupants retain privacy. Where possible, utilize planting strips to buffer paths and sidewalks from cars. Pedestrian paths should be wide enough to accommodate at least two people walking side-by-side.

Pedestrian networks should be designed with adequate landscaping that still allows for usable amounts of green space within the site. (See Section 8, Open Space and Landscape Design, for ideas of natural elements to include.) Some paths can cut along green spaces to create shortcuts through the site and enhance and incentivize walking.

Street crossings should be marked by painted crosswalks on internal streets. Also consider including bulb-outs, signage, and textured or raised pavement at these locations. Crossing designations integrated into the pedestrian network show where pedestrians and cars should travel. Visible pedestrian networks have traffic-calming effects and provide an inherent right-of-way to walkers.

43% of trips by residents living in well-connected multifamily housing are walking trips, compared to only 23% of trips made by those living in less-connected developments.

-Larco et al, 2010. "Overlooked Density: Re-Thinking Transportation Options in Suburbia."

2. Street Network
Creating a System of Well-Connected Streets

A street network refers to the organization of streets through a site; where the streets go, what they lead to, how they relate to each other. A street network should provide many travel choices and create a logical organization for the development. The organization of buildings and internal neighborhoods is dependent upon the street network. Internal street networks should be integrated with neighboring street organizations for logical wayfinding and easy connection. The street network allows for car, cyclist, and pedestrian access to amenities and destinations both inside and outside the development.

Existing Conditions & Challenges

Auto-Dominated Environment

Many developments primarily accommodate auto travel without making provisions for non-auto travel. All areas of the development are accessible by car, but not necessarily by foot. Users rely on cars to get places throughout the site safely and quickly, creating an environment that discourages walking and biking.

Parking Lots Instead of Streets

Often, developments are designed with parking lots acting as the primary circulation through the site. Parking encompasses all areas of the site, making it seem as though buildings are located in a sea of parking. This condition makes it difficult for people to orient themselves and feel comfortable walking throughout the development.

Limited Connections to Adjacent Street Systems

Often dictated by local codes, developments have just one or two motor vehicle connections to adjacent street systems. These connections are usually focused on arterials and rarely on neighboring developments. Limiting street connections does not allow for local travel between neighboring developments.

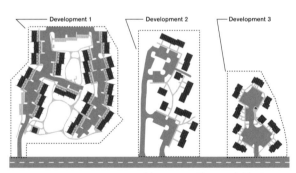

No connections exist between these developments

Inaccessible Streets

Some developments prohibit or discourage the use of the development's internal street network by non-residents. Although this condition provides residents with control over their streets, it creates physical barriers within the city, causing traffic along arterials and long, circuitous routes for both cars and pedestrians.

Recommendations

2.1 Legible System of Streets and Blocks
Using streets to clarify the organization of developments.

2.2 Connection and Continuity to Adjacent Streets and Properties
Multiple and seamless street connections to neighbors.

2.3 Minimize Cul-de-Sacs and Dead-Ends
Use grid patterns to facilitate local travel.

2.4 Local Auto, Pedestrian, and Bike Travel
Encouraging local, non-commuter travel.

2.1 Legible System of Streets and Blocks

Use a legible system of streets and blocks to reduce confusion, increase safety, and create aneighborhood feeling. Poorly defined streets, lack of a street system, and the use of parking lots as primary circulation routes creates a confusing environment for cars and pedestrians. These environments often result in unpredictable travel patterns and decreased comfort, thus discouraging walking and biking.

Create clear, legible streets for cars and pedestrians to travel to units and amenities. A legible system of streets and blocks orients people, shows them how to travel through the site, and can help determine building locations. It should include clear intersections, stops, and pedestrian walkways. Drivers have been shown to adapt to the road they see, thus it is important that the streets clearly demonstrate that they are a residential area. The context of the site should be used to drive the organization of the streets. Doing so allows for connection and continuity with neighboring networks.

In larger developments, it is possible to create a unique network of buildings and streets. Buildings can be grouped into blocks that promote a neighborhood feel and connect to each other

through the street network. Networking buildings and streets can provide natural and useful connections to surrounding housing, commercial areas, or open spaces.

In smaller developments where block systems are more challenging, the existing site conditions and context should be the first consideration. Design the internal street network as a logical extension of the neighboring street network. Utilizing the look and feel of existing motor vehicle and pedestrian connections can help to create a more seamless integration with new circulation systems.

Baldwin Park, Orlando, FL
A well-articulated intersection with a block-like feel.

2.2 Connection and Continuity to Adjacent Streets and Properties

Developments with street networks and connections focused only on arterials miss opportunities to connect with neighboring developments and other local streets. This condition can unnecessarily clog arterials with short-trip vehicle traffic. It can also create barriers to easily accessing neighbors by foot as it increases walking distances, which can force residents to drive when a more-direct connection would have made walking or biking possible. A robust network lets residents get to desired destinations easily and more conveniently.

The street network should make logical connections to adjacent street systems and promote travel through the site. Look to existing street systems, not just arterials, around the development to determine the placement and design of the street network. Use similar design features to create continuity and to cue users that the system is continuous and it is possible to travel there. If adjacent sites are vacant, create street stubs to encourage future connections and the continuation of the network (see Section 3, Access Points).

2.3 Minimize Cul-de-Sacs and Dead-Ends

The use of cul-de-sacs and dead-ends can deter walking or biking because they increase the distance that pedestrians and cyclists have to travel. Avoiding the use of cul-de-sacs provides more route choices for travel and distributes auto traffic rather than allowing it to collect on over-burdened connecting streets. Cul-de-sacs also make it difficult for emergency service providers to navigate quickly and safely.

Create internal street networks that are connected to adjacent street systems, provide travel options, and decrease walking and driving distances. Build shared pathways between the development and neighbors to create more community connection and easier/shorter commutes for residents and neighbors.

If there are instances where cul-de-sacs are desired or existing, strive to make inviting bike and pedestrian-only connections between cul-de-sacs and the street network. These connections will promote walking and biking while still limiting pass-through auto traffic.

Parkside and Crossings, Eugene, OR
These developments' street networks connect to one another, the local streets, and the adjacent commercial area.

2.4 Local Auto, Pedestrian, and Bike Travel

Restricted entries and limited connectivity can make it difficult for residents to access outside amenities located adjacent to the development. Allowing local auto, pedestrian, and bike travel through the site integrates, rather than isolates, the development with its surrounding neighborhoods. Many developments might welcome local auto, pedestrian, and bike trips, but are worried that increased connectivity will increase high speed pass-through traffic. This type of traffic can be limited through the design of the street network. Elements such as curves, on-street parking, raised crosswalks, narrow streets and other traffic calming techniques can discourage cut-through traffic and slow all vehicular traffic.

Using these techniques, while still increasing connectivity, encourages non-commuter, local travel to and through the site. This allows residents and neighbors to feel the development is an extension of the larger neighborhood, not an impassable dead-end.

Bike lanes and sidewalks that connect the development with the larger local system create active and interesting local streets that people will be more inclined to utilize.

Resources:
Street Connectivity

The streets should be part of the city street network. Their continuity should contribute to the overall city goals and standards for connectivity. Street connectivity standards can help achieve this goal.

Street connectivity depends on two key components:
- All streets must connect to adjacent street systems and stub-outs.
- All buildings must face a public street.

All buildings must access a public street by code in Huntersville, NC. (See the Code Appendix for more information regarding this code.) This code enables neighboring developments to be linked directly by a common public realm. It immediately provides a more active street realm for the community.

Map data: Google, DigitalGlobe, Orbis Inc.

Colonial Grand, Huntersville, NC
This aerial photo shows three separate developments, all connected by a public street and to adjacent commercial area to the southeast.

3. Access Points

Creating Connections

Access points connect a development with the areas around it [commercial developments, residential, arterial roads, etc]. Any egress point from the site is considered an access point. They may take the form of a street, sidewalk, or informal pathway. Having an adequate number and distribution of access points is essential to promoting interaction with the outside community and allowing residents to travel to nearby residential or commercial areas on foot or bicycle.

What is an Access Point?

A street

A connected sidewalk

A friendship gate

An informal path

Existing Conditions & Challenges

Limited Number of Access Points

Developments are often designed with only one or two points of entry. Given this limited number, these access points are usually designed with cars as the primary user. Limiting the number of access points forces residents to use longer, indirect routes to go to neighboring residential or commercial developments.

Gated Access

Gated communities control access to the development by blocking free entry and exiting. Often residents can only enter the development in a vehicle. Gated developments create exclusive and inwardly focused communities, limiting interaction with outside neighbors.

Poorly Distributed Access Points

When access points are present they are often poorly distributed around the perimeter of the development. Access points may be located on only one or two sides of the development, preventing travel to adjacent destinations or travel through the site.

No Local or Continuous Travel with Adjacent Developments

Residential and commercial developments and planned open spaces can often be internally focused and have only one point of entry, preventing linking of access points to other multifamily housing. Sidewalks and streets are often disconnected, reducing continuation and consistency, which are needed to create a linked network throughout the community. This condition limits pass through opportunities and increases the distance pedestrians must travel.

Recommendations

3.1 Maximize the Number of Access Points
Create multiple places to enter and exit the development, especially for pedestrians and cyclists.

3.2 Maximize Distribution of Access Points
Evenly distribute access points around the perimeter of the site.

3.3 Provide Stub-Outs for Future Development and Retro-Fits
Create the opportunity for connected neighbors.

3.4 Avoid Gated Communities
Reduce barriers to active forms of transportation.

3.1 Maximize the Number of Access Points

Developments with minimal access points for cars and pedestrians limit route options and often force residents to use longer, indirect routes to access neighboring amenities. Maximizing the number of access points in a development decreases distances from units to amenities, removes physical barriers, and encourages residents to use active transportation for short trips.

Design developments with the maximum possible access points for cars, bicyclists, and pedestrians. Keep in mind that an access point does not need to be a street; it could be a sidewalk, bike path, gravel path, or a simple opening in a perimeter fence. The bike and pedestrian connections do not necessarily need to be part of the street infrastructure. Non-auto connections take up less space, are less expensive to build and maintain than street connections, and are generally more amenable to neighbors.

Remember to create access points to all adjacent amenities, not only to streets and paths. This includes direct connections to commercial areas, parks and open space, and other residential developments.

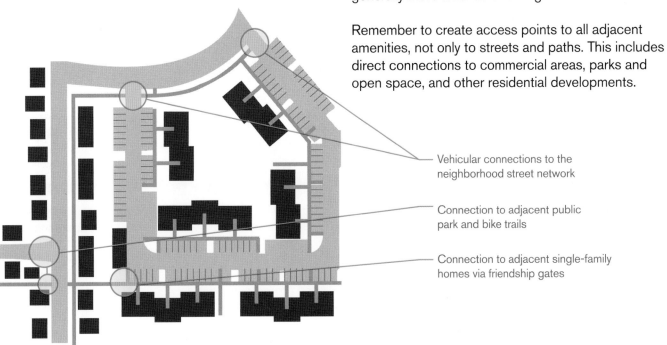

Vehicular connections to the neighborhood street network

Connection to adjacent public park and bike trails

Connection to adjacent single-family homes via friendship gates

3.2 Maximize Distribution of Access Points

An uneven or inappropriate distribution of access points in a development often makes foot or bicycle travel to neighboring amenities difficult or impossible. If a site has numerous access points, these points should be evenly distributed across the site, allowing access in all feasible directions. Residents who wish to walk or bike should not be deterred from doing so by physical barriers around the development. Appropriately distributed access points allow residents to walk or bike through, rather than around, a place, thus shortening the distance and encouraging active transportation.

Where possible, locate one or more access point(s) on each side of the development and to each adjacent use. Provide an adequate distribution of access points so that every resident can easily enter and exit the development near their unit. If the site shape is long and narrow, an access point should be located approximately every 500 feet. In some cases, zoning requirements may include maximum access shadows permitted.

Resources:
How to Calculate the Access Shadow

The Access Shadow represents the largest expanse along the perimeter without entrances. The smaller this angle becomes the greater the distribution of access points throughout the development. This process determines whether access points are concentrated on one side of the development or evenly distributed around the site boundary. It also determines where added access points would be beneficial to site circulation.

To calculate the Access Shadow:

1. Identify the center point of the multifamily housing development

2. Mark each access point within the development

3. Measure the largest angle between egress points (i.e., largest area not served by an access point).

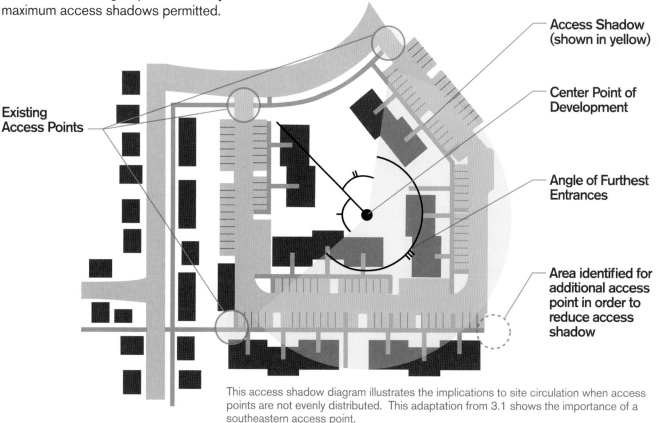

Existing Access Points

Access Shadow (shown in yellow)

Center Point of Development

Angle of Furthest Entrances

Area identified for additional access point in order to reduce access shadow

This access shadow diagram illustrates the implications to site circulation when access points are not evenly distributed. This adaptation from 3.1 shows the importance of a southeastern access point.

3.3 Provide Stub-Outs for Future Development and Retro-Fits

Developments often eliminate the opportunity to create a continuous pedestrian infrastructure by closing themselves off to neighbors with high walls, gates, or other barriers. Due to the nature of suburban developments, adjacent lots can sometimes be vacant. Providing stub-outs to these sites facilitates future connections to adjoining properties and allows those connections to be made more seamlessly. Having a stub-out in place encourages the next development to link to it and also provide additional stub-outs, thus creating a continuous network. Stub-outs can be used for vehicular, pedestrian, or cyclist connections.

Stub-outs can also be used toward existing developments, even if no access points currently exist. Creating stub-outs provides an incentive and location for future, retrofitted connections.

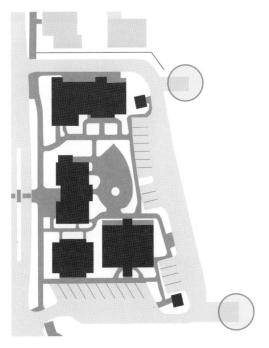

This diagram denotes where stub-outs exist within this development for connection to future neighboring developments.

3.4 Avoid Gated Communities

Gated communities act as barriers between the development and its adjacent community. Generally, they have a connotation of being exclusive and/or unwelcoming and make non-auto travel difficult by limiting access and increasing distances to neighboring amenities. Moreover, they can sever regional bike and pedestrian networks. Avoiding gated communities makes the development more inviting and encourages residents to interact with the larger community.

Where desired, design features can help define neighborhood edges without limiting connectivity. Trees, low fences, or friendship gates create thresholds without becoming barriers. Keeping entries open provides the feeling of access and creates an easier, more acceptable transition from the development to the community. Open entries also encourage active transportation by making it easier to do.

Parkside Crossings, Chelsea, MA
An entrance to the site is not gated and other types of safety features are utilized.

4. Edges

Neighbors, Buffers, Perimeters, and Edge Conditions

Edges refer to the outer boundary of a development and the conditions that comprise it (e.g., shrubs, a wall, entries, exits, etc.). Well-designed edge conditions create pedestrian access to commercial areas and other developments, increase walkability, and create visual continuity between developments. Edges between developments and neighborhoods should be seamless.

Existing Conditions & Challenges

Dividing Walls

Walls, often higher than seven feet, are erected between multifamily developments and single-family residences and/or commercial areas. These walls act as a buffer and are usually meant to block sound and sight. This creates discontinuity within neighborhoods with unattractive blank walls.

Buffered By Major Arterials

Multifamily developments are often located along auto-dominated, typically unattractive arterials. Structures that border the arterials rarely engage the street and are often designed to buffer noise, the speed of cars, and the unattractive corridor.

Buildings and Spaces That Do Not Face Adjacent Streets

Even in development edges along local, low-speed streets, multifamily developments rarely address the street through building entries or open space. This condition closes off developments, forces residents to be internally focused, and creates unsightly edge conditions which detract from the larger neighborhood.

Rough Transitions

As development occurs at different times, rough transitions (e.g., a one-story building next to a three-story building) often exist. Rough transitions decrease the continuity of the urban fabric and discourage single-family homeowners from supporting connections with multifamily housing.

Recommendations

4.1 Decrease Wall Height and Increase Wall Transparency
If walls are necessary they should not block visual connection to neighboring developments.

4.2 Create Visual Appeal and Continuity Between Developments
Use attractive and native design elements.

4.3 Create Developments that Engage Neighboring Streets
Site buildings along edges.

4.4 Create Smooth Transitions Between Developments
Use context to create thoughtful transitions.

4.1 Decrease Wall Height and Increase Wall Transparency

While using walls is sometimes appropriate and desirable (for instance to provide a buffer from a high-speed arterial), they should not be a default element in site design. High, opaque walls don't allow for "eyes on the street," a visually interesting streetscape, or easy access to neighbors and amenities outside the development. Often, using walls creates unusable spaces in and around the development as well as a feeling of isolation.

To minimize these effects and promote continuity and ease of walking or biking, only use walls in areas where separation between developments is absolutely necessary. If walls must be erected, in areas where more connection between developments is possible, limit the height to 3 or 4 feet and make the walls both physically and visually permeable and attractive. This increases visual interaction with neighboring developments and decreases concealed, potentially dangerous spaces. Where possible, remove walls and use landscaping and natural elements to create perceived edges that do not physically separate areas.

Villas and Union Hills, Phoenix, AZ
A more transparent wall facing an arterial with balconies overlooking the street.

Baldwin Park, Orlando, FL
A lowered green wall facing a parking area.

4.2 Create Visual Appeal and Continuity Between Developments

Developments are often closed off with high blank walls on all sides. This condition disrupts the neighborhood fabric and discourages walking and biking by making it less convenient and seemingly unsafe to do so. Creating visual appeal and continuity between developments minimizes the perception of barriers and encourages the use of active transportation. Additionally, developments with edges that look open, friendly, and easy to pass through add value to the community by creating a pleasant environment, and reducing distances that pedestrians and cyclists must travel to neighboring amenities.

Visual appeal of edges can include landscaped spaces that are green, neatly kept, and include local species. To create continuity between developments and seamless edges, look at the neighboring and local environment for design elements. The use of local design elements helps the development blend in with the surroundings and can minimize resistance from single-family neighbors.

Briar Ridge, Corvallis, OR
A planted berm, which provides privacy from the adjacent public street, creates a subtle and attractive transition.

4.3 Create Developments that Engage Neighboring Streets

Developments located along quiet, local neighborhood streets should avoid strictly internal organizations that minimize interaction and connection with the larger community. In internally organized developments, buildings face inward with no street-side entries and essentially turn their back on the outside community. Doing so creates dead spaces around the development, decreases "eyes on the street" and discourages residents from interacting with neighbors outside the development. Developments with buildings that face the street feel less secluded, reduce the number of hidden areas, and encourage residents to engage with the community.

1875 Alder Street, Eugene, OR
The front doors to this development open directly onto the street. The stoops and front gardens provide an attractive green edge to the sidewalk and street realm.

Don't ignore neighboring streets. Instead create a physical relationship between the building and the street. Site buildings along the edges of the development. Buildings should be located close to public streets. Entries or social spaces (porches, patios, stoops, etc.) should face the street (see Section 7, Building Orientation and Massing) and be accessible from the street.

4.4 Create Smooth Transitions Between Developments

Rough transitions and buildings sited too close to neighbors may create a backlash to development and the multifamily housing typology as a whole. Rough transitions destroy continuity in the urban fabric. Additionally, buildings too close to neighbors decrease privacy and light for that neighbor and create a feeling of encroachment. Smooth transitions can mitigate these problems and increase the visual appeal of the larger neighborhood.

Provide thoughtful transitions to neighbors that are not visually or physically encroaching. New buildings should respect adjacent buildings by responding to their massing, scale, need for light, natural ventilation, and views. Responding to these contextual cues and needs will yield a more accepted and visually appealing development. Do not create sight lines directly into buildings in neighboring developments since those will decrease privacy. Use landscaping, low fences or walls, and grade changes to aid the transitions and create privacy.

Resources
Kitsap County, Washington: Alternatives to Blank-Fences and Walls

Kitsap County, Washington, provides alternatives to solid or blank-looking fences. The code suggests that developers "employ different textures, color, or materials (including landscape materials) to break up the wall's surface and add visual interest. If fencing is required, repeat the use of building façade materials on fence columns and/or stringers." The code also requires that developers "place pedestrian breaks and/or crossings at frequent intervals where a fence, wall, or landscaped area separates a sidewalk from a building or one development from another."

– County Code of Kitsap County

Baldwin Park, Orlando, FL
A 3-story multifamily housing building actively engaging a street that primarily has single-family homes lining it.

Sheldon Village, Eugene, OR
The multifamily housing development is adjacent to an assisted-living facility and addresses it in scale and architectural articulation.

5. Parking

Think Outside the Lot

Automobile parking is a necessity in any development, but one that needs to be balanced with other modes of travel. Parking can take many forms including: lots, lanes, courts, on-street, covered, and garage bays. Strategically located and designed parking has the ability to increase safety for walkers and bikers.

Existing Conditions & Challenges

Parking-Dominated Landscape

In many developments, parking encompasses the built landscape and is the primary object in site views. Vast amounts of blacktop and lack of shade create heat islands and an unpleasant atmosphere to look at and travel through. Parking-dominated landscapes with large parking lots create a hostile environment for pedestrians and continue to encourage a 'car-to-unit' mentality within the development.

High Parking Space Ratios

Developments are often required to provide between one to two spaces per unit. With poorly designed parking, these ratios can contribute to parking-dominated landscapes.

Large Parking Lots

Developments are often designed like shopping centers, with one large lot comprised of several rows of parking. Rather than having a street based circulation system, parking becomes the primary travel path throughout the site (see Street Network Code Guide).

No Pedestrian Infrastructure in Parking Areas

The lack of designated and protected places for pedestrians to walk creates a hostile walking environment. Additionally, irregular parking lot patterns are confusing for drivers and can cause accidents.

Recommendations

5.1 Use Alternatives to Parking Lots and Lanes
Utilize parallel on-street parking and courts.

5.2 Integrate Pedestrian Infrastructure into Parking Areas
Provide well-designed and protected sidewalks.

5.3 Create More Beautiful Parking
Increase pedestrian friendliness through landscape design.

5.4 Reduce Parking Ratios and Provide Incentives for Active Transportation
Become a less auto-oriented development.

5.1 Use Alternatives to Parking Lots and Lanes

The dominance of parking areas in developments discourages walking and biking by making it unpleasant and seemingly unsafe to do so. Even with high parking ratios, reducing the dominance of parking can be accomplished in several ways. The primary goal is to eliminate long runs of continuous parking and provide shade and visual interest.

Parking Lots: Parking lots are the least desirable form of parking as they create a large barrier to walking and biking. In developments where parking lots cannot be avoided, incorporate pedestrian-friendly and visually interesting features into them (see Recommendation 5.2).

Parking Lanes (with bulb-outs): Lanes of parking are clearer for the driver and pedestrian, but can seem overwhelming and lengthy if uninterrupted runs are too long. Incorporating bulb-outs into lanes is critical. Bulb-outs extend the sidewalk into the parking area creating more easily accessible parking and making drivers more aware of pedestrian presence. They also provide spaces for trees that can create visual interest and shade.

On-street parking: Parallel or diagonal pull-in parking helps to define the street, creates a barrier between the street and sidewalk, and provides a protected area for drivers to access their cars.

Parking Courts: Parking courts complement parallel on-street parking and allow for the large amount of parking necessary in most developments. A parking court is a group of 12-14 parking spaces per side with a single entrance. Often no more than 2 or 3 courts may be linked together. Parking courts are separated from the street, include bulb-outs, and have pedestrian access on all sides. They do not provide pass-through access and therefore lessen the amount of traffic and the speed of the cars within them.

Parking Typologies

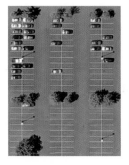

Parking Lot

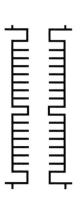

Parking Lane with Bulb-Outs

Recommended Typologies

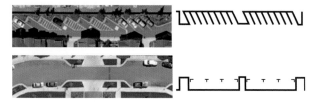

Parallel or Diagonal On-Street Parking

Parking Court

Map data: Google, DigitalGlobe

5.2 Integrate Pedestrian Infrastructure Into Parking Areas

Pedestrians can feel unsafe walking within parking areas. Pedestrians' lack of perceived and actual safety is one of the biggest barriers to walking. To mitigate this, raise the profile of the pedestrian and create an environment where pedestrians can comfortably traverse parking lots and driveways in designated areas.

Provide usable sidewalks to and through all parking areas. Sidewalks should be buffered from traffic by planting strips, parallel parking, and/or curbs. Planting strips provide visual interest, safety, and shade for pedestrians. Parallel parking buffers traffic from pedestrians while helping to meet required ratios. Curbs provide a physical separation between cars and pedestrians and cue drivers of the pedestrian presence. Sidewalks that connect to parking areas should also connect to the larger pedestrian network that allows access to all areas of the site.

Sidewalks and crosswalks in parking areas indicate where pedestrians should be and make drivers aware of them.

Pedestrian amenities should be usable, remove people from vehicle travel lanes, and connect to the larger pedestrian network.

5.3 Create More Beautiful Parking

Unattractive and invasive parking makes walking less pleasurable and desirable. Creating beautiful landscapes that integrate parking promotes an active lifestyle and increases the likelihood of residents using active transportation.

Parallel parking lets the buildings still have a presence on the street while buffering pedestrians and creating opportunities for bulb-outs.

Landscaping in court configurations improves access and makes more attractive parking areas.

Many features can be used to achieve this effect. Trees reduce the heat-island effect by providing shade that reduces temperatures at the surface and, in drier climates, giving off water that evaporates and cools surfaces and the surrounding air.

Planting bulb-outs and strips provide buffers for pedestrians, cue drivers about where to travel, and enhance aesthetics of the parking area. Flowers and lighting fixtures can also be incorporated throughout the parking area to improve the visual appeal and nighttime comfort.

5.4 Reduce Parking Ratios and Provide Incentives for Active Transportation

High parking ratios contribute to parking-dominated landscapes that are unsafe and unpleasant for pedestrians. Residents should feel encouraged that driving, biking, and walking are all safe and appropriate means of travel in their development.

Consider reduced parking ratios or reasonable maximums to reduce the feeling of being completely surrounded by parking. Some developments separate the unit from the car and charge for parking in addition to rent. If charging extra for parking isn't possible, shared parking schemes with neighboring businesses and developments can be used to help reduce parking requirements. Many cities give financial incentives for putting in a bus stop or bike parking to decrease car parking. In addition, car-share companies like ZipCar and WeCar are gaining popularity in many parts of the country.

Legends at Lake Nona, Orlando, FL
Tandem parking reduces paved areas that need to be dedicated to parking while still maintaining a high number of spaces.

6. Street Design
Complete the Streets

Street design refers to the elements that define the street zone. Complete Street design is a practice that is being promoted throughout the world to create streets that enhance efficiency for all users and promote an active and safe street life for people of all ages and abilities. Complete Streets can have benefits that include safety, health, easy access to active forms of transportation and more livable communities around them.

The streets running through multifamily housing developments are typically local neighborhood streets and do not necessarily need to incorporate all of the techniques that define a Complete Street. However, multifamily housing streets should promote a more livable, pleasant and vibrant place and create a more desirable and successful development. Creating amenities that contribute to the street environment can make significant improvements to how residents utilize the street realm.

Complete Streets are designed for everyone, not just speeding cars or creeping traffic. For more information on Complete Streets visit www.completestreets.org/

Existing Conditions & Challenges

Poorly Defined Streets

Designated routes for cars, pedestrians, and cyclists to travel through sites are often poorly defined or nonexistent. Street elements, like curbs and road markings, are often not required in multifamily housing developments. Without these elements, travel patterns can become erratic, and the safety of all users can be compromised.

No Pedestrian and Cyclist Amenities

Streets often lack sidewalks, bike lanes, trees, and other buffers that promote walking and biking by making it safe to do so.

Auto-Dominated Streets

Wide streets without markings encourage cars to travel fast and create the feeling that drivers are not traveling on a real street or do not need to obey driving laws. This condition creates an unsafe environment and discourages pedestrian and cyclist travel.

6.1 Complete Street Design

Complete Streets promote characteristics that create a street 'place' that is useful, safe, and beautiful.

Multifamily housing streets should accommodate all users. As there is a wide range of demographics living in multifamily housing developments, they should all be welcome to enjoy and participate in the street realm. Streets should be well kept, carefully created based on the site conditions, and attractive.

The street is the outdoor room of the development and the first place that people experience as they enter the site. It should be a vibrant street that can be remembered since it represents the feeling and character of the community.

The following places show examples of Complete Street design and elements:

Heron Meadows, Eugene, OR

Sheldon Village, Eugene, OR

Baldwin Park, Orlando, FL

Colonial Grand, Huntersville, NC

7. Building Massing & Orientation
Facilitate Community Through Design and Siting

Building massing and orientation refers to the shape, size, volume, and placement of buildings on a site. As buildings are the primary destination in multifamily housing developments their massing and orientation are integral in creating a sense of community. How people are able to navigate through the built environment and the landscape plays a major role in how residents engage the community. Building siting and the placement of openings can determine whether residents proceed directly from their car to their unit or if they choose to enjoy and engage the broader environment in which they live.

Existing Conditions & Challenges

Massive and Unarticulated Buildings

Multifamily building design is often limited by cost constraints, square-footage requirements, and the need to accommodate many tenants. Massive buildings are often uninteresting, unarticulated, constructed of poor-quality materials, and can be difficult to walk around.

Unfriendly Frontage

Thoughtful building frontage is often overlooked in building design. Street-facing garages, single entries into buildings, a lack of stoops, and reclusive patios or minimally transparent patios result in uninteresting and unused frontages.

Buildings That Do Not Address the Street

Buildings and streets are often considered in isolation from each other. Buildings are often sited with no relationship to internal or external streets, or are set back at awkward, long distances. This creates unusable spaces around the building. Moreover, small openings (entries, windows, and porches) limit the degree to which buildings actively contribute to the street environment.

Inappropriate Building Siting

Buildings are often sited in random arrangements or in layouts solely designed to maximize the number of units and parking. This site design approach can lead to a disassociation between buildings, streets, pedestrian networks, and the natural topography or natural amenities of a site.

Recommendations

7.1 Articulate and Break Up Long Building Lengths
Relate buildings to the human scale.

7.2 All Buildings Face a Street
Orientation can allow for "eyes on the street."

7.3 Activate the Street and Public Spaces
Create direct connections between units and streets.

7.4 Foster Interaction Through Building Groupings
Deliberate building arrangements can promote community.

7.1 Articulate and Break Up Long Building Lengths

Building façades that are long and monotonous can create overwhelming exterior environments that discourage people from being outside. Long, impermeable buildings can become barriers to movement within a development while blank, unarticulated façades can create dull and unpleasant environments. Implement a variety of techniques to create building forms that relate to the human scale and are enjoyable to walk around. The development should add value to the neighborhood through character and a similarity of aesthetic and material choices. Making these decisions thoughtfully can decrease backlash from single-family, multifamily, and commercial neighbors.

Façade articulation and changes in the roof profile can keep a building from looking like a large, singular mass. Articulation can also be achieved by changes in materials and/or colors within different elements on the façade. Openings (entries, windows, etc.) help create a sense that there are occupied units inside the building and activity within the development. Building entries provide opportunities for overhangs, porches, stoops, and other elements that relate to a human scale.

Balconies are a common element employed in multifamily housing to provide articulation to a façade. Balconies should be large enough to be used and can provide an opportunity to add activity to the street. A balcony with people moving in and out of the building can create a sense of vibrancy and consistent "eyes on the street."

In general, shorter building lengths (<150') are recommended, but regardless of length, articulation can create visual interest and scale for a building. Breaking down the building mass into more human-scaled elements makes buildings more approachable and enlivens the surrounding environment. Many city guidelines provide specific information for building massing. Useful resources include San Jose, California and Pasadena, California's regulation regarding overall length and articulation (see the Code Guide and Code Guide Appendix sections of this book).

Cherry Orchard in Sunnyvale, CA illustrates unique and articulated façades of large buildings.

7.2 All Buildings Face a Street

Orienting buildings to face the street provides opportunities for interaction with neighbors, encourages conversation, and promotes a general feeling of community. People may walk in the safety of neighbor's windows and doors and the neighborhood then becomes more pleasant for leisure walking. Developments with buildings facing away from a street do not allow for the increased security of "eyes on the street."

Buildings' primary orientation should be toward streets. All ground-floor building entrances should open directly onto the street and not into internal passageways. This may apply to either streets internal to the development or along adjacent roads. Developments that are situated between internal and adjacent streets should try to address both sides in some way.

Where it is not possible to have the front entrance face the street, units should have a street-facing patio with private and semi-private areas. Other openings, like windows, should also be oriented to face the street. Street-facing windows define the human scale of buildings and reveal the human presence within, all the while maintaining "eyes on the street." These openings provide a sense of importance to the street and encourage activity in it and surrounding it. Porches and stoops are great places for parents to watch children playing or just observe people walking through the neighborhood.

Multifamily units at Town Lake Tempe in Arizona open directly on to the street with front doors and balconies.

7.3 Activate the Street and Public Spaces

Building forms, which define public spaces, should be interesting and create active adjacent outdoor spaces where possible. Buildings should address open spaces. This provides opportunities for residents to utilize the outdoor environment and interact with neighbors. Public spaces that have a direct connection to units provide the feeling of a larger living space. Inactive public spaces create a cloistered environment with limited or no opportunities for residents to be outside or enjoy the outdoor space. The organization of buildings helps define outdoor space.

For outdoor, public places to be useful and add value to the site, they should feel safe, be interesting and useful for activities. Consider how multiple buildings come together to frame open space and avoid small leftover strips between buildings. Where possible, consider the use of the spaces created between buildings. (See section 8, Open Space and Landscape Design.)

Creating openings in buildings, cut-throughs, and other connections to public spaces will increase use and activity within a development. The ease of access to these spaces encourages residents to explore and utilize them.

If there is a neighboring public space, consider creating direct visual or physical connections to it. Creating these connections can take little effort or additional investment but greatly increases actual and perceived value for residents by providing views and access to public spaces.

7.4 Foster Interaction Through Building Groupings

Buildings sited in random or solitary arrangements miss opportunities to create groupings and shared outdoor spaces. Buildings should be grouped in ways that promote connection with neighbors while still providing privacy. Building groupings should be thought of as subsets of the development that are distinct but complementary. Creating a clearer relationship between buildings adds value to their residents' living experience.

When siting buildings, do so in thoughtful and deliberate arrangements that create shared outdoor spaces, including community gardens, patios with furniture, areas for outdoor food preparation and local gatherings.

In larger developments, it may be necessary to create smaller groups of buildings that address neighbors. This can be accomplished by siting buildings in small groups of approximately four to six. This site design creates a more intimate relationship between adjacent buildings. Combining several smaller communities will give the feeling of being part of both a smaller and larger neighborhood. Combinations of buildings create semi-public shared spaces that can make residents feel more ownership over outdoor spaces.

In smaller developments, a contextual site design approach is necessary. Look to create relationships with adjacent developments and the site context.

Consider using distinct, visually interesting materials in different locations within sites. Building distinctions and landmarks act as a wayfinding mechanism and promote walking within and throughout the site.

Sheldon Village, Eugene, OR
Articulated building façades open on to a vibrant central courtyard among this multifamily housing community.

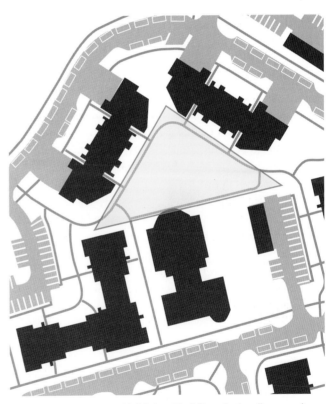

The grouping of highlighted buildings in the diagram above denote a small community among the larger multifamily community at Colonial Grand, Huntersville, NC.

8. Open Space & Landscape Design
Use Natural Elements to Create a More Habitable Development

Creating a usable, attractive, and beautiful natural landscape is paramount to achieving desirable and successful developments. Open space serves as a primary destination and as an environment through which people circulate. It is integral to connectivity and active travel through the site. Landscape design includes the selection and consideration of new and existing trees and other vegetation and site features. Landscaping mediates the transition from the built environment to the outside. Open space and landscape design create interest, excitement, and variation of views throughout the development and make the site more enjoyable.

Existing Conditions & Challenges

Buildings Ignore Existing Site

Buildings are often sited on a landscape with little consideration for how their placement relates to the natural features of the site. The site is typically cleared and modified to a flat plain, which negates the opportunity for buildings to interact with the surrounding landscape and ecologies. This tends to result in spaces that are indistinguishable from one another.

No Hierarchy of Open Space

Many developments consist of a series of open spaces without an order or hierarchy. These spaces are generally similar in size and lack an identity and purpose. It results in a development with homogenous buildings and landscapes. This can be difficult for wayfinding and take away from the general character of the development.

Unusable Open Space

Open spaces that are too small are unusable by residents. These areas are often leftover spaces and are not enjoyable, but are still used to calculate required open spaces. Open space is often poorly programmed and results in vacant outdoor space.

Lack of Street Trees and Green Buffers

Landscape design often neglects to incorporate greening that improves aesthetics and safety, while helping moderate outdoor temperatures. A lack of street trees and green buffers is a missed opportunity to increase the natural look and attractiveness of the site and protect pedestrians, cyclists, and motorists at the same time.

Recommendations

8.1 Create Usable and Attractive Open Space
Scale open space and landscaping to the activities that will take place there.

8.2 Integrate with Existing Site Conditions
Use the natural topography and landscape to create identity.

8.3 Use Natural Elements to Provide Privacy
Create softer exterior edges and attractive scenes to look onto from inside.

8.4 Articulated Landscape Design
Variation in terrain creates interest and identity for developments.

8.1 Create Usable and Attractive Open Space

Creating usable and attractive open spaces encourages a more healthy and active lifestyle via outdoor activities. Open space should not be an afterthought, but rather designed and planned along with new buildings and other site elements. Landscaping should respond directly to the existing site conditions and enhance the outdoor realm. Open spaces should be sensitive to the local climate and create outdoor space that is appropriate for the place where it is located. Landscaped areas should incorporate native plants, creating a more thoughtful relationship to the area.

Scale open spaces and landscaping to users and uses. Smaller open spaces should be sited in logical areas for children to play with appropriate landscaping. Larger open expanses should be thought of as a series of small- to medium-sized areas that can also be used as one large space. Ultimately, areas for activities like picnics should exist along with areas for activities like larger soccer games. Landscaping in these areas should be strategic and not interfere with spaces designated for larger groups to use (i.e., do not place trees in every part of a large field and eliminate the opportunity for team sports). Open spaces are easier to maintain when they occupy a larger area.

Open space presents a great opportunity to deal with stormwater issues. Depending on the climate, these areas can be designed to flood and allow the water to percolate into the soil. Additionally, hard-top areas, which are useful for recreational activities should be considered near pervious areas to mitigate stormwater runoff.

Legends at Lake Nona, Orlando, FL
A playground and yard that acts as a front yard to the multifamily building behind it.

8.2 Integrate with Existing Site Conditions

Building organization is often dictated by what fits on the site and does not consider the existing site conditions. Natural features and amenities are sometimes destroyed or neglected to accommodate the site design, resulting in missed opportunities to integrate with and enhance the natural environment.

Existing site conditions can offer unique opportunities to each site. Their features can define the development's brand and character. Buildings should be sited appropriately to integrate with the existing landscape and topography. Keeping existing trees can add character and value to the development and larger community. Projects can gain goodwill from the neighboring community by taking an approach that respects the natural life that existed before the development.

Adapting to the natural features of the site can also provide a feeling that the development is established in its place. Surrounding open space that continues through the site creates seamless transitions to the public realm and continuity with neighborhoods. Native plants and other terrain features can make the development become part of the local environment more easily.

Buildings sited toward a pond at the development Legends at Lake Nona in Orlando, FL add value to residents and allows for the attractive bike and walking path that runs along it.

8.3 Use Natural Elements to Provide Privacy

The density of multifamily housing can make privacy between units and neighboring buildings difficult to achieve. The landscaped areas between the street and adjacent building can provide a buffer to the private units. Landscaping close to the building can also help to soften the façade and reduce the massive feeling of larger buildings.

Instead of using walls, fences, and other built screening devices, where it is possible use natural elements to provide varying degrees of privacy. Natural elements create attractive barriers for people on the outside as well as those within the building. Use multi-scale plantings, trees, shrubs, or other natural elements to achieve this effect. Natural elements, in conjunction with porches or balconies, create privacy while still allowing for "eyes on the street." Using visually appealing shading devices adds a great deal of value to the residents of the units and can have a positive effect on the thermal comfort of the area.

Units at Baldwin Park in Orlando, FL face out onto a street, but still have private façades through the lush plantings along the façade of the building and the street. This condition is mutually beneficial to those inside and those occupying the street realm.

8.4 Articulated Landscape Design

Open space that lacks any articulation can feel empty, vast, or useless, especially as it approaches buildings. Landscaping, grade changes, and outdoor features demonstrate thought and care for a development. These strategies can provide sensitive transitions to neighboring developments or between individual multifamily buildings.

Well-placed landscaping can also minimize the visual impact of other buildings, define unit entries, and enhance structural elements. The goal is to soften and embellish areas between buildings and adjacent properties with native plant life in a range of scale and cover.

Use trees to provide shade. Grass can be a means of mitigating heat and exposure in parking lots and other paved areas and offer cooling properties to adjacent buildings. Fences higher than 7' should only be used adjacent to high-speed thoroughfares. Thoughtful landscape design around the site encourages residents and neighbors to actively engage with the site.

Site features at Parkside Commons in Chelsea, MA include benches, large planters, and fences. These features provide variation and interest for residents.

9. Bicycles

Accommodations for Cyclists

Bike facilities refer to any amenities that support bicycle travel such as: secure bike parking, air pumps, and bike paths. Adequate bike facilities encourage biking within the development and to neighboring destinations. Creating an infrastructure for bikes in the community can create social interactions between neighbors. It activates streets with people, increasing the level of safety simply through their presence. Cyclists sharing the road with cars can reduce speeds throughout a development and create more balance in travel modes.

Existing Conditions & Challenges

Inadequate Bike Parking

Bike parking in developments is often unlocked, uncovered, and unsafe. Developments often lack bike racks, bike cages, or other secure bike parking. Additionally, unofficial locking areas (e.g., along railings or near unit entries) can create hazardous conditions for others. A lack of secure and easily used bike parking can be a major disincentive to bike use. These conditions create physical and mental barriers to biking.

Hostile Auto-Dominated Environments

Within developments, street and parking design generally do not provide for bicycle travel. This condition can create an environment that discourages biking.

Limited or No Bike Amenities

Developments often do not provide bike maps, air pumps, tools, and connections to local bike paths. The lack of these amenities makes biking less convenient for residents and local riders and acts as a disincentive to biking.

Recommendations

9.1 Make Streets Bicycle-Friendly
Create areas for people to bike.

9.2 Provide Locked and Well-Designed Bike Parking
Design useful approaches to storage.

9.3 Provide Bike Amenities
Consider incentives and basic conveniences for bikes.

9.1 Make Streets Bicycle-Friendly

If people do not feel safe riding a bicycle in the development, they won't. However, when vehicular traffic is minimal, convenient, and comfortable, travel for bikes is possible. Bike travel should take place within the street realm where motor vehicle drivers can expect bicyclists, and not through large parking lots. (Bike lanes are not needed on streets where the speed limit is thirty miles per hour or less.) Bikes should feel comfortable staying within the street realm and avoid the use of sidewalks, so as not to discourage walkers.

Willamette Garden Apartments, Eugene, OR
This biker does not have a designated bike lane on the streets of this development, but the slow motor vehicle speeds allows for roadway use.

Willamette Garden Apartments, Eugene, OR

9.2 Provide Locked and Well-Designed Bike Parking

One of the primary reasons that bikes are not used is a lack of convenient and secure parking. Accessing a bike from a unit should be easier than accessing a car from a unit. Bike parking should be easy and located in areas where they can be protected from the elements and can be monitored from units and other public spaces. The most useful, easily accessible, and safe parking configurations should be determined based on individual site conditions. Within every development, there should be a mix of short-term and long-term bike parking options.

Short-Term Parking:

Provide parking at each unit or shared parking between a small cluster of buildings. This is more convenient for guests and those who wish to ride directly to and from their front door. This type of parking usually accommodates four to six bikes in an area that is directly in view of the units and visible to passersby. Possible locations for this parking is in exterior stairwells, which act as a cover, or along the street entrance of the building. In either case, windows and doors should look directly onto the area where the bike parking is located.

Long-Term Parking:

Create large covered areas logically dispersed throughout the site. These spaces can hold twenty to fifty bikes. They can be caged or fenced, and must be secured areas. These shelters should provide cover to the bikes and, since they are visible throughout the development, they should not be eyesores. Grouped bike parking creates protected areas that are less likely to invite theft and vandalism. Long-term parking areas should be conveniently located for residents near their front doors.

Both short-term and long-term parking should be well-lit and safe for the bike and the rider. Highly visible areas are best for the safety of the bikes and also to remind and encourage others to utilize the amenities. It is unsafe and cumbersome to carry bikes up and down stairs, steep areas, or in places with other obstacles. These types of situations should always be avoided.

Willamette Garden Apartments, Eugene, OR
A large and attractive shelter accommodates long-term parking for residents.

Oak Meadow, Eugene, OR
Racks are conveniently located under the stairs of this building entry. This is directly outside of two unit front doors and below two second floor entries.

9.3 Provide Bike Amenities

One deterrent to cycling is the cost and storage of cycling necessities like pumps and tools. Another deterrent is a lack of connection to public bike paths or local recreation trails that allow cyclists to access locations without traveling on busy arterials. To encourage use of bicycles throughout the site and to neighboring areas, provide cycling amenities that remind residents that alternate forms of transportation are an option. Promoting bike travel throughout a site reduces the need for additional parking at amenities such as pool houses, workout areas, playgrounds, and mailboxes.

Simple items like air pumps and bike tools can provide a feeling of ease and accessibility to biking. Providing vicinity maps to services, shops, and other recreational areas illustrates accessibility by bike. Some multifamily developments have implemented a simple bike sharing program that encourages more residents to bike.

Where possible, connect to surrounding public bike paths or recreational trails. These types of connections provide a high return on a small investment, they are a great benefit to residents, and improve their quality of life.

Some of the bike amenities available at Spencer View in Eugene, OR include the bike pump (top) and the maps that show residents the surrounding public bike paths and trails.

10. Relationships
Connections to Neighboring Developments

This section refers to opportunities where multifamily developments can engage with specific surrounding uses. The section is organized by use types and includes discussion of multifamily housing adjacencies to commercial developments, single-family homes and other multifamily developments, and open space. Integrating multifamily housing developments into their larger context provides opportunities to effectively create mixed-use areas that increase livability and vibrancy.

Issues to Consider

Direct Pedestrian Access to Commercial Strip

When multifamily housing is adjacent to commercial development, there is a large opportunity to connect directly to the pedestrian walkway that typically exists between the commercial parking areas and stores. Making this direct connection both shortens the trip distance for residents and also avoids having residents walk along arterials and through auto-dominated commercial parking lots. This can minimize potentially hazardous conditions and creates a more inviting experience for pedestrians and bicyclists. Making this type of connection has been shown to increase the number of trips residents make to the commercial area and eliminates the need for parking for these trips.

Two means of connecting to the commercial strip can be considered in this situation. The simpler connection is a direct link to the ends of the commercial pedestrian walkway. This should include a continuous walkway from the multifamily site to the commercial walkway and should incorporate marked crossings across any access ways or drive aisles.

For multifamily housing that is behind the commercial development, a connection can be made through a path created between stores in the strip. This is a more complicated connection in that it requires increased coordination with the commercial development and has ramifications for the design of the commercial strip.

Heron Meadows, Eugene, OR
Connection to neighboring commercial development.

This type of connection does, however, provide opportunities for adding storefronts and entrances along the connecting path. Because of safety concerns during the evening, these connections are often well lit and have gates that can be locked during off hours.

Recommendations

10.1 Connect Multifamily Housing to Commercial Areas

10.2 Connect Multifamily Housing to Single-Family Homes and Other Multifamily Developments

10.3 Connect Multifamily Housing to Open Space

Map data: Google, DigitalGlobe

Sheldon Village in Eugene, OR connects by a pedestrian path to the neighboring commercial area.
The path continues through the building to the public pedestrian network (shown on right).

If direct pedestrian access to commercial areas is not possible, access points that link the pedestrian network to external sidewalks should be located to create the shortest possible route. This may require multiple access points depending on the shape and orientation of the development.

10.1 Connect Multifamily Housing to Commercial Areas

Throughout the country, multifamily housing is often used as a buffer between commercial areas and single-family homes. This creates a charged condition where a substantial amount of dense multifamily housing is located within walking distance to commercial areas. In addition, the location of multifamily housing makes it a critical element in the accessibility of the commercial area by surrounding single-family housing. Connectivity in these situations is critical to facilitating walking and biking trips.

In this role, multifamily housing can block safe foot or bike travel to the commercial area or it can facilitate it. There may be greater opportunities for single-family residents to easily access local shopping areas.

Vehicular Connections to Commercial Areas

Vehicular connections are much more complicated than pedestrian paths in that they have the potential to increase traffic through the multifamily development and because developers are generally less receptive to them. Where connections are made, they should be narrow in order to limit travel speeds and in order to limit non-local traffic, should not lead to direct connections to arterials or other major roads.

Parking

Commercial developers often express concern that making pedestrian connections to adjacent multifamily housing will lead some residents to use the commercial parking lot for residential parking or to store extra cars. In interviews with developers who have made pedestrian connections to multifamily developments, they have stated that this is not a problem as this type of parking would typically occur during the night and is easy to locate and control. Towing a single car was enough incentive to remediate the problem for an entire development.

Through Paths for Other Residential Developments

The location of multifamily housing adjacent to commercial areas can make it a barrier or a connection point for other single-family and multifamily developments to access the commercial area. Creating clear, well-lit paths through the multifamily development can make more direct and pleasant paths for neighboring residents, increasing the number of residents that live within walking distance to the commercial area, and reducing the number of auto trips to this area.

While some developers have expressed safety concerns regarding having other residents travel through their multifamily development, many of these concerns can be mitigated through design. Having the through path occur along an internal street, having buildings face this street, and avoiding tall, opaque walls and areas where a person can be hidden can all help mitigate safety concerns. In addition, individuals walking through the multifamily development increase the number of "eyes on the street" that help control an area's safety.

Path Lighting

Some municipal codes limit a site's lighting so that it does not illuminate areas outside of the site boundary. This can create dark gaps in paths to adjacent areas that can become a safety concern. Coordinating lighting with adjacent property owners can eliminate these gaps and create safe, continuously lit paths.

Headlights and Glare

Cars using the commercial parking area in the evening can create disturbing glare within the multifamily development and especially within buildings that are adjacent to the parking area. This glare can be mitigated by orienting buildings so that they don't face the commercial area and/or by the location of low walls or shrubs along the perimeter of the multifamily development.

10.2 Connect Multifamily Housing to Single-Family Homes and Other Multifamily Developments

Multifamily developments often face significant opposition when they are proposed adjacent to existing single-family homes. This is often based on the perception that multifamily housing will increase traffic, increase crime, and burden local schools. While multifamily housing has a higher unit density than single-family homes, residents typically own fewer cars per household and make less auto trips per household. In addition, multifamily housing has no difference in crime rates than lower-density housing, and because the large majority of multifamily households do not include children, they actually are a much smaller load on schools than single-family developments. (For further discussion on these topics, please see: Haughey, Richard M. Higher-Density Development: Myth and Fact. Washington, D.C.: ULI–the Urban Land Institute, 2005.)

One primary concern of single-family residents regarding multifamily housing that is related to site design is a fear that multifamily development will become an eyesore that is incompatible with the existing neighborhood. The design of multifamily housing is critical to mitigating this concern.

Beyond single-family resident concerns, well-connected multifamily housing can also be a benefit to surrounding single-family and multifamily developments. Because multifamily housing is often located between single-family or other multifamily homes and commercial areas, increasing connectivity between these developments can actually increase the accessibility of the commercial area for all residents and give them a protected, pleasant path on which to travel.

Because zoning typically clusters mid to high density housing in suburbia, multifamily housing developments are often directly adjacent to one other. This condition avoids issues of incompatible scale seen with other use adjacencies and instead provides an opportunity to create larger continuity between developments. Creating this continuity not only helps create a larger sense of neighborhood, but also allows residents to access all of the areas beyond any particular development.

Issues to Consider

Smooth Transitions
To mitigate concerns about the compatibility of multifamily and single-family housing, strategies to help smooth transitions between the two housing types are critical. These strategies include creating compatibly scaled buildings, creating edges that engage the surrounding neighborhood, and designing high quality, attractive buildings. Creating smooth transitions between multifamily developments creates a larger sense of neighborhood.

Compatible Scale
As multifamily housing typically includes larger buildings, breaking down the scale of the buildings can help them blend with neighboring developments. This includes articulating the façades, massing large buildings, and bringing down the height of buildings as they approach the perimeter of the site. Mimicking adjacent single-family home set-backs and avoiding units that can look directly into adjacent yards and homes can also help smooth the transition between developments.

Engaging Edges

The perimeter of developments is a primary place of interaction. Creating engaging edges can not only avoid conflict, but can also add to the quality of the neighboring development. In these areas, avoid blank walls or fences that lack articulation or wall openings. Where possible, orient buildings toward neighboring local streets and create façades along those streets that include entry doors and stoops. Activating the street with these elements can help foster "eyes on the street" and a feeling of safety.

Engaging edges and active building façades with stoops, windows and front doors looking out in Baldwin Park, Florida.

Architectural Design and Details

Creating well-designed, attractive buildings is a key component to offering a positive contribution to the larger neighborhood. Avoid low-quality materials that require high degrees of maintenance or that will not weather gracefully. Avoid blank walls or largely unarticulated buildings. Pay attention to building detailing and provide a similar or higher quality of design than the surrounding neighborhood. It is sometimes helpful to use an architectural language that is compatible with surrounding development and creates a feeling of continuity. Consider similar architectural details and articulation as those of surrounding buildings.

Continuous Pedestrian Network

Because of their size, multifamily developments have the potential to act as barriers within larger neighborhoods, increasing travel distances, forcing residents into their cars, and increasing traffic. To mitigate this, connect to the surrounding multifamily pedestrian network both at vehicular access points and also in areas that may only have pedestrian connections. Consider how neighboring residents may be able to walk through the multifamily development to access other residential or commercial areas. Creating a dense network of connections allows residents from both multifamily and single-family developments to walk and bike to destinations.

Continuous Street Network

To create a feeling of continuity and cohesion throughout the area, have internal streets align with surrounding local streets. Look for opportunities to locate multifamily development entries at existing intersections where possible, making the entry an extension of the street system. Also, consider using similar block sizes and layouts as the surrounding neighborhoods and connecting streets all the way through the multifamily development. Consider the use of stub-outs where adjacent areas are currently undeveloped.

Map data: Google, DigitalGlobe

A continuous system of paths and streets at Parkside and Crossings developments in Eugene, Oregon.

10.3 Connect Multifamily Housing to Open Space

City parks, greenways, and waterfront areas provide recreational and social opportunities for multifamily residents that typically do not have access to private yards.

Connections to these areas give multifamily residents direct access to these larger amenities and can significantly improve residents' quality of life.

A connection to a neighboring park in Eugene, Oregon.

Issues to Consider

Direct Pedestrian Links
Where possible, create direct connections between the open space and multifamily housing. This minimizes travel distances for residents and encourages increased use of the open-space amenities. Pedestrian access points should link the open space and multifamily networks. Consider multiple access points if there is a lengthy adjacency. If needed, 'Friendship Gates' – gates that do not lock – can be used to define the edge of the development and create thresholds that can discourage unwanted visitors.

Building Face and Activate the Space
Where possible, buildings should be oriented toward the open-space amenities and should have doors, stoops, and wall openings facing this area. This can provide an attractive view for residents and also allows them to informally monitor the activities occurring within the open space.

Avoid Blocked Views and Hidden Areas
Large, opaque fences and planting located between the open space and multifamily housing can create unsafe conditions within the open space. These barriers can create areas where residents cannot see activities and where individuals can hide. Keeping areas open to "eyes on the street" helps create a safer environment for everyone.

Lighting
Open spaces can feel threatening during evening and nighttime hours if they are not adequately lit. Dark walkways and access points can discourage use of the open space and can create conditions that do not feel safe to residents. Particularly, avoid gaps in lighting continuity at site edges.

Existing, well-connected
developments across the country

Project Profiles

Heron Meadows - Eugene, Oregon

Cherry Orchard - Sunnyvale, California

Colonial Grand - Huntersville, North Carolina

Sheldon Village - Eugene, Oregon

Project Profile:
Heron Meadows
Eugene, Oregon

Map data: Google, DigitalGlobe

Heron Meadows succeeds in many of the areas outlined in this book. It provides particularly good examples of pedestrian and street networks with simple and usable connections to adjacent commercial areas. This project was driven by a new city code and the design has an emphasis on street frontage, parking, access points, and street design.

Heron Meadows is disconnected from the single-family homes to the south and west of the site; although vehicular and pedestrian access is provided at four points along the north and east edges of the development. These links connect to the public street system and an adjacent commercial property.

Since the case study of this development took place, a new multifamily housing development was constructed to the east of Heron Meadows. The existing stub-out that is shown in the map above now connects to new neighbors and a park that is shared with the community.

The Facts:

Total Number of Units:	300
Total Area:	16 acres
Units per Acre:	19
Largest Open Area:	400 sq ft.
Parking Spaces:	440
Year Built:	2007
Unit Types:	1, 2 and 3 BR
Architect:	Reiter Design Group Architects, Inc
Landscape Architect:	Anderson Associates
Developer:	Candle Light Partners, LLC
Total Buildings on Site:	23

Pedestrian Network

There is a extensive network of paths that connect this site internally. There are also pedestrian links between Heron Meadows and its neighbors, specifically to those to the north and east. These pedestrian paths connect to the public street system and allow for walking far beyond the boundary of this site. The pathways are also critical to accessing the parking courts throughout the site.

Access Points

Heron Meadows links directly, by a paved path, to the neighboring commercial area. A crosswalk from the pathway to the sidewalk of the commercial strip has been created for protected pedestrian travel. It is heavily used by residents. The proximity and connection to the adjacent commercial area is touted in promotional material as a key amenity. There are additional access points that create vehicular links to major arterials. More access points are needed to connect to the single-family homes along the west and south edges of the site.

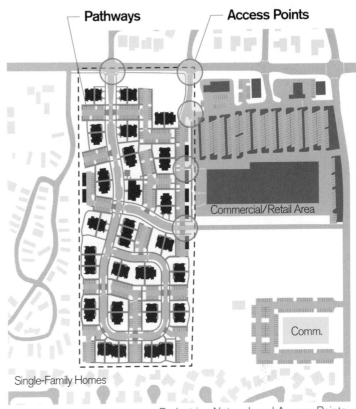

Pedestrian Network and Access Points

Parking

A series of small parking courts are linked to the internal street network and provide residents with parking close to their buildings, without making cars and parking the most dominating feature of the development.

Street Network

Vehicular access is provided to all areas of the site through a loop road. A stub-out (the most southern access point on the east edge of the site) was turned into a through street after the development of an adjacent multifamily housing complex.

Street Network and Parking

Top: Narrow, winding streets provide a neighborhood feel while slowing vehicular traffic. The pedestrian network is an integral component of the street system and allows for "eyes on the street."

Right: Front doors, entry ways, balconies, and windows punctuate the façade of this building.

(Opposite Page)

Top: On-street parking, bulb-outs, sidewalks, and street trees characterize the street design throughout Heron Meadows. It creates a pleasant walking experience for residents.

Left: A protected pedestrian path that is buffered by trees, green planting strips, and parallel parking. Buildings face the street with entrances opening onto and connecting to the sidewalk.

Right: The connection to the adjacent commercial area.

Project Profile:
Cherry Orchard
Sunnyvale, California

Cherry Orchard Apartments place an emphasis on providing ample green space for the residents to enjoy. In addition to grand commons, usable green areas can be found throughout the development, with all units looking out onto one of these common areas. The adjacent commercial area has a fully integrated pedestrian network for residents to easily access the grocery store on foot. This development utilizes the mild climate of California to create a highly connected, walkable, and well-used development.

The Facts:

Total Number of Units:	300
Total Area:	11.2 acres
Units per Acre:	27
Largest Open Area:	37,000 SF
Parking Spaces:	600
Year Built:	2002
Unit Types:	1, 2, 3 BR
Architect:	KTGY Group
Landscape Architect:	The Guzzardo Partnership
Developer:	Irvine Company
Total Buildings on Site:	8

Pedestrian Network

Sidewalks provide a multitude of walking choices within this development. Each building is linked with many landscaped areas to encourage pleasure walking and recreation. The adjacent shopping center is connected by crosswalks and paths which makes it more convenient on foot.

Access Points

Primary vehicular access to Cherry Orchard is provided by connections to two major public roadways with secondary access provided to the shopping center. Pedestrian access points are provided throughout the perimeter, minimizing access shadows and providing direct routes to destinations.

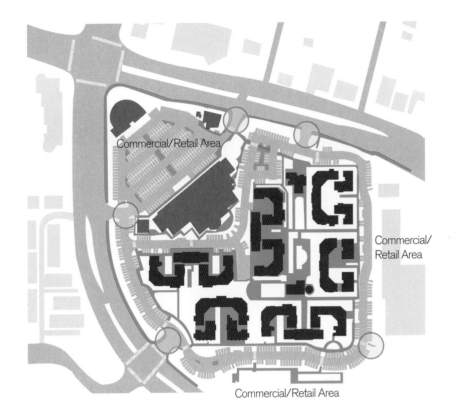

Commercial/Retail Area

Commercial/ Retail Area

Commercial/Retail Area

Street Network

Vehicular traffic within the development is limited to a ring road on the perimeter of the site and has accommodations for pedestrian crossings throughout. There is vehicular access to multiple arterial roads surrounding the development, as well as direct access to the adjacent shopping area.

Parking

Parking is primarily provided along the ring road surrounding the buildings. An area of dense parking in the northern section of the development includes ample plantings and green space and mitigates any feeling of being in a parking lot. There is additional semi-underground parking accessible by elevator from the units. Above ground parking is easily accessible by paths, which keeps pedestrians from passing through high traffic areas. The parking typology allows for a pedestrian dominated development core.

Top: Balconies and windows look out onto recreation areas with walking paths connecting each part of the site.

Bottom: Entries that engage the street and are easily accessible from on-street parking.

(Opposite Page)

Bottom: Buildings relate and address each other on this site. Pathways that are lined with trees provide shade and privacy. Each path leads directly to a building entrance. The entrances are attractive and encourage residents to sit outside.

Highly articulated building façades create interest and reduce the feeling of monotonous and repetitious building design.

Usable green spaces encourage walking and using outdoor spaces.

Project Profile:
Colonial Grand
Huntersville, North Carolina

The site design of Colonial Grand at Huntersville emphasizes its physical location and focuses on providing community features such as outdoor living areas.

Both vehicular and pedestrian access to Colonial Grand are provided at five points along the north, east, and south of the development. Sidewalks run along all of the streets and connect to all buildings and parking areas within the development, helping make walking a good option. A ring road runs along the perimeter of the development and is connected to internal roads that allow more direct access to various parts of the site.

The Facts:

Total Number of Units:	250
Total Area:	14.5 acres
Units per Acre:	17
Largest Open Area:	22,000 sq ft.
Parking Spaces:	455
Year Built:	2002
Unit Types:	1, 2, 3 br
Architect:	Watts Leaf
Landscape Architect:	Design Resource Group
Developer:	Colonial Properties Trust
Total Buildings on Site:	9

Pedestrian Network

An intense network of walkways cross the site and run along all of the streets. This provides residents direct paths to multiple destinations both within and beyond the development, making walking an integral part of the community. Sidewalks and paths outside of the development connect to a bike path and neighboring developments.

Access Points

This development has numerous vehicular and pedestrian access points along its perimeter, giving residents many locations from which to connect to adjacent commercial and residential developments. Access locations are well distributed along the development's north, east, and south edges, minimizing the access shadow.

Parking

Numerous on-street parking spaces make best use of roadway space, while protecting pedestrian pathways and reducing the need for parking lots. This is supplemented by smaller parking courts located near most of the buildings.

Street Network

A continuous street network, based on city code, provides access to all adjacent developments and links directly to the existing street network. Improvements could be made by connecting to the single-family housing development to the southwest.

Top: Street trees, green buffers, and parallel parking make this an enjoyable place for residents to walk.

Middle: A bioswale is highlighted and mitigates rainwater on site.

Bottom: This crosswalk and path lead to the adjacent commercial area.

(Opposite Page)

Top: Parking courts outside of buildings provides convenient parking that does not dominate the entire landscape.

Bottom: Balconies and windows face the street and the entry of the building provides stairs and benches for street on-lookers.

Photos courtesy of Huntersville Planning Department

Project Profile:
Sheldon Village
Eugene, Oregon

Map data: Google, DigitalGlobe

The Sheldon Village design team focused on connectivity throughout the development of the project. As a result, they were able to take advantage of Sheldon Village's proximity to commercial properties and increase the neighborhood feel of the development. This is an affordable-housing project that is widely seen as a successful development with a high demand and happy residents.

The Facts:

Total Number of Units:	78
Total Area:	3 acres
Units per Acre:	26
Largest Open Area:	3800 sq ft.
Parking Spaces:	214
Year Built:	2003
Unit Types:	SROs, 1, 2, 3 br
Architect:	Bergsund DeLaney Architecture & Planning, PC
(in joint venture with)	David Edrington, Architect
Landscape Architect:	Stangeland & Associates, Inc.
Developer:	Housing and Community Services of Lane County
Total Buildings on Site:	13

Pedestrian Network

This project has a dense pedestrian network that serves as the primary means of circulation within the site. The meandering nature of the paths encourages walking inside the development and enhances the sense of community felt by residents.

Access Points

Residents at Sheldon Village benefit from its close proximity to several different commercial properties. Pedestrian paths link the development to a number of the neighboring properties. The connection to the commercial area to the east is made from behind, through a break in the building.

Without access points residents would have to drive or walk out of the development and around the block to access commercial properties immediately adjacent to their homes.

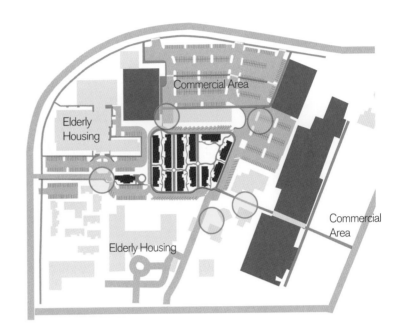

Street Network

A private road loop provides the primary link between Sheldon Village and the public street system. Although this is not ideal, it is supported by an intricate system of walking paths in between the buildings.

Parking

Resident parking is provided along the primary access road along the perimeter of the site, and in concentrated lots to the east. While the lot is not ideal, it frees the core of the site for open, community-enhancing green spaces.

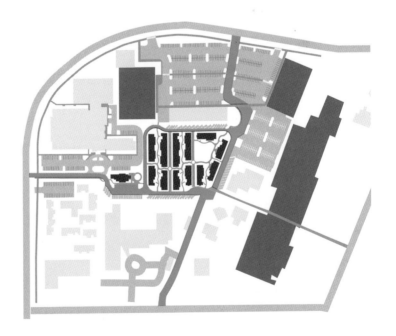

Top: A view of front stoops that face one another and create a welcoming and community-oriented entry.

Left: Buildings at this site are organized around walking 'courts' that are well-used by residents.

Right: Highly articulated façades, which include roof changes, operable windows, and balconies, create interest and an active building façade.

This backyard has balconies, doors, and windows that look onto it so families can watch children at play. This usable outdoor space encourages residents of the building to interact with one another.

Thoughtful site landscaping creates character and interest throughout the community. This encourages pleasure walking and walking to neighboring commercial areas and multifamily developments.

Top: Low stone walls separate green spaces from the pedestrian network. This creates semi-private outdoor spaces and also provides places to sit throughout the development.

Left: Trellises with native plants lead walkers through the pedestrian network.

Right: Connection to adjacent commercial area.

Top: A well-landscaped pedestrian path leads through the development with personalized outdoor seating at the ground level and on elevated decks.

Bottom Left: Buildings face the primary open space with doors, patios, windows, and stoops.

Bottom Right: Balconies and windows overlook walking courts and keep "eyes on the street."

Proposed changes to existing developments
with latent potential for connectivity

Project Retrofits

Riviera Village - Eugene, Oregon

Villas at Union Hills - Phoenix, Arizona

Project Retrofit:
Riviera Village
Eugene, Oregon

Riviera Village is a 168-unit apartment community on the outskirts of a medium-sized metropolitan area in Oregon. Some critical issues exist at this site which make it disconnected internally and externally. There are only two vehicular access points, which are both located on the north side of the site. Pedestrian paths only exist along the front of buildings which face directly onto parking areas and do not connect all buildings. This orientation encourages car-to-unit travel only.

This site is surrounded by an impenetrable fencing. It prohibits access to the neighboring commercial area to the west, the neighboring multifamily to the south, and the public bike path to the east.

The buildings of this development are not oriented to face the street or to take advantage of existing site conditions. The random building placement creates large areas of open space which are not utilized by residents because they are too vast.

Proposed improvements to the site include:
- Careful planning of outdoor spaces to create activity areas for the community
- Vehicle and pedestrian access added at several points around the development
- A more extensive network of paths, linking all parts of the site

Existing Conditions

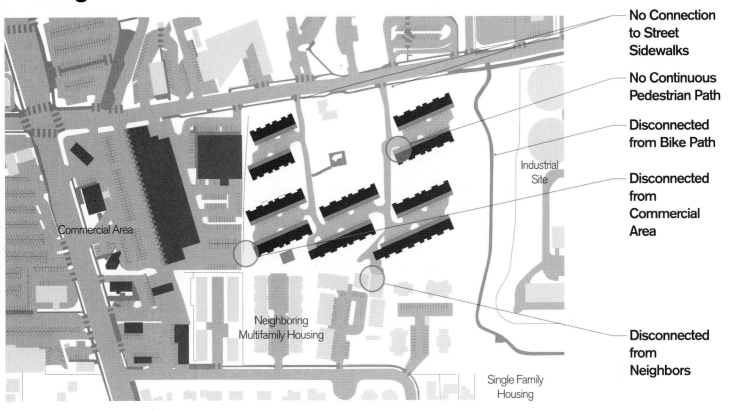

No Connection to Street Sidewalks

No Continuous Pedestrian Path

Disconnected from Bike Path

Industrial Site

Disconnected from Commercial Area

Commercial Area

Neighboring Multifamily Housing

Disconnected from Neighbors

Single Family Housing

Proposed Improvements

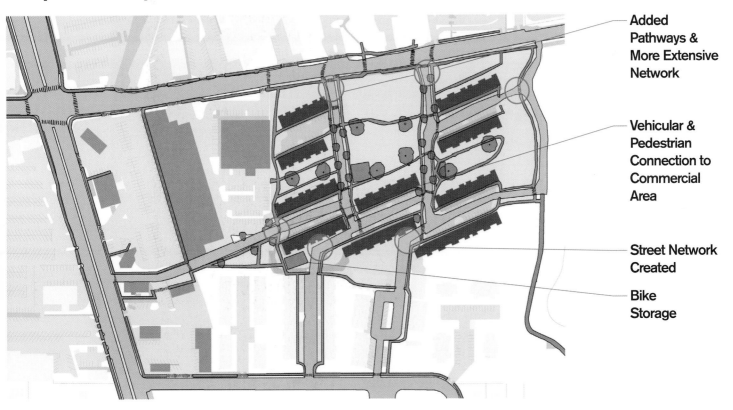

Added Pathways & More Extensive Network

Vehicular & Pedestrian Connection to Commercial Area

Street Network Created

Bike Storage

Existing Conditions

This photo illustrates the existing unfriendly building frontage. The buildings are placed far away from the sidewalk, not providing any direct street access to front doors. The open green space is unprogrammed and not useful to those that live there.

An internal street that leads out to the main arterial does not provide any accommodation for bicyclists or pedestrians. There are no areas that would encourage pleasure walking. This development encourages car-to-unit activity only.

Proposed Improvements

The proposed improvements for this site include a building façade that engages the street and open space, and is connected by a paved path to the existing sidewalk infrastructure. A fenced front yard separates it from the street and can encourage kids to play.

The addition of a sidewalk, crosswalks, green buffers, and street trees makes this street universally accessible and friendly to walk along.

Project Retrofit:
Villas at Union Hills
Phoenix, Arizona

The Villas at Union Hills is surrounded by multifamily housing and commercial buildings. It is an internally focused development which is walled off from all of its neighbors. A four-lane arterial road surrounds the site and cuts off residents from walking to the grocery store and commercial strip to the east.

This development is the epitome of buildings randomly placed within a sea of parking. There is no relationship between buildings and there are no pathways that connect the buildings. The orientation of these buildings and their relationship to the surrounding environment encourages a car-to-unit mentality and certainly does not encourage walking through the neighborhood.

Proposed improvements to the site include:

- Creating through streets connecting to the western and southern adjacent properties
- Developing a pedestrian network that leads directly to relocated front entries or stoops
- Adding bulb-outs and crosswalks to break up long parking lots and provide pedestrians with a place to walk and a right-of-way in the street.
- Make pedestrian connections to the commercial area adjacent to the property on the corner with breaks in the fence and paved paths

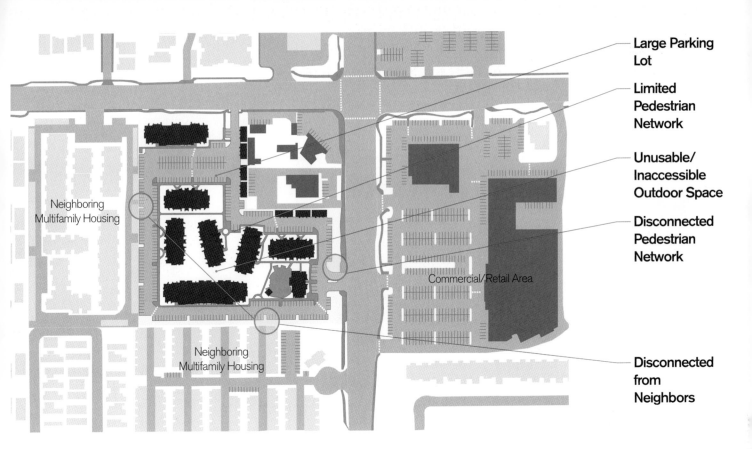

Large Parking Lot

Limited Pedestrian Network

Unusable/ Inaccessible Outdoor Space

Disconnected Pedestrian Network

Neighboring Multifamily Housing

Commercial/Retail Area

Disconnected from Neighbors

Neighboring Multifamily Housing

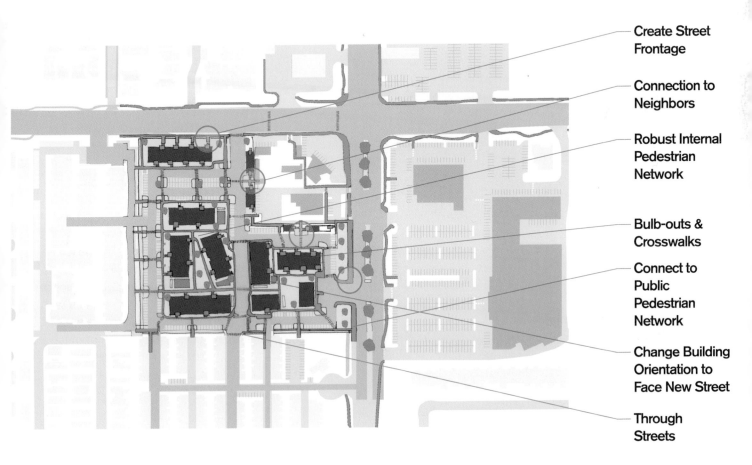

Create Street Frontage

Connection to Neighbors

Robust Internal Pedestrian Network

Bulb-outs & Crosswalks

Connect to Public Pedestrian Network

Change Building Orientation to Face New Street

Through Streets

Existing Conditions

High walls disconnect this development from its neighbors and create large and inaccessible parking lots.

Proposed Improvements - Option I

Changing the building orientation will create more cohesive groupings of buildings and allow for the addition of a through street.

Proposed Improvements - Option II

Clearly defined pedestrian areas and crosswalks connect neighboring developments with green spaces and a friendship gate. Decreased wall height and increased wall transparency further decreases isolation.

This checklist is meant to be a starting point for reviewing suburban multifamily projects and can be used as a guide during design or as an evaluation tool during the permitting/ review process. The issues covered in this list mirror the content covered in the Site Design Criteria section of this book. We recommend that individuals edit and add to this list to coordinate it with the specific code language of their jurisdiction.

We also recommend reviewing the Code Guide section of this book while considering this checklist and local existing codes. The Code Guide Appendix section lists actual code language from cities around the country that are focused on increasing connectivity and livability in suburban multifamily housing.

Project Checklist

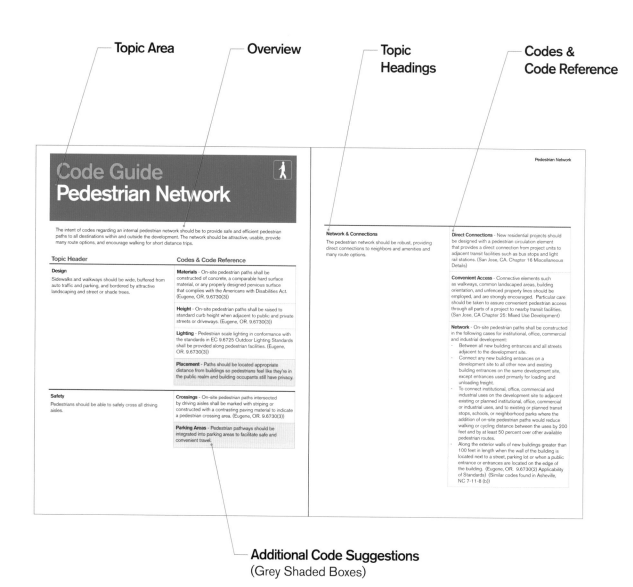

Topic Area

Overview

Topic Headings

Codes & Code Reference

Additional Code Suggestions
(Grey Shaded Boxes)

How to Use the Code Guide

Topic Area — Corresponds to the site design criteria of the book. Codes are organized by the site design criteria to facilitate connection to previously presented material

Overview — briefly summarizes the intent and approach of the codes as they relate to the site design criteria

Topic Headings — organizes codes with similar intents and describes the main idea

Codes & Code Reference — code language from one or more of the five case study cities with a reference that shows where to look for the code in each city's code book

Additional Code Suggestions — ideas from the book that were not seen in codes from the five cities

Introduction to the Code Guide

Some of the current barriers to creating well-connected multifamily housing developments include zoning codes that specifically limit connectivity between dissimilar uses and zoning codes that do not promote or prescribe connectivity. The purpose of this code guide is to present multifamily housing codes from five cities identified as progressive in this area (Eugene, OR; San Jose, CA; Asheville, NC; Arlington, VA; and Huntersville, NC). This guide is meant to provide ideas of how concepts presented in this book can be articulated in code language. It presents several codes related to the site design criteria of the book and provides narrative about the intent and approach these cities have taken with their code. Additional ideas from the book are added as needed. While this code guide has limited excerpts from each code, the following section, Code Guide Appendix, contains more complete code language for each city.

Code Guide
Pedestrian Network

The intent of codes regarding an internal pedestrian network should be to provide safe and efficient pedestrian paths to all destinations within and outside the development. The network should be attractive, usable, provide many route options, and encourage walking for short distance trips.

Topic Header	Codes & Code Reference
Design Sidewalks and walkways should be wide, buffered from auto traffic and parking, and bordered by attractive landscaping and street or shade trees.	**Materials** - On-site pedestrian paths shall be constructed of concrete, a comparable hard surface material, or any properly designed pervious surface that complies with the Americans with Disabilities Act. (Eugene, OR. 9.6730(3)) **Height** - On-site pedestrian paths shall be raised to standard curb height when adjacent to public and private streets or driveways. (Eugene, OR. 9.6730(3)) **Lighting** - Pedestrian scale lighting in conformance with the standards in EC 9.6725 Outdoor Lighting Standards shall be provided along pedestrian facilities. (Eugene, OR. 9.6730(3)) **Placement** - Paths should be located appropriate distance from buildings so pedestrians feel like they're in the public realm and building occupants still have privacy.
Safety Pedestrians should be able to safely cross all driving aisles.	**Crossings** - On-site pedestrian paths intersected by driving aisles shall be marked with striping or constructed with a contrasting paving material to indicate a pedestrian crossing area. (Eugene, OR. 9.6730(3)) **Parking Areas** - Pedestrian pathways should be integrated into parking areas to facilitate safe and convenient travel.

Network & Connections

The pedestrian network should be robust, providing direct connections to neighbors and amenities and many route options.

Direct Connections - New residential projects should be designed with a pedestrian circulation element that provides a direct connection from project units to adjacent transit facilities such as bus stops and light rail stations. (San Jose, CA. Chapter 16 Miscellaneous Details)

Convenient Access - Connective elements such as walkways, common landscaped areas, building orientation, and unfenced property lines should be employed, and are strongly encouraged. Particular care should be taken to assure convenient pedestrian access through all parts of a project to nearby transit facilities. (San Jose, CA Chapter 25: Mixed Use Development)

Network - On-site pedestrian paths shall be constructed in the following cases for institutional, office, commercial and industrial development:
- Between all new building entrances and all streets adjacent to the development site.
- Connect any new building entrances on a development site to all other new and existing building entrances on the same development site, except entrances used primarily for loading and unloading freight.
- To connect institutional, office, commercial and industrial uses on the development site to adjacent existing or planned institutional, office, commercial or industrial uses, and to existing or planned transit stops, schools, or neighborhood parks where the addition of on-site pedestrian paths would reduce walking or cycling distance between the uses by 200 feet and by at least 50 percent over other available pedestrian routes.
- Along the exterior walls of new buildings greater than 100 feet in length when the wall of the building is located next to a street, parking lot or when a public entrance or entrances are located on the edge of the building. (Eugene, OR. 9.6730(2) Applicability of Standards) (Similar codes found in Asheville, NC 7-11-8 (b))

Code Guide
Street Network

Codes related to the street network are primarily intended to promote connections and continuity to adjacent street systems and a legible system of streets and blocks within the development. This is preferable over parking lots being used for streets. Connections should open the development to neighbors and encourage future developments to connect to the street system as well. The approach taken by these cities includes using typical residential streets standards for all circulation areas, emphasizing the continuity of streets, the use of cul-de-sacs and street stubs, and encouraging public instead of private streets.

Topic Header	Codes & Code Reference
Same Standards as Residential Streets The street circulation network in multifamily housing is subject to the same standards as residential streets.	**Standards** - Street standards and connectivity requirements for local residential streets shall be applied to public and private streets within multiple-family developments. (Eugene 9.5500(11)(a) (Refer to EC 9.6815 Connectivity for Streets.))
Continuity of Streets The surrounding street network should help determine the look and placement of streets.	**Alignment** - Public streets should be aligned so that they are continuous through adjacent existing and planned residential development, creating a network of neighborhood streets. (San Jose, CA Chapter 6: Internal Organization Section A)
	Connections - Streets and alleys shall, wherever practicable, terminate at other streets within the neighborhood and connect to existing and projected streets outside the development. (Huntersville, NC Article 5)
	Context - Allow the context of the site to determine a logical street network and block pattern for the development, thus promoting connections to existing street systems.
	Design - Emulate the look and feel of neighboring streets to create continuity.

Use of Cul-de-sacs

Cul-de-sacs should only be used when other configurations are not possible.

Topography - Cul-de-sac shall be allowed only where topographical and/or lot line configurations offer no practical alternatives for connections or through traffic. (Huntersville, NC Article 5.1)

Regulations - Cul-de sacs shall not exceed 250 feet in length, must be accessed from a street providing internal or external connectivity, shall be permanently terminated by a vehicular turnaround, and are permitted where topography makes a street connection impracticable. (Huntersville, NC Article 5)

Alternatives - In most instances, a "close" or "eyebrow" is preferred to a cul-de-sac. Vehicular turnarounds of various configurations are acceptable so long as emergency access is adequately provided. (Huntersville, NC)

Street Stubs

Provide street stubs to encourage future connections and continuation of the network.

Future Connections - Street stubs shall be provided within development adjacent to open land to provide for future connections. The Land Development Map should be reviewed to locate potential connections in new neighborhoods. (Huntersville, NC Article 5.1)

Public vs. Private Streets

Keep developments open to neighborhoods by making streets public.

Public Access - Private streets are not permitted within any new development. Alleys will be classified as public or private depending on function, according to the street acceptance policy. (Huntersville, NC Article 5.5)

Code Guide
Access Points

Codes regarding access points were generally lacking in the codes reviewed. The intent behind the few codes found is to provide residents direct access to nearby amenities. The approach of these codes focuses on specific amenities that should be connected to.

Topic Header	Codes & Code Reference
Direct Connections Access points should be located near existing amenities	**Pedestrian Access** - Mixed use projects should include direct and attractive pedestrian access to all nearby commercial areas, transit stops and transit stations. (San Jose, CA Chapter 25: Mixed Use Development (A) Pedestrian Orientation) **Pedestrian Paths** - On-site pedestrian paths shall be designed and constructed to provide a direct connection to existing public right-of-way and public accessways. (Eugene, OR 9.6730(2)(a)(1))
Number and Distribution Create multiple, well-dispersed places to enter and exit the development.	**Number of Access Points** - Maximize the number of access points for cars, bicyclists, and pedestrians to reduce distances from units to amenities and remove physical barriers to active transportation. **Distribution of Access Points** - Locate at least one access point on each side of the development and to adjacent uses where possible.
Future Connections New developments should be able to easily connect to yours.	**Stub-outs** - Street stubs shall be provided within development adjacent to open land to provide for future connections. The Land Development Map should be reviewed to locate potential connections in new neighborhoods. (Huntersville, NC Article 5.1)
Relationship to Neighbors Support community interaction and active transportation through an open development.	**Edges** - Avoid gated communities. Use transparent materials or natural elements to create permeable edges if needed.

Code Guide
Edges

The intent behind codes regarding edge conditions is to promote neighborhood cohesion, consistency in the urban fabric, and active streets. Where possible and desirable, the development should be connected to adjacent uses and residents should have easy access to amenities and neighbors outside the development. The approach these cities have taken is to have codes around setbacks, street frontage, and various components of fences and walls.

Topic Header	Codes & Code Reference
Setbacks Appropriate setbacks should promote consistency in the neighborhood.	**Building Location** - No structure shall be located closer to the centerline of any street or officially designated street right-of-way (as defined in this ordinance) than fifty (50) percent of the height of the building. For the purpose of determining setbacks, a limited access highway shall be considered as an abutting lot and not as a street or street right-of-way. (Arlington, VA Section 32D. Placement.1 Setbacks.) (Similar codes found in San Jose, CA Chapter 5: Perimter Setbacks - Relationship to Surroundings A. Setbacks from Perimeter Streets & B. Perimeter Setbacks From Adjacent Uses)
	Transitions to Neighbors - Provide smooth transitions to neighbors that are not visually or physically encroaching.
Street Frontage Street frontage should activate local streets and create visual continuity in the neighborhood.	**Street Definition** - On development sites that will result in 100 feet or more of public or private street frontage, at least 60 percent of the site frontage abutting the street (including required yards) shall be occupied by a building(s) or enhanced pedestrian space with no more than 20 percent of the 60 percent in enhanced pedestrian space, placed within 10 feet of the minimum front yard setback line. (Eugene, OR 9.5500 (4)(b))
	Community Interaction - Developments located along quiet, local streets should avoid strictly internal organization. Units along these streets should front onto these streets.
	Continuity - Create visual continuity between the development and surrounding neighborhood; use local design elements.

Fences and Walls

Uses fences and walls appropriately to provide safety, privacy, and access to neighboring amenities.

Height - Fences and walls should be no more than 7 feet high, except when adjacent to freeways, expressways, railroads, incompatible uses, or when they are required for sound attenuation. (San Jose, CA Chapter 4: Perimeter Walls & Fences - Relationship to Surroundings A. Height Fences)

In a residential or mixed use district, a fence or wall in an established rear or side yard which abuts a street or alley may not exceed 6 feet in height unless placed 15 or more feet inside property boundary. (Huntersville, NC 8.11.2)

In a residential or mixed use district, a fence or wall in an established rear or side yard which does not abut a street or alley may not exceed 8 feet in height. (Huntersville, NC 8.11.2)

Material - Solid walls and fences are not permitted between public streets and common open spaces including public or semi-public areas within a project. (San Jose, CA Chapter 4: Perimeter Walls & Fences - Relationship to Surroundings C. Non-Permissible Locations)

Gates in walls or fences over 100 feet in length between public streets or open spaces and public or semi-public areas within a project are encouraged. (San Jose, CA Chapter 4: Perimeter Walls & Fences - Relationship to Surroundings E. Pedestrian Gates)

Within the first 15 feet of the property line, fences of chain link or similar material are permitted only if screened on the exterior side by evergreen shrubs planted no farther apart than 6 feet on center, minimum height 3 feet at installation, or if obscured from view by the screening method(s) set out in the paragraph immediately above. (Huntersville, NC 8.11.2)

Neighborhood Compatibility - Front yard fencing higher than 3 feet should not be introduced on streets that have an existing pattern of residences fronting onto the street. Such fencing should be avoided or minimized to continue the front yard pattern of the surrounding neighborhood. (San Jose, CA Chapter 4: Perimeter Walls & Fences - Relationship to Surroundings J. Neighborhood Compatibility)

Code Guide
Parking

The intent behind these parking codes is to help reduce the dominance of parking in the site and to create a comfortable and safe environment for pedestrians to travel from car to unit. The approach taken by these cities includes a combination of language around desirable types of parking and locations, integration of a pedestrian infrastructure into parking, aesthetics, and some effort to reduce parking ratios. See the Open Space and Landscape Design Code Guide section for a discussion of landscaping requirements in parking areas.

Topic Header

Codes & Code Reference

Use Alternatives to Lots and Lanes
Parking should not be the dominant feature in the development and, where possible, should not be the primary means of circulation. Eliminate long runs of continuous parking.

Types - The city shall allow on-site parking to be provided as part of any multiple-family development project in the form of garages (private or common), carports, open parking areas. (Eugene, OR 9.5500(12) (a))
All parking, except common garages, should be designed as parking courts (Eugene, OR 9.5500(12)(a))

Where considerations preclude parking beneath or within residential buildings, combinations of partial and interrupted parking drives; on-street parking; and small, dispersed parking courts are an acceptable alternative. (Eugene, OR EC 9.8030(8)(f))

Location - No parking lots shall be permitted in required setbacks (Asheville, NC Sec. 7-8-3. RS-4 Residential Single-Family Medium Density District. (f)(9))

Parking lots shall be placed behind buildings; side of building parking will be permitted only as indicated by Building Type and shall be measured along the build-to line. (Huntersville, NC Article 6)

To strengthen the presence of buildings on the street, parking and vehicle use areas and garages adjacent to any public or private street frontage shall extend across no more than 50 percent of any street frontage. (Eugene, OR 9.5500(12)(c))

Parking areas shall not be located between buildings and the streets. (Eugene, OR 9.5500(12)(c))

Every cluster housing project should have a restricted parking zone on all sides that commences at the required setback and extends 18 feet into the site.

Use Alternatives to Lots and Lanes (Continued)

(The percentage of the total area within this zone that may be devoted to parking drives, parking courts, and all areas for parking not within residential buildings should not exceed 50%.) (San Jose, CA Chapter 23: Cluster Housing H. Restricted Parking Zone)

Parking is an appropriate separation between dwelling units and incompatible uses. (San Jose, CA Chapter 23: Cluster Housing H. Restricted Parking Zone)

Entries to parking levels should never be placed in prominent location in primary building façades. Parking entries should be placed in less visible locations at the sides or rears of buildings or at least at a far end of a front elevation. (San Jose, CA Chapter 25: Mixed Use Development (J))

Dimensions - Individual parking courts shall be no more than 9,000 square feet and shall be physically and visually separated by a landscape area a minimum of 20 feet in width. (Eugene, OR 9.5500(12)(b))
No more than 3 individual parking courts may be connected by an aisle of driveway. (Eugene, OR 9.5500(12)(b))

A parking court of any length shall consist of no more than 1 double-loaded parking aisle. (Eugene, OR 9.5500(12)(b))

Integrate Pedestrian Infrastructure into Parking (maintain pedestrian comfort)
Create an environment where pedestrians can move through cars without being overwhelmed.

Parking lots shall be designed to allow pedestrians to safely move from their vehicles to the buildings. On small lots, provide a sidewalk at the perimeter. On larger lots, integrate corridors, delineated by a different paving material, into the lots. (Huntersville, NC Article 6)

To maintain pedestrian comfort and calm the speed of entering traffic, driveways to parking areas should be no wider than 24 feet. (Huntersville, NC Article 6)

Pedestrian Access Landscape bulbs should, wherever possible, align with major building entrances to provide pedestrian access to the building entrance from the parking court or drive. Bulbs that align with entrances should be at least 2 cars spaces wide and should include a pathway as well as a vertical landscape element (trellis or a tree) (San Jose, CA Chapter 7: Driveways L. Pedestrian Access)

Create More Beautiful Parking
Parking should be welcoming and pedestrian-friendly.

Planting Islands - Planting islands shall be placed between parking courts to visually interrupt rows of parked vehicles and to separate individual parking courts. Planting islands between parking courts shall have a minimum width of 20 feet and a minimum area of 360 square feet. Each of these islands shall provide at least 1 canopy shade tree having a clear trunk height of 9 feet. Architectural elements such as trellises, porches, and stairways may extend into planting islands between parking courts. (Eugene, OR 9.5500(12)(b))

Parking courts should be separated from project street, parking drives, and access roads they face by landscaped areas. (San Jose, CA Chapter 7: Driveways K. Parking Court Landscaping)

Landscape buffers should be at least 10 feet in courts with 18 or fewer parking spaces and 20 feet in court with more than 18 spaces. (San Jose, CA Chapter 7: Driveways K. Parking Court Landscaping)

Reduce Parking Ratios
Reduce the feeling of being completely surrounded by parking.

Shared residential and commercial parking is encouraged to reduce the number of parking spaces required for the project. (San Jose, CA Chapter 25 (K.) Alternating Parking Opportunities)

Sharing parking with adjacent sites can also be considered.
(San Jose, CA Chapter 25 (K.) Alternating Parking Opportunities)

On-street parking spaces maybe counted toward the fulfillment of the off street parking requirements for a development. (Asheville, NC)

Code Guide
Street Design

The intent behind these street design codes is to strengthen the presence of buildings on the street, create safe and inviting areas for all users to travel, and reduce the speed of cars in the development. The approach taken by these cities includes codes around street frontage, the streetscape, pedestrian and bicycle amenities, and speed reduction strategies. See the Street Network section of this Code Guide for additional information on streets.

Topic Header	Codes & Code Reference
Street Frontage Street frontage should strengthen the presence of buildings on the street.	**Building Setbacks** - Front building setbacks are required for most housing types to buffer living areas from the public activity of the street and to provide space for landscaping in the configuration associated with traditional residential neighborhoods. Buildings containing living areas should be set back at least 35 feet from major streets, freeways, and expressways (25 feet minimum if average is 40 feet, or 25 feet behind a sound attenuation wall). The 35-foot setback may be reduced on major streets if such a reduction is consistent with the existing or projected urban character. (San Jose, CA Chapter 2: Street Frontage - Relationship to Surroundings GUIDELINES A. Building Setbacks)
	Reduced Setbacks - Zero or reduced building setbacks from the street may be more appropriate for higher density housing types in areas near downtown, along streets with established reduced setback patterns and in areas with specific plans which call for reduced setbacks to reinforce the planned urban character of the neighborhood. (San Jose, CA CA Chapter 2: Street Frontage - Relationship to Surroundings GUIDELINES B. Reduced Building Setbacks)
	Presence of Buildings - To strengthen the presence of buildings on the street, circulation elements and parking areas in the front setback area and/or adjacent to the street should extend across no more than 50 percent of the street frontage. Parking areas should not comprise more than 50% of the elements along a project's street frontage. (San Jose, CA Chapter 2: Street Frontage - Relationship to Surroundings GUIDELINES E. Limitations on Parking Frontage)

Bicycle Amenities

Consider cyclists in street design

Street Expansion - For larger streets (other than Limited Access Streets, Narrow Residential Streets and Minor Residential Streets) as determined appropriate by the Department of Streets and Traffic and City Council Policy, the width of one travel lane in each direction should be expanded by an additional five feet to provide space for bicycle travel. (San Jose, CA Chapter 2: Street Frontage - Relationship to Surroundings GUIDELINES H. Provisions to Accommodate Bicycle Traffic)

Speed Reduction Strategies

Streets should be designed with safety in mind.

Methods -To prevent the buildup of vehicular speed, disperse traffic flow, and create a sense of visual enclosure, long uninterrupted segments of straight streets should be avoided. Methods:

1. a street can be interrupted by intersections designed to calm the speed and disperse the flow of traffic (Article 5) and terminate vistas with a significant feature (building, park, natural feature);

2. a street can be terminated with a public monument, specifically designed building façade, or a gateway to the ensuing space;

3. perceived street length can be reduced by a noticeable street curve where the outside edge of the curve is bounded by a building or other vertical elements that hug the curve and deflect the view;

4. other traffic calming configurations are acceptable so long as emergency access is adequately provided. (Huntersville, NC Article 5.6)

Streetscape

Incorporate attractive and pedestrian-friendly elements into streets.

Street Features - Streetscape including curb, gutter, sidewalk, street light, street furniture, landscaping and other elements, shall be provided as contained in the Rosslyn Station Area Plan Addendum, and other plans and policies established for the area by the County Board. (Arlington, VA SECTION 25 C-0)

Street Trees - The developer should plant street trees of an approved species and size along all public and private streets. There should be at least one tree for approximately every 25 feet of street frontage, depending on species, or at least one tree for each lot abutting the street. (San Jose, CA Chapter 2: Street Frontage - Relationship to Surroundings GUIDELINES F. Street Trees)

Streets should be lined with street trees on both sides, with the exception of rural roads, lanes, alleys, and the undeveloped edge of neighborhood parkways. Private drives are permitted only as described in the Rural and Transitional zone. (Huntersville, NC Article 5.4)

Use 'Complete Street' ideals within the development (curbs, crosswalks, sidewalks, green strips, street trees, lighting, benches, narrow, winding streets, etc.)

Sidewalks

Create a safe environment for pedestrians and drivers.

Requirements - Setback sidewalks shall be required along any public or private street adjacent to or within the development site. (Eugene, OR 9.5500(11)(d) Setback Sidewalks)

Location - Street should be bordered by sidewalks on both sides, with the exception of rural roads, lanes, alleys, and the undeveloped edge of neighborhood parkways. Sidewalks on one side of the road may be permitted in the Rural zone as an incentive to protect water quality. (Huntersville, NC Article 5.3)

Width - In street rights-of-way serving higher density residential development or located in more urban, pedestrian oriented areas of the City, sidewalks should be at least 6 to 10 feet in width, depending on adjacent densities and expectations for pedestrian activity. (San Jose, CA Chapter 2: Street Frontage - Relationship to Surroundings GUIDELINES I. Wider Sidewalks to Accommodate Heavier Pedestrian Demand)

Code Guide
Building Massing & Orientation

These building massing and orientation codes are intended to: 1) promote interesting, aesthetically pleasing buildings that have many front facing openings, are easy to walk around, and have a functional relationship with neighboring buildings and 2) create direct connections between units and streets thus activating the street and public spaces. The approach to achieve these goals includes codes around building dimensions, orientation, articulation and façade, materials, openings, relationships, and street presence.

Topic Header	Codes & Code Reference
Building Dimensions Buildings should be easy to walk around and should relate to the human scale.	**Length** - Extremely long buildings, if they are richly articulated, may be acceptable; however, buildings (including garages and carports) exceeding 150 feet in length are generally discouraged. (San Jose, CA Chapter 11: Building Façade C. Building Length)
	Height - The maximum height of structures shall be 40 feet. (Asheville, NC Sec. 7-8-5) A building may have a maximum height of one hundred thirty-six (136) feet, including penthouses and parapet walls, measured from the average elevation at the perimeter of the site. (Arlington, VA Section 32 RA4.8(C))
	Ratios - For good definition, the ratio of one increment of height to six of width is the absolute maximum, with one to three being a good effective minimum. (Huntersville, NC Article 5.6) Neither the maximum length nor width of any building within 40 feet of a front lot line can exceed 100 feet in the R-1 and R-2 zones and 150 feet in all other zones. (Eugene, OR 9.5500(6)(a))
Building Materials Use material choice to articulate and add interest.	**Materials** - The exterior materials and architectural details of a single building should relate to each other in ways that are traditional and/or logical. For example, heavy materials should appear to support lighter ones. (San Jose, CA Chapter 11 Building Façade D. Building Materials And Details)

Building Orientation

Building orientation should promote "eyes on the street" and interaction with neighbors.

Buildings should be oriented parallel to the street particularly at corners. (San Jose, CA Chapter 25: Mixed Use Development E. Building Orientation)

The major orientation of buildings nearest the street should be parallel to that street or to the prevailing pattern of existing property lines. (San Jose, CA Chapter 25: Mixed Use Development E. Building Orientation)

Multiple-family residential buildings located within 40 feet of a front lot line shall have their primary orientation toward the street. (Eugene, OR 9.5500(5)(a))

Generally, buildings should be oriented with the main façades and primary building entrances facing main and secondary streets and service and parking access points facing tertiary streets. (Arlington, VA Clarendon Sector Plan)

Building Openings

Openings should allow for "eyes on the street".

Main Entrances - The main entrance(s) of ground floor units of any residential building located within 40 feet of a street must face the front lot line. Main entrances may provide access to individual units, clusters of units, courtyard dwellings, or common lobbies. (some exceptions apply – see matrix) (Eugene, OR 9.5500(5)(b))

Windows - Street façades shall contain windows covering a minimum of 15% of the façade on each floor level. (Eugene, OR 9.5500(6)(b))

Adjacency to Public Streets

Continue the neighborhood by connecting to adjacent streets.

Public Streets - Any lot on which a building (or buildings) is to be erected or use is to be established shall abut a public street. (Huntersville, NC Section 8.1)

Building Articulation & Façades

Buildings should add value to the neighborhood and have character.

Articulations - All building façades containing 3 or more attached dwellings in a row should incorporate at least one of the following: 1. At least one architectural projection per unit. Such a projection must project no less than 2 feet 6 inches from the major wall plane, must be between 4 feet 6 inches and 15 feet wide, and must extend the full height of a one-story building, at least one-half the height of a two-story building, and two-thirds the height of a three-story building. On buildings three stories in height, projecting elements may be linked by one level of living space at the top or bottom floor 2. A change in wall plane of at least 3 feet for at least 12 feet every 2 units. (San Jose, CA Chapter 11: Building Façade A. Façade Articulation)

Side Design - If a side or rear elevation faces or is substantially visible from a street, it should be designed with the same care and attention to detail, and in the same material, as the front. (San Jose, CA Chapter 25: Mixed Use Development D. Building Façades)

Wall Surfaces - To preclude large expanses of uninterrupted wall surfaces, exterior elevations of buildings shall incorporate design features such as offsets, projections, balconies, bays, windows, entries, porches, porticos, or similar elements.
1. Horizontal Surface. At least 2 of the design features outlined above shall be incorporated along the horizontal face (side to side) of the structure, to be repeated at intervals of no more than 40 feet.
2. Vertical Surface. At least 2 of the design features outlined above shall be incorporated along the vertical face (top to bottom) of the structure, to be repeated at intervals of no more than 25 feet.
(Eugene, OR 9.5500(7)(a))

Entry Ways - Individual and common entry ways shall be articulated by roofs, awnings, or porticos. (Eugene, OR 9.5500(7)(c))

Relationship to Surrounding Buildings

Buildings should have a clear relationship to each other and surrounding areas.

Relationship - Buildings should have a positive functional relationship with each other as well as an aesthetically pleasing spatial relationship. (San Jose, CA Chapter 25: Mixed Use Development H. Building & Site Design, Horizontal Mixed Use)must project no less than 2 feet 6 inches from the major wall plane, must be between 4 feet 6 inches and 15 feet wide, and must extend the full height of a one-story building, at least one-half the height of a two-story building, and two-thirds the height of a three-story building. On buildings three stories in height, projecting elements may be linked by one level of living space at the top or bottom floor 2. A change in wall plane of at least 3 feet for at least 12 feet every 2 units. (San Jose, CA Chapter 11: Building Façade A. Façade Articulation)

Continuity - The exterior building design, including roof style, color, materials, architectural form and detailing, should be consistent, or at least compatible, among all buildings in a complex and on all elevations of each building to achieve design harmony and continuity within the project and with its surroundings. (San Jose, CA Chapter 25: Mixed Use Development H. Building & Site Design, Horizontal Mixed Use)and in the same material, as the front. (San Jose, CA Chapter 25: Mixed Use Development D. Building Façades)

Street Presence

Orient buildings to the street to promote a community feeling and safety.

Connections - Active connections between buildings and the street, for example residential and retail entries, porches, stairs, decks, courtyards, and windows, should be maximized. (San Jose, CA 25: Mixed Use Development F. Relationship to the Street)

Placement - Residential buildings located away from the street, as on flag lots, should maintain a presence to the street. This may be achieved by placing the rear building so that it is visible from the street. (San Jose, CA 25: Mixed Use Development G. Street Presence)

Street Frontage - On development sites that will result in 100 feet or more of public or private street frontage, at least 60 percent of the site frontage abutting the street (including required yards) shall be occupied by a building(s) or enhanced pedestrian space with no more than 20 percent of the 60 percent in enhanced pedestrian space, placed within 10 feet of the minimum front yard setback line. (Eugene, OR 9.5500(4)(b))

Code Guide
Open Space & Landscape Design

The intent of these open-space and landscape codes is generally focused on deterring randomly placed patches of unusable open space, to encourage use of natural screening materials to provide privacy and hide unattractive features such as dumpsters, to connect with adjacent open space, and to create beautiful parking and streets.

Arlington defines the purpose of its open-space and landscape codes more broadly by stating:

"The purpose of this section is to provide landscaping in order to better control and ameliorate problems of air and noise pollution, afford wind protection, help moderate temperature extremes, to increase property values and attract prosperous business activities into the County and to make the County a healthier and more aesthetically pleasing place to live, shop and work."

The approaches these cities have taken include codes around open-space requirements, screening, relationship to adjacent open spaces, parking lot landscaping, and street trees and buffers.

Topic Header	Codes & Code Reference
Size and Amount of Open Space Designate an appropriate amount of open space and landscaping in developments.	**Landscape Requirement** - Twenty (20) percent of total site area is required to be landscaped open space in accordance with the requirements of Section 32A, "Landscaping". (Arlington, VA Section 25 C-O)
	Minimum Landscaping - Landscaping is required according to the applicable base zone minimum landscape area standards. If there are none specified, the minimum landscape area shall be equal to the amount of area required as open space specified in EC 9.5500(9). (Eugene, OR 9.5500(8)(a))
	Private Open Space - There should be a minimum of 60 square feet of private open space and 200 square feet of usable common open space for every dwelling unit. (San Jose, CA Chapter 23: Cluster Housing F. Open Space) Private open space should be provided at a minimum of 60 square feet per unit with a minimum dimension of 6 feet. Common open space should be provided at a minimum of 100 square feet per unit. (San Jose, CA Chapter 25: Mixed Use Development L. Residential Open Space)

Size and Amount of Open Space (Continued)

Amount of Open Space - All residential districts, 500 square feet of open space per unit or 15% of lot area, whichever is greater. In no case shall the amount of open space devoted to active recreational facilities constitute more than 10% of lot area. (Asheville, NC 7-11-4 (c) Open space requirement)

Minimum Dimensions - The minimum area of any single space shall be 250 square feet, with no dimension being less than 15 feet. (Eugene, OR 9.5500(9)(a))

Common Open Space - Interior common open space shall be at least 10 feet in floor to ceiling height; glazed window and skylight areas shall be provided in the proportion of 1 square foot for each 4 square feet of the floor area of the common space. (Eugene, OR 9.5500(9)(a))

Size & Use - Scale open space and landscaping to the activities that will take place there. Create open space for small numbers to use (e.g., for picnics or reading) with table or tress and use those areas as components to spaces for higher occupancy use (e.g., soccer games)

Landscaping in open spaces should be strategic and not interfere with spaces designated for larger groups to use (i.e., do not place tress in every part of a large field and eliminate the opportunity to play team sports there).

Street Trees & Buffers

Use trees to reduce the heat-island effect and make walking more pleasurable.

Requirement - The developer should plant street trees of an approved species and size along all public and private streets. There should be at least one tree for approximately every 25 feet of street frontage, depending on species, or at least one tree for each lot abutting the street. (San Jose, CA Chapter 9: Landscaped Areas Developer Responsibility D. Street Trees)
Street trees are required along the frontage of all developments abutting newly created public or private streets in accordance with provisions of Chapter 7 of this code regarding the Street Tree Program - Policies, Standards, and Procedures. (Eugene, OR 9.5500(8)(c))

Parking Lot Landscape Design

Create beautiful, pedestrian-friendly parking areas.

Areas to Landscape - All end islands of parking rows and all areas not otherwise used for ingress, egress, aisles or parking must be landscaped. (Arlington, VA SECTION 32A. 3. Parking Lot Landscaping Design Criteria)

Dimensions - The interior space of any planting area shall be no less than nine (9) square feet and not narrower than two (2) feet across its center. (Arlington, VA SECTION 32A. 3. Parking Lot Landscaping Design Criteria)

Materials - The primary landscaping materials used in parking lots shall be deciduous trees which are capable of providing shade at maturity. Shrubbery, hedges and other live plant materials are to be used to complement the tree landscaping. Effective use of berms and existing topography is also encouraged as a component of the landscape plan. (Arlington, VA SECTION 32A. 3. Parking Lot Landscaping Design Criteria)
Trees and shrubs are required in and around parking lots in order to provide attractive views from roads and adjacent properties, provide shade to reduce the heat generated by impervious surfaces, reduce glare from parking lots, and to help filter exhaust from vehicles. (Asheville, NC 7-11-3 (d)(2))

Protection from Vehicles - All interior planting areas shall be protected from vehicle intrusion by a permanent barrier not less than four (4) or more than eight (8) inches high. (Arlington, VA SECTION 32A. 3. Parking Lot Landscaping Design Criteria)

Amount of Planting Required - One deciduous tree and four shrubs are required for every 1,500 square feet of vehicular use area (VUA). At least 75 percent of the required deciduous parking lot trees must be large-maturing trees. Trees and shrubs must be planted within 15 feet of the vehicular use area to count as parking lot landscaping. (Asheville, NC 7-11-3 (d)(4)(b))
When more than four trees are required in a parking lot with interior rows, 50 percent of the trees and shrubs must be planted in islands or medians located within the parking lot. (Asheville, NC 7-11-3 (d)(4)(c))
Each parking space shall be located within 60 feet of a tree as measured from the trunk of the tree to the closest point of the parking space. (Asheville, NC 7-11-3 (d)(4)(h))

Parking Lot Landscape Design (Continued)

Landscape Bulbs - Except where architectural elements extend into required landscape bulbs in parking drives and courts, each landscape bulb should be planted with one or more trees as well as shrubs and/or groundcover. (San Jose, CA Chapter 9: Landscaped Areas Developer Responsibility F. Landscape Bulbs)

Screening

Use natural elements to provide privacy.

Visual Separation - Private Open Space shall be physically and visually separated from common open space through the use of perimeter landscaping and/or fencing. (Eugene, OR 9.5500(8)(c))

Screen & Protect - Tall shrubs or vines should be planted to help screen walls and fences and provide protection from graffiti. (San Jose, CA Chapter 9: Landscaped Areas Developer Responsibility B. Landscaping In Front Of Walls And Fences)

Features to Screen - All dumpsters, loading docks, or utility structures visible from a public street or adjacent property line shall be screened unless already screened by an intervening building or bufferyard. All enclosed outdoor storage areas greater than 25 square feet shall also be screened from adjacent properties and streets. (Asheville, NC Sec. 7-11-3. (6))

Screening Materials - A continuous hedge of evergreen trees and/or densely twigged deciduous trees planted in a seven-foot strip spaced no more than eight feet apart. (Asheville, NC Sec. 7-11-3. (6))
Fence or wall with a minimum height of six feet with the finished side of the fence facing the abutting property or street. Fences longer than 25 linear feet shall be landscaped with trees and/or shrubs planted in a minimum five-foot planting area, except around access areas, spaced no farther than eight feet apart in order to screen at least 50 percent of the fence or wall. (Asheville, NC Sec. 7-11-3. (6))

Relationship with Adjacent Open Space

Capitalize on and integrate with neighboring open space.

Open Space Credit - An open space credit, not to exceed 25 percent of the total open space requirement, may be applied toward compliance with that requirement, for developments that are located within one-quarter mile of a public park. (Eugene, OR 9.5500(9)(c))

Adjacencies - New residential developments adjacent to existing or planned open space should take full advantage of the space and provide maximum visibility. (San Jose, CA Chapter 3: Open Space Interfaces – Intent)

Public Frontage Roads - All new projects adjacent to open spaces (i.e., parks, school fields, riparian corridors, open hillsides) should strive to include adjacent public frontage roads. (San Jose, CA Chapter 3: Open Space Interfaces - Relationship to Surroundings GUIDELINES A. Frontage Roads)

Creeks - Developments along natural creeks are subject to City's Riparian Corridor Development Guidelines. (San Jose, CA Chapter 3: Open Space Interfaces D. Riparian Setbacks)

Setbacks - New buildings should be set back a minimum of 25 feet from parks and public open spaces to reduce the risk of vandalism and theft. Active uses, such as entry walkways or recreation activities, in the setback area are encouraged in order to foster casual surveillance of the transitional area between public and private uses. (San Jose, CA Chapter 3: Open Space Interfaces - Relationship to Surroundings B. Setbacks From Parks)

Integration - Urban open space shall be integrated into the design of the site. (Huntersville, NC Article 7.10.2)

Fences and Walls - No walls or fences are permitted between public open space and roads adjacent to them within a development. (San Jose, CA Chapter 3: Open Space Interfaces C. Limitations on Walls/Fences) Landscaping should be provided by the developer in all setback areas between project walls and/or fences and the rights-of-way of public streets and sidewalks. (San Jose, CA Chapter 9: Landscaped Areas Developer Responsibility B. Landscaping In Front Of Walls And Fences)

Code Guide
Bicycles

Bicycle codes are intended to encourage the use of bicycles by providing safe, convenient, and attractive areas for the circulation and parking of bicycles. The approach taken by the case study cities includes language around bicycle parking requirements, kinds of storage that can be used, the location and specifications of storage, and bicycle access to right of ways.

Topic Header	Codes & Code Reference
Minimum Requirements Require bicycle parking spaces as well as car parking spaces.	**Requirements** - Each city settled on different minimum requirements for bicycle parking. Examples are listed below: 　- One bicycle space per two units (San Jose, CA Chapter 8: Parking L: Bicycle Parking) 　- Equal to 5% of the total number of automobile spaces (Asheville NC, 7-11-2(c)(3)) 　- One bicycle space for every three residential units, one visitor space for every 50 residential units (Arlington VA 'Standard Conditions for High Density Office, Residential and/or Mixed Use Developments' referenced in Zoning Ordinance, Section 36.H) 　- One (1) resident bicycle parking space for every three (3) residential units, or portion thereof, of residential units and one (1) visitor space for every 50 residential units, or portion thereof, of residential units. (Arlington VA 'Standard Conditions for High Density Office, Residential and/or Mixed Use Developments' referenced in Zoning Ordinance, Section 36.H)
Long Term versus Short Term Parking Bicycle parking should be designed with the user in mind.	**Long Term** – Long term bicycle parking space requirements are intended to accommodate employees, students, residents, commuters, and other persons who expect to leave their bicycle parked for more than 2 hours. Long term bicycle parking shall be provided in a well-lighted, secure location within a convenient distance of a main entrance (Eugene, OR 9.6105 (2)(a)) **Short Term** - Short term bicycle parking spaces shall be provided to accommodate visitors, customers, messengers, and other persons expected to depart within approximately 2 hours. (Eugene, OR 9.6105.(4)(b))

Storage Specifications

Accessing and parking a bicycle should be convenient and safe.

Type of Storage
- Inverted-U design bicycle racks (Arlington, VA Clarendon Sector Plan, 2.8)
- Hoop rack (can be used to reduce the required width) (Eugene, OR 9.6105 (2)(b))
- Bicycle locker or other lockable enclosure - (short term doesn't have to be secure but must be a fixed structure that supports the bicycle frame in a stable position without damage) (Asheville, NC 7-11-2(c)(3), Eugene, OR 9.6105 (3)(a))

Location - It is desirable to locate bicycle shortage and parking in locations with these characteristics:
- Highly visible (Arlington, VA, Eugene, OR)
- Convenient to building entrances - shall not be located further than the closest automobile parking space (except disabled parking) (Arlington, VA, Eugene, OR)
- Ground level (Eugene, OR)
- Well-lighted (Eugene, OR)
- Secure (San Jose, CA, Asheville, NC)
- Sheltered from precipitation (Eugene, OR)

Dimensions - Bicycle storage facilities should be at least 6 feet long, 2 feet wide with an overhead clearance of at least 7 feet and a 5 foot access aisle. (Eugene, OR 9.6105 (2)(b))

Access to Right of Ways and Buildings - Bicycle parking should have direct access to right of ways and buildings – direct access with ramps and pedestrian access from parking area to building entrance. (Eugene, OR 9.6105 (2)(d))

Ease & Safety

Bicycling in the development and to neighboring amenities should be convenient and safe.

Consider the use of bike lanes, decals or signage to designate where it is safe for cyclists to travel in the site and remind drivers to use caution and look for cyclists.

Provide basic bike amenities like air pumps, tools, and maps to lower the cost of owning a bike and encourage cycling.

Where possible, connect to neighboring public bike paths and recreational trails.

The Code Guide Appendix is designed to show codes each of the five cities has related to the site design criteria. While the Code Guide earlier in this book deconstructs the intent and approach of the codes and excludes codes if the idea has already been presented, the Code Guide Appendix presents the information without interpretation and in its entirety so you can see how each city's codes work together. This appendix demonstrates the differences between these five progressive cities and can be a resource for other cities considering revisions to their multifamily housing codes. If your city is considering adopting or modeling its code after one of these cities, we suggest you contact them for a complete and updated copy of their development code.

Code Guide Appendix

Arlington, Virginia

San Jose, California

Eugene, Oregon

Huntersville, North Carolina

Asheville, North Carolina

Code Appendix
Arlington, Virginia

Claredon Sector Plan: http://www.arlingtonva.us/departments/CPHD/forums/clarendon/CPHDForumsClarendonMain.aspx

Zoning Ordinances: http://www.arlingtonva.us/Departments/CPHD/planning/zoning/CPHDPlanningZoningOrdinanceCode.aspx

Pedestrian Network

Service/loading and parking access points should not typically be located where build-to lines are specified and should be located along tertiary streets. Where a project does not have frontage on a street designated for a Service/Alley Frontage Type, consideration can be given to alternative locations for service access points where the alternative locations minimize pedestrian and vehicular conflicts. (Clarendon Sector Plan Chapter 3)

Crosswalks. A good pedestrian circulation system continues through each street to the next block with a clearly defined and visible pedestrian walkway. In the R-B Corridor, crosswalks should be marked with white reflective material in a ladder pattern or by a pair of parallel lines. The crosswalk width should be either10-, 12-, or 15-feet wide depending upon the pedestrian volume, traffic speed, and visibility constraints. In most instances, two curb ramps should be placed on each corner with each leading directly into the crosswalk. The path itself should be oriented to be as short as possible, while also directing pedestrians towards the intended corner. (Clarendon Sector Plan Chapter 3)

Street Network

SEE SPECIFIC AREA DISTRICT PLAN for more details

SECTION 25 C-O ROSSLYN COMMERCIAL OFFICE BUILDING, RETAIL, HOTEL AND MULTIPLE-FAMILY DWELLING DISTRICTS

I. Streetscape including curb, gutter, sidewalk, street light, street furniture, landscaping and other elements, shall be provided as contained in the Rosslyn Station Area Plan Addendum, and other plans and policies established for the area by the County Board.

Access Points

None found.

Edges

SECTION 32

D. Placement.

The following regulations shall govern the placement on a lot of any building or structure, or addition thereto, hereafter erected, except as may be allowed by site plan approval:

1. Setbacks: No structure shall be located closer to the centerline of any street or officially designated street right-of-way (as defined in this ordinance) than fifty (50) percent of the height of the building. For the purpose of determining setbacks, a limited access highway shall be considered as an abutting lot and not as a street or street right-of-way. Structures shall be set back from streets no less than as follows: (8-18-79)

a. For all ""C"" and ""M"" Districts excepting ""C-1,"" ""C-1-O,"" "" C-O,"" ""C-H"" and ""C-S-C"": Forty (40) feet from said centerline except for properties located within the "Clarendon Revitalization District" on the General Land Use Plan and zoned "C-3"".

b. For all ""RA4.8"" and ""C-O"" Districts: Fifty (50) feet from said centerline.

c. For all properties that are: (1) located in the "Clarendon Revitalization District" on the General Land Use Plan; and (2) zoned "C-3": 50 feet from the centerline of Fairfax Drive or any street containing more than five lanes, including travel lanes and on-street parking lanes, and 40 feet from the centerline in all other cases. (5-23-06)

d. For all residential structures and all structures in all other districts except for one-and two-family dwellings and their accessory structures regulated by subsection 32.D.1.e.: Fifty (50) feet from said centerline but in no case less than twenty-five (25) feet from any street right-of-way line.

e. For all one- and two-family dwellings and their accessory structures:

(1) No structure shall be located less than twenty-five (25) feet from any street right-of-way line, except that the distance between any street or officially designated street right-of-way line and the front wall of a structure, with the exception of stoops and covered or uncovered but unenclosed porches, may be reduced as follows:

(a) The distance shall be at least the average of the distances between the street right-of-way line, and the edges of the front walls of existing structures located on the frontage where the structure is proposed to be located;

(b) The distance shall be at least fifteen (15) feet, provided, however, that no parking garage shall be located closer than eighteen (18) feet to the street right-of-way line; and

(c) No structure located within twenty-five (25) feet of a street right-of-way line shall exceed two and one-half (2 1/2) stories. (6-9-07)

2. Side and Rear Yards: No structure shall be located closer to side or rear lot lines than as follows:

a. For all ""RA4.8,"" ""C,"" and ""M"" Districts, not including ""C-1-O"": No side or rear yard shall be required except that no wall either on the side or rear of a lot abutting an "" R"" or ""RA"" District or containing openings or windows, whether or not they can be opened, shall be located closer to side or rear lot lines than eight (8) feet for the first ten (10) feet of building height, plus two (2) additional feet for each ten (10) additional feet of building height, or fraction thereof.

b. For all single-family dwellings and their accessory structures: Ten (10) feet, provided that one (1) side yard may be reduced to eight (8) feet. The aggregate width of both side yards on any lot shall not be less than thirty (30) percent of the required width of the lot, provided that on interior lots no structure shall be located closer than twenty-five (25) feet from a rear lot line."

c. For all nonresidential main buildings in ""R"" and ""RA"" Districts: Double the side and rear yard requirements for the district in which said structures are located.

d. For all other residential buildings and for structures in all other districts: Ten (10) feet plus one (1) additional foot for each two and one-half (2 1/2) feet, or fraction thereof, of building height above twenty-five (25) feet, provided that on interior lots no structure shall be located closer than twenty-five (25) feet from a rear lot line.

e. For accessory buildings in ""R"" Districts:

(1) For additions to existing main buildings: No addition shall be located closer than eight (8) feet to any part of an existing accessory building.

(2) For new construction of accessory buildings with heights lower than one and one-half (1 1/2) stories or twenty-five (25) feet, whichever is less, and footprint smaller than five hundred and sixty (560) square feet in ""R-5"" or ""R-6"" Districts, or six hundred and fifty (650) square feet in any other zoning district: No accessory building shall be located closer than eight (8) feet to any part of a main building; on interior lots, no accessory building shall be located closer than one (1) foot to a side or rear lot line and on corner lots, no accessory building shall be located closer than one (1) foot to any side lot line. The provisions of this subsection shall not apply to air-conditioning units.

(3) For accessory buildings of two (2) or more stories, or taller than twenty-five (25) feet, in ""R"" Districts: No such building shall occupy any part of a required rear yard or be located closer than ten (10) feet to any lot line. In addition, no such accessory building shall be located closer than fifteen (15) feet to a main building.

f. For the purpose of side yard regulations, a semidetached dwelling shall be considered as one (1) building occupying one (1) lot.

Parking

SECTION 33. AUTOMOBILE PARKING, STANDING AND LOADING SPACE

Virtually every land use in the County now requires, and in the foreseeable future will require, access by motor vehicles. For the purposes of reducing and avoiding congestion of streets and providing a more suitable living and working environment, it is hereby declared to be the policy of the County that: For every land use hereafter established, there shall be provided sufficient space for access by, and for the off-street standing and parking of, all motor vehicles that may be expected to come to the establishment at any time under normal conditions for any purpose, whether as patrons, customers, purveyors, guests, employees or otherwise.

SECTION 16. RA4.8(C) MULTIPLE-FAMILY DWELLING DISTRICTS

As specified and regulated in Section 33, except that the following may be approved by site plan:

1. Multiple-family dwelling: One (1) off-street space per dwelling unit.

2. The parking provided under the provisions of paragraph C.1., above, shall be located below grade or within the structure housing the use to which the parking is appurtenant, except as may be allowed in an approved site plan.

SECTION 18. RA-H-3.2 MULTIPLE-FAMILY DWELLING AND HOTEL DISTRICTS

C. Parking Requirements

As specified and regulated in Section 33, except that the following may be approved by site plan:

1. Multiple-family Dwelling: One (1) off-street parking space per dwelling unit.

2. Hotel: One (1) off-street parking space for each guest room and dwelling unit.

3. Commercial Uses: One (1) off-street parking space for each three hundred (300) square feet of gross floor area of commercial space provided.

4. The parking provided under the provisions of paragraphs 1., 2., and 3., above shall be located below grade or within the structure housing the use to which the parking is appurtenant, except as may be allowed in an approved site plan.

SECTION 25. C-O COMMERCIAL OFFICE BUILDING, HOTEL AND MULTIPLE-FAMILY DWELLING DISTRICTS

C. Parking Requirements

As specified and regulated in Section 33, except that the following may be approved by site plan: 2. Multiple-family Dwelling: One (1) off-street parking space for each dwelling unit. 4. The parking provided under the provisions of paragraphs 1., 2., and 3., above, shall be located below grade or within the structure housing the use to which the parking is appurtenant, except as may be allowed in an approved site plan.

SECTION 25B. C-O ROSSLYN COMMERCIAL OFFICE BUILDING, RETAIL, HOTEL AND MULTIPLE-FAMILY DWELLING DISTRICTS

F. Parking Requirements

Parking shall be regulated as specified and regulated in Section 33, and as specified below, except that the County Board may specify and modify parking regulations by Site Plan Approval:

1. Dwelling unit: One (1) off-street parking space shall be provided for each dwelling unit.

2. Transportation Demand Management plans shall be required to be approved as part of any site plan approval unless determined otherwise by the County Board. Office, retail and service commercial parking may be approved within a range between the rate of one (1) off-street parking space for each five hundred thirty (530) square feet of office, retail and service commercial gross floor area and the rate of one (1) off-street parking space for each one thousand (1,000) square feet of office, retail and service commercial gross floor area depending on the adequacy of the

Transportation Demand Management plan in addressing the need for parking. Short-term, convenient parking shall be provided for customers of commercial tenant retailers when the business premises are open to the public for business.

3. Hotel: Seven-tenths (0.7) off-street parking space for each guest room and dwelling unit.

4. The parking provided shall be located below grade or within the structure housing the use to which the parking is appurtenant, except as may be allowed in an approved site plan.

5. Off-street loading spaces for all permitted uses shall be provided as specified in SECTION 32A. 3. Parking Lot Landscaping Design Criteria: SEE LANDSCAPING

Section 33. Section 33 General Requirements: The requirements set forth in this article with respect to the location or improvement of parking, standing and loading space shall apply to all such space that is provided for any use, whether said space is provided in accordance with the requirements of this ordinance, or said space is voluntarily provided. Off-street parking, standing and loading space shall comply with the following regulations:

1. Use and Parking on Same Lot: Off-street parking and off-street loading space appurtenant to any use permitted in "R" and "RA" Districts shall be provided on the same parcel of land occupied by the use to which said space is appurtenant or on common areas in the same subdivision.

2. Off-site Parking: All off-street parking space appurtenant to any use other than a use permitted in an ""R"" and ""RA"" District shall be on the same parcel of land with the use to which it is appurtenant or on common areas in the same subdivision; provided, however, that where there are practical difficulties in the way of such location of parking space or if the public safety or the public convenience, or both, would be better served by the location thereof other than on the same parcel of land with the use to which it is appurtenant, the Zoning Administrator, acting on a specific application, shall authorize such alternative location of required parking space as will adequately serve the public interest, subject to the following conditions:

a. Such space shall be located on land in the same ownership as that of the land on which is located the use to which such space is appurtenant or, in the case of parking for certain restaurants, shall conform to the requirements in Section 33.C.3. of the Zoning Ordinance.

b. A pedestrian entrance to such space shall be located within a distance of six hundred (600) feet, by the shortest route of effective pedestrian access, entrance to entrance.

c. Such space shall be conveniently usable without causing unreasonable:

(1) Hazard to pedestrians.

(2) Hazard to vehicular traffic.

(3) Traffic congestion.

(4) Interference with safe and convenient access to other parking areas in the vicinity.

(5) Detriment to the appropriate use of business property in the vicinity.

(6) Detriment to any residential neighborhood.

Street Design

SEE SPECIFIC AREA DISTRICT PLAN for more details

SECTION 25 C-O ROSSLYN COMMERCIAL OFFICE BUILDING, RETAIL, HOTEL AND MULTIPLE-FAMILY DWELLING DISTRICTS

I. Streetscape including curb, gutter, sidewalk, street light, street furniture, landscaping and other elements, shall be provided as contained in the Rosslyn Station Area Plan Addendum, and other plans and policies established for the area by the County Board.

Building Massing & Orientation

2006 CLARENDON SECTOR PLAN

C. 2. Building Orientation and Frontage Types. Address the rhythm of building entries, level of transparency, relationship of building entries to sidewalk grade, minimum structural clear heights and minimum interior ceiling heights, and permitted projections beyond the specified build-to lines Generally, buildings should be oriented with the main façades and primary building entrances facing main and secondary streets and service and parking access points facing tertiary streets. Consideration may be given to adjusting orientation in order to make a new structure compatible with an historic structure and/or façade.

SEE SPECIFIC AREA DISTRICT PLAN for more details

SECTION 32. BULK, COVERAGE AND PLACEMENT REQUIREMENTS

Virtually every land use requires an appropriate relationship between lot area and intensity of use, and sufficient open space surrounding such use, to secure safety from fire, panic and other dangers; to ensure privacy; to lessen congestion in the streets; to promote health and the general welfare; to provide adequate light and air; to prevent the overcrowding of land; to avoid undue concentration of population; to facilitate adequate provision for transportation, drainage and other public requirements; to conserve the value of buildings and encourage the most appropriate use of land.

RA4.8(C) MULTIPLE-FAMILY DWELLING DISTRICTS

D. Height Limit. As regulated in the ""RA14-26"" District, except that by site plan approval, a building may have a maximum height of one hundred thirty-six (136) feet, including penthouses and parapet walls, measured from the average elevation at the perimeter of the site.

RA-H-3.2 MULTIPLE-FAMILY DWELLING AND HOTEL DISTRICTS

D. Height Limit. As regulated in the ""RA14-26"" District, except that by site plan approval, a building may have a maximum height of one hundred eighty (180) feet, including penthouses and parapet walls, measured from the average elevation at the perimeter of the site.

C-O COMMERCIAL OFFICE BUILDING, HOTEL AND MULTIPLE-FAMILY DWELLING DISTRICTS

D. Height Limit. Thirty-five (35) feet, except that the following may be approved by site plan:

1. Office and commercial buildings: A maximum height of one hundred fifty-three (153) feet, including penthouse and parapet walls, measured from the average elevation at the perimeter of the site.

2. Multiple-family and hotel buildings: A maximum height of one hundred eighty (180) feet, including penthouses and parapet walls, measured from the average elevation at the perimeter of the site.

**Open Space &
Landscape Design**

SEE SPECIFIC AREA DISTRICT PLAN for more details

SECTION 32A. LANDSCAPING

The purpose of this section is to provide landscaping in order to better control and ameliorate problems of air and noise pollution, afford wind protection, help moderate temperature extremes, to increase property values and attract prosperous business activities into the County and to make the County a healthier and more aesthetically pleasing place to live, shop and work. It is the further intent of this section to provide minimum standards for the selection of plant materials to ensure their survival.

SECTION 25 C-O ROSSLYN COMMERCIAL OFFICE BUILDING, RETAIL, HOTEL AND MULTIPLE-FAMILY DWELLING DISTRICTS

H. Landscaping. Twenty (20) percent of total site area is required to be landscaped open space in accordance with the requirements of Section 32A, ""Landscaping"". The County Board may modify landscaping requirements by site plan approval when the County Board finds that the proposed site plan accomplishes the policies and recommendations contained in the Rosslyn Station Area Plan Addendum and other plans and policies established for the area by the County Board.

SECTION 32A.

B. Additional Landscaping Requirements for Parking Areas, Public and Private.

3. Parking Lot Landscaping Design Criteria:

a. All end islands of parking rows and all areas not otherwise used for ingress, egress, aisles or parking must be landscaped.

b. The interior space of any planting area shall be no less than nine (9) square feet and not narrower than two (2) feet across its center.

c. The primary landscaping materials used in parking lots shall be deciduous trees which are capable of providing shade at maturity. Shrubbery, hedges and other live plant materials are to be used to complement the tree landscaping. Effective use of berms and existing topography is also encouraged as a component of the landscape plan.

d. All interior planting areas shall be protected from vehicle intrusion by a permanent barrier not less than four (4) nor more than eight (8) inches high.

e. In those instances where plant material exists on a parking lot site prior to its development, such landscape material may be used if approved as meeting the landscaping requirements of this subsection.

Bicycles

Fairfax County Department of Planning and Zoning Arlington Bicycle Storage Facility Requirements

Bicycle Storage Facilities. The developer agrees to provide, at no charge to the user, secure bicycle storage facilities in locations convenient to office, residential (except for townhouses) and retail areas on the following basis at a minimum:

Office and Residential Bicycle Storage Facilities:

One (1) employee bicycle parking space for every 7,500 square feet, or portion thereof, of office floor area and one (1) additional such visitor space for every 20,000 square feet, or portion thereof, of office floor area.

One (1) resident bicycle parking space for every three (3) residential units, or portion thereof, of residential units and one (1) visitor space for every 50 residential units, or portion thereof, of residential units.

Install "Inverted-U" design bicycle racks in highly visible locations convenient to building entrances in retail and office centers; and Enhance bicycle parking.

Retail Bicycle Storage Facilities:

Two (2) retail visitor/customer bicycle parking spaces for every 10,000 square feet, or portion thereof, of the first 50,000 square feet of retail floor area; one (1) additional retail visitor/customer space for every 12,500 square feet, or portion thereof, of additional retail floor area; and one (1) additional retail employee space for every 25,000 square feet, or portion thereof, of retail floor area. The retail visitor/customer bicycle spaces shall be installed at exterior locations that are convenient to the retail visitors/customer.

Code Appendix
San Jose, California

http://www.sanjoseca.gov/documentcenter/home/view/439

Pedestrian Network

Chapter 16: Miscellaneous Details. A. Access To Transit Facilities New residential projects should be designed with a pedestrian circulation element that provides a direct connection from project units to adjacent transit facilities such as bus stops and light rail stations.

Chapter 23: Cluster Housing. E. Balcony/Corridor Circulation Common exterior balconies and corridors that provide access to units should not require circulation past adjacent unit windows and entries. (I) Security Fences And Gates Security fences and gates are strongly discouraged in any residential project. If extraordinary circumstances warrant security fences they should comply with the guidelines in Chapter 4 "Perimeter Walls and Fences".

Chapter 25: Mixed Use Development. (A) Pedestrian Orientation Mixed use projects should include direct and attractive pedestrian access to all nearby commercial areas, transit stops and transit stations. Sidewalks and walkways should be wide, separated from conflicting activities and bordered by attractive landscaping, most importantly by street and/or shade trees. (G) 2. Connective elements such as walkways, common landscaped areas, building orientation, and unfenced property lines should be employed, and are strongly encouraged. 3. Particular care should be taken to assure convenient pedestrian access through all parts of a project to nearby transit facilities.

Street Network

Chapter 6: Streets - Internal Organization Guidelines. A. Continuity of Streets Public streets should be aligned so that they are continuous through adjacent existing and planned residential development, creating a network of neighborhood streets.

Access Points

Chapter 25: Mixed Use Development. (A) Pedestrian Orientation.

Mixed use projects should include direct and attractive pedestrian access to all nearby commercial areas, transit stops and transit stations.

Edges

Chapter 4: Perimeter Walls & Fences - Relationship to Surroundings. A. Height Fences and walls should be no more than 7 feet high, except when adjacent to freeways, expressways, railroads, incompatible uses, or when they are required for sound attenuation. Where the fence is engaged to a retaining wall, this guideline may require special interpretation.

C. Non-Permissible Locations Solid walls and fences are not permitted between public streets and common open spaces including public or semi-public areas within a project.

E. Pedestrian Gates: Gates in walls or fences over 100 feet in length between public streets or open spaces and public or semi-public areas within a project are encouraged.

J. Neighborhood Compatibility Front yard fencing higher than 3 feet should not be introduced on streets that have an existing pattern of residences fronting onto the street. Such fencing should be avoided or minimized to continue the front yard pattern of the surrounding neighborhood.

Chapter 5: Perimeter Setbacks - Relationship to Surroundings
A. Setbacks From Perimeter Streets identifies setback standards for key project elements that are adjacent to existing and proposed perimeter streets. Setbacks identified in Chapter I "Existing Neighborhoods" may supersede setbacks identified on this table. Exceptions to the setbacks listed in this table may be appropriate for projects covered by approved specific plans such as Communications Hill, Tamien, Midtown and Jackson-Taylor.

B. Perimeter Setbacks From Adjacent Uses Table 5.b identifies the setback standards for key project elements from existing uses immediately adjacent to the project perimeter. Setback dimensions are measured from common property lines. Setbacks identified in Chapter 1 ""Existing Neighborhoods"" may supersede setbacks identified in this table.

Parking

Attached unit projects, which do not include enclosed garages, should provide secure parking facilities (one bicycle space per two units) to encourage the use of bicycles instead of automobiles

Chapter 8: Parking. L. Bicycle Parking Attached unit projects, which do not include enclosed garages, should provide secure parking facilities (one bicycle space per two units) to encourage the use of bicycles instead of automobiles.

Chapter 16: Miscellaneous Details. C. Bicycle Parking Attached unit projects, which do not provide private enclosed garages, should provide secure bicycle parking facilities (one bicycle space per two units) to encourage the use of bicycles instead of automobiles (Fig. 16-2).

Street Design

Chapter 2: Street Frontage. Guidelines. A. Building Setbacks Front building setbacks are required for most housing types to buffer living areas from the public activity of the street and to provide space for landscaping in the configuration associated with traditional residential neighborhoods. Buildings containing living areas should be set back at least 35 feet from major streets, freeways, and expressways (25 feet minimum if average is 40 feet, or 25 feet behind a sound attenuation wall). The 35-foot setback may be reduced on major streets if such a reduction is consistent with their existing or projected urban character

B. Reduced Building Setbacks Zero or reduced building setbacks from the street may be more appropriate for higher density housing types in areas near downtown, along streets with established reduced setback patterns and in areas with specific plans which call for reduced setbacks to reinforce the planned urban character of the neighborhood.

E. Limitations On Parking Frontage To strengthen the presence of buildings on the street, circulation elements and parking areas in the front setback area and/or adjacent to the street should extend across no more than 50 percent of the street frontage (Fig. 2-1). Fig. 2-1: Parking areas should not comprise more than 50% of the elements along a project's street frontage.

F. Street Trees The developer should plant street trees of an approved species and size along all public and private streets. There should be at least one tree for approximately every 25 feet of street frontage, depending on species, or at least one tree for each lot abutting the street.

H. Provisions to Accommodate Bicycle Traffic For larger streets (other than Limited Access Streets, Narrow Residential Streets and Minor Residential Streets) as determined appropriate by the Department of Streets and Traffic and City Council Policy, the width of one travel lane in each direction should be expanded by an additional five feet to provide space for bicycle travel.

I. Wider Sidewalks to Accommodate Heavier Pedestrian Demand In street rights-of-way serving higher density residential development or located in more urban, pedestrian oriented areas of the City, sidewalks should be at least 6 to 10 feet in width, depending on adjacent densities and expectations for pedestrian activity.

Building Massing & Orientation

Chapter 11: Building Façade A. Façade Articulation All building façades containing 3 or more attached dwellings in a row should incorporate at least one of the following: 1. At least one architectural projection per unit. Such a projection must project no less than 2 feet 6 inches from the major wall plane, must be between 4 feet 6 inches and 15 feet wide, and must extend the full height of a one-story building, at least one-half the height of a two-story building, and two-thirds the height of a three-story building. On buildings three stories in height, projecting elements may be linked by one level of living space at the top or bottom floor 2. A change in wall plane of at least 3 feet for at least 12 feet every 2 units.

C. Building Length Extremely long buildings, if they are richly articulated, may be acceptable; however, buildings (including garages and carports) exceeding 150 feet in length are generally discouraged.

D. Building Materials And Details The exterior materials and architectural details of a single building should relate to each other in ways that are traditional and/or logical. For example, heavy materials should appear to support lighter ones.

Chapter 25: Mixed Use Development H. Building & Site Design, Horizontal Mixed Use Horizontal mixed use projects will typically have multiple buildings as well as multiple uses. Buildings should have a positive functional relationship with each other as well as an aesthetically pleasing spatial relationship: 1. The exterior building design, including roof style, color, materials, architectural form and detailing, should be consistent, or at least compatible, among all buildings in a complex and on all elevations of each building to achieve design harmony and continuity within the project and with its surroundings.

Chapter 25: Mixed Use Development

E. Building Orientation. Buildings should be oriented parallel to the street particularly at comers. Buildings and, in particular, entrances should be oriented toward light rail stations and bus stops for convenient access by public transit passengers.

F. Relationship to the Street Active connections between buildings and the street, for example residential and retail entries, porches, stairs, decks, courtyards, and windows, should be maximized.

C. Building Orientation The major orientation of buildings nearest the street should be parallel to that street or to the prevailing pattern of existing property lines. This guideline is not intended to limit either the inclusion of architectural elements, articulation, or embellishments that may not align with the street or the inclusion in large projects of minor buildings that do not align with the street.

D. Building Façades If a side or rear elevation faces or is substantially visible from a street, it should be designed with the same care and attention to detail, and in the same material, as the front (see Chapter 11 "Building Design").

G. Street Presence Residential buildings located away from the street, as on flag lots, should maintain a presence to the street. This may be achieved by placing the rear building so that it is visible from the street (Fig. 2-2).

Open Space &
Landscape Design

"New residential developments adjacent to existing or planned open space should take full advantage of the space and provide maximum visibility. All new projects adjacent to open spaces (i.e. parks, school fields, riparian corridors, open hillsides) should strive to include adjacent public frontage roads. No walls or fences are permitted between public open space and roads adjacent to them within a development.

When a frontage road is not possible, residential buildings should be oriented to the open space, with a minimum setback of 25'. It is intended to encourage a neighborhood watch and garages that block these areas should be avoided.

Development along natural creeks are subject to City's Riparian Corridor Development Guidelines.

1. Minimum setback of 100'.

2. Public recreation areas/passive use areas may be located adjacent to the riparian corridor, subject to site inspections

3. Any vegetation within setback area should be native/compatible with the trees, shrubs, groundcover with the riparian corridor type

4. Areas with night lighting must have a 200' separation

5. Where lighting is required for safety, low light and light directed down and not visible from the riparian corridor is preferable

6. Fences along riparian corridors should be intended for the protection of the area from public or pets, or critical to security of development. Fences should be no higher than 3' or 4' and should not obstruct views.

Chapter 3: Open Space Interfaces - Relationship to Surroundings GUIDELINES

A. Frontage Roads All new projects adjacent to or which include parks, school playfields, riparian corridors and open hillsides should be designed to incorporate public frontage roads adjacent to such features.

B. Setbacks From Parks Where a frontage road is not feasible, residential buildings and the private open spaces associated with them should be oriented to the park. New buildings should be set back a minimum of 25 feet from parks and public open spaces to reduce the risk of vandalism and theft. Active uses, such as entry walkways or recreation activities, in the setback area are encouraged in order to foster casual surveillance of the transitional area between public and private uses. Garages and carports that substantially block visibility between proposed residential units and parks are discouraged.

C. Limitations On Walls/Fences No walls or solid fences will be permitted between public open spaces and roads adjacent to them within a project.

Chapter 23: Cluster Housing F. Open Space There should be a minimum of 60 square feet of private open space and 200 square feet of usable common open space for every dwelling unit. Required common open space per unit may be reduced by an area equivalent to the amount of private open space in excess of 60 square feet. Projects with fewer than eight units need not have common open space, provided that each ground floor unit has at least 120 square feet of private open space.

Chapter 9: Landscaped Areas Developer Responsibility

A. Landscaping should be provided by the developer in all planted areas except within private rear yards or patios and within single-family detached lots which are 4,000 square feet or larger. For single-family detached lots less than 4,000 square feet and for paired dwellings, rowhouses and courthomes, the developer should install landscaping and irrigation in the front yards, parkstrips and common areas. All landscaping should be planted and maintained in accordance with the City's Landscape and Irrigation Guidelines.

B. Landscaping In Front Of Walls And Fences Landscaping should be provided by the developer in all setback areas between project walls and/or fences and the rights-of-way of public streets and sidewalks. This landscaping should be generous and should include trees and/or shrubs as well as groundcover. Tall shrubs or vines should be planted to help screen walls and fences and provide protection from graffiti. All slopes should include sufficient erosion control measures to prevent the loss of topsoil.

C. Frontage Roads And Landscaping Islands or medians that separate frontage roads from public streets should be planted with trees and shrubs of sufficient density to form a solid screen at least 5 feet high and a continuous tree canopy.

D. Street Trees The developer should plant street trees of an approved species and size along all public and private streets. There should be at least one tree for approximately every 25 feet of street frontage, depending on species, or at least one tree for each lot abutting the street. The City's street tree planting standards should be used. Solid screen and continuous tree canopy between frontage road and street.

E. Open Space Setback Landscaping Private rear yards, patios, and balconies should be provided with an extra 10 to 20 feet of landscaped setback when adjacent to incompatible uses or close existing decks or balconies.

F. Landscape Bulbs Except where architectural elements extend into required landscape bulbs in parking drives and courts, each landscape bulb should be planted with one or more trees as well as shrubs and/or groundcover.

Chapter 23: Cluster Housing. C. Landscape Areas (Interior Use Separations) Within a cluster housing project, landscaped areas of the following dimensions should be provided to separate the following site elements: Residential building from parking areas, drives, Residential building (unit entrance side) from drives without parking 10 feet (1) (unit entrance side) carports or parking, 15 feet Residential building (garage entrance side) from drives 0 feet (2) Residential building faces having no entries from parking areas, drives or sidewalks 10 feet (1) This 10 feet should remain clear of stairways and patios. (2) A nine (net) square-foot planter area containing a tree or large shrub located between every two parking stalls or at least every 20 feet should be provided. Due to the small size of these landscape pockets, no utilities or meter boxes should be placed in them. Walkways or sidewalks between buildings and parking areas, carports and driveways may not be counted as part of the minimum dimension for a landscaped area.

Chapter 25: Mixed Use Development. L. Residential Open Space Private open space should be provided at a minimum of 60 square feet per unit with a minimum dimension of 6 feet. Common open space should be provided at a minimum of 100 square feet per unit (see Chapter 10 "Common and Private Open Space").

Bicycles

Attached unit projects, which do not include enclosed garages, should provide secure parking facilities (one bicycle space per two units) to encourage the use of bicycles instead of automobiles)

Chapter 8: Parking L. Bicycle Parking Attached unit projects, which do not include enclosed garages, should provide secure parking facilities (one bicycle space per two units) to encourage the use of bicycles instead of automobiles.

Chapter 16: Miscellaneous Details

C. Bicycle Parking Attached unit projects, which do not provide private enclosed garages, should provide secure bicycle parking facilities (one bicycle space per two units) to encourage the use of bicycles instead of automobiles (Fig. 16-2).

Pedestrian Network

9.6730(1) Purpose of Pedestrian Circulation On-Site.
These standards are intended to provide safe and efficient circulation for pedestrians within all developments.

9.6730(2) Applicability of Standards.
As more specifically provided in this section, the standards in this section apply to any development that creates a new building entrance, but not to a building alteration or change in use.

a. In any zone, except I-2 and I-3, on-site pedestrian paths shall be constructed in the following cases for institutional, office, commercial and industrial development:

1. Between all new building entrances and all streets adjacent to the development site. On-site pedestrian paths shall be designed and constructed to provide a direct connection to existing public right-of-way and public accessways.

2. To connect any new building entrances on a development site to all other new and existing building entrances on the same development site, except entrances used primarily for loading and unloading freight.

3. Along the exterior walls of new buildings greater than 100 feet in length when the wall of the building is located next to a street, parking lot or when a public entrance or entrances are located on the edge of the building, except in the following cases:

a. When the edge of a building is within 20 feet of a public sidewalk and the building entrance is connected to the public sidewalk by an on-site pedestrian facility, no on-site pedestrian facility on the edge of the building adjacent to the sidewalk is required.

b. When the edge of the building is bordered by a perimeter of landscaping which does not exceed 30 feet in width, and an on-site pedestrian facility is constructed at the edge of the landscaping, no on-site pedestrian facility immediately adjacent to the landscaped building edge is required.

4. To connect institutional, office, commercial and industrial uses on the development site to adjacent existing or planned institutional, office, commercial or industrial uses, and to existing or planned transit stops, schools, or neighborhood parks where the addition of on-site pedestrian paths would reduce walking or cycling distance between the uses by 200 feet and by at least 50 percent over other available pedestrian routes.

5. Along any development site, an on-site pedestrian facility connecting the street to the main building(s) shall be provided for every 300 feet of street frontage or for every 8 rows of vehicle parking, or for whichever standard requires the most on-site pedestrian paths.
(b) In industrial developments on I-1 zoned property, on-site pedestrian paths shall be constructed in the following cases:

1. Between the main building entrance and all streets adjacent to the development site. On-site pedestrian paths shall be designed and constructed to provide a direct connection to existing public right-of-way and public accessways.

2. To connect the main building entrance on the development site to adjacent existing or planned office, commercial or industrial uses, and to existing or planned transit stops where the addition of the on-site pedestrian facility would reduce walking or cycling distance between the uses by 200 feet and by at least 50 percent over other available pedestrian routes.   (c)
In all zones, on-site pedestrian paths shall be constructed within new multiple-family residential developments with 3 or more units to insure that access is provided:

1. From every unit to all other units within the residential development.

2. From every unit to all laundry, recreational and other community facilities in the residential development.

3. From every building located within 40 feet of a public or private street to the street right-of-way line.

9.6730(3) Design of On-Site Pedestrian Facilities. All on-site pedestrian paths provided for the purposes of complying with this land use code shall conform with the following standards:

(a) On-site pedestrian paths shall provide direct access from public ways to building entrances.

(b) On-site pedestrian paths shall be constructed of concrete, a comparable hard surface material, or any properly designed pervious surface that complies with the Americans with Disabilities Act.

(c) On-site pedestrian paths shall be raised to standard curb height when adjacent to public and private streets or driveways.

(d) On-site pedestrian paths intersected by driving aisles shall be marked with striping or constructed with a contrasting paving material to indicate a pedestrian crossing area.

(e) Pedestrian scale lighting in conformance with the standards in EC 9.6725 Outdoor Lighting Standards shall be provided along pedestrian facilities.

9.6730(4) Adjustment. These standards may be adjusted if consistent with the criteria of EC 9.8030(22) See Block Requirement EC 9.8030(8)(d)(1).

Street Network

9.5500(11)(a) Streets

Street standards and connectivity requirements for local residential streets shall be applied to public and private streets within multiple-family developments. (Refer to EC 9.6815 Connectivity for Streets.). (See Figure 9.5500(12) Multiple-Family Parking.)

9.5500(11)(b) Driveways

Driveways and parking drives are private roadways for projects or portions of projects not served by streets. Driveways and parking drives shall be designed in accordance with the following standards:

1. Driveways. Driveways provide vehicular access to parking and dwelling units but do not provide primary pedestrian access to units. Driveways are intended to be used primarily for vehicular circulation and dwelling access and should be visually distinct from streets. (See Figure 9.5500(11)(b) Multiple-Family Driveways). The following standards apply:

a. Two-way driveways shall be a minimum width of 20 feet, one-way driveways shall be a minimum width of 12 feet. The maximum driveway width is 28 feet.

b. All driveways shall be perpendicular to the street they connect to and shall be constructed with a 10- to 15-foot curb radius.

c. On lots without alley access, driveway connections to public streets shall be limited as specified in Table 9.5500(11)(b)1.c. Multiple-Family Driveway Standards for Lots Without Alley Access.

2. Parking Drives. Parking drives are driveways lined with head-in parking spaces, diagonal parking spaces, garages, or any combination thereof along a significant portion of their length. Parking drives for multiple-family developments with more than 20 units shall be designed so as to permit no through-motor vehicle movements. (See Figure 9.5500(12) Multiple-Family Parking.)

9.5500(11)(c) Alley Access

Development sites with alley access, either at the rear yard or along the side yard, shall use the alley to provide access to the development site. In these instances, no direct access to the street, other than by the alley, shall be permitted. (See Figure 9.5500(11)(b) Multiple-Family Driveways.)

Access Points

On-site pedestrian paths shall be designed and constructed to provide a direct connection to existing public right-of-way and public accessways.

To connect institutional, office, commercial and industrial uses on the development site to adjacent existing or planned institutional, office, commercial or industrial uses, and to existing or planned transit stops, schools, or neighborhood parks where the addition of on-site pedestrian paths would reduce walking or cycling distance between the uses by 200 feet and by at least 50 percent over other available pedestrian routes.

Edges

9.5500 (4) Minimum and Maximum Building Setbacks.

(a) Required Setbacks. The required building setbacks are those required in the applicable base zone.

(b) Street Frontage. On development sites that will result in 100 feet or more of public or private street frontage, at least 60 percent of the site frontage abutting the street (including required yards) shall be occupied by a building(s) or enhanced pedestrian space with no more than 20 percent of the 60 percent in enhanced pedestrian space, placed within 10 feet of the minimum front yard setback line. (See Figure 9.5500(4)(b) Multiple-Family Minimum Building Setback Along Streets.) On development sites with less than 100 feet of public or private street frontage, at least 40 % of the site width shall be occupied by a building(s) placed within 10 feet of the minimum front yard setback line. Building projections and offsets with an offset interval of 10 feet or less meet this standard (excluding required yards). "Site width," as used in this standard, shall not include areas of street frontage that have significant natural resources as mapped by the city, delineated wetlands, slopes greater than 15%, recorded easements, required fire lanes or other similar non-buildable areas, as determined by the planning director.

Parking

9.5500(12)(a) Parking Element Types
The city shall allow on-site parking to be provided as part of any multiple-family development project in the form of garages (private or common), carports, open parking areas. All parking, except common garages, shall be designed as parking courts according to EC 9.5500(12)(b) Parking Courts.

9.5500(12)(b) Parking Courts

1. Maximum Size of Parking Courts. Individual parking courts shall be no more than 9,000 square feet in size and shall be physically and visually separated by a landscape area a minimum of 20 feet in width. No more than 3 individual parking courts may be connected by an aisle or driveway. (See Figure 9.5500(12) Multiple-Family Parking and Multiple-Family Parking Continued.)

2. Parking Court Width. A parking court of any length shall consist of no more than one 1 double-loaded parking aisle.

3. Parking Court Separation. Planting islands shall be placed between parking courts to visually interrupt rows of parked vehicles and to separate individual parking courts. Planting islands between parking courts shall have a minimum width of 20 feet and a minimum area of 360 square feet. Each of these islands shall provide at least 1 canopy shade tree having a clear trunk height of at least 9 feet. Architectural elements such as trellises, porches, and stairways may extend into planting islands between parking courts. Other parking area landscape standards in EC 9.6420 Parking Area Standards also apply. (See Figure 9.5500(12)(b) Multiple-Family Parking Courts).

9.5500(12)(c) Limitations on Parking Frontage
To strengthen the presence of buildings on the street, parking and vehicle use areas and garages adjacent to any public or private street frontage shall extend across no more than 50 percent of any street frontage. No parking spaces, with the exception of underground parking, shall be placed within any required front yard area. Parking areas shall not be located between buildings and the street. A single-story street level parking garage may not occupy the street frontage of a multiple-family development, except for parking garage driveways.

EC 9.8030(8)(f). Vehicle Parking.

The requirements set forth in EC 9.5500(12) may be adjusted if the proposal achieves to the same degree as would strict compliance with the standards all of the following:

1. Limitations on the use of continuous parking drives in large-scale multiple-family developments.

2. Limitations on the size of individual parking lots in multiple-family development.

3. Minimal negative aspects of parking uses in multiple-family developments.

Where cost considerations preclude parking beneath or within residential buildings, combinations of partial and interrupted parking drives; on-street parking; and small, dispersed parking courts are an acceptable alternative.

Street Design

9.5500(11)(a) Streets

Street standards and connectivity requirements for local residential streets shall be applied to public and private streets within multiple-family developments. (Refer to EC 9.6815 Connectivity for Streets.) (See Figure 9.5500(12) Multiple-Family Parking.)

9.5500(11)(d) Setback Sidewalks
Setback sidewalks shall be required along any public or private street adjacent to or within the development site.

9.5500(11)(e) Adjustments to the standards in this subsection may be made, based on the criteria of EC 9.8030(8)(e).

EC 9.8030(8)(e). Site Access and Internal Circulation.

The requirements set forth in EC 9.5500(11) may be adjusted in accordance with the criteria in this subsection. In the case of an adjustment, all of the following standards apply:

1. Sidewalks may be designed as curbside walks only along those portions of the private streets providing parallel on-street parking.

2. Street trees may be placed in tree wells or adjacent to the sidewalk.

Building Massing & Orientation

9.5500 (3)

The maximum building heights allowed are those permitted according to the applicable base zone.

9.5500(4)(b)

On development sites that will result in 100 feet or more of public or private street frontage, at least 60 percent of the site frontage abutting the street (including required yards) shall be occupied by a building(s) or enhanced pedestrian space with no more than 20 percent of the 60 percent in enhanced pedestrian space, placed within 10 feet of the minimum front yard setback line. (See Figure 9.5500(4)(b) Multiple-Family Minimum Building Setback Along Streets.) On development sites with less than 100 feet of public or private street frontage, at least 40 % of the site width shall be occupied by a building(s) placed within 10 feet of the minimum front yard setback line. Building projections and offsets with an offset interval of 10 feet or less meet this standard (excluding required yards). "Site width," as used in this standard, shall not include areas of street frontage that have significant natural resources as mapped by the city, delineated wetlands, slopes greater than 15%, recorded easements, required fire lanes or other similar non-buildable areas, as determined by the planning director.

9.5500(5)(a)

Multiple-family residential buildings located within 40 feet of a front lot line shall have their primary orientation toward the street.

9.5500(5)(b)

The main entrance(s) of ground floor units of any residential building located within 40 feet of a street must face the front lot line. Main entrances may provide access to individual units, clusters of units, courtyard dwellings, or common lobbies. The following exceptions shall apply: 1. On corner lots the main building entrance(s) may face either of the streets or be oriented to the corner.

2. For buildings that have more than 1 entrance serving multiple units, only 1 entrance must meet this requirement.

3. For buildings proposed to be "side oriented" to public streets due to access requirements and/or dimensional constraints not created by the applicant, main entries may face up to 90 degrees away from the street provided both of the following apply:

a. They are visible from the street.

b. The building side facing the street shall not include windows or views into a parking area or garage and shall contain windows that occupy a minimum of 15% of the façade.

9.5500(5)(c)

The main entrance of upper story units shall be provided from the interior of the building or from an exterior walkway that serves no more than 2 units. Stairways to upper floors shall be adequately lighted and protected from the elements. Access to upper-story units may be provided at the front, side or rear of a building.

EC 9.8030(4) Building Orientation and Entrance Standards Adjustment.

Where this land use code provides that building orientation and entrance standards may be adjusted, the standards may be adjusted upon finding that the proposal complies with one of the following:

(a) Promotes compatibility with adjacent property.

(b) Creates building orientations and entrances that achieve all of the following:

1. Support and augment the building setback, massing and architectural details.

2. Achieve an attractive streetscape with a strong building presence on existing and future streets.

3. In the case of multiple-family developments, provides socialization benefits to residents.

9.5500(6)(a) Maximum Building Dimension
Neither the maximum length nor width of any building within 40 feet of a front lot line can exceed 100 feet in the R-1 and R-2 zones and 150 feet in all other zones.

9.5500(6)(b) Windows

Street façades shall contain windows covering a minimum of 15% of the façade on each floor level.

9.5500(6)(c)
Adjustments to the standards in this subsection may be made, based on criteria of EC 9.8030(8)(a).

EC 9.8030(8)(a). Maximum Building Dimension.

The requirements set forth in EC 9.5500(6)(a) may be adjusted if the proposal creates building massing and/or façades that:

1. Create a vibrant street façade with visual detail.

2. Provide multiple entrances to building or yards.

9.5500(7)(a)

To preclude large expanses of uninterrupted wall surfaces, exterior elevations of buildings shall incorporate design features such as offsets, projections, balconies, bays, windows, entries, porches, porticos, or similar elements.

1. Horizontal Surface. At least 2 of the design features outlined above shall be incorporated along the horizontal face (side to side) of the structure, to be repeated at intervals of no more than 40 feet.

2. Vertical Surface. At least 2 of the design features outlined above shall be incorporated along the vertical face (top to bottom) of the structure, to be repeated at intervals of no more than 25 feet.

9.5500(7)(b)

When offsets and projections are used to fulfill articulation requirements, the offset or projection shall vary from other wall surfaces by a minimum of 2 feet. Such changes in plane shall have a minimum width of 6 feet.

9.5500(7)(c)

Individual and common entry ways shall be articulated by roofs, awnings, or porticos.

9.5500(7)(c)

Individual and common entry ways shall be articulated by roofs, awnings, or porticos.

9.5500(7)(d)

Adjustments to the standards in this subsection may be made, based on criteria of EC 9.8030(8)(b).

EC 9.8030(8)(b). Building Articulation.

The requirements set forth in EC 9.5500(7) may be adjusted if the proposed building design: 1. Utilizes architectural masses, features or details to distinguish elements of the building. 2. Defines entryways in appropriate scales.

9.5500(8)(a) Minimum Landscape Area

**Open Space &
Landscape Design**

Landscaping is required according to the applicable base zone minimum landscape area standards. If there are none specified, the minimum landscape area shall be equal to the amount of area required as open space specified in EC 9.5500(9).

1. Any required landscaping, such as for required front and interior yard setbacks and to comply with parking landscape standards, shall apply toward the development site area landscaping requirements.

2. Common open space areas required under EC 9.5500(9) Open Space also apply toward meeting the minimum landscaped area requirements of this section, if they are uncovered.

3. Any portion of a private, ground level open space area exceeding one hundred square feet shall be counted toward the minimum landscape area requirement.

9.5500(8)(b) Compliance with Landscape Standards
Except as may be otherwise provided in this subsection (8), all required landscaping shall comply with the standards beginning at EC 9.6200 Purpose of Landscape Standards. In the event of a conflict between the standards beginning at EC 9.6200 and this subsection, the standards in this subsection shall control.

9.5500(8)(c) Landscape Requirements
Site landscaping shall conform to the following:

1. Required Landscaping in Yards Abutting Streets. Landscaping shall be installed and maintained in yards abutting streets that complies, at a minimum, with the standards in EC 9.6210(1) Basic Landscape Standard (L-1). The required landscaping shall be placed within the required front yard setback area and may be pierced by pedestrian and vehicular access ways.

2. Private Open Space Screening. Where provided, ground-level private open space required under EC 9.5500(9) Open Space (b) Private Open Space shall be physically and visually separated from common open space through the use of perimeter landscaping and/or fencing. If landscaping is used, such landscaping shall apply toward the minimum landscape requirement.

3. Street Trees. Street trees are required along the frontage of all developments abutting newly created public or private streets in accordance with provisions of Chapter 7 of this code regarding the Street Tree Program - Policies, Standards, and Procedures.

9.5500(8)(d) Adjustments to the standards in this subsection may be made, based on the criteria of EC 9.8030(3) Landscape Standards Adjustment.

EC 9.8030(3)Landscape Standards Adjustment.

Where this land use code provides that the landscape standards may be adjusted, the standards may be adjusted upon finding that the proposed landscape is consistent with the following applicable criteria:

(a) General Landscape Standards. Standards establishing a minimum percent of landscape area on the development site, may be adjusted upon a finding that the proposal achieves all of the following:

1. Where necessary, provides visual separation between adjacent development.

2. Provides clearly defined entries and pedestrian pathways.

3. Enhances and softens structural elements.

4. Breaks up large expanses of parking.

5. Protects and enhances the value of adjacent or on-site natural areas.

6. In the case of multiple-family developments, buffers dwellings from views that are unattractive and creates areas for outdoor privacy for residents.

(b) Basic Landscape Standard (L-1). The standards of EC 9.6210(1) may be adjusted if the proposal enhances a development site by providing attractive, open landscaped areas where distance is the primary means of separating different uses or developments.

(c) Low Screen Landscape Standard (L-2). The standards of EC 9.6210(2) may be adjusted if the proposal achieves at least one of the following:

1. A landscape treatment that uses a combination of distance and low-level screening (minimum 30 inches, maximum of 42 inches) to separate uses or development and the screening is adequate to soften the impact of the use or development.

2. In those instances where visibility between areas is more important than a total visual screen, the alternative landscape treatment is appropriate for the site.

(d) High Screen Landscape Standard (L-3). The standards of EC 9.6210(3) may be adjusted if the proposal uses landscape screening to provide a physical and visual separation between uses or development.

(e) High Wall Landscape Standard (L-4). The standards of EC 9.6210(4) may be adjusted if the proposal continues to provide extensive screening of both visual and noise impacts to protect adjacent users.

(f) Partial Screen Fence Landscape Standard (L-5). The standards of EC 9.6210(5) may be adjusted where the proposal achieves at least one of the following:

1. A moderate level of screening, adequate to soften the impact of the use or development.

2. In those instances where visibility between areas is more important than a total visual screen, the alternate landscape treatment is appropriate for the site.

(g) Full Screen Fence Landscape Standard (L-6). The standards of EC 9.6210(6) may be adjusted if both of the following are achieved:

1. The proposal provides a tall, complete visual separation to protect abutting uses.

2. Living plant landscaping is not practical for the site.

(h) Massed Landscape Standard (L-7). Adjustments may be made to the standards of EC 9.6210(7) if the proposal provides a landscape treatment appropriate for interior yards of large development sites adjacent to arterial and collector streets or to non-residential uses adjacent to residential development as the case may be.

9.5500(9)

Open space that complies with Table 9.5500(9) and the standards in this subsection (9) shall be provided unless exempt under other provisions of this land use code.

9.5500(9)(a)

Common open space may include any of the following:

1. Outdoor areas incorporating:

a. Lawn or hard surfaced areas in which user amenities such as trees, shrubs, pathways, tables, benches or drinking fountains have been placed.

b. Ornamental or food gardens.

c. Developed and equipped adult recreation areas.

d. Developed and equipped children's play areas.

e. Sports courts (tennis, handball, volleyball, etc.).

f. Swimming pools, spas and adjacent patios and decks.

g. Roof terraces.

h. Picnic areas.

i. Covered, but unenclosed, patios.

j. Internal courtyards.

2. Common open space may also include up to 30% of the required area in natural resource areas, such as steep slopes greater than 25%, forested areas, conservation areas and delineated wetlands.

3. Up to 30% of common open space may be located in indoor recreation areas fitted with game equipment, work-out equipment, court sports facilities, swimming pools, plant greenhouse, wood shop, or other designated project or game equipment, if the facility conforms to the following standards:

a. The minimum area of any single space shall be 250 square feet, with no dimension being less than 15 feet.

b. Interior common open space shall be at least 10 feet in floor to ceiling height; glazed window and skylight areas shall be provided in the proportion of 1 square foot for each 4 square feet of the floor area of the common space.

c. The space shall be accessible from a common lobby, courtyard or exterior common open space.

4. The minimum area for any common open space shall be 250 square feet.

5. The minimum dimension for any common outdoor open space shall be 15 feet.

9.5500(9)(b) Private Open Space
Private open space is outdoor space directly adjacent to dwelling units providing an outdoor area for private use by the occupants. Private open space, where provided, shall meet the minimum standards in the following Table 9.5500(9)(b).

9.5500(9)(c)   Open Space Credit
1. An open space credit, not to exceed 25 percent of the total open space requirement, may be applied toward compliance with that requirement, for developments that are located within one-quarter mile of a public park.

2. Required setback areas and areas required to comply with perimeter parking lot landscape standards may be applied toward the minimum open space requirements when the minimum dimension of such space is 15 feet or greater."

9.5500(9)(d) Adjustments to the standards in this subsection may be made, based on the criteria of EC 9.8030(8)(c).

EC 9.8030(8)(c). Open Space.

The requirements set forth in EC 9.5500(9) may be adjusted if the proposal will achieve better overall compliance with the purpose of the open space standards than what would result from strict adherence to the standards.

Bicycles

9.6105 Bicycle Parking Standards. (2) Bicycle Parking Space Standards.

(a) A minimum of 4 bicycle parking spaces shall be provided at each development site.

(b) A bicycle parking space required by this land use code shall be at least 6 feet long and 2 feet wide with an overhead clearance of at least 7 feet, and with a 5 foot access aisle. This minimum required width for a bicycle parking space may be reduced to 18"" if designed using a hoop rack according to Figure 9.6105(2) Bicycle Parking Standards. Bicycles may be tipped vertically for storage, but not hung above the floor. Bicycle parking shall be provided at ground level unless an elevator is easily accessible to an approved bicycle storage area.

(c) All required long term bicycle parking spaces shall be sheltered from precipitation. Shelters for short term bicycle parking shall be provided in the amounts shown in Table 9.6105(2)(c) Required Sheltered Bicycle Parking Spaces.

(d) Direct access from the bicycle parking area to the public right-of-way shall be provided with access ramps, if necessary, and pedestrian access from the bicycle parking area to the building entrance.

(a) Long term bicycle parking required in association with a commercial, industrial, or institutional use shall be provided in a well-lighted, secure location within a convenient distance of a main entrance. A secure location is defined as one in which the bicycle parking is:

1. A bicycle locker,

2. A lockable bicycle enclosure,

3. Provided within a lockable room, or

4. Clearly visible from, and within 30 feet of the employee's work station.

Bicycle parking provided in outdoor locations shall not be farther than the closest automobile parking space (except disabled parking). Long term bicycle parking required in association with a multiple-family residential use shall be provided in a well-lighted, secure ground level location within a convenient distance of an entrance to the residential unit. A secure location is defined as one in which the bicycle parking is provided outside the residential unit within a garage, a lockable room, a lockable bicycle enclosure, or a bicycle locker.

(b) Short term bicycle parking shall consist of a securely fixed structure that supports the bicycle frame in a stable position without damage to wheels, frame, or components and that allows the frame and both wheels to be locked to the rack by the bicyclist's own locking device. The required spaces for each use category are listed in EC 9.6105(4) Minimum Required Bicycle Parking Spaces. Short term bicycle parking shall be provided within a convenient distance of, and clearly visible from the main entrance to the building as determined by the city, but it shall not be farther than the closest automobile parking space (except disabled parking).

Sections 9.6100 through 9.6110 set forth requirements for off-street bicycle parking areas based on the use and location of the property. Bicycle parking standards are intended to provide safe, convenient, and attractive areas for the circulation and parking of bicycles that encourage the use of alternative modes of transportation. Long-term bicycle parking space requirements are intended to accommodate employees, students, residents, commuters, and other persons who expect to leave their bicycle parked for more than 2 hours. Short term bicycle parking spaces accommodate visitors, customers, messengers, and other persons expected to depart within approximately 2 hours.

Code Appendix
Huntersville, North Carolina

http://www.huntersville.org/ZONING_TOC.htm

Pedestrian Network

Off-street parking areas should be designed to minimize breaks in the pedestrian environment along the public street and create safe and comfortable passage for pedestrians. (Article 6 Off –Street Parking Design Standards)

Main pedestrian access to the building and to individual units is from the street (indicated by larger arrow), unless specifically exempted by one of the provisions of Section 8.1. Secondary access may be from parking areas (indicated by smaller arrow). (Article 4 Encroachment/Pedestrian Access)

Main pedestrian access to the building is from the street. Secondary access may be from parking areas. (Article 4)

Street trees and sidewalks are required on both sides of public streets except rural roads, lanes, alleys, and the undeveloped edge of neighborhood parkways except that sidewalks may be permitted on only one side of the street to accommodate low impact design in the Rural district. Planting area for street trees should be a minimum of 7' in width and sidewalks shall at a minimum be 5' in width unless otherwise provided. On Commercial Town Streets, sidewalks should be a minimum of 7' in width. A 10' minimum width sidewalk with tree grates or cut-outs is encouraged on Commercial Town Streets. Generally, canopy trees shall be planted at a spacing not to exceed 40' on center. Where overhead utility lines preclude the use of canopy trees, small maturing trees may be substituted, planted 30' on center. (Article 5 Street Design)

Safe and convenient pedestrian access to the open space from all lots not adjoining the open space shall be provided (except in the case of farmland, or other resource areas vulnerable to trampling damage or human disturbance). (Article 7 Landscaping and Open Space)

Accordingly, the town shall evaluate proposals to determine whether the proposed subdivision plan: Includes a pedestrian circulation system designed to assure that pedestrians can walk safely and easily on the site, between properties and activities or special features within the neighborhood open space system. All roadside footpaths should connect with off-road trails, which in turn should link with potential open space on adjoining undeveloped parcels (or with existing open space on adjoining developed parcels, where applicable). (Article 7 Landscaping and Open Space)

Street Network

Article 5 1. Interconnect within a development and with adjoining development. Cul-de-sac shall be allowed only where topographical and/or lot line configurations offer no practical alternatives for connections or through traffic. Street stubs shall be provided within development adjacent to open land to provide for future connections. The Land Development Map should be reviewed to locate potential connections in new neighborhoods.

5. Be public. Private streets are not permitted within any new development. Alleys will be classified as public or private depending on function, according to the street acceptance policy.

Public streets shall provide access to all tracts and lots. Streets and alleys shall, wherever practicable, terminate at other streets within the neighborhood and connect to existing and projected streets outside the development. Cul-de sacs shall not exceed 250 feet in length, must be accessed from a street providing internal or external connectivity, shall be permanently terminated by a vehicular turnaround, and are permitted where topography makes a street connection impracticable. In most instances, a "close" or "eyebrow" is preferred to a cul-de-sac. Vehicular turnarounds of various configurations are acceptable so long as emergency access is adequately provided. The average perimeter of all blocks within the TND should not exceed 1,350 feet. No block face should have a length greater than 500 feet without a dedicated alley or pathway providing through access.

A hierarchical street network should have a rich variety of types, including bicycle, pedestrian, and transit routes.

Access Points

Streets and alleys shall, wherever practicable, terminate at other streets within the neighborhood and connect to existing and projected streets outside the development. (Article 3 TND Districts)

Where connectivity between subdivisions is appropriate for high quality neighborhood design, the Town Board may reduce or waive the required buffer yard. (Article Landscaping and Open Space)

Accordingly, the town shall evaluate proposals to determine whether the proposed subdivision plan: Includes a pedestrian circulation system designed to assure that pedestrians can walk safely and easily on the site, between properties and activities or special features within the neighborhood open space system. All roadside footpaths should connect with off-road trails, which in turn should link with potential open space on adjoining undeveloped parcels (or with existing open space on adjoining developed parcels, where applicable). (Article Landscaping and Open Space)

Edges

8.11.2 In a residential or mixed use district, a fence or wall in an established rear or side yard which abuts a street or alley may not exceed 6 feet in height unless placed 15 or more feet inside property boundary. Within the first 15 feet, fences of chain link or similar material are permitted only if screened on the exterior side by evergreen shrubs planted no farther apart than 6 feet on center, minimum height 3 feet at installation, or if obscured from view by the screening method(s) set out in the paragraph immediately above.

In a residential or mixed use district, a fence or wall in an established rear or side yard which does not abut a street or alley may not exceed 8 feet in height."

Consistent build-to lines shall be established along all streets and public space frontages; build-to lines determine the width and ratio of enclosure for each public street or space. A minimum percentage build-out at the build-to line shall be established on the plan along all streets and public square frontages.

Parking

Article 6: Parking lots shall be placed behind buildings; side of the building parking will be permitted only as indicated by Building Type and shall be measured along the build-to line. Parking lots shall be designed to allow pedestrians to safely move from their vehicles to the building. On small lots, this may be achieved by providing a sidewalk at the perimeter of the lot. On larger lots, corridors within the parking area should channel pedestrians from the car to the perimeter of the lot or to the building. These corridors may be delineated by a paving material which differs from that of vehicular areas and planted to provide shade. Small posts or bollards may be included. To maintain pedestrian comfort and calm the speed of entering traffic, driveways to parking areas should be no wider than 24 feet.

Street Design

Article 5 1. Interconnect within a development and with adjoining development. Cul-de-sacs shall be allowed only where topographical and/or lot line configurations offer no practical alternatives for connections or through traffic. Street stubs shall be provided within development adjacent to open land to provide for future connections. The Land Development Map should be reviewed to locate potential connections in new neighborhoods.

2. Be designed as the most prevalent public space of the town and, thus, scaled to the pedestrian.

3. Be bordered by sidewalks on both sides, with the exception of rural roads, lanes, alleys, and the undeveloped edge of neighborhood parkways. Sidewalks on one side of the road may be permitted in the Rural zone as an incentive to protect water quality.

4. Be lined with street trees on both sides, with the exception of rural roads, lanes, alleys, and the undeveloped edge of neighborhood parkways. Private drives are permitted only as described in the Rural and Transitional zone.

5. Be public. Private streets are not permitted within any new development. Alleys will be classified as public or private depending on function, according to the street acceptance policy.

6. Be the focus of buildings. Generally, all buildings will front on public streets. For good definition, the ratio of one increment of height to six of width is the absolute maximum, with one to three being a good effective minimum. As a general rule, the tighter the ratio, the stronger the sense of place. Very tight relationships of one to one can create special pedestrian places.

To prevent the buildup of vehicular speed, disperse traffic flow, and create a sense of visual enclosure, long uninterrupted segments of straight streets should be avoided. Methods: (1) a street can be interrupted by intersections designed to calm the speed and disperse the flow of traffic (Article 5) and terminate vistas with a significant feature (building, park, natural feature); (2) a street can be terminated with a public monument, specifically designed building façade, or a gateway to the ensuing space; (3) perceived street length can be reduced by a noticeable street curve where the outside edge of the curve is bounded by a building or other vertical elements that hug the curve and deflect the view; (4) other traffic calming configurations are acceptable so long as emergency access is adequately provided.

Building Massing & Orientation

8.1 Any lot on which a building (or buildings) is to be erected or use is to be established shall abut a public street.

4. A site specific development plan may be considered for approval in the TC, NC, NR, R, TR, HC, CB and both TND districts where residential and/or non-residential lots and/or structures front upon a private courtyard, carriageway, mid-block private alleyway with courtyard, or pedestrian way, or urban open space as defined in Article 7, Part B, where adequate access by emergency vehicles is maintained by way of a street or alley and where the off-street placement of uses does not diminish the orientation of building fronts to the public street.

6. Be the focus of buildings. Generally, all buildings will front on public streets. For good definition, the ratio of one increment of height to six of width is the absolute maximum, with one to three being a good effective minimum. As a general rule, the tighter the ratio, the stronger the sense of place. Very tight relationships of one to one can create special pedestrian places.

Open Space & Landscape Design

Article 7.10.2 Urban Open Space shall be planned and improved, accessible and usable by persons living nearby. Improved shall mean cleared of underbrush and debris and may contain one or more of the following improvements: landscaping, walls, fences, walks, statues, fountains, ball fields, and/or playground equipment. Walls and fences shall be made of brick, stone, wrought iron, or wood and shall not exceed 3.5 ft. in height.

Article 7.10.3 In major subdivisions and multi-building developments in all zoning districts except Rural, urban open space shall be integrated into the design of the site. Such open space, whether on-site or off-site, shall be located within ¼ mile of each building lot as measured along the rights-of-way of streets providing access between the two. In large-lot subdivisions such urban open space shall be integrated into the design of the site so that, whether located on-site or off-site, such open space is located within ½ mile of all building lots, as measured along the rights-of-way of street providing access between the two.

Article 7 - All residential development fronting a major or minor thoroughfare shall provide a 20-foot landscape easement located within common area between the future right-of-way and any proposed lots or public streets.

Dumpsters shall be set on a concrete bed and shall be hidden by an opaque fence or wall of sufficient height to screen the bin and any appurtenances, but not less than 6' in height. Wooden shadow box fences are recommended. Trash containers such as dumpsters shall not be located abutting residential property. Wherever used, fences and walls should be constructed to match the architectural detail of the main building(s).

Bicycles

Article 6 - All non-residential buildings should include an area for parking bicycles. This area may be a designated parking space within the parking lot near the building or an area outside the parking lot adjacent to the building. The bike parking area must include a bike rack with locking area.

Code Appendix
Asheville, North Carolina

http://www.ashevillenc.gov/government/subpage.aspx?id=576

Pedestrian Network

7-11-8 (b) Guidelines for requiring sidewalks. Sidewalks shall be required for all new construction and for renovations, additions and/or expansions to existing structures which fall into one of the following categories:

(2) All new multi-family residential development, except for the construction of less than ten units; (5) All new streets, improved streets or extension to streets.
(c) Additional conditions for requiring sidewalks. Notwithstanding (b) above, the following findings must be made prior to the city engineer/designee requiring the construction of a new sidewalk or a ""fee in lieu of"" constructing a sidewalk for an applicable project. One of the following conditions must be met, as determined by the city engineer/designee.

(1) The applicable project area, including the street frontage, is identified as a needed pedestrian linkage within an adopted City of Asheville transportation or corridor plan, including but not limited to such plans as the Transportation Improvement Program (TIP), greenway, small area, pedestrian thoroughfare plans.

(2) The current or projected (within five years) average daily traffic count (ADT) for the street is 300 vehicles per day or more as determined by the city Traffic Engineer. Traffic generated from the applicable project or any additions to the applicable project will be included in calculating the ADT for this condition."

Street Network

General. Except as set forth in subsection (i)(2) below, all residential lots must abut a public street or an approved private street built to public street standards: Residential lots shall meet the minimum lot width requirements of the applicable zoning district where they abut a public street, except for lots on a cul-de-sac or flag lots. (Sec. 7-11-2. Parking, loading, and access standards (j)(1)a.)

b. Lots on a cul-de-sac. A lot on a cul-de-sac shall be a minimum of twenty-five (25) feet at the front property line, and shall be 80 percent of the required lot width at the front setback line. (Sec. 7-11-2. Parking, loading, and access standards (j)(1)b.)

Access Points

Minimum distances between access points and street intersections shall be determined by the access triangle. No access points shall be permitted within the access triangle. The access triangle is that triangle formed by the intersecting undisturbed right-of-way lines ("A" and "B" in the graphic below) and a line connecting the ends of the undisturbed right-of-way lines. (Sec. 7-11-2. Parking, loading, and access standards (g)(2)a.)

Distance from other access points. The distance measured along the right-of-way line between the tangent projection of the inside edges of adjacent access points shall be at least 25 feet. (Sec. 7-11-2. Parking, loading, and access standards (g)(3).)

Distance from property line. Unless the access point will be shared between two or more adjoining properties, all access points shall be located at least five feet from all property lines perpendicular to the street. (Sec. 7-11-2. Parking, loading, and access standards (g) (4).)

Edges

7-8-5.f.5 The following minimum setbacks shall be required for uses in the RM-6 District.

Front: 15 ft.

Side: Single family detached and multi-family less than 4 units/building: 6 ft.

Rear: Single family detached and multi-family less than 4 units per building: 15 ft.

The landscape and buffering standards (section 7-11-3) may require additional setback; if so, the most restrictive requirement shall apply.

The minimum spacing between structures shall, in addition, be as per the Asheville Fire Prevention Code.

Parking

Parking and loading facilities shall be provided as required by section 7-11-2 of this chapter. No parking lots shall be permitted in any required setback.(One Parking Space Required for Each):

Dwellings, multi-family with 2 bedrooms or less: Min = 1 unit, Max = 0.5 unit

Dwellings, multi-family with 3 bedrooms or more: Min = 0.5 unit, Max = 0.33 unit

On-street parking spaces may be counted toward the fulfillment of the off-street parking requirements for a development. Any on-street parking space meeting these standards shall count as 0.75 of a required off-street parking space.

Street Design

Street buffers. Street buffers are designed to provide for a separation of activities and a more comfortable pedestrian environment. The street buffer is required in addition to the street trees planted in a ten-foot planting strip as required in subsection 7-11-2(d) (3)(c). a. Street buffer determination. Vehicular use areas greater than 4,000 square feet that are located within 50 feet of the edge of a street must be buffered from the street. b. Calculating the requirement. One evergreen or deciduous shrub planted for every five linear feet of buffer required. Species selected must achieve a minimum of three feet in height at maturity. (Sec. 7-11-3. Landscape and buffering standards (2))

Street trees. Street trees are required for all new developments except for single- or two-family homes. This requirement is designed to create or enhance an attractive streetscape pattern while contributing to Asheville's urban forest and a more comfortable pedestrian environment. (Sec. 7-11-3. Landscape and buffering standards (3))

Street tree spacing. Trees may be evenly spaced or staggered to accommodate other site features. In no case shall a required street tree be closer than 15 feet or farther than 65 feet from another required tree. No street tree shall be farther than 20 feet from the edge of pavement or, in cases of planned road widening, 20 feet from the proposed edge of pavement. Existing trees credited towards street tree requirements shall meet spacing requirements. (Sec. 7-11-3. Landscape and buffering standards (3)(c))

Planting strip. Trees shall be placed in a planting strip the width of which may vary but shall maintain a minimum of not less than seven feet and an average width of ten feet. The planting area must be covered with living material, including groundcover and/or shrubs, except for mulched areas directly around the trees so that no soil is exposed. No stone much is permitted in the planting strip. Sidewalks may interrupt the planting strip provided the width on either side of the sidewalk totals ten feet. (See the City of Asheville Standards and Specifications Manual for detail(s)). (Sec. 7-11-3. Landscape and buffering standards (3)(d))

Building Massing & Orientation

The maximum height of structures in the RM-6 District shall be 40 feet.

Open Space & Landscape Design

7-11-4 (c) Open space requirement. Open space shall be provided in accordance with the following table for: initial residential development containing eight or more units or redevelopment or additional development that adds eight or more units; for initial nonresidential or mixed use development of lots containing one acre or more in area; or for redevelopment or additional development that adds 25 percent more nonresidential or mixed use floor area on lots containing one acre or more in area. The CBD district and single-family residential subdivisions with a minimum lot size of one acre or more are exempt from the requirements of this section.

All residential districts, 500 square feet of open space per unit or 15% of lot area, whichever is greater. In no case shall the amount of open space devoted to active recreational facilities constitute more than 10% of lot area. ."

7-11-3 (d)(2) Street buffers. Street buffers are designed to provide for a separation of activities and a more comfortable pedestrian environment. The street buffer is required in addition to the street trees planted in a ten-foot planting strip as required in subsection 7-11-2(d)(3)(c).

a. Street buffer determination. Vehicular use areas greater than 4,000 square feet that are located within 50 feet of the edge of a street must be buffered from the street.

b. Calculating the requirement. One evergreen or deciduous shrub planted for every five linear feet of buffer required. Species selected must achieve a minimum of three feet in height at maturity.

(3) Street trees. Street trees are required for all new developments except for single- or two-family homes. This requirement is designed to create or enhance an attractive streetscape pattern while contributing to Asheville's urban forest and a more comfortable pedestrian environment.

a. Street tree determination. Street trees are required along all street frontages. b. Calculating the requirement. Street tree requirements are as follows:

• Overhead utilities present -- One small maturing tree (less than 35 feet in height at maturity) for every 30 linear feet of property abutting a street.
• All other conditions -- One large maturing tree (greater than 35 feet in height at maturity) for every 40 linear feet of property abutting a street.

c. Street tree spacing. Trees may be evenly spaced or staggered to accommodate other site features. In no case shall a required street tree be closer than 15 feet or farther than 65 feet from another required tree. No street tree shall be farther than 20 feet from the edge of pavement or, in cases of planned road widening, 20 feet from the proposed edge of pavement. Existing trees credited towards street tree requirements shall meet spacing requirements.

d. Planting strip. Trees shall be placed in a planting strip the width of which may vary but shall maintain a minimum of not less than seven feet and an average width of ten feet. The planting area must be covered with living material, including groundcover and/or shrubs, except for mulched areas directly around the trees so that no soil is exposed. No stone much is permitted in the planting strip. Sidewalks may interrupt the planting strip provided the width on either side of the sidewalk totals ten feet. (See the City of Asheville Standards and Specifications Manual for detail(s))

(4) Parking lot landscaping. Trees and shrubs are required in and around parking lots in order to provide attractive views from roads and adjacent properties, provide shade to reduce the heat generated by impervious surfaces, reduce glare from parking lots, and to help filter exhaust from vehicles.

a. Parking lot determination. Parking lots with six or more spaces shall require parking lot landscaping.

b. Calculating the requirement. One deciduous tree and four shrubs for required for every 1,500 square feet of vehicular use area (VUA). At least 75 percent of the required deciduous parking lot trees must be large-maturing trees. Trees and shrubs must be planted within 15 feet of the vehicular use area to count as parking lot landscaping.

c. Interior rows of parking. When more than four trees are required in a parking lot with interior rows, 50 percent of the trees and shrubs must be planted in islands or medians located within the parking lot.

d. Multiple parking bays. When more than four bays of parking are proposed, an interior island with an average width of 20 feet and a length equivalent to the length of the average parking bay is required. This island must be planted and include a pedestrian walkway no less than five feet wide and placed in a location that enhances pedestrian circulation, preferably leading directly to a building entrance or sidewalk.

e. Perimeter parking spaces. All continuous runs of 15 or more parking spaces shall be interrupted by a tree island.

f. Minimum island size. The minimum island size shall be 200 square feet of pervious planting surface per tree. Islands must maintain an average width of ten feet with a minimum width no less than five feet.

g. Protection of trees. Curbing, bollards, or parking barriers shall protect trees and shrubs within five feet of the edge of the pavement. Trees and shrubs in islands should be set back at least three feet from the curb so as not to interfere with car doors opening.

h. Canopy coverage. Each parking space shall be located within 60 feet of a tree as measured from the trunk of the tree to the closest point of the parking space.

i. Parking decks. Exposed parking decks are required to plant a minimum of one tree and two shrubs for every 30 linear feet of the parking structure's perimeter. Trees shall be planted within 20 feet of the structure. This requirement shall be waived for any side of the structure where the property line buffer standards of subsection 7-11-2(d)(1) require a greater number of plantings.

j. Additional landscaping required for parking lots exceeding the maximum number of parking spaces. When the number of parking spaces exceeds the maximum city parking standards as set forth in section 7-11-1, one tree and two shrubs per 1,000 square feet of the additional vehicular use area shall be required in addition to the minimum requirements of this subsection.

k. Landscaping of parking areas and other uses by right, subject to special requirements and conditional uses. All parking areas required for specified uses outlined in article XVI shall be screened from adjacent properties with a mix of evergreen and deciduous trees and shrubs to result in a vegetative screen that is 75 percent opaque year round.

(5) Building impact landscaping. Building impact landscaping shall be required for new or existing buildings in order to soften views "

"from roads and adjacent properties, provide shade to reduce the heat generated by impervious surfaces, reduce glare, and to help enhance the urban landscape.

a. Building impact determination. All new developments with an existing or proposed building with a footprint greater than 3,000 square feet. Developments with more than one building shall combine the total footprint areas.

b. Calculating the requirement. One tree and two shrubs for every 1,000 square feet of building footprint. Trees and shrubs may be planted anywhere on site.

(6) Screening of dumpsters, loading docks, outdoor storage areas, and utility structures. All dumpsters, loading docks, or utility structures visible from a public street or adjacent property line shall be screened unless already screened by an intervening building or bufferyard. All enclosed outdoor storage areas greater than 25 square feet shall also be screened from adjacent properties and streets. Screen types include:

• A continuous hedge of evergreen trees and/or densely twigged deciduous trees planted in a seven-foot strip spaced no more than eight feet apart.

• Fence or wall with a minimum height of six feet with the finished side of the fence facing the abutting property or street. Fences longer than 25 linear feet shall be landscaped with trees and/or shrubs planted in a minimum five-foot planting area, except around access areas, spaced no farther than eight feet apart in order to screen at least 50 percent of the fence or wall."

Bicycles

7-11-2(c)(3) Bicycle parking shall be provided for all uses except single-family and two-family dwellings. The minimum number of bicycle parking spaces required shall be equal to five percent of the total number of automobile parking spaces in the lot. Bicycle parking facilities shall include standard bike racks or other secured, lockable facilities.

Image Credits

All images and graphics were taken or created by the authors, except:

CIONET COOKBOOK

RECIPES FOR DIGITAL SUCCESS

Copyright © CIONET, 2022

The right of CIONET to be identified as the author of this book has been asserted in accordance with the Copyright, Designs and Patents Act 1988.

First published in 2022 by
Infinite Ideas Limited
www.infideas.com

A CIP catalogue record for this book is available from the British Library

ISBN 978–1–913022–30–3

Brand and product names are trademarks or registered trademarks of their respective owners.

Printed in Great Britain

MENU

Foreword   v
The Master Chefs   vi
Introduction: setting the context for the IT cookbook   1

**Section 1: What does it take to create and
operate a five-star restaurant?**   5

1. Win the customer: scoring five stars on Tripadvisor   11
   Sainsburys: delivering world-class digital
   experiences   12
   The UK Ministry of Defence: building a
   connected organisation   16
   Port of Antwerp: putting innovation at the
   centre of the organisation   19

Starter: Nikkei-style tuna ceviche   23

2. Reinventing the business: new concepts and
   menus   24
   Munich Re: becoming a serial innovator of
   new digital businesses   25
   Tate & Lyle: reinventing business, redesigning
   work   29
   Signify: mastering the customer experience   33

Starter: Paneer tikka   36

3. Structure the business enterprise: winning the
   best restaurant of the year award   37
   dunnhumby: human-powered business
   transformation   38
   Proximus: delivering five-star customer
   experience   42
   mBank: escaping technical legacy to build
   modern platforms for change   45

Starter: Broad bean tortilla tapas   48

**Section 2: How to build a five-star kitchen
that satisfies your most discerning customers**   49

4. Digital operating models: optimising your
   kitchen to provide tasty new IT recipes   55
   BW Paper Systems: letting joined-up ecosystems
   create big business value   56
   KBC Bank: change the context if you want to
   transform IT operations   59
   Telefónica: Teaching elephants to dance   63

Main Course: Chicken and mushroom cream
   with an avocado and green salad   67

5. New business methods: changing the kitchen
to suit a digital landscape 68
Prudential: creating a fully digital business 69
KfW: how to turn a crisis into an opportunity 73
Orange: leading through open innovation 77
Main Course: Barbecue cedar-plank salmon 80

6. Digital technologies: the best ingredients and
suppliers 81
Red Hat: embracing open transformation to
accelerate change 82
PKO Bank Polski: be brave and humble on
your digital journey 85
MAPFRE: adopting a parallel design path to
enterprise automation 88
Main Course: Tofu with black beans and
red pepper 92

**Section 3: What is expected of top-ranking IT
chefs and their supporting teams?** 93

7. Deciphering the DNA of the Master Chef 99
Ferrovial: a chef for all seasons 100
Kensington Mortgages: designing an agile and
adaptive operating model to support growth 103
Restoration and Renewal Authority:
no challenge is too big for a Master Chef 107
Dessert: Gluten-free dark chocolate torte 111

8. A dream team for your digital kitchen 112
Euronext: managing and empowering a busy
kitchen to deliver great results 113
Maersk: empowering a world-class kitchen team 117
AstraZeneca: leveraging technology as a
competitive advantage 121
Norway Post: learning to innovate greater
value faster 125
Dessert: Sweet curd dumplings with
plum compote 128

9. Winning cultures promote better collaboration
and communication 129
SD Worx: building an organisational culture
for digital transformation 130
Morgan Stanley: employing diversity to
accelerate change 134
Randstad Group Belgium: agile portfolio
management in dynamic environments 138
Dessert: Pears poached in rooibos tea 142

Conclusions and a call for action 143
About the authors 145
About CIONET 147
Index 149
Photo credits 152

FOREWORD

As we witness an unprecedented quickening in the rate of change across the emerging digital world, we at CIONET have a unique vantage point. We listen and interact everyday with our 10,000 CIO practitioners and business partners as they navigate this fast-developing landscape together. With over 1,000 local events each year in more than 20 countries, complemented by our online app, we capture and share best practices direct from IT and business leaders. In the wake of the pandemic, and the acceleration in digitisation that this crisis has invoked, we believe that now is the right time to bring together our community's collective learning: welcome to our IT cookbook.

As part of our analysis, we use the five-star restaurant to symbolise the very best IT kitchen. We believe this analogy fits nicely within the context of how IT can best serve its customers. Appetites and habits are changing fast within the business community as new infusions of technology offer exceptional opportunities to improve the consumer experience. Equally, IT vendors are transforming themselves through the extensive use of cloud platforms, open-source technology and software as a service (SaaS). Poised amid this dynamic is the IT organisation, which must respond to changes on both sides – in both the demand and supply of IT products and services.

In our quest to understand and help replicate the DNA of the Master Chef, we conducted 'deep dive' interviews with over 50 digital leaders across Europe. We have documented each carefully and selected 28 to appear in this cookbook.

We believe that our IT cookbook offers IT practitioners and their business partners a powerful set of insights and tools to become the world-class restaurateurs of high-quality digitisation, both now and in the years to come.

Hendrik Deckers

Hendrik Deckers,
Founder and Chair of CIONET International

THE MASTER CHEFS

Phil Jordan 12

Sainsburys

Charlie Forte 16

UK Ministry of Defence

Erwin Verstraelen 19

Port of Antwerp

Sanjay Patel 29

Tate & Lyle

Kurt De Ruwe 33

Signify

David Jack 38

dunnhumby

Geert Standaert 42

Proximus

Krzysztof Dabrowski 45

mBank

Nino Messaoud 56

BW Paper Systems

Rudi Peeters 59

KBC Bank

Angel Valero 63

Telefónica

Tarun Kohli 69

Prudential

Melanie Kehr 73

KfW

Koen Vermeulen 77

Orange

Margaret Dawson 82

Red Hat

Adam Marciniak 85

PKO Bank Polski

Vanessa Escrivá García 88

MAPFRE

Dimitris Bountolos 100

Ferrovial

Mark Foulsham 103

Kensington Mortgages

Martin Bellamy 107

Restoration and Renewal

Manuel Bento 113

Euronext

Rui Pedro Silva 117

Maersk

Cindy Hoots 121

AstraZeneca

Dr Bijna Kotak Dasani 134

Morgan Stanley

Gunther Ghijsels 138

Randstad Group Belgium

INTRODUCTION

Setting the context for the IT cookbook

In these uncertain times, one thing is certain: IT has captured the board's attention like never before. In response to the coronavirus pandemic, which created a once-in-a-generation challenge for businesses, societies and governments around the globe, IT was called on to deliver radical changes in operating and business models. From establishing hybrid working and online shopping, to providing virtual meetings, streamed entertainment, remote healthcare and online banking, chief information officers (CIOs) were tasked by their boards to deliver digital transformation in weeks and days rather than years and months. Time and again, CIOs and their technology teams delivered great results.

This period of rapid digitisation has been a wake-up call for many incumbent businesses. During the past decade, large enterprises have seen at first hand the disruption to established sectors caused by fleet-of-foot digital natives, such as Amazon and Google. At times, incumbent businesses have been slow to respond. In comparison, the past 20 months has been a period of unprecedented change, where being slow to respond was anathema.

The prize for technology-driven innovation has never been more visible or quantifiable. As a result, digital natives have seen their stocks double or quadruple in just a short period, setting a high bar for incumbent organisations. As we emerge from the pandemic, these traditional enterprises face a new challenge: not just surviving, but thriving in the digital age. As the executives responsible for leading business technology, CIOs will need to meet this challenge head-on.

Change in the rate of change

In March 2020, 2.7 billion employees globally relocated from their usual place of work to the home, requiring the establishment of virtual connections and a wide range of collaborative tools. At the same time, the volume of online enquiries and transactions across all businesses mushroomed in a matter of days, requiring scalable solutions. This shift required an acceleration in the deployment of digital platforms and tools, such as hybrid cloud, robotic process automation (RPA) and predictive data analytics. Cybersecurity also took an elevated position within the CIO's crowded agenda.

Not just 'doing digital' but 'being digital'

Across all the C-suite interviews that we have conducted in 2021, one aspect stands out above all others: the historic focus on operational excellence, and an associated modernisation of the core business, has had to take second place to innovation on behalf of the customer. In response to the pandemic, organisations scrambled to engage with and satisfy their end customers. All IT effort was directed to enhancing the customer journey, whether this was on behalf of external clients or internal employees. Emerging technologies, such as the Internet of Things (IoT), machine learning and 5G connectivity, contributed to these customer-focused developments. This focus on the customer will remain central as we move into the post-COVID age. Without innovation around the customer experience, organisations of all kinds will fail to survive the decade.

A new role for the Master Chef

The transformation of incumbent organisations into digital businesses has thrown a bright spotlight on what the CIO's role should be during this decade and beyond. In the recipes for IT leadership success that are contained within this IT cookbook, we see several common themes emerging. We believe pioneering digital leaders are focusing on three main areas:

- Corporate governance based on appropriate enterprise architectures that align with the purpose and value of truly digital organisations;

- Communities of practice that encourage the widespread dissemination of digital skills across IT and the rest of the organisation;

- Appropriate tooling such as artificial intelligence (AI), robotics, blockchain and quantum computing that can be applied in a consistent fashion across business and functional boundaries.

Most interviewees recognise that the days of running complex infrastructures and undertaking large-scale developments are over. Instead, public cloud platforms are replacing internal facilities, and low-code/no-code development tools can help businesses to devise their own solutions.

How to use this IT cookbook

Our IT cookbook describes the impact of dramatic and prolonged change on organisations of all kinds, both public and private. By drawing on strong use case examples, we describe how your organisation can create and operate a five-star restaurant, and provide all the IT ingredients necessary to support this establishment. The book is divided into three main sections:

- Section 1 (Chapters 1–3): What it takes to create and operate a five-star restaurant;

- Section 2 (Chapters 4–6): How IT can best provide a five-star kitchen to support the enterprise;

- Section 3 (Chapters 7–9) – What is expected of a top-ranking IT chef and their supporting team.

"Without innovation around the customer experience, organisations of all kinds will fail to survive the decade."

In the chapters we describe the critical factors for success in achieving a five-star rating as a restaurant (Section 1), as a kitchen (Section 2) and as a top ranking team (Section 3). Each chapter contains three representative recipes taken from the most relevant Master Chefs. By reading the recipes you will have access to the very best practices across Europe that you can replicate within your own organisation. For those who are already in the most senior positions and for others who are climbing the executive ladder, we hope that this IT cookbook provides valuable insights into what it takes to succeed in the new digital era.

SECTION 1

WHAT DOES IT TAKE TO CREATE AND OPERATE A FIVE-STAR RESTAURANT?

*"Placing new emphasis on the customer rather than
operational efficiencies has a galvanising impact
on corporate investment."*

Digital leaders, especially the CIO, must help elevate and maintain their organisations at a five-star rating if they are to survive and flourish in the emerging digital economy. There is no room for mediocrity with digital natives and start-ups biting at your heels. So, what does it take to be a five-star restaurant? First, you must win and retain the loyalty of your best customers. To do this, you will need to constantly enhance and vary your menus by adding the very latest ingredients and flavours. This will require you to work in a highly flexible and responsive manner by adopting contemporary structures, methods and tools, such as DevOps and Agile working.

In the wake of the coronavirus pandemic, it's time to dispose of your legacy constraints and swim in the fast lane. Let's examine each of the preconditions that will ensure that you operate the best restaurant in town.

Build a five-star reputation – focus exclusively on your best customers

Let's be honest: most organisations have paid lip service to their customers in the past few decades, with only a few placing the customer centre stage in their day-to-day operations. Instead, most businesses have pursued an operational excellence strategy, focused firmly on internal efficiency where they have applied digital techniques to core processes, such as finance, human resources (HR) and IT. This work has made up the bulk of so-called digital transformation efforts by incumbents. The outcome has been a race towards commoditisation of product and service. Digital natives, such as Amazon, have taken full advantage of this internal preoccupation with operational excellence and have instead taken a disruptive stance, placing the customer centre stage. Amazon's inexorable rise, and the near-destruction of slower-moving high-street retailers during the past 18 months, is testament to the digital native's successful customer-focused strategy.

COVID-19 and the associated move to online everything have created a rude awakening for incumbents who have seen both market share and equity value crumble in comparison with digital leaders. Prompted by the crisis, executive attention has switched from factory modernisation to enhancing the customer journey. This switch has involved the simplification of outward-facing processes to make organisations more accessible and relevant to each customer's specific context, in what we call the process of hyper-personalisation. Time and money in incumbents are now both firmly focused 'outside-in' rather than 'inside-out', ensuring that every diner in the restaurant has a truly satisfying experience. What takes place in the kitchen is usually invisible to the end customer. If the food arrives hot, fresh and tasty, the means of production is entirely irrelevant to the diner.

So, what does service in this five-star restaurant look like? Here are three specific areas of best practice that support the move to genuine customer centricity:

- Getting closer to the consumer. By establishing direct, online links with the consumer, many organisations are seeking to influence choice and increase loyalty.

- Improving the customer journey. Providing multi-channel access gives consumers better visibility and ease of access to products and services, as well as support throughout the life cycle.

- Engaging customers in co-development. With fast-changing consumer needs and increasing pressures to innovate around products and services, companies are seeking new ways to bring the customer into the development cycle.

Reinvent the business – deliver new concepts and menus

The pandemic has helped organisations focus on what is important – the end customer, whether that's an employee or an external consumer. Key drivers for action include the recent move to home working by more than 2.7 billion staff and an associated growing dependence on everything digital, from online shopping and education to entertainment, healthcare and sport.

These drivers for change have important consequences in terms of the post-COVID economy. Business leaders will have to deal with both the increasing uncertainty around customer needs in a VUCA (volatile, uncertain, complex and ambiguous) world and also the growing dominance of digital players that can adapt readily to fast-changing circumstances. Two examples:

1. Apple is now worth more than the combined value of all incumbents in the FTSE 100 stock exchange;

2. The FAANG companies are worth more combined than the entire European stock market.

Being digital, it would seem, pays off handsomely.

Companies are beginning to recognise that they will need to change tack over the next five years to accommodate the digital imperatives that will characterise the emerging post-COVID business environment. Here are three strategic imperatives that industry leaders are following:

■ Do fewer things. Organisations are currently pulling back on internal change initiatives to focus all efforts on the end customer. This implies a shift from operational excellence to customer-centric ways of doing things. The customer should become the sole focus of all corporate decisions.

■ Do things differently. In the next two to three years, organisations will take advantage of emerging technologies, such as big data, cloud, AI, 5G, IoT and

---

FAANG is an acronym referring to the stocks of the five most popular and best-performing American technology companies: Meta (formerly known as Facebook), Amazon, Apple, Netflix and Alphabet (formerly known as Google).

intelligent automation, to help transform the way they operate, especially as a means of hyper-personalising products and services.

■ Do different things. Beyond these time horizons, organisations will need to adopt entirely new business models to compete effectively with digital natives. It is conceivable that these moves will require a focus on edge-based innovations in preference to core transformation projects.

Restructure the business enterprise – become the best restaurant of the year

The pandemic and the likely direction of travel in the post-COVID age has emphasised the need for speed and agility, so that businesses can respond effectively to rapid changes in the external environment. Nowhere has this been more pronounced than in the pharmaceuticals sector, where the development of new vaccines has been compressed from 10 years to 10 months. It's a similar story at the cutting edge of technological development, where digital leaders such as Amazon and Google can continuously innovate and test new products and services in a matter of minutes and hours compared to traditional incumbents that often take months or years. Speed rather than efficiency is the new 'new-norm'.

The customer is now at the heart of every corporate decision. Placing new emphasis on the customer rather than operational efficiencies has a galvanising impact on corporate investment. Companies have increased their spend on automation within back-office areas, with the adoption of software as a service (SaaS) solutions, such as Salesforce and Workday, as well as encouraging further outsourcing to global service companies, many of whom are adopting RPA to reduce their headcount. Even government organisations understand that they must reduce bureaucracy, so that decisions on behalf of citizens can be made rapidly in days rather than months or even years.

Most incumbents recognise that modernising the core of their operations will only produce incremental benefits over the longer term. These business leaders are eschewing an investment in operational efficiencies and are instead turning to edge-based ventures that depend on new business models, partnerships and technologies. The challenge here is to scale such edge-based activities and to move the revenue needle in the right direction. Ultimately, success will require new partnerships with the core that can help enterprises to extend the lifetime value of established customers and global supply chains. We see three areas of focus for businesses and their IT partners:

1. Accelerating product innovation: Traditional approaches to product innovation have revolved around sequential processes, handing new ideas progressively down the supply chain, from research and development (R&D) through manufacture and on to sales. Modern management techniques take a parallel approach, involving all parties from day one in so-called 'two-pizza' teams.

2. Automating operations: Many attempts have been made to reduce bureaucracy and headcount. Enterprise resource planning (ERP) has helped businesses to automate most of their core functions, but it has also created rigid structures that are often fragmented and resistant to change. SaaS is gradually replacing many of the functions normally ascribed to ERP systems with public, web-based solutions that are maintained remotely. Outsourcing continues to reduce permanent staff numbers.

3. Innovating at the edge: Many organisations have introduced incubators to test out new business models and technologies. Few of these labs have produced significant results so far. Other enterprises are acquiring successful start-ups to inject new energy into stagnant cultures and to challenge established ways of operating. Perhaps the most successful approach to date has been to source innovation through joint ventures with external start-ups, rather than via acquisitions.

In all these respects, businesses are under increasing pressure to apply new technologies, methods and tools to transform the way they deliver their products and services. Success in these endeavours will be ever-more dependent on the ability of enterprises to operate modern and efficient IT kitchens. In this section, we provide valuable recipes from Master Chefs who have contributed to the success of their respective enterprises.

ONE
WIN THE CUSTOMER
Scoring five stars on Tripadvisor

The number-one priority for any digital leader is to understand who the customers of their business really are. In this set of three recipes, we see a broad spectrum of customers that range from instore and online shoppers to front-line military personnel and on to business partners, including shipping and logistics companies. However, what's common across all three recipes is a shift in emphasis away from internal customers, such as corporate functions, and towards external parties.

In the words of the Sainsbury's CIO, this shift has required a decisive move away from systems of record and engagement to a focus on digital as the very heart of the retail business. He recognises that we are now entering a new era of hyper-personalisation, where companies must extract insights from every customer interaction using modern tools such as data analytics.

What becomes evident through this chapter is the need for constant innovation around the customer experience. In the words of the CIO of the UK's Ministry of Defence (MoD), this concentration on innovation requires new conversations. Central here is the need

for closer integration between all four military divisions: air, land, sea and cyber. Silos need to be dismantled to enable greater speed and adaptability. The MoD's CIO speaks of the 'integration glue' that is an essential component of a modern military organisation. Such is the importance of integration that his role is evolving to become a 'chief connection officer'.

Service innovation can also help to improve the work that organisations undertake with external business partners and customers. The CIO of the Port of Antwerp joins 12 other global ports each year to conduct hackathons. These events aim to improve outward-facing logistics processes and metrics, such as boosting a port's ability to accurately report the expected time of arrival of a ship. The CIO recognises that innovation has become a vital means of securing and retaining business customers as adjacent ports fight hard to attract new business.

Overall, the message from these Master Chefs is clear. In a world of growing competition, innovation around the customer experience is now front of mind for digital leaders in all businesses.

Sainsbury's
Delivering world-class digital experiences

Ingredients

- Innovation at the heart of the corporate DNA
- Democratisation of data across all brands
- Drive for insight-driven decision reengineering
- Seamless consumer experiences across channels

Preparing the dish

Innovation around the customer proposition has been part of retailer Sainsbury's DNA since its inception more than 150 years ago. In the words of Sainsbury's group CIO, Phil Jordan: 'Combining great technologies with great people is the recipe for great customer experiences.'

As the UK's second largest supermarket chain, with 1,400 stores, as well as being owner of Argos, Nectar and Sainsbury's Bank, the firm has to ensure it always puts the customer first. Sainsbury's has pioneered the development of self-service checkouts, smart scanning technology, the production of healthy foods and is a leader in ethical and responsible supply chains.

A combination of the rapid shift to online channels during the COVID-19 crisis, plus aggressive competition from Amazon and discount retailers such as Lidl and Aldi, has placed added pressure on Sainsbury's to deliver outstanding customer experience across all its channels and brands. This delivery has been achieved by strengthening the business–IT partnership in three areas: restructuring IT services around products; democratising and leveraging the use of customer data; and adopting open-source standards and platforms.

Restructuring IT services

Like many comparable IT organisations operating at scale, the efforts of Sainsbury's 1,600-strong IT staff were focused traditionally on modifying and extending core systems within the various businesses. This effort was driven by a project-based approach to investment and service delivery.

In recent times, Phil has implemented a productised approach. This strategy leverages developments across all business units and employs a different financing regime, which is based on half-yearly cycles. Phil believes this approach provides an escape route from legacy practices and is the best way to serve the demands of his internal customers. The strategy also helps IT to allocate its resources more efficiently.

Phil has split his Product Engineering into two sections, each headed by a chief technology officer (CTO). Both have end-to-end life-cycle responsibility for all Sainsbury's products, one facing into customer and data; the other into colleagues, suppliers and operations. These units are supported by three other organisations: Platform Engineering and Services, Information Security, and Supplier Management. Phil's role within this new organisational context is to deliver business transformation, maintain the impetus for change and to promote technology as a key business differentiator.

Leveraging customer data

In a world where technology itself is commoditising rapidly, Phil has adopted the mantra of 'the three "I"s' – innovation, information and integration. He believes information, or 'connected customer data', is the key differentiator for Sainsbury's across all its businesses. He has used Snowflake to build a cloud-based data platform and democratised data access across the brands.

This platform has led to some significant innovations within the business. For example, by applying machine learning to instore data, Sainsbury's can reduce the walk time of employees who are restocking shelves. By mapping data throughout the different business units, Phil has created a digital/data twin of the business that derives insight to deliver speed and efficiency gains in every aspect of the group's operations.

Data analytics is also helping Sainsbury's customers to make better buying decisions. Predictive analytics can help the company to personalise weekly shopping orders. This personalisation nudges customers towards more relevant products that offer better value. Sainsbury's seeks to continually

"Combining great technologies with great people is the recipe for great customer experiences."

Phil Jordan, CIO, Sainsbury's Group

Scan code to watch the full interview.

increase customer intimacy and trust. These improvements result in bigger basket size, both instore and online, and improved sales figures.

Embracing open source and other innovations

Sainsbury's enjoys a strong engineering culture that is a constant source of new techniques. The firm's 800-strong engineering community looks for ways to exploit its technical expertise across a broader range of markets. Open-source technology has been embraced by the company's engineering community. The team uses open-source technology to share innovative ideas across the group as well as with external parties. One example is in increasing levels of e-commerce capability that was pioneered in-house and is now a showcase for what is possible.

Cloud has been central to Sainsbury's IT agenda for many years. The retailer has fostered a strong relationship with Amazon Web Services (AWS). The strength of this relationship is unusual amongst retailers given the potential for competitive overlaps, but Phil is pleased with the support Amazon provides. Line-of-business functions have adopted software-as-a-service solutions, and new IT products have been developed on public cloud platforms. Phil believes Sainsbury's will continue pursuing a hybrid cloud strategy as he consolidates internal data centre resources.

A strong technological ecosystem is crucial to delivering results against 'the three "I"s'. Phil believes cloud is the essential platform from which to encourage partnering with external parties. His team now works with Google Cloud and Microsoft Azure in addition to AWS.

Sainsbury's continues to search for new innovations. Augmented reality (AR) and virtual reality (VR) present fascinating opportunities to retailers. Consumers can expect to enjoy fully immersive experiences both at home and in store. Sainsbury's is experimenting already with AR and VR and is investigating how the technologies can be used to enhance shopping missions. The company is also experimenting with imaging and video behaviour analytics to see what is possible in creating new customer experiences and to continue transforming the store operating model.

Defining the qualities of a Master Chef

The role of IT has already evolved from maintaining systems of record and systems of engagement to becoming the very heart of the modern retail business – yet further change is coming. Phil believes the CIO role will evolve from a focus on service production to helping peers identify new digital businesses. He is building on the heritage of innovation at Sainsbury's to create an integrated business architecture that focuses on the end consumer across the company's brands and channels.

Tips

- Adopt the mantra of information, innovation and integration
- Help shape the business agenda as well as focusing on IT

The UK Ministry of Defence
Building a connected organisation

Ingredients

- A passion for getting stuff done
- Persistence and patience
- Connecting people internally and externally
- A diverse and inclusive team

Preparing the dish

Charlie Forte was appointed CIO of the UK's Ministry of Defence (MoD) in 2018 . With an annual IT budget in the multiple billions, he holds one of the largest and most complex IT positions in Europe. Charlie's belief at the time of his appointment was that a fresh approach to digital and IT could bring entirely new possibilities and opportunities to UK defence: he believes that 'All that is ever missing is a conversation.'

Forte's vision was to put transformational game-changing digital and information technologies on the front line and into core operations, making these tools integrated, simple to use and highly secure. He knew the key to success would be helping to increase organisational cohesion and integration in what is a very large and complex defence organisation, breaking down stovepipes and moving to work in much more integrated ways. He has worked tirelessly with the leaders of the four main military front-line commands – army, navy, air force and strategic command – and with the leaders of the other large enabling units that make up the UK defence family. He describes this part of his role as the 'chief connecting officer'.

Charlie believes the three main ingredients for a successful transformation of the UK's military backbone are: cohesion (working together to increase connectedness and alignment); integration (building outcomes that work together); and adaptability (responding with speed and agility).

Putting theory into practice

Charlie has developed an operating plan with five 'swim lanes' to achieve his vision of a highly connected, agile and innovative organisation:

- Exploiting data as a strategic asset at scale and speed – the digital foundry;

- Building a modern digital platform – the digital backbone;

- Resetting and modernising cyber defence;

- Creating a step change in digital delivery with new levels of trust and consistency in delivery;

- Investing in building talent, diversity and a new way of working across defence as 'one function'.

Defence is large and complex and to achieve this Charlie has used persistence and patience to establish the right conversations across divisional boundaries as well as with outside parties: 'Getting stuff done and making things happen is all about connecting people and ideas,' he says. He sees that being successful in today's technology landscape is a team sport needing multidisciplinary teams working to clear outcomes and avoiding being process focused. This is a big cultural shift.

Creating a new IT operating model

Charlie's new IT operating model is based on the ancient Chinese metaphor, yin and yang. He sees the two key forces (described below) as complementary rather than opposing, interacting to form a dynamic system in which the whole is greater than the sum of its parts:

- Yin: speed; an ability to build capability and to be close to the customer (which in the MoD's case means delivery at the front line),

- Yang: the need for the various parts of the organisation to give something up by adopting open standards and platforms.

Charlie leads an IT organisation that consists of three main sections. The first section contains the senior IT directors who serve each military service or function directly, and who have a matrix reporting relationship to Charlie. The second section is what he refers to as 'the engine room'; a set of shared services on which all defence systems and related programmes are managed. The third and new section is 'the integration glue'. Established by Charlie, this section focuses on the technologies and standards that are required in a

"Getting stuff done and making things happen is all about connecting people and ideas."

Charlie Forte, CIO, MoD

Scan code to watch the full interview.

modern and effective army. This section works across all service areas.

Becoming the chief connecting officer

Charlie says transforming and innovating a complex and sizeable organisation means he must position himself less as a technologist and more as a chief connecting officer. He also recognises that change is a 'team sport' that requires the full collaboration of parties across the organisation.

Charlie's role is to help his peers understand and connect with new potential opportunities due to rapid developments in technology. He says there has never been a better time to apply the technologies emerging from the pipeline of innovation both in the UK and elsewhere. He believes IT creates a spark of possibility and must build strong partnership to achieve what is 'doable'. Combining the possible and the doable is the key to success in any large organisation, especially within the military.

When Charlie joined the MoD, he spent a great deal of time visiting the front line to understand the different businesses. He was fortunate that his peers gave him access to important operational areas, which made his task both rapid and productive. This introduction to the work of the MoD allowed Charlie to draw on the best resources across the businesses as he built his transformation teams. As he built these teams, Charlie focused on diversity and inclusiveness.

Defining the qualities of a Master Chef

Charlie recognises that transforming an organisation with strong traditions and more than 60,000 uniformed and civilian staff is an enormous task. However, his deep-seated belief is that, with persistence and patience, any leader can transform any organisation successfully.

He says the best leaders have a passion for their role and a clear vision about where the organisation should be heading. Given the emphasis on technology and innovation, Charlie also believes that success in digital leadership is powered by a deep sense of inquiry and the patience to use that to create aligned commitments to new outcomes.

His final advice for leaders is to, 'never avoid a hard conversation and to be open minded to listen to diverse perspectives and views'. That human connection is the key underpinning principle.

Port of Antwerp
Putting innovation at the centre of the organisation

Ingredients

- New chief executive and leadership team
- Inspired talent – sprinters and runners
- Innovative technology tools – smart cameras, sensors, drones, RPA, data science
- Open-source platforms
- Ecosystems for continuous 'outside-in' inspiration

Preparing the dish

Antwerp is Europe's second largest port. Being able to sustain its leadership position in the face of formidable competition is a constant challenge for the executive committee, including the port's chief digital and innovation officer (CDIO), Erwin Verstraelen. Geopolitical challenges, such as Brexit, and exponential technology growth, create further challenges. The port aims to turn these challenges into opportunities.

To survive and thrive, the Port of Antwerp must have an innovative culture that is embraced by every member of the organisation and the extended port ecosystem. Erwin says this integrated approach is essential: 'I don't believe in an approach where we create a separate innovation team. Innovation should be everywhere, but we must give it an opportunity to surface and blossom. This requires a structured approach to avoid innovation leading to chaos.'

His formula for innovation success includes: transforming the organisational culture into an opportunistic rather than a risk-averse mentality; experimenting constantly with new ideas and technologies; and building strong capabilities and

"Innovation should be everywhere, but we must give it an opportunity to surface and blossom."

Erwin Verstraelen, CDIO, Port of Antwerp

Scan code to watch the full interview.

partnerships. Erwin's digital and innovation team (DI), which includes the traditional IT department, has provided the vision and inspiration to transform the port as an innovation platform. For the Port of Antwerp, success means working closely with internal and external business partners.

Creating an innovation culture

Erwin says his department fulfils a central role in helping to enable an innovative culture to emerge and prosper within the port and across its trading partners. This is dependent on three preconditions:

- Be clear and articulate about your strategic goals as a leading port;

- Have all the competencies in place to sustain leadership;

- Empower the entire workforce to take risks and experiment with new ideas.

As mentioned above, building an innovative team is critical to success – but not sufficient in isolation. IT must take its best-practice techniques, and enable and inspire an innovative culture across the organisation. IT can engender the trust of the business by performing consistently on its core tasks, such as running a complex infrastructure and building

new applications rapidly. But IT must also go beyond this remit and support innovation across every aspect of the port's operations.

Supporting innovation through IT

There are many ways in which a leading port can apply new technologies to sustain its leadership position. IT can inform the business about the potential that technological innovation holds and assist in setting up proof of values, where the potential of a technology can be sensed in the context of the organisation. Recent examples include:

- Drones to provide situational awareness over the 120 km^2 port area, detecting oil spills and asset inspection;

- Smart cameras that can extract data from video for surveillance and asset detection;

- Robotic process automation to help streamline traditional processes, thereby improving speed and efficiency across the port.

At the end of the day, innovation has to support the realisation of strategic business objectives, aiming to differentiate Antwerp in its battle against other leading ports and stay competitive.

Building the necessary capabilities

Since arriving at the Port of Antwerp, Erwin has expanded the digital and innovation capabilities of the port. In addition to digital business solutions and infrastructure services, IT now has four new competencies:

- Cyber resilience that is designed to deal with cyber incidents more effectively, as well as actively averting attacks;

- Innovation enablement that constantly places new ideas on the organisational radar and supports early-stage experiments;

- Data and analytics that looks for predictive patterns amongst the huge amount of data that is produced by the port and its partners;

- A CDIO office that coordinates the many IT vendor relationships and contracts that exist across the organisation, and manages resources as well as the overall budget.

The successful operation of core systems and services is a necessary condition for success in these new areas. Keeping the lights on, even in the digital age, is still the foundation for credibility and trust from the organisation, a stepping stone towards authority and impact in the digital transformation.

Developing innovation talent and opportunities

It can be difficult for large, traditional enterprises to attract and retain innovative talent and leaders. Erwin has taken steps to ensure his vision spreads far and wide, both within and outside the organisation. The result? He has encouraged younger employees to join the port.

Erwin recognises that any organisation has four different types of staff – sprinters, runners, walkers and those 'who will not move'. Instead of focusing efforts on the latter two groups, he identifies and enables the port's sprinters and runners. He has created several new organisational units and functions, such as enterprise architecture, that help to encourage staff and skill development.

Participating in a global hackathon

One of the most exciting areas of innovation at the port is the harvesting of data to feed predictive and prescriptive algorithms. In 2019, a consortium of leading ports from around the world, called Chainport, came together to conduct a hackathon around several potential use cases leveraging operational data. One of the themes was a better prediction of the expected time of arrival (ETA) of a ship into port.

The hackathon teams examined how combining different sources of data could improve the accuracy of predictions for the ETA of every vessel entering a port. More accurate ETAs would produce big benefits for stakeholders inside and outside the port. Such joined-up activity shows that collaboration is as critical as competition in helping businesses to maintain commercial leadership.

Defining the qualities of a Master Chef

The creation of an innovative culture is not a one-time task. It requires a continual process of enabling experimentation, strengthening capabilities, and motivating staff. Erwin says digital leaders are instrumental in helping to create a better future for their organisations. They should be visionary and active relationship builders, working alongside their C-suite peers and external partners, such as customers and suppliers.

Nikkei-style tuna ceviche

Serves 2 hearty eaters

- 500g very fresh, raw tuna
- zest of 1 lime
- 2 tbsp ginger juice
- 2 tbsp Peruvian chilli paste
- juice of 6 limes
- 6 spring onions, finely chopped
- 1 handful of coriander leaves, chopped
- 1 small red chilli, finely chopped (optional)
- 2 tsp sesame oil
- 2 tbsp light soy sauce
- salt and pepper

Nikkei cuisine has been taking the foodie world by storm, helped by support from renowned chefs like Ferran Adrià. But what is it? At the end of the nineteenth century, Peru became one of the first countries to have formal diplomatic relations with Japan; the first Japanese immigrants arrived in Lima in 1899. 'Nikkei' is the word given to them and their descendants around the world, and they had an immediate impact on Peruvian food culture – one which has continued and thrived there, and has also flourished in Brazil.

Nikkei cooking has been described as a Japanese take on South American food, with the combined influence and ingredients giving rise to something which both looks and tastes different to either cuisine.

Prepare all the ingredients first because you need to be quick. Chop the tuna into small cubes and put them in a bowl. Add the lime zest, ginger juice and Peruvian chilli paste, and stir. Now add the lime juice, stir, and marinate the tuna for just a single minute; the lime will cook the fish, and do so quickly – you can see it changing colour. Add the remaining ingredients, and stir everything together again. Check the mix for seasoning, add salt and pepper if needed, and serve immediately.

The favourite dish of Dimitris Bountolos

TWO
REINVENTING THE BUSINESS
New concepts and menus

The challenge for large incumbent organisations across Europe in the post-pandemic age is to grow revenues and increase profits, especially as digital natives remain stock-market darlings around the globe. In this chapter, our recipes focus on three major organisations that have accelerated growth and generated new products and services through the use of digital technologies and the reinvention of business models.

Our first recipe comes from Munich Re, which has identified exciting new opportunities in the insurance sector, such as mitigating cyber risk. Rather than disturbing its core business, Munich Re has adopted a greenfield approach to innovation. It has established a portfolio of new digital businesses that are backed by £100 million of venture funding. IT has created its own innovation unit to support this initiative, known as Business Technology, which provides a digital platform and tool set to accelerate business formation.

Tate & Lyle provides our second recipe. Over the past 10 years, the company has sold off its sugar division and focused instead on food ingredients that can be used to improve the lives of people around the world. One of the key components of this new model is giving global customers the ability to test out ingredients in virtual kitchens. This shift has been enabled by IT, which has developed new ways of working that allow employees to harness the power of data.

Our final recipe in this chapter focuses on Signify. This recipe illustrates how technology can help transform commodity products – in this case lightbulbs – into sophisticated tools that can be used to support smart homes, offices and cities. Signify has introduced a new concept known as 'Li-Fi', which enables LED lamps to provide high-capacity bandwidth using light modulation. This transformation has added new sources of value to Signify's business.

The key message of this chapter is that IT can enable and accelerate business innovation by providing new tools, digital platforms and skills.

Munich Re

Becoming a serial innovator of new digital businesses

Ingredients

- A distinct group within IT dedicated to new digital business initiatives
- Value-based target portfolio and simplified access to funding
- Dedicated expertise from a pool of experts
- Platform of reusable technological components

Preparing the dish

To thrive in the digital economy, firms must diversify how they make money. Over the past few years, leading reinsurance company Münchener Rückversicherungs-Gesellschaft Aktiengesellschaft (Munich Re) has ramped up its customer-facing digital innovation efforts significantly. Those efforts have led to, among others, Munich Re Ventures, cyber-insurance offerings, and several new internally developed business-to-business-to-consumer (B2B2C) digital offerings that provide new sources of revenue.

Two new digital offerings, Munich Re Internet Risk Assessor (MIRA) Digital Suite and Realytix, grew their revenue and customer base in just two years. The MIRA Digital Suite is a range of services that allow insurance companies to automate the process of handling complex life applications, including those that rely on lengthy manual processing due to pre-existing conditions. The Realytix platform uses cloud-based technology to reduce the time it takes an insurance company to underwrite non-life risks, such as in the case of factory construction.

Becoming a serial innovator of new digital businesses

Munich Re was keen to experiment with a range of digital offerings simultaneously. After launching several initiatives, the company noticed that many experienced similar challenges. In 2016, Munich Re started to build a foundation to help its internally developed digital offerings to succeed. The foundation provided prioritised and staged funding, dedicated, hands-on expertise, and a digital platform of shared services. By 2020, more than 70 initiatives were relying on this foundation.

Creating a new approach to innovation

Senior management defined a target portfolio to prioritise initiatives and ensure that they would help the company realise its strategic objectives. Munich Re's portfolio looked beyond typical three-stage innovation time horizons, prescribing which customers' needs to address and what business value to create. Munich Re's global head of innovation communicated the target portfolio in roadshows and online, encouraging employees across the company to pitch ideas related to the company's priorities.

Munich Re created a separate fund for digital innovation of about €100 million annually. Employees could apply for a limited budget to jump-start an initiative by answering five questions. Munich Re then employed a stage-gated funding process: if an initiative reaches the jointly set goal for a stage, the initiative becomes eligible for an additional, larger, round of funding.

In 2018, Munich Re's IT leadership team created a new unit within IT, called Business Technology, dedicated exclusively to helping innovation initiatives build digital offerings. Business Technology gave these initiatives a range of experts, such as software developers, data scientists, and design-thinking and agile coaches. In addition to contributing their domain expertise to build, test and adapt prototypes, these experts helped innovators to develop sales pitches and navigate Munich Re's organisational structure.

At the ideation stage, major digital offering initiatives were assigned a senior architect to act as co-founder to the full-time, business-based product owner. Business Technology formalised the senior architect role through the introduction of chief innovation and technology officers (CI&TOs). Having complementary co-founders also helped build buy-in across multiple stakeholder groups, making it easier for qualifying initiatives to gain greater investment.

Building a digital platform with shared software components

In its prior innovation efforts, Munich Re built a digital platform and expected initiatives to use the software components that were available. This time, Munich Re decided to first let digital offering initiatives experience what shared components they might need. As a result of this approach, lessons were learnt continuously. Early initiatives observed that developing capabilities, such as non-differentiating functionality for customer identity management or compliant cloud data storage, strained their limited resources and prolonged time to market.

Munich Re used the demand for capabilities from these early initiatives to create Excite, which is its platform for digital offerings. The platform evolved as initiatives progressed and sought help. A year after it was launched, Excite comprised more than 30 shared software components.

Business Technology compelled, rather than forced, its digital offering initiatives to use Excite components. The platform was pitched as a set of managed shared services that unburden initiatives from building essential yet non-differentiating functionality. For each component, the Excite team developed service level agreements that make it clear to initiatives what they will get in exchange for the fee they pay.

Munich Re's digital foundation has evolved as it learns what factors help initiatives to thrive. The team at Munich Re responsible for developing the platform of shared resources measures its success along four objectives: accelerated time to market for digital products; improved experience for customers using offerings relying on Excite; revenue growth; and cost savings with component reuse.

Defining the qualities of a Master Chef

To develop a successful digital offering, an initiative's team must learn how to address customer needs in a manner that is feasible and profitable. To become a serial innovator of digital offerings, as with Munich Re, a company will have to learn how to address systematically the common challenges of multiple initiatives in regard to funding, expertise and technological capabilities.

For funding:
- Define a targeted portfolio of digital offering initiatives;
- Extend funding in stages based on progress along jointly agreed goals, regarding both deliverables and value creation.

For expertise:

- Install an architect as a co-founder to the business for each major initiative;

- Provide each initiative with technology and methodology experts who are fully dedicated to its success.

For technological capabilities:

- Build a digital platform from the bottom up as initiatives recognise the benefits of shared components;

- Promote the platform to initiatives as managed shared services that provide relief from developing non-differentiating functionality.

Sources (available at https://cisr.mit.edu/):

Fonstad, Nils and Martin Mocker (2020), 'Becoming a Serial Innovator of Digital Offerings', *MIT CISR Research Briefing*, Vol. XX, No. 9, September 2020.

Fonstad, Nils and Martin Mocker (2020), 'Munich Re: Building a Foundation for Innovating Digital Offerings'.

Tate & Lyle
Reinventing business, redesigning work

Preparing the dish

Tate & Lyle PLC is a British-headquartered, global supplier of food and beverage ingredients. It was originally a sugar-refining business, but it began to diversify from the 1970s, eventually divesting its sugar business in 2010. Today, Tate & Lyle specialises in turning raw materials like corn, tapioca and stevia into ingredients that add taste, texture, fibre and nutrients to food and beverages.

In the words of Sanjay Patel, Group CIO at Tate & Lyle: 'Our purpose of improving lives for generations is why we do what we do. It guides every action we take and every decision we make.' As global head of Strategic Business Transformation and then as CIO, Sanjay has been actively engaged with his C-suite and business peers in redesigning the business to suit its purpose.

Changing the way we work

Prior to COVID-19, IT had focused on addressing infrastructure opportunities like global network access, refreshed user devices and secure desktop and mobile

"Our purpose of improving lives for generations guides every action we take and every decision we make."

Sanjay Patel, Group CIO, Tate & Lyle

Scan code to watch the full interview.

collaboration software that would enable the company's 4,500 employees to work safely from anywhere. This groundwork, appropriately titled 'Better Ways of Working', enabled the group to respond to the initial lockdown quickly and to roll out universal home working in a matter of weeks. In March 2020, Tate & Lyle was able to close its year-end books remotely and provide virtual support to its many food, beverage, paper and packaging customers who had to adapt to the pandemic quickly.

In the post-COVID age, Sanjay and his team are enabling a hybrid model that encompasses both home and office working. This approach includes:

- Utilising office space around the globe for collaboration and teamwork, which provides an opportunity for a physical redesign of traditional office layouts and ways of working, e.g. smaller offices with mobile enabled booking apps, advanced video and collaboration tools;

- Enabling work from anywhere outside the office, including home and customer locations, by supplying virtual reality devices, video-enabled collaboration tools and home equipment including stand-up desks and wide split-screen monitors.

This hybrid approach allows Tate & Lyle's customers to join the company's staff in virtual tasting events and means Tate & Lyle employees can use travel kits (aka 'meeting in a box') to connect disparate co-workers at a customer site to help design and evaluate new food ingredients. Sanjay is proud that these capabilities have enabled his company to keep working and collaborating with customers to create new products and share knowledge and experience globally.

Building pathways to enterprise automation

In addition to redesigning the workplace, the team also focused on continuing to simplify the way people work. Tate & Lyle employs SAP for back-office automation but also uses software as a service (SaaS) products, including Workday in HR and Salesforce in customer relationship management, to enhance efficiency and global consistency. Sanjay is establishing a Digital Centre of Excellence, leveraging an AWS 'data lake' for consolidating all corporate information into one place and Power BI analytics and visualisation tooling so that staff can easily access and gain insights across recipes, finances and other information. The team is also establishing a 'bot factory' with process mining capability, leveraging early use cases from finance and supply chain functions to drive further automation, removing manual work and paper-based processes and driving further automated workflow. The company's board recognised the strategic importance of artificial intelligence (AI) for its future growth and has been investing in emerging areas as an opportunity to secure the company's future as far forward as 2030.

Sanjay's approach to RPA is to 'crawl before you walk before you run'. His team has started a number of small projects with simple use cases. He envisages that bots will eventually manage bots within the factory environment, leaving humans to oversee this network of bots. This managerial approach will mean that employee administrative activities will be replaced by automation. This will allow employees to focus on higher-value tasks and help support non-linear growth in future revenues, with the prospect of higher group profitability.

Approaching citizen development

In the past few years, Sanjay has focused on eliminating 'grey IT' by imposing standards across the group and by consolidating data into one place in the form of a cloud-based data lake. Looking ahead, he welcomes the advent

of a low-code/no-code era, where a business's end users will be able to develop their own solutions, as well as buying cloud-based services. He believes this shift towards end-user empowerment will add speed and agility to overall business processes.

However, empowerment does not mean handing off responsibility. Sanjay is insistent that, for now, IT must own anything that touches code, so that his team can control data integrity across the group. He has deployed Power BI to foster a data-driven culture and is developing appropriate data-insight tools to support decision-making processes. One target for the future is around predictive forecasting. By using machine learning to understand past demand forecast accuracy, the 'machine' can supplement human insights and improve demand forecast accuracy, improving supply chain yields, reducing inventory and improving customer satisfaction. Sanjay believes that IT can help optimise many other complex business processes like this through AI and related automation technologies.

Reorganising the IT kitchen

To keep pace with the reinvention of the group, Sanjay's first task was to reorganise the way IT provides its services to the group's business units. He reduced IT costs by consolidating and rationalising IT activities across the globe, keeping competitive and intellectual property (IP)-based activities internally driven, and outsourcing everything else. His next step was to engage strategic partners to work closely with his function in four main areas:

- Secure operations that include infrastructure and applications maintenance;

- Strategy and solutions, where IT works with the businesses to develop new applications;

- Enterprise architecture and user experience that ensures standard deployments;

- A new digital tower that oversees data analytics and RPA.

Today, Sanjay employs around 120 internal IT staff, supplemented by over 250 external partner staff. This sourcing strategy means he and his team can spend more time on strategic issues rather than being preoccupied with all the operational, executional aspects of IT.

Defining the qualities of a Master Chef

Having been the former head of transformation at Tate & Lyle, Sanjay believes that successful CIOs must work closely with C-suite peers to understand the priorities and bottlenecks of the business. His key task is to listen to heads of business functions and understand their problems, matching these challenges to technology-based solutions. Building credibility through rapid delivery of value will earn IT the right to be an equal partner at the table. He believes curiosity and strategic thinking combined with an ability to operate at a granular level are key qualities of the IT Master Chef.

Tip
- Follow in the style of Mahatma Gandhi, who valued humility and dedication to cause above all else

Signify
Mastering the customer experience

Preparing the dish

With a background in economics and experience in the chemicals sector, Kurt De Ruwe took a career turn by joining Philips Lighting in 2013. Just one year later, Philips demerged into two primary business areas: medical technologies and lighting. The latter undertook an initial public offering (IPO) in 2016 under the new name of Signify.

Signify focuses on the rapid growth of LED lighting, with the potential for new connected customer solutions using light as an 'intelligent language'. Internet signals passed through the network cables can modulate light emissions from LED bulbs. Each lighting source has its own IP address, and can connect directly with smartphones, laptops and sensors. Next to this Signify also has Li-Fi, a communication technology that transmits data through light. Li-Fi offers a viable alternative to Wi-Fi with the following benefits:

- ■ High-speed connectivity of around 150 megabits per second;

- ■ Improved physical security by limiting connections to a defined space;

- ■ Low latency of information transmission.

Estimates suggest there could now be as many as 50 billion devices connected to the internet. In a new age

"CIOs must help their businesses employ data analytics and artificial intelligence to personalise the customer experience."

Kurt De Ruwe, CIO, Signify

Scan code to watch the full interview.

of connectivity, Li-Fi opens new possibilities for the Internet of Things. This opportunity has helped Kurt position digital at the forefront of Signify's business strategy.

Creating new sources of revenue

The lighting industry has consolidated rapidly during the past decade. Many leading brands have disappeared from the professional and consumer landscape. Today, Signify occupies the number one position in its sector and is a leading innovator of LED-related products, solutions and services. Signify has shifted its focus towards 'customer experiences' by transitioning from the large-scale manufacture of traditional lightbulbs towards the development of digital lighting solutions.

The prospects for growth in connected lighting are significant. From smart cities to smart homes, Signify's smart services provide vital intelligence on physical location, from how many people occupy an office to whether there's an intruder in a home. Such developments have sponsored a shift in lighting away from commodity products and towards customer services and associated user interfaces.

Signify spotted this trend quickly, investing in new lighting applications and introducing venture financing. This backing

has created a flow of start-ups and new product features, such as an app that controls the local lighting environment. Kurt has played a key role in helping Signify to shift from a focus on traditional, analogue products to a new era of smart, connected lighting.

Considering the master of enterprise service

Prior to the demerger in 2014, Philips Lighting was driven by a culture of operational efficiency that enabled market leadership. The company was firmly focused on global manufacturing and local marketing through national organisations. The role of IT at this time was to implement and run global ERP systems, including an SAP platform that helped to integrate production hubs and automate functions such as finance, HR and procurement. IT responsibilities also extended out into the global supply chain. The technology team worked with suppliers and channel partners.

By helping to integrate operational processes under an SAP regime, the global CIO was seen as the 'Master of Enterprise Services'. IT projects were run on a waterfall approach. As SAP took root across the business, IT helped to streamline manufacturing and back-office processes. National organisations were expected to find their own marketing solutions to local challenges.

Becoming the master of customer experience

The IT organisation had to pivot in response to Signify's shift towards LED technologies and customer solutions. Recognising the fast pace of development in this new field, Kurt promoted the widespread use of Agile and DevOps techniques. These techniques helped the company respond quickly to front-end and back-end challenges. He divided the IT organisation into three areas, which he calls 'tribes':

- Process tribes, which are aligned to key business processes, such as order to cash and invention to marketplace

- Enabling tribes, which continue to support back-office functions, such as finance, procurement and HR

- Technology tribes, which operate the core infrastructure, such as data centres, networks and office environments

This new tribe-led organisation helps IT to engage more closely with front-end business functions and deliver customer experience solutions, such as phone and web-based applications.

Streamlining the IT organisation

Kurt has consolidated IT operations into three geographic hubs: Poland, Mexico and India. He has also improved operational efficiency by automating repetitive jobs and introducing collaborative tools, such as Yammer, to encourage the sharing of information. Signify also deploys RPA and chatbots to bring further automation to back-office functions.

Since demerging from Philips, Kurt has reduced the number of applications from 4,300 to 1,400. He has promoted a cloud-first strategy for new applications, especially those focused on the customer experience. This consolidation and transformation has reduced the number of on-premise servers dramatically. Overall, IT costs and headcount are now down by as much as 40%.

Defining the qualities of a Master Chef

Kurt says the role of the CIO has changed dramatically during the past 10 years. Traditionally, the CIO role was about ensuring that everything worked. Today, CIOs must focus attention on the user experience, whether that's in terms of the end customer or the employee. CIOs must help their businesses employ data analytics and artificial intelligence to personalise the customer experience.

Most importantly, Kurt believes that successful CIOs engage closely with business peers and are proactive in promoting new techniques. He has established a digital board with his business counterparts to develop roadmaps and priorities. He is proud to say that IT has increased its visibility considerably by helping to shape the company's vision for a connected future.

Paneer tikka

Serves 4

- 500g paneer
- 3 red peppers
- Spray oil

For the marinade:

- 1 tbsp lemon juice
- 2cm piece of fresh ginger, grated
- 1 large garlic clove, grated
- A generous pinch each of turmeric, ground cumin, ground coriander and paprika
- 50ml Greek yoghurt
- Black pepper

For the raita:

- 250ml yoghurt
- A small handful of fresh mint or coriander

Put the marinade ingredients in a large bowl, stir together well, and add a good grinding of black pepper. Cut the paneer into slices or cubes no larger than 3cm, then chop the peppers into similarly sized pieces. Add these to the marinade and mix them together carefully. Cover the bowl and set it aside for at least 2 hours – it can also be left in the fridge overnight.

Soak some bamboo skewers in water for 20 minutes, and preheat the oven to a high temperature – paneer tikka is traditionally cooked in a tandoor which can reach over 230°C. While the oven heats up, make a raita to serve with the paneer – finely chop the leaves from a handful of mint or coriander, and stir them into the yoghurt. Cover and set aside.

Line a baking tray with foil. Thread the paneer onto the skewers, alternating each piece with a chunk of red pepper. Brush the completed skewers with any leftover marinade and spray them lightly with oil – this should help prevent the paneer from going rubbery in the oven. Cook them in the oven for 10 to 12 minutes (timing will depend on the thickness of the pieces of paneer), then put the tray directly under a very hot grill for a further 2 to 3 minutes to char the paneer and peppers, turning the skewers as you do so.

Serve, accompanied by the raita and a green salad.

The favourite dish of Tarun Kohli

THREE
STRUCTURE THE BUSINESS ENTERPRISE

Winning the best restaurant of the year award

Customer expectations and preferences are advancing at breakneck speed in our digital economy. If large organisations want to outperform their competitors and become the restaurant of the year, they must restructure rapidly to deal with this fast-changing external environment.

In the case of data analytics specialist dunnhumby, the chief product and information officer has recognised the need to productise his offerings to match the variations in maturity of the company's retail customers around the globe. Open-source standards and scalable cloud platforms have enabled dunnhumby's 3,000 staff to employ common tools and share vital data resources. The result of this work is that the company can address customer variations with speed and efficiency.

The focus of the CIO at telecommunications firm Proximus was somewhat different. To help the business retain its two million customers, he recognised Proximus would need to emulate Toyota and deliver a fault-free experience for home-based customers. Starting small with a five-person team, IT helped the organisation to develop customer 'data' profiles. The company used these profiles to apply predictive maintenance tools. The result has been the introduction of proactive service measures that have led to an impressive 30% fall in reported faults.

In all three recipes in this chapter, legacy systems and tooling continue to haunt incumbent and digital organisations. In the case of digital native mBank, this reliance on older technology came as an unwelcome surprise to the recently appointed chief operating officer. Despite being just 10 years old, mBank was operating core systems on COBOL. These systems needed to be converted to modern, cloud-based platforms. By making this transition, mBank's retail and corporate banking operations could create innovative customer offerings ahead of their competitors and set the direction of travel for the banking sector in Poland.

The overriding message is that industry leaders need to please their customers by adopting flexible business structures and IT systems based on open sourcing and Agile development methods.

dunnhumby
Human-powered business transformation

Preparing the dish

dunnhumby is a 30-year-old data sciences company employing more than 2,500 staff worldwide. It provides data monetisation and analytics services to leading retailers such as Tesco and Walmart and hundreds of the world's consumer packaged goods (CPGs). It processes the contents of more than a billion shoppers' baskets every day, which is worth half a trillion dollars in value.

David Jack, the company's CTO, has a passion for putting the customer first. And by customer he means the end consumer, the person that gets the right product at the best price with the most appropriate mix in their basket. He does this by not only influencing the retailer but by also participating across the supply chain, whether that's consumer product companies, wholesale distributors or onto the retailer's till and beyond. He believes every participant in this ecosystem can and should draw value from the insights that can be extracted from the transactional data.

David has led, with the other executives, a company-wide transformation. The transformation encompasses the science, the products and services, the processes and technologies that support the products, and the culture that builds and nurtures exceptional talent.

He has adopted the mantra of 'let people do people things and ensure that machines do all the machine things'. He loves the 'human-powered engine', which harnesses more than an aggregate of 3,000 years of data science experience that the business has gained. He aims to challenge his staff constantly: 'If you act like a parent, the team will behave like children. If you act like a peer, the team will challenge you and take you to a better place.'

Engineering the best set of products

The demand for breadth and richness across dunnhumby's products and services is due to the company working with a wide and varied range of retailers and CPGs across Europe, the Americas and Asia with different levels of data maturity, diverse business pressures and complex global regulatory frameworks.

Rapid product development, high-fidelity deployment and operational repeatability are key to dunnhumby's success. There is a strong focus on productisation of the rich set of services that have been developed over the years. This means that standardisation, code reuse and adoption of industry platforms (where appropriate) are essential. The organisation makes widespread use of open-source standards and platforms.

This openness allows David's 500 data scientists to share resources and capabilities easily, which accelerates product and science development. It also means that, over time, more retail customers will be able to use and contribute directly to dunnhumby's open-source ecosystem. The result is an efficient and agile science product organisation which will constantly evolve and refine.

Nudging the culture forwards

David recognises that no single individual can transform the culture of a large organisation. Instead, his role is to 'nudge the organisation forward' by celebrating successes and addressing weaknesses. This approach requires a new style of leadership that continues to reinforce dunnhumby's long-held values, such as celebrating courage and collaboration.

David says that going beyond simple understanding of consumer intent and really getting to the heart of the psychology (and even the language) behind the buying decision is a fascinating area of research for dunnhumby and that they have a rich academic programme that supports some of the long-term science and machine-learning innovation.

Aligning corporate processes

The data-ingestion process at

"If you act like a parent, the team will behave like children. If you act like a peer, the team will challenge you and take you to a better place."

David Jack, CTO, dunnhumby

Scan code to watch the full interview.

dunnhumby might be focused on the retail transaction, but the insights and value gained from such data are valuable to all the stakeholders in the ecosystem. One priority for David and his team is to carefully manage the growing number of rich data sources. Consumers purchase their goods through a multiplicity of channels and dunnhumby has adopted a single, open platform to simplify the data-ingestion process.

The crucial role of data at dunnhumby means its management and protection is always a huge priority for the company. Effective data governance is a key tool when it comes to maintaining retail and consumer trust. Suppliers, retailers and their customers will only trust organisations that can demonstrate a respect for their

data and a deep understanding of the complexities of how to protect it.

The ability to draw insights without the need for the processing of sensitive personal data, the use of multiple layers of aggregation, anonymisation and encryption are just some of the aspects of delivering this respectful treatment of consumer data.

Applying appropriate technologies

dunnhumby has created its own data standards over time and worked with a number of key industry players to ensure that more and more clients are writing to dunnhumby's standards. These 'common domain

models' (CDMs) are crucial to dunnhumby's success and have been refined over years of experience working with many of the world's leading retailers. As David puts it, 'our CDM is common enough to enable all the downstream products and services but extensible enough to accommodate change and new client needs.'

dunnhumby has also welcomed the emergence of public cloud platforms such as Google Cloud and Microsoft Azure. It believes both platforms are well suited to absorbing not just the seasonal peaks associated to online retail but more importantly they are perfect for the intense and transient computational loads that are required to execute its rich science models. Cloud also provides the perfect environment for applying the open-source tools for data analytics and machine-learning processes. David is always interested in technology trends that will help take the business forward, including:

- Commoditisation of computer power and storage, enabling complex calculations to be achieved in minutes or seconds rather than days;

- Open platforms that encourage the sharing of resources, skills and tools across an ever-expanding data science and product community;

- Location and visualisation techniques that highlight consumer buying habits, helping retailers to identify what categories are performing or underperforming, what is the perfect mix of products (and which can be substituted for each other) and what the optimum pricing should be.

Defining the qualities of a Master Chef

David believes top-down intervention is no longer a successful formula for orchestrating large-scale change at a global level. Instead, dunnhumby has evolved to be an organisation of (largely) independent teams which are led by product, development and science leaders who have large amounts of autonomy, creative licence and accountability for delivering change.

David nudges his leadership team on a peer-to-peer basis rather than forcing a parenting relationship. It's often uncomfortable but he enjoys being challenged by his executives and believes that this dynamic is the secret to a successful transformation. He also spends much of his time working with the executive committee to help shape and influence the direction of travel for the wider business. He sees his 'people-powered' mantra as being widely applicable beyond the technology divisions – focusing on freeing up time for people to think rather than do.

Tips

- Have a bifocal view of life, ensure that they have eyes on all the day-to-day things, and are looking to what comes next

- Let machines do repetitive work and focus humans on thinking and high-value activities

- Focus on technology trends rather than individual techniques

Proximus
Delivering five-star customer experience

Preparing the dish

Geert Standaert is the CTO of Proximus, Belgium's leading telecommunications and information and communications technology (ICT) services company. In a fast-changing and technology-driven environment, Geert's mantra is 'always look forward, never look back'.

Proximus's fibre and wireless networks support a wide range of consumer devices in more than two million homes. One of the biggest challenges facing the company is to help its customers experience fault-free operations across both fixed and mobile platforms. One way of helping to deal with this issue is to create a tech-led solution that anticipates and prevents points of failure before customers notice disruptions in service.

That's where Geert and his team are having an impact. By applying big data, machine learning (ML) and AI to fault-detection processes, Proximus has achieved a 33% reduction in calls to its service centres. This recipe describes how a small, five-person project was the genesis of a much larger transformation across the entire organisation.

Starting small but thinking big

Geert set out to achieve transformational levels of improvement in network and software performance. The aim was to give every home outstanding network quality and reliability across a full set of multimedia services, including phone, TV and house alarm. He created a small team of five people to build a comprehensive dataset of devices in every home that Proximus serves. This 'big data' process, as Geert refers to it, generates more than five terabytes of information every day.

His team uses AI and ML to analyse this big data and has created a 'galaxy of stars' that illustrates visually each home's constellation of devices. At the centre of this graphical representation is a cloud that depicts on-target performance. For those devices that sit outside the data cloud, the possibility of a malfunction is identified, such as an imperfect reboot of TV software.

Proximus uses this data analysis to create a proactive approach. It can push out new software downloads or send out technicians before the customer experiences any sign of a disturbance. Proximus subscribes to the lean philosophy of 'shifting left', which is a practice that aims to find and prevent defects early in the software delivery process. The company can also post out components, such as powerful routers or high-quality cabling, to improve the quality of customer experiences.

The company's proactive use of data has benefits in three key areas:

- Reducing volumes of complaints to call centres by a third;
- Informing field staff of possible issues ahead of a home visit;
- Improving the customer experience across all multimedia services.

Initiating a comprehensive transformation programme

Proximus has brought its mobile and fixed service businesses together to transform network operations. It has placed speed and efficiency at the core of its ambitions. This initiative has changed every aspect of how Geert's more than 2,000 technical staff work, from the way they deliver new services through to how teams are empowered to work more closely with their business partners.

Geert believes in taking 'strategy to action' and has re-architected his technical organisation to boost the speed of delivery. The organisation has been assembled around eight strategic priorities that are empowering people to improve the customer experience

"Always look forward, never look back."
Geert Standaert, CTO, Proximus

Scan code to watch the full interview.

through proactive maintenance and continuous service innovation. Each strategic priority is led by an executive team member who oversees end-to-end strategic programmes.

One crucial component of this cluster-led approach has been the adoption of Agile working. Geert focused initially on digital front-end activities, such as omni-channel working. However, he is now applying Agile techniques to core network operations. The merger of the company's mobile and fixed service businesses has made it possible to create a single platform for technical development. This consolidation process has led to higher levels of staff satisfaction.

Mobilising the workforce around change

Geert believes Proximus could do better at describing its transformational activities to prospective employees, including graduates. In his view, Proximus is 'a candy store' for people with technical curiosity. Geert says he discovers a new technology to apply to the business every day. Once new recruits see this inherent curiosity, it becomes much easier for Proximus to retain its talent.

Geert has created self-empowered teams that are tasked with completing projects quickly. He recognises that front-line staff are the key value creators for the organisation. Senior managers should focus on empowering these employees. This focus on empowerment is an inversion of traditional top-down hierarchies and mirrors developments in manufacturing such as 'The Toyota Way', which is a set of principles focused on continuous improvement and respect.

Defining the qualities of a Master Chef

Geert says successful transformation is about making small steps up a high mountain. First, you need to define the destination – in the case of Proximus, customer service excellence is the peak of the ascent. Second, you need to understand the topography of the landscape and create a map of the capabilities needed to complete the journey. By applying lean thinking and Agile methods, such as short sprints, Geert believes digital leaders can guide the team successfully up the mountain to reach the summit. In doing so, he believes that teams will enjoy unparalleled satisfaction.

Geert understands that he can't determine the pace of travel alone. Instead, he says digital leaders should energise their people – in his case, the more than 2,000 staff members in his function. His style as a Master Chef is to act as an amplifier or energiser. He translates commercial pressures into positive action. His own personal experiences, both as an actor and rock musician, lead him to suggest that successful leaders touch the heart as well as the mind of their audiences.

mBank

Escaping technical legacy to build modern platforms for change

Ingredients

- Access to modern programming languages such as C#
- Migration to a cloud platform for operational flexibility
- Agile development to support changes in customer features

Preparing the dish

Born as a digital native before the term FinTech was even coined, mBank was the first fully internet-based bank in Poland. Today, it sets the direction of travel for the future development of mobile and online banking. The digital bank's former CIO and CTO and now chief operating officer (COO), Krzysztof Dabrowski, describes mBank as a disruptive player, offering free products, such as cards and accounts, that help to democratise banking.

When Krzysztof took up the role of COO two years ago, which also includes responsibility for back-office functions, security and IT, he was able to apply many of the techniques that he had learnt from IT to operations and vice versa. At the centre of his combined approach to IT and operations is 'one culture, one way of doing things'. This approach requires the introduction of standard workflow practices and measurement systems.

Despite mBank being a digital native, Krzysztof discovered that the key obstacles to realising his plans were the legacy systems that had accumulated during the previous 20 years. As a COO, his secret sauce for success has been to tackle this problem across both the retail and corporate banks simultaneously.

"Legacy is a universal problem that all CIOs must tackle."

Krzysztof Dabrowski, COO, mBank

Scan code to watch
the full interview.

Tackling retail banking legacies

mBank has experienced exceptional growth since its inception – with an impact on IT. In Krzysztof's words: 'We often had to prioritise growth over perfection'. At its inception, the digital bank implemented a mainframe-based core system with its programs written in COBOL. This system provided critical customer features but was costly and slow to modify. It also became increasingly difficult for the digital bank to find COBOL programmers.

Krzysztof's solution to this challenge was to create a COBOL compiler that converted code to a .NET environment for Microsoft Windows. This conversion process allowed mBank's source code to run on a modern platform and to support the high-growth trajectory of the business. Krzysztof hired a local IT boutique to help with the conversion process and to provide ongoing support. Today, mBank runs a mainframe and a Windows platform in parallel. The benefits are:

- Most workloads can now run in the cloud, with the benefits of scalability and efficiency;

- A mix and match approach eliminates the need to rewrite old code-based features;

- New features can be written in a modern language using Agile techniques such as DevOps.

Tackling corporate banking legacies

From the inception of the digital corporate bank, mBank adopted Temenos banking software, running on an IBM Unix platform. As in the case of the retail banking operation, Krzysztof realised that this approach was both costly and inflexible to changing customer needs. Once again, he adopted a translation method and converted prevailing code based on J-BASIC to C#. This conversion meant the Bank could cut its ties with COBOL and adopt modern languages such as C# and C++.

Both the retail and corporate projects were completed at the same time, allowing the bank to operate in a more responsive and agile manner to rapidly changing market conditions, especially during the recent coronavirus pandemic.

Reorganising the kitchen

Krzysztof has arranged the IT organisation to align more closely with key customer segments and associated business units. These combined IT and business teams apply modern development methods. However, he has retained the established IT team to run operations across the group or what he refers to as 'keeping the lights on'.

In retail banking, there has been a complete reorganisation of

IT based on new development techniques such as Agile and Scrum. This reorganisation was enabled by mBank's escape from its legacy mainframe environment. Krzysztof recognises there is always constructive tension between the business and IT, where the former is driven by creativity and the latter hindered by system constraints. However, the move to a Windows environment has helped narrow the gap.

Within corporate banking, Krzysztof recognises that progress has often been slower due to structural and regulatory complexities. He has adopted a step-by-step approach that breaks complex workflows down into smaller chunks. Every month, his team delivers two or three redesigned processes into production. In this way, mBank has avoided a big-bang implementation that is risky within a highly regulated environment.

Acquiring appropriate talent

Being a digital native, mBank has had less difficulty attracting IT talent than the incumbent banks in Poland. However, Krzysztof recognises that he faces a tough fight for the best resources. He has chosen, where possible, to train his own talent. He believes start-ups offer graduates more freedom to develop skills, but there is clearly

more risk involved when only one in ten start-ups survive. Banks and more established organisations offer greater job security, but at the price of greater role rigidity.

mBank has launched an incubator to test out new ideas and to encourage collaboration with start-ups. This link helps Krzysztof expose his staff to both traditional and emerging business environments. He also sees value in extracting experiences from the older workforce and passing knowledge to younger employees.

Defining the qualities of a Master Chef

Krzysztof says effective CIOs should be on a par with business colleagues. He believes IT should generate the necessary flow of new ideas to help the businesses cope with challenges and opportunities. It took him two years to understand the finance business when he arrived at mBank from a non-financial career. Yet he says banks are not dissimilar to other organisations when it comes to their levels of complexity. Legacy is a universal problem that all CIOs must tackle.

His mantra, which has helped him move from CIO and CTO to COO, is to give people space to come up with new ideas. It's vital that CIOs trust and support their people.

Broad bean tortilla tapas

Makes approximately 20 bite-sized pieces

- 500g broad beans, podded
- A small handful of flat-leaved parsley
- 5 eggs
- Salt and pepper
- 1 tbsp olive oil

Bring a pan of water to the boil and slip the beans into it for a couple of minutes, then lift them out, retaining the water. The skins will have started to split, revealing the bright green beans. Peel them and discard the skins. This takes time, but is worth it. Discard the stalks from the parsley and chop the leaves finely; put to one side.

Return the beans to the pan and cook them until they are soft but not disintegrating; this will not take long. Drain them thoroughly.

Break the eggs into a large bowl and beat them together well, adding salt and pepper. Then stir in the beans.

Heat the oil in a small frying pan or omelette pan over a low heat, and preheat the grill. Pour in the mixture and, as it begins to cook, push up the sides with a wooden spoon to make a deeper edge – square it off, if you wish (this makes the tortilla easier to cut into uniform pieces).

When the tortilla looks firm you can turn it by inverting the pan over a plate before sliding the tortilla back into the pan for another few minutes, but you can also ensure the top is cooked by popping the pan under a hot grill. Don't let it overcook; when it feels lightly set, slide it out of the pan onto kitchen paper to drain off any excess liquid. Scatter the finely chopped parsley over it.

Cut the tortilla into pieces and serve as a tapa, cool or still warm, each one pierced with a cocktail stick.

The favourite dish of Mark Samuels

HOW TO BUILD A FIVE-STAR KITCHEN THAT SATISFIES YOUR MOST DISCERNING CUSTOMERS

"IT organisations that score a five-star rating understand that their end customers are ultimately a consumer or an employee."

Within a rapidly changing business context, IT must be fleet of foot if it wants to maintain a five-star rating. High-quality IT often requires radical transformation followed by periods of continuous innovation. IT organisations that fail to adopt this approach risk becoming irrelevant, as end users increasingly choose to self-serve due to the wide availability of tools that make this shift possible, such as software as a service (SaaS) and low-code/no-code development tools.

Optimising your kitchen to provide tasty new IT recipes

Any IT organisation that describes its customer as the 'business unit' would, at best, receive a three-star rating on Tripadvisor. In a world of digitally enabled supply chains and online interactions, IT organisations that score a five-star rating understand that their end customers are ultimately a consumer or an employee. These end customers might be soldiers on the battlefield, citizens claiming unemployment benefits, shoppers on the web or in a retail store, first-time homebuyers awaiting mortgage approval, or patients sitting in a doctor's surgery. Every actor within the supply chain must endeavour to improve the experiences for end customers by harvesting and then acting upon the data that emerges at every point of their journeys.

In a business environment where digital and data play an increasingly important role, IT organisations must help shape customer experiences. Great CIOs and their teams provide the tools and platforms to make sense of customer data. They help their business colleagues generate appropriate and timely responses in the form of tailored products and services across the connected supply chain. Digital leaders recognise that we are moving rapidly from a business-to-business (B2B) to a B2B2C world, where success is all about working directly with customers to meet their needs.

Business leaders that want to take advantage of these opportunities will need to optimise their IT kitchens. This optimisation requires a great deal of effort and might require the refurbishment or even reinvention of the IT kitchen. Here are three tasty recipes that can help to satisfy today's most sophisticated diners.

IT is helping businesses to create a digital vision

In the modern world of mobile apps, streamed content, online shopping and remote working, business executives must place digital at the centre of their strategic visions and operating models. Chief digital officers (CDOs), CTOs and CIOs should be considered as key partners to help shape tomorrow's successful enterprises.

IT is driving today's digital agenda

The move to 'everything online' during the coronavirus pandemic has accelerated plans to transform traditional government and commercial organisations. IT has been instrumental in sponsoring new ways of working. IT is also helping to integrate complex supply chains, so they are responsive to changing customer needs.

IT is changing its products and services

The traditional manner through which IT supports the business is less relevant in a digital world. Customised development programmes can be too lengthy and often produce the wrong outcomes. Instead, successful CIOs are productising their offerings to replicate the success of software as a service (SaaS) providers, such as Salesforce.

In all these recipes, CIOs and their teams are repositioning themselves away from a pure focus on operations and towards becoming critical business partners, in terms of working with both internal peers and external parties.

Adopting new methods to suit a digital landscape

To qualify as a legitimate and respected business partner, IT must adopt new policies, methods and tools that are appropriate to working in a fast-moving digital environment. Traditional waterfall methods are too cumbersome and slow to meet new external conditions that are typified by the VUCA (volatile, uncertain, complex and ambiguous) world.

The good news is that IT does have certain advantages when set against other corporate functions. Technology vendors are highly innovative in the ways they support their customers. Key examples include the growth of the public cloud and SaaS-based offerings. CIOs have learnt a great deal from the adoption of these approaches. Now, the IT department must emulate – if not supersede – its key vendor partners to retain the loyalty of the business.

A growing number of CIOs are replacing legacy systems with web-based applications that can flex to meet fast-changing external demands. Even for digital businesses, such as Telefónica, this replacement process is an enormous but necessary task, according to the company's CIO. Ultimately, IT faces an existential challenge: either reinvent itself to become digital end-to-end or find itself circumnavigated by vendors that will then sell direct to its business customers.

As our recipes demonstrate, successful CIOs and their IT teams are facing this challenge head-on and adopting new methods to deliver service excellence. Here are three key examples:

- Working together with business partners. Most CIOs today recognise the need to embed staff deep inside their internal customers' functions. This embeddedness involves a matrix structure, where line-of-business CIOs have dual reporting lines.

- Adopting new delivery methods. Perhaps the most visible development in IT practices is to employ Agile methods to accelerate the delivery of new business

solutions. This widespread adoption of Agile ways of working is causing a constructive tension between people and departments that rely on traditional waterfall methods.

- Increasing IT governance. Agile working has many business merits, but it can create fragmentation if left unsupervised. Group CIOs suggest that developing and enforcing common standards is critical to preserving coherence across all new business applications.

Our conversations with CIOs around the globe make it evident that traditional IT structures and methods cannot keep up with the fast-developing pace of modern business requirements.

Choosing the best ingredients and business partners

During the past two decades, emerging technologies – such as cloud computing, social media, data analytics and mobile applications – have revolutionised operational activities in many sectors. These technological advances have also provided the foundations for the rapid growth of digital leaders, such as the FAANG group.

It is worth remembering that Apple's iPhone only appeared in 2007 and the cloud first moved into common business parlance in 2008 – that's a relatively short time span from emergence to acceptance, especially given the disruption these technologies have caused, particularly to the IT sector itself. Yet more is to come. The pace of change continues to quicken, and we expect a further surge of new technologies in the coming decade. These technologies include AI, the Internet of Things, 5G and 6G mobile, blockchain, 3D printing, edge and quantum computing, and augmented, virtual and mixed reality.

Experience suggests that the expectations for new technologies are often overstated in the short term

but vastly underestimated in the long term. The digital leaders that we spoke with all recognised the potential impact of the fast-approaching second wave. Their task now is to inform peers at board level about the likely consequences of these technological advances.

Open source is the way to go

Many CIOs are turning to open-source strategies, both within their organisations and out across their partnerships with external parties. The combination of application programming interfaces and open-source architectures is encouraging the reuse of modern applications and accelerating the adoption of microservices.

Cloud changes everything

Virtually all CIONET members have adopted a cloud-first strategy. However, many are encountering difficulties when it comes to implementation, especially with respect to legacy applications that are often based on ageing code and mainframe systems. The cost, complexity and risk of re-platforming such core systems often hinders their best intentions. At the same time, all Agile developments are concentrated in the cloud. The result is often a bi-modal, two-speed regime.

The vendor landscape is evolving rapidly

The combination of public cloud platforms and open-source technologies has transformed the IT services sector during the past decade. The speed of change has left many major incumbents on the back foot. The phenomenal success of AWS, Azure and Google Cloud has brought into question the traditional IT practice of outsourcing service towers, such as data centres, networks and applications maintenance. Smart CIOs are instead pursuing a mix-and-match approach to service sourcing, with the prospect of lower-cost, more scalable infrastructures.

Technology-fuelled innovation

Alongside these seismic developments, CIOs are exploiting a broad range of emerging technologies to ensure that their organisations remain ahead of the curve. The use of RPA and AI is being piloted as an effective way of creating a fully automated enterprise. Artificial intelligence is also being used extensively in data analytics.

The pressure is on CIOs to evaluate technologies and then inform their boards about how these advances will push dramatic change during this decade. Corporate survival will depend on early action to embrace these developments and fend off newcomers.

FOUR
DIGITAL OPERATING MODELS

Optimising your kitchen to provide tasty new IT recipes

All organisations – even digital businesses – are beset by legacy systems, skills and cultures. Radical new business designs and ways of working are required if we are to genuinely transform the customer experience and undertake continuous innovation of products and services. As we will see in the three recipes in this chapter, IT plays a central role in helping businesses to optimise organisational structures and to innovate products and services.

The CIO of BW Paper Systems discovered he could create a multi-fold increase in collaboration and connectivity between suppliers and customers by building a digital layer across a highly fragmented supply chain. This layer represents 'one source of the truth', which has enabled BW to move from a reactive to a highly proactive treatment of customer needs, helping the company to increase loyalty and boost revenue streams.

The CDO of KBC Bank, meanwhile, has supported the replacement of physical branches with omni-channel routes to market. This digitisation allowed the bank to compete with the services offered by fleet-of-foot FinTechs. This transformation process also created a one-time opportunity to integrate separate banking and insurance platforms, providing a single view of the customer. Subsequently, KBC has been able to attract third-party vendors to its integrated platform, increasing cross-selling opportunities and customer stickiness.

Finally, Telefónica's CIO took a hybrid approach to dealing with the enormous challenge of transforming one of the world's leading telecommunications companies. The CIO has helped organise global business hubs to consolidate back-office functions, such as finance and procurement. At the same time, he has introduced a common architecture to enable national organisations to build systems that suit the requirements of their respective local marketplaces.

Common to all these approaches is the move to semi-autonomous teams of IT and business staff. These teams undertake change programmes at breakneck speed using Agile development methods and sprints. In all respects, our Master Chefs are helping to bring about rapid and fundamental change to their organisations. This change will inspire greater creativity and innovation in the longer term.

BW Paper Systems
Letting joined-up ecosystems create big business value

Preparing the dish

When Nino Messaoud arrived at BW Paper Systems five years ago as chief digital officer, he discovered a successful and growing business that comprised more than 100 companies worldwide. The one thing missing was a digital infrastructure to connect all the firm's warehouses and manufacturing sites to thousands of suppliers and customers across the globe. Nino saw a unique chance to question everything: 'I wanted to build a roadmap into a digital future where markets and customer requirements would be changing at an ever-faster pace.'

He has built a digital layer above prevailing systems and applications to support full connectivity between all parties in the BW ecosystem. This approach has transformed how BW anticipates and responds to customer needs, harnessing the power of its trade partners in a truly digital manner.

Building a digital ecosystem

Nino's earlier leadership experience highlighted how no company can survive without intensive collaboration with both its customers and suppliers. Common datasets and processes help to bind customers into the supply network and, in BW's case, lower the cost of servicing their maintenance needs. Automated ordering, across 100 geographically disparate companies within BW, supports speedy and seamless customer service.

Nino chose Paper Systems as a test case for how BW would build an integration layer between applications across the globe. At the heart of his design is the ability to ingest data from different sources and produce a single version of the truth. He describes this layer as 'the sauce on top of the spaghetti'. His approach is characterised by:

- Standardised data that creates genuine independence over local systems and applications, which is crucial as BW continuously acquires new companies into its ecosystem;

- An integrated database that operates on an intersystem platform, IRIS, which has helped to simplify merger activities;

- A custom-built Java system for data integration and a presentation layer, provided by Salesforce, that provides a unified interface for mobile and fixed devices.

These activities are supported by a workbench in Ukraine, which takes advantage of local skilled talent and is culturally aligned with BW. In Nino's view, the results of this data-led approach have been even better than might have been anticipated. Parties across the supply chain, from suppliers to customers, receive replies to their enquiries in milliseconds rather than hours or days.

Designing processes for the future

Nino chose to ignore historic ways of operating in favour of a genuine reengineering of critical processes across the supply chain. He saw this as a once-in-a-lifetime opportunity to question how the business operated. He convened a team of experienced staff from three geographic regions to undertake this momentous task. He also co-opted customers and suppliers on to this team to ensure a seamless view of data across the supply chain.

The first area of attention was the supply of spare parts to customers. Historically, front-line BW workers would ring warehouses to locate parts. Nino's team envisaged a more efficient future, where spare parts could be 3D-printed by customers. His team designed a process to transmit designs electronically to customers. This process enabled a near real-time response to breakdowns. It delighted BW's customers as it reduced disruption in their own manufacturing facilities.

Nino's team then went further.

"No company can survive without intensive collaboration with both its customers and suppliers."

Nino Messaoud, CDO, BW Paper Systems

Scan code to watch the full interview.

They developed tools that tracked component life cycles to automatically sense when parts might need to be replaced. Instead of waiting for a breakdown, BW now supplies new parts ahead of potential interruptions. It also furnishes customers with vital information on the health of their manufacturing operations. This has been a gamechanger for customer loyalty, and their willingness to pay for BW services.

Aligning the IT organisation to new practices

Nino was keen to build a new foundation for his IT organisation. He implemented a five-part programme that included Agile working, multidisciplinary business and IT teams, a 360-degree view of the customer, and connected processes. Nino believes successful business innovation is more about people than technologies: 'You need to take the people with you, including customers, suppliers and internal staff. Everyone must be included right from the start of a change programme.'

He has built a close working relationship with an implementation partner in Berlin to help build Agile techniques and cultures. Nino has also strengthened links with his Ukraine-based workbench to accelerate technical projects. In all these respects, Nino has transformed the structure and mindset of what was a traditional IT organisation.

Currently, about 70% of the IT organisation is engaged in keeping the lights on, or what Nino calls 'the silent running organisation'. Encouragingly, the remaining 30% focuses on building the future roadmap, which draws on small, diversified teams of business and technical staff. Nino uses success stories to convince BW executives of the merit of his novel approach.

Defining the qualities of a Master Chef

Nino sits on a global board of five digital leaders who oversee IT across the BW group. It took him two years to gain their full trust in his future-oriented approach to change and innovation. As with his own IT staff, this trust was earned by demonstrating successful outcomes.

Now, Nino is on a quest to find 'tomorrow's people' to support his transformation efforts. He works with leading universities to develop a taste of the future, and to attract the talent to help modernise his IT organisation. Nino believes IT should be a value contributor rather than a cost centre.

His personal style is to be the conductor of change, with an orchestra staffed by business and technical experts. Nino's qualification to lead the orchestra is that he knows what sounds best.

Tips

■ Gain the trust of your peers to deliver fundamental change

■ Adopt a human-centric approach to change

■ Collaborate with the entire ecosystem when developing new schemes

KBC Bank
Change the context if you want to transform IT operations

Ingredients

- Emphasise cultural change ahead of technology
- Adopt a collaborative approach to IT and business
- Develop an innovation pipeline sponsored by the business

Preparing the dish

As both a marketeer and digital leader, Rudi Peeters has been driven by curiosity and a constant desire to innovate everything around him. A notable career achievement was the launch of KBC's internet bank in 1996. KBC is a universal multi-channel bank–insurer, focusing on private clients and small and medium-sized enterprises in Belgium, Ireland, Central Europe and Southeast Asia.

Rudi recognised quickly on becoming CIO at KBC that changing the banking culture would be the most difficult part of his job: 'You can have the best plans, road maps and technologies but if the culture doesn't fit, it just won't fly.' Rudi believes firmly that you must first change the context if you want to change how people operate. This has been his guiding principle in realigning the IT organisation to support KBC's transition to becoming a digital bank.

Starting the journey to digital banking

Physical branches have given way to multi-channel operations across web and mobile channels. This movement has changed the relationship between the bank and its customers. Front- and back-end processes are under constant development. A case in point: the bank recently introduced Kate – a virtual assistant that gives its customers the best financial advice anywhere, anytime.

"You can have the best plans, road maps and technologies but if the culture doesn't fit, it just won't fly."

Rudi Peeters, CIO, KBC Bank

Scan code to watch
the full interview.

The coronavirus pandemic added even greater impetus for change at a business level, says Rudi: 'What we tried to do in three to five years, we had to do in just two months following lockdown in March 2020.' The pandemic made the bank's customers more receptive to digital banking channels. It also meant 60,000 members of staff had to transition to home working quickly. Being able to arrange this transition in days raised IT's credibility enormously.

Becoming the WeChat of European banking

Since the 1990s and the advent of internet banking, KBC's business has been in a state of constant evolution. It has integrated its banking and insurance businesses to become a leader in both sectors. KBC now has single IT and finance functions serving these two businesses. This integrated approach has proven invaluable in helping the bank to collaborate closely with third-party providers and expand customer services.

By offering an expanded range of day-to-day services and features, such as travel tickets, on the KBC mobile app, the bank and its partners encourage customers and prospects to interact with them. This extension in service provision has enabled KBC to gain

the data to understand customer needs. Big data analytics and artificial intelligence have taken on a strategic role here, and this specialist group reports directly to the bank's chief executive.

Changing the IT model

KBC's traditional approach to IT was to stand apart from the business. Business projects were 'thrown over the IT wall' to be priced and placed in an orderly queue that often took years to deliver. This traditional approach became untenable in a constantly changing business environment. Instead, Rudi organised cross-functional teams of business and IT staff to focus on product features and value streams. This joined-up approach meant IT could contribute directly to enhanced business performance. The current approach includes:

■ Placing new features into a pipeline that is prioritised by business leaders monthly;

■ Organising two-week sprints to test out new ideas and develop proof of concepts;

■ Co-opting customers into IT projects to encourage an outside-in mentality.

Innovating at scale

The current IT model is supported by the constant drive to innovate the business – and this drive is based on seamless collaboration between IT and its business partners. Rudi chairs the KBC innovation board and has introduced a formal innovation process, which consists of:

- An R&D budget to encourage staff (IT and business) to pitch ideas to the innovation board;

- Pilots and proof of concepts that are supported by the board, and that include customers;

- Co-creation with business partners in areas such as the impact of climate change.

Kate was one of the innovations that emerged through this approach. Activities are reviewed monthly by the innovation board. To further stimulate innovation within the enterprise, Rudi organises 'inspiration days' that bring start-ups and vendors into the bank. Staff are encouraged to attend these days and interact with the visitors.

Reforming the IT operating model

Rudi says three essential elements help to reform IT so that it is closely integrated with the business: culture, architecture and technology.

Culture

Rudi believes that you can only change people if you change the

context in which they operate, which he describes as 'the smell of the place'. IT staff in the bank's old operating model were sitting with businesspeople, but not working together. Rudi introduced business DevOps tools to bring the two parties together in mixed teams of up to 12 people.

Architecture

Rudi has adopted GitHub, an open-source platform that encourages the development and use of open-source software. This process accelerates software delivery and ensures consistency across the group. As well as open sourcing the IT organisation, the bank is moving to cloud as its preferred development and run platform.

Technology

Rudi is happy with the current banking system, based on mainframe technology. While this platform has not constrained digital transformation projects to date, he recognises that new developments, such as artificial intelligence and machine learning, will present new challenges and opportunities over the coming years, especially regarding customer experience.

Defining the qualities of a Master Chef

Rudi sees a future where IT provides the run platform on which the business develops its own applications. He recognises that IT is core to the bank and must transition to business ownership. This movement will require greater digital maturity across the group – a key role for the CIO.

Tips

- Celebrate success and use storytelling to engage the organisation

- Do what is best for the company rather than what is best for you

---

Rudi left KBC to become CEO at Vandersanden in October 2021.

Telefónica
Teaching elephants to dance

Preparing the dish

With a 30-year background of senior executive positions within global banks, such as Santander and Barclays, Angel Valero is now using his unique experiences to help Telefónica make the challenging but vital journey to becoming a digital leader in telecommunications and media.

Telefónica, which is a Spanish multinational group headquartered in Madrid, is one of the largest telephone operators and mobile network providers in the world. The company provides fixed and mobile telephony, broadband and subscription television across Europe and the Americas.

As Corporate CIO of Telefónica's Spanish business-to-business division, Angel is providing the strategic vision to help transform the organisation into a digital leader. Angel recognises the scale of this task, especially when it comes to converting generations of legacy systems, processes and skills: 'You can only teach an elephant to dance one step at a time,' he says.

"I give each team 100% independence, but I give 100% personal dedication to helping them solve a problem."

Angel Valero, Corporate CIO, Telefónica

Scan code to watch the full interview.

Understanding what drives the transformational agenda

Telefónica must upgrade its products and services almost constantly to maintain its competitive advantage. The company must also focus continually on how it engages and cares for its customer base, which includes 343 million fixed-line subscribers and 272 mobile customers in 17 countries spread across Europe and Latin America (LatAm).

Angel says three specific areas of digital transformation are crucial: enhancing the customer experience, providing industry-leading customer care post-sale and undertaking internal transformation of national and global operations. Fixed and mobile technologies continue to advance at rapid speed. Angel recognises that the platforms his company uses to support its customers must also evolve alongside these advances. Relevant developments include:

- The introduction of an end-to-end fibre network infrastructure (already 100% in EMEA, and 50% in LatAm);

- The network is becoming software-defined, which eliminates the requirement for a significant proportion of traditional switching equipment;

- Mobile is evolving from 4G to 5G, and there is already hype about the long-term shift to 6G;

- Low-orbit satellite networks are entering service and competing with terrestrial networks.

Baking a multi-layered cake

Angel has layered Telefónica's transformation programme geographically to reflect the multi-national nature of the company. He says a combined global and local approach is necessary to create a fully digital organisation.

Globally, Angel is standardising many back-office functions, such as finance and procurement, to exploit internal synergies across the group. He envisions the creation of a global business platform that is common to all national subsidiaries. Building this platform requires the redesign of end-to-end business processes, including lead to order, order to cash, and cash to collection.

For client-facing commercial systems and processes, Angel expects to create a localised approach, where the group establishes a common architecture, but allows national organisations to implement technological solutions that fit the prevailing cultures and regulations. One of the key areas of attention here is data analytics, where he expects national organisations to exploit the most advanced tools available in their respective markets. He encourages developers to adopt open sourcing to maximise creativity as well as to use market platforms such as Salesforce and Velocity.

Infrastructure modernisation is another challenge at the global level, especially given the ongoing move to fibre and software-defined networks. Once again, Angel expects the group to set standards that support national-level roll-out programmes. The rise of the digital infrastructure is helping to bridge the traditional separation between IT and network operations. In Angel's view, IT is now the key enabler for digitisation.

Adopting a greenfield approach to transformation

Angel says a greenfield approach to building digital businesses can help CIOs avoid being constrained by heritage systems and processes. He has selected skilled individuals from across Telefónica's IT and business functions to lead digital programmes around the globe. With strategic guidance from the centre, these highly skilled teams are deployed at every level of the multi-layered transformation.

Cloud has been a key focus of the company's journey to digital. Practical experience from earlier in his career has led Angel to concentrate on quick wins, such as implementing the cloud in multimedia communications. He has also tapped into the selective use of robots to automate

repetitive processes. However, Angel envisages a phased approach to other areas, including:

- Migrating enterprise systems to the cloud with appropriate software modernisation;

- Implementing big data solutions in the cloud with appropriate tools;

- Rebuilding core systems and software-defined networks in the cloud.

The latter rebuilding phase is likely to take a few years due to the complexity of this programme of work. Even further out, Angel expects to draw on edge-based computing, where servers are located close to clients.

Defining the qualities of a Master Chef

It's an enormous task to make change happen across a group that spans 17 countries with 120,000 staff. Success depends on the quality and creativity of the 'change the business' teams that Angel has selected and deployed. His philosophy is simple: appoint the best individuals, give each team a large degree of autonomy to complete their missions, but support them along the way: 'I give each team 100% independence, but when they come to me, I give 100% personal dedication to helping them solve a problem.'

As the Master Chef overseeing 20,000 IT staff worldwide, and with 500 IT staff at the centre of the group, Angel takes full responsibility for the success of the change programme at Telefónica, stating: 'You can delegate the job but you cannot delegate the responsibility.'

He believes effective staff development comes from a combination of education and experience during execution. He asks teams to submit annual plans and milestones, and conducts monthly reviews. The most important thing for Angel is to see results.

Tips

- Empower your teams but be prepared to offer support

- Encourage individuals to take risks and try different approaches

- Treat people with respect and always be truthful

Chicken and mushroom cream with an avocado and green salad

Serves 2

- 2 chicken breasts
- 1 lemon
- 1 bay leaf
- 300g mushrooms
- 1 clove of garlic
- 200ml crème fraîche
- 1 tsp Dijon mustard
- 1 tbsp olive oil
- Salt and black pepper

For the salad:

- 1 large ripe avocado
- Juice of half a lemon
- Olive oil
- Salad leaves

Preheat the oven to 200°C. Skin the chicken breasts, and squeeze the lemon into a baking dish. Add the bay leaf and the chicken breasts and cook for approximately 45 minutes or until any juices run clear, turning them over to make sure they are cooked. Take the chicken out of the oven and set it aside to cool slightly.

Chop the mushrooms and finely chop the garlic. Mix the crème fraîche with the mustard in a small bowl. Cut the chicken into pieces no bigger than 3cm.

Then prepare the salad as the chicken doesn't take long to finish. Peel the avocado, chop it into cubes and sprinkle them well with lemon juice. Make up a couple of salad plates with leaves but don't add the avocado until the last minute.

Put the oil in a large frying pan, add the mushrooms and garlic and let them cook until the mushrooms are starting to brown. Add the chicken and cook everything together, stirring, for a couple of minutes until the chicken is hot again. Then spoon in the crème fraîche and mustard mixture, turn the heat right down, and mix together until everything is coated in the sauce. Check for seasoning and add salt and black pepper as needed.

Scatter the lemony avocado on the salad leaves, drizzle over a little olive oil and grind some black pepper on top. Serve alongside the chicken, accompanied by some crusty bread.

The favourite dish of Mark Foulsham

FIVE
NEW BUSINESS METHODS
Changing the kitchen to suit a digital landscape

At the start of this decade, many incumbent businesses were adopting a cautious approach to digital transformation. The start of the coronavirus pandemic in early 2020 changed attitudes at all levels of business. Billions of employees transitioned to working from home; customers, meanwhile, completed all transactions online. This transition pushed digital leaders into taking big leaps forward in regard to digital-led business transformation.

Some organisations were already ahead of the curve. When a new CTO was appointed at insurance giant Prudential in 2014, he discovered a startling lack of digital awareness and a strong resistance to change. A radical approach was needed to shift mindsets and set the firm on a course to digital leadership. He immediately entered strategic partnerships with leading IT vendors, including Apigee and Diligenta, to accelerate adoption of new methods such as data analytics and digital platforms.

The pandemic crisis hit KfW, Germany's leading promotional bank, in a different manner. The government had to react suddenly and organise billions of Euros of loans to support vulnerable businesses. KfW was called upon to manage this process in weeks rather than months or years. This programme of work required new Agile development methods that could help KfW meet tight timescales. Having already introduced Agile within controlled pilots, the CIO was able to scale agile teams to cope effectively with the crisis.

The rise of digital competitors brought a new sense of urgency to telecommunications giant Orange. The CIO's response was to promote open innovation as a way to maintain global leadership across a range of convergent technologies. He recognised that successful innovation involves converting good ideas into new sources of revenue and profit. To put this into practice, he adopted open sourcing and open processes to support a culture of open collaboration.

Across these different experiences, one common factor is evident: Master Chefs must be accomplished storytellers if they wish to energise and transform prevailing cultures.

Prudential
Creating a fully digital business

Ingredients

- A cloud platform as the digital foundation
- Conviction at board level about being digital
- A humility to accept failures alongside successes

Preparing the dish

Tarun Kohli, the recently appointed Managing Director and Head of New Propositions at Swiss Re, describes the main course of the leadership feast he's preparing: 'We don't need a digital strategy for business, we need a business strategy for a digital future.'

Swiss Reinsurance Company Ltd, commonly known as Swiss Re, is a reinsurance company based in Zurich, Switzerland. It is the world's largest reinsurer, as measured by net premiums written, and provides Tarun with a unique platform to create new digital businesses in the years to come.

However, it's in Tarun's earlier role, as CTO at financial services giant Prudential, that we get a tempting taste of how he has already converted a traditional insurance company into a fully digital business. Tarun's success in this endeavour, which we detail below, helped set the context for his move to Swiss Re.

Laying the digital foundations

When Tarun joined Prudential from BP in 2014, nothing could have prepared him for the analogue business practices that persisted throughout the company. The organisation was still building new data centres. The firm's business model was epitomised by 'the man from the Pru', who used to walk from house to house selling

"We don't need a digital strategy for business, we need a business strategy for a digital future."

Tarun Kohli, ex-CTO, Prudential; MD, Swiss Re

Scan code to watch the full interview.

a conglomeration of insurance and wealth management products.

In 2014, there was no evidence of a cloud strategy or any widespread adoption of data analytics to drive business decisions. The IT organisation itself was resistant to change of any kind, and senior business executives had little grasp of how digital could change the business for the better. As his first step, Tarun established a partnership strategy to begin to convert Prudential into a digital business. The key elements of the Digital Foundation programme included:

- Adopting public cloud with open APIs, through a partnership with Apigee, so that applications could be migrated away from legacy, on-premises mainframes.

- Adopting a platform approach: life and pensions applications were migrated from in-house mainframes to Diligenta's BanCS platform, asset management applications were transformed into Blackrock's Aladdin platform and wealth management applications moved into Bravura's Sonata platform. Thousands of legacy applications were decommissioned as part of this move.

- Establishing digital labs that could act as innovation hubs to address board-level challenges

by leveraging emerging digital technologies.

Tarun embraced software as a service (SaaS) and platform as a service (PaaS) as the future foundation for digital business in Prudential. In so doing, he reduced the dependency on legacy hardware and software.

Bringing a digital business mindset

His next step was to launch the Reconnection Programme, which aimed to illustrate the power of data analytics and artificial intelligence (AI) in helping both Prudential customers and internal business units to achieve greater value from the company's range of insurance and wealth management products.

Tarun chose a practical use case to launch the programme. Talking to people in the industrial branch of Prudential, he discovered there were millions of lost insurance policies dating back to the Second World War. These policies represented an outstanding liability to the business, but also a loss of benefits to the next of kin of the original policy holders.

Tarun leveraged his connections with a leading big data and analytics provider and set up an agile team to work on this problem. The team was able to develop a solution in three months that ingested more than 500 million records across 11 different mainframes and married those records with publicly available data, such as the government's death registry, to source next of kin details. This not only helped in identifying over a million next of kin beneficiary contact points, details that otherwise could not be located, but also enabled an accurate liability of the industrial branch book to be put into the records.

This successful project helped to illustrate the power of data analytics as a problem-solving tool to the rest of the business. Executives welcomed the positive impact of the project, both in terms of the beneficiaries and on the company's bottom line. In Tarun's view, this data-led project created a fundamental shift in mindset across the organisation.

Achieving quantum leaps into the future

Solving historic problems, such as the use case above, has clear economic value. But Tarun saw that bigger steps were needed to achieve a fully digital mindset. He believed the key was to explore fundamental business issues and opportunities rather than focusing on the technology itself.

Tarun cites an example of how, with the shift in mindset, Prudential moved

from optimising the claims process in health insurance to preventing claims by striking a partnership with Babylon Health, leveraging AI and analytics technology.

Tarun's guiding philosophy is that technologies, including cloud and big data, are merely tools to help businesses solve their problems. Hyping a technology such as blockchain for its own sake is a lost cause unless businesses have defined needs. We need to have business-led innovation and start with business problems or business opportunities that technology can serve to solve or enable growth.

Defining the qualities of a Master Chef

Tarun's personal style is very much hands-on. During his early days at Prudential, he took time to visit call centres and observe how staff were interacting with customers.

This helped trigger new thinking about the ways in which technology could streamline operations and increase both customer and staff satisfaction.

He also promotes high-performance team thinking, where he prefers to guide rather than dictate the direction of travel. In this respect, he believes successful Master Chefs empower and inspire their trusted teams. Tarun is a big promoter of servant leadership which he feels is needed in leading teams in the digital world.

Tips

■ Adopt a lifelong learning approach to your career

■ Enjoy the journey, not just achieving an end goal

■ Show humility and practise authenticity

KfW
How to turn a crisis into an opportunity

Preparing the dish

With a distinguished career in consulting and IT, Melanie Kehr was appointed as member of the executive board (CIO and COO) of KfW in 2019. One of the world's leading promotional banks, KfW is committed to improving economic, social and environmental living conditions across the globe on behalf of the Federal Republic of Germany and the federal states.

At KfW, Melanie advocated to transform how IT engages with the business to produce beneficial outcomes for all parties. She focused on creating closer integration between teams through the application of Agile practices, such as Scrum, to business projects. The outbreak of the coronavirus pandemic in March 2020 was the trigger to accelerate her plans and to complete the transformation journey across six steps, which are outlined below.

Step 1: Building an Agile way of working

Prior to the pandemic, Melanie and her leadership team had already begun to introduce Agile practices in an attempt to address the pervasive gap between IT and the business. The aim was to encourage IT and business lines to team up and look at business problems together

"It's about starting an agile movement bottom up, letting employees participate in defining the setup."

Melanie Kehr, CIO and COO, KfW

Scan code to watch the full interview.

rather than relying on IT to propose solutions. She started small, with single pilots to demonstrate results. The benefits were evident: the projects went better, faster and delivered precise results. Above all, the most valuable outcome was that the projects increased the motivation of all involved employees as they worked for common, meaningful goals.

The pilot was then encouraged to propagate the approach more widely across the bank. Melanie also provided resources for Scrum masters and coaches to accelerate this take-up process: 'This was about starting an agile movement bottom up, letting employees participate in defining the setup.' By 2020, 80% of all IT projects were employing Agile techniques. Across all areas, IT has elevated itself from being a cost centre to a change agent, driving the Agile culture into the whole bank.

Step 2: Taking the journey to the cloud

Melanie also recognised that strong cloud-based foundations are needed to support the rollout of an effective Agile approach. Here, KfW's digital office got things started by trying out different application ideas using cloud and testing them with the business lines. Once the major benefits for KfW were identified, Melanie and her leadership team took the next step for getting the bank cloud-ready by bundling the

cloud expertise into a dedicated IT team, the so-called Tech Foundation. Given the regulated nature of financial institutions, skills had to be built in various fields of the bank, such as IT security, compliance and procurement. Development skills are also key for a successful cloud journey.

Step 3: Making sure you can reach your customers quickly

KfW does not have any branches for its domestic activities and, therefore, relies on about 1,400 on-lending bank partners, who interact directly with end customers in Germany. In 2014, KfW started to set up a platform with automated interfaces for its sales partners. The bank subsequently migrated its products to the platform. This new platform allows the majority of commitments to be processed automatically within seconds.

Bringing the dish to the boil: in the epicentre of a crisis

In March 2020, it became evident that the COVID-19 pandemic had arrived in Germany and urgent action was required. As a government-owned bank, KfW was called upon immediately by the German Ministry of Economics and Ministry of Finance to set up large, domestic aid programmes to provide liquidity and financial support to German companies that were facing an existential crisis due to the pandemic.

Melanie's task as a member of the executive committee was to ensure that the KfW Special Programme went live at lightning speed. This task was complicated by major contact restrictions, forcing the majority of KfW employees to work from home, and banks to close parts of their local branches and instead rely on telephone and web-based channels.

Step 4: Putting agility on a new scale

The KfW employees were highly motivated to contribute to the Special Programme: many volunteered to participate in the task force, despite juggling with various challenges such as working from home and providing home-schooling to children. Business lines and IT worked in cross-functional teams, applying Scrum methods to deliver fast and precisely tailored results. The executive committee instituted a daily 'corona call' to take quick and immediately binding decisions, which enabled the teams to continue working on solutions. As a result, while new programmes usually take nine to eighteen months before going live, this time it took less than a month from the initial idea to the first automated payment. The experience of acting in concert to reach ambitious targets had a galvanising effect on the prevailing culture of the bank in the shorter term and has continued to align mindsets with a new post-pandemic normal.

Step 5: Letting platform benefits play out

A huge benefit of the platform became evident during the pandemic. In times of contact constraints and closed bank branches, the platform enabled KfW to stay connected to its banking partners, implement the new programme quickly, and handle a large amount of traffic. As many as 99% of loans up to €3 million were granted automatically, thereby reducing the response time significantly and providing certainty to applicants. This resource-efficient process also enabled KfW to employ staff for the handling of more complex financing.

Step 6: Using cloud-readiness to speed things up

KfW faced immense interest in its programme. Customers flooded the KfW call centre. There was a tenfold increase in the number of calls with requests for information in March 2020. Therefore, KfW developed the funding assistant app, which allowed businesses to check their eligibility for KfW programmes and prepare the application form. Based on acquired cloud skills and the use of predefined cloud services to significantly improve development speed, the first release of the app was ready in just 12 days. The app handled 60,000 customer requests in the first two months.

Overall, the Corona Support Programme turned out to be the largest Special Programme in KfW's history, with domestic commitments amounting to €44 billion in 2020, thereby doubling KfW's business activity in Germany.

Defining the qualities of a Master Chef

Melanie has driven a change in the bank's perception of IT. She transformed the role of IT, which was previously measured in 'IT man-days'. Now, with the advent of Agile working, executives recognise that IT has become a team partner in all business-related activities.

Melanie recognises that her role is evolving rapidly. She is the primary change agent, helping the board to define the digital future of the bank. She acts as a connector, working across silos and hierarchies to eliminate obstacles that block change. This activity takes an external dimension, as KfW also examines other organisations and sectors for techniques to help innovate the bank.

Tips

- Think big but start small: changing organisations and setting a digital agenda is a learning journey, which requires a step-by-step approach

- Love the problem, not the solution: focus on solving the business problems rather than applying a certain technical solution

- Make IT a change agent: enable IT and business lines to work towards a joint goal in cross-functional teams

Orange
Leading through open innovation

Preparing the dish

Orange is a French multinational telecommunications corporation with 580 million customers worldwide, employing 89,000 people in France and 59,000 throughout the rest of Europe, Middle East and Africa. It has an annual turnover of €42 billion.

Koen Vermeulen is the group CIO of Orange Group and senior vice president of Orange Innovation IT and Services. He has oversight of more than 25,000 staff in IT and service platforms and innovation teams across 27 countries, working with local CIOs. He is responsible for global IT governance, strategy and development, and oversees all group-level innovation in service and product offerings, from home connectivity to Wi-Fi, TV, commercial and financial services for business-to-consumer (B2C), B2B and wholesale markets.

Understanding the forces of disruption

Massive technological and economic change is occurring. As the lines between industries have become blurred, the emergence and convergence of technologies provides opportunities for the cross-fertilisation of solutions across sectors. Major industry players are experimenting outside of their core niche areas, such as Toyota building smart cities and Google building self-driving cars. As these innovators enter fresh markets, they benchmark their businesses against new players. Emerging start-up and scale-up businesses add to

"The best way to innovate is to use open technology, have open processes and create an open culture."

Koen Vermeulen, group CIO, Orange Group; senior vice president, Orange Innovation IT and Services

Scan code to watch the full interview.

the rate of market disruption. These new entrants exploit their inherent agility and awareness of emerging technology to render redundant the business models of incumbents, sometimes at breakneck speed.

That narrative is as true in the telecommunication industry as any other sector, where large incumbents have had to diversify their product offerings to navigate a rapidly shifting and highly competitive environment. The exponential growth in demand for faster, cheaper and higher quality broadband connectivity does not mean customers are willing to pay more for services. Incumbents have had to explore ventures in new areas, such as mobile banking services, and new industries, including on-demand television services and home- and cyber-security.

Innovating on behalf of customers

Telecommunication operators must invest heavily in their networks – in the case of Orange, to the tune of €7 billion annually with a massive deployment of fibre and 4G/5G – to satisfy their customers' insatiable demands for connectivity and services, while maintaining historical networks for a long period of time. This perfect storm of tech-led disruption means fundamental and ongoing change in the DNA of telecoms organisations is crucial. Agility and innovation is the way to deliver this change.

Koen is keen to push an agenda of open innovation at Orange, yet he says R&D is not necessarily the same as innovation. He says innovation is about connecting the dots between R&D, IT and the functions of an organisation, and then across the business as a whole, with its ultimate goal being the creation of value for customers. Koen believes the best way to innovate is to use open technology, have open processes and create an open culture.

Embracing open technology

Open-source technology is the default choice for Koen. He believes Red Hat is the 'inventor of open source', where the merits of collaboration and the contributions from users consuming the services have helped to cement open technology as the default development model.

Koen has what he refers to as a 'four-quadrant approach' to managing legacy and technical debt in an incumbent company. In the case of Orange, he has mapped more than 1,200 applications into four quadrants that must be dealt with through corresponding actions:

- First Quadrant: modern technology with strategic purpose – invest;

- Second Quadrant: older technology with strategic purpose – migrate;

- Third Quadrant: legacy technology applications that no longer have strategic purpose – phase-out;
- Fourth Quadrant: non-strategic but sound technology stack – manage in the most cost-effective way and tolerate.

Koen has also made a distinction between innovation in new technology and applied technology. In the case of new technology, Orange has created energy-autonomous objects, such as microcomputer components that rely on solar, wind or ambient energy. These objects can then be integrated into powerful networks to aid agriculture in rural areas. In the case of applied technology, Orange has applied augmented reality and virtual reality to smartphones to create object-recognition systems that provide real-time information.

Developing open processes

Koen believes that successful innovation requires the creation of connections or serendipitous encounters between technology, people and problems. He has created an internal open process of innovation with his 5,000 IT staff.

He sets no limitations – except that ideas must be ethical and legal – and follows start-up practices, where staff can launch their ideas, invest their 'Orange coin' to fund the building of prototypes, and then test these products and services internally before launching to customers externally. His Orange Innovation has to date incubated more than 500 collaborations in 18 countries.

Creating an open culture

Koen says that transformation and change in culture is the most important element of innovation – however, he also recognises that the necessary shift in mindset is the most difficult part to achieve.

Changing cultures is fundamentally about changing habits. It requires constant reinforcement and it needs

senior managers to lead by example, accepting that cultural change takes time and cannot be rushed or dictated. Koen says CIOs looking to change culture must change the context – and changing that context starts at the very top of the business.

Defining the qualities of a Master Chef

Koen's commercial engineering background has helped build his digital leadership credibility. While he is a business executive, he is also genuinely interested in understanding how technology works. He emphasises consistency and transparency in communication with his team. Koen believes the management team should be capable of explaining the full strategy, also outside their domain expertise.

Many senior executives can talk about how much IT costs annually, but few can explain the value technology brings in terms of revenues and growth. Koen is dedicated to providing this clarity around value, leading his IT team from being a cost centre to become a profit-generating unit.

Tips
- Learn to trust and articulate your instincts
- Have a plan but be realistic enough to keep your options open

Barbecue cedar-plank salmon

Serves 4 to 6

- 900g to 1kg salmon fillet, about 4cm thick, skin on
- 2 tbsp grain mustard
- 2 tbsp clear honey or maple syrup
- Grated zest of a lemon
- Salt and pepper

The cedar plank should be large – approximately 14cm x 37cm. Immerse the plank in water and soak it for 2 hours. Prepare the barbecue grill for direct cooking over medium hot charcoal, or a medium to high heat for gas. Open the vents on the lid and bottom of the grill.

Put the mustard, honey or maple syrup and lemon zest in a bowl, and add a good pinch of salt. Grind in some black pepper and mix everything together well. Put the salmon on a large plate, skin side down, and spread the mixture on top. Leave it to stand at room temperature for 15 minutes.

Put the soaked cedar plank on the grill over direct heat and wait until it begins to crackle and smoke. Turn it over and place on indirect heat. Carefully put the salmon on the plank, skin side down. Cover it with the lid and grill it for approximately 15 minutes until the salmon is just cooked through. Check the core temperature of the fish; it should be 62°C – don't let it overcook. Let the salmon rest on the plank before serving.

The favourite dish of Melanie Kehr

SIX
DIGITAL TECHNOLOGIES
The best ingredients and suppliers

The race to implement digital business models and processes in recent times has necessitated the adoption of new IT architectures and tooling. This shift has called for corporate intervention to coordinate experimentation and learning across large and devolved organisations.

The CDO of technology giant Red Hat has taken an industry-leading approach to this challenge by promoting open sourcing both internally and to all her clients. The result is a process that enables rapid transformation and continuous innovation. The approach has also fostered an open culture that encourages collaboration across organisational silos, open processes that employ modern tooling such as DevOps and RPA, and open architectures that can integrate data and associated analytics techniques.

The CIO of PKO Bank Polski recognised the unifying effects of public cloud at an early stage of his journey to digital banking. The move to mobile- and online-banking services required a complete overhaul of traditional infrastructures. This revamp coincided with the transition to hybrid working as the pandemic swept across the globe in 2020. Partnerships with hyperscalers, such as Microsoft Azure and Google Cloud Platform, have enabled a smooth transition to frictionless customer and employee experiences.

The group CIO of MAPFRE Insurance was grappling with margin pressures in a highly devolved structure. Recognising the need to modernise and consolidate business processes on behalf of her 29 national subsidiaries, she chose a two-pronged programme. The first stage was to establish regional hubs for back-office processes such as finance. She was fortunate that the group had just one instance of SAP. The second stage was to adopt a greenfield approach to two front-office processes: insurance quotations and claims processing. She used common tooling, such as optical character recognition, robotic process automation and speech recognition, to engineer these new processes.

In all these recipes, group coordination under strong digital leadership has enabled rapid and cost-effective deployment of new techniques that have helped to speed up the transformation of traditional business structures and ways of working.

Red Hat
Embracing open transformation to accelerate change

Ingredients

- A clear vision and supporting metrics
- Open culture, processes and architectures
- Staff diversity and gender equality

Preparing the dish

For the past six years, Margaret Dawson has been vice president and chief digital officer at Red Hat, a company founded in 1993 that provides open-source software to enterprises worldwide. With a background in marketing and journalism, Margaret offers a unique perspective on how open transformation delivers outstanding customer experiences. Working with her team of more than 100 employees, she promotes the benefits of open transformation both internally and externally.

Margaret says there are three vital ingredients for digital leaders who want to bake open transformation into an organisation: open culture, open processes and open architectures. She believes this 'three-legged stool' will be the foundation for all enterprise strategies in the future: 'I am passionate about inspiring teams and colleagues to change the world for good. What is needed is courageous leadership and a shared vision.'

Building an open culture

Building an open culture at Red Hat means breaking down organisational silos and hierarchies. The result? Great ideas can surface from anywhere in the 15,000-employee organisation and be shared amongst thousands of customers. The spirit of an open organisation is to foster individual passion, encourage collaboration between teams and develop a risk-taking appetite.

'Open leadership is all about focusing on people and behaviour rather than pure technology,' says Margaret. Open leadership also requires a clear vision, which has been demonstrated by Barclays and its attempt to become 'the bank of the future', in an echo of its earlier innovations such as being the first bank to introduce credit cards and cash machines. Airline Cathay Pacific has also fostered an open culture by adopting DevOps practices. This approach produces innovation through collaboration at ten times the speed of traditional methods.

Margaret says an open culture requires diversity across gender, colour and background. Recent benchmarking exercises show organisations that encourage diverse collaboration can double the speed to innovation in only half the number of meetings. Margaret is on a mission to increase diversity within the IT sector, which remains disproportionately balanced towards men. She traces this imbalance to childhood inputs that encourage girls to steer away from science, technology, engineering and maths (STEM) subjects.

Creating open processes

Open processes demand open ways of working. This openness must be baked into an organisation-wide view of what it wants to achieve, and its measurement via clear metrics. That's where modern tools, such as agile teams, DevOps and a fail-fast philosophy, can serve up dramatic improvements in workflow speed and efficiency, as well as genuine innovation in the way things get done.

A second important factor for creating open processes is to define where human effort should be focused and how repetitive and low-value tasks can be automated. Margaret believes that a large portion of office work can be automated, leaving humans to undertake high-value tasks that align with the company's broader strategic vision.

Developing open architectures

Software is at the centre of modern business activities. The central role of software means application development experience is fluid and often distributed across the enterprise and beyond. Open architectures can help developers to use the tools they want and to foster collaboration with any individual or team, regardless of location. Infrastructure is the enabling force for this openness, but it should remain out of sight of work teams.

Just as data is at the heart of modern business operations, so it is becoming the essential ingredient that helps enterprises make key decisions. However, many

"I am passionate about inspiring teams and colleagues to change the world for good. What is needed is courageous leadership and a shared vision."

Margaret Dawson, vice president and chief digital officer, Red Hat

Scan code to watch the full interview.

incumbents have accumulated multiple IT stacks over time, each containing different applications and data structures. Open architectures allow organisations to consolidate their data into a single integrated resource that is accessible by all. Such openness makes it much easier for organisations to use data to optimise business performance and customer experience.

Margaret says cloud, which gives developers the opportunity to move across different environments, is the critical platform for architectural openness. Red Hat is using containers and Kubernetes to make it easier to move and run applications and workloads across a range of cloud platforms. This approach also reduces the possibility of becoming locked in to a single cloud vendor.

Identifying key technologies for the future

As CDO, Margaret sees a rapidly growing pipeline of new technologies that will help digital leaders to achieve innovations in customer service while also overcoming current obstacles such as technical debt. She points to the following trends:

- Distributed or edge-based computing that moves data ingestion closer to customers and associated work processes. This trend will be accelerated by 5G connections and sensors.

- Quantum computing, robotics, AI and ML technologies, which are beginning to intersect as we reach a point of singularity.

- Microservices that encourage productisation and reuse of IT services, as well as supporting infrastructure as code.

The rapid application of emerging technologies requires an open architecture that makes it easier to integrate these tools seamlessly with more traditional systems and services.

Defining the qualities of a Master Chef

Margaret says the CDO is responsible for every aspect of a customer's digital journey. They should inspire their companies to produce a highly personalised omni-channel experience across the web, social media platforms, and physical, face-to-face interactions.

To achieve her ambitions as CDO, Margaret sets clear objectives for her team and discourages hierarchical behaviour. At an individual level, she helps people discover their identity and purpose. She is also religious about achieving an operational cadence that gets things done.

Margaret says success is dependent on attracting, training and retaining the best talent from across the globe. This can be achieved through a combination of demonstrating continuous growth, operating an open culture, and 'doing cool stuff'. She recognises that her objective of changing the world can only be achieved by focusing on one person at a time.

PKO Bank Polski

Be brave and humble on your digital journey

Ingredients

- Learn to trust your colleagues
- Accelerate digital with new techniques
- Envision new working practices

Preparing the dish

With 17 years of banking experience, Adam Marciniak has spent the past decade as CIO of PKO Bank Polski. He is helping to transform Poland's largest bank into a digital behemoth. He believes digital will transform lives profoundly. He says technology leaders must assist boards as they transition towards a digitally enabled future.

PKO was founded in 1919 and has a long tradition of giving both strategic and practical support to Poland's wider economy. Today, it is recognised globally as a digital leader in banking practices. The three drivers that necessitated the bank's digital transition were: growing competition from non-traditional players such as FinTech, tighter regulation and business assurance, and low interest rates that had reduced margins and affected returns on equity.

Adam believes successful CIOs are brave, but also humble within the organisations they serve: 'Humility is about listening, observing, finding the best values and demonstrating the best behaviours.'

Embarking on a digital journey

Adam says digital banking must provide customers with a frictionless experience. This requirement has guided the bank's 10-year journey from e-banking to mobile apps and beyond. The early development of these

"Humility is about listening, observing, finding the best values and demonstrating the best behaviours."

Adam Marciniak, CIO, PKO Bank Polski

Scan code to watch the full interview.

electronic channels was crucial in 2020 when the physical branch network had limits for a long period due to the coronavirus pandemic.

PKO holds a 20% share of the Polish retail banking market, but a 30% share of all mobile interactions. Ready access to mobile banking channels means customers with simple banking issues can now 'self-serve'. This digitisation frees up banking staff to focus their time on high-value tasks, such as advising customers on financial matters.

One of the basic steps in PKO's digitisation journey was the adoption of public cloud services. This was not a straightforward shift, as tight local regulations discouraged investment from hyperscaler providers such as Google and Microsoft. True to his mantra, Adam was brave – and was convinced that PKO could make progress. He worked with external parties, such as Microsoft, Google, Accenture and BCG, to undertake a world tour and examine the cloud in other countries. The outcome of this tour was a commitment by Google and Microsoft to invest in local facilities that conformed to Polish regulations.

The shift to the cloud paid big dividends in March 2020 when it provided the foundations for the bank's shift to home working. As many as 13,000 staff were able to work remotely within just two

days thanks to a combination of Microsoft Teams and Azure cloud services. The cloud also helped PKO to support the rollout of the COVID-19 vaccine programme. In just six weeks, Adam organised joint teams from the Ministry of Health, PKO, Polish Cloud Operator, Google, Microsoft, Accenture and PwC to develop and deploy a comprehensive, complete system that enabled Polish citizens to book vaccine appointments in real time.

Taking a digital approach to workflows

Adam says data analytics and AI are the key tools in helping his team to transform organisational workflows. The bank has introduced intelligent robots to help customers make their own financial decisions. PKO is experimenting with chatbots that listen to customer enquiries using natural-language recognition. These bots then reply with personalised advice or conduct the requested action. In 2020, over one million bot-enabled conversations took place.

The bank has also used robotics to help automate repetitive work processes. PKO has installed about 110 robots to take on the workload of 500 full-time human equivalents. Adam says RPA is a powerful tool that can help business staff to undertake their own software development projects. He believes non-IT staff will use low-code and no-code tools on a regular basis within the next five years. This adoption will have a big impact on the future role of IT.

Embracing a digital workplace

For 100 years, PKO's operating model relied on the physical proximity of its staff. The recent adoption of remote working during the pandemic changed such assumptions forever. Now, there is a long-term preference for hybrid-working models. The IT team has worked with Microsoft to ensure employees have access to the tools that will make hybrid working a success. The IT team has also focused on making both office- and home-working environments as comfortable as possible.

One example of how the adoption of hybrid working will affect the workplace is the plan for PKO's new head office. For the first time, the bank is adopting a hot-desking policy that will enable 3,000 staff to work in a flexible fashion across just 2,000 desks. Mobile apps will be an essential component to making this practice work, with staff deciding where to work each week.

Reimagining the IT organisation

For much of the bank's history, IT has been a servant to the business. For a digital bank, this approach is unworkable. Instead, PKO bravely established 18 tribes that draw on both IT and business staff across the main divisions and functions. These tribes work on business challenges in combination and they have had a radical impact on organisational culture. Non-IT people are becoming familiar with how technology works; IT staff are gaining a much deeper understanding of business processes.

The IT department has expanded dramatically during the past 10 years from 600 to 2,000 staff. Adam has placed ever greater trust in his management team and the tribes. Such empowerment means he can spend more time listening to individual IT staff and peers across the business. He says that being on the board has been invaluable to helping him guide the bank into the digital world.

Defining the qualities of a Master Chef

Adam sees IT evolving primarily into a governance role as the business becomes more self-sufficient in software development techniques. IT will be more about frameworks than solutions, especially in the case of PKO as it becomes digital to its core. However, Adam also recognises that security and business continuity will remain the foundation stone and purpose of the IT organisation.

MAPFRE
Adopting a parallel design path to enterprise automation

Preparing the dish

Vanessa Escrivá García, corporate CIO of MAPFRE, is designing a technology strategy aimed at digitisation, modernisation of systems, redesign of technology processes and a new IT operating model, all in parallel with the maintenance of existing systems.

A key example includes building a hub instead of modernising current operations. Here, MAPFRE is adopting new architectures based on microservices and the open-source orchestration system Kubernetes. The aim of this work is to extract full functionality from heritage processes as the company builds new ones.

MAPFRE is a global insurance company with a worldwide presence. It is the benchmark insurer in the Spanish market and the largest Spanish multinational insurance group in the world. It is the number one non-life insurance group in Latin America and one of the 15 largest European groups in terms of premium volume.

Changing the operating model

As an insurance group operating throughout the world, MAPFRE has depended historically on a decentralised organisational structure for IT operations. Of the company's 2,000 IT resources, only 400 are located at the corporate centre under Vanessa's direct control.

However, several factors are now challenging this decentralised approach to business and IT operations in insurance, including:

- The commoditisation of products through the emergence of comparison websites;

- The associated erosion of margins and the need to streamline operations;

- The rise of sophisticated consumers who are used to exploiting online channels.

This combination of market-disrupting factors means MAPFRE must undertake an end-to-end redesign of core processes and systems. This redesign will allow the company to deal with the challenges of dramatic improvements in speed and efficiency that characterise the new market environment in insurance.

Vanessa also recognises that local conditions vary considerably according to market maturity. This variability is particularly clear across Latin America. She understands that to be successful, the company will need to maintain a broad range of product sets and channel activities. As Vanessa says: 'There is no single

solution to a global marketplace.'

Vanessa must help MAPFRE to balance these demands. As corporate CIO, she says the group centre will play a crucial role in helping the company's local subsidiaries to reengineer IT and associated business operations in the coming years.

Laying out the vision for a future operating model

Vanessa's vision for the group focuses on two main components. The first element recognises that transforming legacy systems in the countries in which MAPFRE operates will take too long and cost too much. Instead, she is executing a parallel strategy.

In this parallel strategy, legacy processes will still be supported but at the same time there will be development of greenfield technology platforms. This parallel strategy will lower any potential risks to the business and will mean the IT organisation can focus on delivering entirely new IT operating models for each national organisation.

The second element of Vanessa's vision is to establish processing hubs that will serve each region and create a common business platform for each subsidiary. These hubs will deliver economies of scale and ensure a standardised approach to technology across variable markets.

"There is no single solution to a global marketplace."

Vanessa Escrivá García, corporate CIO, MAPFRE

Vanessa gives as examples the financial process that is homogeneous for all operations and has allowed having a single version of SAP for more than 10 years, and the human resources processes, where the group has adopted the Success Factors cloud-based platform for general use in all its subsidiaries.

Understanding the two targets for process reengineering

Vanessa has selected two key business processes for a greenfield development programme that will address end-to-end functionality:

- Online insurance quotations that can help MAPFRE respond effectively to the challenges posed by comparison websites, where multiple quotations are required in quick succession;

- Claims processing, where new technologies such as optical character recognition (OCR) can be applied to help speed up claims settlements.

As part of the process reengineering, Vanessa is applying automation, such as intelligent OCR, artificial intelligence and machine learning, to read incoming documents automatically and make better decisions on behalf of the business. The capturing of images associated with car crashes, for example, can be automated by using image-recognition technologies.

When it comes to legacy systems, Vanessa recognises that many of these processes will remain in operation for some time and will require incremental treatments. She is piloting RPA as a means of streamlining existing systems and processes. She has installed several robots already in an attempt to measure potential business outcomes.

Transforming the IT operating model

To enable the reengineering of vital business processes and the consolidation of back-office activities within regional hubs, Vanessa has taken a radical approach to

IT operations across the group that centres on two key areas:

- A cloud strategy for all new applications and business services, with limits to the number of cloud vendors that are used to help reduce complexity. She is also exploiting IT partnerships across regions to carry out core-system upgrades.

- The adoption of modern techniques, such as software as a service, microservices, open sourcing, and Kubernetes, to provide the foundations for reengineered systems and processes that will operate in the cloud. This adoption opens the door for the implementation of DevOps and Agile methods across the group.

Defining the qualities of a Master Chef

Vanessa is now adopting a coordinated approach to group IT policy, where she develops strategy and technical architecture for all subsidiaries. She is also assembling an associated toolset that will be used across the group to encourage knowledge-sharing and the movement of expertise.

Many global organisations find it difficult to harmonise IT policies across an organisation that is set up as individual national units. The fast-changing nature of modern business, including the establishment of effective operations in the post-COVID age, means CIOs must adapt radical change. The only route to success is tighter central control and active investment in modern methods.

Tips

- Avoid betting on legacy upgrades as a future business strategy

- Pilot new techniques at the corporate centre rather than allowing local experimentation

- Use software as a service as an evergreen solution to back-office challenges

Tofu with black beans and red pepper

Serves 4, with rice

- 400g extra-firm tofu
- 2 heaped tbsp fermented black beans
- 2 red peppers
- 10 spring onions
- 1 red chilli (optional)
- 2 tbsp sunflower oil
- 2 tbsp dark soy sauce

For the marinade:

- 2cm piece of fresh ginger, grated
- 1 clove of garlic, grated
- 2 tbsp rice wine
- 2 tbsp light soy sauce

To serve:

- A few coriander leaves, chopped
- Boiled rice

Marinate the tofu first. Drain it and cut it into 1.5cm cubes, put them in a large bowl and then add the marinade ingredients. Stir gently, cover the bowl and set the tofu aside for at least 30 minutes. Soak the black beans in warm (not hot) water for 10 minutes or follow the instructions on the pack.

Chop the peppers into small pieces or fine strips, slice the spring onions and prepare and finely slice the chilli (if using). Drain the beans. Put a wok over a high heat and add the sunflower oil. Carefully lift the cubes of tofu out of the marinade; cook them in batches, or they will steam instead of frying. Put the tofu cubes in the wok – it will spit – and allow them to sizzle on each side, crisping them up. Lift them out and set them on kitchen paper to drain.

Once they are all done, add the chopped vegetables and dark soy sauce to the wok and stir fry for a few minutes. Carefully add the tofu cubes and any remains of the marinade, and cook the tofu until it is tender but not breaking up. Scatter with the coriander and serve immediately, accompanied by boiled rice.

The favourite dish of Jenniffer Gearheart-Tang

SECTION 3

WHAT IS EXPECTED OF TOP-RANKING IT CHEFS AND THEIR SUPPORTING TEAMS?

"Every member of the IT kitchen team plays a pivotal role in enabling sustainable and successful change"

As the journey towards digital continues to accelerate across the globe, CIOs are expected to play a central role in helping their peers navigate the emerging digital terrain. The increasing pace of technology-driven innovation calls for closer engagement between IT staff and their business counterparts. In this respect, the CIO becomes the orchestrator of change across the business. Working under this orchestrator, every member of the IT kitchen team plays a pivotal role in enabling sustainable and successful change.

Deciphering the DNA of the Master Chef

The style of IT management is changing and so is the DNA of successful technology leaders. CIOs can no longer continue to adopt a static, top-down approach, with many moving parts to manage. On the one hand, CIOs must put in place effective governance to ensure the cohesion of all IT-related activities. On the other, they need to encourage local experimentation and ideation to help the business embrace change. Charlie Forte, CIO of the UK's MoD, described this dual role as the 'yin and yang of IT management'. Here's how the best IT chefs are adapting their leadership styles.

Sharing the vision – propagating the big 'why'

In an increasingly uncertain world, CIOs must put forward a compelling vision that is credible to all business partners and that helps motivate IT staff to achieve moon shots rather than incremental steps. Getting people to buy into this vision requires full trust and understanding from peers at the executive level. CIOs must also develop an ability to tell compelling stories.

Leadership is about nudging and coaching

Several CIOs that we interviewed have split their large IT organisations into small units of just five to ten staff, or what Amazon calls the 'two-pizza team'. This approach enables the teams to be more agile when generating and testing ideas. It also places a different responsibility on the shoulders of the CIO – one of nudging and coaching, rather than commanding. Top IT chefs encourage continuous learning and curiosity among their staff.

Personal qualities are all-important today

The profile of the CIO has never been more critical to achieving an effective leadership approach. IT is frequently ahead of other functions in applying new methods and tools. In a world dominated by technological innovation, this focus on personality remains a prerequisite for top IT leaders.

The rapid churn in top-level IT appointments illustrates both the shortage of top chefs and the increasing number of prizes on offer to attract pioneering CIOs to large and complex organisations. CEOs would be well-advised to recognise and reward unique talent as we enter the digital era.

Assembling a dream team for your digital kitchen

The role of IT, and its structure within the broader business, has evolved constantly for decades as new technologies, tools and vendors have swept into the sector, often generated by innovative start-ups. Computer science is still a relatively young profession, blossoming in the 1980s and maturing in the third millennium. However, there is little indication that developments have slowed down recently, as illustrated by the transition to the cloud, the rise of big data and the uptake of Agile development. In fact, IT leaders believe the coming decade will generate even more demand for technology talent than preceding periods.

A new breed of talent is now required that can bridge the gap between technology and business. This capability needs to understand the potential of new technologies, but at the same time relate these advances directly to the specific business context. In the words of Tarun Kohli of Swiss Re, we must learn, unlearn and relearn constantly to maintain our capabilities.

Expanding IT competencies for the digital age

Leading CIOs constantly expand and improve the range of capabilities they offer to their business partners. Attention is often focused on developing specific areas of competence with appropriate leadership. In many leading organisations, the CIO has chosen to establish a digital 'community of practice' that encourages the sharing of techniques and experiences within a continuous learning context.

Sourcing and retaining talent

Many large organisations struggle today to recruit and retain the talent they need to fuel their digital transformation programmes. This is especially true in the government sector, where wages might not be as high as in some private industries, such as financial services. Equally, ambitious millennials see start-ups and digital natives as exciting places to work. Leading CIOs within large incumbent organisations must offer compelling visions to the market to win the battle for talent.

Setting the pace

There are notable variations among IT staff when it comes to pace and ambition. Take the CIO of a large public sector organisation, who recognised he has sprinters, runners, walkers and those who don't move. His preference is to encourage the sprinters and runners in the hope that the rest will catch up. The severe shortage of digital skills means CIOs must develop closer partnerships with academia to harvest new talent as it emerges into the market.

There are few professions that compare to IT. Imagine a constantly changing menu, which is supported by a kitchen that demands new skills monthly and replaces its top chef at two-year intervals. Running this kitchen successfully is no easy task. The IT cookbook approach that we offer here provides valuable lessons for all those who simultaneously work in the kitchen, manage their staff and contribute to the success of the broader establishment.

Developing winning cultures that promote better collaboration and communication

Culture pervades every organisation, large and small, and has a strong influence on how staff behave – especially when change takes place. Within the context of digital transformation, culture can be an unhelpful roadblock unless it is addressed head-on. As many executives will admit, culture is hard to decipher and even tougher to change.

But do we understand what culture is? According to the dictionary, culture is an umbrella term that encompasses the social behaviour and norms found in any human society, as well as the knowledge, beliefs, arts, laws, customs, capabilities and habits of the individuals in such groups. Culture is a complex topic and its effective management requires both empathetic and analytical skills. While many CIOs have had successful careers by applying well-tuned analytical skills, social and empathetic qualities are equally important to IT leadership excellence today.

Here are some of the most enlightened examples of how leading practitioners are helping their organisations to build winning cultures that can promote collaboration and communication.

Bringing the voice of the customer into every conversation

In times of economic turmoil and rapid change, many organisations look inwards to try and discover their future. This inward-looking approach has been compared to arranging the deckchairs on the Titanic. In contrast, the most successful Master Chefs and their teams use an 'outside-in' approach that brings the voice of the customer into every conversation. This approach has a galvanising effect on culture and is often seen as the most effective way to deal with a volatile and uncertain world.

Learning a few tricks from our Asian friends

By adopting a culture of continuous improvement, leading Japanese car manufacturers such as Toyota have long succeeded in building reliable cars that outstrip their competition. Although newcomers such as Tesla might upset this apple cart once in a while, most industries can evolve progressively by emulating cultures that promote continuous learning and improvement. This approach is akin to organic life, which has survived through adaptation for many millennia.

Promoting diversity to encourage higher levels of innovation and creativity

Traditional IT organisations have followed a well-trodden path for hiring and developing engineering talent. However, this talent is often male-dominated and frequently middle aged. This recruitment policy has supported a stable regime of waterfall development and optimised underpinning infrastructures. In the emerging world of design thinking and Agile development, organisational approaches to diversity and inclusivity must extend across individual characteristics, values, beliefs and backgrounds.

To be successful in the emerging digital era, Master Chefs need to address many of the softer issues that have been noticeably absent in stable market situations. Dealing with these concerns includes developing adaptive cultures, digital skills and agile organisations. This focus on softer issues calls for a balance of left- and right-brain capabilities that are defining the next generation of successful digital leaders.

SEVEN
DECIPHERING THE DNA OF THE MASTER CHEF

This cookbook showcases the achievements of Europe's digital leaders. But what are the personal capabilities that support the outstanding accomplishments of these Master Chefs? This chapter reveals the many qualities that characterise a successful leader. Foremost are curiosity and passion for business innovation and transformation.

Ferrovial is a global leader in construction, which is a sector known for its conservative approach to technology-led innovation. The group chief information and innovation officer (CIIO) recognised that the corporate centre must be the active eyes and ears around which emerging technologies can add value in a highly decentralised global organisation. To operationalise this vision, he established centres of excellence for automation, knowledge-sharing and artificial intelligence. These centres helped transform the operational activities across the different businesses within the group.

The COO of Kensington Mortgages, a leading UK provider of specialist loan products, recognised that exceptional business circumstances, such as the coronavirus pandemic, also create opportunities for growth. He completed a root-and-branch review of the organisation covering workplace, workforce and workflow. This review ensured that the best resources and technologies are deployed to help the business maintain market leadership. His approach is encapsulated by a three-pillar model that is based on data analytics, technology and digital capability.

To identify the essential ingredients for success in digital leadership, it is also useful to turn back the clock and examine how senior careers have evolved over the decades. In the final recipe in this section, the CIO of the Houses of Parliament Restoration and Renewal project typifies how a wide range of past experiences prepare a leader for success in today's turbulent and fast-changing world. One of the key strands in his story is an elucidation of the way in which cloud platforms have contributed to improvements in government performance.

The consistent theme across our digital leaders' recipes is the breadth and depth of digital experience they have gained across a multitude of public sector and private business capacities. These experiences have added new flavours to winning menus.

Ferrovial
A chef for all seasons

Ingredients

- Curiosity and a passion for everything new
- Ability to simplify complex problems so they become simple solutions
- Follow ideas through to execution

Preparing the dish

Take a well-seasoned executive with wide experience in consultancy, large corporates and start-ups, and place him as CIIO in a global environment, and you have the recipe for innovation and transformation. That's the perfect description of Dimitris Bountolos, who joined Ferrovial in 2020 to take up his current group role as CIIO. Ferrovial is a Spanish multinational company involved in the design, construction, financing, operation and maintenance of transport infrastructure and urban services.

A taste for transformation means Dimitris is always on the search for fresh ingredients for success: 'I feel like a free electron, bouncing left to right and up and down to keep the atom moving towards its target.' With a deep curiosity for everything new, he and his central team are addressing complex problems and opportunities on behalf of the group. He brings a unique ability to simplify and execute business solutions across a highly distributed landscape that includes semi-autonomous businesses such as Heathrow Airport.

Making changes from the top

One of Ferrovial's primary functions as a construction and operating company is to manage risk. In a post-COVID world, where change has become a new constant, the future has never been more uncertain for all the company's distributed businesses, from aviation and transportation to roads and utilities. This uncertainty poses unprecedented challenges when it comes to predicting demand for services. Rapid technological change adds another radical ingredient to that mix. From 5G to 3D printing and on to AI, blockchain and IoT, Ferrovial faces a tech-led inflexion point that could transform the construction sector, which has traditionally been stable and conservative, in the coming years.

On his arrival, Dimitris was presented with a five-year corporate strategy, Horizon 24, that set out a new path for the company. His challenge was to convert this far-ranging strategy into manageable chunks that could produce great results across a widely dispersed set of national organisations and local construction projects. Overcoming this challenge means his staff have had to work at group level to connect more closely with local communities and partners to execute fundamental changes.

Building momentum for change

Given the highly decentralised nature of the company's global operations, Dimitris has adopted a multi-layered approach to disseminating his recipes for change across the group. This approach has fostered a connected change environment:

■ Establishing centres of excellence at group headquarters in Madrid, which includes both technical experts and product managers;

■ Connecting operating units such as large construction sites by providing knowledge-sharing tools enabled through a digital workspace;

■ Working with external partners such as MIT to harvest the latest techniques within construction, including 3D modelling and asset management;

■ Encouraging gender diversity to help accelerate innovation.

Creating a three-level approach to business innovation

Dimitris believes innovation takes place at three levels: workplace, workforce and workflows. He recognises that a hybrid way of working will persist well beyond the coronavirus pandemic. This new form of workplace will require far higher levels of electronic connectivity within and between operating units to share best practices. His vision is to create a group platform for knowledge-transfer that will operate on any device at any location across the globe.

Dimitris is a fan of workforce centralisation, where his core team of 150 experts based in

"Innovation takes place at three levels: workplace, workforce, and workflows."

Dimitris Bountolos, CIIO, Ferrovial

Scan code to watch the full interview.

Madrid can fashion new ideas and oversee execution across the group. He recognises that large operating companies such as airports will need their own IT staff. However, they can also benefit from group-led ideas and investments. Given the ever-expanding pipeline of technological innovation in construction, he says innovation activity needs to be coordinated to maximise commercial returns.

One of Dimitris's priorities is the automation of workflows. He believes the potential for RPA is exponential and is keen to keep a tight grip on the technology's implementation, particularly given the diversity of suppliers and techniques in today's market. He is already selecting partners such as UiPath to guide RPA developments across all business units. He recognises that AI will be a powerful tool in helping to break down organisational silos and is keen to manage how this technology is exploited from the centre on behalf of the group.

Defining the qualities of a Master Chef

As head of both innovation and IT, Dimitris is keen to preserve a careful balance between ideation (right brain) and execution (left brain). He achieves this balance by helping to stimulate individual initiatives within the company's businesses, while also capturing and amplifying successes through his human networks and centres of excellence. He believes that group functions should be catalysts for innovation because of the pressures on operating units for short-term performance outcomes.

Driven by curiosity, Dimitris constantly looks for weak signals in emerging areas of technology such as AI. Spotting these signals early and testing their viability enables his team to stimulate business innovation in a timely fashion. Once again, this approach exemplifies how he believes the need for coordination at group level is apposite, especially given the potential for replication within relatively autonomous business units.

One of the critical capabilities of a Master Chef is to structure the solutions to complex problems. This is something Dimitris learnt as a consultant at McKinsey. He uses frameworks to convert these problems into simpler solutions that can be executed in practical situations. This approach provides a bridge between the centre (ideation) and operating divisions (execution). Each new idea that is treated in this way can produce compelling narratives that encourage adoption across the company's many operating units. Storytelling is a principal asset of today's digital leaders in all aspects of innovation and transformation.

Tips
- Stimulate individual innovation
- Listen for weak signals
- Harness all such innovations at group level

Kensington Mortgages
Designing an agile and adaptive operating model to support growth

Preparing the dish

As a respected CIO, CDO and CTO, Mark Foulsham was well prepared for his next step up the career ladder when he became COO at Kensington Mortgages in 2019. With a 25-year heritage, Kensington is the UK's leading specialist mortgage lender. It serves fast-growing segments, such as self-employed individuals, people with multiple incomes and those aged over 55.

Mark recognised the exceptional opportunities for Kensington to deal with increased demands for specialist mortgages, loans and servicing in an ever-increasing digital ecosystem. He also knew that big high-street banks were not well equipped to deal with such specialist needs.

'The challenge from the outset was to accommodate growth whilst increasing efficiency and remaining compliant in a highly regulated sector,' says Mark. The solution was to design a new operating model that was both agile and adaptive to fast-changing market requirements.

"Leaders of the future will be able to adjust rapidly to changing circumstances."

Mark Foulsham, COO, Kensington Mortgages

Scan code to watch the full interview.

Reinventing the business

Mark says Kensington's business strategy is all about establishing a model for growth that takes advantage of societal shifts due to the pandemic, including home working and technical advances in areas such as automation and data analytics. His plan includes three connected elements:

- Remodelling the workplace to reflect a new era of hybrid working

- Realigning the workforce to create an agile and adaptive organisation

- Introducing new technology, including automation to increase growth-related functionality and to reduce the administrative workload

The unifying factor linking all these elements was a shared vision of how technology could help the company meet its objectives and support the creation of a more flexible and collaborative culture.

Changing the workplace and workforce

The move to home working during the pandemic was an important catalyst for re-examining the role of the workplace. Mark says corporate offices in the post-pandemic era will have a specific purpose around building teams, encouraging collaboration and developing people. Other types of work, such as administration and meetings, can be undertaken at home effectively.

He recognises there are wide variations in terms of where people live and how much space they have in their homes. To access new sources of talent, Kensington has broadened its recruitment beyond south-east England to the whole of the UK. Despite greater geographic dispersion, Mark feels that all employees should meet occasionally to maintain cohesion and ensure less-experienced staff gain from working alongside more senior colleagues.

The extensive use of video-conferencing technology has helped to flatten hierarchies and made it possible for managers to check-in regularly with their teams regardless of location. This access has boosted flexibility and helped create a more adaptive workforce within Kensington during the past two years. In this increasingly virtual organisation, Mark says leaders must trust their staff to do their jobs: 'Supervision is all about measuring outcomes rather than inputs.'

Automating workflows

Mark has paid special attention to the core processes that underpin Kensington's business operating model, such as loan authorisation, customer acquisition and retention, and performance reporting to investors. The latter is especially important as the firm is backed by private equity.

During his first months as COO, Mark restructured his teams to support improvements in process performance. Two case examples illustrate how he was able to introduce tangible improvements:

- Extending RPA to support colleagues at the front end of the business. Robotic process automation has minimised administrative tasks such as document management and helped to maximise time spent with brokers and end customers. This successful application reinforces the firm's overarching culture of customer centricity.

- Using data analytic tools such as Microsoft's Power BI to generate insight that improves the quality and granularity of decisions that affect internal operations and external customer experiences. The company used these techniques to shorten the loan approval time from twenty to five days – a key competitive advantage in the mortgage marketplace.

Aligning IT to support the new operating model

Mark has adopted a three-pillar model to ensure that IT supports fast-evolving business requirements. The three pillars are: technology, data analytics and digital capabilities.

When it comes to technology, Mark wants to build strong external partnerships. He believes key partners such as banking-technology specialist Sopra can provide contemporary core infrastructure solutions in an increasingly commoditised world.

In contrast, Mark believes data is a core asset of the organisation. He says any tools and capabilities, such as Power BI and data science skills, should reside within the organisation. Finally, Mark has focused on developing digital capabilities around tailored customer solutions. This focus helped the company to meet the requirements of both brokers and customers, increasing the relevance of products matching customer needs and supporting brand loyalty.

Defining the qualities of a Master Chef

Earlier in his career, Mark used his IT leadership position to help pull solutions together from across different functions. He refers to his tactic as 'joining the dots'. Since he always looks to work across functional boundaries, Mark has often been asked to take responsibility for closely related activities, such as procurement and risk management. This cross-boundary working has served him well before and now as COO at Kensington Mortgages.

Mark believes the right language is crucial to gaining greater responsibility and influence within an organisation. Instead of talking about technology stacks, he prefers to focus on business phrases such as earnings and customer impact. His attention is centred on the three key outcomes that relate to his revised business model: growth in revenues and profits, operational efficiency and regulatory compliance.

His guiding principle is to be open and honest, and to have an ability to listen to others. He believes the leaders of the future will be able to adjust rapidly to changing circumstances.

Tips

- Learn to ignore functional boundaries
- Recognise that not making a decision is the worst thing you can do
- Trust people to do their jobs and focus on outcomes
- Be mindful of context – consider the impact of decisions on others

Restoration and Renewal Authority

No challenge is too big for a Master Chef

Ingredients

- A constant search for areas where technology has a transformation impact

- Recognition that cloud platforms will transform both IT and business effectiveness

- Ability to combine strategy and vision with a strong focus on execution and outcomes

Preparing the dish

As we search for the DNA of Europe's most successful Master Chefs, we roll back the clock to discover the primary ingredients that have helped shape and form the successful career of Martin Bellamy. Martin is now CIO of the Houses of Parliament Restoration and Renewal Authority where he is putting digital at the heart of restoring the Palace of Westminster. His career achievements across more than 40 years illustrate the steps necessary to achieve a top rank in every field of endeavour.

Understanding that no challenge is too big

Martin's career has been guided by a simple adage: 'seek out the big challenges and plan for success'. By design rather than by chance, he has chosen jobs in sectors where he has been able to foresee technology having a high impact. This has enabled him to contribute to some major changes.

His career began in the financial services sector prior to the introduction of personal computers. At that time, in the 1980s, Martin predicted the dramatic changes that he could help shape:

- He led an undergraduate project at Imperial College

"Seek out the big challenges and plan for success."

Martin Bellamy, CIO, Houses of Parliament Restoration and Renewal Authority

Scan code to watch the full interview.

London to build a business case for a UK cash-dispensing network for a leading bank;

■ At Reuters, he was involved in the development of a pioneering digital TV service, and a news search engine, well in advance of Google, to provide traders around the world with up-to-date news throughout the business day.

After nearly 20 years in financial services, Martin believed his next move should be into the public sector, where historic under-investment in technology offered major opportunities for innovation and development. This was supported by his personal commitment to public service:

■ At the UK's Department for Work and Pensions, he helped orchestrate a dramatic transformation that reduced the elapsed time for claiming state pension from six weeks to 15 minutes, simultaneously enabling a 50% reduction in workforce at the department.

■ In Her Majesty's Prison and Probation service, he oversaw the national deployment of a case and risk management system that improved the overall efficiency of the department.

■ At the University of Cambridge, he established what was the UK's most powerful academic

supercomputer, accommodating petaflop processing on petabytes of data.

■ At the Financial Conduct Authority, he instigated a cloud programme to enable the organisation to respond to rapid changes in the regulatory environment.

Having pioneered many developments in financial services and the public sector, Martin has chosen now to focus on construction through his new role as CIO of the Houses of Parliament Restoration and Renewal Authority. While construction has traditionally not been one of the leading investors in digital transformation, a rapid catch-up is now underway.

Pioneering UK government cloud policy

One of Martin's landmark achievements has been his contribution to cloud policy across the UK public sector. Appointed by the Cabinet Office in 2010 as inaugural director of the G-Cloud framework, he developed a comprehensive government strategy for adoption and deployment of public cloud services. This development was necessary to enable government departments to release the vice-like grip of just a few dominant IT vendors on lucrative IT contracts.

To undertake this task, Martin succeeded in co-opting 120 external, voluntary resources to establish a cloud policy and develop a government cloud services store. This approach has become a gamechanger for suppliers and government departments in their quest for more flexible and responsive partnerships with the vendor community.

Imperial College London took an academic interest in Martin's work, and he completed a PhD in cloud computing in 2014.

Demonstrating the benefits of cloud platforms

Through his work with G-Cloud, Martin was early to recognise the strategic value of cloud as an all-pervasive IT and business platform.

In this respect, cloud has opened the door to replacing individual responses to user requirements with a more generic capability based on cloud services, especially in the case of software as a service (SaaS), which offers 'evergreen' solutions to functions such as finance, HR and customer relations.

Cloud also provides a modern architecture that can support Agile development tools – reducing IT responses from years to months

or even weeks. Generic capabilities can help productise IT services, with subsequent quantum improvements in efficiency.

Detailing the changing role of the CIO

By adopting cloud and simplifying service delivery, the CIO can focus on business-related opportunities. Martin foresees an evolving portfolio of responsibilities for the modern CIO:

- Business innovation – how can technology contribute to business outcomes?

- Building capability to implement the vision – empowering people to get things done;

- Establishing and sustaining a technical community of practice to support business;

- Focusing on delivery to ensure that full value is achieved in every project;

- Strengthening IT governance at every level by engaging top executives.

Defining the qualities of a Master Chef

Martin is confident that IT and the position of the CIO remains stable and secure over the coming decade due to the innovation challenges that organisations must resolve as they become digital businesses.

He recognises that with the advent of quantum computing, cybersecurity will remain high on the CIO's agenda. He believes that we are approaching a pivot point for automation as new tools such as RPA and ML become commonplace. He also foresees the convergence of IT and operations in areas such as manufacturing, distribution and construction.

In all these respects, the challenges of applying and securing IT systems will continue to demand specialist expertise within businesses of all kinds.

Tips

- Seek out the big challenges and plan for success. Agree achievable goals, construct a realistic plan and never be deterred by challenges, as you might be just a step away from success

- Choose sectors where technology has yet to have a fundamental impact

- Be participative – recognise that the whole is often greater than the sum of the parts

- Balance in life is essential, including family, physical wellbeing and personal integrity

Gluten-free dark chocolate torte

Makes a 23cm diameter torte

- 450g dark chocolate, minimum 85% cocoa
- 225g unsalted butter, or 100ml coconut oil and 125g butter
- 50g coconut sugar
- 6 tbsp clear honey or coconut nectar
- 1 tsp vanilla extract
- A pinch of ground sea salt
- 50ml coconut milk or Bailey's
- 6 medium eggs

Preheat the oven to 180°C/fan 160°C/GM 4, and lightly grease a 23cm ceramic flan dish with butter or spray with coconut oil. Do not use a loose-bottomed tin.

Break up the chocolate into small pieces and put them in a large mixing bowl. Cube the butter and add that to the bowl (with the oil, if using a mixture), then add the coconut sugar. Cover the bowl with cling film, pierce a few holes in it and microwave the chocolate mixture very briefly until it is soft but not molten.

Whisk the mixture until smooth. Add the honey and the vanilla extract, plus a little salt, and whisk thoroughly again. Then add the coconut milk or Bailey's and stir that in. Now add the eggs, one at a time, and whisk the mixture smooth after adding each one. Stir the mix gently to make sure everything is blended together.

Pour the mixture into the prepared flan dish using a rubber spatula to ensure nothing is wasted. Put the dish in the oven and bake the torte for 20 to 25 minutes. Check at 20 minutes; it should still be a bit glossy and wet in the middle. If you wait until it looks fully baked, it will be too dry; it will continue cooking and solidifying after it is removed from the oven.

The favourite dish of Margaret Dawson

EIGHT
A DREAM TEAM FOR YOUR DIGITAL KITCHEN

As the pace of digital transformation hots up in the aftermath of the coronavirus pandemic, IT is being challenged to deliver great results across an ever-increasing pipeline of work. CIOs have adopted new approaches to recruit, deploy and support the best digital resources available globally.

For Euronext, Europe's largest equity trading organisation, the combination of a new microsecond-based trading platform and the integration of several acquisitions called for a rapid expansion of IT and related business resources. This was met in part by a new centre of excellence based in Portugal, combined with expanded links with leading universities that encourage accelerated learning.

At Maersk, the world's largest logistics company, the CIO inherited a fragmented team of IT professionals that was failing to meet business needs. To address this shortfall, he developed a mission and set of processes that have enabled staff to engage more actively with end customers, backed up by Agile methods and a clear focus on business outcomes. The turnaround has been decisive and has won huge recognition from Maersk and its customers.

At leading pharmaceutical company AstraZeneca, the need to develop a vaccine in months rather than years posed a formidable challenge for innovation teams. Automation tools such as RPA and AI have provided a practical way of amplifying the contribution of human talent to meeting stretched business goals.

Traditional waterfall development methods were found to be inadequate at Norway Post, an organisation with a 400-year heritage. The CIO has introduced new methods based on design thinking and Agile development to enable his cross-functional teams to create innovative solutions faster and more effectively than through traditional methods.

Across all these four recipes, team empowerment, shared learning and cross-functional working feature heavily, as does the need to focus available resources on the most value-intensive tasks.

Euronext
Managing and empowering a busy kitchen to deliver great results

Preparing the dish

Manuel Bento is the CEO of the Technology Centre of Euronext, based in Portugal. Manuel is also CTO of the group holding transversal functions such as managing diverse global teams that include Cybersecurity, IT Operations, Infrastructure and Cloud Services, Enterprise Architecture and Corporate Functions.

Euronext is the leading pan-European market infrastructure and it operates regulated exchanges in Belgium, France, Ireland, Italy, The Netherlands, Norway and Portugal. As of the end of September 2021, it had close to 1,920 listed issuers and around €6.5 trillion in market capitalisation. Since his arrival at Euronext four years ago, Manuel has been busy supporting the development of the next-generation trading system, integrating new acquisitions, mainly stock exchanges and other companies that operate in the capital markets, and expanding his team to more than 300 staff across Europe. He says access to fresh talent is critical for the business: 'The only way to grow skills is to empower people and guarantee that they have success.'

Preparing the team to develop and support a new trading system

One of the biggest challenges facing Manuel and his IT organisation since his arrival was to make sure the team

"The only way to grow skills is to empower people and guarantee that they have success."

Manuel Bento, CEO, Technology Centre of Euronext

Scan code to watch the full interview.

was ready to develop and support the next-generation trading system. The trading system is the core of the stock exchange, and the new-generation trading system was essential to support the acquisitions of new stock exchanges. Creating new systems was a complex task because of the need to implement trading algorithms and the requirement to add new expertise. Manuel recruited 150 staff in Portugal, where he was able to take advantage of fast-improving economic conditions.

One of the key attributes of the new trading system is the speed of operation. The platform can run transactions in microseconds rather than milliseconds, which is the situation in other parts of the business. These super-fast speeds can only be achieved by adopting specific software languages, such as C++, and by running trading calculation in solid-state rather than using disk memory. In order to find specialist expertise and to attract appropriate skills, Manuel reached out locally to both universities and companies.

A key success factor for the project was the constant support that Manuel has offered, together with colleagues in other locations. He attended daily progress calls with multinational teams in Porto and Paris, and weekly calls with customers. He believes a close connection with customers is

vital for business leaders who want to innovate.

Growing the IT kitchen

In addition to the introduction of the new trading platform, named Optiq, the IT organisation has been working on the integration of stock exchanges across Europe. Manuel has adapted the size of his original team in order to cope with these new demands. Once again, he also ensured that he maintains constant communication with Euronext's customers. His tactics to attract and retain talent include:

- Exploiting the Euronext brand, which is well known across Europe and generates a constant pipeline of talent;

- Placing staff into challenging projects, with sufficient freedom and empowerment to enable them to learn constantly on the job;

- Expanding the scope of the IT team's projects to include business as well as technical aspects, which offers workers the opportunity to expand their expertise.

One distinct advantage of being located in Portugal is the country's ready availability of multilingual talent, especially MBA students. Manuel says that this broad base of languages is an essential ingredient for a company looking to create a multicultural team

that is able to operate seamlessly across national boundaries.

Establishing a security team

Manuel also supported the chief security officer (CSO) role at Euronext. He is responsible for a dedicated security team that has four main duties:

- Regulation and risk assessment;
- Engineering security into IT solutions;
- Penetration testing and risk mediation;
- Security operations to monitor infrastructure.

Manuel is keen to encourage diversity within his team and has recruited talent from a variety of sectors. To enable the team to reach critical mass quickly, he has combined young, high-potential staff with mature and experienced professionals. This mix gives younger staff the opportunity to develop rapidly on-the-job and to learn from their more experienced colleagues.

Defining the qualities of a Master Chef

In a high-growth and increasingly digital environment, Manuel has focused on building a capable team that is constantly learning and adjusting to its new environment. As responsibilities broaden from trading operations and security to the central role of data within Euronext, Manuel has worked hard to ensure his staff are involved in every aspect of the business – and that includes a constant dialogue with key customers.

His view is that the team will only manage to constantly improve and adjust if they are empowered to make important decisions. Manuel has a combination of personal qualities that contribute to the success of his team:

- A strong focus on execution. Manuel believes that tough challenges are an essential ingredient for personal and team development. He also recognises that control is necessary to keep projects on track and to deliver stretching outcomes.

- A concentration on constant study. Manuel believes education and experience are crucial to helping people grapple with changes in business and technology, and says, 'Success in the past does not guarantee success in the future'.

- An honest approach to situations. Being honest helps teams to communicate more effectively and avoid blind alleys. Manuel believes honesty and pragmatism

are guiding principles when it comes to leading his teams in a challenging business environment.

Manuel advises future leaders to take account of context and to be adaptable to change. As a person who thrives on change, he welcomes the ever-more complex and innovative environments of trading markets as we move closer to a digital world.

Tips

- Having strong leadership qualities such as honesty and commitment

- Grasping the potential of emerging technologies

- Taking a pragmatic and results-driven attitude to team management

- Staying close to the business

Maersk
Empowering a world-class kitchen team

Ingredients

- Use data to speed up decision making across global IT
- Adopt Agile and Scrum to improve responsiveness
- Seek new technology-enabled opportunities to grow revenues

Preparing the dish

Rui Pedro Silva joined Maersk Logistics and Services in 2016 as global head of customer technology. Maersk is a Danish integrated shipping company, which is active in ocean and inland freight transportation and associated services, such as supply chain management and port operations. It has been the world's largest container shipping line and vessel operator since 1996. The company is based in Copenhagen with subsidiaries and offices in 130 countries, employing 83,000 staff.

In his global IT role, Rui (who was recently appointed chief digital and information officer at ERIKS Group) was responsible for all aspects of technology relating to major customers such as Nike and Samsung. Despite the critical nature of the IT function, Rui was dismayed to find that the reputation of his team was extremely poor, with some businesses describing it as a cancer. His task on joining the company in 2016 was to make rapid and sweeping changes to the IT organisation to redeem its reputation both internally and with external customers.

Breathing life into the patient

Rui inherited an unstructured global IT team, with decisions made in a slow and arbitrary manner. Despite

"If you have a competent and experienced team, you just have to get them to work right."

Rui Pedro Silva, former global head of customer technology, Maersk

Scan code to watch the full interview.

high levels of IT expertise, with some individuals boasting more than 30 years with the company, the teams were scattered across the globe with little coordination and no meaningful roles. There was a significant lack of data about current projects. It took Rui two months to gain a full picture of ongoing activities, which was unacceptable for a customer-facing IT function.

Rui's first priority was to develop a roadmap to clarify the purpose of his function. At the heart of the roadmap was Rui's desire for his team to be close to major customers. He wanted his staff to be able to respond quickly to changing customer requirements. Rui avoided being too prescriptive about steps along the roadmap, preferring his team to assume responsibility for individual tasks: 'If you have a competent and experienced team, you just have to get them to work right.'

Building trust across the global team

The first stop on the roadmap was to ensure that everyone in the IT function embraced the mission of becoming a recognised centre of excellence for technology, both within and outside Maersk. There were four essential elements to achieving this mission:

- Building trust within the team by applying an empathetic

approach. Rui was keen to understand the sources of pain within the team, and to address them.

- Adopting modern methods such as Scrum and Agile to speed up project delivery and to engage customers throughout the development process.

- Focusing individuals on individual tasks rather than having them dispersed across multiple projects. The efficiency ratio, which measured this focus, improved from 7% to over 80%.

- Supporting the team with accurate and timely data that meant decisions could be made in minutes or hours rather than days or months.

Rui placed emphasis on empathy and trust as the means to improving his team's performance. His approach paid off handsomely. Using the same internal resources, he was able to increase team performance by more than 250%. At the same time, a customer satisfaction survey across Maersk indicated a high performance score of 4.3 out of 5.0.

Creating new levels of personalisation

Having empowered his team to achieve top-level performance in day-to-day operations, Rui's next step was to concentrate on areas that would truly differentiate Maersk as a global leader. Rui recognised that availability of goods in sectors such as fashion and electronics was becoming a key competitive factor. Fortunately, Maersk boasted full visibility across the entire supply chain, from raw materials and factories to shops and warehouses.

Equipped with predictive data techniques, Rui was able to offer his retail customers tools to locate and pre-assign goods at every stage of the supply chain. This process helped Maersk's retail clients to provide tailored solutions to individual customer requirements, such as pre-ordering a good when on vacation. This personalisation has boosted delivery reliability and cost efficiency.

Reorganising the kitchen

Rui rapidly organised his function into two main streams across 14 countries:

- Requirement engineers or business partners who could work directly with internal and external customers to propose solutions;

- Staff who worked on technical products, which covered classical IT systems, such as ERP, and digital capabilities, including e-commerce and data analytics.

To make the new organisation effective, Rui introduced a range

of collaboration and communication tools to increase connectivity between his staff. Rui favoured face-to-face and video collaboration tools over audio because of his emphasis on empathy.

With a diverse and multicultural staff spanning 14 countries, Rui recognised that everyone in his team had their own opinions. He believes that encouraging people to think as well as act is an important motivator for success, especially in new areas such as e-commerce.

Defining the qualities of a Master Chef

The logistics sector is famed for its conservative approach towards the application of technology. In this context, Maersk might appear to be a less attractive destination for job-seeking graduates than digital natives and start-ups.

However, Rui has always stressed the potential for new entrants to make a difference. Maersk is a market-leading company and technology staff at the company have significant opportunities to help innovate the customer experience.

His message to new recruits during his time at the company was clear: 'You can work in any job, but you cannot always make a difference.' This mantra helped Rui to attract people who understood his mission and were committed to making a big difference.

Tips

- Step up to what you believe in and don't give up
- Give people the benefit of the doubt – trust them
- Apply critical thinking to every aspect of your job
- Spend your time right – recognise that time is our most valuable asset

Rui is now CEO at ERIKS Digital

AstraZeneca
Leveraging technology as a competitive advantage

Ingredients

- Purpose-led mission and values
- Leverage technology to identify new business opportunities
- Bring your C-suite executives and board with you on your digital journey
- Engage strategic partners to work across ecosystems to co-create and co-innovate

Preparing the dish

AstraZeneca is a British–Swedish multinational pharmaceutical and biotechnology company. It has a portfolio of products for major diseases in areas including oncology, cardiovascular, gastrointestinal, infection, neuroscience, respiratory and inflammation.

Most recently it became known for its partnership in developing the Oxford–AstraZeneca COVID-19 vaccine. At the close of 2020, the company reported an annual turnover of $26 billion, with 76,000 employees globally.

AstraZeneca has a predominantly insourced IT organisation comprising 4,800 internal staff. There are five separate verticals: R&D, Operations, Commercial, Alexion (AstraZeneca's rare diseases subsidiary) and Corporate Services. Additionally, a number of horizontal technology services oversee innovation, architecture, data and AI, infrastructure, cybersecurity and enterprise capabilities.

In a post-pandemic world, the measure of digital success will be in how technology is used to identify new business opportunities and new therapeutic modalities. Cindy Hoots, CDO and CIO of AstraZeneca, identifies four key pillars as part of the company's IT-2025 strategy:

"When you focus on the people, you will get the results."

Cindy Hoots, CDO and CIO, AstraZeneca

Scan code to watch the full interview.

- Lead with AI and insights;
- Accelerate delivery and innovation
- Optimise how we run
- Be a great place to work

Lead with AI and insights

One of the IT organisation's top priorities is embedding AI to fundamentally change the way they approach science, make a meaningful impact for patients, and run their business.

AI has played an integral role from advancing areas of drug discovery to enhancing their operations and 'smart factories' and providing data-led insights that help AstraZeneca gain a better understanding of the dynamics of their workforce. Additionally, AI plays an increasingly important role in the organisation's cybersecurity efforts, enabling the IT team to proactively identify threats and risks at a much greater speed and sharpen their risk and management processes.

Accelerate innovation and delivery

Delivery in pharmaceuticals is measured in days and weeks not months and years. The organisation's employees must acquire new skills and capabilities to rapidly meet the growing demand for innovation and speed of delivery. Successful teams are increasingly agile, proficient in navigating ambiguity, and have a strong focus on outcomes.

The best teams are able to quickly identify products and services that can be enhanced over time instead of stalling decisions until the perfect solution is found. Leveraging AI, they are able to iterate different hypotheses rapidly with limited hesitancy to pivot at speed. Successful CIOs are those who create the right culture within their teams to embrace this mindset and help accelerate the innovation process.

Optimising processes in IT and the rest of the company

Optimisation involves looking at all the processes within a company with a fresh pair of eyes. IT teams should partner closely with business units to analyse processes with the intent of identifying areas of complexity, driving out waste and finding new ways of applying technology, such as RPA and AI.

One example at AstraZeneca has been the recent development of an AI assistant to extract medical terms from any adverse events during clinical trials. These are required for regulatory authorities but this task is traditionally incredibly manual and time consuming. Early estimates indicate this approach may lead to a 50% reduction in time taken (with potential cost savings). This tactical use of AI frees up staff to focus on

strategic rather than operational matters.

Making the organisation a great place to work

The key to attracting and retaining great talent is finding people whose passion and purpose mirrors that of your organisation. CIOs must connect these people to the company's values at a deeper level and bring to life a purpose-driven mission that is aligned with personal goals.

One of AstraZeneca's key values is 'doing the right thing' and with employee engagement measured at 92%, it's a clear indicator that the combination of a clear company purpose and the empowerment of teams to believe they can change the lives of patients through their work is critical to sustaining a great work environment.

This engagement manifests itself in staff becoming good stewards of company money. Every dollar spent must be impactful and deliver clear value. IT employees must work with partners to find cost-effective ways of delivering technology that ultimately increases overall patient access to cheaper and better healthcare. Essentially, every dollar spent to support the process has the potential to make the treatment less expensive for the patient.

Cindy has built and championed diversity within her team, where differences in cultural and personal characteristics are embraced and celebrated. Employees at every level are encouraged to build learning moments into their daily schedules and to seek on-the-job learning experiences to build breadth and depth of expertise. Cindy ensures that teams across her organisation have access to the right job opportunities, and encourages employees to move around different roles in the IT organisation and other business functions: 'When you focus on the people, you will get the results,' she says.

Defining the qualities of a Master Chef

Cindy believes that CIOs should focus on driving innovation and leveraging technology as a competitive advantage across the broadest spectrum of business functions. At AstraZeneca, Cindy's focus is to leverage technology to drive better patient outcomes, modernise the business to be equipped for the future, simplify the lives of employees and define how the business ultimately works in a broader ecosystem to tackle some of the world's most difficult problems.

CIOs continue to be uniquely positioned to help businesses navigate the world of digital and the impact this will have. While in many instances they still play a key role in running company infrastructure, applications, etc., the pandemic means CIOs and the transformative work they do have been pushed to the forefront. These CIOs have fresh opportunities to bring essential thought leadership to the boardroom, helping the business understand how to leverage technology as a competitive advantage and identifying new business models and potential adjacencies.

Successful CIOs combine vision with execution. Cindy is an inspirational leader who shares her vision of where she sees the company in the future. However, she is also grounded and results-oriented, with an eye on the sharp execution of strategy. Rather than focusing on theory for too long, she believes value is created at the point of execution.

Cindy is passionate about her strong work ethics, integrity and above all her love for lifelong learning. She believes it is important to be a mentee as well as a mentor, and works with digital natives under the age of 25 to help ensure she and her skills remain relevant in a rapidly evolving landscape. Cindy's aim for life is to leave things better than when she found them.

Tips

- Be inquisitive, curious and ready to learn

- Step outside your core job and participate in other areas to increase your breadth of knowledge

- If you do not have the confidence to do new things, have a healthy dose of courage and do it anyway

- Do not limit yourself; push the boundaries

- Focus on co-creating and networking with others

Norway Post
Learning to innovate greater value faster

Preparing the dish

Established in 1647, Norway Post is a Nordic postal and logistics group that develops and delivers integrated solutions in postal services, communications and logistics, with the Nordic region as its home market.

Traditionally, business innovation at Norway Post focused on operational improvements. Leaders allocated funds in response to business cases developed by individual business units. The business unit then handled IT-related requirements. IT then developed the innovation using waterfall methods. Based on specifications set up at the start of a project, a team committed to a budget, scope and delivery date. The IT team was rewarded for meeting its commitments.

This anticipate-then-build approach produced valuable innovations. Using advanced digital technologies and algorithms, such as neural networks, Norway Post developed a system that could read handwritten addresses faster and more accurately than any other system in the world. On the mail side of the business,

Norway Post was considered to be one of the most efficient and automated mail companies in the world. The company's successes reinforced its commitment to its approach to innovation.

Understanding what didn't work well amidst constant flux

Despite all the benefits, an anticipate-then-build approach wasn't right for the logistics side of the business. The delivery needs of logistics customers are unique and change frequently. A process of testing and learning was essential to figuring out what kinds of offerings would be desirable to end users, which were feasible to Norway Post and which made good business sense for all parties concerned.

Inspired by a successful effort within the company to develop a set of services in logistics, Norway Post adopted a new approach to digital innovation that delivered valuable offerings faster. The new approach discouraged pursuing innovations of little or no value, increased the likelihood of creating competitively advantageous innovations and helped Norway Post become more agile.

Developing a new recipe for innovation: defining value

Norway Post introduced two fundamental changes to how it approached innovation. First, drawing on design thinking, Norway Post anchored the new approach in a careful definition of a valuable innovation. Valuable innovations can be measured by the degree of overlap of three attributes:

- Desirable – customers/end users wanted it;

- Feasible – Norway Post could provide it;

- Viable – it made business sense.

Traditionally, a team could develop an offering that was simply feasible. However, because the concepts of desirability and viability were evolving as frequently as uses of digital technologies, it was important to revisit all three attributes and examine whether they overlapped to produce valuable innovations.

To put this new approach into practice, the company also redefined the innovation process into three phases, each generating a distinct set of insights:

- Boundaries of an opportunity (What do end users want? What is feasible for the organisation? Is there an overlap?);

- Offerings within an opportunity (If there is an opportunity, then what services are desirable, feasible and profitable?);

- Limits of an offering (If there is an offering, then to what extent is it scalable?).

Developing a new recipe for innovation: empowered decision-making processes

The second change to how Norway Post approached innovation involved shifting decision-making processes from a top-down system to one built on empowered cross-functional teams. By giving a team of experts across the three key attributes – desirable, feasible, viable – decision rights over what offerings to develop and how, Norway Post expected to increase the velocity and speed of the value generated by individual efforts.

In the first phase, Explore, the team leading an innovation effort articulates and tests assumptions regarding the boundaries of an opportunity for valuable innovations. The team finishes the Explore phase when it has developed insights that either identify an opportunity that is desirable, feasible and seemingly viable, or reveal that such an opportunity no longer exists. If there is an opportunity, then it receives funding for the next phase, Create.

In the Create phase, the team develops and tests several potential solutions within the opportunity, building

minimum viable products (MVPs), testing how desirable, feasible and viable each is, and adapting them based on learnings. The team persists until it settles on one or more solutions to implement and scale, or until it reaches a point where it believes there are no viable solutions.

During the Implement stage, the team scales an MVP iteratively by incrementally adding new types of users and functionality.

Defining the qualities of a Master Chef

Most companies are starting to empower cross-functional teams and encouraging them to take a test-and-learn approach. However, their outcomes often remain questionable. Norway Post's approach offers lessons on how companies can drive benefits from their teams by changing their targets and decision rights – and ensuring they fund and reward teams accordingly.

> ## Tips
> - Invest incrementally in hypotheses and reward teams based on outcomes. If not, it is time to rethink how your organisation funds and rewards innovation efforts
> - Embrace the paradox that to innovate greater value faster, cross-functional teams need to take time to learn
> - Make it safe to learn, rather than to fail

Sources (available at https://cisr.mit.edu/):
Nils Olaya Fonstad (2020), 'Innovating with Greater Impact at Posten Norge', MIT Sloan CISR Working Paper, No. 440, January 2020.
Nils Olaya Fonstad (2020), 'Innovating Greater Value Faster by Taking Time to Learn', *MIT Sloan CISR Research Briefing*, XX, No. 2, February 2020.

Sweet curd dumplings with plum compote

Serves 4

For the dumplings:
- 250g curd cheese
- 1 large egg
- 1 tbsp sugar
- About 2 tbsp plain flour

For the compote:
- 500g red plums
- 1 tbsp clear honey
- 50ml water
- 2 tsp brandy (optional)

First, prepare the dumplings. Beat the cheese, egg and sugar together in a bowl and add as much flour as necessary to bring them together in a soft but firm dough. Put the bowl in the fridge for 30 minutes.

Then make the compote. Chop the plums, discarding the stones. Put them into a non-stick pan over a moderate heat and add the honey and water. Stir thoroughly. As the plums cook they will begin to break up; add the brandy if using, allow the compote to cook down a little, and remove the pan from the heat. Pour the plums into a bowl to cool a little.

Put a large pan of lightly salted water on the heat and bring it to a boil, then reduce the heat to a gentle simmer. Take the dumpling dough out of the fridge.

Form the dumplings using two spoons – dip the spoons into cold water first and then use them to mould the dumpling mixture into ovals; this will make approximately 16 using teaspoons. Drop them into the water carefully and cook them for approximately 7 minutes with the water at a gentle simmer – if you use larger spoons and make fewer dumplings this takes about 10 minutes. They will rise to the surface; when they are just firm take them out of the water with a slotted spoon and drain them on kitchen paper. Serve with the compote, and some cream if wished.

The favourite dish of Nils Fonstad

NINE
WINNING CULTURES PROMOTE BETTER COLLABORATION AND COMMUNICATION

In almost every conversation about digital transformation our CIONET community stresses the importance of having a well-aligned organisational culture. Implicit within this dialogue is a diversity of thought and a strength of vision that inspires people to participate in the fundamental changes needed for success in the fast-emerging digital age.

At global HR services organisation SD Worx, change is brought about by embedding the customer into every conversation – whether that's in the front or back office. This insertion has a galvanising effect on corporate culture. It induces a sense of common purpose and value at every level of the organisation. Equally, the focus on constructive dialogue between established and new operations helps to achieve a balanced business outcome.

One might expect global banks to feel threatened by enterprising start-ups operating in an open-banking environment. But in the case of Morgan Stanley, the change director is confident that a process of continuous improvement aligns well with the prevailing culture. By introducing the concept of guilds, she has accelerated collaboration and learning across the bank to help accelerate change. She is also introducing a mentoring programme entitled 'career allies', which encourages tighter inclusion within a highly diversified workforce.

The Randstad Group in Belgium has an extensive global network of 360 offices. The CIO recognised the need to combine global capability with local solutions to compete effectively in every national market. A well-articulated portfolio management framework that incorporates Agile methods has helped to align cultures and skills across the company's diverse geographic landscape.

Throughout the recipes in this cookbook, there are numerous references to diversity as a core competence for digital leaders who want to deliver a winning culture. This requirement for diversity extends beyond gender equality in IT departments, which remains out of balance in most parts of the world. Organisational approaches to diversity and inclusivity must extend across individual characteristics, values, beliefs, and backgrounds to ensure corporate cultures align with the emerging digital world.

SD Worx

Building an organisational culture for digital transformation

Ingredients

- Digital transformation requires an appropriate organisational culture

- Organisations need to give explicit attention to culture in a digital transformation journey

- Certain cultural values are key enablers for digital transformation success

Preparing the dish

SD Worx is a leading European payroll and human resource (HR) services provider. The company has its roots and headquarters in Belgium and provides solutions and services relating to the employment of personnel that cover the whole employee life cycle: payroll calculation and administration, social legislation, international payroll and tax, and human resources in the broadest sense. Businesses can also turn to SD Worx for outsourcing their remuneration and all HR activities. More than 76,000 small and large companies around the world rely on the services of SD Worx. The company offers its services in 150 countries, calculates the salaries of around five million employees, and is one of the top five HR service providers worldwide. Its more than 5,300 employees are active in 18 countries: its headquarters in Belgium, Austria, Denmark, Estonia, Finland, France, Germany, Ireland, Italy, Luxembourg, Mauritius, Netherlands, Norway, Poland, Spain, Sweden, Switzerland and the UK. In 2020, SD Worx achieved a consolidated turnover of more than €825 million (pro forma).

SD Worx recognises the necessity of digital transformation. More specifically, SD Worx's services are digitised and will undergo further digitalisation in the future. The company considers this a logical and necessary response to changing customer expectations and behaviours.

In the context of this journey, SD Worx explicitly recognised the importance of organisational culture as an enabler of digital transformation success. The company took appropriate action to ensure that its organisational culture acted as an enabler of digital transformation. To this end, SD Worx focused on three cultural values: customer centricity, willingness to learn and communication.

Focusing on customer centricity

At SD Worx, the customer perspective is carefully considered in every decision. Net Promoter Scores (NPS) are frequently surveyed and communicated throughout the organisation. If deemed necessary, actions are planned to increase these scores, and the results monitored. SD Worx also connects back-office departments to customer perspectives by showing customer testimonials, such as videos. These videos show back-office employees how their work contributes to customer experience. SD Worx's

back-office employees are proud their work is perceived as valuable.

SD Worx believes a customer-centric attitude is crucial to a successful digital transformation. The customer is the burning platform for change, and the need for a digital transformation is linked to changes in customer behaviour and expectation. The business model must transform in response to these changes.

To stimulate a culture of customer centricity, SD Worx keeps close to its customers. The company brings its products and services to customers as early as possible. It develops minimum viable products swiftly and then seeks customer opinions. The company uses customer panels, where customers discuss features they would like added or removed. The customer, therefore, has a direct impact on the development of products and services at SD Worx.

Focusing on willingness to learn

SD Worx believes that the willingness to learn is an essential cultural value to enable successful digital transformation. The company has a strong skill development and training-oriented culture. For example, mentorships are organised for employees. The company also offers access to e-learning platforms. SD Worx ensures that sufficient training

budget is available. Job rotation is also stimulated, but not obligatory. Management will support employees who would like to rotate to a different role, while also identifying and offering supportive training.

SD Worx believes people learn best when they have to perform actual tasks. The company has identified essential skills that need to be developed and acquired by its employees. These skills are described in a skills framework for different organisational roles. The company believes it is necessary to map out the necessary skills that people have to acquire in order to support the ongoing development of capabilities.

Focusing on communication

SD Worx believes that the success of any transformation boils down to an open and convincing communication about the need for change. It is crucial that people in the organisation understand the need for transformation, and do not perceive it as merely a 'new way of working' imposed by management. In other words, effective communication can help to manage employee resistance.

An important aspect of this communication is managing the possible tension between the people who are working on the existing business and the people working on innovative products and services. The former group generates the financial means that makes innovation possible. If the first group does not understand the benefits and necessity of innovation, they can perceive it as a wasted expense. Businesses must emphasise an appreciation for the people in the existing business departments, who are running the business as cost efficiently as possible, which makes innovation and growth possible in the first place. These people who generate cash need to be proud of their achievements and their value should not be underestimated.

At SD Worx, the management team organises town-hall meetings and strategic update seminars to communicate the 'why' behind investments and the need for organisational transformation. The gap between C-level executives and operational people needs to be bridged by line managers. While executive management sets the good example, managers at all

layers in the organisation should communicate directly to their people. As a result, every employee in every department needs to understand why transformation is necessary, and how their work contributes to success.

Defining the qualities of a Master Chef

Organisational culture is one of the most important differentiating factors that separate successful digital transformations from unsuccessful ones. SD Worx understands this importance, and gives explicit attention to organisational culture in the context of its digital transformation journey.

SD Worx believes the most important cultural values are customer centricity, willingness to learn, and communication. Organisations should understand that a digital transformation is a logical and necessary response to a change in customer behaviours and expectations. To do this successfully, an organisation needs to understand the behaviours and expectations of its customers.

Internally, the company needs to understand the importance of communicating why the organisation needs to transform, which is a crucial aspect in managing resistance to change. Focusing on these cultural aspects ensures a good breeding ground for the digital transformation to ultimately succeed.

Tips

- Give explicit and appropriate attention to organisational culture in a digital transformation journey.

- Focus on customer centricity, willingness to learn and communication, as these are the key enabling cultural values for digital transformation success.

Tim Huygh, PhD; Steven De Haes, PhD; Anant Joshi, PhD. Antwerp Management School, Antwerp, Belgium

Morgan Stanley

Employing diversity to accelerate change

Preparing the dish

With a distinguished career in global banking and financial services, Dr Bijna Kotak Dasani MBE, FRSA was this year voted one of the top 100 female business leaders in the world (from across industries and sectors), for the fourth consecutive year by Yahoo Finance and Involve People. She recently earned an MBE in the UK for her services to the areas of diversity and inclusion. She has also been awarded the title of 'Digital Leader of the Year 2021' by Seamless Middle East which hosts 12,000 participants, under the patronage of HH Sheikh Saif Bin Zayad Al Nayhan.

Bijna is currently Morgan Stanley's Executive Director, focusing on Transformation in the Asian region and Global Automation. Additionally, she serves over a dozen groups internally on the diversity, equity and inclusion (DE&I) agenda.

Morgan Stanley is an American multinational investment bank and financial services company headquartered in New York City. With offices in 42 countries and with more than 60,000 employees, the firm's clients include corporations, governments, institutions and individuals.

Leading a revolution in banking

In Bijna's words: 'Banking is essential, but banks are not'. With the advent of open banking and the rapid rise of FinTech companies and non-financial services players entering the financial services ecosystem, global banks such as (her former employer) Lloyds Banking Group need to find ways to stay relevant and close to their clients. Digital start-ups are chipping away at traditional banking franchises and are threatening to erode margins. This situation is particularly true in the case of middle-income customers who constitute rich pickings for newcomers.

Bijna believes established players have the necessary scale and scope to respond to the FinTech onslaught, but they must remain vigilant. Established banks are increasingly seeking to exploit their data lineage to retain and gain customers in a renewed effort to increase revenues. At the same time, these institutions need to streamline their global operations to reduce costs and increase margins. The bank's global change programmes address all these factors.

Adopting a measured approach

Given regulatory constraints and the reduced appetite for risk following the 2008 financial crisis, global banks such as Deutsche Bank and Goldman Sachs (both also former employers of Bijna) are adopting a measured approach to business innovation. In many cases, this approach is centred on modernising existing factories rather than building new ones. Goldman Sachs has put its toe in the water with its recent launch of Marcus, its new retail-banking business. However, the majority of mainstream global banking players are adopting a continuous improvement strategy that is geared to optimising their current operations.

At the core of Morgan Stanley's transformation is the adoption of Agile ways of working that provide a test and learn environment for teams across the globe. This approach focuses on the ability to fail fast and learn from every experience. This measured approach has helped the organisation to embrace new ways of mobilising change at a global level that relate to the future of the workforce and the workplace.

Leading the rise of the corporate guilds

Bijna has led the introduction of a new concept in business transformation that is based on the formation of guilds within her working environment. These guilds bring technology, business strategy and innovation experts together as agile teams that are an integral

"If you don't understand the problem, you will never reach a satisfactory solution."

Dr Bijna Kotak Dasani, Executive Director, Morgan Stanley

element of the bank's change programme. Her vision is to create guilds of technical and business staff who can share experiences on a regular basis to ensure that any lessons learnt are communicated rapidly around the globe.

The first guild was launched in Asia in 2020. This guild aimed to build case studies around process improvement. Members of the guild used monthly video sessions and online communication tools to discuss topics of interest and to share experiences. This collaboration has accelerated innovation and prompted continuous improvement across the region. These benefits have drawn the attention of senior stakeholders in the firm, says Bijna: 'It is all about getting buy-in from the top. The guilds must be empowered to work collectively at a time of immense commercial disruption.'

Introducing diversity to accelerate change

Bijna is fully conversant with the many differences in race and gender that pervade the Asian region. In many respects, the region remains conservative, with women accounting for less than 20% of the workforce in populous countries such as India. Bijna envisages a workforce and workplace of the future that is more evenly balanced. One of the mechanisms that helps promote a positive diversity policy is the use of 'career allies'. Becoming a career ally is now a critical component of a leader's role within the bank. Career allies such as Bijna actively identify and encourage the development of ethnic and gender minorities.

Bijna believes the coronavirus pandemic has provided new possibilities to elevate industry's culture by exposing weaknesses that were less of a priority in stable times. Bijna is positive that the combination of guilds, agile teams and career allies will help the banks make the necessary changes to excel in the coming years.

Defining the qualities of a Master Chef

To be effective, business leaders within the bank need to articulate their vision for the future by giving the guilds and other communities of practice crucial knowledge, which includes:

- An understanding of the business strategy and associated measures that matter to the bank at board level;

- An awareness of the way in which the workforce and workplace of the future will evolve to fulfil this strategic vision;

- A comprehension of the role that each key function will play in the new banking landscape and the contribution of technology.

To meet these conditions, Bijna has placed strong emphasis on demystifying and simplifying many of the digital concepts that permeate the bank and the finance sector. She is keen to ensure that everyone works from a common foundation of knowledge. This foundation strengthens the prevailing culture and invites open conversations about issues that need to be resolved. In Bijna's words: 'If you don't understand the problem, you will never reach a satisfactory solution.'

Tips

- Embrace collaboration and inclusion to accelerate business value creation

- Emphasise the overlap between strategy, technology and innovation

- Introduce new schemes to overcome current limitations in diversity

Randstad Group Belgium
Agile portfolio management in dynamic environments

Preparing the dish

Randstad Group Belgium is a leading global HR services firm. With around 1,800 employees in over 320 offices and client locations, the company employs about 43,000 temporary staff on a weekly average through its clients. The company outperformed its market and earned €1.4 billion in revenues last year despite the coronavirus pandemic.

Gunther Ghijsels, CIO/CDO of Randstad Group Belgium, says technology is critical to sustaining the firm's market leadership position through effective digital capabilities. He aims to 'bring digital to the DNA of the company'. The company's data-driven, cloud-native technology platforms combine global IT capabilities and localised solution delivery. This approach creates efficiencies in existing business models and supports new opportunities to serve clients, talent and consultants.

Driven by a need to increase the speed of solution delivery, Gunther and his team embarked on an Agile transformation journey in 2016 using the Scrum framework. Over time, they adopted the Scaled Agile Framework (SAFe), which was tailored to the company and its capability maturity. Randstad Group Belgium evolved a portfolio management capability to support its Agile adoption and address six key aspects impacting IT agility.

Using portfolio management capability to support agility

Portfolio strategic alignment

The company maps its ICT efforts into four strategic domains: three domains aligned to business strategies and one foundational IT domain. Domain managers define each domain's roadmap and track progress, which promotes transparency and alignment across business and IT. The Business Excellence function analyses trends in the talent market, evaluates competitor product offerings, and coordinates the technological response. The Shared Services Direction Board (SDB), a cross-functional leadership group, reviews portfolio roadmaps every quarter to commit investments to prioritised feature requests.

Enabling continuous delivery

Alongside quarterly portfolio reviews, Randstad Group Belgium conducts Program Increment (PI) Planning events to synchronise solution delivery cycles and ensure developers have adequate information on upcoming features. Portfolio reviews are timed with this planning process to maintain a consistent cadence.

Adaptive planning

The domain managers define epics and features in their domain roadmaps as 'mini business cases', with just enough information to determine investment viability, which are progressively refined before the next PI Planning event. The domain managers also participate in the delivery process as product owners for the features they request. They work with agile teams to adapt to changes or uncertainties they encounter while delivering the features. The ICT team maintains an architectural runway, allowing developers to quickly build solutions based on agreed principles.

Organisational learning

The transparency of the portfolio process helps business and IT teams to better understand dependencies in solution delivery and to plan more collaboratively. The Business Excellence function contributes to organisational learning because it explores business demands to identify strategic opportunities instead of merely translating requests as features scheduled for delivery.

Financial processes

Randstad Group Belgium adapted its portfolio budgeting to reflect funding for team-level capacity. The SDB collectively approves features based on available capacity and business value. Instead of elaborate return on investment evaluations, Gunther brings the business stakeholders closer to technical delivery processes to minimise value leakage.

"Keep the internal world as simple as possible to handle the complexity in the outside world."

Gunther Ghijsels, CIO/CDO, Randstad Group Belgium

Scan code to watch the full interview.

Performance indicators

The ICT team continues to evolve its performance indicators and metrics. The Business Excellence function monitors business outcome measures with each released feature, including implementation, usage and operational KPIs, while the IT team tracks PI efficiencies and team effectiveness.

Organising the agile portfolio capability

Project investment portfolios are inherently complex and rely on a range of interactions. Gunther drives home the need for an agile portfolio to foster a mindset that balances internal and external complexities: 'We should keep the internal world as simple as possible, just to make sure that we can handle the complexity in the outside world,' he says. The agile portfolio capability is organised through a system-thinking approach across five structural sub-systems:

- Portfolio operations. Gunther says at the core of the agile portfolio capability is the process of 'getting everything ready to keep the teams occupied and to deliver as much of the business value as we can, given certain priorities and given the capacity that we have within ICT.' Portfolio refinements through the feature intake process and the portfolio prioritisation during the PI Planning events are crucial portfolio operations activities.

- Portfolio coordination. The strategic domain roadmaps act as guardrails for the portfolio planning process and

guide the Business Excellence function to coordinate portfolio epics and features across business functions.

- Portfolio management and control. The annual planning process and the quarterly portfolio reviews help with portfolio cohesion and alignment to business strategies. The oversight and approval of epics and features by the SDB reflects the broader strategic objectives. Aggregated funding at the portfolio level allows the company to make informed trade-offs during feature prioritisation. Finally, visibility of progress at the executive committee level ensures the necessary focus on outcomes.

- Portfolio intelligence. The ICT team monitors operational and strategic environments by tracking market developments, regulatory expectations, competitor actions, technology advances, and global ICT architecture directions. The agile portfolio capability balances changes sensed in the environment with internal capabilities to formulate appropriate responses.

- Portfolio identity. Gunther and the executive committee play a significant role in guiding Randstad Group Belgium's digital transformation and related cultural changes. They define the overall portfolio directions by defining the high-level strategic domains and key objectives that are the 'true north star' for solution delivery.

Tips

- Allow the portfolio to reflect a holistic view of the organisation's context

- Shorten planning cycles and align funding to solution-oriented teams

- Continuously adapt the portfolio to reflect environmental dynamics

- Communicate the portfolio roadmap broadly

- Focus on outcome measures to drive decisions

- Prioritise around broader strategic objectives, as opposed to individual demands

- Deploy formal and informal mechanisms to sense changes within environments

Joseph Puthenpurackal; Tim Huygh, PhD; Steven De Haes, PhD.
Antwerp Management School, Antwerp, Belgium

Pears poached in rooibos tea

Serves 4

- 4 underripe pears (Comice, Williams, Anjou, Bosc or Bartlett)
- 150g sugar
- 50g clear honey
- 6 rooibos tea bags
- 1.5 litres water

To serve:

- Greek yoghurt or vanilla ice cream

Prepare the syrup first. Put the sugar, honey and tea bags in a pan with the water. Bring to the boil, then take the pan off the heat and set it aside for 10 minutes while you prepare the pears.

Peel the pears, leaving the stalk on. Extract some of the core by cutting a small hole in the base (and cut a small slice off the base if you want to serve them standing upright).

Take the tea bags out of the pan, squeezing them well to extract more flavour. Bring the liquid back to the boil, then carefully add the pears. Cover the pan and cook the pears for 15 to 20 minutes. Check during this time; pears vary enormously and they should be tender but not over soft. They may need cooking more, or less, and a little more liquid may need to be added accordingly.

Remove the pears from the liquid and put each one in a serving bowl. Increase the heat under the pan and cook the remaining liquid down until it reduces to a light syrup, being careful not to let it reduce too much or catch.

Pour the syrup over the pears. They can be served at any temperature, and are delicious chilled with a spoonful of Greek yoghurt or ice cream.

The favourite dish of Roger Camrass

CONCLUSIONS

And a call for action

As we have witnessed in every chapter of this IT cookbook, a new digital landscape is emerging at an unprecedented speed. Within this environment, our Master Chefs are being placed centre stage in the business as a revolution plays out, comparable in its scope and scale to the Renaissance that took place in Europe during the fifteenth and sixteenth centuries. Perhaps we should think of the internet as a 'steroid-fuelled', modern-day equivalent of Gutenberg's printing press? What we can be sure of, however, is that further, radical change will come. No one can predict where we will end up even 20 years from now. However, we already know that the corporate world of the future will be very different from the one we all grew up in.

How, as leaders and active participants in this revolution, do we navigate safe passage for our families, organisations and nations in these turbulent times? At CIONET, we have a deep belief in the power of the community to assist in this endeavour. Across almost two decades, we have established leading communities of practice in more than 20 countries across Asia, Europe and the Americas. With the active support of our national advisory boards, we have built a flourishing community of 10,000 technology executives.

The power of this community of practice lies in the constant interaction between our members. CIONET holds more than 1,000 community events annually, ranging from roundtable events and national community programmes to large international gatherings, including CIONEXT and CIOFEST. Our members testify to us that this constant sharing of experience and best practice has helped to elevate the CIO role to full parity with those positions held by their C-suite peers.

Every year, we undertake 'deep dive' TV interviews with 50 of Europe's most influential digital leaders. We publish these interviews on YouTube. These personal stories provide the community with unique and valuable insights into the DNA of its most accomplished Master Chefs. They also help our business partners to engage more effectively with IT leaders at the highest levels of their organisations. We encourage you to access these interviews on the CIONET TV YouTube channel.

In addition, we undertake a constant stream of research programmes to capture and document the insights that arise from our community events and executive interviews. This IT cookbook is just one outcome of our research. We hope that you will take full advantage of the many other

"The corporate world of the future will be very different from the one we all grew up in."

reports that we publish each year in areas spanning technology strategy, innovative methods and tools.

In conclusion, we hope that by reading our IT cookbook and tasting its successful recipes you will be better equipped to deal with the many challenges and opportunities ahead of you on the journey to becoming digital. As we continue to capture and document recipes from digital leaders, especially via CIONET TV and our

many events, we plan to publish further editions of this book as we travel through a unique moment of digital development. In this respect, we acknowledge our gratitude to Red Hat and Intel for sponsoring this first edition of the IT cookbook.

We thank you for your interest and participation in this exciting adventure and encourage you to join us at our many local and global events during 2022.

ABOUT THE AUTHORS

Roger Camrass

A pioneer of today's internet at MIT in the early seventies, Roger has spent over fifty years helping global corporations harness the power of digital technologies such as cloud, mobile, voice recognition and Space networks. He led a strategic study, Business in the Third Millennium, whilst at SRI International and was a senior partner at Ernst & Young, responsible for e-commerce during the dot.com boom. He is now director of research for CIONET International. Roger is a graduate of Cambridge University and MIT, and the author of numerous papers and books. See www.rogercamrass.com.

Jenniffer Gearheart-Tang

Jenniffer has over 25 years of international experience specialising in Innovation, Brand Marketing, Market Research and Senior Executive Recruitment at Shell International, Korn/Ferry International and Research International.

As Head of Global Innovation and Research at Shell, Jenniffer created an award-winning global digital platform – Shell Ideas360 – which attracted over 62 million views and a cross-industry and sector collaboration across 140 countries.

As Managing Director of !nnov8 Ltd, Jenniffer has coached over 100 start-up founders, helping them conceptualise products, develop go-to-market strategies, collaborate with and connect to corporations, and scale their businesses internationally. Visit www.i-nnov8.com.

Dr Nils Olaya Fonstad

Nils is a Research Scientist, Europe and LATAM, at the MIT Center for Information Systems Research (MIT CISR). Drawing on both in-depth qualitative data and survey data from hundreds of firms, he has identified which investments and innovation practices distinguish the most competitive firms. In 2010, he co-founded with CIONET the annual European CIO of the Year Awards (http://ecoty.eu/) to raise awareness of the expanding strategic roles of digital leaders. Nils regularly conducts workshops for cross-functional groups of top-level executives, during which he presents and discusses MIT CISR research findings. Visit http://cisr.mit.edu or email nilsfonstad@mit.edu.

Antwerp Management School

Antwerp Management School (AMS) delivers state-of-the-art management knowledge, anchored in a business and organisational context. One of the key thought-leadership domains of AMS focuses on leading the digital transformation journey, with a special focus on digital governance, architecture and security. Together with its international academic and business partnership, the ambition of AMS is to positively impact the digital transformation of society. Contributors to the SD Worx and Randstad recipes are:

- **Steven De Haes**, PhD, Dean and full-time Professor of Management Information Systems at AMS.

- **Tim Huygh**, PhD, an Assistant Professor of Information Systems at the Department of Information Science of the Open Universiteit, The Netherlands, and Visiting Professor at AMS, University of Antwerp, Belgium.

- **Anant Joshi**, PhD, Assistant Professor of Information Management at the Department of Accounting and Information Management at Maastricht University's School of Business and Economics, Maastricht, The Netherlands.

- **Joseph Puthenpurackal**, an information technology leader with over three decades of experience in application development, infrastructure management, IT strategy, architecture, IT governance, and project/program execution.

Mark Samuels, Chief Editor

Mark is a business writer and editor, with extensive experience of the way technology is used and adopted by CIOs. His experience has been gained through senior editorships, investigative journalism and postgraduate research. Editorial clients include the *Guardian*, *The Times*, the *Sunday Times* and the Economist Intelligence Unit. Mark has written content for a range of IT companies and marketing agencies. He has a PhD from the University of Sheffield, and master's and undergraduate degrees in geography from the University of Birmingham. Visit marksamuels.co.uk.

ABOUT CIONET

CIONET is the leading community of 10,000 senior digital and IT executives in more than 20 countries across Asia, Europe and the Americas. Through this global community CIONET helps orchestrate peer-to-peer interactions focused on the most important business and technology issues of the day. CIONET holds over a thousand international and regional live and virtual events annually, ranging from roundtables, community events and tribe meetings to large international gatherings, including CIONEXT and CIOFEST. Our members testify that CIONET is an impartial and value adding platform that helps each member to advance their professional development and accelerate beneficial outcomes within their organisations. For more information, please visit www.cionet.com or follow us on LinkedIn and YouTube.

INDEX

3D printing 53, 57, 100
4G 64, 78
5G 53, 64, 78, 84, 100
6G 53, 64

Accenture 86
Agile 52–3, 95, 97
   BW Paper Systems 58
   KfW 73–4, 76
   Maersk 118
   MAPFRE 91
   mBank 46, 47
   Morgan Stanley 135
   Proximus 44
   Randstad Group Belgium 138
   Red Hat 83
   Restoration and Renewal Authority 109
   Signify 35
Amazon 1, 7, 9, 12, 95
   Web Services (AWS) 14, 15, 30, 53
Antwerp, Port of 11, 19–22
Apigee 70
Apple 8, 53
application programming interface (APIs)
   53, 70
artificial intelligence (AI) 53, 54
   AstraZeneca 122
   Ferrovial 100, 102
   KBC Bank 60, 62
   MAPFRE 90

PKO Bank Polski 86
Proximus 42–3
Prudential 70, 72
Red Hat 84
Signify 35
Tate & Lyle 31, 32
AstraZeneca 112, 121–4
augmented reality (AR) 15, 53, 79
automation
   Kensington Mortgages 104–5
   MAPFRE 90
   Munich Re 25
   PKO Bank Polski 86
   Red Hat 83
   Signify 35
   Tate & Lyle 30–1
   see also robotic process automation

Babylon Health 72
Barclays 83
Bellamy, Martin 107–10
Bento, Manuel 113–16
big data 42–3, 60, 66, 70, 72, 95
Blackrock 70
blockchain 53, 72, 101
Boston Consulting Group (BCG) 86
Bountolos, Dimitris 100–2
Bravura 70
BW Paper Systems 55, 56–8

C# 46
C++ 46, 114
Cathay Pacific 83
chatbots 35, 86
cloud 52, 53, 95
   dunnhumby 41
   Financial Conduct Authority 108
   KBC Bank 62
   KfW 74, 76
   MAPFRE 90, 91
   mBank 46
   Munich Re 25, 27
   PKO Bank Polski 86
   Proximus 43
   Prudential 70, 72
   Randstad Group Belgium 138
   Red Hat 84
   Restoration and Renewal Authority 108–10
   Sainsbury's 13–14
   Signify 35
   Tate & Lyle 31–2
   Telefónica 65–6
communication 97
   Euronext 114, 115, 116
   Maersk 120
   Morgan Stanley 136
   Orange 79
   Randstad Group Belgium 141
   SD Worx 132–3
   storytelling 62, 68, 95, 102

communities of practice 2, 96, 110, 137, 143
continuous improvement 44, 97, 135, 136
culture 97, 129
    AstraZeneca 122
    dunnhumby 38, 39
    KBC Bank 59, 61–2
    Kensington Mortgages 104
    KfW 74, 75
    mBank 45
    Ministry of Defence 17
    Morgan Stanley 137
    Orange 79
    PKO Bank Polski 87
    Port of Antwerp 19, 20, 22
    Randstad Group Belgium 141
    Red Hat 82–3
    SD Worx 131, 133
    Signify 34
    Tate & Lyle 32

Dabrowski, Krzysztof 45–7
Dasani, Bijna Kotak 134–7
data analytics 54
    dunnhumby 41
    KBC Bank 60
    Kensington Mortgages 104, 105, 106
    Maersk 119
    PKO Bank Polski 86
    Port of Antwerp 21
    Prudential 70–1, 72
    Sainsbury's 13
    Signify 35
    Tate & Lyle 32
    Telefónica 64
data protection 40
Dawson, Margaret 82–4
De Ruwe, Kurt 33–5
design thinking 27, 97, 126
Deutsche Bank 135
DevOps 35, 46, 62, 83, 91
digital natives 1, 7, 24, 96, 124
    mBank 45, 47
Diligenta 70
distributed computing 84
diversity and inclusiveness 97, 129
    AstraZeneca 123
    Euronext 114–15
    Ferrovial 101
    Maersk 120

    Ministry of Defence 18
    Morgan Stanley 134, 136–7
    Red Hat 83
drones 20
dunnhumby 37, 38–41

edge computing 9, 53, 66, 84
enterprise resource planning (ERP) 9, 34, 119
Escrivá García, Vanessa 88–91
Euronext 112, 113–16

Ferrovial 99, 100–2
FinTech 45, 55, 85, 135
Forte, Charlie 16–18, 95
Foulsham, Mark 103–6

Ghijsels, Gunther 138–41
GitHub 62
Goldman Sachs 135
Google 1, 9, 77
    Cloud 15, 41, 53, 86
governance 2, 53, 87, 110
guilds 135–6

heritage systems *see* legacy systems
home working 1, 7–8, 68
    KBC Bank 60
    Kensington Mortgages 104
    KfW 75
    PKO Bank Polski 86, 87
    Tate & Lyle 30
    see also hybrid working
Hoots, Cindy 121–4
Houses of Parliament Restoration and Renewal Authority 99, 107–10
humility 32, 72, 85
hybrid working
    Ferrovial 101
    Kensington Mortgages 104
    PKO Bank Polski 87
    Tate & Lyle 30
    see also home working

IBM Unix 46
inclusiveness *see* diversity and inclusiveness
integration
    KBC Bank 60
    Ministry of Defence 16–17

    Port of Antwerp 19
    Red Hat 84
Internet of Things (IoT) 34, 53, 101

Jack, David 38–41
Java 57
Jordan, Phil 12–15

KBC Bank 55, 59–62
Kehr, Melanie 73–6
Kensington Mortgages 99, 103–6
KfW 68, 73–6
Kohli, Tarun 69–72, 95
Kubernetes 84, 88, 91

lean 43, 44
legacy systems 13, 52, 53
    MAPFRE 89, 90, 91
    mBank 45–6, 47
    Orange 78–9
    Prudential 69–70
    Telefónica 63, 65
Li-Fi 33–4
Lloyds Banking Group 135
low-code development tools 3, 32, 51, 86–7

machine learning (ML)
    dunnhumby 39, 41
    KBC Bank 62
    MAPFRE 90
    Proximus 42–3
    Red Hat 84
    Restoration and Renewal Authority 110
    Sainsbury's 13
    Tate & Lyle 32
Maersk 112, 117–20
MAPFRE 81, 88–91
Marciniak, Adam 85–7
mBank 37, 45–7
mentorships 124, 131
Messaoud, Nino 56–8
microservices 53, 84, 88, 91
Microsoft
    Azure 15, 41, 53, 86
    PKO Bank Polski 86, 87
    Power BI 30, 32, 105, 106
    Teams 86
    Windows 46, 47
Ministry of Defence (MoD), UK 11, 16–18

mission
    AstraZeneca 123
    Maersk 118, 120
mixed reality 53
Morgan Stanley 129, 134–7
Munich Re 24, 25–8

neural networks 125
no-code development tools 3, 32, 51, 87
Norway Post 112, 125–7

open source 53
    dunnhumby 39, 41
    KBC Bank 62
    MAPFRE 88, 91
    Orange 78–9
    Red Hat 82
    Sainsbury's 14
    Telefónica 64
optical character recognition (OCR) 90
Orange 68, 77–9

Patel, Sanjay 29–32
Pedro Silva, Rui 117–20
Peeters, Rudi 59–62
personality of IT leaders 95, 97
Philips Lighting 33, 34
PKO Bank Polski 81, 85–7
platform as a service (PaaS) 70
Port of Antwerp 11, 19–22
PricewaterhouseCoopers (PwC) 86
proof of concepts 60, 61
Proximus 37, 42–4
Prudential 68, 69–72

quantum computing 53, 84, 110

Randstad Group Belgium 129, 138–41
recruitment see talent sourcing and
    retention
Red Hat 78, 81, 82–4
remote working see home working
Restoration and Renewal Authority 99,
    107–10
robotic process automation (RPA) 9, 54
    AstraZeneca 122
    Ferrovial 102

Kensington Mortgages 105
MAPFRE 90
PKO Bank Polski 86
Port of Antwerp 20
Red Hat 84
Restoration and Renewal Authority 110
Signify 35
Tate & Lyle 30–1, 32
Telefónica 65–6

Sainsbury's 11, 12–15
Salesforce 9, 30, 51, 57, 65
SAP 30, 34, 90
Scaled Agile Framework (SAFe) 138
Scrum
    KfW 73, 74, 75
    Maersk 118
    mBank 47
    Randstad Group Belgium 138
SD Worx 129, 130–3
self-driving cars 77
Signify 24, 33–5
smart cameras 20
smart cities 77
smart factories 122
smart lighting 34
Snowflake 13
software as a service (SaaS) 9, 51, 52
    MAPFRE 91
    Prudential 70
    Restoration and Renewal Authority 109
    Sainsbury's 14
    Tate & Lyle 30
Sopra 106
Standaert, Geert 42–4
start-ups 95, 96
    banking sector 135
    disruption 77–8
    partnerships 9, 47
    survival rate 47
storytelling 62, 68, 95, 102
Success Factors 90
Swiss Re 69

talent sourcing and retention 95, 96
    AstraZeneca 123
    BW Paper Systems 57, 58

Euronext 113, 114–15
Kensington Mortgages 104
Maersk 120
mBank 47
Red Hat 84
SD Worx 131
Telefónica 66
Tate & Lyle 24, 29–32
Telefónica 52, 55, 63–6
Temenos 46
Tesla 97
Toyota 44, 77, 97
trust 95
    BW Paper Systems 58
    dunnhumby 40
    Kensington Mortgages 104, 106
    Maersk 118, 120
    mBank 47
    PKO Bank Polski 87
    Port of Antwerp 20, 21
    Sainsbury's 14

UiPath 102
UK Ministry of Defence (MoD) 11, 16–18
Unix 46

Valero, Angel 63–6
Velocity 65
Vermeulen, Koen 77–9
Verstraelen, Erwin 19–22
virtual reality (VR) 15, 53, 79
vision 18, 95, 129
    AstraZeneca 124
    digital 51
    MAPFRE 89
    Morgan Stanley 137
    Port of Antwerp 22
    Red Hat 83
    Restoration and Renewal Authority 110
    Signify 35

Workday 9, 30
working from home see home working

Yammer 35

PHOTO CREDITS

EYES
of the
RAF

A History of Photo-Reconnaissance

By the same author

Woe to the Unwary
Torpedo Airmen
The Strike Wings
Target: Hitler's Oil (with Ronald C. Cooke)
Arctic Airmen (with Ernest Schofield)
Failed to Return
An Illustrated History of the RAF
RAF Records in the PRO
    (with Simon Fowler, Peter Elliott and Christina Goulter)
The Armed Rovers
The RAF in Camera 1903–1939
The RAF in Camera 1939–1945
The RAF in Camera 1945–1995
RAF Coastal Command in Action 1939–1945
RAF: An Illustrated History from 1918
Britain's Rebel Air Force
    (with Dudley Cowderoy and Andrew Thomas)
The Flight of Rudolf Hess
    (with George van Acker)
RAF in Action 1939–1945
The Battle of Britain
The Battle of the Atlantic
Missing Believed Killed

EYES
of the
RAF

A History of Photo-Reconnaissance

ROY CONYERS NESBIT
ASSISTED BY JACK EGGLESTON

Foreword by Air Chief Marshal Sir Neil Wheeler GCB, CBE, DSO, DFC & BAR, AFC

SUTTON PUBLISHING

This book was first published in 1996

This new revised edition first published in 2003 by
Sutton Publishing Limited · Phoenix Mill
Thrupp · Stroud · Gloucestershire · GL5 2BU

British Library Cataloguing in Publication Data
A catalogue record for this book is available from the British Library

ISBN 0 7509 3256 2

Typeset in 10/13 Sabon.
Typesetting and origination by
Sutton Publishing Limited.
Printed and bound in Great Britain by
J.H. Haynes & Co. Ltd, Sparkford.

CONTENTS

Foreword   vi
Acknowledgements   vii
Introduction   ix

1.   The Other Side of the Hill   1
2.   Cameras at War   14
3.   Above the Trenches   27
4.   Between the Wars   54
5.   Sidney Cotton's Air Force   80
6.   British Intelligence   100
7.   Africa and Malta   127
8.   The New Squadrons   146
9.   Europe's Underbelly   164
10. Photography and the Invasion   179
11. Night Bombing and Photography   198
12. South-East Asia   214
13. Behind the Iron Curtain   238
14. Near and Middle East Commands   267
15. The Far East   282
16. Strike Command   295

Bibliography   322
Appendix I: Second World War Photo-reconnaissance
   Strategic Units and Squadrons   324
Appendix II: Adrian Warburton   329
Index   335

FOREWORD

BY

AIR CHIEF MARSHAL SIR NEIL WHEELER
GCB, CBE, DSO, DFC & BAR, AFC, FRAeS, RAF (RET'D)

Since the Second World War there have been many books about air operations but the vast majority have confined themselves to the Battle of Britain, the strategic bombing offensive and the Battle of the Atlantic. The general public could be forgiven for presuming that there must have been few other operations of importance. During the early years of the war I was involved in photographic reconnaissance, mostly in Spitfires, as both a Flight Commander and a Squadron Commander. I am, therefore, delighted that a book has been written on the history of photographic reconnaissance, starting even before the First World War. Moreover, it has been written by an author who is experienced in air operations and is also a painstaking researcher. Arguably, photographic reconnaissance made one of the greatest contributions to the Allied victory in the Second World War. I was, therefore, extremely pleased when Roy Nesbit invited me to write the Foreword to his book.

I first came across photographic reconnaissance in the early days of the war when staying with my brother in the Army. In his office I saw an aircraft recognition notice portraying a blue Spitfire. At the time I was a flying instructor on Fairey Battles in Bomber Command, stationed at Benson, and on my return to my unit I decided to find out about blue Spitfires. It was not easy because the unit, then based at Heston just outside London, was regarded as very secret. However, it was the early summer of 1940 and I thought it about time, as a permanent regular officer, that I took a more active part in the war. So, by a highly

irregular visit to the Air Ministry, I managed to wangle a posting to the Photographic Reconnaissance Unit at Heston in the late summer. The unit by then was commanded by Wing Commander Geoffrey Tuttle, although Sidney Cotton still seemed to be on the scene! Roy Nesbit's book refers to 'Sidney Cotton's Air Force' but, rest assured, Heston was a strange place and by then 'Sidney Cotton's Air Force' had become 'Geoffrey Tuttle's Air Force'. Certainly, I had been in the RAF for over five years and Heston bore little resemblance to the RAF stations on which I had served. But there was a terrific spirit!

As this book so graphically portrays, although the operational activity was essentially individual, the morale in PRU was very strong – and not only among the pilots. People speak of the dangers of penetrating deep into enemy-held territory without guns but frankly I do not recall that the dangers loomed large in the minds of the pilots. Moreover, at least we knew that our masters wanted us to get back with the photographs!

I have found reading Roy Nesbit's book most interesting and very nostalgic. It is thorough in its cover of what in the Second World War became a very large area of operations, developing in six years of war from a mere Flight to a Group. The author has clearly carried out exhaustive research into his subject. But it is definitely not a dreary history. Roy Nesbit has made photographic reconnaissance a live and fascinating subject and his book is long overdue. It is a fine tribute to those who did not return with their photographs.

ACKNOWLEDGEMENTS

This book was begun several years ago at the request of the Chairman of the Association of Royal Air Force Photography Officers, who at the time was Squadron Leader Don F. Barltrop RAF. It is based partly on the accumulated material of this association. I was encouraged by their historians, the late Squadron Leader Paul Lamboit RAFVR and the late Squadron Leader Jack E. Archbald RAFVR, and also urged to embark on the book by the late Air Marshal Sir Geoffrey Tuttle.

In researching and writing the book I have received a great deal of help from the Joint Air Reconnaissance Intelligence Centre (UK) at RAF Brampton, the Joint School of Photography at RAF Cosford, the Joint School of Photographic Interpretation at RAF Wyton, the Air Historical Branch (RAF) of the Ministry of Defence, the Imperial War Museum, the Museum of Army Flying, the Royal Air Force Museum, the Science Museum, the Tangmere Military Aviation Museum, the USAF Archives, the US 8th Air Force Historical Society, the South African Air Force Association, the Italian Ministry of Aviation, 39 (No. 1 PRU) Squadron RAF, 42 Squadron RAF, 47 Squadron RAF, RAF Coltishall, RAF Finningley, RAF Leuchars, RAF Lossiemouth, RAF Waddington, RAF Wittering, *Aeroplane Monthly*, *Jet & Prop* in Germany, and members of such bodies as the Medmenham Club and the Boy Entrant Photographers' Association. I have also carried out much research at the Public Record Office at Kew, although of course official documents within the last thirty years are not released to the public.

My thanks are due to the following, who have helped with the narrative or contributed photographs from their private collections. Decorations are omitted from this long list.
Mrs Ann Archbald; Brian J. Attwell; Peter Batten; Squadron Leader J.D. Braithwaite RAFVR; Squadron Leader Brian A. Broad RAF (Ret'd); The late Jack M. Bruce; The late Wing Commander F.E. 'Monty' Burton RAF; The late Wing Commander Geoff J. Buxton RAF; A. Richard Chapman; Squadron Leader Ian M. Coleman RAF; Mrs Jane Cowderoy; J. Sebastian Cox; Wing Commander Gordon J. Craig RAFVR; Warrant Officer Phil G. Crozier RAF (Ret'd); Flight Sergeant E.T. Davies RAF (Ret'd); Sergeant Graham Dinsdale RAF (Ret'd); Bob Docherty; Peter J.V. Elliott; The late Flight Lieutenant G. Alan Etheridge RAFVR; Wing Commander E.A. 'Tim' Fairhurst RAF (Ret'd); G. Flowerday; The late Corporal Alan Fox RAFVR; Roger A. Freeman; Squadron Leader Don R.M. Furniss RAFVR; Barry Gray; M.H. Goodall; Dr Christina J.M. Goulter-Zervoudakis; Senior Aircraftman Nigel Green RAF; Hans Grimminger; Dave Hatherell; Dr Eric V. Hawkinson USAF (Ret'd); Roger Hayward; The late Squadron Leader Norman Hearn-Phillips RAF; Flight Lieutenant John P. Hygate RAF; The late Flight Lieutenant W. Mike Hodsman RAFVR; Ted Hooton; Malcolm Howard; Sergeant Dave J. Humphrey RAF (Ret'd); Flight Lieutenant Norman Jenkins RAF (Ret'd); Sergeant Dave Jenkins RAF (Ret'd); Corporal L. Jewitt RAF (Ret'd); Mrs Patricia Fussell Keen; Brian Kervell; Squadron Leader Vic Kinnin RAF; Robert E. Kuhnert USAAF (Ret'd); Paul Lashmar; Art K. Leatherwood USAAF (Ret'd); Squadron Leader Howard W. Lees RAFVR; Bernard Lefebvre; G. Stuart Leslie; Flight Sergeant Ken Loweth RAF (Ret'd); Wing Commander Mike D. Mockford RAF (Ret'd); Sergeant Jim Muncie RAF (Ret'd); The late Squadron Leader Don J. Munro RAF; Ken Murch; John K. Nesbit TA; Flight Sergeant A.W. Orford RAF (Ret'd); Wing Commander David D. Oxlee RAF (Ret'd); The late Flight Lieutenant George H. Parry RAF (Ret'd); Flight Lieutenant Stan G.E. Payne RAF (Ret'd); Chris Pocock; Dr Alfred

Price RAF (Ret'd); Sergeant Alf Pyner RAF (Ret'd); Squadron Leader E.A. 'Tony' Robinson RAF (Ret'd); Squadron Leader Tom N. Rosser RAFVR; The late Corporal Norman Shirley RAFVR; Squadron Leader Peter H.R. Singleton RAF (Ret'd); The late Flight Officer Constance Babington Smith WAAF; Mrs K. Stevens WAAF; Squadron Leader A. Stevenson RAFVR; Squadron Leader Andy S. Thomas RAF; Geoff J. Thomas; Squadron Leader Peter J. Thompson RAF (Ret'd); Wing Commander R.G.M. 'Johnny' Walker RAF (Ret'd); Sergeant David T. Watson RAF; Sergeant George M. Webb RAF (Ret'd); Leading Aircraftman Reg F. White RAFVR; The late Group Captain S.G. 'Bill' Wise RAF; G.J. Zwanenburg RNethAF (Ret'd).

My thanks are also due to Air Chief Marshal Sir Neil Wheeler for writing the Foreword. Two friends who have painstakingly checked and corrected the narrative and captions of this book while it was being written are Squadron Leader Dudley Cowderoy RAFVR and Warrant Officer Jack Eggleston RAF (Ret'd).

Any errors which remain after all this expertise are my own responsibility.

INTRODUCTION

Intelligence of the enemy's strength and dispositions has always played a vital role in warfare. The first major use of air reconnaissance for these purposes by the British armed services occurred in the so-called Boer Wars, when manned balloons were raised above army lines to observe the location of enemy forces. The advent of powered airships coupled with air photography gave impetus to this form of intelligence acquisition in the early years of the twentieth century. With the development of aircraft and the formation of the Royal Flying Corps in 1912, followed by the Royal Naval Air Service two years later, air photography became an established function in these branches of the armed services.

In the First World War, air reconnaissance and photography were employed primarily for tactical purposes by both the RFC and the RNAS. Reconnaissance proved extremely useful for artillery spotting or the location of enemy warships, while air photography enabled interpreters to pick out details of enemy trenches, supply depots and so on behind his lines. As the war progressed, air cameras became more efficient and glass plates began to give way to rolls of film. But the use of aircraft for the gathering of stratgeic intelligence remained in its infancy, since the only long-distance aircraft built were engaged mainly on bombing operations.

Aircraft and air cameras developed considerably in technical terms in the interwar years, but the use of air photography remained largely tactical in order to provide 'army co-operation'. By 1937, before the Second World War, the only RAF aircraft considered suitable for strategic photography was the robust Bristol Blenheim. However, its range, level of altitude and armament were soon found to be inadequate for this purpose.

Fortunately a small unit of strategic aircraft was formed in the RAF on the declaration of war in September 1939, staffed by far-seeing flying and ground personnel. The first unit dedicated solely to photo-reconnaissance was born, and its most effective aircraft was the superb Supermarine Spitfire, stripped of armament and fitted with long-distance fuel tanks and automatic air cameras. With the fall of France and the isolation of Britain from mainland Europe, this unit assumed paramount importance in the prosecution of the war. It was expanded into several squadrons within Britain, while similar squadrons were formed in the Middle East and in India. As the war progressed, the de Havilland Mosquito, with its longer range, joined the Spitfire in strategic work. Equally significant, the interpretation of air photographs was carried out by dedicated teams of experts, many recruited from academic circles.

The RAF led the world in this sphere, surpassing the efforts of its allies and even its powerful enemies. The intelligence obtained from these highly dangerous air operations (which required a special kind of courage from those who crewed the aircraft) was coupled with the outstanding achievement of the Government Code and Cypher School at Bletchley Park in decrypting the German 'Enigma' signals. Thus British Intelligence had the edge on its enemy throughout much of the war, facilitating the re-entry of the Western Allies into mainland Europe in June 1944 and leading to the ultimate victory.

These lessons have not been forgotten in the long postwar period, although this has not been attended by any major world conflict. The Cold War, with the threat of nuclear missiles from Soviet Russia, resulted in air photo-reconnaissance of that country by RAF strategic aircraft as well as by the American Lockheed U-2 fitted with high resolution cameras. Tactical reconnaissance aircraft were also permanently active from bases in West Germany. The conflicts within Malaya and Indonesia were resolved with the aid of air cameras. The Falklands War and the Gulf War were won with the aid of even more sophisticated surveillance equipment. At the time of the latter, electronics and optical imagery were beginning to replace 'wet' films and relay pictures direct to analysts on the ground, both by day and night.

The intelligence value of good air photography is immense. The old adage that one picture is worth a thousand words can be multiplied a hundredfold or more. No part of the terrestrial world is now immune from this vital form of intelligence gathering.

CHAPTER ONE

THE OTHER SIDE OF THE HILL

From the beginning of warfare, military commanders have sought to know the disposition and strength of enemy forces, by intelligence or observation. Sometimes visual reconnaissance of a potential battlefield could be obtained by simply climbing up a suitable hill and looking down the other side, provided the enemy had not already occupied that advantageous position. The observer then raced back to report his findings or used some method of signals communication. This was one of the functions of light cavalrymen, while their heavier counterparts were used as shock troops against the enemy. Victory or defeat in battle depended to a great extent on the success or failure of such reconnaissance. Moreover, when the range of artillery increased considerably in the second half of the nineteenth century, an observation post on high ground was often essential if the gunners were to determine whether their shells were falling on the enemy or being wasted.

The first manned ascent in a tethered balloon, by the Frenchman Jean-François-Pilâtre de Rozier on 15 October 1783 over Paris, provided an obvious improvement in military observation. A manned flight of 27 miles by two Frenchmen in a balloon on 1 December of the same year, from the Tuileries in Paris, seemed to offer a new dimension for the art of warfare. A more startling example of the possibilities took place in January 1785, when Jean-Pierre Blanchard crossed the English Channel in a balloon.

The British were somewhat slower to experiment with this form of aerial endeavour, even though it was the English physicist Henry Cavendish who had in May 1776 discovered the density of hydrogen, the flammable gas with which the more successful of the French balloons were filled. An Italian, Vincenzo Lunardi, was probably the first person in Britain to ascend in a balloon, when he made a 20-mile flight from the grounds of the Honourable Artillery Company at Moorfields in London in May 1784. The first military test took place on 3 June when Major John Money, together with George Blake, ascended from Tottenham Court Road in London and came down at Abridge in Essex, a distance of 20 miles. But, by and large, the military establishment in Britain seems to have regarded ballooning as an amusing sport rather than a means of gaining advantage in warfare.

The French took a different view for, in the war against Austria and Prussia which followed their Revolution of 1789, they developed a mobile apparatus for producing hydrogen in the field of battle and so employed military balloons with some success. However, the destruction by Nelson of a ship carrying a balloon company at Aboukir Bay in Egypt in 1798 seems to have discouraged the French from further efforts. With the peace in Europe which followed the defeat of the French at Waterloo in 1815, the military development of aerial observation came to a halt, although in England Sir

The French town of Sèvres, photographed from a balloon by Paul Nadar, the son of the pioneer photographer Gaspard Félix Tournachon, better known as Nadar. (Flight Lieutenant G.H. Parry RAF (Ret'd))

Photograph of the Army camp at Lydd in Kent, taken in 1886 by a camera operating automatically from a small balloon released by Major H. Elsdale of the Royal Engineers. Lydd was an artillery practice camp. (Flight Lieutenant G.H. Parry RAF (Ret'd))

Colonel James L Templer, one of the pioneers of military ballooning from 1878 to 1905, in the wicker car of one of his observation balloons.
(Museum of Army Flying)

George Cayley carried out studies into heavier-than-air flight coupled with the design and testing of gliders.

It was not until 24 September 1852 that the next major development took place, when Pierre Jullien successfully flew a powered airship, 144 feet long and with a 3-hp steam engine, from Paris. A few years later, experiments with aerial photography from balloons began in both France and the USA. A Parisian photographer, Gaspard Félix Tournachon, who was also a caricaturist and journalist with the pseudonym of 'Nadar', attempted in 1858 to take out a patent on his examples of aerial photographs from balloons, although without success. His initial results were disappointing, partly since balloons tended to spin in high winds and partly because the release of hydrogen from the vent valve of the balloon contained impurities which affected the wet collodion plates used in his cameras. These plates needed to be sensitised, exposed and then developed while the balloon was in the air. On subsequent flights, Nadar overcame most of these problems.

In 1859 the enterprising Nadar was offered a commission in aerial photography and by 1863 had built a very large balloon named *Le Géant* for this purpose. Its two-storey wickerwork car contained a photographic darkroom and a small printing room, as well as a dining room. The life of this enormous balloon was short, for it was damaged beyond repair in October of the same year, when its nine occupants attempted to land in a high wind after a journey of 400 miles. But Nadar's enthusiasm was not diminished and he took many successful photographs in the following years.

Similar experiments took place in the USA, where the first satisfactory photographs from a tethered balloon were taken by J.W. Black and S.A. King from an altitude of 1,200 feet over the city of Boston in October 1860.

However, there do not appear to have been attempts to use photography from the balloons employed by the Federal side during the American Civil War of 1861–5.

Balloons were employed extensively by the French during the Siege of Paris in the Franco-Prussian War of 1870. Three tethered balloons were used for reconnaissance, while many others were released to float over the Prussian lines, carrying people and letters. Soon afterwards, the British War Office asked its Royal Engineer Committee to look into the practicability of using balloons with the Army. The War Office was doubtless influenced by the example of the French although two Royal Engineer officers, Captains Grover and Beaumont, had been carrying out many experiments with civilian balloons at their own expense and trying to get ballooning adopted by the British Army. In this period, the problem of sensitising and developing wet photographic plates in the air was overcome by the introduction by the English physician Richard L. Maddox of gelatine dry plates instead of collodion; this improved the sensitivity of the plates and also allowed them to be developed after return to earth.

Initial progress in Britain was slow since no funds were forthcoming from the War Office, but the purse-strings were loosened slightly in 1878 with the setting up at Woolwich of an establishment to develop military ballooning and the employment of an experienced balloonist, Captain James L. Templer, as an instructor. The first Army balloon, named *Pioneer*, made its ascent in the same year, and before long the store at Woolwich Arsenal contained five balloons. In 1882 the balloon establishment moved to Chatham, where the School of Ballooning was formed as part of the School of Military Engineering. Officers and men of the Royal Engineers were trained in aerial reconnaissance, photography and signalling.

The pigeon camera, patented in Germany by Dr Julius Neubronner in 1903. It weighed only 2½ ounces and took negatives of 1½ inches by 1½ inches automatically every 30 seconds. (Flight Lieutenant G.H. Parry RAF (Ret'd))

A man-carrying kite designed by S.F. Cody being raised by a detachment of Royal Engineers at Aldershot, probably in 1906. (Museum of Army Flying)

Stonehenge, taken from a balloon by Lieutenant P.H. Sharpe of the Royal Engineers. This photograph was first published on 6 December 1906. (B. Gray)

Preparing an observation balloon, around 1912 or 1913. (Museum of Army Flying)

The GI building of the Defence and Research Agency at Farnborough (formerly the Royal Aircraft Establishment), photographed in April 1993. This was built in 1907 as the headquarters of the Army's School of Ballooning. It became the headquarters of the RFC in 1913. (B.M. Harris)

The cupboard under the stairs in the GI building of the Defence and Research Agency at Farnborough (formerly the Royal Aircraft Establishment), photographed in April 1993. This was the darkroom used in 1912 by Air Mechanic F.C. Victor Laws of the RFC, who became known later as the 'Father of RAF Photography'. (B.M. Harris)

When in Nova Scotia in 1883, Major H. Elsdale of the Grenadier Guards also experimented with cameras fitted around free balloons and timed by clockwork to take exposures. At long last, balloon flights dedicated to reconnaissance had arrived in the British Army.

One of these units, commanded by Major Elsdale, travelled to Bechuanaland in 1884 as part of an expedition sent to repel Boer incursions, with results which were considered beneficial. Another unit, under Major Templer, was sent to the Sudan the following year, after the fall of Khartoum and the death of General Gordon. The use of balloons in the British Army became assured when successful experiments to correct artillery fire from balloons took place at Lydd in Kent.

The School of Ballooning moved to Aldershot in 1891–2, where there was more space for training. Tethered balloons were flown at altitudes of about 1,000 feet and in winds of up to 20 mph; the operators were also taught how to handle the free-running if the balloons came adrift. Experiments with kites also took place, and in 1894 the first man-carrying kite was raised over Pirbright Camp in Surrey, although this method of aerial observation remained in the experimental stage for some years. Meanwhile the military airship with a rigid frame, developed by Count Ferdinand von Zeppelin, made its first flight in Germany on 2 July 1900 and, after early set-backs, proved successful.

On 17 December 1903 an event occurred which heralded the eventual eclipse of the use of balloons and airships as observation platforms. This was the first powered flight of the biplane *Flyer*, designed by Wilbur and Orville Wright, near Kitty Hawk beach in North Carolina. Although at first this invention received little encouragement from the military in America or Britain, a French syndicate purchased the patent and, with help

from Wilbur Wright, took the lead in aeronautical progress.

In Britain, private enterprise began to wake up to the potentialities of powered flight, and experiments were carried out by engineers such as Charles Rolls, Robert Blackburn, A.V. Roe, Thomas Sopwith, and the brothers Horace and Oswald Short. At this time, these men were not constructing warplanes but were seeking to improve techniques for personal interest coupled with commercial possibilities. Very substantial rewards were offered by newspapers to those men who came first in flying events.

Meanwhile the military establishment continued flying experiments with lighter-than-air craft, its factory moving from Aldershot to Farnborough in 1906. In the same year, a man-carrying kite invented by S.F. Cody was added to the Army equipment. In 1907 the Army's first powered airship, or dirigible as it was sometimes called, made its appearance; it was named *Nulli Secundus* and had a semi-rigid gas envelope. Cody then designed and built an aeroplane powered by a 50-hp engine, which made a flight of about 400 yards on 16 October 1908 and later became Army Aeroplane No 1. The War Office banned further experiments with aeroplanes because of the cost, but events were moving at such a pace that it was soon forced to reverse this decision.

On 25 July 1909, Louis Blériot took off in a monoplane from Les Boraques, near Calais, and landed near Dover thirty-seven minutes later. This startling achievement caused a great stir in the British press, for newspaper editors foresaw thousands of armed Frenchmen, the country's traditional enemies, soaring above the Royal Navy to take coastal defences in the rear. While remaining phlegmatic about this possibility, the War Office set up an Air Battalion in April 1911, consisting of No 1 Company for balloons, airships and kites, and No 2 Company for

The Watson Air Camera was the first camera specially designed for the RFC. It had a 6-inch lens and carried twelve 5-inch by 4-inch plates which were moved into position by pulling a lever. In 1913, the first series of vertical and overlapping photographs was taken with this camera, from HMA *Beta* over the Basingstoke Canal. The airship was flown by Captain J.E. Fletcher and the photographer was Sergeant F.C.V. Laws. (Squadron Leader P. Lamboit RAFVR, courtesy Photogrammetric Record)

The Army airship HMA *Beta* was completed in June 1910, rebuilt from the airship *Baby*. She was a non-rigid machine with a length of 104 feet, powered by a 35-hp Green engine, used mainly for wireless experiments. The airship was rebuilt in late 1912 after an accident, enlarged to 108 feet and fitted with a 50-hp Clerget engine, and renamed *Beta 2*. She was transferred to the RNAS in late 1913. (Museum of Army Flying)

aeroplanes. A White Paper issued by the Secretary of State for War gave details of the Air Estimates: £85,000 for new aeroplanes and dirigibles, with £28,000 for a new shed at South Farnborough in Hampshire to house them. The name of the factory – H M Balloon Factory and Balloon Section, Royal Engineers – was changed to the Army Aircraft Factory, and its engineers began to design and construct aeroplanes.

The Air Battalion formed part of the Royal Engineers, the most innovative and forward-looking branch of the British Army, and of course the principal roles of both Companies were those of reconnaissance and artillery spotting, coupled with aerial photography. No 1 Company received non-rigid airships such as *Beta*, *Gamma* and *Delta*, while 2 Company began to acquire an assortment of aeroplanes, both French and British. The Royal Navy received naval 'Blimps', non-rigid airships of different types, and also began to experiment with aeroplanes.

Public alarm in Britain at the increase in numbers of German Zeppelins and the growing strength of the French Air Force, which in 1911 was able to join in Army manoeuvres with over 200 aeroplanes, forced the War Office to step up the pace of aerial development. It announced a grant of £75 for any officer who learned how to fly an aeroplane, this being the amount charged by private flying schools for tuition. There was no shortage of adventurous young men willing to join this novel, if dangerous, branch of the armed services.

On 13 April 1912, the Royal Flying Corps was formed with the granting of a Royal Warrant by King George V, while the factory at Farnborough became the Royal Aircraft Factory. It was intended that the RFC would have a Military and a Naval Wing, with a Central Flying School common to both. However, the Admiralty refused to take part in such an arrangement and the Naval Wing

became known unofficially as the Royal Naval Air Service, a title which eventually became official on 1 July 1914. The Admiralty also set up its own Flying School.

Criticisms of the Royal Aircraft Factory began to appear in journals and newspapers, accusing it of being a government monopoly engaged in unfair competition with private enterprise. In August 1912 a Military Aeroplane Competition, intended to encourage private designs of military aeroplanes, took place at Larkhill on Salisbury Plain. A BE2, built by the Royal Aircraft Factory and flown by Geoffrey de Havilland, gained the highest marks but was considered to be *hors concours* since it was a government design. The competition was officially won by S.F. Cody with his biplane powered by a 120–hp Austro-Daimler engine, but the design was not considered suitable by the Army.

In June and July of 1912 the War Office sent letters to every regiment in the British Army, asking for volunteers to join the Military Wing of the RFC, which was short of ground personnel. One branch which the RFC was anxious to improve was air photography, particularly the adaptation to aeroplanes of the methods of photography used in balloons. In August of that year a young guardsman who was to have a profound effect on the development of air photography was accepted as a First Class Mechanic Air Photographer in the RFC. He was Frederick Charles Victor Laws, twenty-five years of age, who transferred from the 3rd Battalion Coldstream Guards after approximately seven years of Army service. He was a keen photographer who had been able to set up his own darkroom and augment his service pay by selling copies of his photographs, mostly to officers in the Coldstream Guards.

Laws found that photographic facilities at Farnborough were amateurish and ill-equipped, consisting of two men and himself working in a small room under some stairs. However, after a few months he was promoted to sergeant and put in charge of the photographic section of No 1 Squadron and thus became the first non-commissioned officer in charge of photography in the RFC. This squadron had taken over the airships, balloons and kites of No 1 (Airship) Company of the Air Battalion, Royal Engineers. Laws was also disappointed with his first duties, for instead of aerial photography the only use of cameras seemed to be taking pictures of airships emerging from or entering the large hangars at Farnborough. He was keen to become an air photographer, spurred on partly by the extra two shillings a day he would receive whenever he could get into the air, but also genuinely anxious to create a specialised photographic branch for his squadron. He made friends with officers who could allow him to ascend in an airship, a balloon or even a man-carrying kite. Other photographers joined the squadron during the next six months, and he was then in charge of a section of five men.

There were no specialised air cameras in those days and the only adaptable equipment available was the press camera, usually a Pan Ross with a 6-inch lens using 5-inch by 4-inch glass plates. The two methods of air photography were, and still remain, the taking of oblique and vertical photographs. The former are comparable to those exposed from high terrain or a high building, while the latter involve overlapping photographs taken directly downwards. One major advantage of the vertical picture is that it gives an image similar to that of a map, so that the results can be employed for map production. In these early days most air photographs were oblique views, but by mid-1913 it became apparent that verticals were also required for military purposes. A special

camera was needed for airborne use, and this had to be capable of being mounted in the aeroplane as well as sufficiently automatic to provide a series of overlapping photographs in order to ensure continuity of cover for mapping.

The Watson Air Camera, designed in 1913, was the first camera specially produced for air photography in the RFC. It was with this apparatus that the first series of vertical photographs was taken, from the airship *Beta* with Captain J.E. Fletcher as pilot and Sergeant F.C.V. Laws as photographer, together with a sergeant engineer. The photography, carried out along the Basingstoke Canal, marked a major advance in the application of air photography for mapping purposes.

In October 1913 a decision was made to transfer all the airships from the RFC to the Royal Naval Air Service, together with much of the other equipment and many of the personnel. A war in Europe seemed possible by this time, and No 1 Squadron of the RFC was reorganised into an 'Aircraft Park' for the proposed British Expeditionary Force. Laws was more interested in aeroplanes than airships and asked to remain with the RFC. He was transferred to the Experimental Flight at Farnborough under Major Herbert Musgrave. This officer had served in the South African war and, after witnessing the arrival of Blériot at Dover in 1909, had also urged the War Office to interest itself in military aviation. The Farnborough unit carried out experimental work with wireless, ballooning, kiting, bombing, meteorology, photography, armament and artillery co-operation. There were many opportunities for flying and Laws gained much experience in the next few months. With his pilot, Lieutenant F. Joubert, Laws took pictures of such areas as the Royal Aircraft Factory, the Isle of Wight defences and the Solent. Exposures were made from 3,000 feet in a two-seater

F.C. Victor Laws, as a captain in the RFC. He enlisted as a private in the Coldstream Guards in February 1905 and was seconded to the RFC as an air mechanic and photographer in August 1912. He became a sergeant-major and was commissioned in November 1915, rising steadily in rank and prestige, serving after the war and then in the Second World War, before retiring as a group captain in May 1946. He died in October 1975 at the age of eighty-eight, being renowned as the 'Father of RAF Photography'. (Squadron leader P. Lamboit RAFVR)

The Maurice Farman 11, known as the 'Shorthorn', entered service with the RNAS and the RFC shortly before the beginning of the First World War for reconnaissance and bombing duties. In the earlier machines, the observer sat in the rear cockpit with a hand-held machine gun while the pilot sat in the front cockpit, but later these positions were reversed. It was in one of these machines that Sergeant Laws photographed the gathering of the Military Wing of the RFC at Netheravon in Wiltshire, a few days before war was declared. The Shorthorn was withdrawn from front line duties by the end of 1915, but continued in use for training purposes. (*Aeroplane Monthly*)

Blériot XI–2 monoplane and Laws processed the pictures in the back of the aircraft.

In June 1914 the Military Wing of the RFC was gathered into a 'Concentration Camp' at Netheravon in Wiltshire, for a trial mobilisation and practice flying over Salisbury Plain. At the end of July, Laws was transferred to 3 Squadron at Netheravon, and took off from Farnborough with his pilot Lieutenant T.O'B. Hubbard to make the journey. They were flying in an Henri Farman pusher biplane, with the Watson Air Camera mounted in the nose. The engine cut out when they were over Odiham and they came down in a hop field, ending up with the fragile aircraft looking like a broken matchbox, although neither occupant was seriously hurt.

Laws took off again two days later in a Maurice Farman 'Shorthorn', this time piloted by Lieutenant Fitzjohn Porter, and arrived over Netheravon when a great parade and inspection was in progress, for the Secretary of State for War was reviewing the Royal Flying Corps. Photographs were taken

of this historic event, and Laws was very pleased with the results, for some of them were so sharp and clear that they showed a sergeant-major chasing an inquisitive dog off the parade ground. The erratic track of the dog and the footprints of the sergeant-major could be seen, where crushed grass presented different angles to the light. These marks were still visible in a later photograph and it was realised that, for example, the overnight movement of troops or vehicles over grass or soft ground might be visible in an aerial photograph up to several days afterwards, even when the tracks were not evident at ground level. The art of photographic interpretation had begun in the RFC.

Laws now felt confident that these results augered well for the future of air photography, and indeed this became a requirement several hours later when, on 4 August 1914, Britain declared war against Germany, the day after that country declared war against France. Nobody could have foreseen the terrible carnage which was to follow.

CHAPTER TWO

CAMERAS AT WAR

The British Expeditionary Force under General Sir John French which arrived in France at the beginning of the First World War was small but, for its size, was a first-class and professional fighting force. Within its ranks were well-trained soldiers, some of whom had had considerable experience of mobile warfare, although not in Europe. The Army had used observation balloons in the past and knew about man-carrying kites, but had little practical experience of the use of aeroplanes or even dirigibles as instruments of war. The idea of photographing the enemy from the air was barely considered. If discussed, some officers even expressed the view that it would be an ungentlemanly intrusion into private affairs, breaching the unwritten code of chivalry in warfare which existed in those days. On the other hand, the French Army had no such inhibitions, and the British notions of a chivalrous enemy were to be shattered when the Germans launched their first gas attack, at Ypres on 22 April 1915.

Most of the Royal Flying Corps, consisting of 2, 3, 4 and 5 Squadrons and their aircraft park, accompanied the British Expeditionary Force to France. There were sixty-three aeroplanes in all, a collection of BE2s, BE8s, Blériot XIIs, Henri Farmans, Sopwith Tabloids and Avro 504s. They concentrated on Amiens and then, leaving the aircraft park there, moved to Mauberge near the Belgian border. The headquarters went with them, commanded by Brigadier-General Sir David Henderson. Meanwhile the Royal Naval Air Service, which consisted of seventy-one aeroplanes and seven dirigibles, began to patrol the North Sea and also operated a small wing at Dunkirk in France.

During August and September 1914, the British fought an open and mobile campaign against the Germans. They were positioned on the left flank of the French Army, where there were no trench lines up to the Channel coast, and the fighting took place on Belgian and French soil. The Germans had planned a wide sweep through Belgium and around the northern flank of the French, gaining Paris and trapping the French Army on two sides. Britain's 'contemptible little army', as the Germans called it, stood in their way.

When the RFC squadrons flew to Mauberge they were fired upon by British columns and thus, on arrival, painted Union flags on the undersides of their wings. Since these were not easily distinguishable the insignia were altered later to the roundel which became so familiar. Meanwhile, Sergeant-Major Victor Laws had accompanied 3 Squadron to France and was fully expecting to be sent up in the air to take photographs of the enemy. But nobody seemed to think of this and instead he was sent up the line to work with the first anti-aircraft battery which had arrived in the BEF. This was a horse-drawn carrier on which pom-pom guns were mounted, and Laws's job was to indicate to the gunners which aircraft belonged to the RFC.

The Henri Farman HF20 first appeared in 1913, designed primarily as a reconnaissance aircraft. During the First World War it also served in France, Belgium, Holland, Italy, Romania and Russia. This example was photographed in March 1915 on the island of Tenedos, near Gallipoli. (J.M. Bruce/G.S. Leslie Collection)

The Short 184 seaplane was designed as a torpedo bomber and entered RNAS service in the summer of 1915. On 12 August 1915 one of these machines sank a Turkish merchant vessel in the Dardanelles, achieving the first success of any air-launched torpedo. However, the Short 184 was not wholly successful, being tricky to fly as well as difficult to take off with the load of a torpedo. It served until the end of the war, but primarily for reconnaissance and anti-submarine work. The machine in this photograph, serial 8033, was being hoisted on board the seaplane carrier *Vindex* of 2,950 tons. (J.M. Bruce/G.S. Leslie Collection)

The RFC sent up its first two reconnaissance aircraft on the morning of 19 August 1914, both manned solely by pilots. They were told to keep in company but, intent on looking for signs of the enemy, first lost each other and then themselves. Both landed to ask the way back and eventually returned to Mauberge. After this air observers flew with the pilots, and advancing German columns were spotted on the following day. The British moved into position at Mons in Belgium on 22 August and were ordered to hold this position for a day, in order to guard the left flank of the French Army. Reconnaissance aircraft were sent up and brought back accurate reports of the German dispositions. No wireless sets had been installed in the aircraft, and reports were written in the air and handed in on return. One aircraft crashed, killing both occupants, but the partially written report was brought to the British by Belgian civilians.

On 23 August the Germans attacked the British Expeditionary Force with what appeared to be overwhelming strength but were held back by the accuracy of the British fire. The soldiers had practised rapid firing with their bolt-action rifles to such effect that the Germans believed that every man had been issued with a machine gun. However, the French on their right withdrew unexpectedly, a matter which caused some bitterness with the British. Thereafter, Sir John French gave the RFC the additional task of reporting on the dispositions of the French Army.

The British Expeditionary Force then began a skilful fighting withdrawal and the RFC moved back with them, from Mauberge to Le Cateau, then in turn to St Quentin, La Fère, Compiègne, Senlis, Juilly, Serrit, Pezearches and, finally on 4 September to Mélun, 30 miles south of Paris. During this period the reconnaissance aircraft continued flying over the changing battlefield, where fierce fighting took place with gallant rearguard actions against superior forces. By 4 September the British Expeditionary Force had reached the River Marne and the Germans were unwittingly advancing into a trap, for a new French Army had been mustered and was ready to attack them in the rear. The Battle of the Marne began two days later. The Germans still attempted to attack but communication with their forward area was poor. By then, some of the RFC's aircraft were fitted with wireless sets and the crews were thus able to report immediately on the German dispositions. The Germans were defeated and forced to abandon the battlefield.

In a dispatch of 7 September to the War Office, Sir John French paid a glowing tribute to the work of the RFC during the campaign and also congratulated the squadrons on their air fighting. Although this consisted of little more than firing at German machines with rifles, sporting guns and revolvers, the RFC did succeed in shooting down about five German aircraft. This marked the beginning of aerial combat, for which the RFC is best remembered in the First World War although it comprised only part of its work.

Further battles of movement took place but by November both sides were exhausted. They dug in and a series of trenches extended from near Nieuport in Belgium to the Swiss border. A longer and even bloodier phase of the war was about to begin.

The anti-aircraft battery which Laws accompanied did not shoot down any aircraft at all, friend or foe, but as a result of this exercise he was offered a commission with the Royal Artillery and a letter to that effect was sent to the RFC. In turn, the RFC advised him to stay with them and he agreed readily, for his interest still lay in air photography. In December 1914 he was transferred from 3 Squadron, which by then

The Royal Aircraft Factory BE2c was built to satisfy the requirement of the War Office for an extremely stable reconnaissance aircraft. The first arrived in France in late 1914 but later proved unable to out-manoeuvre German monoplane fighters and too slow to escape them. It was more successful where the opposition was less severe, such as against the Turks in the Middle East. This BE2c was photographed in 1915. (*Aeroplane Monthly*)

was based at Houges, to 9 Squadron at St Omer. This was the same experimental flight in which he had previously served, but enlarged and formed into a squadron. It was equipped with BE2as, Blériot XIs and Maurice Farmans, and still commanded by Major Herbert Musgrave. The squadron came under the direct control of the headquarters of the RFC. Its main occupation was the development of wireless communications but Laws was given the duties of a carpenter, then a motor driver, and finally a motor mechanic. There was still no mention of photography.

A few days before Laws arrived, a new officer joined 9 Squadron. This was 2nd Lieutenant J.T.C. Moore-Brabazon, thirty years of age and a person of considerable experience and influence. He was a skilled mechanic, a balloonist, an acclaimed motor-racing driver, a sportsman, and an aviator who had won many competitions and who held Certificate No 1 issued by the Royal Aero Club, dated 8 March 1910. One of his many friends had been the eccentric genius Charles S. Rolls of Rolls-Royce fame, for whom he had worked as an unpaid mechanic. When Rolls was killed tragically in a Wright aircraft on 12 July 1910, Moore-Brabazon's wife was expecting her first baby and she asked him to cease flying, for he had already suffered a number of accidents in balloons, aeroplanes and on the motor-racing track. He agreed, but on the outbreak of war volunteered to serve as an ambulance driver in France. After several rather unpleasant weeks in that capacity, he decided that he should serve in the RFC and then used his influence in England to obtain a commission and his wings, without any military experience at all.

Moore-Brabazon was not altogether happy with his duties in 9 Squadron, which was non-operational at the time, although he admired most of the other officers, many of

whom later achieved great distinction in the RFC as well as in the RAF. However, he did not get along well with Major Musgrave and, on one occasion when he queried an order, was told, 'You will obey your superior officers.' His response was cutting: '*Superior* officer? Senior, if you please, sir.' No disciplinary action was taken against him, and in fact when the various flights of 9 Squadron were dispersed to other squadrons in February 1915, Major Musgrave left the RFC and returned to the Army; he was killed on a patrol behind the German lines on 2 June 1918. His old squadron was re-formed at Brooklands on 1 April 1915 under one of its previous officers, Major Hugh C.T. Dowding, who later commanded the headquarters wing of the RFC in France and twenty-five years on was to earn undying fame as the C-in-C of Fighter Command during the Battle of Britain.

Meanwhile Moore-Brabazon, who was both inventive and enterprising, yearned to do something positive to further the progress of the RFC and help win the war. His opportunity came in early January 1915 after Sir John French had been impressed by a map of the enemy trenches constructed from clear photographs obtained by the French Air Force. The RFC's 3 Squadron had attempted to take photographs of German dispositions during the previous September, during the time Laws was serving with the Royal Artillery, but the results were indistinct. The French map was passed to Sir David Henderson of the RFC, and a staff officer, Major W.G.H. Salmond, was instructed to study the French photographic organisation. Salmond found that the French squadrons were fully staffed with expert photographic personnel, and he recommended to Sir David Henderson that an experimental photographic section be set up in the RFC.

By this time, four of the operational squadrons of the RFC in France had been

The SS (Sea Scout) airship was supplied to the RNAS in March 1915 for coastal patrols around the British coast. It carried a crew of two in a control car constructed from a fuselage such as an Armstrong Whitworth FK3, slung from the non-rigid envelope. This SS airship was photographed on 18 December 1917 while flying over the snow-covered airfield of Waddington in Lincolnshire. (J.M. Bruce/G.S. Leslie Collection)

The Henri Farman HF27 was a variant of the HF20, slightly bigger and with a steel airframe. This example of the RNAS, serial 3618, was photographed in early 1915 on the island of Mafia, near the delta of the River Rufiji in German East Africa, where it was engaged on a hunt for the cruiser *Königsberg*. (J.M. Bruce/ G.S. Leslie Collection)

Above, left: Lord Brabazon of Tara, photographed here as Lieutenant John T.C. Moore-Brabazon MC of the RFC, was a pioneer aviator who held No 1 Certificate of the Royal Aero Club. Born on 8 February 1884, he was responsible for the RFC/RAF Photographic Section in the First World War, rising to the rank of Lieutenant-Colonel. He became an MP in 1918 and remained very prominent in aviation circles until his death on 17 May 1964. *Above, right:* Lieutenant Charles D.M. Campbell MBE, who was a founder of RFC photography in the First World War, together with J.T.C. Moore-Brabazon and Sergeant-Major F.C.V. Laws. He rose to the rank of major but died of tuberculosis on 9 March 1918. (Both photos: B. Gray)

The RE5 was the first of the Royal Aircraft Factory's 'Reconnaissance Experimental' biplanes to be put into production. This example, serial 380, was completed in March 1914 as a single-seater with an unequal wingspan. It joined 2 Squadron in France in November 1914, probably converted to a standard two-seater. Most production RE5s were equal-span two-seaters. The air observer sat in the front, armed only with personal weapons. The RE5s was a stable aircraft, but so unmanoeuvrable that it was soon withdrawn from front-line service. (J.M. Bruce/G.S. Leslie Collection)

The A-type camera was built to specifications given to the Thornton-Pickard Camera Company by Lieutenants J.T.C. Moore-Brabazon and C.D.M. Campbell on return from the Western Front in early 1915. It was a tapered and brass-bound wooden box which took 5-inch by 4-inch plates, inserted one after the other by hand. The lens was initially an 8½-inch set at infinity focus. The camera could be mounted on a bracket for vertical photography or the operator could hold it by the straps, leaning over the side into the slipstream. The sight was a simple brass tube with cross-wires. (Flight Lieutenant G.H. Parry RAF (Ret'd))

Lieutenant C.E. Tinne, an air observer in the RFC who was formerly an officer in the Royal Field Artillery, holding an A-type camera in a Nieuport 12 of 46 Squadron. This aircraft also carried a Lewis gun mounted on a Scarff ring. In October 1916, 46 Squadron moved to the Western Front, where it was employed on air reconnaissance and artillery spotting. (Flight Lieutenant G.H. Parry RAF (Ret'd))

formed into two wings, each to operate with two of the four Army Corps of the BEF. The First Wing, commanded by Lieutenant-Colonel Hugh M. Trenchard, comprised 2 and 3 Squadrons while the Second Wing, commanded by Lieutenant-Colonel C.J. Burke, controlled 5 and 6 Squadrons. This arrangement was made in anticipation of a huge expansion of the RFC, for new wings and many new squadrons were planned to co-ordinate with additional Army Corps. The wireless unit, 9 Squadron and 4 Squadron remained temporarily attached to RFC Headquarters, but the new experimental photographic section was set up under the First Wing in the middle of January 1915.

Lieutenant-Colonel Trenchard was an extremely formidable officer who was held in awe and respect by all those who served under him. His Army service had been mainly in India and Africa. During 1912 at the age of thirty-nine he had qualified privately as a pilot at the Sopwith School, paying for his tuition himself. When Sir David Henderson left to take command of the RFC in France, Trenchard commanded the Military Wing at Farnborough, where he had been responsible for much of the planning that led to the later expansion. Confronted with his tall figure and broad shoulders, coupled with his booming voice, junior officers could be reduced to abject misery when subjected to his rebukes. But he was not an unkind person and his attributes of wisdom and farsightedness became startlingly evident as the war progressed and afterwards in the inter-war years. He will always be remembered as the 'Father of the RAF'.

Trenchard sought men with knowledge and experience of photography to staff the new section, and three were available. One of these was 2nd Lieutenant Moore-Brabazon, who had already made up his mind that photography was bound to become an important function for the RFC and had asked Sir David Henderson's General Staff Officer, Lieutenant-Colonel F.H. Sykes, if he could be considered for work in this specialism. In addition to his other accomplishments, he had previously practised photography on the ground and also experimented with colour systems, X-ray work and high-speed photography in his laboratory. Thus he felt that he was well-qualified in the art of photography. The other candidate was Lieutenant Charles D.M. Campbell, of whom little has been recorded save that he is known to have been proficient as a photographer; he eventually rose to the rank of major but died of tuberculosis before the end of the war.

Neither Moore-Brabazon nor Campbell had had any experience of aerial photography but one man who was proficient in that field was Sergeant-Major Laws. Trenchard sent for the three men, all of whom were based on the airfield at St Omer but had scarcely met before, and asked Laws for his recommendations. Laws suggested that photographic sections should be set up in each wing, and that he should be sent to them in turn, in order to form, equip and run them until they were capable of continuing on their own. The two junior officers supported his opinion, which was accepted by Trenchard. Soon afterwards, Laws began three months with the First Wing. This was followed by three months with the Second Wing and then three months with the Third Wing, which was formed in March 1915.

At the headquarters of the First Wing, which was based within St Omer, Trenchard gave Moore-Brabazon and Campbell the encouragement they needed to develop air photography, and there was much work ahead of them. The majority of cameras in use with the RFC were the folding type with bellows, which were usually held over the side of the cockpit and took rather unsatisfactory oblique pictures, although one

An A-type camera being handed to the air observer of a Vickers Fighting Biplane FB5, a two-seater with a pusher engine which first reached France in July 1915. It was armed with a single Lewis gun and thus the first specialised British fighter, but could also be used for photo-reconnaissance. (Flight Lieutenant G.H. Parry RAF (Ret'd))

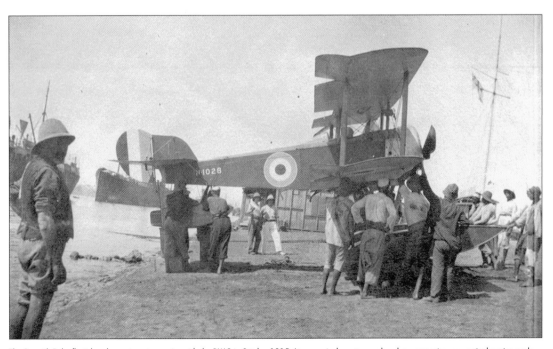

The Sopwith Baby floatplane began to enter service with the RNAS in October 1915. It was a single-seater employed on reconnaissance, anti-submarine work, bombing and fighter patrols. In addition to operating from bases around the British coast, it served on aircraft carriers in the North Sea and the Mediterranean. Serial N1028 seen here operated in the Mediterranean. (J.M. Bruce/G.S. Leslie Collection)

The Caudron GIII was widely used as a photo-reconnaissance aircraft in the early years of the First World War. Most were manufactured in France, and were supplied to the RFC and the RNAS, as well as to Belgium, Russia and Italy. The machine was unusual since it was fitted with a tractor engine but used the nacelle and tailbooms configuration of a pusher aircraft. Like many reconnaissance aircraft, it was vulnerable to enemy fighters. This Caudron GIII, photographed in 1915, carried a vertical A-type camera. (J.M. Bruce/G.S. Leslie Collection)

The Morane-Saulnier BB biplane was developed as an alternative to the parasol monoplanes, as a reconnaissance aircraft. It entered service with the RFC in December 1915. The armament consisted of two Lewis guns, one firing through the propeller and one in the rear cockpit. It was considered a heavy aircraft to handle but continued in service until January 1917. This example was fitted with an asymmetrical bulge on the starboard side for a camera housing. (J.M. Bruce/G.S. Leslie Collection)

The Franco-British Aviation flying boat first appeared in 1915. Some were supplied to the RNAS and were used for photo-reconnaissance and naval patrols. A camera mounting was fitted to the starboard side of this example, serial 3646. (J.M. Bruce/G.S. Leslie Collection)

enterprising observer of 2 Squadron cut a hole in the bottom of his cockpit in a BE2a and took some verticals.

A more robust camera was required, one which could be either hand-held or mounted on the aircraft. Moore-Brabazon and Campbell set about designing one and visited England to invite co-operation with the Thornton-Pickard Manufacturing Company. It was a box-type, built to withstand rough usage, which made use of the Mackenzie-Wishart plates and a Zeiss Tessar lens, and became known as the A-type camera. It could be employed for both oblique and vertical photography and was first used by 3 Squadron over the enemy trenches on 3 March 1915. Although each exposure required ten operations, the results were excellent, and the invention went into production for the RFC.

Even before the introduction of this new camera, however, the tutelage given by Victor Laws to the photographic section of the First Wing bore fruit. In advance of the battle of Neuve Chapelle which began on 10 March, 2 and 3 Squadrons successfully photographed the entire German defences from a depth of 700 to 1,500 yards, in an area where a salient jutted out into the British positions near the junction with the French Army. The enemy trenches shown on the photographs were then traced on a skeleton map in a scale of 1:8,000, and details of the British plan of attack were superimposed.

Copies of the map were used by the artillery, the infantry and the aircrews. The gunners subjected the German forward trenches to a short but intense bombardment and then lifted their fire to fall on the communication trenches and support positions while the infantry attacked. This battle was also notable for the introduction of the 'clock-code' system of artillery spotting by the reconnaissance aircraft. The air observer was handed a celluloid disc with concentric circles radiating from the centre, each circle given a letter, together with the numbers of a clock shown round the outer rim. When the disc was centred on an enemy target shown on the map, he was able to send a wireless message to the battery, giving in letter and figure form the position where the shells were falling, thus enabling the gunners to correct their aim.

Under cover of accurate artillery fire, the British infantry successfully attacked the village of Neuve Chapelle from two sides and consolidated their positions, although further progress was hampered by bad weather, lack of sufficient artillery shells, and stiffening German resistance. For the RFC, the battle was also notable since it marked the first systematic attempt to bomb German positions, using newly introduced bomb racks. These attacks took place at low level behind the German front lines, mainly against railway lines and troop trains, with considerable success.

These beginnings led to the extensive use of photography, interpretation, map construction and artillery spotting in the RFC, and later in the RAF. Before long, Trenchard began carrying aerial photographs in his pockets, displaying them on every possible occasion as evidence of the success of his reconnaissance aircraft and their aerial photography.

CHAPTER THREE

ABOVE THE TRENCHES

The limited success at Neuve Chapelle convinced the British commanders that they had found a formula for defeating the Germans on the Western Front. Firstly, the enemy trenches and supply lines should be covered continually by photo-reconnaissance aircraft, followed by military interpretation of the photographs and the construction of accurate maps. Next, the enemy positions should be subjected to enormous artillery bombardment, as soon as sufficient supplies of ordnance became available from munition factories. This bombardment would be guided by artillery-spotting from aircraft and balloons, enabling the gunners to knock out all German strong points. Then waves of infantry would attack the demoralised defenders and occupy their positions, leading to a breakthrough of the enemy lines. Unfortunately, this planning was to prove tragically flawed, mainly because the Germans were capable of anticipating the British intentions and taking effective counter-measures.

To play its part in these plans, the RFC continued a rapid expansion. By April 1915 there were three wings in France, consisting of seven squadrons and one flight, and an aircraft park. There were about eighty-five aeroplanes in the front line and about twenty in reserve. A much greater expansion had been authorised, now that the vital role of aerial reconnaissance and photography had been recognised. When it was proposed in early 1915 to increase the number of RFC squadrons to fifty the Secretary of State for War, Lord Kitchener, doubled the figure. A similar increase was under way in the RNAS.

However, the Germans did not wage war by the same rules as the British. The Second Battle of Ypres opened in the evening of 22 April 1915 with the infamous release of chlorine gas by the Germans towards a salient occupied by French colonial troops. It was seen from above by a reconnaissance aircraft of 6 Squadron, based at Poperinghe in Belgium, as a bank of yellow-green cloud emerging from the German trenches and drifting in the wind towards the French positions. The victims were not equipped with gas masks and those who were not suffocated fled, leaving a wide gap on the British right flank. German reinforcements moving up to the front were spotted by RFC reconnaissance aircraft and duly bombed, while the 1st Canadian Division counter-attacked and held the line in an epic defence, in spite of enormous casualties.*

This gas attack did not deter the British and the French from continuing a spring offensive, although with limited success. In early May, kite balloons began to arrive on the Western Front, manned by the RNAS but

*The author's uncle, Company Sergeant-Major Thomas O. Nesbit of B Company 10th Battalion, 2nd Brigade, 1st Canadian Expeditionary Force, was killed in this battle. His battalion was one of two which led the counter-attack and of its 750 men only 150 remained after four days of fighting.

A kite balloon, used for spotting by both the RFC and the RNAS, photographed over trenches dug into farmland where the harvest had been gathered. The elongated 'sausage' shape and the drogues on the wire helped to steady the balloon, but observers frequently suffered from airsickness. These balloons were usually flown 3 miles from enemy lines but could be set on fire by gunfire from aircraft or artillery shells. Balloon observers were provided with parachutes. (East Anglian Photographic Collection)

The Royal Aircraft Factory FE2a was a two-seat biplane with a pusher engine which first flew in January 1915. The FE2b, with a more powerful engine, began to arrive in France during the following October. With two Lewis guns, one firing forward and the other upwards towards the rear, the aircraft proved effective against Fokker monoplanes. This FE2b serial 4903 of 18 Squadron, which was equipped with these machines from April 1916 to June 1916, was fitted with a C-type camera. (J.M. Bruce/G.S. Leslie Collection)

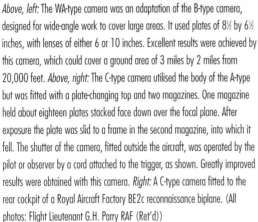

Above, left: The WA-type camera was an adaptation of the B-type camera, designed for wide-angle work to cover large areas. It used plates of 8½ by 6½ inches, with lenses of either 6 or 10 inches. Excellent results were achieved by this camera, which could cover a ground area of 3 miles by 2 miles from 20,000 feet. *Above, right:* The C-type camera utilised the body of the A-type but was fitted with a plate-changing top and two magazines. One magazine held about eighteen plates stacked face down over the focal plane. After exposure the plate was slid to a frame in the second magazine, into which it fell. The shutter of the camera, fitted outside the aircraft, was operated by the pilot or observer by a cord attached to the trigger, as shown. Greatly improved results were obtained with this camera. *Right:* A C-type camera fitted to the rear cockpit of a Royal Aircraft Factory BE2c reconnaissance biplane. (All photos: Flight Lieutenant G.H. Parry RAF (Ret'd))

The Royal Aircraft Factory RE7 was designed with a wider wingspan and a more powerful engine than its predecessor, the RE5, to carry a new and large 336-lb bomb as well as to carry out photo-reconnaissance duties. The first RE7 went to France in September 1915 to join 12 Squadron, and many squadrons had a few RE7s by the end of that year. The aircraft was slow and armed with only a single machine gun mounted in the front cockpit. Withdrawal from front-line service began at the end of 1916. This example was fitted with a vertical camera, possibly a WA-type. (J.M. Bruce/G.S. Leslie Collection)

working in co-ordination with the RFC. These balloons were modelled on the German *Drachen*, a sausage-shaped design with the forward segment filled with gas and the rear section with air. The mooring cable was attached to the nose while the observation car was slung from the rear. For stability, the balloon was fitted with a rudder and wind sails, as well as drogue streamers flying from the tail. This design was a great improvement on the spherical balloon, which could not ascend in winds of more than 20 mph and also rotated on its axis, making observation difficult. At the same time, the man-carrying kite could not be flown in winds of less than 20 mph and was also an unsteady platform, so that the kite balloon combined the best attributes of both. They proved of great use for artillery spotting at first, but those employed on both sides later became favourite targets for fighter aircraft.

By the Battle of Loos, which began on 25 September 1915, the three wings of RFC on the Western Front had grown to twelve squadrons with about a hundred and sixty aeroplanes, plus forty aeroplanes in reserve in two aircraft parks, as well as four RNAS Kite Balloon Sections in the front line. The three photographic sections were also equipped with mobile darkrooms, built on the backs of Leyland lorries, which supplemented the darkrooms improvised in cellars and sheds. Five weeks earlier, Sir David Henderson had returned to the War Office and Brigadier-General Trenchard had taken over command of the RFC in France.

The attempts of the British and the French to break the German lines made little progress, and it was in this period that air fighting developed significantly. The summer of 1915 had seen the introduction of a German machine which, for several months, was to prove the scourge of British reconnaissance aircraft. This was the Fokker E-type monoplane, designed by the Dutchman Anthony Fokker before the war but steadily improved until it combined clean lines with a good performance. It was armed with a forward-firing machine gun linked with an interrupter gear, so that the bullets passed the blades of the revolving propeller and enabled the pilot to take direct aim in the line of his flight. A new tactic was evolved for this machine, whereby the German pilot cruised at relatively high altitudes looking for prey and then dived down very steeply, preferably from out of the sun. The pilot fired at his victim and then shot past at high speed, usually before any retaliation could take place. An improvement on this tactic was introduced by Leutnant Max Immelmann, who developed a method of rolling off the top of a loop after the first pass, thus regaining altitude and repeating the attack.

The Royal Aircraft Factory and the Royal Flying Corps had shunned monoplanes after several fatal accidents had occurred in experimental machines, even though they were known to be very manoeuvrable as well as faster than biplanes. Stability and safety for air reconnaissance were the main criteria for new machines rather than air fighting qualities. Even the Blériot monoplane was redesigned as a biplane, being known as a BE, or Blériot Experimental, a type with a tractor engine; the early types had no armament. Another type was the FE or Farman Experimental, with a pusher engine at the rear of the cockpit; this enabled the observer to sit in the front cockpit and fire his machine gun without obstruction by the propeller. The third type was the most stable of all, the RE, or Reconnaissance Experimental, with a tractor engine and the observer sitting in front, supplied in the early machines with only small arms for defence. The last type was the SE, or Scouting Experimental, a single-seater with a tractor engine; the early type was fitted with no more than a couple of rifles angled to fire outside the propeller arc,

A wooden shed built on the side of 'Bocket Winckel' in the Belgian village of Eecke served as a 'cabine photographique' in May 1916. (East Anglian Photographic Collection)

A Leyland mobile photographic 'Prime Mover' of II Wing RFC in France. (East Anglian Photographic Collection)

Ground photographers at the entrance to a photographic workroom at Abeele in Belgium, close to the border with north-east France, in March 1916. RFC photographers were known as 'stickybacks'. (East Anglian Photographic Collection)

A 'Field Developing Box' used by the RFC in France during the First World War. The operator put his arms through the 'sleeves' to develop the plates. Printing was done by light reflected through the mirror. (Squadron Leader P. Lamboit, courtesy Photogrammetric Record)

The Sopwith 1½-Strutter was used widely for photo-reconnaissance as well as for bombing, ground strafing and coastal patrols. It first entered service with the RNAS in April 1916 but was soon in demand by the RFC, being popular as the first British aircraft with a machine gun efficiently synchronised to fire through the propeller. Strutters were replaced with Sopwith Camels on the Western Front during the summer of 1917 but were employed on home defence and on training duties, while others continued on Fleet charge. This example was serial 7777. (J.M. Bruce/G.S. Leslie Collection)

The twin-engined Caudron R4 was designed as a three-seater bomber, with the pilot in the centre cockpit and gunners in the other two. However, it proved too underpowered to carry the intended load and, from April 1916 to April 1917, was used by the French mainly for photo-reconnaissance. This machine had made an unconventional landing on top of a large shed. The French NCO underneath was smoking a cigarette. (J.M. Bruce/G.S. Leslie Collection)

The C (Coastal) airship was another non-rigid and first flew with the RNAS in June 1916. It carried a crew of 5 and had an endurance of about 11 hours at its full speed of 48 mph, or considerably more at lower speeds. This photograph of C9 was taken at Mullion in Cornwall in 1917. (J.M. Bruce/G.S. Leslie Collection)

but the later SE5a proved one of the most formidable fighters of the war.

The Royal Aircraft Factory BE2c was the type which most often fell victim to the Fokker monoplane, when the crews were flying over enemy lines for reconnaissance and photography. Its operational ceiling was 10,000 feet compared with the 11,500 feet of the Fokker, while its maximum speed in level flight was about 72 mph compared with 83 mph. By this time, the BE2c was fitted with a Lewis gun in the front cockpit, but the observer had a very limited field of fire above the propeller and wings, or to port and starboard. An additional hazard was the weather, for the crews usually encountered head winds on their return journeys against the prevailing westerlies.

There had always been enemy aircraft, but now the unfortunate BE2c earned the nickname of 'Fokker fodder'. The menace of the Fokker reached its height in October 1915 and continued for several months. The supremacy of this German fighter began to wane when the Nieuport Scout appeared in the spring of the following year and better-armed British reconnaissance machines such as the FE2 and the DH2 were introduced. For the rest of the war, control of the skies over the battlefields swung from one side to the other as new types were introduced, but life expectancy for RFC fliers always remained short, save for the most skilled or the very lucky. While British reconnaissance aircraft usually flew over enemy positions, the method of air photography employed by the Germans consisted mainly of flying low over their own lines and taking distant oblique shots of the Allied positions.

The expansion of the RFC and the replacement of aircrew losses could not have taken place without a huge increase in training facilities. Air photography was one of the subjects which needed to be taught, as well as the equally difficult photographic techniques required on the ground. Here it was Victor Laws who came to the fore once more. After nine months spent forming the photographic sections of the three wings in France and commanding these for six months, he returned to England in September 1915 at his own suggestion to set up a School of Photography at Farnborough.

At this time Laws was still a sergeant-major, having resisted offers of a commission, since this involved a drop in pay as well as the cost of bills in the officers' mess. However, in his new appointment his trainees were to include experienced photographers who had been recruited into the RFC to serve in the new function of photographic officer and in turn become instructors. It was clear that he would have to accept a commission, and on 7 November 1915 was discharged as a non-commissioned officer to become a 2nd Lieutenant in the Lincolnshire Regiment, seconded to the Royal Flying Corps. He was appointed immediately as commandant of the newly created RFC School of Photography at Farnborough.

Meanwhile, Moore-Brabazon and Campbell continued to develop cameras. The B-type was introduced as a modified and enlarged version of the A-type. This used 8½-inch by 6½-inch plates instead of 5-inch by 4-inch and had the means of fitting a tubular extension to the main body, giving longer lenses. This new camera was used mainly for oblique work, but a further adaptation known as the WA-type employed the same plate size and was used for wide-angle work. Another camera, the C-type, used the body and the plates of the A-type but was fitted with a semi-automatic device for changing the plates, using two magazines; this was introduced in the summer of 1915. At the end of 1916 the E-type followed the C-type, being made of metal and fitted with a remote control which facilitated the operation.

The Curtiss H12 flying boat, derived from the American H4, was assembled at Felixstowe for the RNAS, from 1916 onwards, from parts made in the USA. It was fitted with Rolls-Royce engines in place of the original Curtiss engines and carried a crew of four. The airman in this photograph was holding a Houghton-Butcher naval camera. This was a light hand-held camera used mainly for obliques, which employed glass plates and took 7-inch by 5-inch photographs. The cockpit was fitted with twin Lewis machine guns. (J.M. Bruce/G.S. Leslie Collection)

The SSZ (Sea Scout Zero) airship was introduced in 1916. It was provided with a control car modified so that it could float like a boat, in case of landings in the sea. The crew was increased to three and the pusher engine could be started by a mechanic standing inside the rear cockpit. This photograph of SSZ 25, showing a Houghton-Butcher naval camera, was taken at Mullion in Cornwall on 9 January 1918. (J.M. Bruce/G.S. Leslie Collection)

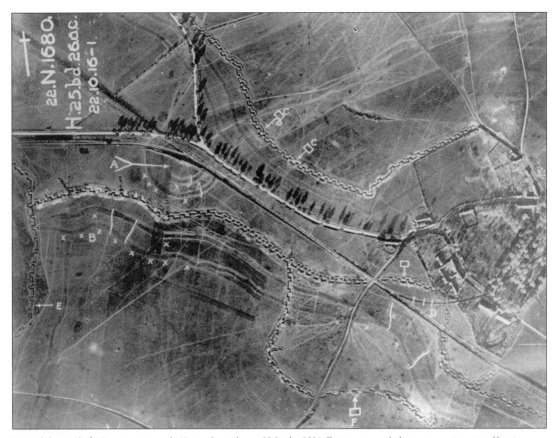

A vertical photograph of a German position on the Western Front taken on 22 October 1916. The interpreters picked out a strong point protected by wire defences at 'A', a passage through the wire at 'B', dugouts in reserve trenches at 'C', trenches marked out but not dug at 'E', and a series of dugouts connected by a trench at 'F'. (The late Squadron Leader J.E. Archbald)

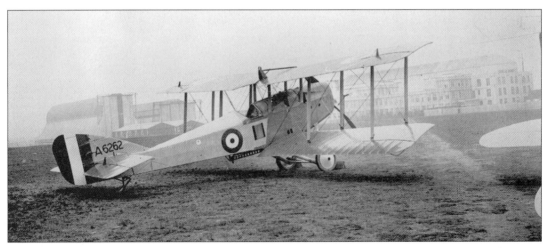

The Martinsyde 'Elephant' was a single-seater biplane designed for long-range escort duty, but it proved too heavy and unresponsive for this role. It first appeared on the Western Front in early 1916, and was soon employed as a bomber, for ground attack and air reconnaissance. In this photograph of serial A6262, a camera mount can be seen fitted beside the pilot's cockpit. (J.M. Bruce/G.S. Leslie Collection)

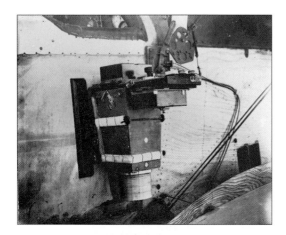

Above, left: The E-type camera, made from metal, succeeded earlier wooden types which sometimes suffered from distortion during changes of temperature and threw the lens out of focus. It was fitted with a remote control and could be mounted alongside the observer or behind his seat, with the lens through a hole in the fuselage. This E-type camera was photographed on the side of a Martinsyde 'Elephant'. *Below, left:* The L-type camera, which succeeded the E-type, required less attention than any previous models. It could be fitted either inside or outside the cockpit and was operated either by hand or automatically. When working on power, the plate changed every four seconds. This L-type was suspended in a spring mounting which converted vibrations into a mainly vertical movement, minimising blurring of exposures. (Both photos: Flight Lieutenant G.H. Parry RAF (Ret'd)) *Above, right:* An L-type camera fitted to a Sopwith Pup. The flexible cable was connected to a small windmill fitted to the aircraft, providing power drive for the mechanism of the camera. (J.M. Bruce/G.S. Leslie Collection)

The Royal Aircraft Factory FE2d, with a more powerful engine than the FE2b, began to enter service in June 1916. This FE2d serial A6516 of 20 Squadron, which was equipped with these machines from June 1916 to September 1917, was fitted with an L-type camera. (J.M. Bruce/G.S. Leslie Collection)

The Sopwith Pup was a small but robust fighter first delivered to the RNAS in the autumn of 1916, and then in large quantities to the RFC. Fitted initially with a single Vickers gun firing through the propeller, it was well-liked for its excellent flying and fighting qualities. The Sopwith Camel was introduced in the summer of 1917 and the Pup began to be withdrawn at the end of that year. Large numbers of Pups were transferred to training units, such as the example here. (J.M. Bruce/G.S. Leslie Collection)

In January 1916 the RFC in France underwent reorganisation to meet the growing needs of the BEF. It was formed into two brigades, each to support an army in the field. In turn each brigade was divided into two wings, a corps wing and an army wing. The corps wing carried out tactical photographic reconnaissance and artillery spotting for a distance of up to 5 miles beyond the enemy lines, while the army wing carried out strategic photographic reconnaissance and bombing duties beyond this distance. A third brigade was added in mid-February, so that by then there were six wings, each with its own photographic section. In addition, there was the headquarters wing.

By the opening of the notorious Battle of the Somme on 1 July 1916, the RFC in France had grown to four brigades, consisting of twenty-seven squadrons with a front-line strength of 421 aeroplanes, as well as four kite balloon squadrons. There were also 216 aeroplanes in reserve at aircraft parks, while further squadrons were forming in England. By then, the demand for constantly updated photography had become so enormous and urgent that the wing sections could not cope quickly enough. A small photographic section, usually consisting of one NCO and three men, had been established at every front-line squadron. The men had been trained at the School of Photography at Farnborough in such matters as developing and printing of plates, the mixing of chemicals, enlargement of prints, their lettering and numbering, lantern slides, the use and maintenance of aerial cameras, and the method of preparing maps from photographs. The techniques of photographic interpreters had also improved, with the use of shadows to determine height and depth playing an important part. As well as distinguishing trenches and strong points, the interpreters could pick out batteries, mortar and machine gun emplacements, wire, sniper posts, headquarters, tracks of troops and many other points of interest.

In preparation for the British and French assaults, all the German positions had been photographed by tactical and strategic aircraft, and maps had been constructed. A tremendous artillery bombardment opened, with the fire accurately directed from balloons and aeroplanes. This bombardment lasted for a week before 1 July, and then the infantry came out of the trenches and attacked. Unfortunately, the element of surprise which had been so crucial at Neuve Chapelle was lost, for the long bombardment had given the Germans ample warning of what was to follow. Their survivors rose up from their deep dugouts and mowed down the attackers.

These frontal assaults in the area of the Somme continued at intervals until the following November, with little territorial gain. Almost four hundred British aircraft were lost, including many of those employed on photographic reconnaissance duties. The Germans appear to have lost almost the same number of aircraft although, being outnumbered, they ventured over enemy lines far less frequently than the British or the French. Casualties on the ground were appalling: 450,000 British, 340,000 French and 530,000 German.

Back in England, Laws's promotion was rapid, for in September 1916 he was posted as a captain from the School of Photography to the headquarters of the Training Brigade, which had been formed two months earlier. His previous position was taken over by an air observer, Lieutenant Cyril Porri. On arrival in his new post, Laws realised that it would be preferable if he wore pilot's wings, since one of his functions was to give lectures to officers under training for flying duties. Before receiving his commission, he had been the only NCO entitled to wear the air

The NS (North Sea) airships were the last non-rigids constructed in Britain, the first of the series of twelve entering service in February 1917. They had a duration of about 21 hours at the full speed of 57 mph while carrying a crew of ten. This photograph of NS1 was taken at Longside in Aberdeenshire, a crew member seemingly balanced precariously on the gondola. (J.M. Bruce/G.S. Leslie Collection)

The Royal Aircraft Factory RE8 was designed to provide the RFC with a reconnaissance aircraft which was better defended than the BE2 series. It carried a machine gun firing through the propeller and either one or two machine guns mounted on a Scarff ring in the air observer's position. The RE8 entered service in November 1916 and continued until the end of the war. As with other designs from the Royal Aircraft Factory, the insistence on stability resulted in an aircraft which could be out-manoeuvred by enemy fighters. The machine shown here carried a camera mounted vertically. (J.M. Bruce/G.S. Leslie Collection)

Above, left: The LB-type vertical camera was developed when improved anti-aircraft defences forced reconnaissance aircraft to fly higher. The lens cones were up to the length of 20 inches, as shown in this photograph. However, the plates were only 5 inches by 4 inches in size, so that some definition of photographs was lost during enlargement of photographs taken from high level. *Above, right:* An LB-type vertical camera with a shorter focal length, shown here with RFC photographers in 1918. Such cameras were used for reconnaissance at lower level over enemy trenches. (Both photos: Flight Lieutenant G.H. Parry RAF (Ret'd))

observer's brevet, since he had made a number of photographic flights over enemy lines. He applied for a flying course and permission was granted provided he agreed to remain in the photographic branch; he duly passed his course as a pilot and was granted his wings. Within eleven months of obtaining his commission, Laws attained the rank of major.

Laws also took a hand in designing cameras, recognising the need for a type that required as little attention as possible by aircrews who were menaced by enemy fighters. The result was the L-type, which was introduced in early 1917 and represented a further improvement in aerial cameras, for it could be operated either by hand or automatically. The camera could be fitted in any position in the aircraft, since power for changing the plates and resetting the shutter was obtained through a flexible drive connected to a 'windmill' turned by the airflow. The pilot or observer simply pressed a trigger to take an exposure and start the

mechanism. When the camera was set to automatic feed, a locking device ensured that the trigger could not be pressed again until the camera was reset.

The L-type was followed by the LB-type, in which both Laws and Moore-Brabazon collaborated. This employed lenses with much longer focal lengths, up to 20 inches, which enabled aircraft with improved performance to fly above anti-aircraft fire and still obtain reasonable results. The camera was also easier to maintain, since the various sections of the mechanism could be removed with less difficulty for overhaul.

The heavy losses of photo-reconnaissance aircraft in 1916 resulted in some rethinking of tactics by the RFC. Fighters were employed to escort the camera-carrying aircraft but, when losses continued in the whirl of dogfights, cameras were mounted in some of the fighters on the assumption that these were better able to look after themselves. However, this did not prove satisfactory, for it was always necessary to fly straight and level while photographing and at such a time any aircraft was vulnerable. The idea of stripping a single-seater fighter of its armament, fitting it with a camera and then flying at altitudes which armed fighters could not reach, does not seem to have occurred to the planners. It was not until the Second World War that this very successful method was employed.

The Russian Revolution began in March 1917 and it became apparent to the Allies that the Germans would be able to transfer troops to the Western Front. Although the USA declared war on Germany the following month, she was unable to train and equip a large expeditionary force immediately. The RFC had increased its strength to about fifty squadrons by this time, and the Allies continued their attacks throughout the year, through the Battle of Arras, the Third Battle of Ypres and the Battle of Cambrai. Enormous losses were sustained while little was gained. By December, when the Russo-German Armistice was signed, the exhausted troops of the Allies faced a very ominous situation. In the same month, Major Victor Laws was posted to France as Senior Photographic Officer in General Headquarters, replacing Moore-Brabazon who returned to England as a lieutenant-colonel in order to take charge of photographic requirements at the War Office. By this time a vast photographic map of the whole of the Western Front had been built up, constantly amended as new photographs were brought in almost daily. With the aid of this map, the Allied commanders watched enemy preparations while battle-hardened German troops poured across from the Eastern Front.

When the Germans began their spring offensive on 21 March 1918, their movements behind the lines had been shrouded by fog for several days, enabling them to bring forward in secrecy troops and aircraft to key sectors. Their assault was heralded by an intense but short artillery bombardment: the infantry attack broke through the Allied lines and threatened to roll up and entrap whole armies. Suddenly, trench warfare was replaced by mobile battles, with the German positions reported only intermittently in the continuing bad weather. For a while, it seemed that even the fall of Paris was possible.

On 1 April 1918 the Royal Air Force was formed by merging the RFC and the RNAS, partly to unite their heavy bombers in an 'Independent Bombing Force' which it was expected would exact retribution on Germany for the bombing of London by Gothas. This RAF bombing force was located in France and commanded by Major-General Hugh Trenchard, who had been replaced during the previous January by Major-General John Salmond as General Officer Commanding the RFC. However, it was the less dramatic work of the photo-reconnaissance aircraft over the Western Front which was to prove of far greater importance to the Allies. Ten days after the formation of the RAF the Allied position on the Western Front had become so perilous that the British commander, Field Marshal Sir Douglas Haig, delivered a somewhat desperate 'backs to the wall' order of the day to his troops. On the following day the weather cleared and RAF photo-reconnaissance aircraft brought back precise details of the German positions, which were bombed and machine-gunned with considerable effect, and then subjected to artillery bombardment which was accurately directed from the air. More photographs were taken on that day than on any other since the outbreak of war. From this time, air surveillance was continuous. The German attacks were checked and, although further thrusts were made over the next three

The BM-type camera was an enlarged version of the LB-type, with a plate size of 9½ inches by 7 inches. It gave results of fine detail but its disadvantage was the weight, 85 lb with one magazine and 12 plates by comparison with 52 lb for the LB-type and 18 plates. This BM-type camera was installed in a Bristol F2B Fighter. (Flight Lieutenant G.H. Parry RAF (Ret'd))

months, enemy casualties became so severe that a halt was made in a salient between Soissons and Reims.

When the British and the French, reinforced by American divisions, began the first of their counter-attacks on 18 July, they possessed an air superiority of about five to one. The Germans had lost about half a million men during 1918 in their final bid to win the war, and could only fall back while fighting stubbornly. Their positions were recorded assiduously by photo-reconnaissance aircraft. In the course of 1918, over 10 million prints were delivered to the armies on the Western Front. Assaults fell on the Germans from different sectors in turn, by Allied armies who by then enjoyed

such an overwhelming strength with tanks, artillery and aircraft that they could frequently achieve surprise. The German artillery commanders knew that they had lost the war and that it would be only a matter of time before the fighting reached the Fatherland. The Armistice of 11 November 1918 ended the bloodiest fighting recorded in the history of mankind.

Of course, the Western Front was not the only theatre of the First World War in which the British carried out aerial photography, although by comparison the others were known as 'sideshows'. Of these, the débâcle of the landings at Gallipoli which began on 25 April 1915 is perhaps the most notorious. This operation was intended to deal a blow

The Royal Aircraft Factory BE12a was designed as a single-seat fighter and began to appear in December 1916. However, the few that were sent to France were not successful in their intended purpose and were transferred to the roles of photo-reconnaissance and light bombing. They served in Palestine, Macedonia and in some Home Defence squadrons. The aircraft shown here, serial A579, was fitted with a camera which may have been a LB-type for high-level photography. (J.M. Bruce/G.S. Leslie Collection)

The Hythe gun camera was invented in the First World War by Major David Geddes of the RFC, the commanding officer of the Hythe Gunnery School. It incorporated a shutter and a lens in a barrel casing which replaced the normal barrel of a Lewis gun. A film box contained a ruled glass screen on which the position of the target was recorded each time the gun was cocked and the trigger depressed. From the photographs, it could be ascertained whether the trainee was allowing the correct amount of adjustment for distance and deflection when aiming at a target aircraft, either from a stationary position on the ground or from a moving aircraft during training flights. (J.M. Bruce/G.S. Leslie Collection)

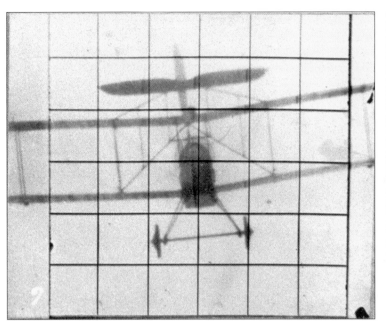

Above, left: An air-to-air practice shot with a Hythe gun camera on a DH2 of 20 Squadron. It was taken in July 1917 during training at Bailleul in France. (East Anglian Photographic Collection) *Above, right:* A vertical photograph of RAF Boscombe Down in Wiltshire, taken on 24 February 1918. This station was opened in 1917 as a training unit but closed at the end of 1919. It was re-opened in 1930 as a bomber station but on the outbreak of the Second World War became the home for the Aeroplane and Armament Experimental Establishment, which moved from Martlesham Heath in Suffolk. (J.M. Bruce/G.S. Leslie Collection)

The Airco DH4 was designed for day bombing and photo-reconnaissance at high speed, being capable of climbing above enemy fighters and thus operating without fighter escort. The first machines arrived in France in March 1917, when some were allocated to 2 Squadron. This was renumbered 202 Squadron on 1 April 1918. This DH4 of 202 Squadron was photographed at Bergues, near Dunkirk. It carried a camera housing beneath the fuselage. (J.M. Bruce/ G.S. Leslie Collection)

The Curtiss JN series was produced in the USA and Canada in response to a requirement of the US Army in 1914 for a biplane trainer with a tractor engine. The JN–3 was the first major version, becoming known as the 'Jenny'. This example, serial A3277, was fitted with a camera and employed at the School of Photography at Farnborough. (J.M. Bruce/G.S. Leslie Collection)

The Armstrong Whitworth FK8 arrived in France during January 1917, designed for photo-reconnaissance and bombing. Well-defended with a machine gun firing through the propeller and another on a Scarff ring, it was liked by aircrews, who considered it superior to the contemporary Royal Aircraft Factory RE8. The cameras in this photograph were an L-type mounted vertically beside the pilot and a P-type being handed to the air observer. (J.M. Bruce/G.S. Leslie Collection)

against Turkey after she entered the war in October 1914 as well as to relieve pressure on the Russians on the Eastern Front. Air reconnaissance and photography were carried out by the RNAS, which at the outset could muster only six seaplanes of dubious reliability, together with two aeroplanes which flew from the nearby island of Tenedos. The aircrews were inexperienced and communications with the ground were poor, so that the British and ANZAC troops who made the first landings were given little idea of the Turkish dispositions in the hills above and suffered heavy casualties. Thereafter reconnaissance improved until by June the enemy trenches had been photographed and maps prepared. Further landings, at Sulva Bay on 6 August, were almost unopposed, but the favourable situation was not exploited and the Allies evacuated their positions during the following December and January.

Reconnaissance aircraft of the RNAS and RFC supported the British, South African, and Belgian forces in German East Africa, now Tanzania. On 25 April 1915 an RNAS seaplane located and photographed the cruiser *Königsberg* in the Rufiji river, where she had been hiding since the previous October. The German cruiser was badly damaged by monitors on 4 July and then sunk a week later. Air photographs were also taken of the German forces, while routes through the featureless bush were mapped by the aircraft for use by the Allied troops. Nevertheless, the Germans waged a skilful guerilla campaign and some elements were able to continue fighting until the Armistice.

British and French divisions arrived in southern Macedonia, or Salonika, to help the Allied cause against the Bulgarians, who entered the war on the side of the Central Powers on 12 October 1915. The early air reconnaissances were made by the RNAS, but RFC aircraft arrived in July 1916. In addition to reconnaissance, photography and artillery spotting, the BE2cs and BE12s of the RFC carried out bombing attacks and air combats. The Bulgarian positions in the mountains were so well concealed, however, that the Allies were unable to detect the true deployment of artillery from dummies until winter, when tracks in snow showed up in photographs. The fighting continued until Bulgaria surrendered on 29 September 1918.

Italy entered the war on the Allied side in May 1915 and fighting took place in the mountains and plains against Austrian troops. The Italians held their ground for over two years but began to collapse when German forces joined the Austrians in October 1917. British and French troops were sent to reinforce the Italians, together with the RFC in brigade strength. Air superiority over the Austro-German Air Force was gradually achieved and the RFC's reconnaissance of enemy positions helped the Allies to regain lost ground and check further advances by the enemy.

In Palestine, the Turkish forces advanced across the Sinai Desert in early 1915 with the objective of taking the Suez Canal. Their movements were detected by a small number of British and French aircraft, and the attack was repulsed. An RFC wing arrived in November 1915, but the BE2cs were outclassed a few months later by German fighter aircraft which arrived to support the Turks. Nevertheless, the RFC continued its work of reconnaissance and photography, and the British began to advance in the spring of 1916, assisted by Arab guerilals who were in rebellion against Turkish rule. The RFC in the area was built up to brigade strength by 1 July 1916 and slowly began to gain ascendancy over the German fighters. In the following year the RFC commenced photographing the whole of the area facing the British, which hitherto had not been surveyed in detail. In spite of primitive

A vertical photograph of Valenciennes taken on 2 February 1918, with pit slag heaps showing as conical shapes. (The late Squadron Leader J.E. Archbald)

An oblique view of the airfield of Coudekerke, near Dunkirk, photographed in 1918. This was the home of the Handley Page 0/100 and Short landplane bombers of the RFC's 5th Wing. (J.M. Bruce/G.S. Leslie Collection)

Airmen of 15 Squadron, commanded by Major H.V. Stammers, receiving reconnaissance reports on 25 March 1918, during the first battle of Bapaume. The squadron was equipped with Royal Aircraft Factory RE8s and based for that day only at Le Houssoye in France. (Flight Lieutenant G.H. Parry RAF (Ret'd))

Towards the end of the First World War it was decided to give all plate cameras the prefix 'P', all film cameras the prefix 'F', and gun cameras the prefix 'G'. The LB-type camera, as in this photograph, became the P7. (Flight Lieutenant G.H. Parry RAF (Ret'd))

The P18 camera was similar to the P14, but it was made from metal and wood and could be fitted with 6-inch, 8-inch and 10-inch lenses. The P18 (without magazine) in this photograph was demonstrated in April 1993 by Brian C. Kervell, Curator and Archivist of the Museum at the Defence and Research Agency, Farnborough. (B.M. Harris)

The P14 camera was developed as a replacement for the A-type hand-held camera, for the purpose of taking oblique photographs. It was made entirely of metal and fitted with a 10-inch lens. The P14 (without magazine) in this photograph was demonstrated in April 1993 by Brian C. Kervell, Curator and Archivist of the Museum at the Defence and Research Agency, Farnborough. (B.M. Harris)

Photographic processing in the desert during the First World War. (Flight Lieutenant G.H. Parry RAF (Ret'd))

A mobile photographic laboratory employed by the RFC in Palestine. (The late Wing Commander H. Hamshaw Thomas MBE)

A photographic mosaic, prepared by the RFC in Palestine, being rephotographed. (The late Wing Commander H. Hamshaw Thomas MBE)

conditions in the desert, the photographic officer of V Wing, Lieutenant Hugh Hamshaw-Thomas, earned a high reputation for his work in building up mosaics from which accurate maps were constructed. The British advance continued and by early 1918 the Turkish forces had been ousted from Palestine.

In Mesopotamia, a small force from India landed at Basra in November 1914, in order to protect the oil wells in the area of the Persian Gulf, and advanced up the Tigris and Euphrates rivers towards Baghdad during the following spring. Air reconnaissance was rewarding in the flat terrain, but only a handful of RFC and RNAS aircraft were available and these flimsy machines suffered from the extreme heat while a high sickness rate among the airmen caused additional problems. The arrival of German fighter aircraft gave the enemy temporary air superiority. One Indian division was surrounded at Kut on the Tigris and forced to surrender in April 1916. It was not until early in the following year that the British troops, aided by reconnaissance aircraft which photographed and mapped extensive areas of enemy territory, resumed the offensive. The Allies occupied Baghdad on 10 March 1917, and newly arrived aircraft such as Spads, Bristol Scouts and SE5As steadily overcame the German Air Force. The Turks withdrew northwards in good order and the fighting continued until, in September 1918, two of their armies were trapped in defiles and the men, bombed and machine-gunned by the RAF, were slaughtered in their thousands. Turkey surrendered the following month.

CHAPTER FOUR

BETWEEN THE WARS

The RAF ended the First World War with over 25,000 aircraft, more than 100 airships, and about 316,500 uniformed personnel, including airwomen. It is estimated that there were some 4,000 aerial cameras in the front line areas in addition to about 5,000 being used for training in England. However, the RAF was rapidly run down from about 200 squadrons to only 33, with those based in the UK being divided into a Northern Area, a Southern Area and a Coastal Area. The Independent Bombing Force, which was still being built up at the end of the war, was disbanded. It seemed that the RAF could no longer remain as a separate force, for the War Office coveted the old RFC squadrons as an air arm while the Admiralty hoped that it would resume control of the old RNAS squadrons. Hugh Trenchard was given a gratuity and a baronetcy, and contemplated retiring to civilian life.

In January 1919 Winston Churchill became Secretary of State for War and Air, and had the foresight to see the potential of the RAF. He invited Trenchard to resume the position of Chief of Air Staff which he had held briefly in April 1918. Trenchard set about the task of revitalising the RAF and raising its esteem in the eyes of the public. He was aided by events abroad, for it became apparent that control of territories such as Iraq, which had been mandated to Britain, could be exercised most effectively by the combination of RAF squadrons and armoured cars. Moreover, this method

proved far less expensive than maintaining a considerable force of ground troops in parts of the British Empire, and was thus favoured by the government. Trenchard, who was eventually successful in expanding the RAF, occupied the position of Chief of Air Staff for nearly eleven years, before retiring with the undying reputation as the 'Father of the Royal Air Force'.

Within the post-First World War RAF, air photography did not receive a high priority, in spite of a memorandum written by Trenchard in 1919 which recognised that photography was one of the 'prime necessities' for which training was 'of extreme importance'. Training continued at the School of Photography at Farnborough but Trenchard decided that all photographic officers should be recruited from the General Duties, or flying, branch. Those officers who qualified from the long course were entitled to appear in the Air Force List with the letters PH after their names. Very few pilots or navigators were interested in this subject, however, preferring to qualify in subjects such as engineering, armament or wireless, as their specialisms. Similarly, the non-commissioned ranks who qualified at the School of Photography found that there were few opportunities for promotion. Military interpretation of aerial photographs remained in the hands of the Army, and officers were attached to RAF units for this purpose.

Nevertheless, the RAF gained a high reputation for its ability to provide

The F5 was the last of the Felixstowe flying boats, entering service soon after the end of the First World War. It became the standard flying boat of the RAF for the next seven years. This Felixstowe F5 serial N4198 was on the strength of 480 (General Reconnaissance) Flight at Calshot in Hampshire. (J.M. Bruce/ G.S. Leslie Collection)

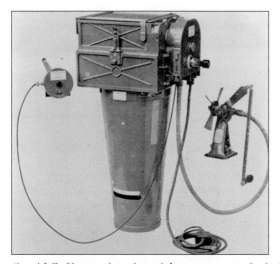

Above, left: The F8 camera, designed primarily for air survey, was introduced in 1919. It could be used for automatic overlapping of vertical photographs or for individual exposures. Power was supplied by either a windmill or an electric motor. Fixed-focus lenses of 7, 10, 14 and 20 inches could be fitted to the camera body. The film magazine contained 100 exposures of 7-inch by 7-inch, plus space for flight instrument recording, taken on a mean exposure of 1/90th of a second. Exposure was set by adjusting the lens aperture. The camera used a fixed-slit focal plane shutter and was fitted with a capping blind which screened the film during the shutter rewinding and film-changing operation. It was built on the unit principle, each unit being inter-changeable with the corresponding unit of any F8 camera. *Above, right:* An F8 camera on a gun mounting. (Both photos: Flight Lieutenant G.H. Parry RAF (Ret'd))

The Supermarine Southampton entered RAF service in August 1925 with 480 (Coastal Reconnaissance) Flight, replacing the long-serving Felixstowe F5s. This flight became 201 Squadron in January 1929. Four other maritime squadrons were also equipped with Southamptons, which remained in service for over ten years. They became famous for their long-distance flights, particularly a cruise to the Far East in 1927. This photograph is of Southampton II serial S1123. (J.M. Bruce/G.S. Leslie Collection)

The F24 camera, first introduced in 1925, could be either hand-held or installed in vertical and oblique positions with the operation fully automated. The picture size was 5-inch by 5-inch and the magazine contained rolls of film which gave up to 125 exposures. Three lenses were initially available, 6-inch, 8-inch and 10½-inch. The focal plane shutter speeds could be adjusted between 1/40th and 1/120th of a second, by adjusting the shutter spring tension. It was a reliable instrument which became the RAF's main general-purpose camera during the Second World War, and remained in service for thirty years. (Flight Lieutenant G.H. Parry RAF (Ret'd))

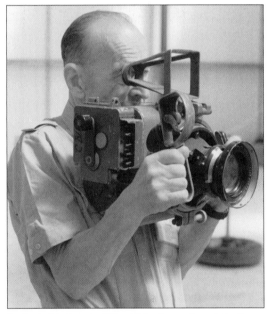

Ken Murch of the Tangmere Military Aviation Museum demonstrating the use of a hand-held F24 camera, without magazine. The rubber eye-piece is missing from the camera sight and the front of the lens has been modified. (B.M. Harris, courtesy Tangmere Military Aviation Museum)

A photographer handing a camera magazine to the air observer of an Airco DH4. (*Aeroplane Monthly*)

Lawrence of Arabia, photographed as an aircraftman. He joined the RAF on 30 August 1922 under the assumed name of John Hume Ross and, after basic training at Uxbridge, was posted in November 1922 to the RAF School of Photography at Farnborough where he began training as a photographer, a trade which interested him. His identity was discovered by the press and he was forced to leave the RAF in January 1923. He joined the Tank Corps as Thomas Edward Shaw in March 1923 but in the following year was hounded again by the press. Under this name (confirmed by deed poll in 1927) he transferred back to the RAF in August 1925. He then served at clerical duties and on seaplanes and motor boats, at home and abroad. His last station was RAF Bridlington in Yorkshire, where this photograph was probably taken. He left the RAF at the end of his engagement on 25 February 1935 and was killed in a motorcycle accident on 19 May 1935, at the age of forty-seven. (The late Wing Commander G.L. Buxton MBE)

photographs for the construction of mosaics, maps and charts. In one project from 1920 to 1922, the Egyptian Government funded a survey of the Nile. This was carried out from 14,000 feet by the DH9As of 47 Squadron and the Bristol fighters of 208 Squadron, over a stretch of 618 miles. The main objectives were to provide the Department of Irrigation of the Public Works Ministry with hydrological records of the behaviour of the Nile with respect to its ever-changing sandbanks, erosion of the river banks and the effect of the annual flood on the protection works.

In another scheme, the DH9As of 60 Squadron based at Risalpur in India undertook during 1923 a photographic reconnaissance of vast areas of the Baluchistan and Afghan borders. Three years later the DH9As of this squadron, by then based at Kohat, photographed an area of the Indus river from 12,000 feet, using P7 cameras with glass plates. A mosaic was prepared from the results, to assist the Indian Government in building dams to conserve water for agricultural purposes.

Another mapping survey was carried out in 1924 by the DH9As of 84 Squadron based at Shaibah in Iraq, when the Anglo-Persian Oil Company requested a mosaic of their Abadan refineries. Such photographic survey flights made in difficult conditions by overseas squadrons of the RAF preceded the work undertaken in later years by civil air survey companies.

Meanwhile, Squadron Leader Victor Laws was posted after the war to a newly created branch of the Directorate of Scientific Research at the Air Ministry, with the brief of producing a specification to meet the photographic necessities of the post-war RAF. His first step was to design a camera with a larger picture format and to replace glass plates with roll film.

Before the war, the companies of Dallmeyer in Britain, Goerz–Anschutz in Germany and Kodak in the USA, had dominated the field of lens and camera making. In the course of the war various British companies improved the difficult techniques of making the lenses and also produced most of the cameras used in British aircraft. Together with Harry B. Stringer of the Royal Aircraft Establishment, Laws designed in 1919 the excellent F8 camera, which used roll film with a 7-inch by 7-inch picture format and could be fitted with lenses of various focal lengths.

To the disappointment of Laws, the Air Ministry considered that the camera was too large and heavy for the aircraft in service at the time, as well as too expensive at £200 each, and by 1924 only thirty had been made. Some of these were sent to India for testing under tropical conditions, where, as will be seen later, they proved of immense value when the Japanese invaded Burma in 1942. Others were used in a photographic survey of the boundaries of British Somaliland in 1929. For this work an Air Survey Flight was formed under Flight Lieutenant G.S. Shaw, consisting of two Fairey IIIFs with seventeen personnel including four aircrew. The length of the survey area was 350 miles and excellent results were obtained, despite extreme climatic conditions. With day temperatures of 50°C, processing was carried out in tents at night when photographic solutions dropped to 25°C.

The Air Ministry required a smaller and lighter camera than the F8, and in 1925 the Royal Aircraft Establishment produced the F24, which gave a picture of 5 inches by 5 inches. This proved a highly reliable camera which, although it was not capable of the higher definition which Laws knew would be required in times of war, became the mainstay of the RAF's photographic equipment for many years. It fulfilled only limited requirements for military mapping, but the Archaeological Office of the Ordnance

Fairey IIIF Mark IVs of 47 Squadron, serials J9796, J9809 and J9802, fitted with floats, on the River Nile. The squadron was equipped with these general-purpose machines from December 1927 to January 1933 while based at Khartoum in the Sudan. It was employed on photo-reconnaissance while exploring the Cape to Cairo route. (The late Squadron Leader J.E. Archbald)

King George V and Queen Mary visiting the RAF's School of Photography at Farnborough on 16 May 1928, accompanied by the commanding officer, Wing Commander Victor Laws. (The late Group Captain F.C.V. Laws CB, CBE, FRPS)

Group Captain F.C. Victor Laws CB CBE FRPS. He was also mentioned in despatches twice and awarded the US Legion of Merit and the French Croix de Guerre. (The late Group Captain F.C.V. Laws CB, CBE, FRPS)

The Armstrong Whitworth Atlas, the first aircraft designed for Army co-operation, entered service in October 1927. Its duties included artillery spotting, photo-reconnaissance, reporting by W/T, picking up messages by means of a hook on the undercarriage, and attacking with bombs or machine guns. The observer in this Atlas serial J9956 was busy taking photographs from his exposed position. (*Aeroplane Monthly*)

The Hawker Audax entered RAF service in 1931, as the Army co-operation version of the Hawker Hart. It had a message-collecting hook on the undercarriage and could be distinguished from the Hart by its long exhaust pipes. In this photograph of an Audax trainer and photography pupils at Farnborough, taken in 1934, Flight Sergeant Don Munro had his hand on the leading edge of the lower wing while the engine was running. (The late Squadron Leader D.J. Munro)

An F24 camera being handed to a leading aircraftman photographer in a Hawker Audax trainer, with another F24 (manually operated, with sight) on the ground. (*Aeroplane Monthly*)

The Vickers Vildebeest, originally designed in 1928, remained the only torpedo bomber available to front-line squadrons of the RAF in the years immediately before the Second World War. It was also employed on maritime reconnaissance. This Vildebeest III serial K4589 was a three-seater on the strength of 22 Squadron before Bristol Beaufort torpedo bombers arrived at the end of 1939. (The late Squadron Leader N. Hearn-Phillips AFC, DFM)

Vickers Vincent serial K6364 of 47 Squadron, one of those which replaced Fairey IIIFs from July 1936 onwards and continued in service with the squadron until July 1940. This modified version of the Vickers Vildebeest could carry a long-range tank in the place normally occupied by the torpedo. With an endurance of up to nine hours, Vincents helped survey the route along the Nile used by flying boats of Imperial Airways. (*Aeroplane Monthly*)

Survey used the camera for recording sites from the air. Almost all aircrew trained with this camera before, during, and even after the Second World War, and looked upon it with considerable affection.

Victor Laws became dissatisfied with his lack of advancement at the Air Ministry but in October 1924 was posted back to Farnborough, once more to take charge of the School of Photography, where he remained for six more years. He was promoted to wing commander in January 1927 and became a revered figure to his staff and the trainees, being known as 'Daddy' Laws – although not to his face, for he was a severe but fair disciplinarian. His next posting was in October 1930 when he moved away from the photographic branch to become the commanding officer of the Aircraft Depot at Hinaidi in Iraq.

When Laws returned to England in February 1933 to take up the post of station commander of Farnborough, he decided that RAF photography was, in his own words, 'at a dead end'. Very little was being done to develop cameras and air photography, while the skill of photographic interpretation remained with the Army. The only minor encouragement had occurred the previous year when the Under-Secretary of State for Air, Sir Philip Sassoon, announced an annual competition and trophy for 'any regular unit in the home commands normally carrying out air photography', other than the School of Photography.

At this time Britain had not yet recovered from the Great Depression, and all public spending was severely restricted. The RAF still numbered only about forty squadrons, in spite of a proposed expansion to fifty-two which had been decreed in 1923. It was still equipped with biplanes and, although some of these machines were beautiful in appearance and a pleasure to fly, most were little more than advanced versions of those which had

flown in the First World War. In September 1933, Laws retired from the service to take up a lucrative civilian post in charge of a photographic survey in Western Australia.

As it happened, Laws left the RAF at a time when public awareness of the need for strong armed services was beginning to stir. The assumption of power in Italy during 1922 of Benito Mussolini and the fascist dictatorship had caused little disquiet in Britain, but the appointment of Adolf Hitler as Chancellor of Germany in January 1933 was potentially a different matter. It soon became known that German aircrews were receiving military flying training as 'civilians' and that German civil aeroplanes were easily capable of conversion to warplanes, in spite of the conditions of the Treaty of Versailles which prohibited the formation of a German Air Force. The National Socialist philosophy of the German rulers, with its extreme nationalism and overtones of race hatred, gave people in Britain pause for thought. Perhaps the terrible conflict of 1914–18 had not been a 'war to end all wars' after all. RAF bomber stations were concentrated in the south of England, against any enemy across the Channel, but in the mid-1930s it became apparent that a far greater threat was developing from across the North Sea.

In 1934 the British Government decided to increase the strength of the RAF as rapidly as possible to seventy-five squadrons, and then to one hundred and twenty-eight squadrons within five years. Specifications for new aircraft were prepared, and these were to lead eventually to the development and construction of monoplanes such as the Hawker Hurricane, the Supermarine Spitfire, the Bristol Blenheim, and the Short Stirling. In February 1935 Hitler defied the League of Nations by creating the Luftwaffe, and the race to re-arm began. Mussolini invaded Abyssinia in October of that year and started bombing villages as well as using poison gas.

Fairey Gordon serial K1776 of 35 Squadron, which was equipped with these machines from July 1932 to August 1937 and based in the Sudan for part of this period. The Gordon was employed as a day bomber and as a general-purpose aircraft, including reconnaissance. The aircraft in this photograph was converted from a Fairey IIIF, being fitted with a Panther radial engine in place of the Napier Lion. (*Aeroplane Monthly*)

A photographer handing an LB-type camera with a 4-inch or 6-inch lens to the air observer of a Fairey Gordon of 40 Squadron, which was equipped with these aircraft from April 1931 to November 1935. The photograph is dated 13 May 1932, when the squadron was based at Upper Heyford in Oxfordshire. It seems that some squadrons of the RAF were still using this camera of First World War vintage (renumbered the P7 after the war) although the F24 had come into service a few years earlier. (*Aeroplane Monthly*)

Hawker Harts of 39 Squadron flying over the Himalayas from their base at Risalpur in India. These were light day-bombers which first entered RAF service in 1930, and their duties also included photo-reconnaissance. Harts proved very successful and continued with 39 Squadron until July 1939. (The late Wing Commander F.H. Isaac DFC)

Hawker Hind serial K5558 of 107 Squadron, photographed at Andover in Hampshire in 1936. The Hind was a general-purpose aircraft, developed from the Hart, and was employed on Army co-operation work as well as on light bombing duties. (Flight Lieutenant S.G.E. Payne C Eng., MRAeS, RAF (Ret'd))

The RAF moved squadrons to Malta, Somaliland and Egypt. Requests were received from the Chiefs of Staff for vertical and oblique photographs of a number of Italian islands in the Mediterranean and areas of land along the coast of North Africa and the Red Sea. Some results were achieved by 1936 and then, in the following year, there were reports that the Italians were building an underground air base on the island of Pantellaria. On 15 May 1937 the Air Officer commanding RAF Malta was asked to obtain distant air photographs to determine the state of construction. The Italians had imposed a 6-mile prohibited zone around the island and care had to be taken to avoid any infringement. Two Supermarine Scapa flying boats of 202 Squadron from the seaplane base of Kalafrana were allotted the work but the first results, taken on 25 May with F24 cameras, were too indistinct to be of any use. Another attempt on 15 July by two Scapas of the same squadron proved somewhat more successful.

In the same year anxiety arose about threats to passage through the Suez Canal, and British Forces Aden requested photographic coverage of the island of Dumeirah in the Red Sea to verify reports of Italian military construction. The task was given to 8 Squadron, equipped with Vickers Vincents and based at Khormaksar in Aden. Pictures were taken in July from outside a 6-mile radius from 10,000 feet, using F24 cameras with 14-inch lenses, but the definition was so poor that they were almost useless. Fresh supplies of panchromatic film and filters were ordered, but did not arrive for two months. Better coverage took place on 1 October and the negatives were sent to the School of Photography for interpretation, perforce by an Army officer. In the subsequent report sent to the Air Ministry, Wing Commander Cyril Porri, who was once more the Commandant of the School of Photography, pointed out that there were no RAF officers trained in photo-interpretation. This revelation followed a report earlier in 1937 when, at a conference of Command and Group photographic officers held on 16 April, it had been stated that the RAF had little knowledge of photographic requirements in times of war.

One person who was alerted to the inadequacies of RAF photography was Squadron Leader Fred W. Winterbotham of the Air Ministry. Winterbotham had flown as a pilot with the RFC and on 13 July 1917 had been shot down in a Nieuport 17 of 29 Squadron behind German lines. After the war he had entered RAF Intelligence and became involved with MI6, a branch of the Secret Intelligence Service. He had met many of the German military leaders and had even become a honorary member of the Luftwaffe Club which was formed in Berlin in 1935.

Winterbotham was convinced that air photographs could provide a prime source of intelligence concerning the German defence system in the west, and discussed the matter with his French counterparts. The French were also interested in extending their espionage system in western Germany, and their Deuxième Bureau de l'Armée de l'Air approached Alfred J. Miranda Jr of the American Armament Corporation for advice. In turn, Miranda was a friend of Lieutenant F. Sidney Cotton, an Australian pilot who had flown on reconnaissance flights with the RNAS during the First World War. He was the inventor of the warm 'Sidcot' flying suit which later became standard issue to RAF aircrews.

After the war, Cotton had pursued an adventurous career in civil aviation and had also been a director of Dufaycolor, the camera film company. Miranda flew over from the USA to London in September 1938 and took Cotton to Paris to meet Paul Koster, the European representative of the American

The Westland Wapiti first appeared in 1927 as a replacement for the DH9A, which had given faithful service for many years. It was a general-purpose aircraft, employed on reconnaissance and light bombing. This all-metal Wapiti V serial J9754 was on the strength of 5 Squadron, which was equipped with Wapitis from May 1931 to June 1940 while on the North West Frontier of India. The photograph was taken at Miramshah in March 1938, during Army co-operation sorties, with Pilot Officer C.D. Lavers as pilot and Aircraftman S.G.E. Payne as gunner. (Flight Lieutenant S.G.E. Payne C Eng., MRAeS, RAF (Ret'd))

The airfield, on the upper left, at RAF Quetta, photographed in June 1935 from a Wapiti IIA of 5 Squadron. (Flight Sergeant A.W. Orford RAF (Ret'd))

Ground practice with the Mark III Hythe gun camera mounted on a Scarff ring, being carried out by a leading aircraftman in the mid-1930s on a day when the weather was obviously very chilly. (The late Squadron Leader N. Hearn-Phillips AFC, DFM)

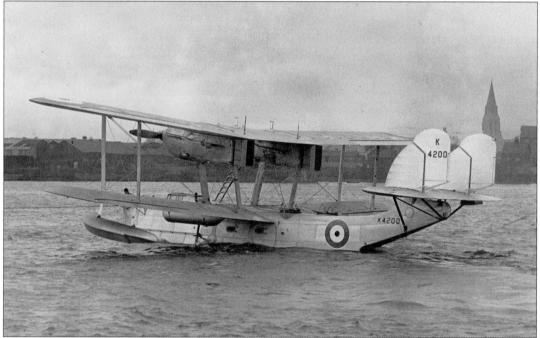

The Supermarine Scapa was an improved version of the Southampton, first entering squadron service in May 1935 and continuing until December 1938. This Scapa, serial K4200, served with 202 Squadron. (*Aeroplane Monthly*)

The Saro London entered service with 201 Squadron in April 1936, replacing the Southampton flying boat. It continued in squadron service until June 1940. (*Aeroplane Monthly*)

The Vickers Wellesley entered squadron service in April 1937 as a long-range bomber and became famous the following year when three aircraft broke the world's long-distance record, flying non-stop from Egypt to Australia. After the outbreak of the Second World War it was employed by 47 Squadron on reconnaissance work in Egypt. (The late Squadron Leader J.E. Archbald)

When the Westland Lysander entered service in May 1938, the RAF believed that it was the most suitable aircraft for carrying out tactical reconnaissance and photography for the Army. This Lysander II serial L4742 was on the strength of 4 Squadron, which went to France on the outbreak of war as part of the Air Component. By 1942 most Lysanders had been withdrawn from front-line duties, although they continued for the remainder of the war in air-sea rescue squadrons, as target-towers, and in special duty units. (*Aeroplane Monthly*)

Fitting an F24 camera in an oblique position beside the observer of a Westland Lysander. (*Aeroplane Monthly*)

Armament Corporation. The men discussed the possibilities of clandestine reconnaissance flights over Germany and agreed that these should be carried out in a civil aircraft.

The day after Cotton returned to London, he received a telephone call from Winterbotham, and the two men met on several occasions. They decided that the Lockheed 12A was the most suitable aircraft for the proposed flights. Although the normal range of this civil aircraft was about 700 miles, it could be fitted with extra fuel tanks which added another 900 miles. It was in a modified Lockheed 12 that during the previous year Amelia Earhart had attempted to circle the world along an equatorial route, although the enterprise ultimately led to her death. Miranda arranged for one of these machines to be sent from America, and it arrived at Southampton in January 1939. A pilot with engineering qualifications was required to work with Cotton and Winterbotham chose a Canadian who was nearing the end of his short-service commission with the RAF, Flying Officer Robert H. Niven. A private company was formed as a cover, the Aeronautical Research and Sales Corporation.

Cotton and Niven flew from Heston to Toussus-le-Noble, a small airfield about 15 miles south-west of Paris, where they were welcomed by a liaison officer from the Deuxième Bureau. On 25 March 1939 the two men flew at an altitude of about 15,000 feet over Krefeld, Hamm, Munster and the Dutch border, using a French camera with a focal length of 30 cm. The Black Forest was covered on 1 April and Wurtemburg six days later. On 9 April they covered the outskirts of Karlsruhe, Bruchsal, Heidelberg, Mannheim, Ludwigshafen and Eberbach, taking evasive action from an approaching German fighter at one stage. Later in the month they flew to Tunis and, on 25 April, covered the Italian port of Tripoli, the airfield of Castel Benito,

several other airfields and a number of gun positions. In the course of this series of flights, Cotton was annoyed to find that the French were not prepared to show him the photographs he had taken and decided that it was impossible to work with them.

The Lockheed was handed over to the French and two more of these machines were ordered, one for the French and one for the British. Winterbotham told Cotton and Niven that their first task would be to carry out photographic reconnaissance in the Middle East. The Lockheed 12As arrived at Southampton in early May and Cotton took charge of one of them, which was given the civil registration letters G-AFTL. He installed extra fuel tanks behind the cockpit, similar to the arrangement in Amelia Earhart's machine, and had three F24 cameras with lenses of 5-inch focal length fitted in the fuselage, one vertically and two obliquely, so that he could photograph a strip 11½ miles wide from an altitude of 21,000 feet. The holes in the fuselage were cut slightly larger than the camera lens, so that warm air from the interior was sucked out over them and prevented condensation. They were covered with small sliding panels when not in use, and these and the cameras were controlled electrically from the cockpit. Next, he invented and installed a Perspex pear-shaped window so that he could look downwards from the cockpit; this 'tear-drop' window proved so successful that over 100,000 were manufactured for RAF aircraft during the Second World War. Finally he had the Lockheed painted in a light duck-egg green, which he considered provided the best camouflage at higher altitudes, and registered this colour as 'Camotint'.

On 14 June 1939 Cotton and Niven flew to Malta, where they met Flying Officer Maurice V. 'Shorty' Longbottom, a pilot who had been involved with the reconnaissance flights during 1937 and was convinced of the

The Short Sunderland I entered service with the RAF in June 1938 as a general reconnaissance and anti-submarine flying boat. It proved an excellent platform for photography and the interior was sufficiently spacious to include an F24 developing tank, enabling a photographer to carry out inflight processing. The films were dried by festooning them along the lower deck. This photograph of a Sunderland of 210 Squadron was taken at Pembroke Dock in 1939. (Flight Lieutenant G.H. Parry RAF (Ret'd))

A Supermarine Stranraer I serial K7292 of 228 Squadron at Pembroke Dock in 1939, with a Sunderland in the background. Stranraers served with 228 Squadron from April 1937 until April 1939, when they were replaced with Sunderlands. (Flight Lieutenant G.H. Parry RAF (Ret'd))

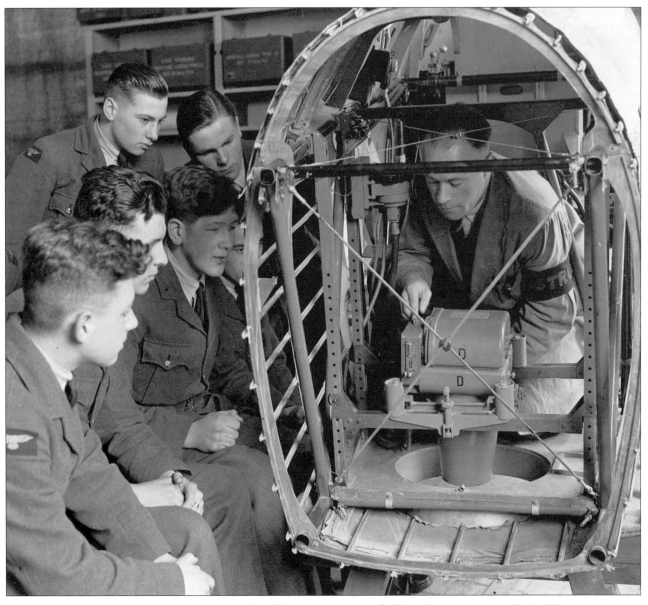

RAF trainee photographers receiving instruction in the installation of the F24 camera in a section of a fuselage, during May 1938. (*Aeroplane Monthly*)

RAF trainee photographers attending a lecture on the construction and assembly of the F8 camera, with a demonstration F24 camera on the right. The photograph was taken in September 1938. (*Aeroplane Monthly*)

importance of air photography in times of war. Cotton, who was now in the guise of a wealthy Englishman with a penchant for photographing ancient ruins, needed someone to help with the cameras and the films, and Longbottom was allowed to join his clandestine team for a single day. On 15 June they flew to Sicily and covered Comiso, Augusta, Catania and Syracuse before returning to Malta, where the photographs proved to be excellent, but Longbottom was not allowed to accompany them on further flights. Nevertheless, the three men were able to discuss their ideas concerning the most suitable RAF aircraft for photographic reconnaissance, and their conclusions were to produce very significant results a few months later.

At dawn on 16 June, Cotton and Niven left Malta to photograph the Italian-held islands of Cos and Leros in the Dodecanese and then headed for Cairo, where they landed. On 19 June they covered the port of Massawa in Italian Eritrea, but after flying inland, found that Asmara was swathed in cloud. They turned to land at the British island of Kamaran in the Red Sea, and then continued to RAF Aden. On the following day, Cotton took off to examine a possible submarine base on the peninsula of Hafun in Italian Somaliland, and returned with some photographs showing the construction in progress. On 21 June they flew back to Kamaran and then, on the following day, photographed some parts of Massawa which they had not covered on their previous run, before landing at RAF Atbara in the Sudan, where the results of their work were collected by a Blenheim and flown to RAF Heliopolis. They then flew to Cairo and headed back to Malta on the following day, en route photographing Italian airfields and military installations at El Adem, Tobruk, Derna, Bernice and Benghazi. From Malta, they landed back at Heston on 25 June.

The next task was to take some further photographs over Germany. Fortunately, Cotton had been given the sales rights for Dufaycolor film in Europe, and a German combine was interested in this product. Cotton and Niven flew the Lockheed to Berlin on 26 July 1939, but did not carry cameras on that occasion. However, the aircraft had been modified to take two Leica cameras in the wings, concealed by sliding panels, and these were carried on a 'business' trip to Frankfurt on 28 July, where there was also an international air meeting. The Lockheed was much admired at Frankfurt, and they took the Commandant of Tempelhof airfield, who was at the gathering, for a pleasure flight during the following day. They passed over Mannheim, where Cotton secretly took a series of photographs. On the return trip to Heston, Cotton and Niven took photographs of the Siegfried Line.

A further flight to Berlin took place on 17 August, and on the return trip the two men managed to take pictures of targets north of Berlin. The cameras were removed from the wings for another trip on 22 August but on the return flight they used hand-held Leicas to take photographs of German warships at Wilhelmshaven. These were received so enthusiastically by the Admiralty that Cotton was asked if he could take some photographs of the German Frisian islands, Heligoland and the island of Sylt. He took off with Niven on 27 August, accompanied by a young lady photographer to help with the Leicas, under the guise of a business group heading for Copenhagen. They photographed airfields in the Frisian group and took some excellent shots of Sylt, but Heligoland was covered with fog.

On the morning of the day that Hitler sent his troops into Poland and received an ultimatum from Britain, 1 September, Cotton was asked by the Admiralty for information about the German fleet in its home ports. A

Before the outbreak of the Second World War, the RAF allocated the task of long-range strategic photography to the Bristol Blenheim IV, known as the 'long-nose Blenheim'. Attempts were made to operate over Germany in daylight but the aircraft was far too lightly armed and could not fly high enough; many were shot down by German fighters. This photograph is of a Blenheim IV of 90 Squadron, a training squadron based at Upwood in Huntingdonshire from 19 September 1939 to 4 April 1940. (The late Squadron Leader J.E. Archbald)

A vertical F24 camera being handed to the observer of a Blenheim IV. (Flight Lieutenant G.H. Parry RAF (Ret'd))

Above, left: F. Sidney Cotton in 1941. (The late Wing Commander F.S. Cotton OBE) *Above, right:* Squadron Leader Maurice V. 'Shorty' Longbottom DFC. In June 1939, when he was a flying officer, he accompanied Sidney Cotton and Flying Officer Robert Niven on a clandestine flight over Sicily in a Lockheed 12A. The following August, he submitted to the Air Ministry a memorandum recommending the use of unarmed Spitfires for strategic reconnaissance deep in enemy territory. After the outbreak of war he joined the new Photographic Development Flight which was formed at Heston. He was later attached to Vickers-Armstrong as a test pilot and in April 1943 was partly responsible for testing 'Upkeep' mines in Lancasters and 'Highball' mines in Mosquitos, the bouncing bombs invented by Dr Barnes Wallis. He was killed at Weybridge on 6 January 1945 when testing Vickers Warwick V serial PN778, one of the general reconnaissance versions used by Coastal Command for anti-submarine work. (Flight Officer Constance Babington Smith MBE, WAAF)

Sidney Cotton's Lockheed 12A at Spaceport Executive Airport, Titusville in Florida, photographed on 11 March 1991 by Graham Dinsdale, who had retired from the RAF a few months previously. It had been restored to flying condition. Although displaying registration NC116IV, the correct registration was N12EJ. Owned by Steve R. Oliver, the former spy-plane is in natural metal overall with an orange cleat line and orange on the nose and engine cowlings. When flown by Sidney Cotton before the Second World War, it was painted in Camotint, a light duck-egg green. (Sergeant G. Dinsdale RAF (Ret'd))

few hours later, Niven took off in a single-engined Beechcraft monoplane, which had been painted in Camotint and added to the Heston flight, on a further flight to these ports and came back with some photographs of Wilhelmshaven. These last three photographic flights impressed on the Admiralty the advantage of frequent coverage in order to determine the movements of enemy units.

While these events were taking place, Longbottom had been recording his discussions with Cotton and Niven in Malta. These were submitted to the Air Ministry in August 1939 in a memorandum entitled 'Photographic Reconnaissance of Enemy Territory in War'. Longbottom concentrated on strategic reconnaissance, which at the time was considered by the RAF to be the province of the new Bristol Blenheim IV. He argued that the use of a single light bomber to photograph deep in enemy territory was extremely dangerous, for it invited the attention of enemy fighters and anti-aircraft fire, and the results might not be brought back to base. He recommended the employment of a fast single-engined machine, stripped of radio and armament so that it could carry extra fuel tanks. The aircraft would be camouflaged and fly high enough to be almost invisible from the ground in clear weather. Its operating altitude would be beyond the reach of anti-aircraft fire while reliance would be placed on speed to avoid enemy fighters. In cloudy weather, it would descend low enough only to take photographs and then take cover once more. Longbottom assumed that the best aircraft for such stategic photographic reconnaissance was the new Spitfire I.

This was a remarkable document to be written by a junior RAF officer, and no immediate action was taken. The proposals seemed revolutionary at the time, although after a few months they were to become standard practice in the RAF. Longbottom was blessed with the gift of foresight, as was Generaloberst Werner Freiherr von Fritsch of the Wehrmacht who forecast in 1938 that 'the military organization which has the most efficient reconnaissance unit will win the next war'. Neither Longbottom nor von Fritsch were to survive the conflict which began with Britain's declaration of war on 3 September 1939, but the words they left behind were to prove absolutely correct.

CHAPTER FIVE

SIDNEY COTTON'S AIR FORCE

The ability of the RAF to reconnoitre and photograph enemy activity on the outbreak of the Second World War was not of the highest order. Of course, most bomber and maritime aircraft could carry the F24 camera on daylight operations and the aircrews were trained in its use. Systematic photography for the purpose of gathering intelligence was, however, vested mainly in two types of aircraft. Within the Air Component of the British Expeditionary Force which was sent to France, tactical reconnaissance and photography was one of the functions of five squadrons of Westland Lysanders, while strategic reconnaissance and photography behind the German lines as far as the Rhine was entrusted to four squadrons of Bristol Blenheim IVs. Whatever the merits of these two aircraft, it is certain that both were very vulnerable to the attentions of Messerschmitt Bf109 fighters, particularly when flying alone. The Lysander depended mainly on manoeuvrability at low level to escape German fighters. The Blenheim was even less fortunate, for its service ceiling was only 22,000 feet, bringing it within the range of heavy anti-aircraft fire on long-distance flights as well as attack by enemy fighters, which were about 100 mph faster than their quarry. Moreover, the use of the F24 camera with its limited definition compelled aircrews of the Blenheim to fly at no more than 12,000 feet, so that in clear weather their missions became almost suicidal; when they were partially protected by cloud cover

photography was often impossible.

However, a few high-ranking RAF officers were aware of the defects in the service's photo-reconnaissance and were receptive to ideas for improvement. In July 1936 the home-based RAF, consisting of the Air Defence of Great Britain and various Area Commands, had been reorganised into Bomber, Fighter and Coastal Commands, to meet the steady expansion of the service. The nucleus of a photographic interpretation section, known as AI 1(h), had been formed at the Air Ministry in March 1938 under Squadron Leader Walter H.G. Heath. Soon afterwards, Bomber Command had set up a similar section, commanded by Squadron Leader Peter J.A. Riddell and staffed by graduates of the Army Interpretation course at Farnborough. A small photographic interpretation team, consisting of three Army officers trained at Farnborough, accompanied the RAF to France.

During the first few weeks of the 'phoney war' which characterised the beginning of the conflict, the photographs brought back by RAF aircraft did not provide adequate intelligence of the enemy's activities and possible intentions. In this early period, Bomber Command was prohibited from attacking the German homeland, for fear of retaliation on British cities by the Luftwaffe, so that its sorties were mostly confined to dropping propaganda leaflets at night. Only the warships of the Kriegsmarine were considered legitimate targets for attack by

The premises of Aerofilms Ltd and the Aircraft Operating Company at Wembley, photographed in 1936 or 1937. The photo-interpretation skills of the staff were used by the RAF's Photographic Development Unit at the beginning of the Second World War, and both companies were taken over by the Air Ministry in April 1940. (Squadron Leader P. Lamboit RAFVR, courtesy Hunting Aerofilms of Borehamwood)

Civilian photo-interpreters using mirror stereoscopes, which gave the impression of depth and solidity to aerial photographs. (Squadron Leader P. Lamboit RAFVR, courtesy Hunting Aerofilms of Borehamwood)

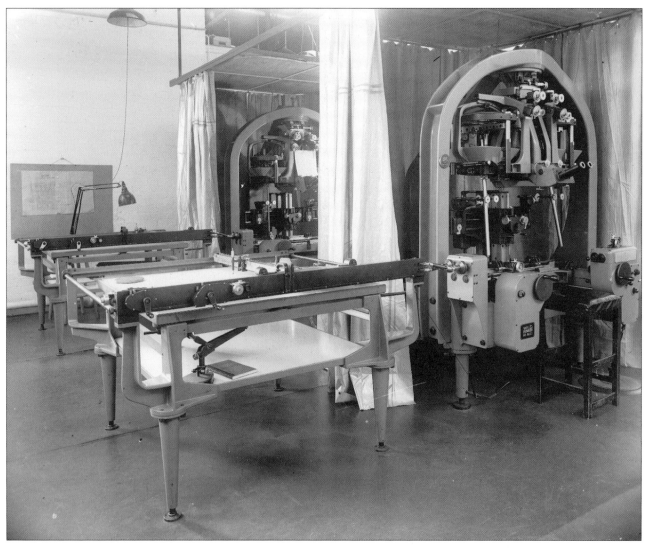

The Wild A5 'Stereo-autograph' machine, manufactured in Switzerland and originally belonging to the Aircraft Operating Company. It was taken over by the Air Ministry and used for map production by the Central Interpretation Unit. (Squadron Leader P. Lamboit RAFVR, courtesy Hunting Aerofilms of Borehamwood)

The Wild A5 'Stereo-autograph' machine being used by a civilian operator. (Squadron leader P. Lamboit RAFVR, courtesy Hunting Aerofilms of Borehamwood)

both the RAF and the Royal Navy. Of course, Sidney Cotton's exploits were known to the intelligence services and the Admiralty had no hesitation in approaching him for help with a somewhat delicate matter. The personal assistant to the Director of Naval Intelligence, Ian Fleming (who was later to achieve fame as the author of the James Bond novels), suggested that Cotton use his private aircraft to investigate the possibility that the Germans had set up refuelling bases for U-boats along the west coast of neutral Eire.

Cotton and Niven made a reconnaissance sortie in the Lockheed 12A at 10,000 feet on 12 September 1939, but no refuelling bases showed up on the photographs. They were asked to make another at 2,000 feet but meanwhile Wing Commander Fred Winterbotham had made an arrangement for Cotton to visit the Director General of Operations at the Air Ministry, Air Vice-Marshal Richard Peck, on 15 September. On the morning after this meeting Cotton was introduced by Peck to the Vice-Chief of the Air Staff, Air Marshal Sir Richard Peirse. The two senior officers discussed with Cotton the difficulty the RAF was experiencing in obtaining photographs of Dutch ports, where movements of German naval units had been reported, primarily because the F24 cameras kept 'freezing up' at medium level.

Cotton explained that the trouble was probably caused by condensation, not freezing, and decided to demonstrate his own proficiency. Without obtaining authority, he took off with Niven in his Lockheed during the same afternoon and came back with excellent photographs of Flushing and Ymuiden, which he showed on 17 September to a meeting of RAF officers, all of whom were astonished and some rather indignant. The outcome was Cotton's appointment on 22 September 1939 to the RAF, as a squadron leader with the acting rank of wing commander and the duty of commanding a special photographic

reconnaissance flight under Fighter Command's 11 Group, operating from Heston, which at that time was a civil airport. Authority for the formation of this unit, part of the Secret Intelligence Service, had been granted on 15 September. Winterbotham had hoped to assume this command, but Cotton was chosen. The initial establishment provided for a commanding officer, a photographic officer, an adjutant, four officers for flying duties and nineteen other ranks.

The new unit, known as the Heston Flight, was opened on 23 September. Squadron Leader Alfred 'Tubby' Earle, a pilot/photographer who had been an instructor at the School of Photography at Farnborough where he had done a great deal to launch and foster a Boy Entrant's training scheme, was appointed to take charge of the photographic development. Flying Officers Bob Niven and 'Shorty' Longbottom were the first of the four operational pilots, and they were later joined by Flying Officers Hugh C. Macphail and S. Denis Slocum, as well as other pilots when the unit expanded.

The first photographers in the unit were Sergeant S.R. 'Wally' Walton and Leading Aircraftmen Whinra Rawlinson, Ron Mutton and Jack Eggleston, all of whom had passed through the School of Photography at Farnborough and were also available for aircrew duties. There were also five fitters, three flight mechanics, two flight riggers, an electrician, an instrument maker and three general aircraft hands.

The only aircraft on the strength of the new unit were Cotton's Lockheed and Beechcraft, both of which carried out further flights along the west coast of Ireland as well as off Belgium and Holland. Although Cotton had protested that they would be of little use, two Blenheim IVs were sent to Farnborough on 21 September for modification. These were rubbed down to a smooth finish, with all airflow spoiling cracks blocked up.

Group Captain Fred Winterbotham CBE. Born on 16 April 1897, he served as an RFC pilot in the First World War and became a PoW after being shot down behind German lines while flying a Nieuport fighter of 29 Squadron. He entered RAF Intelligence at the Air Ministry in the 1920s and managed to ingratiate himself with prominent Nazis in Berlin during the 1930s. He was associated with Sidney Cotton's clandestine flights over Italian and German installations before the Second World War and later helped to organise the RAF's new Photographic Development Unit. In April 1940 he organised the decryption of German 'Ultra' signals at the Government Code and Cypher School at Bletchley Park and then he liaised with the Allied high command with the flow of information from these decrypts. He died in January 1990. (Flight Officer Constance Babington Smith MBE, WAAF)

The Avro Anson, which first entered service in 1936, was the standard reconnaissance aircraft in Coastal Command at the outbreak of the Second World War. With a range of only about 790 miles and an armament consisting of a single machine gun firing forward and another in the turret, it was not adequate for its duties. After the German Blitzkrieg it was relegated to the roles of trainer and transport. Nevertheless, it was liked for its reliability, being known as 'Faithful Annie', and remained in RAF service until 1968. The Anson on convoy duties in this photograph was from 502 Squadron, which was equipped with these machines from January 1939 to November 1940 when based at Aldergrove in Northern Ireland. (The late Squadron Leader J.E. Archbald)

The Lockheed Hudson, modified from the Lockheed 14 Super Electra civil aircraft, began to replace Coastal Command's Avro Ansons in May 1939 for maritime reconnaissance and anti-shipping work. With a range of 2,160 miles and an armament of seven machine guns, it was a great improvement on its predecessor, the Anson. The Hudson in this photograph was on the strength of 48 Squadron when operating from the north of Scotland and the Shetlands. (The late Squadron Leader J.E. Archbald).

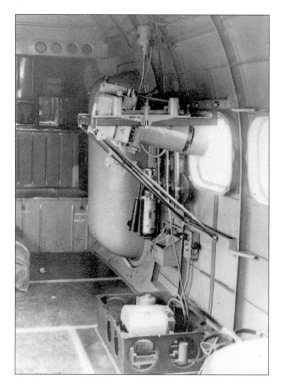

Oblique and vertical F24 cameras fitted in the fuselage of a Lockheed Hudson. (Flight Lieutenant G.H. Parry RAF (Ret'd))

Spinners were fitted to the propellers, the tail-wheels were made retractable, and tear-drop windows were installed. It was found these measures increased the airspeed by about 20 mph, and Cotton believed that the commander-in-chief of Fighter Command, Air Chief Marshal Sir Hugh Dowding, was so impressed by this result that he agreed to allocate two Spitfires Is to the new unit. In fact these two aircraft, serials N3071 and N3069, did not come from Fighter Command but were delivered to Heston on 30 October from Maintenance Command, by arrangement with Air Vice-Marshal Peck.

In his memoirs written in 1991 one of the airmen photographers, Jack Eggleston, wrote:

'The modification of aircraft for wartime photography involved experimenting with different cameras having focal lengths from five to forty-eight inches and varous camera fits. This was done in liaison with Mr Harry Stringer together with the aircraft and photographic experts of the Royal Aircraft Establishment at Farnborough, about twenty miles south-west. F24 cameras were fitted in vertical positions, as split pairs, forward-facing, and as side obliques. Cameras could be mounted in the wings, housed in small pods, or positioned in the fuselage. They were protected from condensation and the effect of cold by electrically-heated muffs or by air ducted from the engine. Particular attention was paid to obtaining vibration-free mountings for the fixed cameras. All experiments aimed for a camera fit which would be best for the particular conditions of air photo recce anticipated.

Modification also consisted of stripping the aircraft of all armament facilities and unwanted weight. An extra twenty to forty knots was obtained by minimising air-spoiling protuberances and by creating a smooth-polished skin surface. Even rivet heads were smoothed over. This task was carried out with a will by all airmen of the unit regardless of rank or trade. The Spitfires in particular were treated in this way and were experimentally sky-camouflaged for high or low level photography with variations of pale pink, light blue, duck-egg green and later a darker blue which was generally adopted. The pilot's cockpit canopy was modified with tear-drop extensions each side for visual navigation, and with marks to aid oblique target sighting. Extra fuel tanks were fitted and on later Spitfires the wing units were converted to hold many more gallons of fuel. It was said that the PR Spitfire was like a flying petrol bowser with cameras attached. This aircraft modification for wartime air photo recce was called "Cottonising".'

The Heston Flight was renamed No 2 Camouflage Unit on 1 November, in an additional attempt to preserve secrecy. The first two Spitfires retained only the normal tanks of 84 gallons, however, being known as Spitfire PR IAs. It was decided to test N3071 in operational conditions and the aircraft was flown on 5 November by Longbottom to Seclin, near Lille in France, while other personnel arrived in the Lockheed. The unit in France was named the Special Survey Flight and was kept isolated from RAF squadrons. Longbottom flew the first sortie in the Spitfire on 18 November, refuelling at Challerton near the Luxembourg border and then flying over the German frontier as far as Aachen. He brought back some excellent pictures from 33,000 feet, although Aachen itself was covered by cloud. After a period of settling into the French environment, part of the unit moved on 20 November to Coulommiers, about 30 miles east of Paris. The photographic section, under Sergeant S.R. Walton, was also based near there, at the village of Tigeaux. Jack Eggleston described the morale of the personnel back at Heston:

This example of the excellent photographs taken by the Luftwaffe shows part of Hamburg in February 1938. Of particular interest is the battleship *Bismarck* under construction in the Blohm & Voss shipyard, to the right of the six corrugated roofs at the bottom of the photograph. To the right of this shipyard is the armed yacht *Grille*. The cruise liner *Wilhelm Gustoff* is immediately above the six roofs. On the left of her is the heavy cruiser *Admiral Hipper*.
(The late Squadron Leader J.E. Archbald)

This photograph of the entire shipyard of Bremen was taken by the Luftwaffe in the early summer of 1939. The slipways top left are of particular interest. They show the ocean-going tug *Atlantis*, the SS *Rheinfels*, the keel of the battleship *J* (never completed) and the heavy cruiser *Lützow*. In the top centre is the heavy cruiser *Seydlitz* (never completed). (The late Squadron Leader J.E. Archbald)

'In the early days the unit was very informal, not at all like the regular air force we were used to. Some pilots, particularly the ex-bush pilot types, often wore desert boots, spotted neck scarves, and wore their caps at jaunty angles with their tunic top buttons undone. We young airmen delighted in this informality. No Station Warrant Officer to harass us, no working parades, no kit inspections and minimum saluting. We were "Sid Cotton's Air Force", working on and with the aircraft, all mucking in together and the end product was good quality intelligence-producing photography.'*

Although the pilots were flying fighter aircraft, they were expected to possess qualities which were different from those required by the men who flew on short missions hunting for enemy aircraft to attack. Their sorties were for long distances in conditions of extreme cold, while breathing oxygen most of the time. They needed to fly very steady compass courses and to be capable of pilot-navigation without any aids other than map-reading. Above all, they were expected to avoid combat and to bring their precious magazines of photographs safely back for interpretation.

Some RAF officers did not approve of Cotton's working methods, especially when the unit began to expand. The photographic officer at Heston, Squadron Leader 'Tubby' Earle,† asked to be transferred, leaving Cotton with the problem of finding a replacement. He selected a civilian

photographic technician, Paul Lamboit, who was then working with Dufaycolor in the USA. Lamboit was asked to return to Britain and duly commissioned as an acting pilot officer on 23 November but found, on Cotton's insistence with his superiors, that he was elevated to the rank of squadron leader in early January 1940.‡

Another who disapproved of Cotton was Victor Laws, who had finished his work in Australia and returned home to become managing director of the Williamson camera company. He was called up soon after the outbreak of war and posted as a wing commander on 24 November to the headquarters of the Air Component of the British Expeditionary Force in France, where he took charge of photography. In his own words, Laws regarded Cotton as 'quite out of control', although he rather grudgingly admitted that the 'one good thing Cotton did' was to introduce Spitfires into photographic reconnaissance.

In the knowledge that the static 'phoney war' could not last indefinitely, the Royal Aircraft Establishment at Farnborough formed its Mobile Photographic Printing Unit. This consisted of a 'J'-type trailer for processing and printing contact prints, a generator mounted on another trailer, and a vehicle containing a Graber multi-printing unit for mass production. Another vehicle carried a copy camera for enlarging or reducing, mounted on rails for ease of scaling. A stores vehicle completed this mobile unit, which moved to France in December with Sergeant Len Eades in charge, and set up in a village near Arras. Very bad weather hampered activity in the last weeks of 1939 and Eades received orders to move

---

* After retirement from the RAF, Jack Eggleston became an instructor and also worked in a voluntary capacity as the curator of the museum at the Joint School of Photography at RAF Cosford. In 1993–5 he helped the author to write his book.

† Alfred Earle continued his distinguished career in the RAF and also opened the School of Photography at RAF Cosford in 1965. He retired with the rank of Air Chief Marshal in 1966 and died in 1990.

‡ It was Paul Lamboit, as the historian for the post-war Association of RAF Photography Officers, who first persuaded the author to embark on this book.

A photo-reconnaissance Spitfire of 212 Squadron on an airfield in France, possibly Seclin or Coulommiers. It seems to have been a warm day in late spring, with some of the airmen in shirt-sleeves. (Squadron Leader P. Lamboit RAFVR)

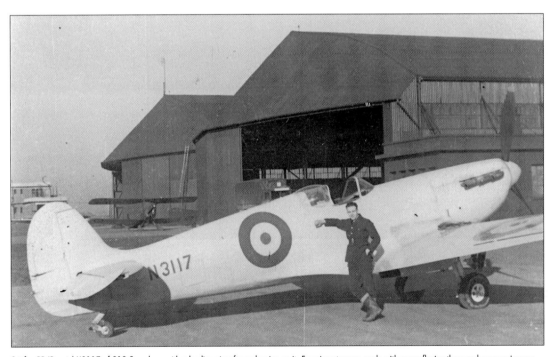

Spitfire PR IB serial N3117 of 212 Squadron, with a leading aircraftman leaning on it. Experiments were made with camouflaging these early reconnaissance Spitfires in light blue, light green and even light pink. This photograph was taken at Seclin in France before the German Blitzkrieg of May 1940. (Warrant Officer J.H. Eggleston RAF (Ret'd))

Two of the earliest pilots of the Photographic Development Unit, photographed at Heston in 1940. Left to right: Pilot Officer Spencer L. Ring, Pilot Officer S.G. 'Bill' Wise. Later, both commanded photo-reconnaissance squadrons. (The late Group Captain S.G. Wise CBE, DFC).

The Lockheed Hudson which was given the civil registration G—AGAR and used for the spy flights over Baku and Batum in March and April 1940. Conversion of a Hudson for photo-reconnaissance was made by removing the gun turret and other armament so that the aircraft's configuration closely resembled the original Lockheed 14 Super Electra civil aircraft. It was then fitted with cameras and an extra fuel tank in the fuselage. This aircraft was flown back to the Middle East in June 1940, where it was sometimes known as 'Cloudy Joe'. It was written off on 4 April 1941 after being badly damaged by an Italian CR42 while on the ground in Crete. (Wing Commander R.G.M. Walker DFC, RAF (Ret'd))

into Arras, where the equipment was installed in a building while the vehicles were jacked up. This move proved to be unwise in the light of later events.

The bad weather restricted the operations of the solitary Spitfire PR IA in France, but by 26 January 1940 Cotton was able to claim that it had photographed 5,000 square miles of enemy territory without loss, whereas up to the end of 1939 the RAF Blenheim IVs had photographed only 2,500 square miles and lost 16 aircraft in the process, while the French had photographed 6,000 square miles with the loss of 60 aircraft. In order to obtain the photographs, however, the Spitfire had frequently flown without authority over the neutral countries of Belgium and Holland. These statistics, which Cotton had obtained partly from the French, made a deep impression on the Air Staff as well as Air Marshal Sir Arthur S. Barratt, who commanded the British Air Forces in France.

Meanwhile, on 16 January 1940, the first Spitfire fitted with an auxiliary fuel tank of 29 gallons, behind the pilot, arrived at Heston. This was known as the Spitfire PR IB, the radius of action being increased from about 240 to 325 miles. It was painted in medium blue, which became the standard camouflage for photo-reconnaissance aircraft. On 10 February, Longbottom flew it from Debden in Essex and photographed Wilhelmshaven, for the Admiralty was particularly anxious to verify whether the powerful new battleship *Tirpitz* was still in dry dock.

Cotton had begun to fall out with the Air Staff, who pointed out that RAF interpreters could not cope with photographs taken from 33,000 feet with the F24 camera, since the small 5-inch by 5-inch format lacked definition. However, Cotton was equal to any problem. He had already made contact with Major Harold 'Lemnos' Hemming, AFC, the managing director of a survey organisation located at Wembley in Middlesex. This was the Aircraft Operating Company, which had considerable experience of surveys for oil companies in the Middle East and employed a number of photo-interpreters. Together with its associated company Aerofilms, it was equipped with a sophisticated photogrammetric mapping machine made in Switzerland, the Wild A5. This remarkable machine gave eight times magnification, so that far more information could be obtained from the F24 photographs than by using a hand stereoscope.

Without obtaining permission, Cotton had already begun to use the staff in these two civilian companies for the interpretation of RAF photographs, the work being carried out in strict secrecy. One of the photo-interpreters, Michael Spender, was able to verify that the *Tirpitz* was still in dock. Cotton passed this information to the Admiralty, where it came to the attention of the First Sea Lord, Winston Churchill. The Air Staff had little option but to accept the approval of the Admiralty, but resentment of Cotton's unorthodox methods was growing. Negotiations began for bringing the Aircraft Operating Company and Aerofilms, together with their staff, under the authority of the RAF, but were not completed until 31 May.

The titles of the reconnaissance units were changed yet again. On 17 January 1940, No 2 Camouflage Unit was renamed the Photographic Development Unit, and on 10 February 1940 the detachment in France known as the Special Survey Flight became 212 Squadron. To the cheerful and industrious airmen in both units, however, these alterations were made solely to confuse the enemy, and they still served in 'Sid Cotton's Air Force'. A step was taken to bring both units in conformity with regular RAF practice by the appointment on 9 February of Squadron Leader Geoffrey W. Tuttle as second-in-command. Tuttle was a former fighter pilot who had earned his DFC in north-west India and was also a qualified aeronautical engineer. He proved the ideal choice for the position, handling the administration with great skill but at the same time ensuring that the spirit of enterprise was not stifled.

In the first months of 1940 the Spitfires in France were employed on essential work for the British Expeditionary Force under Lord Gort. It was fully appreciated that the Germans would try to attack through Belgium, around the northern flank of France's Maginot Line, but the maps available dated back to 1914. A photographic survey was required and this was begun by the Spitfires of 212 Squadron, operating from Seclin, without authority from the neutral country of Belgium. The 'cover story' was that the pilots were engaged on training flights but made errors in navigation or experienced compass trouble. The whole of Belgium was photographed in this way and up-to-date maps were duly constructed.

Meanwhile, the unit at Heston concentrated mainly on work for the Admiralty. In February, it was allocated three Lockheed Hudsons, the RAF's name for the Lockheed Super Electra 14 civil airliner. Cotton devised a scheme whereby these aircraft, without gun turrets or armament but with auxiliary tanks in the fuselage, went out and reported on weather conditions over enemy territory. If the skies were sufficiently clear, a Spitfire then took off and continued at high level over German targets. In cloudy weather, the Hudson came down briefly to take photographs and then climbed back into cover. But a tragedy occurred on 3 March when one of the aircraft, with its livery of duck-egg green, was shot down over Kent by a puzzled Hurricane pilot. The machine was flown by Flying Officer Denis Slocum, who was killed with the photographer Leading Aircraftman Mutton and the wireless operator LAC Butcher, although the co-pilot Sergeant Peid managed to bale out.

On the day before this tragedy, 2 March, the new Spitfire PR IB was employed on a task which the short-range Mark IA had been unable to perform. Bob Niven took off from Heston and flew over neutral Holland making for the Ruhr, a target which had been too distant and too dangerous for the reconnaissance Blenheims of Bomber Command. He photographed Duisburg from 30,000 feet, turned east as far as Dortmund and then made a reciprocal run back to the Rhine. German fighters pursued him over Luxembourg but he managed to outstrip them and landed safely at Heston. A mosaic of the photographs was prepared from this successful sortie, which Cotton showed triumphantly to the Commander-in-Chief of Bomber Command, Air Marshal Sir Edgar Ludlow-Hewitt. The C-in-C was so astonished and impressed that he put forward a proposal that his command should take over the whole photographic unit, but this was not accepted by the Air Staff.

The first loss of a Spitfire occurred on 22 March when Flying Officer Claude M. Wheatley took off from Stradishall in Suffolk for north-west Germany but did not return. He was reported to have been shot down by an enemy fighter and lost his life. It is possible that his 'tell-tale' condensation trail, which was one of the inevitable hazards of the high-flying Spitfires, was spotted by the Germans in time to arrange an interception.

One of the Hudsons at Heston, serial N7364, was fitted with extra fuel tanks in the fuselage and used for an exploit which in retrospect seems almost bizarre. At the time, Russia was still bound by the Non-Agression Pact which had been signed with Germany on 24 August 1939 and was supplying large quantities of oil from the Caucasus region to Germany, which had almost no natural sources of its own and was forced to rely mainly on synthetic oil derived from coal for its military forces. Russia was regarded as a potential enemy by the British

Above, left: Squadron Leader Hugh C. Macphail DFC, one of the early pilots in the Photographic Development Unit. In March and April 1940 he commanded an expedition to spy on the Russian oilfields at Baku and Batum. In March 1941 he took over command of No 2 Photographic Reconnaissance Unit at Heliopolis in Egypt. (The late Squadron Leader H.C. Macphail DFC). *Above, right:* Flying Officer Frederic E. Burton DFC. He was the captain of the Hudson, or Lockheed 14 Super Electra serial N7364, which was given the civil registration G–AGAR and made spy flights from Iraq over the Russian oilfields at Baku and Batum in March and April 1940. (The late Wing Commander F.E. Burton OBE, DFC). *Right:* Flight Lieutenant R. Idris Jones, who made detailed interpretations of the photographs taken during the spy flights over Baku and Batum in March and April 1940. The Germans sentenced him to death *in absentia* following their discovery of the Anglo-French plans after the fall of France, but could not carry out their sentence. Afterwards, RAF interpretation reports were no longer signed. (The late Squadron Leader R.I. Jones)

and French, and their Combined Chiefs of Staff devised a scheme which they thought might knock out both Germany and Russia in a single blow. This was no less than the destruction of the Caucasus oil supplies by bombing, employing five squadrons of Martin Marylands of the French Air Force to be moved to northern Syria, and four squadrons of Blenheim IVs and one of Vickers Wellesleys of the RAF to be moved to northern Iraq. Both the French and the British expressed optimisim about the likely results, probably unwisely, and the British ordered the Photographic Development Unit to carry out a preliminary photo-reconnaissance of the main Russian production centres at Baku, Batum and Grozny.

Slocum had been the only pilot in the unit qualified to fly the Hudson, but 224 Squadron at Leuchars in Fifeshire had been equipped with these machines since May 1939. A call was sent to this squadron for a pilot to fly on a secret mission and Flying Officer Frederic E. 'Monty' Burton, DFC, was chosen. Burton had flown Hudsons operationally since the outbreak of war and had participated in the destruction of two Dornier flying boats, including a Dornier 18 which was shot down on 5 September 1939, the first victory of the RAF in the war. He travelled to Heston and crewed up with Squadron Leader Hugh Macphail, who was put in charge of the mission whereas Burton was the captain of the aircraft. Together with a photographer, Leading Aircraftman Alan J. 'Tubby' Dixon, and a fitter, Leading Aircraftman Bissett, they took off in the early morning of 23 March 1940 for the destination of RAF Habbaniya, near Baghdad in Iraq.*

* Before his death in 1984, Wing Commander Freddie Burton, OBE, DFC, discussed this matter in great detail with the author, using his pilot's log book and other memorabilia. Details of the plan of attack can be found in the Public Record Office, under AIR 14/770 and AIR 23/980.

They arrived at Habbaniya three days later, having made overnight stops at Marseille, Malta, and Helwan in Egypt. Here they changed into civilian clothes and put aside their service documents, for they had been issued with civilian passports. The RAF markings were painted out of the machine, using a pot of Camotint brought with them for the purpose, and the civil registration G-AGAR was painted on the fuselage and wings. Burton took the aircraft up for a fuel consumption test on the following day, and it was decided that Baku and Batum were within range but that they could not make a return trip to Grozny.

They photographed the whole of Baku on the coast of the Caspian Sea, in brilliantly clear weather on 30 March, making a series of line overlaps to provide a mosaic, although the town proved to be far bigger than it appeared on the thirty-year-old map which had been given to them. The photographs were developed on their return to Habbaniya and they flew them down to the RAF headquarters in Heliopolis. Returning once more to Habbaniya they took off on 5 April and crossed the neutral country of Turkey making for Batum on the coast of the Black Sea. On this occasion flak opened up on them as they began their photographic runs at 20,000 feet, although it burst harmlessly beneath them. After the first run Macphail spotted an Me109, probably one of a batch provided to Russia by Germany, climbing towards them. They beat a hasty retreat to the safety of the Turkish border and returned to Habbaniya with the target only partially covered. The RAF men returned to Heston, arriving on 13 April. Three copies of the developed photographs were brought back and interpreted by Flying Officer R. Idris Jones for distribution to the Intelligence Section of the Air Ministry, the British Secret Service and the French Secret Service. The photographs were accompanied by a target map and details of the plan of attack.

While these strange events were taking place, a new long-distance version of the Spitfire arrived at Heston. This was fitted with a 30-gallon blister tank under the port wing as well as the 29-gallon tank behind the pilot, giving a radius of action of about 410 miles. The wing tank was counter-balanced by a blister under the starboard wing, housing two F24 cameras with 8-inch lenses. On 7 April, Longbottom took off in one of these machines, which was known as a Spitfire PR IC, and photographed Kiel for the first time, to the intense interest of the Admiralty, for the pictures disclosed preparations for the anticipated invasion of Norway which began two days later. One result was the shelving of the proposed attacks on the Russian oil fields, for the British and the French became engrossed in matters of more immediate importance.

The Germans began their anticipated attack through Belgium on 10 May and the British and French Armies advanced to meet them. In the campaign which followed, the front-line strength of the Blenheim and Battle squadrons was wiped out and the Lysander squadrons also suffered badly, in spite of the astonishing bravery of the aircrews. The Allied Forces reeled back from the Blitzkrieg and on 16 May Cotton received orders from London to evacuate to Heston. He chose to ignore this order but it was repeated on the following day and some of the personnel were flown back by various means.

Cotton's photo-reconnaissance aircraft continued to operate over the German lines for the next three weeks, even after Dunkirk fell on 4 June, and some aircraft which were sent down to Corsica and the south of France to photograph targets in Italy did not return home until 15 June, four days after that country entered the war. Unfortunately, Spitfire PR IB serial P9331 was left behind in

France and captured intact by the Germans, giving them a clear appreciation of the techniques developed by the RAF's reconnaissance unit. On 16 June, in a railway train at La Charité-sur-Loire, the Germans captured the French copies of the photographs taken over Baku and Batum by Burton and Macphail, together with the Allied plan of attack. They duly sent copies to Stalin and made a great show of righteous indignation on behalf of their 'ally', causing some embarrassment to the British Government. The photo-interpreter who signed these reports, Flying Officer R.I. Jones, was sentenced to death *in absentia* by the Germans. Future interpretation reports were therefore not signed, but of course the Germans were never able to carry out their threat.

Meanwhile, the RAE's Mobile Photographic Printing Unit was put back on the road and the vehicles set off towards Boulogne and then Cherbourg. However, the men were forced to abandon their vehicles and eventually returned home in a French aircraft, with their films, or from ports in western France.

The men of 212 Squadron set off on 9 June in the direction of Poitiers, while Cotton circled above in his Lockheed 12A. Cotton flew down to Marseille on 11 June to arrange the evacuation of his party by Hudson and also made other flights back to Heston. Some of the men patched up a damaged Battle which they found at Poitiers and then drove on to a small grass airfield at Fontenay-le-Comte, near the port of La Rochelle, arriving on 16 June. Cotton flew to this airfield to see that all was well with the men, whose morale remained astonishingly high, and then flew on to the airfield at Le Luc, near Marseille. Here he found that a Hudson sent to evacuate his men had been destroyed on the ground by an Italian air attack, but he arranged for them to be brought back by the

Photographic vehicles in June 1940 at the airfield of Fontenay-le-Comte, near the port of La Rochelle, ready to be blown up by the RAF men. They consisted of photographic trailers, trucks, a petrol bowser, a power unit and a van. After destroying the vehicles, the RAF men who were unable to take off in aircraft headed for Bordeaux. They boarded a collier and reached the UK in July. (The late Corporal C.E. Lloyd)

On 20 June 1940, five men from 212 Squadron escaped from France in Fairey Battle I serial L5360 of 88 Squadron. The aircraft had been attacked and forced down at Poitiers airfield, where it was abandoned. Some of the men from 212 Squadron patched up the bullet holes and replaced a damaged wing tip with a tree branch and some fabric. The aircraft was flown down to Fontenay-le-Comte, north-east of La Rochelle, by Flight Lieutenant L.D. 'Tug' Wilson, where the ground personnel cut cards for the privilege of flying back to England. The winners were (left to right): Leading Aircraftman Cook, Sergeant Walton and Sergeant Ward. The other was Leading Aircraftman Jim Muncie, who took the photograph. Wilson took off with his four passengers and reached Heston after a flight of four hours. (Sergeant J. Muncie RAF (Ret'd))

Fleet Air Arm. Back at Fontenay-le-Comte later that day, he and his men slept in the open and he then arranged for the evacuation of some of the party in a Bristol Bombay transport aircraft, while a few returned in the Battle and others in a collier from Bordeaux. By these and other means, all the men managed to return to England.

Cotton flew back to England on 17 June, together with Niven and four other passengers, landing at Jersey for the night and then on to Heston the following day. He sent his two remaining Hudsons back to Bordeaux to pick up other passengers and opened a letter which had been written to him on 16 June by the Permanent Under-Secretary of State for Air, Sir Arthur Street. The content was terse but polite, expressing appreciation of his work but informing him that the Photographic Development Unit was to be removed from his command and taken over by Wing Commander G.W. Tuttle, to serve under the orders of the Commander-in-Chief, Coastal Command.

CHAPTER SIX

BRITISH INTELLIGENCE

The replacement of Sidney Cotton as the commanding officer of the Photographic Development Unit was inevitable. He was a good master, to whom most of his RAF officers and airmen were devoted, but he was also a bad servant. A photo-interpreter who met Cotton when she was a young trainee in the WAAF, Constance Babington Smith, described him in her very readable book* as 'tall, quick, wolf-like, with horn-rimmed glasses and thick grey-white hair'. It is unlikely that a man of Cotton's entrepreneurial talents and impatient nature could have fitted into a service environment for the duration of the war, obeying orders he thought unsuitable or misguided. He was unable to accept the delays which were inevitable in an organisation which had been drastically run down between the wars. In his own words, attempts to make the RAF satisfy his requirements for equipment was 'worse than trying to extract diamonds from the Crown Jewels'.

Whatever his defects as an RAF commanding officer, however, Cotton deserved better treatment than was meted out to him. He was placed on the RAF Reserve List and made an Officer of the Order of the British Empire. This award, although prestigious, was not thought by his friends to have been sufficient recognition of the value of his achievements. After months of frustration he was invited on 3 March 1941 by Sir Arthur Street to resign his commission, and had no alternative but to do so. Thereafter, all his attempts to offer help with various ideas for improving Britain's prosecution of the war were steadfastly blocked by the authorities, which was considered to have been a shameful waste of his talents.

On the other hand, the appointment of Wing Commander Geoffrey Tuttle[†] to succeed Cotton was wholly admirable. He had been responsible for running the unit at Heston for several months and was highly respected by his officers and airmen. He was an experienced pilot, a qualified aeronautical engineer, and an excellent administrator. He was also fortunate in some respects, for the way ahead had been charted by Cotton while the value of his unit had come to be recognised at the Air Staff and even by the War Cabinet headed by the new Prime Minister, Winston Churchill. On 13 May 1940 the Commander-in-Chief of the Home Forces had advised the Chiefs of Staff that 'the most effective method of keeping a watch by air on German movements will be high altitude reconnaissance as often as practicable'. With the threat of an imminent invasion after the fall of France, the RAF heeded this advice.

---

* Constance Babington Smith, *Evidence in Camera*, London, Chatto and Windus, 1958.

† During several meetings before his death in 1989, Air Marshal Sir Geoffrey Tuttle KBE CB DFC FRAeS, was kind enough to encourage the author to write this book.

Above, left: Group Captain Peter J.A. Riddell, who commanded Bomber Command's air photographic section at the beginning of the Second World War. He devised the highly successful photo-interpretation procedures which were later followed by the RAF. In May 1944 he became the Senior Air Staff Officer for No 106 (Photo-Reconnaissance) Group when it was formed to co-ordinate and control all RAF and USAAF strategic reconnaissance work. *Above, right:* Air Marshal Sir Geoffrey W. Tuttle CBE CB DFC FRAeS, photographed as a Wing Commander. Born on 2 October 1902, he was awarded the DFC in 1937 while serving on the North West Frontier of India. After the outbreak of the Second World War, he served with the Advanced Air Striking Force in France. He took over command of the Photographic Reconnaissance Unit at Heston in June 1940 and was mainly responsible for its expansion before he was promoted and moved to other duties in November 1941. His distinguished career in the RAF continued until he retired in 1960. He died on 11 January 1989.

Wing Commander Douglas N. Kendall, a former staff member of the Aircraft Operating Company Ltd, who was commissioned in the RAF in January 1940. He was sent to join the small detachment of 212 Squadron in France, engaged on photo-reconnaissance over German territory. After the fall of France, he devised the procedures for the RAF's photo-interpretation and trained its personnel, with great success, and commanded the Photographic Interpretation Section at Medmenham in Buckinghamshire. From mid-1943 onwards, he co-ordinated the reconnaissance work on German 'V' weapons. (All photos: Flight Officer Constance Babington Smith MBE, WAAF)

The Spitfire PR ID entered service in October 1940. It was a modification of the Spitfire V, carrying 114 gallons of extra fuel in wing tanks as well as 29 gallons behind the pilot. It carried two F24 or F8 cameras. The type was later designated the Spitfire PR IV and became the mainstay of No 1 Photographic Reconnaissance Unit during 1941 and 1942. This photograph was taken in a blast pen at St Eval in Cornwall in 1941, where B Flight No 1 Photographic Reconnaissance Unit was based. (Sergeant J. Muncie RAF (Ret'd))

Spitfire serial N3117, converted to a PR IE from a PR IB, with two cameras in the wings pointed outwards for low-level work. It is believed that this was the only Spitfire converted to this configuration. It was first flown in this form on 3 July 1940 by Wing Commander Geoffrey Tuttle of No 1 Photographic Reconnaissance Unit. On 7 July 1940, Flying Officer Alistair Taylor flew the machine to Boulogne, where he took some excellent photographs below cloud at 300 feet. (The late Squadron Leader J.E. Archbald)

A Spitfire PR IV of B Flight, Photographic Reconnaissance Unit at St Eval in Cornwall, with the photographer Leading Aircraftman Jim Muncie sitting on the nose. This aircraft, serial P9385, began life as a Mark I but was later converted to a Mark IV. The 'teardrop' window on the cockpit hood, which gave the pilot a much better view, was invented by Sidney Cotton; over 100,000 were made. (Sergeant J. Muncie RAF (Ret'd))

Above: Split F24 cameras with 8-inch lenses, installed forward-facing in a 90-gallon 'slipper-type' drop-tank fitted to a reconnaissance Spitfire. (Flight Lieutenant G.H. Parry RAF (Ret'd))

Tuttle took over the unit on 21 June 1940. Seventeen days later, on 8 July, there was yet another change of name when it became the Photographic Reconnaissance Unit. On the same day, it was placed under the control of Coastal Command's No 16 Group. This was also a wise choice, for a number of reasons. By this time, the Germans controlled the whole of the European coastline from the north of Norway to the Franco-Spanish border. The likelihood of invasion necessitated continual reconnaissance of enemy ports while the seriousness of the threat to Britain's shipping lanes from German U-boats and capital ships was equally acute. If the Spitfires were to achieve maximum radius of action, it was necessary for them to operate from coastal airfields. Moreover, if the unit had been transferred to Bomber Command, there is little doubt that its limited resources would have been concentrated on bombing assessment flights, the matters being of less immediate importance than reconnaissance devoted to Britain's survival in her most critical period.

British Intelligence inherited from Cotton the nucleus of another organisation which was to play a prominent part in the war. This was the photo-interpretation unit which had been set up on 31 May 1940 when the Aircraft Operating Company at Wembley was taken over by the RAF. Originally known as the Photographic Development Unit (Interpretation), its name was changed on 6 July to the less clumsy Photographic Interpretation Unit. The functions of photographic processing and interpretation, hitherto carried out by the Royal Aircraft Establishment at Farnborough, were transferred to this unit. It had been joined on 26 June 1940 by Squadron Leader Peter Riddell, the most experienced interpreter in the RAF, who had already been recruited by Cotton from Bomber Command.

Riddell set about organising this strange new unit with an unquenchable energy, knowing that he had to satisfy the demands of the Admiralty and the Army as well as the three operational Commands of the RAF. It had already been recognised that women possessed the qualities of patience and perception which were required by photo-interpreters, and a number of young women in the WAAF had been recruited as trainees.

At the outset, Riddell was the only RAF officer in the unit, and one of his first actions was to ask for the Army interpreters who had escaped from France. He was also able to use the services of the civilian experts who had previously worked for the Aircraft Operating Company, some of whom were commissioned into the RAF. With the help of one of these men, Michael Spender, he was successful in attracting into the RAF unit a number of eminent academics who specialised in such subjects as cartography, mathematics, archaeology, geology and geography. In addition, Flight Lieutenant Hamshaw Thomas, who had been responsible for the success of photo-interpretation in the Middle East in the First World War and had since worked as a botanist at Cambridge, eventually joined the unit. One of Thomas's first tasks was to revise the Air Ministry's manual of photographic interpretation.

Riddell devised a method of interpretation which he divided into three phases. In the first phase, a preliminary report was prepared almost immediately after the aircraft had landed and the contents of the camera magazines were developed, sometimes from the negatives before they were printed. The second phase resulted in a report which was made within the following twenty-four hours, giving a more detailed appreciation of the enemy activity by comparison with earlier photographic cover. The third phase was made by the experts who specialised in various fields, providing discerning reports of

Gun cameras were superseded by ciné cameras when Hurricanes and Spitfires entered service. Although designed to assist in training, they also provided a record of air combat. The first to be electrically operated was the G42B, which carried a magazine containing 25 feet of 16-mm film and took 1,000 exposures. It was usually installed in a fixed forward position and operated automatically when the pilot pressed the firing button, but it could also be used as a free-handling camera by an air observer. (B.H. Harris, courtesy Tangmere Military Aviation Museum)

The G45 ciné camera was designed to replace the G42B ciné camera after numerous RAF fighters had been lost in the Battles of France and Britain. The intermittent drive of the latter was difficult to machine and production could not keep up with requirements. The G45 was designed to be loaded from the top or the side and could also be fitted in turrets in addition to the fixed-forward and free-handling positions. (B.H. Harris, courtesy Tangmere Military Aviation Museum)

This 35-mm ciné camera was donated by the film industry and fitted to the Spitfire VA serial W3185 flown by Wing Commander Douglas Bader. It was lost when this celebrated pilot was shot down or collided over Béthune on 9 August 1941 and taken prisoner. (Flight Lieutenant N. Jenkins RAF (Ret'd))

This posed photograph was intended to encourage recruitment into Group 2 trade of the WAAF, which included the maintenance of photographic equipment. The young lady was aiming a G28 gun camera, which was based on the Vickers K machine gun and produced negatives of 2½-inch by 2½-inch from a roll film. (The late Squadron Leader J.E. Archbald)

strategic value. For the second and third phases, these experts were eventually put in charge of interpretation sections entitled Airfields, Aircraft and Aircraft Industry, Army, Naval, Industries, Wireless, Communication, Camouflage, Damage Assessment, Plotting, Enemy Decoys and Photogrammetric. Supporting sections dealing with models and target material, press and public relations, and a print library were also added to this growing organisation.

The interpreters used small stereoscopes to view stereo pairs of vertical photographs, so that buildings and other objects stood up quite startlingly in three dimensions. Each became familiar within his or her specialised subject from a succession of photographs, and learnt to look for any unusual alteration among a mass of other details. Shadows were particularly important, and one of the interpreters, Squadron Leader Claude Wavell, later invented a spheroid device which he named an 'Altazimeter' for measuring the heights of objects in relation to the shadows they threw on the ground. On this the interpreter set the declination of the sun (i.e. the angle above the horizon) for the date, time and latitude of the object, together with the azimuth of the sun (i.e. its direction). These details were readily available from Air Almanacs and Astronomical Navigation Tables. The device then gave the height of an object by comparison with the length of its shadow, which was known from the scale of the photograph.

The Photographic Interpretation Unit soon became an indispensable source of intelligence for the Chiefs of Staff. The other main provider of intelligence was the Government Code and Cypher School, the nucleus of which had been set up by the Cabinet in 1919 and moved to Bletchley Park in Buckinghamshire on the outbreak of the Second World War. Its purpose was the protection of British cyphers and the decryptanalysis of enemy cyphers, usually obtained from the Britith 'Y' service which monitored enemy wireless transmissions.

In the 1920s the Germans had introduced a commercial version of an 'Enigma' machine, an electro-mechanical device which encyphered messages with a system of wired drums and wheels. This machine was adopted by the German Navy in 1926, the Army in 1929 and the Air Force in 1935, after some modifications had been made which were considered to render the system safe even if a machine was captured. The Germans were too sanguine in this belief, for considerable advances in breaking the various codes were made by Polish mathematicians before the war and this information was passed to the French and the British. However, the Germans made certain additional changes to the wheels and the codes, and it was not until their invasion of Norway that the British succeeded in breaking the codes used by the Army and the Air Force, although the Enigma used by the Navy, which employed additional wheels, remained impenetrable at this time.

Decryptanalysis and photo-interpretation, in both of which Wing Commander Winterbotham was closely involved, provided the Allies with their main sources of intelligence throughout the war. Of course, additional information was obtained through diplomatic channels, as well as from agents and very courageous resistance fighters in occupied countries, but these sources could not cover the great spectrum of information gleaned by the two main intelligence bodies.

Meanwhile, the photo-reconnaissance Spitfires and Hudsons continued to fly. On 1 July 1940, Tuttle moved A Flight to Wick on the north-east tip of Scotland for operations over the Norwegian coast, while B Flight was sent to St Eval in Cornwall to cover the west coast of France. C and D Flights remained at Heston to cover the enemy ports in the English Channel as well as the Belgian,

Dutch, Danish and German coasts. E Flight, formed for training on 27 July, was also based at Heston. Six months later, sections engaged on first phase interpretation were also set up at Wick and St Eval.

At the beginning of July 1940 a Spitfire IA was modified to carry an F24 in a blister under each wing, angled outwards at about 15 degrees below the horizontal so that photography could be carried out at extremely low level. On 3 July Tuttle flew the first operation in this machine, Spitfire PR IE serial N3117, but cloud covered the target. Flying Officer Alistair L. Taylor took off three days later and photographed Boulogne from 300 feet, then making a run in the other direction with the other camera.

At the end of July, another variant of the Spitfire arrived. This was the 'super long-range' Spitfire PR IF, which carried a 30-gallon tank in each wing as well as the 29-gallon tank behind the pilot. Fitted with two F24 cameras in the fuselage, it had a radius of action of about 650 miles, but this was still not sufficient to meet the demands of the Air Ministry or the Admiralty. By this time the unit consisted of only twelve Spitfires, of which eight were PR IBs, three were PR ICs and one was the PR IE. Nevertheless, these could carry out a surprisingly large number of sorties.

While the Battle of Britain raged in the summer and early autumn of 1940, the men of the Photographic Reconnaissance Unit flew 327 sorties, 183 of them in September. Reports that invasion fleets were being assembled in western France, Belgium, Holland, Germany and even southern Norway were checked by the Spitfire pilots, and their photographs revealed that invasion barges were assembling at Channel ports such as Dunkirk. Bomber Command carried out a number of daylight raids with light bombers against enemy ports and airfields, suffering severe losses on occasions. These attacks were made in addition to night operations over Germany itself. The threat of invasion petered out when intelligence reports confirmed that Hitler had suspended the military operation on 12 October 1940, after the Luftwaffe had failed to overcome the RAF.

Of course, there were casualties among the Spitfire pilots and Hudson crews, but the morale and spirit of the unit remained high, for the men were very proud of their role in the war. Some of these men lost their lives but others fell into enemy hands. Flying Officer Peter L. Dakeyne failed to return in a Spitfire on a low-level operation over the Belgian coast on 14 September 1940 and wrote to Tuttle from Dulag Luft, the German interrogation centre for the RAF at Oberursel near Frankfurt:

'I rather foolishly ran into AA fire whilst preoccupied and also distracted by a third factor. A direct hit stopped the prop, so rolled and fell out to land among troops! The machine made a spectacular crash full out! The prospect of a year or two here is infuriating but I hope that I will see you again – the last month or two had been to me – ideal! The best of luck!'

A letter also arrived from the same German PoW centre, from Flight Lieutenant James R.T. Smalley DFC, who had been shot down in a Spitfire over Kiel on 8 October 1940:

'Sorry I couldn't finish the job, Sir! Don't quite know what happened – big bang and fireworks. I just managed to get out, a bit battered but safe and sound and as happy as can be expected. Very good treatment, good quarters, food and company here – but of course I'm worried about and anxious for all my friends back home and long for news and long to be back with you all again. My love to all the boys, Sir – thank you for a very happy stay in your unit.'

The Consolidated PBY-5 of the US Navy was known as the Catalina I when it entered RAF service early in 1941. In spite of its slow speed, it proved a very effective reconnaissance aircraft in home waters and abroad. When fitted with long-range tanks, it had an endurance of up to twenty-seven hours. This example, Catalina IVA serial JX574 of 210 Squadron, was fitted with a Leigh Light for illuminating U-boats detected at night by radar. The photograph was taken in 1944, at a time when the squadron was based at Sullom Voe in the Shetlands. (*Aeroplane Monthly*)

The effect of a German parachute mine on the Imperial Airways hangar at RAF Heston on the night of 19/20 September 1940. Five reconnaissance Spitfires were badly damaged, as well as Sidney Cotton's Lockheed 12A which had to be shipped back to the USA for rebuilding. Most of the photographic equipment was recovered. (The late Corporal C.E. Lloyd)

Danesfield, the country house at Medmenham taken over by the RAF after the Photographic Interpretation Unit at Wembley received a direct hit from a German bomb on 2 October 1940. Nissen huts and other temporary buildings were erected as expansion continued. After the war the house was occupied by several organisations. It was opened as a five star hotel by a Dutch chain in 1989 but severely damaged by fire. (Squadron Leader P. Lamboit RAFVR, courtesy Hunting Aerofilms of Borehamwood)

Hudson N7301 was shot down on 26 October 1940 on an operation over the Scheldt estuary and the pilot, Flight Lieutenant Arnold A. Rumsey, wrote to Tuttle from Oflag IXA on 7 November:

'You will be glad to know Phillips, Williams, Dixon and Broome, also myself, landed by parachute. I have not seen Broome since he landed but all the others are well. We jumped between 600 and 200 feet so were lucky to escape from the burning kite. Sorry to disappoint you in not turning up for the party.'

Unfortunately, Pilot Officer Charles G. Broome did not survive. Leading Aircraftman Alan Dixon was the photographer who had flown with Burton and Macphail over Baku and Batum during the previous March and April, and he and the others remained in PoW camps for the rest of the war.

By this time, the Germans were fully aware of the photo-reconnaissance flights, from the presence of high-flying Spitfires over Europe and the wreckage of some aircraft. They also used the device of hidden microphones in their interrogation centre, as did the British in their centre at Cockfosters, and ensured that there were two prisoners in the same cell so that they could eavesdrop on their conversations. They were also experts at breaking the British codes used in wireless transmissions. Heston airfield and the Photographic Interpretation Unit at Wembley became obvious targets, and these were doubtless picked out by photo-reconnaissance Ju86 P2s. The German *Knickebein* system of radio beacons provided accurate navigation for bombers, not yet having been jammed by the British, while the winding Thames enabled bomb aimers to make good visual checks at night. Attacks against Heston culminated in a raid on the night of 19/20 September 1940, when the main hangar was hit by a parachute mine and five Spitfires as well as Cotton's Lockheed were badly damaged. In the early hours of 2 October 1940, the interpretation section at Wembley was almost demolished by a bomb. St Eval on the north coast of Cornwall was also bombed on frequent occasions, although these attacks were probably directed mainly against the bomber aircraft of Coastal Command which were operating from this airfield.*

It became evident that the units at Heston and Wembley would have to move to safer localities. The airfield at Benson in Oxfordshire was chosen by Coastal Command, but the aircraft and crews did not begin moving to this new base until 27 December 1940. The photo-interpreters continued to work at Wembley, in a row of shabby and unheated houses opposite their bombed premises. On 7 January 1941 it was renamed the Central Interpretation Unit and the first section moved to Danesfield House at Medmenham in Buckinghamshire, the main party following on 23 May 1941.

Meanwhile, two new variants of the Spitfire were employed at Heston. One was the Spitfire PR IG, which was inspired by the PR IE which took large-scale photographs from low level. This retained the eight machine guns of the fighter version, since it was recognised that the pilots might be involved in combat or be able to take a quick squirt at ground targets. The machine was fitted with the 29-gallon tank behind the pilot and three F24 cameras, two verticals and one in the fuselage arranged obliquely to either port or starboard. From early October 1940 these PR IGs were employed on dangerous short-range sorties, most being painted in a very light pink instead of blue or the light green Camotint.

*In the evening of 25 January 1941, a few days after the author arrived at St Eval as a newly commissioned pilot officer, a bomb fell on an air raid shelter and killed twenty-one RAF men. Another man died the next day.

Personnel of the WAAF working on a continuous film processing machine at Medmenham, with the drying drum on the right. (The Medmenham Club)

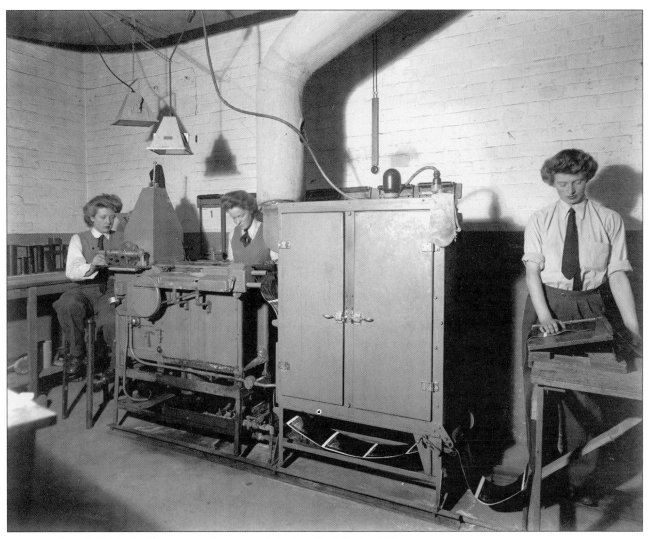

Personnel of the WAAF working on a multiprinting machine at Medmenham. (The Medmenham Club)

The other was the Spitfire PR ID, two of which were completed in late October 1940. This variant arrived out of alphabetical sequence since the structural alterations originally requested by Sidney Cotton took more than three months to complete. It was the type known as the 'extra-super-long-range' Spitfire or the 'flying petrol bowser', since it carried 114 gallons of petrol in special tanks fitted into the leading edges of the wings. Together with the extra tank containing 29 gallons behind the pilot, they gave a radius of action of about 875 miles. The machine carried two F24 cameras with 8-inch or 20-inch lenses or two F8 cameras with 20-inch lenses, the latter having been designed by Victor Laws and built in the early 1920s. On 29 October 1940 Flying Officer Samuel J. Millen took off in Spitfire PR ID series P9551 and covered the distant targets of Stettin and Rostock in the Baltic, a sortie of five hours twenty minutes which earned him the DFC. Sadly, Millen lost his life the following month.

There was a strange episode at Heston on 21 November 1940 when a Polish pilot, Flying Officer Richard Drygalla, taxied Spitfire I serial P9426 out over the grass airfield with a fitter, Aircraftman H. Rhodes, sitting on the tail and then took to the air before the airman got off. The pilot managed to avoid a spin on two occasions, unaware that someone was clinging desperately to the tail, and finally dropped the machine back on the ground from 100 feet. Rhodes shot into the air and rolled over and over, breaking two ribs and suffering concussion. The Spitfire was badly damaged and Drygalla was also knocked out but, when he came to, complained that the aircraft was 'tail heavy and not stable'.

In the latter part of 1940, the activities of the PR Spitfires were directed primarily at naval targets. This concentration of effort gave rise to some annoyance on the part of Bomber Command, who justifiably required damage assessments after their raids. On 16 November, No 3 Photographic Reconnaissance Unit was formed at Oakington in Cambridgeshire, consisting of a number of Spitfires transferred from Heston under Squadron Leader Pat B.B. Ogilvie. Two Wellingtons were added for night photography. The unit came under the authority of Bomber Command's No 3 Group, and it began work over targets in Germany and occupied Europe. The results began to cause considerable perturbation, for it seemed that many of the bombing attacks were ineffectual.*

The unit at Heston was renamed No 1 Photographic Reconnaissance Unit, No 2 being reserved for the Middle East, as will be recounted in the next chapter. The flights at Wick, St Eval and Heston (later at Benson) were rotated every three months or so, to give the air and ground crews a change of environment. The pilots were required to bring back evidence of U-boat construction, and a steady stream of photographs was provided for the photo-interpreters. They also confirmed the Admiralty's worst fears when they discovered that the battleships *Scharnhorst* and *Gneisenau* had left Kiel on 27 December 1940, thus adding to the perils of Britain's life-line, the Atlantic convoy system. In the words of Winston Churchill, these were 'dark days' for Britain.

When these warships were photographed in Brest on 28 March 1941, having sunk about 120,000 tons of British shipping, they received almost daily attention from No 1 PRU as well as nightly bombing attacks. On 5 April *Gneisenau* was photographed outside the safety of dry dock at Brest, having been moved into the harbour to avoid danger from an unexploded bomb, and a flight of Beauforts from 22 Squadron was despatched from St Eval early the following morning.

*See Chapter Eleven, Night Bombing and Photography.

Constance Babington Smith joined the WAAF in July 1940 and was commissioned six months later. In April 1941 she began work as the only photographic interpreter in the aircraft section of the RAF's Central Interpretation Unit (later the Allied Central Interpretation Unit), and continued in charge of this section until VE-Day. She was mentioned in despatches in January 1942 and was awarded the MBE in 1945. She was then attached to the USAAF for interpretation work in the Pacific theatre and in December 1945 became the first British woman to receive the US Legion of Merit. (Flight Officer Constance Babington Smith MBE, WAAF)

Charles Sim, who served as a photographer/air gunner in the pre-war RAF, joined the *Aeroplane* magazine and later served as a photo-interpreter during the Second World War. He is seen here as a flight lieutenant, checking air photographs with a factory plan at Medmenham. (The Medmenham Club)

A leading aircraftman of the Support Section at Medmenham, annotating a map showing the movements of the battleship *Tirpitz* from Germany to Norwegian fjords. (The Medmenham Club)

A Norwegian officer working in the Shipping Section at Medmenham, examining photographs of German coastal vessels and U-boats. Coupled with the decrypting of German signals at the Government Code and Cypher School at Bletchley Park, precise information of enemy movements was made available to the Royal Navy and strike aircraft of Coastal Command. The lighthouse charts on the wall were compiled from photo-reconnaissance and were used by aircrews for navigational purposes along the indented coast of Norway. (The Medmenham Club)

First-phase interpretation being carried out on reconnaissance photographs at Medmenham by a WAAF section officer with a pocket stereoscope.
(The Medmenham Club)

Only one aircraft, flown by Flying Officer Kenneth Campbell, found the target in atrocious weather. He dropped a torpedo which blew a 40-foot hole in the side of the battleship before his aircraft was destroyed by flak. The battleship was out of commission for six months and Campbell was awarded a posthumous Victoria Cross.

The Spitfire PR ID ranged far afield, and Flight Lieutenant Peter Corbishley flew P9551 to Malta in a single hop on 19 January 1941, in order to photograph the Italian battle fleet. Unfortunately, he was shot down over Genoa on 2 February, but survived to become a prisoner of war. In April 1941, when fitted with the more powerful Merlin 45 engine instead of the Merlin III but still without the comfort of cockpit heating, the Spitfire PR ID was redesignated the PR IV. A total of 229 of these Spitfires were built, becoming the standard single-engined machines employed by photo-reconnaissance units until the end of 1942. They were painted in cerulean blue, a deep shade which became known as 'PR blue'.

In March 1941 a new unit was formed at Hendon, on the insistence of the Army. This was No 1416 Flight, equipped initially with six Spitfire PR IGs, their main task being to reconnoitre British beaches in the event of invasion. This was soon extended to include photography of the enemy coastline, and the unit became 140 (Army Co-operation) Squadron on 17 September 1941, based at Benson.

On 21 May 1941 the most powerful battleship in the world, *Bismarck*, arrived at Grimstadfjord, south of Bergen. Her companion, the heavy cruiser *Prinz Eugen*, sailed further north to Kalvanes Bay. These two warships had already been spotted by a Swedish cruiser while en route from Gdynia and the information had been passed to British intelligence. On the same day as their arrival, two Spitfires of No 1 PRU were

despatched from Wick for a sweep over the Norwegian fjords. One of these, Spitfire PR IC serial X4496 flown by Flying Officer Michael F. Suckling, located both vessels and brought back photographs from high level. It became evident that the Atlantic convoys faced their greatest threat of the war, and the Royal Navy ordered heavy warships to patrol the Denmark Strait between Iceland and Greenland. The German battleship was damaged during an engagement in which she blew up the battle cruiser HMS *Hood*, and headed for St Nazaire. The Royal Navy lost contact with her during the subsequent chase but she was located in the morning of 26 May by Catalina I serial AH545 of 209 Squadron from Loch Erne in Northern Ireland, flown by Pilot Officer Dennis A. Briggs. The British warships closed in and, after being crippled further by torpedoes dropped by Fairey Swordfish from HMS *Ark Royal*, the enormous German battleship was destroyed by gunfire and more torpedoes. She went down with her colours flying.

No 3 PRU and its interpretation section were disbanded on 21 August 1941 and their resources brought back into No 1 PRU, in spite of bitter protests from Bomber Command. It was discovered that the two units were duplicating their operations to some extent, although it was recognised that some additional effort would have to be put into bomb damage assessment in future. More distant targets came within range of the unit a week later when de Havilland Mosquito PR Is began to arrive at Benson. Ten of these new machines, serials W4053 to W4062, were the first to enter RAF service in any capacity, although a lengthy fitting-up process took place. This machine had a radius of action of about 1,100 miles, carried one oblique and two vertical cameras in the bomb bay, could reach 35,000 feet, and was capable of outstripping any German fighter sent up to intercept it.

The heavy cruiser *Admiral Hipper* in dry dock at Brest, photographed by a Spitfire of No 1 Photographic Reconnaissance Unit from St Eval in Cornwall on 26 January 1941. The warship entered the port with machinery defects and slight damage inflicted by British cruisers, after commerce raiding in the Atlantic. The hull, funnel and bridge were dazzle-painted, while the hangar (which housed three aircraft) was open. (The late Squadron Leader J.E. Archbald)

An oblique photograph of a model of Lorient, facing south, used by the author in 1941 as a target map for low-level bombing attacks agains the port. (R.C. Nesbit)

A strange event with beneficial consequences for British intelligence took place on 27 August 1941 when a Hudson of Coastal Command's 269 Squadron from Kaldadarnes in northern Iceland straddled a U-boat in the Atlantic with depth charges. This was a Type VIIC, *U-570*, and the inexperienced crew decided to surrender. This was accomplished with the aid of a Catalina from 209 Squadron and an armed trawler of the Royal Navy, the U-boat being towed to Iceland. The intelligence obtained from this U-boat added to the information obtained from *U-110*, which had been abandoned by her crew after being depth-charged by the Royal Navy on 9 May 1941; British seamen had been able to board her before she sank, and vital code books used in the German naval Enigma machine were obtained.

By September 1941, No 1 PRU was equipped with thirty-seven Spitfires, two Mosquitos and two Marylands, the latter being used occasionally for high-level photography. The first successful sortie in a Mosquito took place on 20 September 1941, when Flight Lieutenant Alistair L. Taylor in serial W4055 covered Bordeaux, Pauillac, Le Verdon and La Pallice. Three Mosquitos were sent up to Wick during the following month, but serial W4055 was lost on a sortie to Trondheim and Bergen on 4 December. It was flown by Alistair Taylor and both he and his navigator Sergeant Sidney E. Horsfall were killed. Taylor had been regarded as the 'ace pilot' of the unit, for he was the first officer in the RAF to have been awarded the DFC and two bars.

On 5 December 1941, an audacious sortie was carried out by Flight Lieutenant A.E. 'Tony' Hill in Spitfire PR IV serial R7044 from Benson. During a visit to the Central Interpretation Unit at Medmenham, he had learned that a Scientific Officer on the staff of the Air Ministry, Dr R.V. Jones, was intensely interested in an object which had been photographed from high level near the village of Bruneval at Cap d'Antifer near Le Havre. It had been known since 22 February 1941, from photographs taken from a Spitfire flown by Flying Officer K. Manifould in a low-level sortie over Auderville, near Cherbourg in the Hague peninsula, that the Germans employed radar equipment known as the *Freya*. It seemed to British scientists that this radar gave the direction of an aircraft but not its altitude. Another radar known as the *Würzburg* had been identified from its transmissions and was believed to give range, direction and altitude to German nightfighters.

Tony Hill made his first low-level sortie over Bruneval on 4 December, but his camera did not function. Undeterred, he went back the next day and returned with perfect photographs. It was evident, however, that more information was required about the nature of the German equipment than could be disclosed from photographs. The newly formed 1st Airborne Division was alerted and the Model Section at Medmenham began work on a model of the locality, including the coastal cliffs at Cap d'Antifer.

Wing Commander Tuttle finished his long stint as commanding officer on 24 November 1941 and was replaced by Wing Commander J.A.C. Stratton, who in turn was replaced on 25 April 1942 by a Canadian with much experience of flying with the unit, Wing Commander Spencer L. Ring.

In January 1942 the first new camera of the Second World War was fitted to aircraft. This was known as the F52, and by coincidence the prototype took fifty-two days from design to completion. It utilised the mechanism of the F24 but was fitted with lenses of up to 40 inches for high-altitude photography, while the format was increased to $8\frac{1}{2}$ inches by 7 inches. Most of the credit for this very successful camera went to Harry Stringer of the Royal Aircraft Establishment but Group Captain Victor Laws, who had

Right: Flying Officer Michael F. Suckling, the Spitfire pilot who photographed the battleship *Bismarck* and the heavy cruiser *Prinz Eugen* in the Norwegian fjords on 21 May 1941. He was known as 'Babe', owing to his name and youthful appearance. He lost his life on a photographic sortie over La Pallice on 21 July 1941. (Flight Officer Constance Babington Smith MBE, WAAF).

Below, left: The heavy cruiser *Prinz Eugen*, with destroyers and auxiliary vessels, photographed at Kalvanes Bay in Norway by Pilot Officer Michael F. Suckling on 21 May 1941. *Below, right:* The battleship *Bismarck*, with attendant vessels, photographed at Grimstadtfjord in Norway by Pilot Officer Michael F. Suckling on 21 May 1941. (Both photos: Squadron leader P. Lamboit RAFVR)

become the Deputy Head of Photography at the Air Ministry and frequently lectured at Farnborough, also contributed to the design.

Britain entered 1942 with higher hopes for a successful conclusion to the war, with the entry of the USA into the conflict on 8 December 1941 and the knowledge that Germany was expending great efforts in the east after her attack on Russia on 22 June 1941. Nevertheless, there was national humiliation when the battleships *Scharnhorst* and *Gneisenau* with the cruiser *Prinz Eugen* left Brest on 12 February 1942 and made a successful dash through the English Channel to their home ports. However, the move gave the reconnaissance aircraft more opportunity to devote their growing resources to other tasks such as Bomber Command's requirements for bomb damage assessments. They also provided essential photographic information so that models could be made for the combined operation against St Nazaire on 28 March 1942, when the lock gates were blown up to destroy the only potential Atlantic anchorage for the huge battleship *Tirpitz*, as well as for the raid on Dieppe of 19 August 1942, when a rehearsal for an eventual invasion of France took place at the cost of very heavy casualties.

By this time, the Germans were able to put up effective resistance to RAF photo-reconnaissance aircraft. In November 1942 the RAF calculated that the chances of survival on a tour of operations in a fighter reconnaissance unit was no more than 31 per cent, compared with 44 per cent in a medium or heavy bomber squadron. The most dangerous squadrons for crews were those of Coastal Command equipped with strike aircraft, the survival rate being only 25$\frac{1}{2}$ per cent in light bombers or merely 17$\frac{1}{2}$ per cent in torpedo bombers.*

* See Public Record Office AIR 20/2859 Aircrew: Operational tours.

The near-destruction of Convoy PQ17, which sailed on 27 June 1942 from Iceland to Archangel in north Russia, created a major problem for the Allies. When it became known that the battleship *Tirpitz* and the cruisers *Hipper*, *Lützow* and *Scheer* had been sent northwards to Altenfjord, ready to fall on this convoy in the vicinity of Bear Island, the Admiralty ordered PQ17 to scatter. Only eleven of the original thirty-five merchant vessels reached Archangel, the remainder being picked off by U-boats and aircraft. Only 57,000 tons of supplies reached the Russians from the 156,000 tons carried. The disaster was one of the worst suffered by the Allies at sea.

Something had to be done to protect PQ18, which was scheduled to sail from Loch Ewe in September. Three squadrons of Coastal Command were ordered to fly to north Russia, consisting of the Hampdens of 144 and 455 (RAAF) Squadrons and the Catalinas of 210 Squadron. A daily watch on the German battle units in the Norwegian fjords was required, but the furthest radius of action for the Mosquitos based in Scotland was Narvik. It was decided to send a flight of Spitfire PR IDs to north Russia, to cover the fjords.

The RAF was not unfamiliar with north Russia. Some squadrons had operated from there after the First World War in support of the White Russians. From September to November 1941 a Hurricane wing had operated from Vaenga near Murmansk against the German Air Force, before handing its aircraft over to the Russians. On 7 July 1942, Flying Officer Keith H. Bayley flew from Scotland in Mosquito PR I serial W4054, photographing Altenfjord en route and then continuing to the airfield at Vaenga. After refuelling, he returned on the same day.

Much of the planning for the three Spitfires was carried out by Flight Lieutenant Len J. Cotton, the photographic officer at Benson. He was asked to find out the latest

Squadron Leader A.E. 'Tony' Hill DSO DFC was an audacious pilot who carried out many reconnaissance missions in unarmed Spitfires. Among these was the low-level photography of the German Würzburg radar station at St Bruneval on 5 December 1941. He was shot down on 20 October 1942 (the day after his appointment as commanding officer of the newly formed 543 Squadron) when trying to photograph the famous daylight raid by ninety-four Lancasters on the Schneider armaments factory at Le Creusot in central France. Although rescued from his burning Spitfire by the French, he died shortly afterwards. (Flight Officer Constance Babington Smith MBE, WAAF)

The German Würzburg radar at Bruneval, near Cap d'Antifer, photographed on 5 December 1941 by Flight Lieutenant A.E. 'Tony' Hill of No 1 Photographic Reconnaissance Unit based at Benson in Oxfordshire, flying Spitfire VD (later designated PR IV) serial R7044. The building behind the radar dish was a sanitorium. From this and other photographs, the Model Section at Medmenham constructed an accurate model for study by paratroops, commandos, RAF aircrews and an RAF technician. (The late Squadron Leader J.E. Archbald)

date when photography was possible within the Arctic Circle, and calculated that results could be achieved provided the sun was at least fifteen degrees above the horizon. Thus operations could continue until mid-October, when there should be two hours a day available for photography. The ground party of fitters, riggers, electricians and photographers left by warship on 13 August. They took with them eight packing cases containing film, paper, processing tanks, chemicals, a printer and a drying drum.

The commander of the flight of Spitfires was Flight Lieutenant E.A. 'Tim' Fairhurst, the other two pilots being Flying Officer Donald R.M. Furniss and Pilot Officer G.W. 'Sleepy' Walker. Fairhurst was slightly disturbed to see that the only available maps of Russia contained large tracts marked 'uncharted territory', for they had no navigational aids in their Spitfires. They worked out a 'great circle' route from Sumburgh in the Shetlands to Kandalaska, near the White Sea. On 1 September they flew up to Sumburgh and then took off at five-minute intervals for north Russia. Then they flew in brilliant sunshine to Norway and through thick cloud over Sweden and Finland, in conditions the exact opposite of the meteorological forecast. Coming down though cloud over Russia, they picked up the coast of the White Sea and followed it to the camouflaged airfield of Afrikanda, where they landed after averaging flights of four and a half hours.

They were met by a pretty Russian girl in uniform who directed them in English to the officers' mess, where they were greeted by Flight Lieutenant G.V. Cottam, a language officer who had been born in Russia. Cottam told them that they would have to fly on to Vaenga, about 80 miles to the north-east, since German tanks sometimes attacked Afrikanda and flattened all the aircraft. Arriving at Vaenga the next day, they found that it consisted of two airfields connected by a runway, set in a silver birch plantation. They were billeted in a red-brick country house overrun with mice. The roundels on their Spitfires were painted out and replaced with five-pointed Russian stars, which looked quite attractive against the PR blue. Relations with the Russians were a little strained, and the pressing need was for maps, for the only ones available were in Cyrillic script. However, the photographic officer Flying Officer Len Wager sent a set in a Catalina of 210 Squadron back to the UK, where they were immediately translated and returned.

Meanwhile, 144 and 455 Squadrons also arrived, having lost nine of their thirty-two Hampdens en route. One was shot down by a Russian fighter, while the others ran out of fuel or iced up and crashed. The unenviable role of the remainder, based at the other end of Vaenga, was to try to torpedo the German battle fleet if it put out to sea.

The Germans sighted convoy PQ18 on September 9 and trouble began. The PRU pilots were at lunch with the Russians when General Kusnetsov, their commanding officer, was informed that about twenty Ju88s were approaching from Norway. Kusnetsov did nothing for a while and then invited the RAF men to accompany him to the control tower. He looked at his watch and fired a signal pistol. Suddenly, Yaks, MiGs and even old biplanes emerged from their shelters in the trees and took off in all directions, flying through Russian flak to the attack. They claimed a victory afterwards, but the aircraft which were shot down appeared to be Russian. One of the Spitfires was riddled with bomb splinters and a replacement was flown out via Sumburgh by a New Zealander, Sergeant Donald R.I. Hardman.

On the following day, Fairhurst made the first photo-reconnaissance of Altenfjord, flying through flak at high level. The photographs revealed the presence of the

The F52 camera was an enlarged version of the F24, introduced in January 1942 for high altitude photo-reconnaissance. The format size was increased from 5-inch by 5-inch to 8½-inch by 7-inch, while long focus lenses of 14, 20 and 36 inches were provided. The magazine capacity was either 250 or 500 exposures. The camera continued in use with various modifications into the 1960s. This F52 camera, with a 20-inch lens and control attachments, was photographed at the Tangmere Military Aviation Museum, brought into the adjoining hangar from its normal display position. (B.M. Harris, courtesy Tangmere Military Aviation Museum)

An F52 camera with a 36-inch lens mounted vertically in a Mosquito, and an F24 with a 14-inch lens mounted obliquely to port. (Flight Lieutenant G.H. Parry RAF (Ret'd))

cruisers *Scheer*, *Hipper* and *Köln* with four destroyers, but *Tirpitz* was not there and could not be located anywhere. Every day when flying was possible, the pilots took turns to fly over the fjord, although the Russians did not approve, saying that sorties which did not include bombing were a waste of effort. Walker failed to return from a low-level sortie on 27 September, and it was believed that he had been shot down by flak.

PQ18 continued its journey, harried by the Luftwaffe and U-boats, but the German warships did not come out to attack. On 28 September, a PR Mosquito from Leuchars located *Tirpitz* in Narvik, where it had been out merely for sea trials. Nevertheless, only twenty-seven of PQ18's original forty merchant vessles reached Archangel.

By mid-October, the Hampdens were handed over to the Russians and the Catalinas returned to the UK with some of the airmen. Two of the Spitfires were still serviceable, the third having been used for spares. General Kusnetsov got into the cockpit of one and asked a series of questions through the girl interpreter. Then he taxied down to the runway and took to the air. Leaving their equipment behind, the aircrews and ground parties left for the UK by cruiser and arrived safely in mid-November. Future convoys to Russia would be able to sail under the cover of arctic darkness until the following spring.

On their return, the contingent from Benson found that No 1 Photographic Reconnaissance Unit no longer existed, for it had been broken up into five squadrons, as will be related in Chapter Eight.

The battleship *Tirpitz* photographed by a Mosquito of No 1 Photographic Reconnaissance Unit in February 1942 while sheltering in Aasfjord near Trondheim. Camouflage netting was draped between the port side of the ship and the shore in an attempt to break up the outline. (The late Squadron Leader J.E. Archbald)

CHAPTER SEVEN

AFRICA AND MALTA

When Italy entered the war on 10 June 1940, there was no photographic unit in Egypt comparable to that in the UK. The only aircraft capable of specialised long-distance work was the Lockheed Hudson which in its guise of the civil G-AGAR had been flown over Baku and Batum in the previous March and April. Repainted with RAF markings, this had arrived back in Heliopolis after leaving Heston on 4 June 1940, with Flying Officer R.G.M. 'Johnny' Walker as first pilot and Squadron Leader Hugh Macphail as second pilot. Photo-reconnaissance of the network of roads in both French and Italian Somaliland was required when Italy entered the war, and on 12 June 1940 the two RAF men flew the Hudson to Aden via Khartoum to begin the task, photographing en route the port of Assab and the airfields of Gura and Mindega. After completing their task from Aden, they returned to Heliopolis and then photographed the Italian-held islands of the Dodecanese on 28 June.

The Air Officer Commanding the Middle East, Air Chief Marshal Sir Arthur Longmore, was so impressed with the accomplishments of the Hudson that he retained the aircraft and its crew to supplement his very limited resources for aerial reconnaissance. At the same time he formed an Intelligence Photographic Flight to work directly under the Senior Intelligence Officer at Headquarters Middle East in Cairo, although no other suitable aircraft were available at this stage. Flight Lieutenant R. Idris Jones, who

had interpreted the photographs taken by the Hudson over Baku and Batum, was posted to Cairo to set up an Interpretation Section, this work having hitherto been carried out by NCOs. The creation of No 2 Photographic Reconnaissance Unit at Heliopolis was authorised in September 1940, but a ship which sailed the following January with a crated consignment of Martin Maryland reconnaissance aircraft was sunk. In the event, the new unit did not come into being until 17 March 1941.

Malta was the most vulnerable of the British bases overseas when Italy declared war. Less than seven hours after this declaration a tight formation of Italian bombers dropped bombs on Grand Harbour and the airfield of Hal Far. The only fighters capable of defending the island were four Gloster Gladiators which the RAF had acquired from the Fleet Air Arm and assembled from their packing cases. One of these was soon damaged beyond repair but the other three, nicknamed 'Faith, Hope and Charity' engaged the Italians in combat until Hurricanes began to arrive at the end of June.

The RAF's main photographic section in Malta was situated at the seaplane base of Kalafrana, where the NCO in charge, Flight Sergeant Geoffrey J. Buxton, had been responsible for processing the negatives taken during Sidney Cotton's clandestine flights of June 1939 in his Lockheed 12A. Other photographic work consisted mainly of processing films taken by 202 Squadron's

Wing Commander Geoffrey J. Buxton MBE, who served as an aircraftman photographer with J.H. Ross (Lawrence of Arabia) in 1922. As a flight sergeant in February 1939, he was in charge of the photographic section at Kalafrana in Malta. He commanded the RAF School of Photography in 1953/54. (The late Wing Commander G.J. Buxton MBE)

Sunderlands and some taken by Swordfish of the Fleet Air Arm or visiting RAF aircraft.

The Air Staff in London recognised that a more effective photographic capability was essential in the Mediterranean. On 6 September 1940 three Martin Marylands arrived at Malta, forming 431 General Reconnaissance Flight. The aircraft had been ordered originally from the USA by the French Air Force while the RAF crews had been trained on them when serving with 22 Squadron, a Beaufort squadron based at North Coates in Lincolnshire. The Marylands were capable of a radius of action of about 900 miles and had a service ceiling of 31,000 feet, their main role being to reconnoitre and photograph enemy ports and shipping movements in the Eastern Mediterranean. The Italian ports of Brindisi and Taranto were covered, as well as the Sicilian ports of Messina and Palermo and the Libyan ports of Tripoli and Benghazi.

In the autumn of 1940 Admiral Sir Andrew Cunningham, the C-in-C of the Mediterranean Fleet, decided to launch an attack with Swordfish torpedo bombers of HMS *Illustrious* against the Italian fleet at Taranto, and required photo-reconnaissance of this naval base. Two RAF men in Egypt were briefed to help while the aircraft carrier was at Alexandria. These were an Operations Officer from Headquarters Middle East, Wing Commander Cyril E.J. Baines, and the head of the Interpretation Section, Flight Lieutenant R. Idris Jones. Photography of Taranto was carried out by Marylands based at Malta and showed the unexpected hazard of a balloon barrage over the target.

One of the pilots of the Marylands was Pilot Officer Adrian Warburton, who had joined an Army Territorial Unit in 1937 and transferred to the RAF with a short-service commission in the autumn of 1938. He was so ham-fisted with his take-offs and landings that he had not been allowed to fly a Maryland to Malta but instead had navigated one of them. He was also an eccentric officer, contemptuous of many aspects of RAF authority, but he was to become one of the most renowned photo-reconnaissance pilots of the Second World War. Unknown to his flying assessors, he was a superb pilot once his machine was in the air and he seemed to be quite impervious to fear.

It was only illness of the other Maryland pilots which gave Warburton his chance to begin flying as a pilot. On 10 November 1940, he carried out one of the final flights over Taranto, flying twice round the harbour at extreme low level for preliminary photo-reconnaissances and then heading back for a third run in spite of heavy flak. His Maryland returned with a ship's aerial trailing from the tailwheel. The crew reported that the balloons were down and their photographs showed that 5 battleships, 14 cruisers and 27 destroyers were in the harbour. Many of these went to the bottom after the Swordfish attacked on the following day, giving the Royal Navy a great victory. The remainder of the Italian Navy retreated to safer anchorages.

While these events were taking place, photo-reconnaissance was also required in West Africa. After the fall of France in June 1940, an abortive attempt was made by British and Free French forces to land at Dakar in Senegal, in the hope that this French territory would abandon Vichy France and join the British cause. The expedition included French photographic personnel equipped with RAF apparatus, including F24 cameras and a J-type photographic trailer. Four French airmen photographers were collected at RAF Odiham in Hampshire under the command of a French pilot, Lieutenant de Thuisy. They joined the expedition on a Dutch boat, the *Pennland*, which left Liverpool on 30 August 1940, while General de Gaulle and his staff left on a sister ship, the *Westernland*.

However, the expedition failed in its purpose, following the resistance of the Vichy French at Dakar. The *Pennland* continued to Nigeria, where the photographers transferred to the *Ektian* and on 8 October 1940 landed at Doula in the French Cameroons, a colony which had espoused the Free French and British cause. Air photography began soon afterwards, carried out by a French squadron, but processing of the negatives failed since the air conditioning in the trailer was unserviceable and the emulsion melted in the high temperatures. The photographer in charge, Bernard Lefebvre, was unfairly blamed by his commanding officer, but the air conditioning was never made serviceable.

It was considered necessary by the RAF to form a West African Command, partly since Takoradi on the Gold Coast possessed dock facilities and airfields which were vital for the assembly of crated aircraft and their flights across Africa to Egypt, and partly since strong elements of the Vichy French Fleet were docked at Dakar and constituted a threat to the Allies, if the Germans began to control them. There were also some thirty airfields or landing strips in the Vichy French colonies of the Ivory Coast, Guinea, Senegal and other parts of West Africa, from which there were other potential threats to the Allies. The new Command was not formed until October 1941, however, and for the time being the RAF had to reconnoitre a vast area of West Africa as best it could. Sunderlands of 95 Squadron arrived at Freetown in March 1941 and carried out convoy escort duties as well as some photo-reconnaissance flights. Marylands of No 1 Photographic Reconnaissance Unit at Heston were detached to Gibraltar to carry out other essential duties, covering the south of France and the west coast of Africa.

Back in Egypt, No 2 Photographic Reconnaissance Unit came into being on 17 March 1941 at Heliopolis under the command of Squadron Leader Hugh Macphail. Flight Lieutenant Paul Lamboit, who had spent a period with Bomber

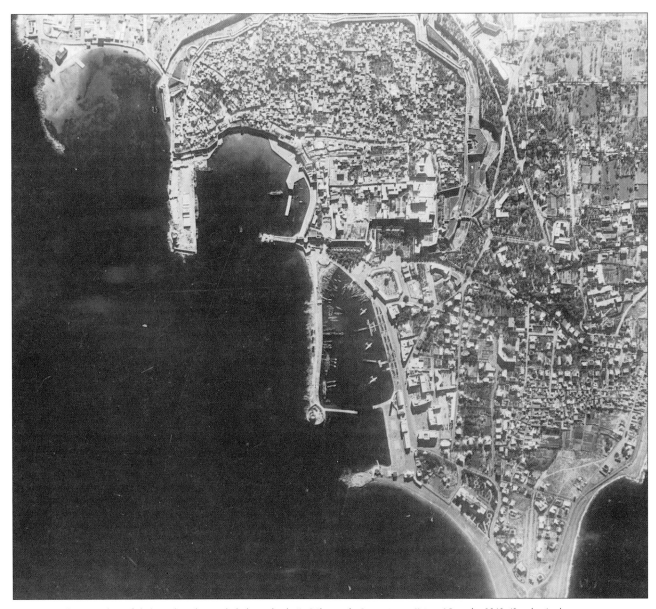

The town and port of Rhodes, with seaplanes in the harbour, taken by No 2 Photographic Reconnaissance Unit on 4 December 1942. (Squadron Leader P. Lamboit RAFVR)

Flight Lieutenant Gerard (Gerry) Glaister in a Spitfire of No 2 Photographic Reconnaissance Unit, still in the cockpit after landing from a reconnaissance mission. (Squadron Leader P. Lamboit RAFVR)

Command and had temporarily lost his acting rank of squadron leader, was appointed as Photographic Officer. Flight Lieutenant R. Idris Jones was appointed as Photo-Interpretation Officer. A consignment of Marylands arrived to equip the new unit, but these aircraft did not prove satisfactory and were transferred to 60 (SAAF) Squadron, a survey unit which had been engaged on work in East Africa with Avro Ansons. As an alternative, three Hurricanes were modified locally with extra fuel tanks in the wings and twin F24 cameras fitted vertically in the fuselages. The area the Hurricanes were expected to cover was vast, for it included airfields, ports, harbours and shipping in North Africa as far as Benghazi, as well as in the eastern Mediterranean.

The Hudson was placed on the strength of the new unit and on the day of its formation was flown to Heraklion in Crete by Flying Officer Johnny Walker, accompanied by one of the Hurricanes flown by a Kenyan, Flight Lieutenant A.C. 'Fatty' Pearson. Their targets for photography were three Italian airfields in Rhodes but soon after this was accomplished a flight of Italian Fiat CR42 biplanes attacked Heraklion. The Hurricane was hit by a single bullet and Pearson flew it back to Egypt. The Hudson was more seriously damaged and a few days later another Fiat CR42 came in so low that its undercarriage knocked 6 feet off the port wing. The Italian pilot flew off minus his undercarriage, leaving Johnny Walker to wonder what sort of landing he would make. After this, the Hudson was beyond repair and had to be written off. Walker got out of Crete in a Sunderland on 15 April 1941, before German airborne forces invaded and captured the island.

The Lockheed Hudson was replaced by a commercial Lockheed 10A Electra, one of three which had escaped from Yugoslavia when the Germans overran that country in May 1941. It was given the serial number AX701 and painted in PR blue, but it was not fitted with cameras since its role was to fly crews and equipment to the various operational bases. The controls were marked in Serbo-Croat, which caused the pilots some difficulty until they had discovered their use by trial and error.

The Lockheed Electra was flown to Iraq in the late spring of 1941, carrying a replacement for the Air Officer Commanding, who had been injured in a motor accident. From 30 July 1941 the Hurricanes also flew to Habbaniya and carried out photo-reconnaissance sorties, in case the Vichy French tried to occupy the area. Another detachment was sent to Shaibah in the Persian Gulf during August 1941, to cover part of Persia prior to the occupation of that country by the British. Other Hurricanes were detached from time to time to Cyprus and Palestine.

The second-in-command of No 2 Photographic Reconnaissance Unit was Flight Lieutenant A.M. 'Tony' Brown, who had previously flown with 208 Squadron, engaged on tactical reconnaissance with Hurricanes and Lysanders in the Middle East. He had the misfortune to become the first casualty of the unit. During a sortie to Benghazi on 2 October 1941, the fuel selection cock of his Hurricane froze up and he could not free it. Unable to switch tanks, he glided down and was captured by the German 21st Panzer Division. His place was taken by a Canadian, Flight Lieutenant J. Roger Whelan.

In Malta, the situation worsened with the arrival of about two hundred German aircraft on Sicilian airfields during January 1941. Bombing attacks against dock installations in Valletta and the airfields of Luqa, Hal Far and Takali were intensified and pressed home far more vigorously. The siege of Malta had begun. On 10 January 1941, 431 Flight was expanded into 69 Squadron, commanded by Squadron Leader E.A. 'Tich' Whiteley. The unit had been equipped with further

Bernard Lefebvre, a photographer with the Free French Forces, at Doula in the Cameroons, standing inside an RAF photographic trailer in late 1940. (Bernard Lefebvre, Photo Ellebé)

A Lysander of 'Arras' Squadron of the Free French Air Force at Pointe-Noir, on the coast of French Equatorial Africa, in 1942. The Free French established two reconnaissance squadrons in the country, the other being named 'Picardie' and based at Libreville. The two squadrons were part of the 'Artois' Group. (Bernard Lefebvre, Photo Ellebé)

Dakar harbour in Senegal, photographed in 1942. The warships *Richelieu, Gloire, Montcalm* and *Georges Leygues*, controlled by the Vichy Government, were picked out from this photograph, as well as anti-torpedo booms and nets. These warships were a constant worry to the Allies until the Anglo-American landings of November 1942 in North-West Africa, when a pact was made with the French authorities in the region. (Flight Lieutenant W.M. Hodsman RAFVR)

consignments of Marylands, and two Hurricanes were added in April, being fitted with twin F24 cameras and used for shorter range sorties. Losses of reconnaissance aircraft continued but replacements arrived, as well as new aircrews.

The photographic section soon outgrew its resources at the seaplane base of Kalafrana. A new section was formed on 5 July 1941 at Valletta in the fortress of St John de Cavalier, which had been built centuries earlier with enormously thick walls and a strong roof. Geoffrey Buxton, by then commissioned as a flying officer, trained local photographers in the use of RAF equipment. The section continued to work throughout the continual bombing attacks, films taken by the Marylands and Hurricanes being rushed from Luqa by dispatch rider. After processing, they were interpreted by Flying Officers Howard Colvin and Ray Herschel.

In addition to the intelligence obtained from these photographs, there was a great advance in 1941 when the Government Code and Cypher School at Bletchley Park made a very important breakthrough. From May of that year, the RAF had been benefiting from the decryption of signals sent by the German Air Force but two months later the codes of the Italian Navy, which had been persuaded to adopt the German Enigma system, were also broken. From this time until Italy surrendered, the British knew the exact composition of the Axis convoys and dates of sailing to North Africa, as well as details of each cargo and its destination. British submarines were able to home in on the Axis convoys, which were tracked and photographed from high level by the Marylands, although for the remainder of 1941 the RAF in beleaguered Malta was able to muster only a few Blenheims to carry out anti-shipping attacks.

By the end of September 1941, Flying Officer Adrian Warburton had carried out 155 sorties in Marylands and Hurricanes from Malta, and had been awarded the DFC and bar. He had been in aerial combat on numerous occasions and he and his crew in Marylands had shot down several enemy aircraft and had even carried out bombing attacks. He was due for a rest and was posted as in instructor to 223 Squadron at Shandur in Egypt, a training unit which was occupied in converting crews to Marylands, Blenheims and Bostons. However, this posting was not to his liking and by early November he had contrived to join No 2 Photographic Reconnaissance Unit in Heliopolis.

In the previous September, two Mosquitos had been flown out from England to join this unit, but both had been damaged by enemy action when they reached Malta and thus were written off. Instead, the unit had acquired two Beaufighters, converting them for photographic work by removing the cannons and some armour plate and then installing three F24 cameras with lenses of 20-inch focal length. They formed a small flight under Flight Lieutenant Johnny Walker, who called for airmen photographers to volunteer as extra crew members. Operating from the forward airfield of Fuka, both Walker and Warburton flew with volunteers on photo-reconnaissance missions over the distant target of Crete, as well as other targets. Then a requirement came through for photographs of potential beach landing sites in Sicily, in anticipation of an eventual Allied invasion of the island, and the two Beaufighters were chosen for this purpose. It was obvious that they should operate from Malta and on 29 December 1941 Walker and Warburton flew the machines for refuelling purposes to Timini, west of Tobruk carrying another pilot, Flying Officer 'Benjie' White, and three airmen photographers. The weather ahead was bad but Warburton pressed on while Walker, who had never before flown to Malta, prudently delayed his flight for several days until the weather cleared.

Malta was undergoing its most intensive aerial bombardment when the Beaufighters arrived, and the men never began their survey of the Sicilian beaches. Instead they were waylaid by the Air Officer Commanding Malta Air Vice-Marshal Hugh Pughe Lloyd, and pressed into other reconnaissance duties. At the end of six weeks, Warburton had been awarded the DSO while two photographers, Corporal Norman Shirley and Leading Aircraftman Ron Hadden, had received DFMs. Shirley, who frequently flew with Warburton and became one of his friends, was wounded but pulled his pilot, Benjie White, from his burning and wrecked Beaufighter after returning to Luqa. The remaining Beaufighter was flown back to Heliopolis by Warburton.

More Hurricanes and Beaufighters had arrived at No 2 Photographic Reconnaissance Unit in Heliopolis, and in addition Spitfire PR IVs began to arrive in April 1942. These Spitfires were fitted with F52 cameras with lenses of either 20-inch or 36-inch focal lengths, but problems arose with the films for these had been stored in high temperatures during their long sea journey. This resulted in fogging of the emulsion, so that it was difficult to obtain clear prints. A remedy was found by adding a special chemical, known as an anti-fogging agent, to the developer. Fortunately humidity was low in the Middle East, so that there were no processing problems in the high temperatures, but there were difficulties when developing at advanced airfields, since sand could blow through the film dryer on to the negatives.

In June 1942 Squadron Leader Macphail was posted from the unit and his place was taken by Squadron Leader J. Roger Whelan. By then a Middle East Central Interpretation Unit, on the lines of the unit at Medmenham, had been set up at Heliopolis. It was commanded by Squadron Leader R. Idris Jones and included a number of WAAF

officers. At the beginning of July, when Rommel had advanced so far in the Western Desert that his *Panzerarmee* was almost knocking on the doors of Cairo, the situation became so tense that an evacuation was ordered. The smell or burning papers pervaded Cairo but the orders for the photographic units to move eastwards were countermanded when the equipment was being loaded on to the transport vehicles.

A detachment of No 2 Photographic Reconnaissance Unit operated in the Western Desert but it was not the only unit of its type. The others were 1437 Flight, which carried out strategic reconnaissance with Martin Baltimores, 208 Squadron and 40 (SAAF) Squadron which were equipped with Hurricanes fitted with oblique cameras and engaged on close support work for the British 8th Army, and 60 (SAAF) Squadron employed on survey and mapping work with Marylands and Baltimores. Their diverse operations sometimes resulted in an overlap of photographic activities and caused problems for the interpreters. In July 1942 all these units were brought under 285 Wing, which was formed under Air Headquarters Middle East and co-ordinated the operations of the aircraft.

On the night of 29 July 1942 the airfield at Heliopolis was bombed for the first time, some aircraft and one of the hangars being damaged. Another attack followed two days later, when the German bombers were met by a box barrage and night-fighters. The airmen's quarters were hit, but the men had been evacuated to temporary accommodation. The Middle East Central Interpretation Unit was moved to the town of Heliopolis to be free of these attacks. In the following month Squadron Leader R. Idris Jones was posted to No 2 Section at Ras el Tin near Alexandria, and his place was taken by Wing Commander Eric L. Fuller.

Meanwhile, West African Command was set up in October 1941 at Freetown in Sierra

Casablanca harbour in the French Protectorate of Morocco, photographed before the Anglo-American landings in North-West Africa of November 1942. The battleship *Jean Bart* of 25,000 tons (bottom left, partly obscured by cloud) took part in opposing the landings but was put out of action by gunfire from British warships. (Flight Lieutenant W.M. Hodsman RAFVR)

Flight Lieutenant R. Idris Jones, Senior Photo-Interpretation Officer of
No 2 Photographic Reconnaissance Unit, at his desk in Heliopolis.
(Squadron Leader P. Lamboit RAFVR)

Airmen photographers laying mosaics at No 2 Photographic Reconnaissance Unit at Heliopolis on 10 September 1941. (The late Squadron Leader R.I. Jones)

Photo-interpreters at work at Heliopolis, probably in 1942. (Squadron Leader P. Lamboit RAFVR)

Members of No 2 Photographic Interpretation Unit, photographed at Heliopolis in 1942. Front row, left to right: Flight Lieutenant Paul Lamboit (Senior Photographic Officer), Squadron Leader J. Roger Whelan (Commanding Officer), Flight Lieutenant R. Idris Jones (Senior Photo-Interpretation Officer). (Squadron Leader P. Lamboit RAFVR)

Leone, under the command of Air Commodore Edward A.B. Rice. It comprised two Sunderland squadrons, No 95 at Fourah Bay near Freetown and No 204 at Half Die near Bathurst in the Gambia, as well as 200 Squadron equipped with Hudsons and based at Jeswang in the Gambia, and finally 128 Squadron equipped with Hurricanes and based at Hastings in Sierra Leone. Fortunately for the improvement of photo-reconnaissance, the post of Senior Air Staff Officer was filled by Group Captain Ronald H. Carter, who had previously commanded the Central Interpretation Unit in the UK and was thus able to form an effective intelligence and photographic organisation.

Carter requested special Hudsons from England to improve essential photo-reconnaissance but the machines were not immediately availabe. A Maryland from Benson arrived as an interim measure and carried out reconnaissance until it crashed on landing in March 1942. Two specially fitted Hudson IIIs arrived in the same month and were attached to 200 Squadron, which was already equipped with other Hudsons. Two Hurricanes of 128 Squadron were converted for photographic duties by fitting extra fuel tanks and F24 cameras, and also began work. The aircraft frequently encountered flak in their sorties and sometimes French fighters were sent up in attempts to intercept them.

Flight Lieutenant Bernard R. Catcheside was appointed as Command Photographic Officer and set up sections in Sierra Leone and the Gambia. Flight Lieutenant A. Macdonald and Flying Officers Jack E. Archbald, Fitzpatrick and Goodall arrived to begin work as photo-interpretation officers, followed by Pilot Officers Mike Hodsman and Fisher. They were dispersed to the airfields in Sierra Leone and the Gambia, as well as to Air Headquarters, and a more systematic photographic organisation began to operate. In addition to the ports and airfields controlled

by Vichy France, discreet cover was also obtained of some of the offshore islands such as the barren coasts of the Portuguese Cape Verde Islands, in case German U-boats were using these as anchorages. On the ground, conditions for the photographers were extremely unpleasant, for they had to work in sweltering darkrooms without air conditioning and with 100 per cent humidity. The men were plagued by insects and there were always the dangers of malaria and yellow fever, although new drugs had been developed in the fight against these infections. Food was indifferent at best and there was little relief from monotony. Some men became lethargic, irritable and debilitated, but the work continued and excellent results were achieved.

An American Photographic Mission arrived at Freetown during April 1942, in the form of a single B–17 Flying Fortress accompanied by Major Elliot Roosevelt, one of the sons of the US President. The aircraft began to operate under conditions of secrecy over the Canary Islands, the Cape Verde Islands, Senegal and the Ivory Coast, continuing over these vast areas until it was damaged beyond repair. Numerous rolls of film were exposed and these were returned to the USA for processing. Copies of the photographs were eventually sent back to the RAF in West Africa but proved of little value for military purposes. However, it is probable that the Americans gained some useful experience in this type of flying and certainly Elliot Roosevelt soon became very prominent in the USAAF as a specialist photographic officer.

By August 1942 the plans for an Allied invasion of North-West Africa, code-named Operation 'Torch', had been crystallised and the small photographic unit in West Africa was given the task of continuous cover of Dakar and other targets. Two Spitfire PR IVs were allocated from a batch in transit at Takoradi and flown to Freetown, where cameras were fitted. The few aircraft

Above, left: Wing Commander Adrian Waburton DSO and bar, DFC and two bars, DFC (USA), who was one of the most daring and successful photo-reconnaissance pilots. He completed over three hundred operational sorties before his death in a Lockheed F-5B on 12 April 1944. In this photograph, he appears to be wearing wing commander tabs with a khaki background on his blue battledress. (Flight Officer Constance Babington Smith MBE, WAAF)

Above, right: Corporal Norman Shirley DFM, who flew as a cameraman with Adrian Warburton. (Corporal N. Shirley DFM, RAFVR)

The Martin Maryland was supplied from contracts placed by the French with the US and was used mainly by RAF and SAAF squadrons in the Mediterranean. It gave good service as a bomber but was also used for photo-reconnaissance. The Marylands of 12 (SAAF) Squadron in this photograph were taking off from a landing ground in the Western Desert. (SAAF Association)

available, two Hurricanes, a Hudson and the two Spitfires, were concentrated at Yundum, a newly completed airfield in the Gambia. The unit was supplied with its own Photographic Interpretation Section, under the main section at Air Headquarters at Freetown. By working intensively until the invasion began on 8 November 1942, the organisation built up an accurate picture of the French Navy and Air Force in West Africa, supplying target maps which could be used if necessary. On 23 November, however, the French in West Africa decided to join the Allied cause and the operations of the RAF photographic contingent ended a few months later.

In Egypt, a great deal of photographic reconnaissance was carried out before the battle of El Alamein began on 23 October 1942. A mosaic of the entire area was completed by 60 (SAAF) Squadron, and this proved of great use in planning the battle and also in the subsequent operations of the 8th Army. Adrian Warburton flew several photo-reconnaissance operations in this period, in Spitfires and Beaufighters, but on 11 August returned to Malta to take over command of 69 Squadron, with the rank of squadron leader. By then the squadron had acquired Martin Baltimores, machines developed from the Martin Maryland to meet the requirements of the RAF, having more powerful engines and better crew communication. The squadron had evolved into an unusual mixture of three flights. A Flight with Baltimores was used for collaboration with anti-shipping squadrons, B Flight employed Spitfire PR IVs on high-altitude photo-reconnaissance, while C Flight was equipped with the remaining Marylands as well as Wellingtons engaged in anti-shipping attacks at night.

Malta played a crucial role before, during and after the battle of El Alamein. Beaufort torpedo bombers had arrived during the previous June and were employed against Axis convoys and naval units while Beaufighters

provided their long-range fighter escorts. These operations were the most dangerous of all RAF activities, but numerous successes were scored at the expense of heavy casualties. On 20 August 1942, the surviving Beauforts of the various squadrons in Malta were grouped into 39 Squadron, providing a 'strike wing' in combination with the Beaufighters of 227 Squadron. The third component of this force was 69 Squadron, for the photo-reconnaissance aircraft identified the enemy convoys en route to North Africa after the Government Code and Cypher School had decrypted enemy signals and warned of their dates of leaving port. A Baltimore of 69 Squadron invariably accompanied the Beauforts and Beaufighters on their attacks from Malta and photographed the results from high altitude. This small RAF force was able to strike effectively at enemy supply ships in this critical period. In combination with the operations of British submarines, the RAF in Malta and Egypt ensured that almost every supply vessel destined for North Africa was sunk. With extended supply lines, the critical shortage for the German and Italian forces was fuel. According to the Germans after the war, lack of sufficient fuel for their armoured units was the major reason for their withdrawal from El Alamein and their retreat to Tunisia.

The invasion of Morocco and Algeria, code-named Operation 'Torch', which began on 8 November 1942, was preceded by intense photo-reconnaissance activity. Mosquitos from Benson were detached to Gibraltar and carried out special tasks in the Casablanca area, while other Mosquitos operated from Benson to keep watch on the French Fleet at Toulon, sometimes flying to Malta in the course of their operations. The Spitfires of 69 Squadron operated over ports in Sicily, southern Italy and the coast of North Africa as far west as Oran. The USA's Western Air Command was also provided with a photo-reconnaissance unit, the 3rd Photo Group under Lieutenant-

The Martin Baltimore was manufactured in the US to British specifications as an improvement on the Maryland, with more powerful engines and better crew communication. It served in the Mediterranean theatre from January 1942 onwards as a light bomber and a photo-reconnaissance aircraft in RAF, RAAF and SAAF squadrons. Here an RAF Baltimore IIIA, serial FA342, is shown taking off from Luqa to bomb enemy positions in Sicily. (SAAF Association)

Lieutenant-Colonel Elliot Roosevelt (left) and Lieutenant-Colonels Powers and Eldridge of the USAAF, with the commanding officer of 682 Squadron, Squadron Leader A.H.W. 'Freddie' Ball DFC (right) and his photographic officer Flight Lieutenant S.R. 'Wally' Walton (centre), photographed at Maison Blanche in Algeria in early 1943. (Warrant Officer J.H. Eggleston RAF (Ret'd))

On the night of 20 November 1942, a German bombing attack destroyed many Allied aircraft and installations at Maison Blanche in Algeria. The photographic section and a type-J trailer were also badly damaged and photographic equipment was destroyed. These items of processing equipment were improvised locally and used for the next few weeks by the photographic section at La Dersa. (All photos: Warrant Officer J.H. Eggleston RAF (Ret'd))

An improvised drying drum for up to 300 feet of F52 film, which was 9 inches wide.

An improvised enlarger made from a biscuit tin and 5-inch by 5-inch contact printer.

An improvised contact printer for 9-inch square negatives.

Colonel Elliot Roosevelt. This was equipped with about twenty assorted aircraft, mostly F-4s, the photographic version of the Lockheed P-38 Lightning, but the crews were not experienced in their work and in any event operated independently from the RAF at this stage. From all the RAF photo-reconnaissance sorties, the Model Section at Medmenham made forty-six models of the landing beaches for the planners of Operation 'Torch', which was successfully executed by American troops in the western sector and the British 1st Army on the east.

On 15 November 1942 the newly formed No 4 Photographic Reconnaissance Unit arrived at Maison Blanche in Algeria, from Benson via Gibraltar. This consisted of six Spitfire PR IVs under Squadron Leader A.H.W. 'Freddy' Ball, under the RAFs new Eastern Air Command. The aircraft began to cover the area of Algiers and Oran, as well as the north-west coast of Africa as far as Casablanca. Five days after arriving, this unit lost several Spitfires and much photographic equipment in a very accurate air attack by the Luftwaffe on the airfield. Replacement aircraft soon arrived via Gibraltar, but the ground photographers had to improvise much of their equipment.

On 1 February 1943 the RAF's Photographic Reconnaissance Units in the Mediterranean theatre were disbanded and formed into squadrons, thus conforming with the arrangements at home. No 2 Photographic Reconnaissance Unit, which by then was based at LG219 near Heliopolis, became 680 Squadron commanded by Wing Commander Roger Whelan. No 4 Photographic Reconnaissance Unit at Maison Blanche became 682 Squadron under Squadron Leader A.H.W. Ball. In addition, B Flight of 69 Squadron in Malta became 683 Squadron under Wing Commander Adrian Warburton, while the other two flights remained in their old squadron, which was taken over the following month by Squadron Leader R.C.

MacKay. These new squadrons were equipped mainly with Spitfire PR IVs, which were becoming outmoded by comparison with the latest Me 109s, but the new Spitfire PR IXs did not begin to arrive for several months.

After their fighting retreat from the British 8th Army in the Western Desert, the Axis forces made a stand during February 1943 at the Mareth Line, built by the French as a fortification between Tunisia and Libya. This was flanked on both the east and the west by salt marshes, and mapping was essential for the attacking 8th Army. Two Mosquito PR IVs were sent out from England and allocated to 60 (SAAF) Squadron. They were fitted with American K–17 cameras, which were ideal for mapping purposes, and the work was carried out admirably before the defensive line was assaulted and breached.

During the Casablanca Conference between Franklin D. Roosevelt and Winston Churchill in mid-January 1943, it was considered essential to weld the USAAF and RAF operations in the Mediterranean under a single command. On 23 February 1943 the Mediterranean Air Command was formed, and within this organisation came the Northwest African Air Forces, which in turn controlled the North African Central Interpretation Unit, consisting of all the RAF photographic interpreters of the RAF's former Eastern Air Command and those of the USAAF's former Western Air Command. In the following month, the US 3rd Photographic Group and the RAF's 682 Squadron were combined into the North African Photographic Reconnaissance Wing under this new organisation, commanded by Lieutenant-Colonel Elliot Roosevelt.

The Axis forces in Tunisia finally surrendered on 14 May 1943, clearing the way for the Allies to invade southern Europe via Sicily. Photographic reconnaissance played a major part in these campaigns, as will be seen in Chapter Nine.

CHAPTER EIGHT

THE NEW SQUADRONS

By the autumn of 1942, No 1 Photographic Reconnaissance Unit at Benson had grown to such a size that it had become administratively unwieldy. Some of its flights had expanded to the size of squadrons, and were considered as such within the unit. On 19 October 1942 it was disbanded and the parts formed into five new squadrons. The Mosquito PR IVs of H and L Flights became 540 Squadron at Leuchars, under the command of Wing Commander Michael J.B. Young, with the main duty of keeping watch on the movements of the German Navy along the coasts of Norway. B and F Flights at Benson became 541 Squadron, commanded by Squadron Leader Donald W. Steventon, and retained Spitfire PR IVs with the duty of covering enemy ports and areas of Germany, Denmark, Holland and Belgium, coupled with bombing assessment sorties. A and E Flights at Benson were formed into 542 Squadron under Squadron Leader David Salway, employing Spitfire PR IVs and operating mainly from nearby Mount Farm over ports in northern France as well as on bombing assessment sorties. No 543 Squadron was formed with Spitfire PR IVs at Benson under Squadron Leader Anthony E. Hill, with A Flight detached to St Eval to cover the west coast of France as well as fly on bomb damage sorties, and B Flight established at Mount Farm to train pilots going overseas. No 544 Squadron was formed at Benson under Squadron Leader William R. Acott, with A Flight at Benson flying Ansons and Wellingtons on

experimental night photography sorties while B Flight was equipped with Spitfire PR IVs and based at Gibraltar.

Many of these duties were to some extent interchangeable, and they altered as the war progressed. In addition, 140 Squadron at Benson, equipped with Spitfire PR IVs, continued its Army co-operation work over northern France and the Dutch and Belgian coasts. Lastly, No 8 Operational Training Unit had been formed on 18 May 1942 at Fraserburgh in Aberdeenshire for training photo-reconnaissance pilots who served on home squadrons and overseas units, this work being supplemented by B Flight of 543 Squadron.

This photo-reconnaissance organisation was a far cry from the tiny unit of three years before, when Sidney Cotton had struggled to obtain suitable aircraft and recognition of its work. After the success of the Allied landings in north-west Africa, Air Vice-Marshal Charles E.H. Medhurst, the Vice-Chief of the Air Staff, stated in January 1943 that 'no Commander will now undertake an operation unless he has been completely equipped with air intelligence, not only with photographs and mosaics but also with models of the beaches he is to land on'. It was recommended that the squadrons should be given Group status, but this was not achieved until May 1944.

Operations by the RAF squadrons continued as before, but more intensively and over a wider range of targets. The Mosquito PR IV had joined the Mosquito PR I, slightly

A Consolidated Liberator I of 120 Squadron, based at Nutts Corner in Northern Ireland. This was the first version to reach the RAF, in June 1941. It carried a row of machine guns below the fuselage, operated manually, as well as 'Air to Surface Vessel' radar aerials mounted above the fuselage. With a range of about 2,400 miles, this was the first of Coastal Command's aircraft which helped to close the 'Atlantic Gap', where U-boats had hitherto been immune from attacks by shore-based aircraft. (The late Squadron Leader J.E. Archbald)

The unarmed Spitfire PR XI replaced the Spitfire PR IV from December 1942 onwards. It was fitted with the Merlin 61 series engine, giving a top speed of 422 mph, and production continued well into 1944. Some Spitfire PR XIs continued in service after the war, such as this serial PA888. (The late Squadron Leader J.E. Archbald)

The Lockheed F-4 and F-5 were photographic versions of the P-38 Lightning fighter employed by the USAAF. This photograph of F-5 serial 006, flown by Major Gerald M. Adams of the 14th Reconnaissance Squadron, 325th Reconnaissance Wing, was taken in late February 1945 from a Douglas B-26 Invader of the 7th Photo Reconnaissance Group based at Mount Farm in Oxfordshire, flown by Colonel George Humbrecht. (Dr E.V. Hawkinson USAF (Ret'd))

The K–20 was employed during the Second World War by the USAAF as a hand-held camera for day reconnaissance. Shutter speeds ranged between 1/125th and 1/500th of a second, while the lens was 6⅜-inch. The picture size was 4-inch by 5-inch, and the magazine gave 50 exposures. This camera was also used by the RAF. (J.K. Nesbit, courtesy RAF Cosford Museum)

modified with longer engine nacelles but still fitted with the twin Merlin XXIs of its predecessor, of which only ten were built. It was proposed to equip all squadrons with these long-range Mosquitos, partly on the grounds that the Spitfire PR IV was outclassed by the new Me109G. This was resisted by the pilots, who argued correctly that the Spitfire was far more manoeuvrable, much quieter, more suitable for low-level work, and possessed a much faster rate of climb than the Mosquito. Thus Spitfires were retained for the shorter range tasks, and a few of the new Mark IX fighters were adapted for photographic work and delivered to 541 Squadron in November 1942. The production version of this adaptation, known as the Spitfire PR XI, entered service with the same squadron two months later. It carried the same amount of fuel as the Spitfire PR IV but mounted a Merlin 61 engine of 1,560 hp with a two-speed, two-stage supercharger, replacing the Merlin 46 engine of its predecessor. This improved the top speed by 50 mph, attaining 422 mph. The new Spitfire PR XI also entered service with 542 Squadron in February 1943 and with 544 Squadron three months later. Some of these aircraft continued operating until the end of the war and beyond, even when new versions of PR Spitfires were introduced.

The squadrons achieved many successes in the last months of 1942 and throughout the following year. A continuous watch from Leuchars was kept on the heavy units of the Kriegsmarine in German ports and the Norwegian fjords as far north as Narvik. The German and Italian blockade runners, which had made audacious runs to the Far East and brought back vital supplies such as natural rubber, were located in the ports of western France and subjected to attacks by the RAF and the Royal Navy. By April 1943 all twenty-two of these vessels had been sunk or bottled up in ports.

The effects of bombing operations on Germany, northern Italy and occupied Europe were photographed assiduously and the results accurately interpreted. The famous attack by Lancasters of 617 Squadron on the night of 16/17 May 1943 on German dams in the Ruhr was preceded by very effective photo-reconnaissance and the results were accurately photographed during daylight. While the effects of the breaching of two dams on the German war economy may have been exaggerated at the time, the boost to the morale of the RAF and the British public generally was enormous. The effects of the huge raid by Bomber Command of 27/28 July 1943 on Hamburg, which created a firestorm and the deaths of about 40,000 people, was also photographed. This raid had been preceded by one of equivalent size on the night of 24/25 July and another by the US Eighth Air Force during daylight on 26 July. Bomber Command then continued these raids on Hamburg with another enormous attack on the night of 29/30 July, but by that time the majority of the inhabitants had fled the ruins of their city.

Of course, not all photographs taken by the RAF derived from the specialist photo-reconnaissance squadrons. All aircraft could carry cameras, some being installed forward-facing in the wings or mounted vertically in the fuselage, while others were hand-held by a crew member. Those taken by Bomber Command, mainly at night, are described in Chapter Eleven, but the daylight photographs taken from aircraft of Coastal Command often provided dramatic evidence for photo-interpreters. Some were taken from F24 cameras mounted vertically but fitted with mirrors angled backwards to record the effect of exploding bombs. G45 gun cameras mounted in the wings of aircraft such as the Beaufighter TFXs, carrying cannons, machine guns, torpedoes or rockets, provided action pictures of the final run-up at low level to

A Lockheed F-5 and a Spitfire, both serving with US reconnaissance units, photographed at a time of day when long shadows were cast. (Dr E.V. Hawkinson USAF (Ret'd))

Ground crew working on a Lockheed F-5 at Mount Farm in Oxfordshire, an airfield at which the 7th Photographic Group of the US Eighth Air Force was based. (Dr E.V. Hawkinson USAF (Ret'd))

This photograph was discovered by the Medmenham Club. It was later identified by an eyewitness, Jack Gabbutt, as Spitfire PR XI serial PL838 of 681 Squadron at Alipore in India. This was in collision with Hurricane LE294 of No 906 Wing during take-off on 24 December 1944. Neither pilot was injured. The Type 35 control on the instrument panel can be seen clearly on the original photograph; this provided a push button for single exposures and a knob for setting the time interval between successive exposures. (The Medmenham Club)

In early 1942 some Boeing B-17Fs were converted to photo-reconnaissance aircraft, designated F-9s, but it was soon discovered that they stood little chance against enemy fighters when operating in unescorted pairs during daylight. This photograph shows B-17Gs in the normal bomber role, part of the 447th Bomb Group of the US Eighth Air Force, based at Rattlesden in Suffolk. (The late Squadron Leader J.E. Archbald)

enemy convoys, while those taken with hand-held F24 cameras through the navigators' cupolas showed the effect of the attacks. Aircraft such as Liberators, hunting for submarines, sometimes brought back photographs showing the effect of depth charges or bombs on their targets, before they submerged or after being blown to the surface.

Meanwhile, the Americans had arrived in England. The US Eighth Air Force began daylight operations on 17 August 1942, although some of the American crews had flown in borrowed RAF aircraft from the previous June. Photographic units of the US Ninth Air Force followed in September 1942, but almost all their squadrons were drawn away a few weeks later to join the US Twelfth Air Force for the invasion of north-west Africa. One which remained was the 13th Photo-Reconnaissance Squadron, which moved to Mount Farm in February 1943, under Major James G. Hall, and began operations over France as part of the US Eighth Air Force. This squadron was equipped with Lockheed F–4s and F–5s, the photographic versions of the P–38 Lightning. The aircraft were fitted with K–17 cameras, the most widely used American camera of the Second World War. Unfortunately, the twin-engined Lockheeds did not possess sufficient speed or manoeuvrability to avoid German fighters, and the inexperienced American pilots suffered heavy losses in the first few weeks. The 14th Photo Reconnaissance Squadron, equipped with Spitfires, joined them in July 1943 to form the 7th Photo Recon Group. Commanded by James G. Hall, who was promoted to lieutenant-colonel, this Group formed the nucleus of a vast US photographic organisation which grew up in England.

American photo-interpreters had also begun to arrive in England, in the autumn of 1942, and joined the Central Interpretation Unit at Medmenham. In the spring of 1941 Lieutenant-Commander Robert S. Quackenbush Jr, of the US Navy's Bureau of Aeronautics Photographic Section, had been sent to the Central Interpretation Unit, together with two captains of the Marine Corps, to gain British experience. On their return to the USA they set up a photo-interpretation school at Anacosta Naval Air Station in Washington DC in order to train units for service on aircraft carriers and with amphibious forces in the Pacific. These three men had been followed at Medmenham by Captain Harvey C. Brown Jr of the US Air Corps. On Brown's return to the USA he set up a school at Harrisburg in Pennsylvania, where trainees who had already passed through the photography school at Lowry Field at Denver in Colorado received further instruction. Nevertheless, on arrival at Medmenham in 1942 these US photo-interpreters required practical experience under operational conditions. They began to acquire the skills necessary for the European theatre of war, and their co-operation with the RAF proved remarkably harmonious. All photographs which arrived at Medmenham received equal priority, whether originating from the RAF or the US Army Air Force (which supplanted the US Air Corps on 20 June 1941), and could be interpreted by officers of either country.

On 26 June 1943 No 106 (PR) Wing was formed, controlling the operations of all photo-reconnaissance units in Britain other than those allocated to the new Second Tactical Air Force, which was formed for the purpose of invading north-west Europe. This new Wing included the US 7th Photo-Reconnaissance Group as well as the RAF's 540, 541, 542, 543 and 544 Squadrons. In the following month, No 34 (PR) Wing was formed under the Second Tactical Air Force, with 140 and 16 Squadrons. The former was equipped with Spitfires and the latter with North American Mustang Is, converted for tactical photo-reconnaissance.

The Eder Dam photographed on 13 May 1943 byFllying Officer G.W. Puttick in Spitfire PR XI serial BS502 of 542 Squadron at Benson in Oxfordshire, with a spot of cloud covering the basin below. (*Aeroplane Monthly*)

An almost identical photograph of the Eder Dam on 18 May 1943, thirty hours after the attack by 617 Squadron, taken by Flying Officer D.G. Scott in Spitfire PR XI serial EN411 of 542 Squadron at Benson in Oxfordshire, showing water still pouring through the breach in the wall. (*Aeroplane Monthly*)

The Möhne Dam photographed by Flying Officer F.G. Fray in Spitfire PR XI serial EN343 of 542 Squadron a few hours after the attack by 617 Squadron on 16/17 May 1943, showing water still pouring through a breach over 200 feet wide and foam covering the remains of the power station. (*Aeroplane Monthly*)

On the night of 17/18 August 1943, the RAF's Bomber Command despatched 596 aircraft on a massive raid against the German rocket research establishment at Peenemünde on the Baltic coast, following extensive photo-reconnaissance and photo-interpretation. Forty bombers were lost, mainly as a result of the effectiveness of German nightfighters newly equipped with air interception radar and upward-firing cannons, but several scientists and numerous other workers were killed at the research station. It was estimated that the German rocket programme was set back by about two months and its scale considerably reduced.

The British Secret Intelligence Service had been aware for several years that the Germans were experimenting with rockets propelled by liquid fuel. From December 1942 reports from agents in neutral countries indicated that these experiments had reached the advanced stage of development at Peenemünde. Meanwhile, an airfield in the vicinity of this target had been photographed on 15 May 1942 by Flight Lieutenant Donald W. Steventon in a Spitfire of No 1 Photographic Reconnaissance Unit, who happened to notice it on the Baltic coast while en route to photograph Swinemünde. The results showed some puzzling circular objects in the nearby woods. The interpreters noted these as 'heavy constructional work' and the photographs were filed.

The Chiefs of Staff became increasingly perturbed by reports from agents of these German rockets, including information from the French Resistance of the construction near Calais of ramps pointed towards London. The Joint Parliamentary Secretary to the Ministry of Supply, Duncan Sandys, was appointed in April 1943 to take control of enquiries, while Wing Commander Hamshaw Thomas, who at the time was in charge of all 'third phase' work at Medmenham, controlled the photographic interpretation.

Peenemünde was photographed on several occasions, and certain earthworks were noted as possible stands for launching missiles. Then large rockets, some standing vertically and others lying horizontally, were identified from photographs taken in June by Mosquitos of 540 Squadron. These became known as V–2 rockets. From the photographs, Flight Officer Constance Babington Smith was also able to measure an aircraft which was later identified as the Me163 rocket fighter, which in May 1944 became the first jet-propelled aircraft to enter operational service anywhere in the world.

Photographs taken over northern France disclosed the existence of large concrete structures in the woods at Watten, near Calais, which were identified as possible launching ramps for rockets. On 27 August 1943, ten days after Bomber Command's night raid on Peenemünde, the US Eighth Air Force despatched 227 Boeing B–17 Flying Fortresses on a daylight raid to these targets, escorted by 137 Republic P–47 Thunderbolts. The sites, which were later known to have been constructed for V–1 flying bombs, were destroyed. The danger of rocket attacks against London seemed to have been forestalled for the time being.

In the late summer of 1943, another detachment of photo-reconnaissance aircraft was sent to north Russia, employing the older Spitfire PR IVs. Sea convoys to Russia had been suspended during the summer months but it was time for their resumption when daylight hours began to shorten. Three Spitfires of 543 Squadron, flown by Squadron Leader F.A. 'Tony' Robinson, Flying Officer B. Roy Kenwright and Flying Officer Johnny H. Dixon, took off on 3 September from Sumburgh in the Shetlands and flew direct to Vaenga. Kenwright's flight lasted five and a half hours and he ran out of petrol as he landed. Airmen photographers, with Corporal J.M. Davies in charge, left by

The pilot of a photo-reconnaissance Spitfire of 541 Squadron, Pilot Officer J.R. Myles from Canada, being debriefed by an intelligence officer in an Operations Room, after returning from a daylight sortie over Frankfurt in which he photographed the results of a raid by Bomber Command during the previous night. (*Aeroplane Monthly*)

Second phase interpretation being carried out on reconnaissance photographs by Z Section at Medmenham. The officer on the right was Lieutenant Xavier Alencio of the USAAF, who in civilian life was an animator of Disney Studios. (The Medmenham Club)

Mass production of town plans from aerial photographs at Medmenham, using a stylograph. (The Medmenham Club)

Captain L.E. Hollinger of the USAAF and Section Officer Kitty Sancto of the WAAF studying photographs of the Binnen Alsten in Hamburg, at the Allied Central Interpretation Unit at Medmenham. (The Medmenham Club)

Flight Sergeant Steve Waring working in the Model Section at Medmenham in 1943. The models were built up with the help of photographs taken by photo-reconnaissance aircraft. (The Medmenham Club)

sea, together with the language officer, Pilot Officer B. 'Booby' Trapp. Two photo-interpretation officers, Flying Officers R.R. Eyre and W.M. Hodsman, flew in a Catalina of 333 (Norwegian) Squadron from Sullom Voe in the Shetlands. A ridiculous episode occurred when the Russians impounded the aircrew's homing pigeons, which were used for conveying distress messages from men in dinghies, and kept the birds under armed guard in a shed until the Catalina departed.

On this occasion the RAF personnel were billeted in two flats on the top floor of a bomb-battered building in the nearby town of Grasnaya, where they lived mainly on tinned food left over from the 1942 detachment. A photographic processing vehicle which had been left in 1942 was pressed back into service, for the Russians had not discovered how to use the equipment. An efficient processing and printing section was set up, although the Russians were inclined to steal the liquid chemicals, under the impression that they were alcohol.

Once again, the pilots carried out their flights over the *Tirpitz* in Altenfjord, for their operations were associated with the forthcoming attack on the battleship by midget submarines of the Royal Navy. Excellent photographs were sent back to the UK, contributing to the attack of 22 September 1943 when the battleship was crippled. Their duties successfully completed, the detachment arrived back in the UK by destroyer on 11 November. The men found that 543 Squadron, which had been commanded for a year by Squadron Leader Gordon E. Hughes, had been disbanded three weeks before they landed, and its Spitfires and personnel distributed among the other photo-reconnaissance squadrons.

The Russians awarded Kenwright and Dixon their medal for Distinguished Battle Service, while Tony Robinson received the Order of the Patriotic War. The latter carried a pension of £1 a year, but this ceased after five years.

During the summer and early autumn of 1943, Spitfires of 541 Squadron continued to comb northern France for enemy positions, and certain installations of a new type began to show up on the photographs. At the end of September a report from the French Resistance gave the positions of 'secret weapon launching sites'. Photo-reconnaissance continued and about a hundred 'ski sites' were discovered from the Pas de Calais to Cherbourg, springing up at an alarming rate but cleverly camouflaged. From 5 December 1943, these were attacked relentlessly by Bomber Command, the US Eighth Air Force and the Second Tactical Air Force, and aerial photographs showed that the majority were destroyed or damaged. However, defensive precautions took place in England, in the form of massed anti-aircraft guns, balloon zones and fighter zones, against an assault by flying bombs and rockets which by then seemed inevitable. Meanwhile, the photo-reconnaissance squadrons in Britain, both RAF and USAAF, were presented with the additional task of preparing for the forthcoming invasion of Normandy.

The bomb-damaged barrack block at Grasnaya in north Russia which housed the RAF's photo-reconnaissance contingent during 1943 and 1944, when operating from Vaenga airfield. This photograph was taken in the autumn of 1943. (The late Squadron Leader J.E. Archbald)

The experimental rocket site on the island of Peenemünde on the Baltic coast. (Flight Officer Constance Babington Smith MBE, WAAF)

The V–2 rocket establishment at Peenemünde photographed in September 1944, showing the damage caused by Bomber Command's heavy raid of the night of 17/18 August 1943, after which much of the work on the site was moved to Blizna in Poland. The arrow marked 'A' indicated that light flak positions on the roof of the damaged building had been removed. (*Aeroplane Monthly*)

CHAPTER NINE

EUROPE'S UNDERBELLY

When the remaining Axis forces in Tunisia surrendered on 14 May 1943, the Allied forces poised to attack the 'soft underbelly of Europe', in the vivid phrase of Winston Churchill, included the North African Photographic Reconnaissance Wing of the Mediterranean Air Command. In July 1943 this Allied Wing was based at La Marsa in Tunisia and commanded by Lieutenant-Colonel Elliot Roosevelt. The RAF's contribution to the Wing consisted of the Spitfire PR IVs and PR XIs of 682 Squadron, based at La Marsa and commanded by Squadron Leader A.H.W. 'Freddie' Ball. The American contribution consisted of the 3rd Photo-Reconnaissance Group, with the Lockheed F–5s of the 5th and 12th Squadrons and the B–17 Fortresses of the 15th Squadron. It should be noted that an American Wing was in command of Groups, the reverse of the RAF's nomenclature.

The Wing also controlled the North African Central Intelligence Unit (NACIU), staffed by RAF photo-interpreters of the old Eastern Air Command and Americans of the US Twelfth Air Force. This became the centre in Tunisia for all Allied photographic interpretation and the resulting intelligence information. Three Mobile Photographic and Interpretation Units were preparing to participate in the invasion of southern Europe.

In addition, there were other RAF photo-reconnaissance squadrons further east in the Mediterranean. The Spitfire PR IVs and PR XIs of 683 Squadron remained at Luqa in Malta under the command of Wing Commander Adrian Warburton, while at the same base were the Baltimores of 69 Squadron, commanded by Wing Commander Terance M. Channon. Covering the eastern Mediterranean were the Spitfire PR IVs and PR IXs of 680 Squadron at LG219 near Heliopolis, commanded by Wing Commander J. Roger Whelan.

Demarcation lines were established for these photo-reconnaissance squadrons in Africa. The North African Photographic Reconnaissance Wing concentrated on the area to the west of longitude 12 degrees East, which included Sardinia and Corsica. The area to the east of 12 degrees East, including Sicily, Pantellaria and Italy, was covered by the RAF's 683 Squadron and 69 Squadron at Malta. From Headquarters Middle East, 680 Squadron covered the Mediterranean eastwards of the Greek island of Corfu.

In addition to these activities, which were primarily strategic, 285 Photographic Reconnaissance Wing, commanded by Group Captain Edward G.L. Millington at Sorman West in Libya, was allocated much of the shorter range tactical work for the invasion of Sicily. This Wing had already carried out skilled photo-reconnaissance work in the Western Desert in support of the British 8th Army. It now came under the North African Tactical Air Force, and consisted of 60 (SAAF) Squadron with Mosquito PR IVs and Baltimores commanded by Major Owen

A model of Palermo in Sicily, constructed from photography taken at 35,000 feet. (Squadron Leader P. Lamboit RAFVR)

Davies, 40 (SAAF) Squadron with Spitfire VBs and commanded by Lieutenant-Colonel J.P. Bleaaw, and 1437 Flight with six Mustang A–36s commanded by Squadron Leader S.G. Welshman. All these aircraft operated from Luqa prior to the invasion. The American contribution to this tactical reconnaissance section of the North African Tactical Air Force was the 111th Tactical Reconnaissance Squadron equipped with Mustang F–6s; this was part of the US Twlefth Support Command.

No 60 (SAAF) Squadron had become adept at mapping future battlegrounds and was equipped with the only Mosquito PR IVs available for photo-reconnaissance in the Mediterranean. The squadron had also managed to borrow from the UK a couple of the new Mosquito PR IXs, the high-altitude photo-reconnaissance version of the latest Mosquito bomber. Fitted with F52 cameras, the Mosquitos' surveys over Sicily were essential in planning the invasion. A detachment of Mosquitos from this squadron had also been sent to Tunisia, from where the aircraft surveyed the beaches of Sardinia, which had been considered as possible landing places, although the invasion of this Italian island was deferred in favour of Sicily. The Mustang A–36 was a development of the famous Mustang P–51 fighter, with two seats in tandem and two oblique cameras. The six Mustang A–36s flown by the RAF's 1437 Flight had been transferred from the US Twelfth Air Force.

There were three main objectives in the photo-reconnaissance operations. The first of these was to obtain vertical photography for large-scale mapping. The second was to take obliques of static positions such as beaches, defended river banks and other military objectives. The third was to discover the activity of the enemy by tactical reconnaissance over changing positions.

The shortage of suitable aircraft for the RAF photo-reconnaissance squadrons continued to give cause for concern. The older Spitfire PR IVs were outclassed by German fighters, especially the FW190, and only a handful of the new Spitfire PR XIs had become available. Mosquito PR IVs and PR IXs were demanded, but none could be supplied at this stage other than the few operated by 60 (SAAF) Squadron. This situation was not remedied satisfactorily for several months.

The joint Anglo-American invasion of Sicily, code-named Operation 'Husky', began on the night of 9/10 July 1943. Although some of the Allied airborne forces met with disaster when gliders were released prematurely by their tugs in adverse weather conditions, the invasion developed into a successful campaign. Meanwhile, the North African Photographic Reconnaissance Wing remained at La Marsa and its squadrons continued to operate from their North African bases. But some of the tactical photo-reconnaissance squadrons began to move to Sicily. The Spitfire VBs of 40 (SAAF) Squadron arrived at Pachino on 15 July. In addition a ground detachment was sent by ship from Bizerta in Tunisia to Syracuse in Sicily. This included photographers and one J-type trailer, together with tentage and equipment. From Syracuse, the detachment established itself at Lentini, south of Catania. The Spitfire VBs of 40 (SAAF) Squadron moved to this base on 27 July and it was also used by a detachment of Mosquitos from 60 (SAAF) Squadron, which by then was based at Sabratha in Libya, together with 285 Wing. The Mustang A–36s of 1437 Flight arrived at Francesco in Sicily on 31 July, but 285 Wing did not move to the island until early September.

The J-type trailer, which had been used by photographic personnel in France during 1939/40, was employed far more effectively in Sicily and later on the Italian mainland. It was a mobile darkroom designed for the hand processing and printing of films. Partly air-conditioned, it was divided into two compartments, a small processing room and a larger printing room. A generator set provided an independent power source in the field. Darkroom accommodation could be increased by the addition of a photographic tent which consisted of a steel framework on the ends of which were suspended one or more darkroom tents, the whole being covered by an outer waterproof canvas. This tent gave a central working space of 11 feet by 8 feet, with each adjoining darkroom section about 6 feet by 8 feet. In addition, a marquee was used to accommodate the washing, drying, numbering, finishing and sorting of the films and prints. The whole arrangement was not perfect, for there were difficulties in maintaining a strict black-out when working at night, and the detachment operated in an area subjected to several enemy air raids.

In addition to this detachment, No 3 Mobile Field Photographic Section (No 3 MFPS) under the command of Flight Lieutenant A. May arrived at Lentini, together with photographic semi-trailers, having left Africa on 19 July. These trailers, first introduced in 1942, provided accommodation for the processing, printing and duplication of films, on the same scale as a static section. A complete unit consisted of five semi-trailers, providing facilities for the continuous film-processing machine as well as the universal multi-printing machine and the enlarging-copying camera. The unit included lithotex print-drying equipment and could cope with contact printing, negative duplicating and film drying.

At Lentini, the photographic sections were set up about a mile from the airfield, adjacent to a stream which provided the nearest available water for washing films and prints. But film drying presented a real problem at first. Strange spectacles were sometimes presented by groups of airmen – photographers, electricians, instrument mechanics and transport drivers – strung out across the Sicilian airfield and holding long wet films, waving them gently in the breeze. Mosquitos stuck to the films like flies to sticky paper, moths settled on them affectionately, while wisps of vegetation draped themselves around them. Nevertheless, good results were achieved.

The Sicilian campaign was the beginning of the end for the Italians, who had entered the war at a time when Hitler had defeated the Anglo-French forces in Western Europe and felt that they could share in the spoils of the German victory. They had not anticipated their own defeats in Africa or the RAF's devastating attacks against their northern cities and ports further south, which were intensified in this period and the results photographed assiduously. By the end of August 1943 only a few Italian diehards had the stomach for further conflict. However, the Germans fought stubbornly and skilfully, eventually retreating in good order across the Straits of Messina to Italy.

The mainland was invaded on 3 September 1943 and Italy surrendered five days later, although the tough Wehrmacht and a few Italian fascist units continued a fierce resistance. No 285 Wing began to move to Sicily on 4 September and nine days later crossed over to Italy and eventually arrived at Foggia near the east coast. No 3 MFPS followed the British 8th Army to Reggio in the toe of Italy and then to a series of positions up the east coast. Flight Lieutenant May fell sick and was posted back to base, command passing to Flight Lieutenant T.J. Mathews, who had previously commanded No 2 MFPS at La Marsa. Both 40 (SAAF) Squadron and 1437 Flight also arrived at Foggia in early October, but 1437 Flight was disbanded on the 13th of that month and its

A group of senior officers examining a photographic mosaic at La Marsa in Tunisia. Left to right: unknown brigadier (British Army), Colonel Elliot Roosevelt (USAAF), General Sir Harold Alexander (Deputy Allied C-in-C North Theatre), unknown major-general (British Army), unknown US officer, Major-General Carl Spaatz (USAAF, C-in-C Northwest African Air Forces). The heavily fortified island of Pantellaria, on the wall map, surrendered to the British 3rd Infantry Brigade Group on 11 June 1943, after a heavy air raid and a bombardment from the sea. (Warrant Officer J.H. Eggleston RAF (Ret'd))

General Dwight D. Eisenhower (Allied C-in-C in the North-African theatre) at the air film negative library of the North African Photographic Reconnaissance Wing at La Marsa in Tunisia, with Squadron Leader S.R. 'Wally' Walton and Colonel Elliot Roosevelt smiling at him. (Warrant Officer J.H. Eggleston RAF (Ret'd))

Left to right: Air Chief Marshal Sir Arthur Tedder (Air C-in-C Mediterranean Air Command), Squadron Leader S.R. Walton (Photographic Officer), Brigadier-General Patrick W. Timberlake (Director of Operations, USAAF), Colonel Elliot Roosevelt (Commander of the North African Photographic Reconnaissance Wing). They were discussing photographs prior to the invasion of the Italian mainland in September 1943. (Warrant Officer J.H. Eggleston RAF (Ret'd))

place taken by 225 Squadron, equipped with Spitfire VCs, another tactical photo-reconnaissance squadron which had been working temporarily with the Allied Tactical Bomber Force.

The North African Photographic Reconnaissance Wing remained at La Marsa for several months after Sicily was invaded. Its commander, Elliot Roosevelt, has been accused of anglophobia and to some extent the allegation is justified. Certainly he resented any British domination of USAAF activities, either in the Mediterranean or in England, but at the operational level he was on cordial terms with RAF aircrews and ground personnel. Aged thirty-two, he had qualified as a civilian pilot before the war, although a minor problem with eyesight prevented his acceptance into the USAAF in that capacity. Instead, he had qualified as a navigator and frequently flew on operations, sometimes taking the controls. He was generous enough to use his B–17 Flying Fortress to carry what were regarded as luxury foodstuffs and even refrigerators to Malta, where shortages still existed in the RAF messes. At both Luqa and La Marsa, the Americans were particularly fascinated by Wing Commander Warburton's vast operational experience as well as his unconventional approach to life.

With the geographical changes in the Allied positions, the Mediterranean Air Command was again reorganised. On 30 October 1943 the new British 336 Wing was formed at La Marsa in Tunisia under the North African Photographic Reconnaissance Wing. This controlled 680 Squadron in Egypt and 682 Squadron at La Marsa, both by then equipped with Spitfire PR IXs in addition to the older machines. Also, 683 Squadron in Malta came under the new Wing, equipped with Mosquito PR IVs and Spitfire PR XIs. Lastly, 60 (SAAF) Squadron, by then at Ariana in Tunisia and equipped with Mosquito PR VIs and PR IXs, was transferred to it from 285 Wing. This British Wing was responsible for the provision of photo-reconnaissance detachments to operate wherever required, either with the North African Tactical Air Force or under the control of the AOC-in-C Middle East.

The new 336 Wing was commanded by Wing Commander Adrian Warburton, who had handed over his 683 Squadron to Squadron Leader Harry S. Smith at the beginning of October 1943 and then spent a leave in England. Decorated with the DSO and bar and the DFC and two bars, Warburton had flown the astonishing total of 390 sorties and achieved the status of the premier photographic pilot of the war. He was also on terms of personal friendship with Lieutenant-Colonel Elliot Roosevelt. Unfortunately, the charmed life that he had enjoyed in the air did not continue on the ground. He had been presented with a personal jeep by Elliot Roosevelt and was involved in an accident on 26 November, which was sufficiently serious to put him into hospital at Algiers until late January 1944. His post was taken over temporarily by Wing Commander Freddie Ball.

In November 1943 a reorganisation of the American photo-reconnaissance units also took place when the 3rd Photo Group was joined by the 5th Photographic Group, consisting of two US squadrons. The Free French *Groupe de Reconnaissance* 2/33 was attached to these, but remained under French command. The 90th Photographic Wing was formed to control the 3rd and 5th Groups which, in addition to their other duties, provided photo-reconnaissance for the US Twelfth Air Force and the US Fifteenth Air Force, the latter having replaced the US Ninth Air Force, which had returned to England.

From LG219 near Heliopolis, the Spitfire PR IXs of 680 Squadron continued to cover

A photographic mosaic of the British 8th Army – the Desert Rats – invading the south-east corner of Sicily on 10 July 1943, in the Gulf of Noto. The United States 7th Army went ashore further to the west. The landings were successful everywhere. (The late Squadron Leader J.E. Archbald)

Receiving film magazines at a J-type processing trailer, at Lentini in Sicily in 1943. (Warrant Officer J.H. Eggleston RAF (Ret'd))

The water supply for washing photographic prints at Lentini in Sicily in 1943. (Warrant Officer J.H. Eggleston RAF (Ret'd))

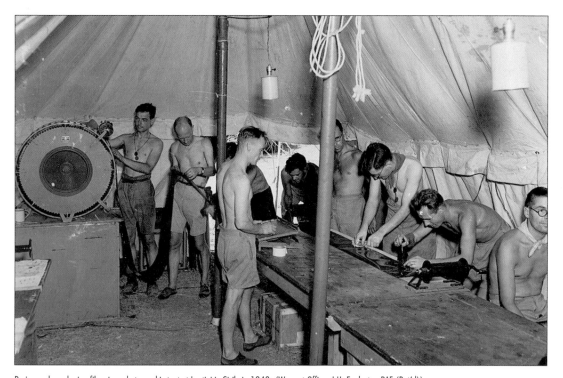

Drying and numbering films in a photographic tent at Lentini in Sicily in 1943. (Warrant Officer J.H. Eggleston RAF (Ret'd))

the eastern Mediterranean, but British military operations in this area suffered a severe setback. It had been decided to seize the Italian-held island of Rhodes in advance of an invasion of Greece and a possible link-up with the advancing Russians in south-east Europe. The island was garrisoned by the Germans. After extensive photographic cover by 680 Squadron, British troops landed by sea on 15 September 1943 on two other islands in the Italian Dodecanese, Cos and Leros, with the intention of cutting off Rhodes from the mainland. Further north, the island of Samos was invaded on the following day. As expected, the Italian garrisons surrendered, but the German reaction was surprisingly swift and effective. They withdrew aircraft from other spheres of operations and, with overwhelming strength and far shorter lines of communications, subjected the airfields on the islands to continual attack. Aided by dive-bombing Ju87s, German seaborne and airborne forces landed on Cos on 3 October and overcame the British. Leros followed on 12 November and Samos ten days later, the defenders becoming casualties or prisoners. Although the Germans also suffered heavy losses of ships, aircraft and troops, the British enterprise had to be classed as an expensive failure.

In December 1943, when the British 8th Army and the American 5th Army had fought their way beyond Naples, the North African Photographic Reconnaissance Wing transferred from La Marsa to San Severo, about 20 miles north-east of the Allied operational air bases around Foggia. Three squadrons of 336 Wing moved to this new base. These were 60 (SAAF), 682 and 683 Squadrons, while 680 Squadron remained in Egypt to cover the eastern Mediterranean. By then, this British Wing was commanded by Wing Commander Gordon E. Hughes, who had commanded 543 Squadron at Benson in

England for a year before its disbandment in October 1943.

There was yet another change in the command structure on 10 December 1943 when the Mediterranean Air Command and the North African Allied Air Forces were merged into the Mediterranean Allied Air Force. The North African Photographic Reconnaissance Wing was placed under the command of the new Allied Air Headquarters and renamed the Mediterranean Allied Photographic Reconnaissance Wing (MAPRW).

By this time the 'European underbelly' had proved far less soft than anticipated, for the Germans formed a very effective defensive line from coast to coast across Italy, backed by the heights around Monte Cassino and protecting the approaches to Rome. The Allied attempt to outflank this line by launching the seaborne landings at Anzio on 22 January 1944 were contained by the enemy. The bombing of the Monastery of Monte Cassino on 15 February, believed to be the hub of the German defences, had no effect. It was not until the opening of their spring offensive on 11 May 1944 that the Allies were able to make any considerable advances up the peninsula of Italy.

Meanwhile, on 25 January 1944, Colonel Elliot Roosevelt, who had been awarded a CBE by the British for his work in the Mediterranean, was recalled to England to take command of the strategic photo-reconnaissance units of the US Eighth Air Force. Command of his MAPRW in Italy was taken over by another American officer, Colonel Karl 'Pop' Polifka of the USAAF, an outstanding and popular pilot with much experience of flying the Lockheed F–5.

In England, Colonel Roosevelt began work on what became, in August 1944, the 325th Strategic Photographic Reconnaissance Wing. He asked for Adrian Warburton to be appointed as his deputy and the British pilot arrived at his headquarters at Mount Farm in Oxfordshire on 1 April 1944. By this time Warburton had been awarded the American DFC in addition to his other decorations. It is possible that he had not fully recovered from his injuries, and certainly he seemed to be suffering from depression. However, on 12 April 1944 he took off in a Lockheed F–5B of the USAAF, serial 42–67325, to photograph the ball-bearing plant at Schweinfurt, 100 miles north of Munich, which was due to be attacked by the US Eighth Air Force on that day. It was intended that he would then continue south and land at Alghero in Sardinia, which had been captured by the Allies. As it happened, the American bombers were forced to turn back owing to dense cloud, but the exact fate of Warburton remains a mystery, for he simply disappeared. It was thought that he might have hit a mountain somewhere high and inaccessible in the Swiss or Austrian Alps, but no trace of him or his aircraft was ever found. He was aged twenty-six and had become a legendary figure in the world of photo-reconnaissance, both British and American.*

On 31 July 1944 another celebrated photo-reconnaissance pilot also lost his life, in the same type of machine as that flown by Warburton. This was Commandant (Major) Antoine de Saint-Exupéry, a 44-year-old Frenchman who had achieved fame as a pilot, a thinker, a novelist and an essayist. He had served in the French Air Force in the 1920s and then as a commercial pilot on African and South Atlantic routes. In spite of injuries sustained in crashes, he rejoined the French Air Force on the outbreak of war and became a photo-reconnaissance pilot. After the fall of France, he escaped to America and eventually joined the *1ère Escadrille* (1st Flight) of the *Groupe de Reconnaissance 2/33*, which was attached to the 23rd Squadron of the US 5th

Photographic Group but remained under Free French command. He took off at dawn on 31 July 1944 from Bastia-Borgo in Corsica in a Lockheed F–5B serial 42–68223, bearing French markings. His duty was a reconnaissance over the Grenoble–Annecy area but, like Warburton, he disappeared and no satisfactory trace of his aircraft has ever been found. Some of his manuscripts and drawings were discovered in his effects and published posthumously.

The US 5th Photographic Group was engaged on reconnaissance of the south coast of France, preparatory to an invasion by the US 5th Army with the object of linking up with the Allied Armies which had already landed in Normandy. In this reconnaissance work it was assisted by several Spitfire PR IXs of 682 Squadron which were detached from San Severo to operate from Alghero in Sardinia. The invasion began on 14/15 August 1944 and the initial landings were almost unopposed.

Back in Italy, the Mediterranean Allied Photographic Reconnaissance Wing continued to operate from San Severo, although its US 3rd Photo Group was based at Naples until the end of the war. When the US operations began from Naples there were no American photographic ground personnel to support them and the work was undertaken by some of the RAF's No 2 Mobile Field Photographic Section, commanded by Flight Lieutenant White. This RAF section was posted away from Naples after a few months.

San Severo was a hive of activity during this period, with day and night shifts turning out prints by the thousand. From Foggia, Spitfire PR XIs and Mosquito PR IXs flew over everything of strategic interest between Munich in Germany and Ploesti in Romania, as well as over Yugoslavia and the south of France. The longest return flight in a single-engined aircraft was attained on 25 June by the commanding officer of 336 Wing, Wing

* See Appendix II.

The town of San Severo, near Foggia in Italy, was the home of the Mediterranean Allied Photographic Reconnaissance Wing from the end of 1943. About a hundred RAF photographers were based in the headquarters, in addition to US personnel. The American units split away in October 1944, and henceforth RAF photography came under 336 Wing. This photograph was taken with an F24 camera in February 1945. (Flight Sergeant K. Loweth RAF (Ret'd))

Commander Gordon Hughes DSO DFC, when he flew in a Spitfire PR XI over Ulm, on the Danube in southern Germany. Although there were accepted limits to the sphere of operations, a Mosquito of 60 (SAAF) Squadron flew on a return flight as far as the southern outskirts of Berlin on one occasion. On other sorties, Mosquitos flew all the way to England in single hops, taking photographs en route and returning later on similar operations.

The Mediterranean Allied Photographic Reconnaissance Wing at San Severo included approximately a hundred RAF photographers. In addition there were the photographic personnel of 60 (SAAF) Squadron, while the American squadrons at San Severo had their own photographic personnel. There was also a USAAF photographic capability at Foggia. Co-ordination between the RAF and the USAAF was carried out by the RAF Senior Photographic Officer, Squadron Leader S.R. 'Wally' Walton, who was posted away later in 1944 and replaced by Squadron Leader B.K. Barber.

When the Allies reached Rome in June 1944, almost complete air supremacy was achieved in Italy, and this lasted until the end of the war. This was of great benefit to the photographic squadrons, and an enormous amount of tactical intelligence information was accumulated. One flight of either 682 Squadron or 683 Squadron operated alongside the tactical reconnaissance squadrons of 285 Wing. All these sorties served the American 5th Army and the British 8th Army by covering German positions and lines of communication. They were backed by the 'cab rank' system of RAF and USAAF fighters circling in the air until called upon to attack enemy positions as soon as located, either from the air or by the troops on the ground. The Allied Armies fought their way up the Italian peninsula with the aid of this method.

The Mobile Field Photographic Sections were also kept constantly busy, moving up with the advance from airstrip to airstrip. Flight Lieutenant White commanded No 2 MFPS on the west side of Italy while Flight Lieutenant Mathews commanded No 3 MFPs on the east. Each MFPS remained for about ten or fourteen days at each location, but was split into three parts to ensure mobility and to maintain continuous operations. On the first day of a move to a new location, an advance party moved up to the new area, to find suitable accommodation and facilities such as water and drainage. On the second day, the main party moved to the new site, and on the third day the rear party completed its work at the previous site and joined the new location.

At the beginning of September 1944, the USAAF decided that its Twelfth and Fifteenth Air Forces should have their own photographic Groups, preparatory to a possible move to another theatre of war, leaving the British photographic and intelligence organisations to meet the needs of the RAF and the 8th Army in Italy. Thus, on 1 October 1944, the Mediterranean Allied Photographic Reconnaissance Wing and the American 90th Photographic Wing were disbanded, and the American 3rd and 5th Photographic Groups were transferred to their Twelfth and Fifteenth Air Forces respectively. The RAF photographic squadrons in Italy were then controlled by their 336 Wing and 285 Wing until the end of the war.

On 29 April 1945 the German and Italian fascist units remaining in Italy, numbering almost a million men, surrendered to the Allies, the ceasefire becoming effective three days later. Among the victors, the RAF and USAAF photo-reconnaissance aircrews who served in Italy were all of high quality, as were their ground crews, not least among whom were the photographers. The

Continuous film processing machines being assembled at San Severo in Italy in early 1944. (Warrant Officer J.H. Eggleston RAF (Ret'd))

Print finishing in a school building at San Severo in Italy in early 1944. (Warrant Officer J.H. Eggleston RAF (Ret'd))

General Mark W. Clark, commander of the US 5th Army, arriving by Dakota at an airfield in Italy. An Auster light monoplane can be seen behind his tall figure. Together with Field Marshal Sir Harold Alexander, the Supreme Allied Commander in the Mediterranean, Clark accepted the unconditional surrender of the German forces in Italy on 29 April 1945, the cease-fire being ordered for 2 May. (Squadron Leader P. Lamboit RAFVR)

combination of strategic and tactical photo-reconnaissance squadrons working in concert with both static and mobile ground photographic sections, all responding to the requirements of the RAF and the Army, was proved correct. Even before the end of the war in Italy, these techniques were to prove invaluable during the invasion of Normandy and the subsequent drive towards the German homeland.

CHAPTER TEN

PHOTOGRAPHY AND THE INVASION

By the late autumn of 1943, the British had good grounds for believing that the war against Germany could be brought to a successful conclusion. The Axis forces had been cleared out of North Africa, Sicily was in Allied hands, the mainland of Italy had been invaded and the Italians had surrendered. The menace of U-boats was receding, following improved intelligence, the bombing of production plants in Germany and the closing of the 'Atlantic Gap' by long-distance aircraft fitted with new equipment. Germany itself was being subjected to 'round the clock' strategic bombing, by the USAAF in daylight and the RAF at night. In all these operations photo-reconnaissance played a prominent part and had become recognised by high-ranking Allied commanders as an essential instrument when making decisions. Further east, the German invasion of Russia had been halted and turned back, with terrible losses. It became evident to the British public that the Allies were preparing to invade western Europe and begin liberating the occupied countries.

Strategic reconnaissance continued under the RAF's No 106 (PR) Wing. By early 1944 this consisted of the RAF's 540, 541, 542 and 544 Squadrons, 543 Squadron having been disbanded in October 1943. These squadrons were equipped with either Mosquito PR IXs or Spitfire PR XIs, although the new

Mosquito PR XVI and Spitfire XIX, both with pressurised cabins and improved performance, were beginning to appear. In addition, the US Eighth Air Force made its contribution to strategic reconnaissance with the squadrons of its 7th and 25th Groups, equipped with Lightnings, together with Spitfires and Mosquitos borrowed from the RAF. Colonel Elliot Roosevelt was transferred to England in January 1944 to command these US Groups, which later became the 325th Reconnaissance Wing.

Relations between the RAF and USAAF units had been very harmonious in 1943, but in January 1944 Lieutenant-General James H. Doolittle, who had previously commanded the US Twelfth Air Force in the Mediterranean and now commanded the US Eighth Air Force, made it known that he would require independent control of his own photo-reconnaissance and photo-interpretation. This demand was strongly backed by Colonel Roosevelt, who acted as his advocate in the matter. Some difficult meetings and negotiations took place, but eventually it was decided to form No 106 (Photo-Reconnaissance) Group on 15 May 1944, to co-ordinate and control all USAAF and RAF strategic photo-intelligence work, other than the squadrons of the Allied Expeditionary Air Force set up in November 1943 for the invasion of Europe.

The Consolidated Liberator GRVI entered Coastal Command in the summer of 1944, joining the earlier versions of this highly successful 'very long range' aircraft. It was fitted with twin .50-inch machine guns in nose, dorsal and tail turrets as well as a single .50-inch in each waist position. This machine, photographed at St Eval in Cornwall, was also fitted with a Leigh Light under the starboard wing, for picking out U-boats at night. A church can be seen in the background of this photograph. This was originally built in Norman times and was within the boundary of the aerodrome during the Second World War. It has now reverted to its function as a parish church, but has been refurbished to commemorate the RAF and USAAF squadrons which served at St Eval. (Flight Lieutenant G.H. Parry RAF (Ret'd))

The Mosquito PR XVI was the first photo-reconnaissance variant to be fitted with a pressurised cabin for high-altitude work. It was adapted from the Mosquito XVI bomber and began to appear at the end of 1943. This photograph shows a Mark XVI painted in the invasion stripes. (*Aeroplane Monthly*)

The Hawker Typhoon IB is best remembered for its role as a rocket-firing fighter-bomber in the RAF's Second Tactical Air Force. The aircraft in this photograph, painted with invasion stripes, was fitted with four 20 mm cannons in the wings but there was provision for eight rockets or two 1,000 lb bombs. A G45 ciné camera was fitted in the nose. (*Aeroplane Monthly*)

Spring 1944 at Grasnaya, near Vaenga airfield in north Russia. Left to right: Flying Officer E.G. Searle (pilot), Flight Lieutenant Nicholas (equipment officer), Squadron Leader D.R.M. Furniss (pilot and commanding officer), Flight Lieutenant H.K. Pusey (photo-interpretation officer). (The late Squadron Leader J.E. Archbald)

This new 106 Group was commanded by Air Commodore John N. Boothman, who was promoted from his position as station commander of RAF Benson, with Group Captain Peter J.A. Riddell as his Senior Air Staff Officer. It remained under the control of Coastal Command but included a very strong American representation. The Central Interpretation Unit at Medmenham was given the prefix 'Allied' on the same date. Lastly, the Joint Photographic Reconnaissance Committee was set up to ensure that duties were equitably apportioned to the British and the Americans, and that all information was pooled.

Meanwhile, another photo-reconnaissance detachment was sent to north Russia, with the objective of keeping watch on the battleship *Tirpitz* in Altenfjord preparatory to an attack by Barracudas of the Fleet Air Arm from aircraft carriers. The ground party was assembled at Benson and left Scapa Flow by warship, together with a convoy, and arrived at Vaenga on 7 March 1944. It consisted of the photo-interpreters Flight Lieutenant H.K. Pusey and an Army officer, Lieutenant T.V. Newmark, together with Sergeant J.M. Davies, two airmen photographers, and other ground staff. Four of the older Spitfire PR IVs were fitted up at Benson with vertical and oblique cameras as well as long-distance fuel tanks. Three of these, flown by Squadron Leader Don Furniss, Flying Officer J.H. Dixon and Flying Officer E.G. Searle, took off on 7 March 1944 from Sumburgh in the Shetlands, heading for Vaenga. Dixon and Searle arrived safely but Furniss experienced carburettor trouble and was forced to descend to 2,000 feet over Norway, with his engine misfiring. He was shot at by the Germans and the Russians successively, until Russian fire hit the tail of his Spitfire. Nevertheless he landed at Afrikanda, left his damaged aircraft there and continued by train.

The detachment occupied the same quarters as during the previous year, but the photographic processing vehicle was found to be frozen up and took three days to thaw out. Vaenga airfield was kept reasonably clear by snow-scrapers and spiked rollers but there was a problem with slush on windscreens and camera lens windows when the thaw set in. Sorties began on 12 March and vertical photographs of *Tirpitz* were obtained from 20,000 feet, with obliques from 6,000 feet. On 2 April the Fleet Air Arm attacked and disabled the battleship, achieving complete surprise. The two Spitfires continued their work but were plagued with unserviceability. Flying Officer V.I. Gorrill of the RCAF set off from Sumburgh with the remaining Spitfire on 19 April. His gyro compass and other instruments went out of action and he crash-landed near the Finnish border, wrecking the Spitfire but emerging unscathed from deep snow. He was rescued by the Russians and flown to Vaenga, where he was put out of action when he scratched an eye in a snowball fight.

The detachment was recalled on 31 May and all the equipment and aircraft were handed over to the Russians. The ground party returned by warship but the pilots contrived a more circuitous route, by train to Moscow and then by civil aircraft to the Middle East, Gibraltar and home.

But the work of the strategic reconnaissance squadrons, which was mostly concerned with attacks by heavy bombers against Germany or targets in the occupied territories, represented only part of the photo-reconnaissance required for 1944. Experience in North Africa and Italy had confirmed that modern armies in the field needed to be supplied with a constant flow of tactical photographs of enemy forces, together with interpretations, if they were to win battles. Planning for the great enterprise of the invasion had begun as early as 1940,

The first North American Mustangs, such as serial AM148 of 26 Squadron in this photograph, were fitted with Allison engines and employed in the RAF on tactical fighter-reconnaissance from January 1942 onwards. Later Mustangs, fitted with the more powerful Merlin engines, became highly successful long-range escorts for bomber formations. (*Aeroplane Monthly*)

These three photographs of beach obstructions were taken about a month before D-Day by a Lockheed F—5 of the US Ninth Air Force, flying at 50 feet. The Germans believed that the Allies would land in this area, but in fact they arrived further west, on the beaches of Normandy.

These obstacles between Le Tréport and Perck-Plage (south of Le Touquet) were anti-tank obstructions about 5 feet high to which mines or explosive charges were fitted. (Squadron Leader P. Lamboit RAFVR)

Rows of stakes surrounding an old wreck along the beach between Dunkirk and Ostend. Some carried holders for explosive charges. (Squadron Leader P. Lamboit RAFVR)

'Hedgehog' obstacles further inland along the beach, with the stakes to seaward. (Squadron Leader P. Lamboit RAFVR)

after the fall of France. For the next three years, photo-reconnaissance took place in order to select the most suitable landing areas.

In 1942, an Army Photographic Interpretation section had been formed at the Central Interpretation Unit, with the task of examining all photographs taken of areas within 30 miles of the European coastline from Den Helder in Holland to the Spanish frontier. Located at Mount Farm in Oxfordshire, a satellite of Benson, 140 Squadron had been engaged for over two years on photographing all coastal defences and beach gradients between Calais and Cherbourg. By early 1944 this squadron was equipped with Mosquito PR IXs and PR XVIs as well as Spitfire PR XIs. The F–52 camera was adapted to take a strip of film which moved at a speed which compensated for image movement when the aircraft flew at low level. Other RAF squadrons allocated to reconnaissance Wings of the new Allied Expeditionary Air Force joined in this work, equipped with Spitfires and Mustangs.

American squadrons also joined in this activity from January 1944. The US Ninth Air Force had been transferred to England from the Mediterranean in the previous September. Its heavy bombers were then taken over by the US Eighth Air Force but the remaining tactical squadrons were built up to become part of the Allied Expeditionary Air Force. Of these, the 10th and 67th Groups, with eight squadrons equipped mainly with photo-reconnaissance Lightnings, combed the potential invasion beaches at the cost of considerable losses to aircraft and crews.

In this period, fighter squadrons of the RAF and USAAF carried out aggressive sorties to ensure that very few Luftwaffe aircraft were able to fly over these coastal areas. All the RAF and USAAF photographs were processed at Benson, and the negatives were then sent to Medmenham for selective printing as needed. The task was immense, both for the photo-reconnaissance squadrons and the photographic interpreters.

The choice of the landing areas was obviously dependent on the suitability of beaches and the strength of enemy defences discovered in the aerial mosaics which were put together at Medmenham. The possible areas selected were the north coast of Brittany and the coast of Normandy between Cherbourg and Le Havre. Of these, Calvados Bay in Normandy proved the most interesting and was finally chosen. To confuse German Intelligence, numerous sorties were carried out over other areas, particularly in the Pas de Calais. A brilliant deception was devised around Dover, consisting of a concentration of troops in the harbour area, together with dummy barges and gliders. These were duly discovered by German photo-reconnaissance aircrews and helped to convince Feldmarschall Gerd von Rundstedt, the commander of Army Group West, that an area somewhere near Calais had been chosen for the Allied invasion.

In order to ensure the success of the enterprise it was essential that the Germans were kept in a state of ignorance as to the true landing places. It was therefore vitally important to eliminate the German radar stations along the coast from the Franco-Belgian border as far as Cap Fréhel in Brittany. Rocket-firing Typhoons and Spitfires made a series of low-level attacks for a period of three weeks from mid-May 1944, and in early June the German Signals Intelligence Unit near Cherbourg was blasted by a heavy bomber raid. However, a few radar stations around Cap d'Antifer and opposite Dover, were conveniently left unharmed.

The great invasion fleet of 6,500 ships and landing craft formed up on the night of 5/6 June 1944, off Littlehampton in Sussex, before setting off due south for the beaches of

Landing craft along Gold beach at Asnelles, photographed at 10.30 hours on D-Day, 6 June 1944. This was one of the beaches on which the British 2nd Army landed. The artificial 'Mulberry' harbour, named Port Winston, was built a short distance to the west of this position. (Squadron Leader P. Lamboit RAFVR)

The headquarters of the 325th Reconnaissance Wing of the US Eighth Air Force at High Wycombe in Buckinghamshire. (Dr E.V. Hawkinson USAF (Ret'd))

Normandy on Operation 'Overlord'. The enterprise had been postponed for twenty-four hours as a result of unseasonable bad weather, but further delays were not practicable even though weather conditions did not improve as much as hoped.

While the troops were afloat, Bomber Command carried out a remarkable series of operations, designed to confirm the German belief that the Allies intended to land further east, between Boulogne and Dieppe. Lancasters of 617 Squadron, the famous Dam Busters, flew between Dover and Fécamp, circling a number of small ships flying balloons fitted with reflectors which the German radar could pick up. These aircraft also dropped strips of aluminium foil 'Window', specially cut into shapes which simulated approaching ships on enemy radar screens. The whole procession moved towards the French coast at about 7 knots, giving the impression of a huge convoy. Meanwhile, the Stirlings of 218 Squadron carried out a similar operation further east, circling gradually towards Boulogne.

At the same time, Stirlings of 199 Squadron and B–17 Fortresses of the USAAF's 803rd Squadron used 'Mandrel' (Monitoring and Neutralising Defensive Radar Electronics) equipment to jam that part of the enemy's radar which might have picked up the true invasion fleet. Further to the west, Lancasters of 101 Squadron and RAF Fortresses of 214 Squadron patrolled between Beachy Head and Paris, jamming the enemy's nightfighter control system by the use of 'ABC' (Air Borne Cigar) equipment, while dropping 'Window' aluminium foil.

Halifaxes and Stirlings of 90, 138 and 149 Squadrons dropped dummy paratroops, fireworks and rifle-fire simulators over the village of Yvetot, north of Rouen, to deceive the Germans into believing that an airborne operation was taking place in that area. A German regiment in reserve was rushed to investigate these 'paratroops', but the true airborne landings were taking place elsewhere. These aircraft also dropped a few SAS troops north of Caen in this operation, to link up with the true airborne landings.

The exact effect of these deception operations is difficult to determine. They certainly confused the Germans and delayed the despatch of Panzers and other reinforcements to the correct landing places. The unfavourable weather also proved beneficial, for the Germans did not believe that any invasion fleet would sail in such rough seas or that airborne operations could take place in such strong winds. Field Marshal Erwin Rommel, the commander of Army Group B which defended the French coast, had even taken a short leave in Germany, while other senior German officers were also absent temporarily from their posts. The British and the Canadians had feared that their casualties might be as high as 30 per cent in the initial landings, but mercifully they were only 3 per cent.

The extent of support by the preliminary photo-reconnaissance to the invading troops proved most gratifying. Firstly, this photography assisted in the accuracy of the final navigation to the beaches. The coxswain of each landing craft was provided with a photograph of his allotted beaching point, taken about 1,500 yards from the shore by an aircraft skimming over the surface of the sea. Once ashore, the troops were able to pick up their bearings, for each infantry platoon commander was given an oblique photograph of the terrain inland from his landing area. It was said that never before in war had military commanders landed on a foreign shore so well equipped with detailed information of the defending troops, equipment and minefields facing them, or of the battlefield terrain beyond the landing beaches.

A vehicle of No 7 Mobile Field Photographic Section backing into Landing Craft T936 at Gosport in Hampshire on 30 August 1944, preparatory to making the crossing to Normandy. (The late Corporal C.E. Lloyd)

Vehicles of No 7 Mobile Field Photographic Section on a landing craft en route for Normandy in August 1944, where they joined No 34 Wing at the headquarters of the Second Tactical Air Force. (Squadron Leader P. Lamboit RAFVR)

A North American B-25 Mitchell of the RAF's 226 Squadron, based at Hartford Bridge in Hampshire, escorting a convoy carrying troops and supplies to the battle front in Normandy. (*Aeroplane Monthly*)

The seaborne forces which landed on the shores of Normandy on 6 June consisted of about 57,500 American troops of the US 1st Army, on Utah and Omaha Beaches, and about 75,000 British and Canadian troops of the British 2nd Army, on Gold, Juno and Sword Beaches. They were preceded by some 27,000 airborne troops who descended by parachutes or gliders, and they were followed by a stream of seaborne reinforcements. By 23 July sufficient Canadians had arrived to form the 1st Canadian Army.

These forces were supported by a massive naval and air effort which included the squadrons of the US Ninth Air Force and the RAF's Second Tactical Air Force. The latter consisted of a Headquarters Section as well as two Groups, No 83 which worked closely with the British 2nd Army and No 84 which supported the Canadian 1st Army.

In turn, the Headquarters Section of the Second Tactical Air Force and each of its two Groups controlled photo-reconnaissance Wings. Of these, No 34 Wing was attached to Headquarters and consisted of three squadrons. These were 16 Squadron equipped with Spitfire PR XIs and PR IXs, 140 Squadron with Mosquito PR IXs and PR XVIs, and 69 Squadron with Wellington XIIIs. The Spitfires had been employed identifying V–1 flying bomb sites in northern France and they continued daylight work at both high and low level, keeping watch on the movements of German reinforcements to the invasion beaches. Some of the sorties of the Mosquitos had already located possible positions for forward airfields, which were soon provided by the RAF's Construction Wings and Servicing Commandos, using portable runways, after the foot-holds had been won in France. The Mosquitos turned their attention to night photography, using K–19 night cameras with exposures triggered by a series of photo-flashes to discover the movements of German military formations,

which were soon forced to move primarily in darkness. They were joined by 69 Squadron, which had returned from Malta in April 1944 and converted to Wellingtons equipped for night photography, becoming operational on D-Day.

No 39 (RCAF) Wing came under No 83 Group and consisted of 168 Squadron, 414 (RCAF) Squadron and 430 (RCAF) Squadron, all equipped with Mustang Is and IAs, and 400 (RCAF) Squadron with Spitfire PR XIs. No 35 Wing formed part of No 84 Group and consisted of 2 and 268 Squadrons equipped with Mustang IAs and IIs, and 4 Squadron with Spitfire PR XIs. The arrangement whereby an RAF Wing supported a Canadian Army while an RCAF Wing supported a British Army seems rather curious in retrospect, but in practice it worked well.

The P–51 Mustangs employed by these reconnaissance squadrons were powered by Allison 1,150-hp engines in the Mark Is and IAs, and Allison 1,120-hp engines in the Mark II. These versions of the American fighter had been the first to reach the UK, but the engines were found to be unsatisfactory at high level. Although they retained their armament of four .50-inch and four .30-inch guns in the Mark I and Mark II, or four 20-mm guns in the Mark IA, these Mustangs were employed by the RAF solely on low-level photographic work, being fitted with an F24 camera behind the pilot on the port side. The long-distance, high-level, versions of this famous aircraft, the Mustangs III and IV, were powered by 1,680-hp Merlin engines built in America and employed by the RAF purely in the fighter role.

RAF and RCAF photo-interpretation officers and men worked in the Army Photographic Interpretation Section (APIS) of all three reconnaissance Wings. One of these parties, attached to No 39 (RCAF) Wing which supported the British 2nd Army, sent its advance party from Odiham in Hampshire on 21 June and embarked on an American landing craft the following day. The craft sailed down the Thames Estuary and beached on the Normandy coast a day later. On 23 June the party arrived at Sommervieu airfield. With the exception of a few specialists, including two RAF photo-interpreters, all the personnel in this Wing were Canadians.

The three tactical reconnaissance Wings also controlled seven of the RAF's Mobile Field Photographic Sections (MFPSs), comprising vehicles with film-processing machines, multi-printers, copy enlargers, water bowsers, copy cameras, enlarging apparatus, generators and photostat machines. Each of these units, with a flight lieutenant commanding photographers and other personnel, had undergone pre-invasion exercises to ensure that they were brought to a high state of efficiency and mobility. Some modifications had been found necessary. Fordson tractors replaced Bedford tugs, 30 kilovolt diesel generators replaced petrol-driven generators, while water supplies were provided by 1,000-gallon bowsers with prime movers. To take an example of the pre-invasion exercises of these mobile units, No 4 MFPS found itself in North Yorkshire before the end of September 1943, training with No 84 Group. During the following winter, motor transport and other personnel went down to Southampton to study methods of loading and off-loading vehicles with the invasion landing craft. The men also learnt how to waterproof vehicles so that neither these nor their contents became water-logged when driven off a ramp into 3 or 4 feet of water and then up a beach to dry land.

Nine MFPSs were in service by D-Day, numbered consecutively. Nos 2 and 3 were in Italy, but the remaining seven were sent to France. Nos 1, 7 and 9 accompanied No 34 Wing and the headquarters of the Second Tactical Air Force, Nos 4 and 8 formed part of No 35 Wing and No 84 Group, while Nos 5 (RCAF) and 6 (RCAF) were allocated to No 39 (RCAF) Wing and 83 Group.

During the first weeks of Operation 'Overlord', the three reconnaissance Wings remained in England, while prefabricated 'Mulberry' harbours were towed across the Channel and moved into positions off the invasion coast to enable the off-loading of armour, artillery, ammunition and other essential supplies. At the end of June, No 39 (RCAF) Wing moved over to Normandy to support the British 2nd Army, together with Nos 5 (RCAF) and 6 (RCAF) MFPS. These two mobile photographic sections went into production within hours of their arrival at Sommervieu airfield. By the end of July, No 5 (RCAF) MFPS alone is recorded as having produced the astonishing total of 302,000 prints, enlargements, mosaics and plots, far more than in the whole of the previous seven months.

Next to follow was the advanced headquarters of No 35 Wing, which flew on 30 July to Plumetot airfield, about 10 miles from Caen, to take up its appointed tactical role with the Canadian 1st Army. The rear echelon of the Wing remained in England a little longer but came over to France in mid-August. No 8 MFPS landed on Juno beach on 13 August 1944, en route to join this Wing. It then drove to airfield B4 at Beny-sur-Mer, about 4 miles to the south, and became operational six hours after landing. Its sister unit, No 4 MFPS, followed on 18 August and became operational at the same airfield five hours after landing. Work had accumulated during the transit periods and the two units jointly produced as many as 30,000 prints in their first twenty-four hours of operation.

The mobile photographic units often worked in pairs, one processing negatives from the sorties on continuous processing machines and multi-printers, with the other producing reprint orders. Photostat machines

The battle against the V-1 flying bombs, with two Army officers at Medmenham studying photographs of launching sites and a chart on the wall showing the plotted tracks of the bombs. (The Medmenham Club)

RAF officers examining the wreckage of one of the first V-1 flying bombs shot down by fighters over southern England in June 1944. (*Aeroplane Monthly*)

Preparing master cover traces at Medmenham for maps of the Arnhem operation in September 1944, from aerial photographs. The officer on the left was Flight Lieutenant Julian Phipps. (The Medmenham Club)

The Production Control Section of the Allied Central Interpretation Unit at Medmenham, staffed by RAF, WAAF and USAAF personnel. (The Medmenham Club)

were also employed, so great was the demand. Tactical requirements were normally met by photographs from oblique cameras facing forward, port or starboard, mostly taken by Mustangs at low level. However, the work often included the preparation of mosaics from vertical photographs, as well as photographs taken by G45 ciné cameras fitted in fighter aircraft.

Nos 35 Wing and 39 (RCAF) Wing supplied close tactical support for the two Armies while they were still in their Normandy bridgeheads. In the weeks before the invasion, much of the railway system of northern France had been reduced to a tangle of twisted wreckage by RAF and USAAF bombing attacks. The Armies placed great store on last-minute cover of pinpoint targets. Requests were often received from Army Liaison Officers, and the pilots of the photo-reconnaissance aircraft were briefed with the intelligence information available for a particular area. Sorties were usually of short duration and the pilots gave R/T reports while in the air, followed by immediate interrogation on landing. Their photographs were rapidly printed by an MFPS and photocopies were circulated to the troops, even down to platoon level.

As soon as enemy forces were identified on roads or fields, rocket-firing Typhoons and Spitfires of the Second Tactical Air Force, flying in the 'cab rank' system developed in Italy, swooped down on them like avenging demons, blasting tanks, artillery and infantry. The Germans soon learnt to detest these aircraft, for their own fighters had been swept out of the sky. They named them 'schreckliche Jabos' (terrifying fighter-bombers). Rommel himself was wounded in one of these attacks, while in his staff car on 17 July, and replaced in his command. However, the German troops continued to fight with their usual courage and tenacity.

No 34 Wing came over to France at the end of August, together with Nos 1, 7 and 9 MFPSs, to join the headquarters of the Second Tactical Air Force, after experiencing two days of very rough crossing. By this time the British and Canadian Armies had broken out of their bridgeheads and begun to fight their way towards the Rhine. The ability of all the mobile photographic units to continue functioning while moving rapidly was severely tested in this period.

As an example of these movements, No 4 MFPS left Beny-sur-Mer airfield on 1 September and travelled through France on the heels of the 1st Canadian Army to airfields at Boisney, Fresnoy Folny, Fort Rouge and St Denis-Vestrem, staying only a few days at each airfield. On 11 October 1944 the unit crossed the Belgian border and reached Antwerp/Deurne, where it operated until late November. It then moved off once more and after a three-hour trip reached Gilze Rizen in Holland, where it caught up with No 8 MFPS and stayed for three and a half months. From Gilze Rizen, both MFPS moved to Mill and from there to Enschede, which proved to be their last wartime location before Germany surrendered. The units sometimes managed to borrow Canadian soldiers who were resting for short periods away from the front line. These men washed, dried and sorted the prints and helped with other duties while the photographers concentrated on the more technical aspects of production.

Meanwhile No 7 MFPS, which had driven with the headquarters of No 34 Wing from Belleroy via Amiens and arrived at Melsbroek near Brussels, suffered casualties when a flying bomb exploded nearby on 22 October. However, the MFPS personnel captured four German soldiers at a farm in Perck on 21 November. The photographic units at Melsbroek suffered a setback on 1 January 1945 when the Luftwaffe made its last great

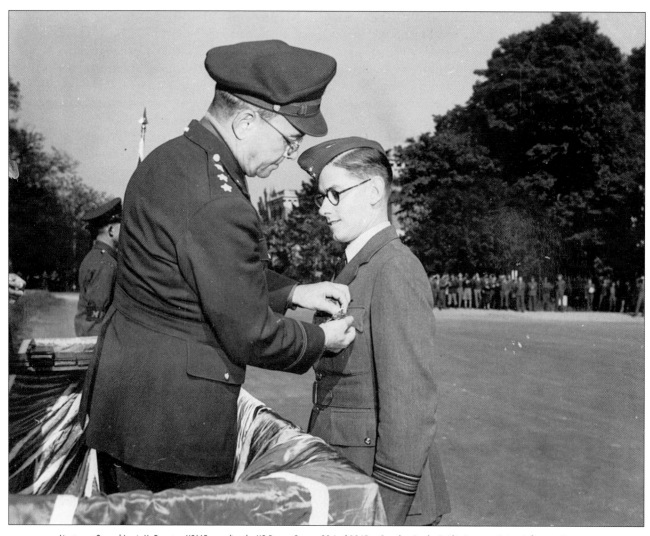

Lieutenant-General Lewis H. Brereton, USAAF, awarding the US Bronze Star on 20 April 1945 to Squadron Leader R. Idris Jones, at Maison Lafitte near Paris. Jones, an RAF photo-interpretation officer, had been seconded to the Allied Airborne Army. (The late Squadron Leader R.I. Jones)

offensive of the war. Six Mosquitos, six Spitfires and eleven Wellingtons of No 34 Wing were destroyed on the ground in this attack.

As an example of the intense work of the mobile units, during the campaign from 6 June 1944 to VE-Day on 8 May 1945, the two MFPSs of No 35 Wing produced about 500,000 exposures, resulting in the production of 4,500,000 prints for the Canadian 1st Army. This enormous effort involved the production of 73,000 feet of ciné film and the use of 60,000 gallons of developer and 51 tons of hypo fixer. This was a very high production rate for the period, especially under such difficult conditions. Equivalent figures for the other units are not available, but there is no reason to suppose that they contributed less to the total effect of the mobile units.

While these events were taking place, the strategic photo-reconnaissance squadrons continued their work from Britain. Some of the aircraft joined in tactical work when the first V–1 flying bombs were launched against London on 12 June 1944. Most of the launching sites had been built underground to avoid detection from the air, and Mosquitos made very dangerous sorties at extreme low level to bring back photographs. Thereafter, the only danger from V–1s occurred when they were launched from He111s over the North Sea, although the results were very inaccurate. A far greater threat was the long-range V–2 rocket, which was first fired on 8 September 1944. Since these rockets stood vertically and needed no launching ramp, they were far more difficult to detect from the air. They remained effective until the last was fired on 27 March 1945.

The watch on the battleship *Tirpitz* in Norway was maintained until, on 12 November 1944, Lancasters of 617 Squadron dropped 12,000-lb 'Tallboy' bombs which capsized the vessel and removed a major threat to Allied shipping. Other photographs, taken over German ports, verified that U-boats were being assembled from pre-fabricated components built elsewhere. This information resulted in heavy bomber attacks against manufacturing bases and assembly yards. Photographs taken over the Augsburg area showed that Me262 jets were being constructed, and in fact a Mosquito of 544 Squadron evaded one of these fighters over Munich on 25 July 1944.

From July 1944 the greater part of the effort of Bomber Command and the US Eighth Air Force was concentrated on oil installations, for by then the advancing Russians were at the point of capturing the Romanian fields, leaving the Germans almost entirely dependent on their manufacture of synthetic oil. Transportation within Germany also received much attention in the closing stages of the war. Strategic reconnaissance aircraft faithfully identified targets and the results of bombing attacks.

The defeat of the German Armies was an achievement in which all branches of the Allied forces can claim a share. There were many reasons for the victory, but the fact that the Allied forces were able to obtain a continuous and clear picture of the enemy's strength and intentions was due in no small measure to the photo-reconnaissance pilots, the intelligence staffs and the photographers of the Mobile Field Photographic Sections.

CHAPTER ELEVEN

NIGHT BOMBING
AND PHOTOGRAPHY

On the outbreak of the Second World War, the RAF relied on gun turrets for protecting its bomber squadrons when operating in close formation during daylight, each aircraft covered by cross-fire from the combined turrets. These power-operated turrets, each fitted with up to four .303-inch Browning machine guns, were considered to be so effective that any enemy fighters which approached would find the defences too formidable. This faith was shattered in the first few weeks of the war when Wellington bombers, often riddled with bullet and cannon shell holes from Messerschmitt fighters, returned from daylight attacks on German warships, leaving many of their number at the bottom of the North Sea. In the absence of suitable long-range fighters for escort duties, it became apparent that strategic bombing would have to be carried out mainly at night, with consequent difficulties in both navigation and air photography. These two problems were not fully overcome in Bomber Command for almost three years.

The use of night photography from aircraft was not new, for experiments over the Western Front during the First World War had been quite successful. The techniques which originated in those days were continued in Bomber Command's night offensive against Germany after the fall of France, when F24

cameras were carried in some aircraft and used in combination with photographic flash-bombs. However, Bomber Command's objective was to carry a camera in every operational aircraft, in order to study the results of each sortie on return and check that the targets had been reached. This became imperative when D.M.B. Butt, who was secretary to Lord Cherwell, Winston Churchill's 'one-man brain's trust', reported in August 1941 that, from an analysis of 650 photographs taken at night between 2 June and 25 July, only one aircraft in three had succeeded in dropping its bombs within a radius of 5 miles of its intended target. The whole future of Bomber Command's strategic bombing campaign was thrown temporarily into doubt.

One immediate result of this disclosure was to accelerate the development of additional navigational aids to be carried in bombers. The first of these was Gee, which came into general use in March 1942. This consisted of a radio receiver fitted in the aircraft, which enabled the navigator to see the difference in time signals from synchronised pulses sent out from three separate ground stations in Britain. The results were then plotted on a special Gee chart, so that the intersection of the three lines determined the aircraft's position with considerable accuracy. Owing to the

The Vickers Wellington, such as this example on the strength of 75 Squadron, was the mainstay of Bomber Command from before the outbreak of the Second World War until late 1942. Some Wellingtons continued in front-line service with Bomber Command squadrons until October 1943. (*Aeroplane Monthly*)

The Short Stirling was the first four-engined bomber to be used operationally by Bomber Command in the Second World War, entering service in August 1940. This Stirling I of 149 Squadron was photographed while being bombed up preparatory to a raid. Stirlings continued in service with Bomber Command until September 1944, while others were employed on supply-dropping, transport work and glider-towing. (*Aeroplane Monthly*)

curvature of the earth, the range was usually confined to about 400 miles, but Gee enabled high-flying aircraft to identify targets in the industrial heartland of the Ruhr, before the Germans began jamming the transmissions towards the end of 1942. It was with the aid of this system that Air Chief Marshal Sir Arthur T. Harris, the newly appointed C-in-C of Bomber Command, was able to launch the first 1,000 bomber raid, against Cologne on the night of 30/31 May 1942. The accurate results of this enormous attack, photographed later in daylight by photo-reconnaissance aircraft, were greeted with elation by the British public and convinced some military experts that Bomber Command was developing the ability to destroy the German war economy almost unaided.

The second of these navigational aids was Oboe, introduced in late 1942. This employed two transmitters in England, one of which sent out a series of radar pulses which the aircraft amplified and returned, so that the transmitter station could tell if the aircraft was to the right or left of its track, and gave instructions accordingly. The second transmitter could tell when the aircraft had reached its target and also gave instructions. Oboe was very accurate, although its range was as limited as Gee's and it could only handle one aircraft at a time. Its main use was to enable a few bombers to drop target indicator markers over the target. An adaptation of Oboe was later introduced under the name of GH. With this, the interrogation and display equipment was fitted in the aircraft itself, so that many aircraft could use the system at the same time. It was not until early 1944 that the Germans were able to introduce counter-measures against Oboe or GH but, thanks to the ingenuity of A.H. Reeves and the scientists at the Telecommunication Research Establishment, the squadrons of Bomber Command were usually able to keep one jump ahead of the enemy with their night-bombing operations.

The third navigational aid was self-contained, of unlimited range and could not be jammed by the enemy. Code-named H_2S, it was first used operationally by the Pathfinder Force at the end of January 1943. The system consisted of a small transmitter in the aircraft, which emitted a radar signal to the ground beneath. This was reflected back and displayed on the screen of a cathode ray tube of about 5 inches in diameter, around which a trace revolved once a second. The image from the trace gave a rough picture of the ground, although sometimes this was not easy to read. However, an operator could usually pick up a distinctive landmark such as a coastline or a river. Most important of all, it operated above cloud. The great raids against Hamburg of July 1943, resulting in enormous devastation, were carried out with the aid of this instrument together with the dropping of 'Window', streams of small aluminium strips which when falling blotted out the display screens of German radar. An American-built version of H_2S, named H_2X, was employed by the USAAF and enabled their Fortresses and Liberators to bomb targets from high altitude above cloud during the latter stages of the massive daylight bombing campaign which developed from small beginnings in June 1942.

All these devices increased the effectiveness of the strategic bombing campaign at a time when heavy four-engined bombers such as the Stirling, the Halifax and the Lancaster were coming off the production lines, with the capacity to strike hard at German industrial centres. In addition, the twin-engined Mosquito was becoming available as a light bomber and photo-reconnaissance aircraft.

However, it was the setting up of the Pathfinder Force which heralded the great improvement in accuracy of the RAF's night bombing operations. In spite of initial opposition from Sir Arthur Harris, this was formed in August 1942 under the command

The Handley Page Halifax was the second four-engined bomber to enter service with Bomber Command during the Second World War, in November 1940. Various marks then continued until VE-Day. This photograph is of a Halifax II serial HR926 of 35 Squadron. (The late Squadron Leader J.E. Archbald)

An F24 camera installed in a Halifax. (Flight Lieutenant G.H. Parry RAF (Ret'd))

The twin-engined Avro Manchester did not fulfil expectations after it entered service with Bomber Command in November 1940, for the engines proved unreliable and under-powered. It was withdrawn at the end of June 1942. The Manchester Ia serial L7427 in this photograph was on the strength of 83 Squadron, which was equipped with these machines from December 1941 to May 1942 before converting to Lancasters and joining the Pathfinder Force. (*Aeroplane Monthly*)

of a dynamic Australian, Group Captain (later Air Vice-Marshal) Don C.T. Bennett. Composed initially of four squadrons, equipped with Stirlings, Halifaxes, Lancasters and Wellingtons, it was formed under No 3 Group and developed steadily into an elite corps, eventually attaining its own Group status.

At first, the Pathfinder method consisted of marking the target with sticks of flares and then dropping showers of incendiaries, slightly in advance of the main bomber stream. After the introduction of Oboe and the acquisition of Mosquito aircraft, this progressed to putting down lines of yellow target indicator (TI) flares along the line of approach and then marking the target itself with a series of coloured target indicators during the period of the attack. This marking was backed up by other Mosquitos dropping target indicators of a different colour, together with high-explosive bombs, while yet more Pathfinder aircraft led the main bomber force to deliver their heavy cargoes of bombs and incendiaries. Very precise planning within Bomber Command resulted in cities and towns in Germany suffering enormous casualties and devastation, bringing disruption to the German war effort.

The results of these attacks were photographed assiduously by high-flying Mosquitos and Spitfires of the photo-reconnaissance squadrons, operating mainly in daylight, and enabled photo-interpreters to make assessments of the damage. But Bomber Command required more than this. Each bomber was required to carry a camera and to operate it simultaneously with the release of the bombs, in order to bring back evidence of an accurate attack. This procedure was intricate as well as far more difficult on operational sorties than during training in the UK, where the bombers flew over blacked-out ranges without interference.

To provide the illumination for the exposure, a photo-flash cylinder of about 30 inches in length and 4½ inches in diameter was employed. This was filled with a special mixture of flash powder which, if wrongly handled, was enough to blow the aircraft apart. The blunt-nosed cylinder was fitted at the tail with a small propeller which was prevented from rotating prematurely by a steel pin through the shaft. During the run-up to the target, it was the duty of the wireless operator to attach a lanyard to this pin so that, when the flash-bomb was launched from the flare chute in the fuselage, it was pulled out of the shaft. It was also the duty of the wireless operator to bring this pin back for interrogation during debriefing, as proof that the photo-flash had been dropped 'live'.

Simultaneous with the release of the flash-bomb together with the high-explosive bombs or target indicators, an electric current was passed to a timing device known as a Type 35 Control, which had been pre-set to the bombing altitude. This control ticked off the predicted time of fall of the flash-bomb to 0.6 of the altitude of the aircraft less four seconds, and then opened the camera shutter for a period of eight seconds, ready for the explosion of the flash. During this crucial eight seconds the pilot was required to keep the aircraft straight and level, regardless of flak and searchlights, so that the resulting photograph would show the position marked or bombed.

The objective of fitting and using a camera in every bomber was not fully attained until the end of 1943, but meanwhile their introduction was certainly not popular among the aircrews. The reasons for the dislike were simple. Firstly, the photographs could determine whether the crew had dropped the bombs over the wrong target or had been guilty of 'creep-back' over the correct target; this was the name used to describe the release of the bombs before the

In February 1943 Bomber Command decided that all its aircraft engaged on night bombing should be fitted with a camera and take at least one photograph to synchronise with a photo-flash released with the first bomb, or with the target indicator flare in the case of Pathfinder aircraft. This objective was achieved by the end of the year. This photograph is of Lancaster I of 83 Squadron, which formed part of the Pathfinder Force from 15 August 1942 and then carried out target-marking for the main bomber streams until the end of the war. (The late Squadron Leader J.E. Archbald)

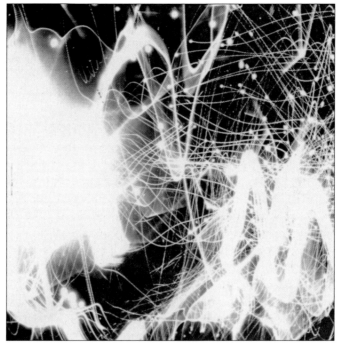

A typical photograph of the heavily defended target of Berlin, taken from 10,000 feet on the night of 29/30 March 1943, before the introduction of the 'master and slave' twin camera system invented by Squadron Leader Howard W. Lees of the Pathfinder Force. Ground details were obscured by the tracks of target indicators, searchlights and flak, all further confused by the evasive action of the aircraft. Such photographs, although dramatic, were of little use to photo-interpreters. (Squadron Leader H.W. Lees RAFVR)

The first heavy attack against the Barmen district of Wuppertal in the Ruhr was made on the night of 29/30 May 1943, when 719 aircraft were despatched and 33 were lost. The target was accurately marked and devastation was complete, with about 3,000 people killed. Interpreters of this photograph could pick out a Lancaster flying north towards a cloud of smoke as well as the round light of a target indicator. The streaks on the picture were caused by a technical fault, the film winding on before being completely protected by the capping blind. (The late Squadron Leader J.E. Archbald)

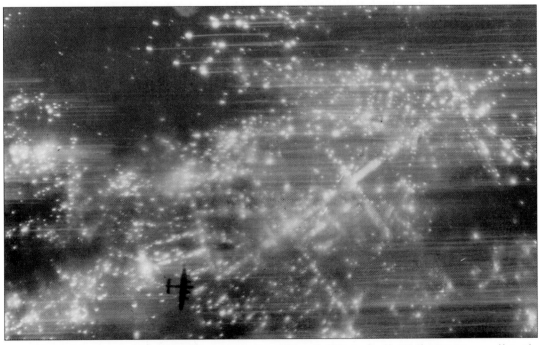

Hannover photographed on the night of 8/9 October 1943, when Bomber Command despatched 504 aircraft and lost 27. Photo-interpreters were able to pick out a four-engined bomber flying over a mass of incendiary fires to the south-south-west of the railway station, while the broad white ribbon running from the nose of the aircraft to the top right of the photograph was the Sallestrasse. The raid resulted in the destruction of almost 4,000 buildings with over 30,000 damaged, as well as the deaths of 1,200 people and 3,345 injuires. (The late Squadron Leader J.E. Archbald)

aiming point had been reached. If there was no satisfactory explanation for such errors, the sortie might be deleted from the build-up to the thirty which each Bomber Command flyer was required to complete in an operational tour. Secondly, photography required the crew to fly directly towards the target for the period between releasing the bombs and the explosion of the flash-bomb, and then to fly straight and level for another eight seconds while the film was being exposed. This long exposure was necessary since an instantaneous exposure would almost certainly miss the brief illumination of the flash, which lasted for a peak of only 1/60th of a second and tailed for a total of 1/10th of a second. It was accepted at first that the long exposure caused 'fire tracks' on the picture from the 'stretched' recordings of light sources such as ground fires and searchlights while the aircraft was moving.

The total period of straight and level flight usually lasted for only about half a minute, but that was a very long time when searchlights were probing and the flak was intense. It is true that more bombers fell to the guns of night-fighters on the outward or return flights than to flak, but the fiery spectacle over the target was often enough to test the courage of the most determined of men.

There were, of course, valid reasons why crews sometimes brought back unsatisfactory photographs. There could be cloud over the target and very occasionally there were mechanical, electrical or flash failures. In addition, another problem arose, for it had not been foreseen that bombing would develop into the saturation of targets by incendiaries dropped by numerous aircraft. With the camera shutter open for eight seconds, the movement of the aircraft over a blazing target resulted in numerous fire tracks on the ground being recorded as irregular traces on the film, thus obliterating other details.

Before the end of the war, Bomber Command had built up to eleven Groups, including No 8 (Pathfinder Force) Group. Each Group appointed its own Photographic Officer, but it was the Pathfinder Force which led the way in the improvements in night photography, just as it led the way in marking the targets. The Group Photographic Officer for this force was Squadron Leader Howard W. Lees, who was posted as a Flight Lieutenant to RAF Wyton in Huntingdonshire during January 1943 and was among the nucleus of the new unit when it attained Group status a few weeks later. Shortly after his arrival, while the new formation was still a lodger unit at Wyton and under the control of No 3 Group, it received a visit from Group Captain F.C. Sturgiss OBE, the Photographic Officer of Bomber Command. Sturgiss asked Lees if he had any suggestions for overcoming the problem of fire tracks which were obscuring much of the evidence that the bomber offensive was improving its accuracy.

Lees immediately came up with the idea of fitting two films and two shutters in the same camera, geared to expose alternately, so that the period of 'standby duty' for each film would be limited to about one second. During one of those periods the vital 1/60th of a second of flash illumination would be recorded. Thus each ground fire would appear only as a fairly small point of light instead of a track, and moreover the photo-interpreters would be able to locate its position.

It was not feasible to design and produce such a camera within a short space of time, although the idea eventually came into being in the shape of the F97 camera shortly after the war. As a more practicable alternative, Lees had two F24 cameras installed in the same aircraft. He modified the camera gear boxes and electrical circuits so that while one camera – the Master – was exposing, the

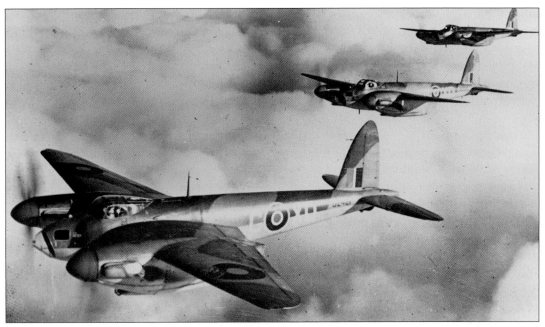

De Havilland Mosquito IV bombers, such as these on the strength of 139 Squadron, formed part of No 8 (Pathfinder Force) Group. They were employed in dropping target indicators for the main bomber stream. (*Aeroplane Monthly*)

Squadron Leader Howard W. Lees, the Group Photographic Officer of No 8 (Pathfinder Force) Group, standing by the turret of a Lancaster. His inventions led to great improvements in the quality of night photographs taken from aircraft of Bomber Command and were adopted in post-war cameras. (Squadron Leader H.W. Lees RAFVR)

other – the Slave – was rewinding. Having rewound, the Slave shutter re-opened and simultaneously energised the solenoid of the Master, so that this rewound in turn. By this means the exposure time was reduced from eight seconds to little more than 1.6 seconds required for the rewinding cycle.

Thus the 'Master and Slave' camera was born, resulting in a great improvement in the clarity of the night photographs. The system was introduced into the Groups of Bomber Command from the spring of 1943 onwards. The clarity of photographs improved further when the American K–24 camera was issued in February of the following year, for this was made with a high-speed gearbox which reduced the exposure time from the 1.6 seconds of the F24 to .33 of a second.

However, there was an associated problem which Lees was anxious to solve. Many of the night photographs gave evidence of having been taken while the aircraft was banking, usually during avoiding action against enemy defences. Lees thought it was unfair to expect aircrews to fly straight and level after continuing to the centre of the target. It troubled him especially since he had to brief aircrews to do this, when he was not subjected to such hazards himself. Staff officers were not permitted to fly on operations, lest they be taken prisoner and interrogated, although he did manage to go on one sortie.

The flash-bomb in use was blunt-nosed and trailed behind other bombs during descent, so that the flash illumination was outside the area of the photograph when it was taken. Lees thought that it would be better to design one which kept pace with the bombs and burst closer to the ground. Thus the flash itself would appear in the picture and be plotted as the position bombed, subject to parallax error wherever it appeared off-centre in the photograph. It was calculated that this would allow the pilot to take evasive action

up to seventeen degrees of bank and still record the flash within the frame.

By hanging with his head out of the entrance door of a Halifax over the bombing range at Rushford in Suffolk, Lees was able to witness the erratic behaviour of the $4\frac{1}{2}$-inch flash-bomb after it had been launched sideways from the flare chute. It was seen to cartwheel, which not only retarded its forward velocity but also must have caused the propeller to rotate in opposite directions and thus delay the release of the firing mechanism and the flash burst.

The flash that Lees had in mind was one which would have the same ballistics and terminal velocity as the bombs, and be dropped from the bomb bay. But he knew that no substitution of bombs would be authorised, for every bomb hook was required for weapons of destruction or target markers. Thus he proposed combining the flash with a target indicator, which was a 250-lb bomb casing filled with about sixty coloured 'Roman candles'. These candles were ejected by a small explosive charge, detonated by a reliable barometric fuse, and cascaded out over the target at a low altitude. Twenty of these candles were removed to make room for a $4\frac{1}{2}$-inch flash, enabling the target to be marked with the remaining forty and to be photographed at the same time. This occurred at 0.2 of the aircraft's altitude instead of the 0.6 previously used. The resulting flash would be seen as a circle of light in the photograph but was unlikely to handicap the photo-interpreters.

Air Vice-Marshal Bennett wasted no time in having a prototype prepared and ordered Lees to collect his 'toy' from the bomb dump at RAF Wyton and take it in his car to the Bomb Development Unit at RAF Feltwell in Norfolk. It was tested successfully from there over Rushford Bombing Range and put into production as the 'TI Flash'. However, it was not used by the heavy bombers, as Lees had

This photograph, the highest taken at night by the RAF during the Second World War, showed Osnabruck in Lower Saxony. It was taken on the night of 18/19 April 1944 from 36,000 feet by Mosquito IX serial ML923 flown by Flight Lieutenant J.W. Jordan of 105 Squadron, part of No 8 (Pathfinder Force) Group, based at Bourn in Cambridgeshire. It was a purely experimental photograph, using a combined indicator and photo-flash devised by Squadron Leader Howard W. Lees, during which the shutter was open for 30 seconds and recorded the progress of a target indicator dropped by another Mosquito. Jordan also dropped one target indicator and red photo-flash as well as three 500-lb bombs, but there was no attack by the main bomber force on Osnabruck on that night. (Squadron Leader H.W. Lees RAFVR)

originally intended. Instead, it was realised that the invention provided the means for Mosquitos, which were not fitted with flare chutes and so far had been unable to take night photographs, to bring back evidence of their success in the bombing war. It was first used by Group Captain Charles E. Slee of 139 Squadron on 8/9 October 1943 to check the accuracy of the GH radar navigational aid, and produced an excellent photograph of Düren in Germany from 25,000 feet.

Thereafter the TI Flash was used almost exclusively by target-marking Mosquitos, dropped with three 500-lb bombs, and unfailingly ensured night photographs of good quality from high altitudes. This was particularly true of those taken over Berlin, while the highest night photograph of the war was taken over Osnabruck from 36,000 feet. These photographs gave support for Air Vice-Marshal Bennett's drive for more Mosquito squadrons in his Light Night Striking Force, which was harassing the enemy while suffering minimal losses. However, production of the TI Flash was never sufficient to supply the heavy bomber squadrons and thus put to the test Lees' contention that it would enable the crews to take evasive action and save lives, as well as providing a more accurate assessment of bombing and target marking.

Another of Lees' inventions was related to the H_2S radar screen. It was decided to photograph this screen over the target at the time the target indicators were released, or at a turning point sharply before. The Radar Officer of the Pathfinder Group had been trying, in utmost secrecy, to obtain photographs of the image on the screen with a Leica 35-mm camera fitted with a close-focusing device but, since anything closer than $17\frac{1}{2}$ inches was out of focus, he was unsuccessful and asked for advice. After being sworn to secrecy and told not even to mention this matter to the Photographic

Section of Bomber Command, Lees was shown the new and highly secret H_2S set. He arranged for Wyton workshops to make some 11.7-mm extension rings, which were then fitted to all the Leica cameras which could be bought from dealers, and in turn these were fitted to lightweight copying stands. The navigator operating the set was required to hold one of these over the H_2S screen and depress the shutter level for one second, the time of the sweep of the trace.

The first results were obtained on the night of 2 October 1943, when the navigator of a Lancaster of 83 Squadron took a very clear photograph of the screen showing Friedrichshafen on the shore of Lake Constance. Leipzig was also recorded by the same squadron in early December, but the main venture in risking this secret took place over Berlin on the night of 1 January 1944, when forty-one successful pictures were taken by eight cameras. Lees had earlier asked Bomber Command to issue a 35-mm enlarger for printing the negatives but this request was refused since he was not allowed to state its purpose. However, he used his own enlarger and developing tanks, installing them in an unventilated cellar at Station Headquarters. Seven enlargements were required from each negative, together with three rows of contact titling information on each print. Thus it was a great relief when secrecy was eventually relaxed and he was able to arrange for processing under normal conditions at Station Headquarters. When the USAAF joined in the battle against Berlin in March 1944, these early H_2S photographs were included in a booklet which was issued to the H_2X operators, to show them what to expect on their screens in the run-up to the target.

However, the results of this rather make-shift method of photography of the H_2S display began to deteriorate when handled in the photographic sections of the various

The Kodak 'Bantam' camera, with a 1-inch lens, was used to photograph the display screen of the H$_2$S radar set when over the target. It was mounted on a hinged bracket so that it could be kept clear of the set when this was being viewed by the operator. However, when the bombardier called 'Bombs gone!' it was swung into position to record the effect of the bombs. The shutter release was held down for one second for each exposure, this being the length of time the radar trace described a full circle. After landing, the camera assembly was removed and handed to the duty photographer for film processing. (Squadron Leader H.W. Lees RAFVR)

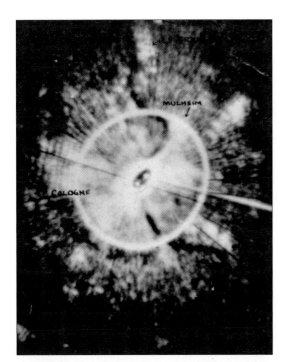

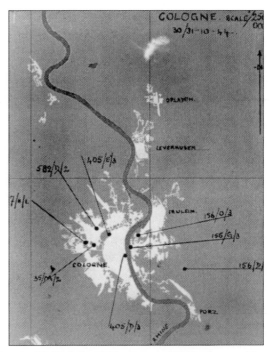

Above, left: This photograph of an H$_2$S radar screen was taken over Cologne on the night of 30/31 October 1944 by a Lancaster of 156 Squadron, part of No 8 (Pathfinder Force) Group, based at Wyton in Huntingdonshire. The photo-interpreters were able to relate this and other photographs to the ground positions, from which the diagram (*above right*) was constructed. The main bomber force of 905 aircraft caused enormous damage to Cologne on that night, without loss of aircraft. (Squadron Leader H.W. Lees RAFVR)

WAAF personnel registering films of night photographs in the negative library at Medmenham. (The Medmenham Club)

Identification of night photographs being carried out at Medmenham, by comparison with large-scale maps of photographs prepared with the aid of aerial mosaics. (The Medmenham Club)

Pathfinder stations. In November 1944 Howard Lees collected 200 Kodak Bantam 35-mm cameras from the Maintenance Unit at Stafford. These had been specially designed in America and fitted with a 1-inch Dallmeyer lens, which enabled the distance from lens to image to be halved. Lees then designed a hinged bracket so that the camera could be swung firmly into position, already correctly focused and aligned, when the photograph was required. This device is now in the RAF Museum at Hendon. By this time an improved version of H_2S had been developed, and the results obtained were excellent. Lees then modified a 16-mm Eyemo ciné camera to take one-second exposures every alternate second, which provided a 'moving picture' of the run-up to Berlin from the Tegel See. In a way, this was a primitive forerunner of the modern video.

Bomber Command also employed colour photography, towards the end of the war. This was required since the Germans, with characteristic resourcefulness, began to light decoy fires in places where bombing could do no harm, together with fake target indicators, to fool the main bomber stream. The Pathfinder Force began to vary the colour of its target indicators, and Bomber Command wished to verify if each bomber had attacked those of the correct colour. In May 1943 attempts at using Kodachrome colour film were made over the bombing range, but the ground detail was poor. Within a few months, a supply of Kodacolour film arrived from the USA, but results were still inadequate.

In early 1944 the Group Photographic Officer of No 5 Group, Squadron Leader Len A. Eades, experimented with laying the Kodacolour film in front of the usual high-speed night film, so that the light of the flash affected both. This worked well, although the colour film showed only the colours of the target indicators. However, the system was introduced gradually until, by the end of the war, over 80 per cent of the bomber force were using this composite film.

While these immense night attacks against the German heartland and targets in the occupied territories were taking place, Bomber Command carried out several daylight raids. The majority of these were short-range sorties made by medium bombers against targets in occupied territories, usually with the escort of swarms of Spitfires. After the invasion of Normandy and the establishment of air superiority over German skies in the summer of 1944, however, Bomber Command resumed daylight attacks against targets in Germany. The heavy bombers flew in close formation, in accordance with the pre-war conception, but with an escort of P-51 Mustang long-range fighters carrying drop-tanks. In these daylight attacks, photographs were taken in the usual way. But the main burden of daylight attacks against Germany and occupied Europe was carried by the USAAF from bases in England and Italy, escorted by their long-distance fighters.

The RAF made night sorties over Germany from the beginning of January 1940 onwards, the final attack taking place on the night of 2/3 May 1945 against Kiel by Mosquitos of the Pathfinder Force. Bomber Command's last effort in the European war was a great errand of mercy. Much of western Holland was still occupied by the Germans and the population was starving. By arrangement with the local German commander a truce was organised, and between 26 April and 7 May 1945, Bomber Command flew nearly 3,000 sorties in daylight to drop food supplies for these civilians, under Operation 'Manna'. Bombers of the US Eighth Air Force joined in this effort, under Operation 'Chowhound'. Thus the Allied Air Forces not only played an enormous part in the liberation of Europe but saved civilian lives towards the end of the war.

CHAPTER TWELVE

SOUTH-EAST ASIA

When the Japanese landed at Khota Bharu on the east coast of the Malayan Peninsula on 8 December 1941, there was a woeful lack of RAF strategic photo-reconnaissance aircraft in the area. Long-range Hurricanes had been requested, but these were not available, for at the time the British were far more intent on supplying aircraft to the Russians than building up the RAF in South-East Asia. Two Brewster Buffalos had been stripped of armament and non-essential equipment so that, fitted with two F24 cameras, their range was considerably increased. There was also a solitary Bristol Beaufort II, one of six built in Australia which had arrived in Singapore shortly before the invasion in order to replace the obsolescent Vildebeest torpedo bombers of 36 and 100 Squadrons. Without trained crews, the Beauforts were not considered suitable for operations but one, serial T9543, was retained for reconnaissance purposes.

Most of the RAF squadrons in Malaya were equipped with aircraft which were at the end of their usefulness for front-line operations. Moreover, the gathering of signals and other intelligence, under the Far East Combined Bureau in Singapore, was in the hands of the Royal Navy and thus biased towards the requirements of that service. There was almost no knowledge about the disposition of the Japanese Air Force which was to play such a crucial role in the forthcoming conflict, and very little information on the performance of its aircraft. Instead, there was a general belief that the Japanese armed forces were inferior in equipment and fighting ability to those of their Western opponents.

The small flight of RAF photo-reconnaissance aircraft, under the command of Squadron Leader C.G.R. Lewis, was based at Seletar in Singapore, where it was known locally as No 4 Photographic Reconnaissance Unit. Of course, it was unable to keep watch on the movements of Japanese forces from their bases in Indo-China or Siam, whereas numbers of the Mitsubishi Ki 46-II 'Dinah' flew regular reconnaissance missions over Malaya, at altitudes which the RAF fighters could not reach.

On the day of the landings in east Malaya, the Beaufort flew into the small RAF airfield near Khota Bharu, carrying films of the Japanese disembarking from troopships at Singora and Pattani in Siam. The machine had been damaged in combat and caught fire when it tried to take off again. It was written off, but the films were processed in a wooden hut by Leading Aircraftman Stan Lewis, using inadequate equipment and guesswork, while the airfield was being strafed by Japanese fighters. They were then flown to Seletar by a Buffalo. Shortly afterwards, the airfield buildings were set on fire and the base was abandoned.

One of a flight of Catalina flying boats present in the area had been shot down a day before the Japanese landed in Malaya. Attempts by RAAF Hudsons and RAF

The RAF's Brewster Buffalo, the equivalent of the US Navy's F2A-2, was rejected as a front-line fighter when it arrived in England during July 1940. As with other machines and equipment which were considered inferior at home, all Buffalos were sent to the Far East where they were allocated to five RAF and one RAAF fighter squadrons as well as to No 4 Photographic Reconnaissance Unit. Although these machines were outclassed by Japanese fighters, the pilots achieved remarkable results. (*Aeroplane Monthly*)

The bridge over the Sittang River, east of Rangoon, after the central spans had been blown up by the retreating British while some of their men were still on the Japanese side. These men had to use improvised rafts or swim to safety, to avoid capture. (Squadron Leader J.D. Braithwaite RAFVR)

The RAF's photographic section in retreat over the Irrawaddy north of Rangoon in early April 1942. The oil fields at Yenangyaung, in the background, were destroyed by the British shortly before they were occupied by the Japanese 33rd Division. (Corporal A. Fox DFM, RAFVR)

The bridge over the Irrawaddy at Ava, near Mandalay, which was blown up by the British on 30 April 1942 to impede the advancing Japanese. Two spans fell in the river and created a sandbank. (Squadron Leader J.D. Braithwaite RAFVR)

Vildebeests based at Khota Bharu to attack the Japanese invasion fleet were partially successful but did not stop the landings. In later attempts to attack Japanese transports, the Vildebeests were almost wiped out.

As the Japanese advanced down the Malayan Peninsula, squadrons of RAF Blenheims, operating from northern airfields which lacked sufficient anti-aircraft defences or radar coverage, were gradually whittled down to a handful of survivors. The Buffalos of RAF, RAAF and RNZAF squadrons suffered in combat against the superior Japanese fighters. During these events the reconnaissance Buffalos flew over 100 sorties and, amazingly, they were not shot down although they frequently returned full of holes. The pilots relied on manoeuvrability to escape the Japanese fighters. Two more were converted and joined in the sorties. But the end came when the Buffalos were destroyed or damaged on the ground in an air attack on 7 February.

Only a handful of Hudsons, Vildebeests, Buffalos and Blenheims remained when the retreating Commonwealth forces reached Singapore. A consignment of Hurricanes arrived in crates and their RAF pilots shot down numerous Japanese bombers, but these machines were also outclassed by the Japanese fighters and the numbers were steadily depleted. When the fall of Singapore became imminent, five officers and twenty-eight other ranks of the photographic sections had gathered on the island. All managed to escape by various means, some experiencing astonishing adventures, and arrived in Palembang in Sumatra. After their departure and that of the surviving aircraft, the surrender of Singapore on 15 February 1942 was undoubtedly the most humiliating defeat suffered by British arms in the war. Inadequate aerial reconnaissance and the failure of intelligence had been among the main reasons for this débâcle.

The British hoped to retain Sumatra, with the help of the Dutch, but the chances of defending an island 1,000 miles long with their depleted forces were nil. On the day before the fall of Singapore, one of the RAAF Hudsons which had flown to Sumatra spotted a Japanese invasion fleet sailing in the direction of the island. The enemy transports were then mauled by Hudsons and Blenheims, but the remaining ships continued their journey. Meanwhile, Japanese paratroops landed on the fighter airfield at Palembang and overcame the defences. The invasion fleet was again attacked by the defending aircraft, supported by Hurricanes which had previously arrived from an aircraft carrier, and the transports and landing barges were almost wiped out. But more Japanese paratroops were dropped and the British, by then desperately short of supplies, were ordered to retreat to Java. The few remaining RAF and RAAF aircraft were flown to the airfield at Semplak in the west of this island, while the ground personnel were evacuated by boat on 18 February, amid scenes of great confusion. The men of the photographic section accompanied them.

By then, the military situation in the Dutch East Indies had become hopeless, with the civilians demoralised by the defeats of the British and Dutch. Nevertheless, the handful of Blenheims, Hudsons and Vildebeests returned to the attack, suffering further losses. It was not long before the relentless Japanese attacked again, beginning their landings on 1 March. A few days later, the evacuation of Java began. The surviving handful of RAF and Dutch aircraft were either destroyed or flown to Australia, while some of the personnel left by boat from the south of the island. Priority was given to aircrews and technical staff, but three photographic men were captured, including Stan Lewis. Another fell sick and was taken off by a destroyer. The remainder were evacuated in various vessels, mostly in the Dutch freighter *Kota Gede* of 7,800 tons, and were lucky enough to reach Colombo in Ceylon. No preparations had been made for their arrival, but local civilians rallied round to help with accommodation.

Meanwhile, Siam had surrendered without resistance to the Japanese and the country was used as a base for the assault on Burma, which began on 23 December 1941 with an air attack on Rangoon. This and subsequent raids caused many civilian deaths and casualties, so that streams of panic-stricken refugees poured out of the capital. Japanese troops crossed the Burmese border on 15 January 1942, and the British forces began a long retreat.

The RAF in Burma had built a chain of excellent airfields and landing fields, but as with Malaya these lacked sufficient anti-aircraft guns or radar warning facilities. Moreover, there were very few aircraft, even counting those types which were regarded as obsolescent in Britain. There were a few squadrons of RAF Buffalos, one squadron of RAF Lysanders and another of the Indian Air Force, while shortly after Christmas a squadron of Hurricanes and about thirty Blenheims arrived. In addition, there were three squadrons of the American Volunteer Group which, equipped with P–40 Warhawks, had flown from China to Mingaladon near Rangoon. Opposed to this force, the Japanese could mount about 400 modern aircraft. Nevertheless, the P–40s and Buffalos attacked the Japanese bombers so effectively that they were forced, at least for the time being, to discontinue daylight raids.

Facilities for strategic photographic coverage in Burma were at first almost non-existent. Some topographic mapping had taken place during 1940 under the direction of Lieutenant-Colonel W. Westland Wright, using the services of the Air India Survey and Transport Company based in Calcutta. Part of the probable invasion route had been mapped during these surveys. A Blenheim I of 60 Squadron had been converted for photographic work and began strategic reconnaissance over Siam. When the Japanese attacked, one Buffalo of 67 Squadron and one P–40 Warhawk were modified for photography. These carried out tactical reconnaissance, and later two Hurricane IIBs of 17 Squadron were also converted for this purpose. The two Lysander squadrons did their best to carry out Army co-operation duties, but were hopelessly outclassed by the Japanese Air Force.

On 25 January two photo-reconnaissance Hurricane IIBs were flown from the Middle East to Mingaladon by Flying Officers F.D. Procter and K.A. Perkin. They began strategic reconnaissance three days later, the pilots covering targets as far afield as Bangkok and Chiengmai in Siam and Tavoy and Moulmein in southern Burma. As the Japanese approached Rangoon on 21 February, these two Hurricanes were withdrawn to Magwe, 300 miles to the north. The ground party of photographers followed with a mobile darkroom and three large trucks, mostly containing supplies abandoned by fleeing shopkeepers.

The photo-reconnaissance Blenheim was destroyed in an air raid on 21 February but other Blenheims of 60 Squadron carried out some photographic sorties. Meanwhile the defending RAF aircraft were steadily being whittled down, although they inflicted heavy casualties on the Japanese aircraft, both in the air and on the ground. Flying Officer Perkin was shot down on 21 March by Japanese fighters. He landed his Hurricane in a lake near the oil wells at Yenangyaung, but skidded to the bank and suffered nothing worse than a cut eyebrow. The other Hurricane was written off after a bombing attack.

The North American B-25C Mitchell II was mainly employed by the RAF as a bomber but also used by No 3 Photographic Reconnaissance Unit for photo-reconnaissance in the Far East theatre. This unit became 681 Squadron in January 1943 but the twin-engined aircraft were transferred to the new 684 Squadron the following September. This B-25C of 684 Squadron was photographed in 1944 at Comilla in India. It was probably N5-145 of the Military Aviation Arm of the Royal Netherlands—Indies Army, one of five which were transferred to the RAF and employed in this role. (F.W. Guy via G.J. Thomas)

Ground crews of No 3 Photographic Reconnaissance Unit (India) in front of one of the North American B-25C Mitchells acquired from the Military Arm of the Royal Netherlands Indies Army. The photograph was taken in May 1941 at Pendevesvar in India. (Corporal A. Fox DFM, RAFVR)

Group Captain S.G. Wise, who arrived as a wing commander in India during May 1942 to command the Photographic Reconnaissance Unit. He had previously flown as a pilot with No 1 Photographic Reconnaissance Unit in the UK and had also commanded 248 Squadron, a strike squadron of Coastal Command equipped with Beaufighters. (The late Group Captain S.G. Wise CBE, DFC*)

Hurricane PR IIC serial BN125, which arrived in October 1942 from the Middle East to join No 3 Photographic Reconnaissance Unit at Dum-Dum, India. The fairing beneath the fuselage enclosed the cameras. The machine was painted in royal blue, with wing and tail markings outlined in yellow, but with the fuselage roundels painted over. (The late Wing Commander F.D. Procter DFC via G.J. Thomas)

All the time the Japanese continued their advance, apparently invincible. Magwe was evacuated and the RAF retreated once more, this time to Akyab, which immediately came under air attack. The photographic ground party set off again, taking the road past Mandalay and Maymyo towards the mountains around Lashio on the route to China. However, they were ordered to return as far as Swebo, where they were picked up by a Dakota and flown to India. By then, the few surviving RAF aircraft had also flown to India, while the ground staff made their way over the hills to Bengal. The surviving P–40s withdrew to China, and almost the whole of Burma fell into Japanese hands.

India seemed to be as vulnerable as Burma, but the Japanese were halted by the onset of the summer monsoon and the mountainous terrain which separated them from their next objective. This breathing space was a godsend to the RAF, which needed to rebuild its shattered squadrons. It was also recognised that strategic photo-reconnaissance was essential, although this had been almost unknown in India before the war with Japan. Some coverage of the military zone on the North-West Frontier had taken place by Army co-operation and bomber squadrons, with interpretation carried out locally by air intelligence liaison officers, but otherwise air photography had been undertaken only for a survey of India.

In January 1942 the Air Staff had agreed that a Far Eastern Photographic Intelligence Unit should be sent to Singapore. Fortunately, the party travelled only as far as India, where in March it was formed into three sections – a School of Photographic Interpretation, a Central Interpretation Section, and a Photographic Library. These were commanded by Squadron Leader J.D. Braithwaite, a pilot who had served with the Burma Volunteer Air Force which carried out liaison duties during the Japanese invasion.

Earlier, he had fitted a camera in a Puss Moth and made a survey of the oil installations south of Rangoon.

After the photographic parties from Singapore and Burma had linked up with these sections, a new unit was formed on 10 April 1942 and given the title of No 5 Photographic Reconnaissance Unit. It came under 221 Group and was commanded temporarily by Squadron Leader A.C. 'Fatty' Pearson, who had arrived from No 2 Photographic Reconnaissance Unit in Egypt. The unit acquired five North American B–25C Mitchells which had been stranded in India when en route to join the Military Aviation Arm of the Royal Netherlands Indies Army, at the time when Java surrendered. These aircraft were converted at Karachi for strategic photography by removing their armament and installing three F24 cameras in the ventral gun position, an F52 camera in the tail, and an extra fuel tank in the bomb bay. On 13 May they were flown to Pandeveswar in Bengal, where the Dutch crews helped the RAF pilots to convert on to them. The unit was renumbered No 3 Photographic Reconnaissance Unit (India) on this date, to follow consecutively after No 1 in the UK and No 2 in the Middle East.

On 16 May Wing Commander S.G. 'Bill' Wise arrived to command the unit. He had flown with No 1 Photographic Reconnaissance Unit in Britain and during the previous year had commanded 248 Squadron, a strike squadron of Coastal Command which was equipped with Beaufighters. During May, three Hurricane IIBs arrived from the Middle East to join the new unit at Pandeveswar. This base was a singularly unattractive place, situated in a sand-blown open plain which was churned into mud when the rains came. Maintenance was difficult and the men suffered from poor food and heat exhaustion. The aircraft carried out photographic missions over

Burma, concentrating on enemy airfields and lines of communication, but the monsoon restricted these operations for several weeks.

At the end of June the unit began to move to Dum-Dum, near Calcutta, a permanent station which was far more suited to their requirements. One B-25C was lost in an accident but more Hurricanes arrived, so that by the end of September the unit had on charge four B-25Cs and six Hurricane IIBs. Three camera mountings for F24s were installed in the latter machines, two forward and one in the rear fuselage, while additional internal fuel tanks increased the range to about 1,100 miles.

The films were taken to nearby Barrackpore for processing and interpretation. Squadron Leader G.J. Craig, who in civilian life had worked for Kodak in London, was posted to Barrackpore as Senior Photographic Officer, while Squadron Leader G.D. Parke took over as Interpretation Officer. At first the sections operated from a trailer, but they soon moved to Tagore Palace, a residence of the Maharajah of Tagore, with their various messes in huts nearby. The effectiveness of the unit increased rapidly, both in terms of the photographic coverage and the work on the ground. There was a great demand by the Army and the RAF for these photographs.

In the extreme heat and humidity, problems arose with the cameras, which were mostly an assortment of F24s with 5-inch, 14-inch and 20-inch lenses. The glass covering the camera portholes of the aircraft was of a lower standard than that used in the UK and gave optical distortion. Fortunately, after some experiments, it was found that this glass was unnecessary in the prevailing hot climate and the covers were removed. Photographic sharpness was also reduced since condensation formed in the lenses of cameras fitted in the Hurricanes, caused by warm air flow from the aircraft radiator

during flight. This problem was overcome by placing the lenses into the Kodak cold store in Calcutta for two days, after which they were filled with dry air and sealed. Camera vibration in the mountings, which also reduced photographic quality, was associated with worn and faulty rubber suspension, and this could be only partially corrected. During film processing, temperature differences between the solutions and the wash water caused 'reticulation', or crinkling of the gelatin emulsion of the negatives. This was corrected by ensuring uniform liquid temperatures during processing. In printing, the photographs often lacked sharpness, resulting from poor contact between the printer pressure pad and the negative, but this was eventually corrected by modifying the pad.

Wing Commander Wise called for volunteers among the ground photographers to fly in the B-25C Mitchells. One of those who put his name forward was Leading Aircraftman Alan Fox, who had been in Mingaladon when the Japanese attacked and taken part in the evacuation from Burma. The other crew members were the pilot, the second pilot and the navigator. The operating altitude was 26,000 to 30,000 feet and Fox found the aircraft freezing cold. His job was responsibility for the cameras, replacing the film magazines and attending to stoppages, but in addition he kept watch from the astrodome for any dot in the sky which might turn out to be a Japanese fighter. Some interceptions were made and the usual method of escape was to build up speed by putting the Mitchell into a steep dive. Fox eventually flew on seventy-five sorties, to targets such as the airfield at Myitkyina in Burma, the docks at Rangoon, the airfield at Chiengmai in Siam, the Andaman Islands and the new Burma-Siam railway which was being built by thousands of British and Commonwealth prisoners. He was awarded a

The main airfield at Toungoo in Burma, photographed in early 1943 after it had been developed by the Japanese. (Squadron Leader J.D. Braithwaite RAFVR)

Spitfire PR XI serial PL773 of 681 Squadron in India. This mark of aircraft replaced the Spitfire PR IV in the UK photo-reconnaissance squadrons towards the end of 1942 but did not appear in India until October 1943. It was powered by a Merlin 61 engine which gave a top speed of 417 mph. Two vertical cameras were installed in the rear fuselage, sometimes with the addition of an oblique. These Spitfires were painted in 'special blue'. (The late Group Captain S.G. Wise CBE, DFC*)

Flying Officer F.D. Procter standing in front of a Spitfire PR IV at Dum-Dum. This was one of the first two Spitfires to arrive at No 3 Photographic Reconnaissance Unit (India), ferried from the Middle East in October 1942. After the unit became 681 Squadron on 25 January 1943, Procter commanded the squadron from December 1943 to April 1945. (The late Wing Commander F.D. Procter DFC via G.J. Thomas)

Spitfire PR XI serial PL776 photographed at Alipore, where 681 Squadron was based from May 1944 to June 1945. This aircraft was flown by Wing Commander F.D. Procter from July 1944 to April 1945, during part of the period when he commanded the squadron. (The late Wing Commander F.D. Procter DFC via G.J. Thomas)

A Spitfire PR XI of 681 Squadron being serviced at Chandina in India, an airstrip constructed in 1943 on paddy fields as a satellite to Comilla, near the Burmese border. It was built without runways, hard-standings or permanent buildings. The squadron was based there from 9 December 1943 to 30 January 1944, returning to Dum-Dum when the surface became unusable with the onset of the winter monsoon. (Squadron Leader T.N. Rosser OBE, DFC, RAFVR)

DFM, and was believed to be one of only three airmen photographers to receive this decoration.

On 10 October 1942 two Spitfire PR IVs were ferried from the Middle East to India, thus improving still further the effectiveness of the unit, and two more arrived within that month. The new aircraft were fitted with pre-war F8 cameras, used for high-altitude photography, and at first these had to be removed until suitable processing equipment became available. In the following month, No 3 Photographic Reconnaissance Unit called for additional volunteers from pilots in the Hurricane squadrons who had had experience in Spitfires, to join those who were already flying the Hurricane IIBs. One who came forward from 72 Squadron was Flying Officer Tom N. Rosser, who then flew on numerous photo-reconnaissance sorties until May 1944, becoming a flight commander and earning a DFC.

The Hurricane and Spitfire pilots carried out extensive strategic sorties over Burma, usually taking in several targets during flights of over four hours. Airfields and railways were of special interest, as were the tracks leading to the Arakan. The aircraft often flew to the limits of their range and the pilots feared engine failure and the violence of the monsoon more than pursuit by enemy aircraft. Tom Rosser recollects that there were no navigation aids, apart from the R/T in the Spitfire. Compass courses were flown over the jungle-clad Arakan range, and then pinpoints were usually made by map-reading over the Chindwin river and then the Irrawaddy. If there was cloud on the return journey, Rosser normally made a generous time allowance over the hills and then let down over the flat ground beyond, hoping to pick up a visual pinpoint.

Unlike the Spitfire PR IV, the Hurricanes IIA and IIB were not designed as long-range reconnaissance aircraft. They were fighters with the guns removed, an assortment of tanks in the wings and no heating. The pilot usually supervised the complex business of filling the tanks, while squatting on a metal wing which was blazing hot. Then he donned a heavy sweater, woollen socks, fleece-lined boots, overalls and gloves. Soaked with sweat, he ascended into the bitter cold of high altitude in order to fly above Japanese fighters and anti-aircraft fire.

While the RAF was carrying out its sorties, the British Army built up its forces and in December 1942 began a gradual thrust down the Arakan with the intention of recapturing Akyab. Tactical photographic support for the ground forces was carried out by Lysanders of 20 Squadron and Hurricanes of 28 Squadron. The objective of taking Akyab was not achieved on this occasion, since the landing craft were not available, but the assault demonstrated the importance of close collaboration with the RAF, both in terms of tactical reconnaissance and supply from the air.

On 25 January 1943 No 3 Photographic Reconnaissance Unit was renumbered 681 Squadron, in common with the policy of giving squadron numbers to all such units. In the same month Squadron Leader Craig was sent to Ceylon to work on camera installations for the B–24 Liberators of 160 Squadron, which by the following May began to supplement the work of 681 Squadron by covering the Andaman Islands, southern Malaya and northern Sumatra.

Early in February, General Wingate began his famous Chindit operations behind the Chindwin river to disrupt Japanese communications, and in the following month was supported by some of the Hurricanes of 28 Squadron and 1 (India) Squadron in the tactical reconnaissance role, the aircraft being fitted with long-range tanks.

By May, only two B–25C Mitchells remained with 681 Squadron, through unserviceability and the loss of aircraft on an operation on 13 February. Help was requested from the US Tenth Air Force in India, and two aircraft were converted and collected by pilots of 681 Squadron in June.

A major hazard in these PR operations was the weather, especially in the monsoon period when close-set pillars of cumulo-nimbus cloud towered from a few feet above the ground to 40,000 feet or more, the tops giving the appearance of boiling steam. On 8 June 1943 Warrant Officer F.D.C. Brown in a Spitfire of 681 Squadron was faced with a wall of these clouds when returning to Chittagong from a sortie. He had insufficient fuel to fly round it and dived straight ahead. His Spitfire went into a spin and he pushed the stick forward and then blacked out. When he came to, he was falling through the air with bits of his aircraft fluttering around him while the main part of the fuselage, minus the engine, wings and tail, was falling several hundred feet below. He pulled his parachute ripcord and landed in a paddy field in the mouth of the Ganges river, where he was dragged along the ground by the strong wind. Some Bengali villagers found him and took him on a twenty-hour journey by sampan and bullock cart to safety, where he eventually recovered from his injuries.

Following the reduction in 681 Squadron's capacity to carry out very long-range reconnaissance, it was decided to supply the squadron with Mosquitos. Two PR IVs arrived on 9 August 1943 and others followed, including Mosquito PR IXs. In addition, two more B-25 Mitchells were supplied by the USAAF in the same month. The operational capacity of the squadron was thus greatly extended, but losses continued. The fates of those who failed to return were not usually known in the squadron, although one Spitfire pilot was led out of Japanese-occupied territory by friendly Burmese. Another Spitfire pilot who was captured by

the Japanese is known to have been hideously tortured to death, and it is possible that the same fate befell others.

On 29 September 1943 all the twin-engined aircraft in 681 Squadron were transferred to the newly created 684 Squadron, also based at Dum-Dum and commanded by Squadron Leader Basil S. Jones. In the following December, with the improvement in the weather, both squadrons moved east over the Brahmaputra River, 684 Squadron to Comilla and 681 Squadron to its satellite Chandina. The photographic section was set up near a dirt road, where dust proved a major problem when drying the negatives, but good results were still achieved. At the same time there was another administrative change with the creation of No 171 Photographic Reconnaissance Wing, controlling both squadrons. Wing Commander Wise was given command of the new Wing while Squadron Leader Paul Lamboit, who had arrived in 681 Squadron the previous summer, became the Photographic Officer. Squadron Leader Freddie D. Procter, one of the two pilots who had flown the Hurricanes in Burma, took over command of 681 Squadron. The strength of the single-engined aircraft in this squadron had been augmented by the arrival of Spitfire PR XIs to supplement the Spitfire PR IVs and the Hurricane IIBs, although losses continued in both squadrons, which were flying intensively on operations.

The arrival of the Mosquitos enabled 684 Squadron to increase the range of its sorties. On 15 December Squadron Leader Jones covered the distant target of Bangkok for the first time, a feat for which he and his navigator were awarded immediate DFCs. Jones left the squadron in the same month and his place was taken by Wing Commander W.B. Murray. In early 1944 Mosquito PR XVIs began to arrive and, with their pressurised cabins, improved further the

Above, left: Squadron Leader Jack E. Archbald was one of the first professional photographers to join the RAFVR after the outbreak of the Second World War. He was posted to No 2 Camouflage Unit (later the Photographic Development Unit and then No 1 Photographic Reconnaissance Unit) at RAF Heston. Later in 1940 he joined Bomber Command, where he was employed training aircrews on photographic procedures. He was posted to South East Asia Command in 1944, where he was employed for a while as Deputy Command Photographic Officer for the Near and the Far East. (Mrs Ann Archbald) *Above, right:* Leading Aircraftman Alan Fox DFM, holding an F24 camera, at Dum-Dum airfield in Bengal in 1944. (A. Fox DFM, RAFVR)

A Consolidated Liberator III of 354 Squadron, based at Cuttack in India during 1944. These 'very long range' aircraft were fitted with extra fuel tanks and employed on general reconnaissance and photographic work, but they also attacked shipping off Burma and carried out anti-submarine patrols. (Wing Commander G.J. Craig RAFVR)

The USAAF Photographic Section at Bally in India, photographed in 1944. Left to right: Air Vice-Marshal T.M. Williams (Assistant to the Air Officer of Eastern Air Command), Group Captain S.G. Wise (Officer Commanding Photographic Reconnaissance Wing), Colonel Milton Kaye (Officer Commanding USAAF Photographic Wing), Air Vice-Marshal R.V. Goddard (on visit from the UK). (Wing Commander G.J. Craig RAFVR)

Commanders of the Eastern Air Command, photographed in May 1944. Left to right: Group Captain S.G. 'Bill' Wise (commanding 171 Photographic Force), Air Marshal Sir Richard Peirse (Allied Air C-in-C), Major-General George E. Stratemeyer, USAAF (Second-in-Command to Sir Richard). (Wing Commander G.J. Craig RAFVR)

A Spitfire PR XI of 681 Squadron, with M. 'Bluey' George of the RAAF in the cockpit, possibly photographed at Dum-Dum. George began flying with the squadron as a flight sergeant and was commissioned by early 1945. The cameras were F8s, used by the RAF in the 1930s for high-altitude photography. These had been withdrawn generally with the introduction of the F52 camera, but several were purchased from the Indian Government for use over Burma. (The Medmenham Club)

effectiveness of the twin-engined aircraft in the squadron. With the approach of the monsoon season in January 1944, the two photo-reconnaissance squadrons returned to Dum-Dum.

The Allies planned advances into Burma in early 1944, the British and Indian 14th Army from the west, the Chinese and Americans from the north, while Wingate's Chindits penetrated behind Japanese lines and harassed their lines of communications. Survey photography of Burma began, so that accurate maps could be constructed for these advances. Yet another administrative change took place in February 1944, when No 171 Photographic Reconnaissance Wing was renamed No 171 Photographic Reconnaissance Force and incorporated into Eastern Air Command. In turn, this was part of Air Command, South-East Asia, which was formed by the amalgamation of the RAF in the area with the US Tenth Air Force. The US 8th Photo-Reconnaissance Group joined this Force, consisting of three squadrons equipped with Lockheed F–5s, P–40 Warhawks and F–7A Liberators, all initially under the command of Group Captain Wise. However, no arrangements were made for a headquarters organisation at this stage, and the RAF and USAAF continued to operate independently although in collaboration.

As it happened, the Japanese commander decided to attack first, in the Arakan during early February 1944, followed by advances further north at Imphal and Kohima during the following month. But by then the Allies had achieved air superiority with their fighter, bomber and reconnaissance squadrons, and above all with their ability to supply their ground forces from the air. Tactical reconnaissance was carried out by the Hurricanes of 28 Squadron as well as those of 1 and 6 (India) Squadrons. After weeks of fighting, during which their lines of supply were cut by Allied air attacks and many of

their aircraft destroyed, the Japanese were repulsed with heavy losses and forced to retreat. At the same time, their reconnaissance 'Dinahs', which hitherto had been immune from air attack, began to fall victim to Spitfire V fighters which had arrived in India.

Paul Lamboit was posted back to the UK in March 1944 and his place was taken once more by Gordon Craig, who had finished his work of equipping 160 Squadron with cameras. The two RAF reconnaissance squadrons moved to Alipore the following month and operations continued at an intense pace.

By May the survey of the battle area had been completed, amounting to 57 per cent of all Burma, an area about three times the size of England. Among many other matters, this survey enabled photographic interpreters to identify jungle clearings formed by former rice fields, where rats carrying the scourge of scrub typhus fed; these were to be avoided by the Allied troops. Holes in landing strips were also identified, dug by the Japanese with the intention of placing a man with a 500–lb bomb in each of them, ready to blow up landing aircraft in kamikaze fashion.

The Allied ground offensive could not be renewed intensively until the end of the monsoon season in October. During the intervening period a detachment of Mosquitos from 684 Squadron was sent to Yelahanka near Madras to help in aerial surveys of southern India. Another detachment was sent in August to China Bay in Ceylon, where it was joined by the first detachment and both were engaged on a survey of northern Sumatra in preparation for an eventual invasion of that island. These detachments returned to Alipore when the major offensive developed on all fronts in Burma, leaving 160 Squadron to continue reconnaissance from Ceylon.

The Japanese evacuated Rangoon towards the end of April 1945 but the British did not realise this until an RAF pilot read messages written by PoWs on the roof of the gaol: 'BRITISH HERE', 'JAPS GONE'. The inmates had painted these partly to avoid the possibility of being bombed by the RAF. (Squadron Leader J.D. Braithwaite RAFVR)

The PoWs in Rangoon gaol added 'EXTRACT DIGIT' to their roof notices, which was an unmistakably RAF expression. An RAF pilot landed at nearby Mingaladon airfield on 2 May 1945 and walked to meet the senior officer of the gaol, an RAAF wing commander. (Squadron Leader J.D. Braithwaite RAFVR)

The Mitsubishi Ki-46-III, known to the Allies as the 'Dinah', was one of the most successful reconnaissance aircraft employed by the Japanese during the Second World War. On the Burma front, it was able to fly above the ceiling of RAF fighters until the Spitfire arrived in the area. This captured Dinah was evaluated by the Allied Tactical Air Intelligence Unit of the South East Asia Air Command after the Japanese capitulation. (J.M. Bruce/G.S. Leslie Collection)

A Japanese mechanic working on an engine at RAF Mingaladon in Burma, photographed by the author soon after the capitulation. The Japanese worked hard and efficiently for the Allies after they had been ordered to surrender by Emperor Hirohito. (R.C. Nesbit)

Life returning to Hiroshima, photographed in January 1947. This shows the mainstreet with the telephone exchange still standing, although the interior of the building was gutted by the heatwave of the atom bomb dropped on 6 August 1945. (Sergeant J. Muncie RAF (Ret'd))

The rebuilding of the Christian church in Hiroshima, 1947. (Sergeant J. Muncie RAF (Ret'd))

The Allies began their advances in northern Burma, supplied from the air. Wing Commander W.E.M. Lowry took over 684 Squadron in November 1944, but unfortunately the Mosquitos had to be withdrawn in that month since defects in their wooden structure had developed in the steamy tropical climate, caused partly by faulty bonding of glue. With the few remaining Mitchells in the squadron well past their prime, the function of very long-range reconnaissance was thus performed mainly by the USAAF during this period, but the Spitfires of 681 Squadron continued flying.

By 2 January 1945 the Japanese had been forced back from many of their positions in northern Burma, and had also evacuated Akyab. They fought to the death when they could not extricate themselves, including those in the garrison of Ramree Island to the south of Akyab, which was reoccupied in March. In the same month, Mandalay fell to the 14th Army after an intense bombardment from the air, and the way to Rangoon down the Irrawaddy was opened.

The formal structure of No 171 Photographic Reconnaissance Force was finally resolved on 9 January with the appointment of Colonel Milton W. Kaye of the USAAF as commander, with Group Captain Bill Wise as his deputy while retaining command of the RAF's squadrons. By then, four American squadrons were engaged on photo-reconnaissance. The Warhawks of one of these squadrons had been replaced with North American P–51C Mustangs, modified with cameras as F–6C Mustangs, and these were engaged mainly on support for the Chinese and American forces advancing from the north.

The Mosquitos of 684 Squadron came back up to strength by the end of February. From advanced bases, the whole of Burma could be covered by both RAF reconnaissance squadrons, while the Mosquitos could also cover the north of Siam and Malaya. The remaining B–25C Mitchells were relegated to courier duties, mainly flying between Alipore and Ceylon, where a detachment of the Mosquitos of 684 Squadron was engaged on reconnaissance of the Nicobar Islands, southern Malaya and northern Sumatra. In the same month, the Spitfires of 681 Squadron flew intensively over southern Burma from advanced bases. There was a change of command when Squadron Leader D.B. Pearson, one of the pilots who had flown the reconnaissance Buffalos in Malaya, took over from Wing Commander F.D. Procter. At the end of March, the Hurricane IICs of 7 (India) Squadron joined in tactical reconnaissance for the 14th Army.

A combined assault on Rangoon, code-named Operation 'Dracula', began in early May 1945, but it became clear from aerial photographs that the Japanese had abandoned the capital before the troops landed. Signs on a jail known to contain PoWs which read JAPS GONE and EXTRACT DIGIT were so unmistakably British that Wing Commander A.E. Saunders landed his Mosquito VI of 110 Bomber Squadron at Mingaladon and walked into Rangoon, where he was met by the senior officer of the PoWs.

Following these victories, the Americans and the Chinese departed from this theatre of war to reinforce their armies in China, leaving the forces controlled by the British to finish off the Japanese in Burma. By this time there remained only about 17,500 Japanese troops, in the district of Pegu. These were intent on crossing the Sittang river into Siam but were bombed mercilessly by the RAF and cut down by guerilla forces, leaving only a few starving and ragged remnants. The British began making arrangements to recapture Malaya, in a combined operation code-named Operation 'Zipper'.

Meanwhile No 171 Photographic Reconnaissance Force was disbanded. Group Captain Wise departed for the UK and the two RAF squadrons then came under No 347 Photographic Wing. This was commanded by Group Captain C.E. St J. Beamish, who had previously commanded RAF Benson. The first Mosquito PR 34s arrived in 684 Squadron during July 1945 and were detached to the Cocos Islands, where a new airfield had been built to give access to southern Malaya and Sumatra. One of the achievements of this long-distance reconnaissance squadron was the identification of the PoW camps where the inmates were living in appalling conditions of brutality. In August 681 Squadron received Spitfire PR XIXs, so that at last the two squadrons were equipped with the most advanced reconnaissance aircraft in existence. But the end of the war came when the Japanese surrendered unconditionally on 14 August 1945, after the atomic bombs had been dropped on Hiroshima and Nagasaki.

CHAPTER THIRTEEN

BEHIND THE IRON CURTAIN

When the Americans in the Allied Central Interpretation Unit (ACIU) returned home with the US Eighth and Ninth Air Forces in August 1945, the unit lost the 'Allied' part of its title and was placed under the control of the newly created Central Photographic Establishment, part of Coastal Command, while 106 Group was disbanded. In August 1947 the CIU was renamed the Joint Air Photographic Interpretation Centre (UK), known as JAPIC (UK). Of course, by this time many of the staff had been demobilised to resume their civilian careers, and the establishment was rapidly whittled down from about 1,700 during wartime to 350 personnel. The majority of these were based at Nuneham Park, near Oxford, which had been used as an overflow section during the war, leaving only the Model Section and the Print Library at Medmenham. Meanwhile the School of Photography at Farnborough, which had trained 6,510 photographers during the war, with the temporary aid of a second school in Blackpool, moved into improvised quarters at Farnham in Surrey, where it remained until a second move during 1948 to Wellesbourne Mountford in Warwickshire.

Some of the RAF's photo-interpreters had been sent to Paris before the end of the European war, as part of the British Bombing Survey Unit, to assess the damage and disruption caused by Allied bombing. After VE-Day, personnel were also sent to Germany, to collect and record those enemy photographs which had not been destroyed. Those of European Russia were of particular interest, although not considered adequate for updated mapping or accurate knowledge of the military and industrial capacity of that vast country. While there, the RAF team was able to gain further information of the German photo-reconnaissance organisation, which had been partly assessed by British Intelligence during the war.

There is no doubt that the Germans appreciated the value of photo-reconnaissance before the war, perhaps to a greater extent than the RAF and British Intelligence. However, the service was designed to conform with the structure of the Luftwaffe, being split among the various Luftflotten (Air Forces) which supported the Armies on the various fronts, with specialised squadrons and mobile field photographic units, somewhat on the lines of the RAF's Reconnaissance Wings which formed part of the Second Tactical Air Force. Thus the work was concentrated on tactical reconnaissance, and light aircraft such as the Henschel 126 and the Focke Wulf 189 produced good results in the early years of the war, during the period when German Armies conquered much of Europe under cover of their air superiority.

Each Luftflotte was also equipped with strategic reconnaissance aircraft, such as the Dornier 17–E which could outfly at high altitude any RAF fighter aircraft at the beginning of the war. However, no competent

The Spitfire PR XIX was the last of the photo-reconnaissance versions of this famous aircraft, replacing the Spitfire PR XI soon after the war. The main production aircraft was powered by a Rolls-Royce Griffon 66 engine and fitted with wing tanks with a capacity of 172 gallons. It was unarmed and employed mainly for strategic work at high altitude. The last operational flight made by any Spitfire was in one of these machines over Malaya on 1 April 1954. This photograph is of serial PM631. (The late Squadron Leader J.E. Archbald)

Fitting an F24 camera in the oblique position of a Spitfire. (*Aeroplane Monthly*)

A Mosquito PR XVI, serial RG116, in post-war markings. A very long-range version of this mark of Mosquito, known as the PR 34, carried 200-gallon drop-tanks under each wing as well as extra tanks in the bomb bay, giving a range of about 2,500 miles (*Aeroplane Monthly*)

organisation such as the Central Interpretation Unit at Medmenham was ever set up in Germany to assess the photographic results. Although a department in the German Air Ministry, known as Air Photos of the Air Inspectorate for Reconnaissance, was formed in 1942, it was given a very low priority and indeed the majority of the photo-interpreters remained NCOs and their work was seldom used for the systematic gathering of intelligence or for high-level military decisions.

In addition, the equivalents of the unarmed and high-performance photo-reconnaissance Spitfire and Mosquito were not developed in Germany. The German cameras were of excellent quality but were too heavy for very high-altitude work, and the aircraft which carried them were eventually outclassed by the new Allied fighters. In short, German strategic reconnaissance and photo-interpretation became little short of disastrous, and the words of General Werner Freiherr von Fritsch, who had said in 1938 'The military organization which has the best photographic intelligence will win the next war', were proved correct.

Even before the war in Europe came to an end, the RAF's strategic photo-reconnaissance squadrons began some peaceful operations. On 21 March 1945 the Secretary of State for Air announced that they would undertake aerial survey work on behalf of Government departments and the Colonial Office. Eight days after this announcement, the Mosquitos of 540 Squadron moved from Benson to Coulommiers, east of Paris, to begin a survey of France. This task was completed by the following November, when the squadron moved back to Benson and began work in Britain on behalf of Ordnance Survey, in order to help update maps. The F49 survey camera had been developed for this work, which was also aided by new equipment such as the Decca Navigator, which provided an accurate position from radio beams.

The survey of Britain produced some unexpected benefits to such experts as the archaeological officer of Ordnance Survey, the former RFC air observer Osbert G.S. Crawford, since the photographs sometimes showed outlines of ancient settlements which were indistinguishable from the ground. Dr Glyn Daniels, a former photo-interpreter at Medmenham who became a well-known TV personality, wrote 'The interpretation of air photographs and visual air reconnaissance has become one of the major instruments of archaeological research'. This survey work was continued for several years, 540 Squadron being renumbered 58 Squadron on 30 September 1946 when it was equipped with the latest Mosquito PR 34 as well as the Anson C19, a version of the venerable aircraft which was particularly suitable for medium-altitude photography.

Requests for overseas surveys proved overwhelming, to the surprise of the Secretary of State for Air. No 541 Squadron was reorganised, with A Flight operating Spitfire PR XIXs while B Flight received Lancasters converted for survey work as PR 1s. In March 1946 the Lancasters were sent to Takoradi for a survey of the Gold Coast, but on their return the following September the squadron was disbanded, B Flight becoming 82 Squadron. These Lancasters were then detached to West Africa and Kenya, in order to carry out further surveys, the tasks not being completed until October 1952.

The other RAF photo-reconnaissance squadrons in Britain did not last long after the war. The strategic 542 Squadron was disbanded on 27 August 1945, followed by 544 Squadron on 13 October 1945. Drastic reductions also took place within the RAF based in Germany. On 14 July 1945 the Second Tactical Air Force was renamed the British Air Force of Occupation (BAFO) and rapidly reduced in strength. By the end of 1947 it had been reduced to ten squadrons,

The destruction of the buildings around Cologne Cathedral, with the Rhine in the top left. This city was the target of the RAF's first 1,000 bomber raid, on 30 May 1942. (Corporal L. Jewitt RAF (Ret'd))

The city of Wiesbaden, with the Rhine bottom left, showing pedestrians and motor vehicles. Some of the buildings seem to have escaped the effect of Allied bombing, although many others are gutted. (Corporal L. Jewitt RAF (Ret'd))

with only 2 Squadron, by then equipped with Spitfire PR XIXs, engaged on tactical photo-reconnaissance work.

Events were to demonstrate that these reductions were unwise, for the uneasy wartime alliance between the Western Allies and the Soviet Union soon deteriorated into hostility. Winston Churchill, who had lost the British election at the end of the war, stated during a speech at Fulton in the USA on 5 March 1946 'From Stettin on the Baltic to Trieste on the Adriatic an Iron Curtain has descended across the Continent'. On the eastern side of this physical barrier, the Soviet Union and the countries dominated by it faced the Anglo-Americans.

One effect of this hostility was the re-formation of two strategic photo-reconnaissance squadrons at Benson, No 541 with Spitfire PR XIXs on 1 November 1947 and No 540 with Mosquito PR 34s exactly a month later. Any hopes that a peaceful co-existence might be resumed were shattered when, on 24 June 1948, the Soviet Union refused to allow further communication by land between West Germany and the sectors of Berlin controlled by the Western Powers, in spite of an international agreement. The result was the Berlin Airlift, carried out by the Americans and the British until September 1949, four months after the Russians lifted their blockade. American squadrons also returned to Britain in 1948 as part of the United States Air Force (USAF), an independent body which had been created on 18 September 1947 on terms of equality with the US Army and Navy.

The appalling threat of nuclear warfare prompted the West into further rearmament. The North Atlantic Treaty Organisation (Nato), consisting initially of the USA, Canada, Britain and nine other European countries, came into effect on 24 August 1949. A formidable bloc was thus formed against Soviet Russia and within this the RAF

was built up again, in spite of the impoverished state of the British post-war economy. It was known that Russian scientists had developed a nuclear bomb in that year and had thus broken the monopoly held by America. The Western powers feared that such terrible weapons might be delivered either by long-distance Russian bombers or as warheads of missiles.

On 1 March 1950 a further reorganisation took place in the RAF, when the Central Photographic Establishment of Coastal Command was disbanded and the photo-reconnaissance squadrons, together with JAPIC (UK), were transferred to No 3 Group of Bomber Command. By then the photo-reconnaissance activities of the RAF were linked with those of the USAF, and in particular its Strategic Air Command. In December of the same year a major conference was held at RAF Benson to discuss the objectives to be attained. This was attended by numerous representatives of the Air Ministry, Bomber Command, the Admiralty, the War Office, the USAF, the RCAF, the US Navy, BAFO, JAPIC, the School of Photography and officers of the various photo-reconnaissance squadrons. It was stated that the primary tasks were to provide photographic evidence of the ability of Soviet long-range aircraft to mount attacks against the UK, the ability of Soviet submarines to attack sea communications, and any movements of Russian troops westwards through Europe. The other tasks were to provide cover of the internal and industrial capacity of the Soviet Union, to carry out general surveys to correct out-of-date maps, as well as reconnaissance for damage assessment and the production of target maps.

There was another aerial reconnaissance objective which was discussed at this conference and which began to assume prime importance. It had become necessary to assess

The Lancaster PR 1 was a version of the famous bomber, with the turrets faired over, employed after the war on photo-reconnaissance duties. During the period it was equipped with this aircraft, from October 1946 to December 1953, 82 Squadron carried out photographic surveys of Nigeria, the Gold Coast, Sierra Leone, the Gambia and Kenya, parts of which were not mapped at the time. Other Lancaster PR 1s were employed by 683 Squadron from November 1950 to November 1953 over Arabia and Africa. This Lancaster PR 1 serial TW904 of 82 Squadron was photographed over a Kenyan game reserve in 1949. (C.F. Scandrett via Flight Lieutenant A.S. Thomas)

The F49 camera was introduced shortly after the Second World War for air survey work of fine definition. It was a heavy camera which, when loaded with a film and fitted with a 20-inch lens, weighed nearly 87 lb. The Mark I and Mark III had shutter speeds between 1/150th and 1/200th of a second, and the magazine held 200 exposures of 9-inch by 9-inch. The camera could be operated electrically or manually. (Flight Lieutenant G.H. Parry RAF (Ret'd))

The Gloster Meteor FR 9 was introduced into RAF service with 2 Squadron in Germany during December 1950, replacing the Spitfire PR XIX for tactical photo-reconnaissance. It was armed with four 20-mm cannons and employed mainly on low-level work, with a nose camera mounted either obliquely or straight ahead. These machines also served in the Middle East. This photograph of Meteor FR 9 serial VZ602 of 226 Operational Conversion Unit was taken in 1951. (Flight Lieutenant A.S. Thomas RAF)

The Gloster Meteor PR 10 first entered RAF service with 541 Squadron in January 1951. It was unarmed and mounted vertical cameras as well as a nose camera, replacing the Spitfire PR 19 for strategic reconnaissance at high altitudes. This photograph of Meteor PR 10 serial WB!65 of 81 Squadron was taken on 17 December 1959, when the squadron was based at Tengah in Singapore. (Flight Lieutenant A.S. Thomas RAF)

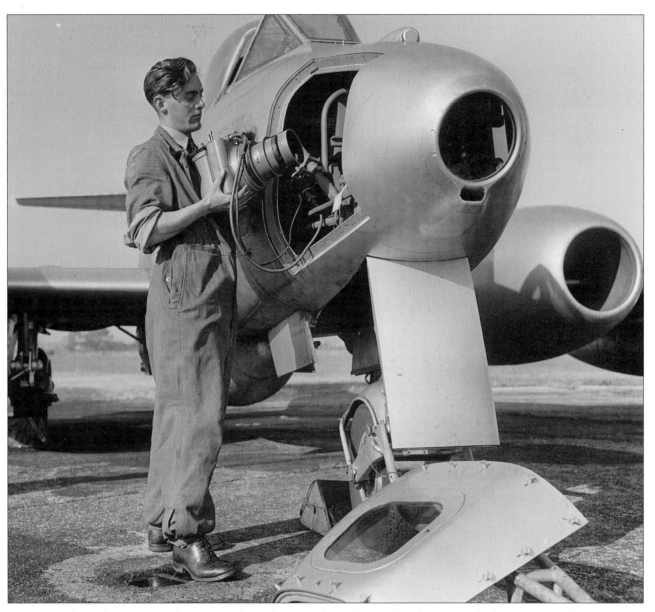

Leading Aircraftman Peter J. Griggs fitting an F24 camera to a Gloster Meteor of 2 Squadron, Second Tactical Air Force, when based in West Germany in the early 1950s. (*Aeroplane Monthly*)

This North American RB-45C was a test-bed machine with an engine bolted underneath the fuselage. It was a photo-reconnaissance version of the four-jet bomber and first flew in April 1950. The nose was adapted for a ciné or an oblique camera, and there was provision for up to ten cameras in all. It was unarmed and could carry a crew of up to five. The maximum speed was 370 mph, the ceiling 37,550 feet and the range 3,450 feet with in-flight refuelling. (*Aeroplane Monthly*)

RAF aircrew, dressed in tropical kit, in front of a North American RB-45C Tornado photo-reconnaissance aircraft, during training in the USA. (P. Lashmar)

any development of radar defences in the Soviet Union, which had been inadequate during the war, so as to provide American and British scientists with information necessary to develop RCM (radio counter-measures), or jamming equipment. This type of work, known as electronic intelligence or 'Elint', had been carried out by the RAF's 100 Group during the war, employing trained radar operators in specialised aircraft fitted up for this purpose. In April 1946, 90 (Signals) Group was formed to take over this work. Aircraft named 'ferrets', equipped with electronic search equipment, cruised the borders of the Soviet Union. They occasionally made passes as though they intended to intrude and thus activated the Russian radar defences, for assessment. This procedure could be highly dangerous if MiG fighters were in the vicinity and the Russian pilots were not too worried about crossing their borders. By 1952 only one squadron of the RAF was engaged on this work, 192 Squadron equipped with Boeing B–29A Washingtons and based at Watton in Norfolk.

To accomplish the photographic objectives, reconnaissance aircraft would need to continue infringing Soviet airspace, and both the USA and Britain were prepared to contravene international law in order to acquire intelligence considered essential for the defence of their countries. From the beginning of 1951 such penetrations were carried out far more intensively. Details of the RAF operations have not yet been released in Britain, but both the USA and Russia have been more forthcoming. Some information has appeared in books published in America and Britain, and a television programme on the subject was shown by BBC TV 'Timewatch' on 16 February 1994.

From the end of the war some British and American photo-reconnaissance aircraft, including Mosquitos from Benson, had 'inadvertently' crossed the Iron Curtain as a result of 'navigation errors'. These aircraft suffered their first casualty on 8 April 1950 when a Consolidated PB4Y–2 Privateer (a version of the famous Liberator) of the US Navy was shot down over Latvia by a Lovochkin LA–11 fighter, resulting in the deaths of all ten crew members. This was the first of a series of losses. However, President Harry S. Truman authorised the establishment of US spy-plane units in England. Among these were the 72nd Strategic Reconnaissance Squadron, equipped with Boeing RB–50 Superfortresses, and a detachment of the 91st Strategic Reconnaissance Group, equipped with North American RB–45C Tornados.

The Tornados were based at RAF Sculthorpe in Norfolk. This American aircraft, powered by four turbo-jet engines, possessed considerable advantages over the RAF's piston-engined Mosquito PR 34. The maximum speed of the Tornado was 570 mph compared with the 425 mph of the Mosquito. There was provision for ten cameras and a crew of up to five, while the Mosquito usually carried three cameras and a crew of two. At 37,550 feet, the ceiling of the Tornado was about 1,500 feet higher than that of the Mosquito, almost beyond the reach of Russian fighters and over the limit of Russian flak. Moreover, the Tornado was equipped with facilities for radar photography, using the technique of photographing H_2S (H_2X in American aircraft) developed by Squadron Leader Howard Lees of the Pathfinder Force during the war, whereas the smaller and cramped Mosquito did not normally carry this instrument. Although 2 Squadron had received the RAF's first jet reconnaissance aircraft in December 1950, in the form of the Gloster Meteor FR 9, this single-seat aircraft had a range of 1,400 miles and could be used only for tactical work. It was employed in

This prototype English Electric Canberra PR 3, serial VX181, first flew on 19 March 1950. It was adapted from the Canberra B2 light bomber as a replacement for the Mosquito PR 34. The first squadron to be equipped with these machines was 540 Squadron, in December 1952. (*Aeroplane Monthly*)

Senior Aircraftman Colin Saunders (left) and Senior Aircraftman Herbert Hinman about to fit an F52 camera with a 36-inch lens in a Canberra, in March 1955. (*Aeroplane Monthly*)

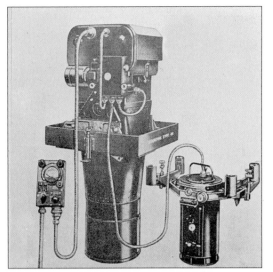

Above, left: The F89 camera, designed for night photography, came into use soon after the Second World War. The Mark 2 (shown here) operated electrically, with a moving film which gave 165 exposures of 7-inches by 8½-inches. Lenses were 20-inch and 36-inch. *Above, right*: The F97 camera was developed after the Second World War for night photography at levels between 500 feet and 3,000 feet and at speeds between 300 knots and 600 knots, using photo-flash cartridges. The camera contained two 5-inch lenses which operated alternately, and it carried a moving film which gave 480 overlapping exposures of 5-inch by 4½-inch. (Both photos: Flight Lieutenant G.H. Parry RAF (Ret'd))

The F95 camera was developed for oblique photography in daylight, at low level and high speed, and was usually mounted on a pod beneath the aircraft. The lenses were 4-inch or 12-inch while the shutter speeds were 1/1,000th of a second at four pictures a second or 1/2,000th of a second at eight pictures a second. The picture size was 2¼-inch by 2¼-inch while the film magazine of the Mark 2 (shown here) gave 500 exposures. (Flight Lieutenant G.H. Parry RAF (Ret'd))

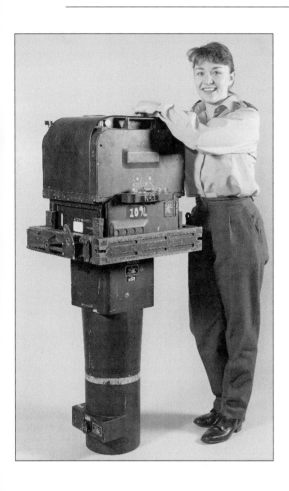

The F96 camera was designed for day reconnaissance at high altitude. The picture size was 9-inch by 9-inch and the film in the magazine ranged from 250 feet to 1,000 feet. Shutter speeds of the Mark 1 were 1/125th, 1/250th of a second, while the lenses ranged from 6-inch to 48-inch telephoto. The camera was the largest employed by the RAF, as can be seen from this example with a 48-inch lens and young WRAF servicewoman 5 feet 3 inches in height. (Sergeant D. Jenkins RAF (Ret'd), courtesy RAF Cosford Museum)

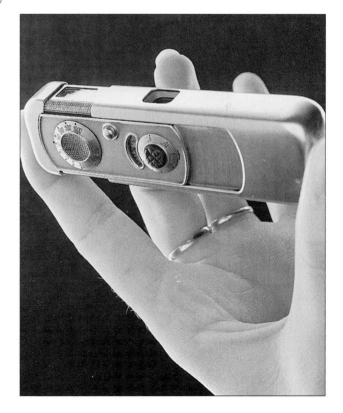

One of the smallest cameras was the ultra-miniature Minox, well-loved by makers of spy movies. It had a lens with a focal length of 15 mm and used a film with a width of 9.5 mm, giving a picture size of 11 mm by 8 mm. (Sergeant D. Jenkins RAF (Ret'd), courtesy RAF Cosford Museum)

Germany where, in September 1951, BAFO had resumed the title of Second Tactical Air Force, to emphasise that the RAF would soon serve alongside that country as an ally instead of as part of an occupying power.

At this stage in early 1951, President Truman had banned further USAF flights over the Soviet Union as too provocative, especially when his country was embroiled in the Korean War. Thus it seemed that the RAF would need to undertake the special photographic tasks with the USAF Tornado. The Strategic Air Command of the USAF approached the Joint Chiefs of Staff of Nato for permission, and agreement was reached with Clement Attlee. This was endorsed by Winston Churchill when he resumed the Premiership in October 1951. A special RAF unit was formed at Sculthorpe by the Vice Chief of Air Staff, Sir Ralph Cochrane, under the command of Squadron Leader H.B. 'Mickey' Martin, one of the pilots who had flown on the famous Dam Buster raid of 1943. When it was found that Martin was medically unfit to fly at such high altitudes, command was passed to Squadron Leader John Crampton of 101 Squadron, who was already experienced with jets, his squadron having been the first to receive the new English Electric Canberra bomber in May 1951.

The first RAF crews went to America in September 1951, where they trained at the Air Force bases of Langley, Barksdale and Lockbourne, gaining experience of flying the Tornado as well as knowledge of the targets required by the Strategic Air Force of the USAF. They returned to Sculthorpe in December 1951 and continued training for a while, flying with crews of three – pilot, co-pilot, and navigator/radar operator. The first mission took place on 21 March 1952, when a single aircraft flew up and down the Berlin air corridor at high speed and maximum altitude, to test the reaction of the Russians. The next operational flights took place on 17 April 1952 when three Tornados, with USAF insignia removed and replaced with RAF roundels, refuelled from Boeing KC-29 tankers and then penetrated Russian air space. One flew to Murmansk, another to the environs south of Moscow, and the third through central Russia. All returned safely with radar photographs of key targets, in spite of flak, and were refuelled over Western Germany on the way out. The success of the missions delighted General Curtis LeMay, who commanded the USAF.

The RAF crews than returned to their normal units and, although other missions were planned, nothing took place until 24 April 1954 when three Tornados were again employed. One flew north of Moscow, another south of Moscow, and the other through central Russia as far as the Ukraine. Once again, all returned safely. Unknown to the crews, the Russian MiG pilots, who had no radar equipment at this stage, had been ordered to ram the intruders, somewhat in the fashion of the Japanese kamikaze pilots but not head-on so as to give them the chance of baling out. However, the Russian pilots were unable to find the reconnaissance aircraft in the dark.

On 8 May 1954, another mission took place when a Boeing RB-47 Stratojet of the USAF took off from Fairford in Gloucestershire, without the authority of the US President, and penetrated Soviet airspace south of Murmansk, photographing airfields. It was attacked by several MiG-15s but these were unable to maintain altitude and the turbo-jet bomber returned safely. Tornados carried out other missions in 1954, without loss. For instance, a flight with RAF crews flew over Moscow on 29 April. However, by then there had been further major developments.

Britain had exploded its first atomic bomb, in Australia on 3 October 1952. The Americans had exploded a hydrogen bomb in the Pacific the following month. This was

The Canberra PR 7 followed the Canberra PR 3 in May 1954, with engines of 7,500 lb thrust compared with the 6,500 lb thrust of its predecessor. The camera ports can be seen in this photograph of serial WJ819. (*Aeroplane Monthly*)

One of the first Canberra PR 9s received by 58 Squadron at RAF Wyton in 1960, undergoing pre-flight checks. The navigator, Flight Lieutenant Peter Thompson, is checking his equipment in the nose. The pilot, Flight Lieutenant Fred Hoskins, is standing on the ladder while a fitter is checking his ejector seat. (*Short Bros & Harland*)

The Canberra PR 9 began to succeed the PR 7 in January 1960, with engines of 11,250-lb thrust instead of the 7,500-lb thrust of the PR 7. These PR 9s of 59 Squadron were lined up at RAF Wyton, with the two nearest visible as serials XH164 and XH136. (Short Bros & Harland)

followed by a report of the explosion of a hydrogen bomb by the Russians in August 1953. The prospect of nuclear war seemed to be looming even larger. It was known that Russia had been experimenting with nuclear bombs in Novaya Zemlya inside the Arctic Circle, but the US Central Intelligence Agency had received information of long-range missile testing at Kapustin Yar, east of Stalingrad, and photographic cover of the site was urgently required. However, Dwight D. Eisenhower, who had been sworn in as President of the USA on 20 January 1953, also refused permission for overflights by the USAF.

By the end of 1954, ten US aircraft of various types had been shot down around the borders of the Soviet Union on ferret missions. An RAF aircraft had also been lost, an Avro Lincoln serial RF531 from the Central Gunnery School at Leconfield in Yorkshire, shot down on 12 March 1953 by MiG fighters near Lüneburg. In this instance, the aircraft seems to have strayed over the border by accident, when on a training flight. There were no survivors from the crew of seven, five of whom fell in the Russian zone, their bodies being returned later.

At this time, photo-reconnaissance versions of the Canberra had been developed. The first was the Canberra PR 3, which entered service with 540 Squadron in December 1952. It was followed by the Canberra PR 7, which first went to 542 Squadron at Wyton in Cambridgeshire, where the former Spitfire squadron re-formed on 17 May 1954. The range of this machine was no better than the Tornado but it possessed the great advantage of a maximum speed of about 600 mph and an altitude of over 50,000 feet. It could thus fly above the ceiling of Russian fighters and flak as well as above the levels at which condensation trails might form and give away its position. With a crew of two, pilot and navigator/ radar operator, it could carry up to

six F52 cameras for daylight work. Alternatively, it could be fitted with two F97 cameras for night photography at low level, or two F89 cameras for night photography at high level, or two F95 cameras for daylight oblique photography at low level, or one F49 camera for survey work. Although it was not normally equipped for radar photography, the new Canberra PR 7 was otherwise ideal for reconnaissance over Kapustin Yar.

One of these machines was especially adapted but details of its flights have never been released, although they are reported to have been approved by Winston Churchill. They were code-named Operation 'Robin' and the Canberra is believed to have borne the serial WH726 and to have been fitted with a 100-inch camera specially made in America. It flew from Giebelstadt in the eastern part of West Germany on daylight operations over the Soviet Union and landed in Iran. A MiG pilot who was ordered to intercept one of these flights, Mikhail Shulga, described on the BBC TV programme how he managed to climb to 48,500 feet and could see a Canberra shining in the sunlight, several thousand feet above. His efforts to reach it became fruitless when the MiG stalled several times. The Canberra always completed its missions successfully. The Russians were understandably furious at these incursions but could not protest too vociferously since they did not wish to confess to the world the inadequacy of their defences.

In May 1955 the military alliance of the Warsaw Pact was formed, consisting of the communist countries of East Europe under the leadership of the Soviet Union, in response to the formation of Nato. Aware of Anglo-American superiority with reconnaissance aircraft but at the same time anxious to reduce international tension, President Eisenhower proposed at a summit meeting in Geneva on 19 July 1955 an 'Open Skies' policy in which both sides would have the right to reconnoitre the other's territory. But Nikita Khrushchev, the leader of the Soviet Union, turned down the proposal, probably since his aircraft could not match the performance of the Americans and the British. Instead, the Russians accelerated development of surface-to-air missiles and brought out fighters with better performance, such as the near-supersonic MiG-17 (Nato code-name Fresco). At a Red Air Force Day display of 24 June 1956, Khrushchev was able to warn General Twining of the USAF that any Canberras which entered Russian airspace in the future were 'flying coffins' and would be shot down.

By this time, however, the Americans had developed a most unusual aircraft which was capable of flying even higher than the Canberra. This was the Lockheed U-2A, a single-engined aircraft with an enormous wingspan. It cruised rather slowly, at about 250 mph, and its range was about 2,200 miles, but it was capable of flying at over 72,000 feet. It was fitted with electronic sensors and a panoramic strip camera named the Hycon-B, which weighed about 500 lb and contained a special lens system. This system, when used with a film of high resolution, gave 60 line pairs per millimetre, about five times that of the cameras used in the Second World War. A special thin film was developed by Eastman Kodak which enabled the camera to carry over 10,000 feet.

The U-2A could cover a wide photographic swathe across the Soviet Union. It was financed by the Central Intelligence Agency and thus its development was conveniently independent of the USAF. The unit was given the cover title of the 1st Weather Reconnaissance Squadron, Provisional (WRSP-1) and the first machines were airlifted to the US airfield at Lakenheath in Suffolk, where they were reassembled and test-flown. Permission to operate from Britain was withdrawn, however, and the first flight

over the Soviet Union took place from Wiesbaden in Germany on 4 July 1956, sanctioned by the US President and supported by the German Chancellor, Dr Konrad Adenauer.

The results of these flights showed that the 'bomber gap' – a belief that bombers of the Soviet Air Force were far more numerous than those of the Strategic Air Force – did not exist. However, they did show that the Russians had made considerable progress in developing strategic missiles, which caused the Americans to divert part of their programme away from their bomber force and on to 'Minuteman' inter-continental ballistic missiles.

The confidence of the Western Allies in their technical superiority suffered a severe shock when the Russian launched their 'Sputnik 1' satellite into orbit in October 1957, thus narrowly beating the United States in the race to develop this new form of reconnaissance. Nevertheless, overflights by U-2s continued. American records show that six RAF pilots also qualified in this machine from June 1958 onwards, at Laughlin Air Force Base in Texas, while another was killed in training. Two RAF navigators and a flight surgeon were also trained in the programme. Operations took place from January 1959 from Incirlik in Turkey, the RAF men being given the cover of employees of the Meteorological Office. Although precise details have not yet been released, it is probable that about eighteen U-2 flights took place over Russia, while others took place over Egypt, Syria and Israel. It would be naive to believe that the RAF pilots did not carry out some of these missions and instead devoted their efforts to sampling the air in the upper atmosphere.

The U-2 flights over Russia came to an abrupt end on 1 May 1960 when a SA-2 surface-to-air missile exploded near one of the machines at an altitude of 68,000 feet

The Supermarine Swift FR 5 was the fighter-reconnaissance version of the earlier Swift interceptors, first entering RAF service in February 1956. The nose was lengthened to include three cameras but it retained its armament of two 30 mm Aden guns. It equipped only two RAF squadrons, being employed on low-level tactical work over Germany. Like its predecessors, it suffered from a high accident rate, but remained in service until March 1961. This photograph is of serial XD904. (*Aeroplane Monthly*)

The Hawker Hunter FR 10, based on the Hunter F6 interceptor, entered RAF service in March 1961 as a replacement for the Meteor FR 9 and the Swift FR 5. In addition to its armament of four 30 mm Aden guns, it carried three cameras in the nose. This Hunter FR 10 serial XF460 of 8 Squadron was photographed in 1969. These machines continued in active service until March 1971. (Flight Lieutenant A.S. Thomas RAF)

The Lockheed U-2A reconnaissance aircraft, painted all-black, first began operations over the Soviet Union on 4 July 1956, under the control of the US Central Intelligence Agency. The U-2R serial 68–10337 shown here was a later version which formed part of the 9th Strategic Reconnaissance Wing of the USAF. (Ex-Warrant Officer 1 (MAD) P.G. Crozier RCT)

The Vickers Valiant was the first of the RAF's 'V' bombers, entering squadron service in February 1955. In July of that year 543 Squadron was equipped with Valiant PR 1s for strategic reconnaissance, machines which continued in service until February 1965. This Valiant PR 1 of 543 Squadron was photographed in 1960, accompanied by a Canberra. (Flight Lieutenant A.S. Thomas RAF)

The Handley Page Victor B/SR2 was a version of the Victor B2 nuclear bomber, adapted for strategic reconnaissance. It entered service with 543 Squadron at Wyton in December 1964 as a replacement for the Vickers Valiant B(PR)1 and continued in this role until May 1974, when the squadron was disbanded. This photograph of serial XH672 of 543 Squadron was taken in 1970. The aircraft was eventually converted into a K2 tanker and transferred to 55 Squadron at Marham. (Flight Lieutenant A.S. Thomas RAF)

Lancaster GR 3s (later designated MR 3s) were employed by Coastal Command after the Second World War on maritime reconnaissance, replacing the lease-lend Liberators which were returned to the USA. They remained in service until Neptunes and Shackletons began to arrive. This photograph of Lancaster GR 3 serial RF307 of 203 Squadron was taken at Gibraltar on 10 March 1947. The RAF's last Lancaster in active service was an MR 3, serial RF325, which was retired on 15 October 1956. (Flight Lieutenant A.S. Thomas RAF)

The Lockheed Neptune MR 1 entered RAF service with 217 Squadron in January 1952 as Coastal Command's long-range reconnaissance aircraft and anti-shipping bomber, eventually equipping four squadrons and one special flight. The aircraft was fitted with Magnetic Anomaly Detector (MAD) equipment in the tail, as well as radar and searchlights. All Neptunes were returned to the US Navy by 1957, when they were replaced by the latest versions of Shackletons. This Neptune serial WX543 of 36 Squadron was photographed over Bermuda in 1956. (Flight Lieutenant A.S. Thomas RAF)

The Avro Shackleton began to replace the RAF's long-range maritime reconnaissance aircraft, such as the Liberator and the Fortress, from April 1951 onwards. The MR 1 carried a chin radome but the MR 2, introduced in late 1952, was fitted with a semi-retractable radome behind the wings. The Shackleton, such as the MR 2 of 42 Squadron shown here, gave excellent service although it was known affectionately as '10,000 rivets flying in close formation'. The MR 2 continued in active service until April 1972, by which time some had been converted into Shackleton Advanced Early Warning aircraft. (Squadron Leader I.M. Coleman RAF)

near Sverdlovsk in the Ural Mountains, causing it to spin down out of control. The civilian pilot, Francis Gary Powers, had taken off from Peshawar in Pakistan and was heading for Bödö in Norway. He baled out and was imprisoned, in the glare of much dramatic publicity, although he was later exchanged for a Russian spy. The affair was a serious embarrassment to the Americans but soon afterwards, in August 1960, the first successful recovery of a capsule from the country's satellite 'Discoverer' took place, adding a new dimension to the watch over the Soviet Union.

During the period of the U-2 overflights, the RAF's photo-reconnaissance squadrons in England were whittled down once again. At Wyton, 542 Squadron had already been disbanded in October 1955, although it was re-formed a month later and a detachment of its Canberra PR 7s sent to Australia during Britain's nuclear tests. Also at Wyton, 540 Squadron with Canberra PR 7s was disbanded in September 1956. No 541 Squadron, which had been sent to Germany with Meteor PR 10s in June 1951, was disbanded in September 1957. However, 543 Squadron was re-formed in July 1955 at Gaydon in Warwickshire with Vickers Valiant B (PR) 1s, the reconnaissance version of Britain's first nuclear bomber, and then moved to Wyton the following November. No 192 Squadron, the electronic intelligence squadron, was renumbered 51 Squadron in August 1958 and equipped with both Canberra B2s and Comet C2s. It continued its highly secret work from Watton and then Wyton, where in July 1971 it received Nimrod R1s with additional electronic equipment.

At the same time, the RAF's photo-reconnaissance facilities in Germany were strengthened, four squadrons being equipped with Canberra PR 7s. No 69 Squadron was the first, in May 1954. It was followed by 31 Squadron in March 1955, 80 Squadron in August 1955, and 17 Squadron in June 1956. Second Tactical Air Force was thus well served with photo-reconnaissance squadrons during this period of the Cold War. In January 1959 this Command was renamed RAF Germany.

Other units also underwent changes. In December 1953, JAPIC (UK) was given the revised title of the Joint Air Reconnaissance Intelligence Centre (UK) and three years later began to move from Nuneham Park to RAF Brampton, close to the reconnaissance squadrons at Wyton. Part of its organisation was the Joint School of Photographic Interpretation. In July 1957 the Central Reconnaissance Establishment was established and occupied the same building. In December 1965 the School of Photography, which in 1963 had moved from its quarters at Wellesbourne Mountford to temporary quarters at RAF Cosford in Shropshire, took over a new building on this station.

Meanwhile, RAF maritime reconnaissance assumed increasing importance with the growth of the Soviet Navy. In common with the remainder of the RAF, Coastal Command had been reduced drastically after the Second World War, but its squadrons were built up again in the early 1950s when it was believed that the Russians were constructing as many as 1,000 submarines, some of which could carry missiles with nuclear warheads. By mid-1953 Coastal Command had increased to eight Shackleton squadrons, four Sunderland flying boat squadrons, four Neptune squadrons, one Hastings squadron for meteorological reconnaissance, and one Sycamore helicopter squadron for search and rescue. Four years later the Sunderlands were withdrawn and the Neptunes returned to America, being replaced by Shackletons as the main aircraft engaged on surveillance of the Warsaw Pact naval and merchant shipping, as well as on fishery protection patrols and on the monitoring of sea pollution. To these were

The F117 cameras were developed as replacements for the hand-held versions of the F24 used by the RAF and the K20 used by both the USAAF and the RAF during the Second World War. The F117A was manually wound, capable of taking 120 exposures of 4½-inch by 4½-inch, with a 6-inch lens and shutter speeds of 1/60th, 1/125th and 1/400th of a second. The F117B was very similar, but it was rewound with an integral electric motor and the handle grips were slightly different. (J.K. Nesbit, courtesy RAF Cosford Museum)

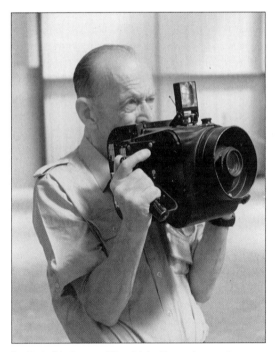 

Ken Murch of the Tangmere Military Aviation Museum demonstrating an F117 from the museum exhibits. (B.M. Harris, courtesy Tangmere Military Aviation Museum)

Many women served as photographers and photo-interpreters during the Second World War. Leading Aircraftwoman Kay Davison, a photographer with Bomber Command at Driffield in Yorkshire, was allowed a flight on 17 July 1945 in Halifax letter Y over the devastated areas of the Ruhr. (Mrs K. Stevens née Davison)

eventually added the surveillance of the UK's offshore energy installations.

In spite of its somewhat ungainly appearance, the Avro Shackleton was one of the most successful and enduring aircraft used for long-range maritime reconnaissance, both at home and overseas. It was armed with cannons and machine guns, and could carry depth charges, homing torpedoes or bombs. As with its predecessors in the Second World War, it carried Air to Surface-Vessel (ASV) radar, the maritime equivalent of H_2S. The later versions were fitted with Magnetic Anomaly Detectors (MAD), used for spotting submarines underwater. In addition, these aircraft monitored innumerable naval and merchant vessels on the surface. Although there were a couple of retractable camera mountings in the rear fuselage, photography at low level was usually carried out by the hand-held F117 camera.

In April 1964 the functions of the Air Ministry, Admiralty and the War Office were absorbed into a reconstituted Ministry of Defence. Four years later (fifty years after its formation) the RAF in the UK began a radical alteration to its command structure when Fighter Command merged with Bomber Command to form Strike Command. No 90 (Signals) Group was incorporated into this new Command on 1 January 1969. Coastal Command followed on 28 November 1969, becoming No 18 Group. The Central Reconnaissance Establishment was disbanded on 1 October 1970 and control of JARIC (UK) was passed to No 1 (Bomber) Group within Strike Command. Finally, the former No 90 (Signals) Group was passed to Maintenance Command on 1 May 1972 and in turn this Command was merged with Training Command on 1 September 1973 to form the new Support Command.

Flying Officer Stan G.E. Payne, the Station Armament and Photographic Officer at RAF Aqir in Palestine, photographed in 1947. He was holding an F24 camera, which was still in service after its introduction in 1930. (Flight Lieutenant S.G.E. Payne C.Eng, MRAeS, RAF (Ret'd))

The Avro Lincoln, designed to replace the Lancaster as the RAF's main heavy bomber, arrived too late to take part in the Second World War but equipped many squadrons of Bomber Command until the last were withdrawn in May 1963. Lincolns served in operations against terrorists in Malaya and Kenya. A detachment of 214 Squadron, of which serial RE295 is shown here, was sent to Eastleigh near Nairobi from June to December 1954, during the Mau Mau uprisings; photographic reconnaissance formed part of their duties. (Squadron Leader P.J. Thompson RAF (Ret'd))

CHAPTER FOURTEEN

NEAR AND MIDDLE EAST COMMANDS

In common with squadrons at home, the photo-reconnaissance squadrons overseas suffered from the drastic cut-backs of the RAF in the immediate post-war years. Indeed, the problems resulting from the reductions overseas became even more acute, since some of the countries in which the squadrons were based entered a period of political turbulence and even armed conflict when released from the constraints imposed by the war. Meanwhile Britain felt compelled to fulfil her obligations to maintain law and order in the countries of the Commonwealth and Empire, while recognising the natural desire of indigenous peoples to govern themselves. At the same time, it became necessary to protect some of these peoples from the threat of international communism and dictatorship emanating from the Soviet Bloc under the guise of freedom from colonialism. The remaining photo-reconnaissance squadrons overseas played a full part in these extremely difficult years.

At the end of the war, the RAF squadrons in the Mediterranean were controlled by the Mediterranean Allied Air Forces, based at Caserta in Italy. This headquarters was disbanded in August 1945 and replaced by RAF Mediterranean and Middle East in Cairo, which covered the enormous area of North Africa, Malta, Greece, the Levant, Iraq, Egypt, the Sudan, Aden and East Africa. Serious trouble was brewing in all these areas, perhaps insufficiently appreciated by a British Government which was wrestling with the immense problems of turning its war economy back to civilian requirements.

Two long-range photo-reconnaissance squadrons in the area were disbanded. In September 1945 at Peretola in Italy, 682 Squadron lost its Spitfire PR XIXs and was disbanded. This fate befell 683 Squadron in the same month at San Severo in Italy, also equipped with these aircraft. However, 680 Squadron, equipped with Mosquito PR XVIs and based at Deversoir in Egypt and then Ein Shemer in Palestine, carried out aerial surveys of Iraq and Persia until September 1946 when it was renumbered 13 Squadron and received Mosquito PR 34s. In addition, 208 Squadron moved to Ein Shemer in June 1946 and was equipped with Spitfire XVIIIE fighter-reconnaissance aircraft two months later, flying on policing sorties.

Two squadrons operated in the maritime photo-reconnaissance role. These were 38 Squadron, which received Lancaster GR IIIs in November 1946 and moved from Luqa in Malta to Ein Shemer the following month, and 37 Squadron which was re-formed at Luqa in September 1947, also equipped with Lancaster GR IIIs, and then moved to Ein Shemer.

The gathering of these four reconnaissance squadrons at Ein Shemer, which lay mid-way between Haifa and Tel Aviv, was no coincidence. Palestine had been mandated by the League of Nations to Britain at the end of the First World War and the British Government was expected to create within it a national home for Jewish people without denying the aspirations of the Arabs who formed the majority of the population. But the Second World War had witnessed the appalling massacre of millions of Jews in occupied Europe and world sympathy had moved strongly in favour of the survivors, many of whom wished to create a new home in Palestine. The unenviable task of the British, including the RAF squadrons, was to prevent the illegal entry of these would-be immigrants and to try to arrange an equitable agreement with the Arabs.

A ship carrying immigrants was located on 17 January 1946 by a Warwick GR V of 621 Squadron, based at Ein Shemer, some months before the squadron was disbanded. The ship was then intercepted by a British destroyer and turned back. Seventeen such ships were located before the end of the year, with the Lancasters of 37 and 38 Squadrons playing a prominent part in the final months. An outcome of these operations was a series of attacks on RAF bases in Palestine by Jewish terrorists, resulting in much destruction and some loss of life.

The two maritime squadrons moved back to Luqa, 38 Squadron in November 1947 and 37 Squadron in April 1948. Malta had been given a certain amount of self-government in 1947 but Britain retained the right to base armed forces on the island. The Lancasters continued reconnaissance from this distant base until the United Nations decreed that Palestine should be partitioned between the Jews and the Arabs, resulting in the creation of the republic of Israel on 30 June 1948. The British forces gradually withdrew before this date, the RAF having located no less than forty-seven immigrant ships in all, to be dealt with by the Royal Navy. Most of the servicemen were glad to leave the country, knowing that the political situation was intractable and that they were leaving behind a divided country which could explode into conflict at any time.

The situation in Egypt was also fraught with problems but the British wished to remain in this country in order to protect the interests of the Western Allies in the Suez Canal. During 1947 British forces in the country were withdrawn to the Canal Zone in the hope of affording a compromise with Egyptian national aspirations. Within the RAF units, 13 Squadron with its Mosquito PR 34s moved to Fayid in February 1947, followed by 208 Squadron with its Spitfire XVIIIEs in November 1948. One of their main functions was to reconnoitre and photograph the border between Israel and Egypt, for there was bitter hostility between the two countries. By this time, the RAF Mediterranean and Middle East had been renamed the Middle East Air Force.

On 7 January 1949, four Spitfires of 208 Squadron were ordered to reconnoitre the incursion of Israeli troops over the Egyptian border. At the end of the operation, one was shot down by anti-aircraft fire and the pilot baled out over Egyptian territory. While the other three pilots were watching his descent they were attacked by Israeli Spitfires with the same camouflage and red spinners as their own aircraft, and all three were shot down. It is probable that the Israeli pilots of these intruding Spitfires had received their training in the RAF. One RAF pilot was killed, one managed to get back to Fayid, and two were captured by the Israelis within Egypt and imprisoned for a while before being released. On the same day as this episode, six more Spitfires of 208 Squadron escorted by seven Tempest VIs of 213 Squadron, searching for

Handley Page Halifax VII serial PP375 of 620 Squadron, at Aquir in Palestine in 1946. This version of the bomber was fitted with carburettor air filters for operations in tropical climates, as well as extra fuel capacity. Among the squadron's duties was maritime reconnaissance, searching for shipping carrying illegal immigrants headed for Palestine. (Flight Lieutenant S.G.E. Payne C.Eng, MRAeS, RAF (Ret'd))

A Canberra PR 9 (left) and a Canberra T4 two-seat trainer (right) of 39 Squadron at Luqa in Malta. The squadron was first equipped with Canberra PR 9s in October 1962, when based at Luqa and engaged on photo-reconnaissance during attachment to Nato. (Squadron Leader P.J. Thompson RAF (Ret'd))

their lost comrades, were similarly attacked. The pilots were also confused by the camouflage of the Israeli Spitfires and one Tempest was shot down.

The Israeli troops inflicted a number of reverses on the Egyptian forces before withdrawing, and serious tension continued. The need for survey and mapping was recognised by the re-establishment during November 1950 of 683 Squadron at Fayid, equipped with Lancaster PR 1s. The squadron carried out these duties before moving to Aden in January 1952 to continue the same tasks. Meanwhile, 208 Squadron was equipped with Meteor FR 9s for fighter reconnaissance in January 1951. Meteor PR 10s were supplied to 13 Squadron in November of that year, tactical photo-reconnaissance being of paramount importance in the Canal Zone.

The unpleasant political situation in the Middle East was further exacerbated in June 1951 by the action of the Persian Government in nationalising the Anglo-Iranian oil refinery at Abadan, with a threat to the safety of British nationals, many of whom were evacuated by air. At the same time, the British forces in Egypt faced increased hostility from nationalist bodies. Some of their number were murdered, local labour was withdrawn and the families of servicemen were evacuated. The RAF in the Canal Zone was reinforced with bomber and fighter aircraft. The situation worsened in July 1952 when King Farouk was deposed and Egypt came under the control of its military, eventually led by Colonel Gamal Abdel Nasser. By then Britain had begun to reassess its obligations and a decision was made to pull out of the country. A treaty was signed in July 1954, agreeing to withdraw British forces provided facilities were kept in the Canal Zone for their return in the event of an attack by the Soviet Union. The RAF decided to base its units in Cyprus, together

with the headquarters of Middle East Air Force, and this was achieved by May 1956.

Before this move to Cyprus was carried out, RAF photo-reconnaissance aircraft were involved in a dispute which, although very minor in military terms, was extremely important for their country's relations with Saudi Arabia. For many years, Britain had maintained a presence in the Trucial States on the Arabian side of the Persian Gulf, a territory which had been known previously as the Pirate Coast. With the development of huge deposits of oil, these Gulf States began to equal Saudi Arabia in significance.

The Buraimi Oasis, on the boundary between the state of Abu Dhabi and that of Muscat and Oman, had always been coveted by Saudi Arabia. In August 1952 a small force of Saudi militia crossed over Abu Dhabi territory and occupied part of the oasis. To avoid armed conflict with Saudi Arabia, it was decided to blockade this force, with Trucial Oman Levies intercepting camel trains carrying supplies. The reconnaissance of the surrounding desert was first carried out by Vampire fighters operating from RAF Sharjah but in April 1953 the work was taken over by four Meteor FR 9s of 208 Squadron detached from Abu Sueir in Egypt. Their range proved insufficient, however, and within a few weeks they were replaced by four Lancaster GR IIIs of 37 and 38 Squadrons from Malta, operating outside their normal maritime reconnaissance role. These returned to normal duties in July and were replaced by Lancaster PR 1s of 683 Squadron, which by then were engaged on a survey of Iraq from their base at Habbaniya. They flew down to Sharjah and carried on the work. However, this squadron was due for disbandment by November, and in September 1417 Flight, equipped with Ansons, was formed to take over the reconnaissance. The blockade was called off for a few weeks while negotiations took place but when these failed the British, tired of the matter and its cost, decided to remove the Saudi party by force. An operation was mounted in October and achieved success with little bloodshed. Relations with Saudi Arabia became even more soured and diplomatic relations were broken off.

In this period a rebellion of the most vicious and brutal kind broke out in Kenya. From 1952 the so-called Mau Mau sect of the Kikuyu people began committing atrocities against other Africans and white settlers, with the intention of occupying land which they believed had been taken from them unfairly. A State of Emergency was declared in October 1952 but the King's African Rifles, reinforced with a British battalion, were unable to contain all terrorist activities over the vast area of central Kenya. They were supported by light aircraft of the Police Air Wing and, from the spring of the following year, a flight of armed North American Harvards of the Rhodesian Air Training Group. These carried out some useful work but this was not sufficient to deal with all the Mau Mau gangs, who moved into the dense forests and rocky defiles of the Aberdare Mountains and Mount Kenya, at altitudes where light aircraft were less effective. In March 1954 two Meteor PR 10s of 13 Squadron were sent from Fayid for a short while to carry out photo-reconnaissance. On their return, vertical photography was undertaken by Lincolns of Bomber Command squadrons which were detached from Britain to RAF Eastleigh, near Nairobi. These photographs were duly interpreted and followed by bombing attacks which were so accurate that they destroyed the morale of the terrorists, who scuttled out of the area in droves to surrender. By early 1955 the Mau Mau activities were greatly reduced, although the work of mopping up the remainder continued for several months.

The renewed interest of the RAF in Cyprus coincided with the signing of the Baghdad Pact on 4 April 1955 by Britain, Turkey, Iraq and Pakistan. The United States became closely associated with this new group of states united in military defence, which provided a welcome extension of Nato's eastern boundary confronting the Soviet Union. The concentration of RAF units in Cyprus included 13 Squadron, which moved to the new airfield of Akrotiri in February 1956 and began to receive Canberra PR 7s three months later to replace its ageing Meteor PR 10s. However, 208 Squadron moved to Malta during January 1956 until sufficient accommodation for its Meteor FR 9s was available at Akrotiri two months later. Canberra bomber squadrons also arrived, providing an offensive capacity.

Living conditions in Cyprus proved far more agreeable than in the Canal Zone, but some Greek inhabitants began to stir up political trouble in the name of 'Enosis' (union with Greece) – a proposal which was bitterly opposed by the Turkish community. The leader of the Greek Cypriots was Archbishop Makarios, but his request for union with Greece was refused by the United Nations in early 1955. The initiative passed to Colonel Grivas who began a 'revolution' on 1 April 1955, leading a band under the acronym of Eoka (Ethniks Organosis Kypriou Agonistou). Bomb explosions and the murder of British servicemen followed, and counter-measures were taken. Nos 37 and 38 Squadrons, still based at Luqa but re-equipped with Avro Shackleton MR 2s, hunted for small vessels carrying arms to the terrorists, with considerable success. A collection of privately owned light aircraft was pressed into service to hunt for terrorists and these were joined by a flight of Bristol Sycamore HR14 helicopters. Two flights of Austers arrived, these 'Air Observation Post' aircraft being flown by Army pilots. When it became clear that Makarios was involved with the terrorists he was arrested and exiled to the Seychelles, but violence and rioting continued in Cyprus.

The RAF withdrew from Iraq in January 1956, following a long association with the country and without ill-feeling on either side. However, relations with Egypt reached crisis point when on 26 July 1956 Colonel Nasser announced that the Universal Suez Canal Company was to be seized, as retaliation for the withdrawal of the United States from a project to build the Aswan High Dam on the River Nile. Western interests, primarily those of Britain and France, were thus destroyed at a stroke, and the two countries decided that military action might have to be taken to counter this illegal seizure.

The first requirement was photo-reconnaissance and in early August 1956 a detachment of Canberra PR 7s of 58 Squadron was sent out from Wyton to Akrotiri, augmenting those with which 13 Squadron was re-equipping. They were followed by Republic F-84F fighter-reconnaissance aircraft of the French Air Force. Hunter Vs and Meteor NF 13s also flew out, reinforcing Venoms already based at Nicosia, the only other usable airfield. There were also transport aircraft such as Hastings and Valettas on the island. The congestion was such that many of the Meteors of 208 Squadron, which did not have the range to operate over Egypt, were sent back to Malta. Meanwhile, an aircraft carrier task group and other warships of the Royal Navy headed towards the eastern Mediterranean.

When diplomatic efforts failed and conflict seemed inevitable, detachments from eight squadrons of Canberra B2s and B6s of Bomber Command were sent to Cyprus, adding to the congestion. No more could be accommodated in the island and four other detachments of Canberra B2s together with four detachments of Vickers Valiant V-bombers were sent to Malta, arriving in the latter part of October. The first reconnaissance was carried out by a Canberra PR 7 of 58 Squadron on 20 October, surveying the Egyptian coastline. Others began eight days later, carried out by both 13 and 58 Squadrons. One Canberra was damaged by a MiG fighter but returned safely.

The British and French plan of attack was given the code name of Operation 'Musketeer'. It began in the afternoon of 31 October 1956, the day after Israel invaded the Sinai Peninsula in north-east Egypt. During the early part of the day, eleven photo-reconnaissance sorties were flown by Canberras and F-84Fs, covering the Egyptian airfields. These airfields were attacked by Valiants and Canberras on the same day and the following night. Ground attacks by land-based and carrier-borne aircraft began the next morning. After a couple of days photo-reconnaissance revealed that 158 aircraft of the Egyptian Air Force, consisting originally of 216 modern aircraft, had been destroyed without loss to the attackers. Moreover, twenty-one of the surviving aircraft had disappeared from the country, possibly fleeing to Russia. Anglo-French attacks then began on other ground targets and one RAF Venom was lost in an accident at low level.

Airborne landings took place near Port Said on 5 November and seaborne forces followed the next day, accompanied by bombardments from the air and sea. However, the action of the Anglo-French intervention was severely criticised by the United Nations, led by the United States. An Emergency Force was raised by the Security Council, while a cease-fire was ordered to take effect from midnight on 6 November. The British and French, who had made rapid progress along the Suez Canal, were forced to cease operations and pull out of Egypt. It was a humiliating and frustrating end to a venture which was within sight of military success, even though politically ill-conceived in the first place. Somewhat incongruously, technical development soon demonstrated that the Suez Canal was of less strategic value than had been believed, for it could not be used by the new breed of supertankers which were coming into service and instead sailed round the Cape of Good Hope.

The work of photo-reconnaissance was not finished, however. Syria had forbidden over-flying on 1 October, in sympathy with Egypt, but the RAF continued clandestine flights over this country and others in the Middle East. On 8 November Canberra PR 7 serial WH799 of 13 Squadron, flown by a crew from 58 Squadron, was attacked while on a reconnaissance over Syria and came down over the Lebanese border. It was believed that the attacking aircraft was a Meteor or a MiG-15 of the Syrian Air Force, probably flown by a Czechoslovakian or a Russian pilot. The navigator of the Canberra was killed, but the pilot and second navigator were taken to the military hospital at Beirut and eventually repatriated.

Further conflicts occurred in the Trucial States in this period. The Sultan of Muscat nominally exercised authority over the vast territory of Oman but for many years had been thwarted in a remote part of the country by the leader of a sect which was supported by Saudi Arabia. In 1955 the Sultan decided to remove this rebel force with the aid of the British. Military operations began, while reconnaissance was carried out from an airstrip by 1417 Flight, which by then was equipped with Hunting Percival Pembrokes as well as the faithful Ansons. Four Lincolns of Bomber Command, formed into 1426 Flight at Bahrein, reinforced this reconnaissance. Some military progress was achieved but in 1956 an 'Oman Liberation Army' was formed and in June of the following year an armed force landed on the

coast and made its way into villages in the mountainous interior. Increased air photography was required, and several Shackleton MR 2s of 37 Squadron, which moved in July 1957 from Luqa to Khormaksar, were brought in from Aden to operate from the RAF station on the island of Masirah. A detachment of Meteor FR 9s of 208 Squadron also flew in from Malta, to carry out shorter range photo-reconnaissance at low level. Air attacks by Venoms were combined with attacks by the Sultan's forces and elements of the British Army but the rebels retreated to higher ground from where they proved more difficult to dislodge. In January 1958, 208 Squadron was transferred to the fighter role back in the UK and then returned to Aden. The campaign in Oman was not wound up until February 1959.

Meanwhile, the measures against terrorists in Cyprus were strengthened by increasing the number of Sycamore helicopters and forming these into 284 Squadron during October 1956. Activities against these terrorists, who moved mainly in remote areas of the Troodos Mountains, became more effective and in March 1957 Eoka offered a truce provided Makarios was released. This was accepted by the British and the archbishop was released a few weeks later, although he was not allowed to return to the island. The violence continued.

The reconnoitring of terrorist activities was best carried out by light aircraft and helicopters, with the crews working visually in the manner of First World War pilots and observers but with the advantage of reporting immediately by R/T. The helicopters could also land small bodies of troops in areas highly inconvenient to the terrorists, who were then harried and often destroyed. Westland Whirlwind helicopters, with their larger carrying capacity, arrived in 284 Squadron the following month. With regard to the fixed-wing light aircraft, numerous Air

The Bristol Sycamore was the first helicopter designed and built in Britain to enter RAF service, in February 1952. The first was the Mark HR12, but the improved versions HR13 and HR14 followed. Sycamores were employed for reconnaissance and casualty evacuation, and saw service at home and overseas. They were withdrawn from front-line duties in October 1964 but continued on communications until August 1972. This Sycamore HC14 serial XG502 saw service with the Joint Experimental Helicopter Unit from March 1955 and was then employed on Operation 'Musketeer' in Suez during 1956. It was then reissued to 225 Squadron, which continued with Sycamore HC14s until March 1962. (Museum of Army Flying)

Observation Post squadrons had been formed in the RAF from 1941 onwards. These squadrons were usually equipped with Austers flown by Army pilots, using small hand-held cameras, and their work of close co-operation with ground troops had proved highly successful in Italy and Normandy. On 1 September 1957 the Army Air Corps was formed, the squadrons at last achieving independence from the RAF, and this new organisation operated with modern Austers in Cyprus. From November 1958 the Austers of the Army Air Corps were backed by RAF light aircraft, Scottish Aviation Pioneers of 230 Squadron and de Havilland Chipmunks of 114 Squadron.

These combined operations contained most of the activities of the Eoka terrorists but some violence continued. On 17 February 1959 an agreement was reached in London by Britain, Greece and Turkey, whereby Cyprus attained sovereign status but Britain retained control of Akrotiri and the Army base of Dhekelia. This agreement became effective the following September and terrorist activities against the British died away. Cyprus soon rejoined the British Commonwealth, but the peace between the Greeks and the Turks remained uneasy.

While these activities were in progress, the Canberras of 13 Squadron at Akrotiri continued their work, some of which was clandestine. Their crews were often joined by others from 58 Squadron from Wyton and their tasks included photo-reconnaissance of airfields in Middle Eastern countries which were being supplied with aircraft from the Soviet Union. Details of these operations have never been disclosed, but there is little doubt that they also included electronic intelligence of radar stations and other activities in the south of the Soviet Union itself.

The situation in Malta in this period was not altogether happy, in spite of the excellent relations which had existed between its people and the British forces during the Second World War. The dependence on Britain as an employer on the island had diminished with the run-down of the armed forces and in 1957 the Maltese Labour Party demanded total separation. The maritime Shackletons of 38 Squadron continued to fulfil their usual role from Luqa but in July 1958 Canberra PR 7s of 69 Squadron flew out to Malta from Laarbruch in Germany. They were renumbered 39 Squadron and also employed primarily on maritime photo-reconnaissance as part of Nato's southern flank, for a Russian fleet was active in the Mediterranean. The Canberras also flew on survey work in Libya and some were sent to Khormaksar in Aden, where they carried out a survey of the country and photographed ports in the Yemen, since arms were believed to be arriving from Egypt to encourage incursions into the Protectorate.

Meanwhile, a coup took place in Iraq during July 1958 and the King and Prime Minister were deposed. The country decided to withdraw from the Baghdad Pact during the following spring and on 20 August 1959 this was replaced with the Central Treaty Organisation (Cento), which worked effectively from headquarters in Turkey. On 1 March 1961 the Near East Command was formed in Cyprus and the Middle East Command in Aden. One of the first problems the latter faced concerned Iraq, for this country claimed that Kuwait, with an oil production which had expanded enormously since the Second World War, was part of its territory. In fact, Kuwait was a small and independent state which for many years had enjoyed friendly relations with Britain, to whom it looked for protection.

Throughout the turbulent post-war years, Aden and its Protectorates had remained fairly quiescent, apart from border incursions from the Yemen and inter-tribal conflicts which had been quelled by air and ground

The Westland Whirlwind entered RAF service in September 1954 as a helicopter with a larger capacity than the Dragonfly, serving with squadrons at home, in Germany, the Near East and the Far East. It was used for tactical transport, ground assault or search and rescue, the last continuing in squadron service until March 1982. This Whirlwind HAR 10 serial XP347 was photographed with a Wessex of the Royal Navy. (P. Batten)

The Hawker Siddeley Nimrod MR 1, evolved from the Comet airliner, entered service with the RAF in October 1969 for marine reconnaissance. Thereafter, the electronic equipment was updated to include 'Searchwater' radar and the aircraft became the MR 2, as with this photograph of XV238 of 42 (Torpedo Bomber) Squadron. In addition to its reconnaissance role, the machine could carry up to nine homing torpedos in its bomb bay and, during the Falklands campaign, was fitted with Sidewinder missiles. (Squadron Leader I.M. Coleman RAF)

operations. Indeed, between 1956 and 1959 the RAF squadrons in Aden had been strengthened considerably, Khormaksar being considered a suitable alternative for the loss of bases in other areas. Among the new arrivals was 37 Squadron, which moved its base from Luqa in July 1957 during the confrontation with the dissidents in Oman.

Kuwait was about 1,500 miles from the headquarters in Aden and it was obvious that operations could not be conducted from that distance. Bahrein, another friendly state in the Persian Gulf, was a suitable choice and RAF squadrons flew to RAF Muharraq in that country, from the UK and East Africa as well as from Khormaksar and a detachment from 13 Squadron at Akrotiri, which by then was equipped with Canberra PR 9s. These kept watch on the border between Kuwait and Iraq as well as the sea approaches. Other squadrons airlifted troops and sent fighter aircraft to Kuwait while Royal Navy vessels headed for the threatened state. A considerable build-up was achieved with such commendable rapidity that the Iraqis decided that discretion was the better part of valour and no attack materialised. The British forces were gradually withdrawn.

The Federation of South Arabia was formed on 11 February 1959 from Aden and its Protectorates, in the hope that a peaceful state would be the outcome. The rush for independence from Britain accelerated during the early 1960s. British and Italian Somaliland combined as an independent state in July 1960. Independence was achieved by Tanganyika in December 1961, by Uganda in October 1962 and by Kenya in December 1963. These moves were peaceful on the whole, but disturbances broke out in the Federation of South Arabia after a republican coup in the neighbouring state of the Yemen during September 1962. This was encouraged and supported by Egypt, which continued to foment incursions across the border.

Canberras of 13 Squadron were brought into Khormaksar from Akrotiri to keep watch on vessels carrying arms from Egypt, and these aircraft were joined by a detachment from 58 Squadron at Wyton. The Shackletons of 37 Squadron also operated in this role. Yemeni aircraft intruded across the border and an insurrection in this area had to be put down by combined operations in the spring of 1964, resulting in the defeat of the rebels. However, this success did nothing to limit terrorism within Aden, which increased alarmingly over the next two years. Heavy casualties were caused, primarily from mortars and the throwing of grenades. Britain determined to pull out of the territory by 1968 at the latest.

While arrangements for this withdrawal were under way, a further commitment fell on 37 Squadron at Khormaksar. The Federation of Rhodesia broke up in 1964, with Nyasaland becoming the independent state of Malawi and Northern Rhodesia becoming the independent state of Zambia. However, the British Government refused to grant sovereignty to the remaining country, Southern Rhodesia. This country, by then named simply Rhodesia, announced a Unilateral Declaration of Independence (UDI) on 11 November 1965. Britain duly declared that the regime was illegal and invoked economic sanctions by members of the United Nations. For the RAF, this move was followed by some bizarre episodes with their former friends and brothers-in-arms in the Rhodesian Air Force. The crew of an RAF Vulcan V-bomber which was unaware of UDI and landed at New Sarum, near the capital of Salisbury, found that the fuselage had been painted with the assegai and roundel motif of the RhAF before they took off the next morning, after enjoying the hospitality of the country. Javelin FAW9s of 29 Squadron, which flew into Ndola in Zambia from Akrotiri, to 'protect' the country from

Rhodesia, used the Flying Information Centre at Salisbury when flying from their base.

The most notable effect of sanctions against Rhodesia was the lack of oil. In March 1966 Shackletons of 37 Squadron were sent from Khormaksar to Majunga in Madagascar to work with the Royal Navy on the Beira Patrol, since it was known that supplies were arriving via Portuguese Mozambique, which was sympathetic to the Rhodesia cause. Thereafter Rhodesia obtained its oil via South Africa. The costly patrols continued, and other Shackletons were sent out from the UK after 37 Squadron was withdrawn.*

The departure of the British from Aden was complicated by the Arab/Israeli War of 3–9 June 1967, which ended in an Israeli victory but closed the Suez Canal. This move was accomplished before the end of the year, with some of the squadrons taking up new bases in the Persian Gulf, although 37 Squadron was disbanded at Khormaksar in September 1967, when its Shackletons were flown back to England. The increased presence of the RAF in the Gulf States remained amicable but the need diminished as the newly rich countries built up their own forces. Reconnaissance continued, with a detachment of Canberras of 13 Squadron from Muharraq keeping watch on the Iraqi/Kuwait border and the formation in November 1970 of 210 Squadron, equipped with Shackleton MR 2s, serving from Sharjah until disbanding a year later. The RAF pulled out of the Persian Gulf at the same time as this disbandment, leaving a high reputation with the rulers of these states and their peoples.

Meanwhile, Malta decided to achieve independence from Britain in September 1964, although an agreement was reached whereby Britain was allowed to retain defence facilities for the next ten years. Thus the Shackletons of 38 Squadron and the Canberras of 39 Squadron were permitted to remain on the island. In addition, the Canberra PR 9s of 13 Squadron moved from Akrotiri to Luqa in September 1965, concentrating the whole Near East photo-reconnaissance force in Malta. But 38 Squadron was disbanded in March 1967 and its place in Malta was not taken until February 1968 when the Shackleton MR 3s of 203 Squadron flew out from Ballykelly in Northern Ireland, continuing the watch on Russian warships in the Mediterranean. This squadron began to receive new Hawker Siddeley Nimrod MR 1s in July 1971, replacing the ageing Shackletons. However, 39 Squadron was sent back to Wyton in September 1970.

All did not go well with the agreement between Britain and Malta, and the Maltese Government insisted on the complete withdrawal of British forces by March 1972. No 203 Squadron transferred to Sigonella in Sicily in January of that year, as part of Nato, but operated partly from Akrotiri. At the same time 13 Squadron, which was partly engaged on a survey of Kenya, moved its headquarters back to Akrotiri. However, the loss of the British forces created such massive problems for the Maltese economy that a reversal of the decision took place and the squadrons returned to Luqa, 203 Squadron in April 1972 and 13 Squadron in the following October.

When Turkey invaded the northern part of Cyprus in July 1974, the Vulcans based there carried out some of their duties from Malta, often in the maritime reconnaissance role. By this time it was clear that the Central Treaty Organisation was of little value, with two members of Nato fighting each other, and the nuclear bombers were withdrawn to the UK

---

* In 1973 the author saw a Royal Navy plaque, on the wall of the Leopard Rock Hotel in the east of Rhodesia, which read: 'With grateful thanks for your hospitality: HMS *Charybdis*, Beira Patrol'.

in early 1975. Only 84 Squadron, equipped with Whirlwind helicopters, remained in Cyprus.

The fairly gentle state of affairs in Rhodesia did not persist, for a bloody and vicious war broke out after the coup in Portugal in 1975. Major incursions were made into Rhodesia from Zambia and Mozambique and the matter was not settled until December 1979, when the white government of Rhodesia relinquished control.

In spite of the renewed presence of the RAF in Malta, relations were far from cordial, with the Maltese Government in sympathy with Libya and its new ruler Colonel Gaddafi, who had staged a military coup in the country during 1969, ousting the British forces from their bases and creating a strongly anti-Western society. It was decided to disband 203 Squadron at Luqa and its Nimrods flew back to Britain at the end of 1977 to be allocated to other squadrons. The Canberras of 13 Squadron flew home to Wyton in October 1979, severing the last formal links of RAF squadrons with the famous George Cross Island. Within the Mediterranean, only the bases of Gibraltar and Akrotiri remained to serve the RAF.

CHAPTER FIFTEEN

THE FAR EAST

The dropping of the atom bombs and the capitulation of Japan came as a complete surprise to almost all servicemen. The Japanese had been defeated in Burma apart from a few starving and harried remnants of their forces, but it was generally believed that those occupying other countries in the Far East and Japan itself would fight to the death. Plans for a huge invasion of the west coast of Malaya had been prepared, under the code name of Operation 'Zipper'. Some British troops had already entered the vessels when VJ-Day and the end of the Second World War was declared on 14 August 1945. Landing beaches had been identified by photo-reconnaissance carried out by Mosquito PR 34s of 684 Squadron and all was ready for the great enterprise, but the troops were able to arrive unopposed in Malaya after surrender documents had been signed by Japanese commanders. The first British to arrive in Singapore were the crew of a Mosquito PR 34 of 684 Squadron, which took off from the Cocos Islands on 31 August 1945 to photograph southern Malaya and developed an engine fault. They were received correctly by Japanese officers, before their commander signed the surrender document.

The area of South-East Asia Command, which already covered India, Ceylon, Burma, Siam, Malaya and Sumatra, was extended on 13 August 1945 to include Borneo, Java, the Celebes, and French Indo-China below the 16th parallel. Parts of the south-west Pacific, including New Guinea and the Solomons,

were handed over to Australian control. The total area was thus immense and the problems faced by the British were almost insuperable, for some of the indigenous peoples had lost faith in the Western countries which had failed to protect them from years of brutal Japanese domination. Some nationalist bodies were intent on getting rid of European control and establishing communist states, even if this meant armed insurrection. At the same time the men of the British forces, particularly those conscripted into the services, were anxious to return home and resume civilian life, and insufficient transport was available for this purpose. These returnees included many ex-PoWs, almost all of whom were in an extremely debilitated condition after their inhuman treatment at the hands of the Japanese.

Although many RAF squadrons were disbanded after VJ-Day, there was still plenty of photo-reconnaissance work ahead. Thus 681 Squadron, equipped with Spitfire PR XIXs, and 684 Squadron, equipped with Mosquito PR 34s, remained operational for the time being. The former was based at Mingaladon in Burma at the time of the surrender and continued photographing roads, railways, airfields and PoW camps. It moved to Kai Tak at the end of the following month, to help with the re-establishment of civil administration in Hong Kong, a matter which was achieved speedily. The squadron then flew down to Kuala Lumpur for a few

Sunderland V serial RN290 of 230 Squadron, in maritime white livery, in the seaplane base at RAF Seletar in Singapore after the Japanese capitulation. (The late Corporal C.E. Lloyd)

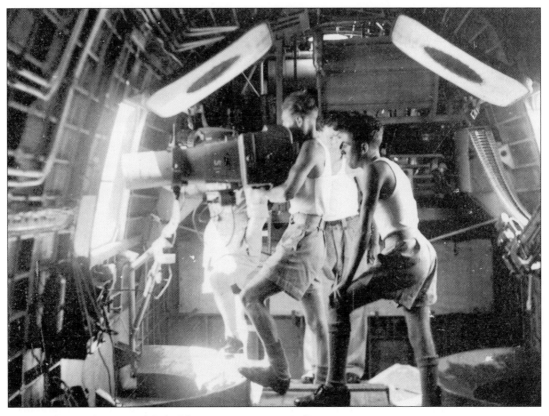

F52 camera oblique installation in a Sunderland. (Flight Lieutenant G.H. Parry RAF (Ret'd))

The RAF airfield at Seletar in Singapore after the Japanese capitulation. (Leading Aircraftman R.F. White RAFVR)

The Westland Dragonfly HC2 was based on the US Sikorski S-51 but manufactured in Britain. It first entered RAF service in 1950 with the Casualty Evacuation Flight (later 194 Squadron) in Malaya. This Dragonfly serial XD649, photographed in the mid-1950s, was fitted up with casevac panniers for jungle rescue work. Versions of this helicopter continued in service with the RAF until June 1956. (The Westland Group)

weeks before taking up its new base at Seletar in Singapore Island, where it arrived on 9 January 1946. Meanwhile the Mosquito squadron, based at Alipore in India at the time of the surrender but with detachments at Mingaladon and the Cocos Islands, moved to Tan Son Nhut near Saigon on 11 October 1945 to begin a photographic survey of French Indo-China. On 27 January 1946 the squadron crossed over to Don Muang near Bangkok to carry out similar work over Thailand (as Siam was more generally known by this time), including the Kra isthmus adjoining Malaya. These surveys were to prove highly beneficial in later years.

At this time, Britain faced the task of assuming control over many island communities of the south-west Pacific, including the Netherlands East Indies. The re-occupation of Sumatra, Borneo, New Guinea, Timor and Bali was carried out reasonably smoothly by the British or the Australians. However, an Indonesian Independence Movement in the Netherlands colony of Java managed to acquire weapons from the Japanese and was prepared to use them against all Europeans, seeing little distinction between the British and the Dutch. The RAF formed 904 Wing in Java, at Kemarojam airfield near Batavia, and a detachment of Spitfires PR XIXs flew down from Kai Tak in late October 1945 to join the fighter and transport squadrons allocated to the Wing. The main duties of the RAF were to help round up the Japanese forces and to locate camps containing internees before flying them to safety, or guarding road convoys. Photo-reconnaissance was an essential part of these tasks.

The situation in Java became unpleasant rapidly, with much of the country out of control. Before the end of the year the Army suffered over 1,000 casualties, and all the occupants of a Dakota which made a forced landing 5 miles from the airfield were captured and murdered. A detachment of Mosquito PR 34s from 684 Squadron arrived, but the high humidity caused problems with the wooden construction of the aircraft. Auster Vs of 656 Squadron made a notable contribution to tactical reconnaissance. The difficulties continued for much of the following spring and the RAF and Army personnel were not sorry when their duties began to wind down in the summer of 1946 and there was a gradual handover to Dutch authorities. The last of the RAF units were withdrawn from the Netherlands East Indies at the end of November 1946. By this time, Java and Sumatra had been surveyed by the detachment of Mosquito PR 34s from 684 Squadron, in spite of the aircraft's structural problems.

In the following three years the area of South-East Asia Command was reduced drastically. India became an independent republic on 14 August 1947, but great tracts of its vast territory were partitioned to become the new Republic of Pakistan. Both countries remained in the Commonwealth. Burma became an independent country outside the Commonwealth on 4 January 1948. Ceylon assumed the status of a self-governing Dominion within the Commonwealth exactly a month later. During this period, 681 Squadron returned from Seletar to India in May 1946 but the squadron was renumbered 34 Squadron three months later. The Spitfire PR XIXs continued with aerial surveys for the next year but then the squadron was disbanded. Meanwhile the Mosquito PR 34s of 684 Squadron at Don Muang continued survey work but the squadron was disbanded on 1 September 1946, being immediately re-formed as 81 Squadron at Seletar, where it also received a flight of Spitfire PR XIXs and later a few Spitfire FR 18s. The squadron continued survey work, moving within Singapore to Changi on 1 October 1947 and Tengah on 1 February 1948. With a detachment at

Mingaladon, it completed surveying the remainder of Burma by August 1947. This was followed by a survey of British North Borneo by the end of the year, carried out by another detachment operating from the island of Labuan off the coast of Brunei.

South-East Asia Air Command left India, Pakistan and Burma. By 1 June 1949 it was whittled down to the Far East Air Force, with main headquarters at Changi in Singapore but with other headquarters in Ceylon and Hong Kong. By this time its manpower had shrunk from about 125,000 at the end of the war to under 9,000. Singapore proved an admirable centre for maintaining British interests in the Far East, in spite of its history of failure in the war against the Japanese. The island possessed four excellent airfields: Seletar, Tengah, Changi and Sembawang. The industrious Chinese and Malays harboured little resentment at the presence of the British while the climate, although hot and subject to heavy reain, was not oppressive. In addition to the photo-reconnaissance surveys completed by 81 Squadron, maritime reconnaissance was carried out by Sunderland squadrons operating from Seletar, which was an excellent flying boat base, as well as an airfield, close to the naval base.

The new Far East Air Force faced a serious problem in the mainland peninsula, however. This arose from the Malayan Communist Party, which had collaborated with the British during the Japanese occupation by providing a resistance movement which by the end of the war consisted of about 4,000 guerillas. These attempted to turn Malaya into a communist republic by a series of strikes and other disruptions but when these failed began a policy of murder, intimidation and sabotage in 1948, with the objective of gradually taking over the country area by area. They were opposed by the great majority of the Malayan and Chinese people of the country, who looked to Britain for

protection. The RAF played a full part in what became known as the 'Malayan Emergency' by providing reconnaissance, by moving troops and police, and by carrying out bombing or rocket attacks against terrorist bases. These were named Operation 'Firedog' and Kuala Lumpur was re-activated as an RAF station to co-ordinate the activities. At the same time, the Sunderlands at Seletar patrolled the Gulf of Siam and the South China Sea, photographing small craft which might be smuggling arms between China and the east coast of Malaya. This work was carried out in collaboration with sloops and destroyers of the Royal Navy.

Fortunately, the surveys previously completed by 81 Squadron gave the security forces accurate knowledge of the interior of Malaya, although much of this was covered by thick jungle which favoured the terrorists. The state of Perak in the north-west was one of the seriously affected areas, and a single photo-reconnaissance Spitfire accompanied by a mobile photographic and interpretation unit was sent to the civil airfield of Taiping in the centre of the state. For about a month, terrorist encampments were identified and photographed. When attacked, however, the survivors simply fled into the jungle. Collections of huts in the interior of several other states were photographed by 81 Squadron's Mosquitos and Spitfires and then attacked by Beaufighters and Spitfires with rockets, cannon fire and bombs, while security forces, transported to landing grounds or parachuted from Dakotas, laid ambushes for the fleeing terrorists. The troops and police were supplied from the air by Dakotas, using the techniques perfected in Burma against the Japanese. These operations achieved some successes but the remaining terrorists split up into smaller groups and hid in deeper jungle where identification was more difficult. Murders and attacks on road and rail convoys continued and even intensified, especially in

The Scottish Aviation Pioneer entered service with the RAF in the Far East during February 1954 as an Army co-operation and communications aircraft, capable of operating from short runways. Squadrons at home and in the Mediterranean were also equipped with this tough and reliable aircraft, which continued in service until January 1970. (*Aeroplane Monthly*)

The Scottish Aviation Twin Pioneer followed the single-engined version, entering RAF service during 1958. It possessed the same attributes as its predecessor, but with a larger carrying capacity and a longer range. Twin Pioneers remained in front-line duties until late 1968. (*Aeroplane Monthly*)

287

the monsoon period when air activity was curtailed. By early 1949 it became evident that a long struggle lay ahead.

No maps had been constructed from 81 Squadron's surveys and it was thought necessary to update its work before these were drawn up. Large-scale maps of 1 inch to 1 mile and 2½ inches to 1 mile were required for use by the Army on jungle patrols and by the RAF in picking out suitable dropping zones. This work was begun in 1949 by 81 Squadron, flying at a lower level in order to produce suitable photographs for these large-scale maps. Some Anson C19s were also employed on this task in the summer of 1949. The squadron moved back to Seletar on 16 March 1950 but detachments were frequently sent to Butterworth in north-west Malaya. The new survey was not completed until 1952.

Terrorist camps were also identified by 81 Squadron, although aircraft flying below about 15,000 feet could often be spotted from the ground and dispersal might take place before air and ground strikes could be carried out. The counter-measures certainly harried and dispersed the terrorists and kept them on the move but their activities did not diminish.

In 1950 the security forces began the far-sighted plan of moving Chinese and Malay settlements in the interior into safe havens where they could be protected and where social amenities were provided. This plan was carried out gradually by British and Gurkha troops and the police, with a kindliness and humanity which contrasted sharply with the brutality of the communists, thus benefiting the government cause. The scheme also had the effect of isolating the terrorists from their supplies of food, for they were unable to grow their own or keep livestock when kept constantly on the move. It also denied to them valuable sources of information, for they were no longer able to intimidate the villagers. Of course it was essentially a long-term plan and for the time being the results

were not conclusive. Nevertheless it was notable that, in a vain attempt to win over the villagers to their cause, the Malayan Communist Party changed its name during 1950 to the Malayan Races Liberation Army.

While the RAF was embroiled in operations in Malaya and the Middle East, war broke out in Korea. The communist state of the People's Democratic Republic north of the 38th parallel, which was fixed at the end of the Second World War as a demarkation line between the areas controlled by the Russians and the Americans, invaded South Korea on 25 June 1950. Although Britain was able to help the South Koreans and the United Nation's Forces, mostly Americans, with Army and Navy support against North Koreans backed by Chinese forces, other commitments prevented the RAF from making a major contribution. By this time, the personnel of the Far East Air Force had been whittled down to no more than 4,000. However, excellent photo-reconnaissance was provided by detachments of Sunderland Vs from 88 and 209 Squadrons which moved from Seletar to Iwakuni on the Japanese island of Honshu, using Hong Kong as an intermediate base. The aircraft were engaged on anti-submarine patrols as well as the photography and identification of surface vessels. Many of the carrier-borne attacks made by the American Navy and the Royal Navy stemmed from these long and tedious reconnaissance sorties. In addition, the RAF provided pilots who flew in US aircraft, as well as two flights of Austers which carried out some of the dangerous work of tactical reconnaissance. The war continued with heavy losses on both sides until a truce was signed on 27 July 1953.

In the course of the Korean War, there were signs that the security forces in Malaya were beginning to gain the upper hand over the communists. The terrorists intensified their attacks against soft targets but

RAF Whirlwind HAR 10 serial XP398, based at Kuching, landing at an Army outpost in May 1964 during the Indonesian confrontation. (P. Batten)

A logging site in Borneo, photographed from 1,500 feet by a Canberra PR 9 of 13 Squadron on 3 February 1966, during the confrontation with Indonesia.
(Squadron Leader P.J. Thompson RAF (Ret'd))

The Westland Belvedere HC 1, with twin engines and twin rotors, entered RAF service in September 1961 as a transport and troop carrier, equipping three squadrons. This Belvedere serial XG456 of 66 Squadron was photographed in June 1964 at Nanga Gaat in North Borneo while transporting a downed Wessex 1 of the Royal Navy's 845 Squadron. Belvederes were retired in March 1969. (P. Batten)

identification of their positions improved and air attacks became more effective while the large-scale maps provided from 81 Squadron's surveys enabled the ground forces to dispose their units more accurately. The policy of gathering villagers into protected encampments began to pay dividends. Increased numbers of terrorists surrendered, and known communist sympathisers in the country were deported. The first Westland Dragonfly HC2 helicopters arrived in April 1950 and assisted in reconnaissance as well as casualty evacuation. By the middle of 1954 it was estimated that 7,500 terrorists had been killed or captured, leaving about 3,500 in the jungles. Some areas of Malaya had been completely cleared of terrorists.

The Far East Air Force was always the last to receive the RAF's new equipment, but at last modern aircraft began to arrive. The fighter-bomber squadrons were equipping with Vampires and then Venoms. Meteor PR 9s arrived to re-equip 81 Squadron in December 1953, and on 1 April 1954 the squadron enjoyed the distinction of flying the last operational sortie of any Spitfire. This was followed by the last operational sortie of any Mosquito on 15 December 1955. The venerable Sunderlands at Seletar were also beginning to wear out. On 1 October 1954, 88 Squadron was disbanded and its remaining flying boats were distributed among the other two squadrons. Then 209 Squadron was disbanded on 1 January 1955 and all the Sunderlands were concentrated in 205 Squadron. Bristol Sycamore helicopters arrived to form 194 Squadron at Kuala Lumpur in October 1954, improving both casualty evacuation and reconnaissance. Scottish Aviation Pioneers of 267 Squadron also supported these operations.

Both reconnaissance and air strikes were intensified in 1954 and co-ordinated even more precisely with ground operations. Large-scale maps were constantly updated by photo-reconnaissance carried out by 81 Squadron. Austers marked targets with smoke or flares and air strikes followed almost immediately, before the terrorists had time to disperse. The terrorists could no longer find hiding places, and by the end of the year it seemed that the security forces were within sight of winning the conflict.

The end came after the new Federal Government of Malaya offered an amnesty to the remaining terrorists in November 1955, in advance of the independence which had been arranged for the country. Sporadic violence continued but, when this independence within the Commonwealth was attained on 31 August 1957, any residual sympathy among the population for the communists evaporated. By 1 April 1959 it became possible for most RAF units to leave Malaya and hand over their duties to the emergent Royal Malayan Air Force and three RAAF squadrons. The Emergency regulations were finally lifted on 31 July 1960, by which time a hard core of only about five hundred communists remained in the interior, waiting impotently for a time when they might become a resurgent force. This brought to an end twelve years of campaigning in which photo-reconnaissance had played a major and vital part.

While Malaya was achieving its independence, a new organisation was formed. This was the South-East Asia Treaty Organisation (SEATO), which was born at a conference held in Manila in September 1954 attended by Australia, Britain, France, New Zealand, Pakistan, the Philippine Republic, the United States and Thailand. It came into force on 19 February 1955 and provided a defensive alliance against communist aggression, with headquarters in Bangkok. There were no standing military forces but joint exercises were held from time to time.

In August 1957 the RAF opened an important staging post on the island of Gan in the Maldives, thus providing a strategic link between the Middle East and the Far East which was independent of India, Pakistan and Ceylon. This was placed three months later under the control of the Far East Air Force. It was not used as a permanent base for any RAF squadrons but detachments could be sent there for exercises, including photo-reconnaissance Canberras.

After leaving the Malayan mainland, the Far East Air Force concentrated its squadrons at Singapore. Among these was 205 Squadron, which was equipped with Avro Shackleton MR 1As in May 1958 and moved from Seletar to Changi, and 81 Squadron, which received Canberra PR 7s in January 1960 when based at Tengah. After a few quiet years, the RAF in the region found itself involved in yet another confrontation, this time in Indonesia. This arose in 1962 from the proposal to incorporate Malaya, Singapore Island and British North Borneo into a new Federation of Malaysia, within the Commonwealth. British North Borneo consisted of the Crown Colonies of Sarawak, Sabah and Brunei, but to the south was the much larger Indonesian state of Kalimantan, and the Indonesian Republic laid claim to the whole island and indeed even to Singapore and Malaya.

Rebellion and terrorism fomented by the Indonesian Government, which included a strong communist influence, began in Brunei and Sarawak during December 1962. British and Gurkha troops were flown from Singapore to support the local police and other forces, landing at the RAF base in the island of Labuan, which was easy to protect. Most of the pockets of revolutionary forces were then suppressed but incursions by bands of armed irregulars from Kalimantan occurred. These intensified when the Federation of Malaya was proclaimed on 16 September 1963, until an undeclared state of war existed between Malaysia and Indonesia. Fortunately the new Federation was supported by the majority of its Malayan and

Chinese population in North Borneo, although the oil-rich state of Brunei chose to remain a separate Sultanate within the Commonwealth. Nevertheless the incursions became so threatening that it was decided to evacuate many British residents to Singapore.

The terrain in North Borneo is similar to that of Malaya but the jungle is even thicker and the mountains are higher, while the climate is wetter. The country had been surveyed by the Mosquito PR 34s of 81 Squadron in 1947 and the defending troops had the additional advantage of experience in Malaya and the use of advanced helicopters. The frontier was enormous, about 800 miles, but the aerial survey disclosed that there were only a few feasible points of entry and these were guarded by troops who were often landed by Westland Whirlwind HAR 10 helicopters of 225 Squadron, which had been sent out from Odiham in 1960 and were based at Kuching in Sarawak but operated from various airstrips. These were reinfoced by a detachment of Westland Belvedere HC 1 heavy-lift helicopters from 66 Squadron sent out from Khormaksar. Supplies were either parachuted to the troops or landed by these helicopters. Naval helicopters also joined in this work, and at a later stage Whirlwinds of 103 and 110 Squadrons also arrived.

Tactical photo-reconnaissance was of course essential, and this was supplied mainly by the Canberra PR 7s of the ubiquitous 81 Squadron, which were detached to Labuan from Singapore, occasionally supported by Canberra PR 7s of 13 Squadron detached from Malta. The earlier photographic survey had been on too small a scale for tactical use on the ground but the great endurance and better performance of the Canberra and its camera equipment provided large-scale photography of jungle tracks and crossing points, as well as longhouses which might harbour the terrorists. Moreover, the processing of the films and photo-interpretation was carried

A Wessex HU 5 of the Royal Navy's 848 Squadron, based at Bario in North Borneo, delivering supplies to troops of the Gurkha Regiment in September 1965. (P. Batten)

out with remarkable speed. The intelligence gained was superior even to that acquired in Malaya, giving the troops an advantage which the Indonesian Air Force did not provide for the invaders.

At the same time, a detachment of Shackletons from 205 Squadron at Labuan provided maritime photo-reconnaissance in liaison with the Royal Navy, although it seems that the Indonesians made few attempts to land insurgents or supplies from the sea in North Borneo. The presence of these aircraft and the Royal Navy persuaded Indonesian naval vessels to retire to safety. However, in August 1964 a party of about a hundred regular Indonesian troops was landed by small craft on the west coast of Johore in Malaya, and about the same number were dropped inland from a Hercules several days later. Some sabotage followed and more Indonesian troops were landed. Their locations were identified by air reconnaissance and air strikes and ground attacks followed. In all, 451 Indonesian soldiers arrived and every one was either killed or captured before the attempts at invasion ceased during the following March. They caused irritation but very little damage.

Meanwhile regular Indonesian troops joined in the infiltration of North Borneo and the defending forces were permitted to cross the border for a distance of up to 10,000 yards as a counter-measure. The Indonesian Air Force took little part in these operations, knowing that RAF fighter squadrons provided an effective defence and would be eager to shoot down their aircraft. Nevertheless the ground incursions continued into 1965, although the troops showed no desire for conflict with the British or the Gurkhas.

In August 1965 Singapore decided to leave the Federation of Malaysia and to pursue its own policy of expansion, but it remained within the Commonwealth and continued to support the counter-insurgency operations.

The conflict dragged on in Borneo, but an important event followed in the next month when the Indonesian Communist Party failed in an attempt to stage a coup in the country. Popular feeling moved against the communists and, although the armed incursions continued into 1966, a peace treaty was signed between Indonesia and Malaysia in August of that year. The campaign ended and the RAF and the other security forces began to withdraw from Borneo.

In spite of the successful conclusion of the Indonesian confrontation, the expense involved caused concern at home, coming as it did at the same time as other conflicts in the Middle East. By 1966 Britain decided that it could no longer afford expensive commitments abroad and must provide for emergencies by retaining at home a 'rapid reaction' force which could be transported quickly by air to any trouble spots. A programme of training the Royal Malayan Air Force and the emergent Singapore Air Force began to achieve success. The area remained quiet, while Britain did not participate in the Vietnam War which began with the direct involvement of American forces in 1965 and ended with the surrender of Saigon in 1975.

RAF squadrons were disbanded or withdrawn to the UK. The remaining forces were withdrawn from Borneo. In January 1970, 81 Squadron, which had performed for so long and so magnificently in the Far East, was disbanded at Tengah. This was followed by 205 Squadron at Changi in October 1971, when the RAF finally left the island. The Far East Asia Command and the Far East Air Force closed down. RAF Gan continued as a staging post until March 1976 and the South East Asia Treaty Organisation was finally wound up in June 1977. Soon afterwards, only 28 Squadron in Hong Kong represented the RAF in the Far East, equipped with Westland Wessex HC2 helicopters.

CHAPTER SIXTEEN

STRIKE COMMAND

When it was formed in April 1968, Strike Command possessed only two long-range strategic reconnaissance squadrons. Both had formed part of Bomber Command, which was incorporated into the new organization as No 1 Group. Of these, 543 Squadron at Wyton had acquired Handley Page Victor SR 2s in January 1966 after its ageing Vickers Valiant B (PR) 1s were grounded in the previous year. These aircraft were normally employed on high-altitude work in daylight, when the bomb bays were fitted with up to eight F96 cameras, each with a focal length of 48 inches, arranged in a fan so as to cover a wide area from horizon to horizon. Improvements in film emulsions, automatic exposure in varying conditions of light, and the introduction of computerised techniques in the design of lenses added to the effectiveness. Radar photography had also improved with later and better versions of the H_2S, and more advanced methods were being developed. Although American satellites were steadily replacing such manned aircraft in the strategic reconnaissance role, 543 Squadron continued as a photograpic unit until it was disbanded in May 1974.

Meanwhile, 27 Squadron at Scampton in Lincolnshire was equipped in November 1973 with Avro Vulcan SR 2s and continued in a similar capacity as the RAF's strategic reconnaissance squadron, with the additional duties of mapping and ocean surveillance. However, the squadron was disbanded in March 1982, although re-formed a few

months later with the new Panavia Tornado GR 1 in the tactical role. Another unit was 51 Squadron, also based at Wyton, equipped with de Havilland Comet R1s in the electronic intelligence and radar reconnaissance roles. As related in Chapter Thirteen, these were supplemented by Hawker Siddeley Nimrod R1s in July 1971 but the Comets continued alongside the new aircraft for three more years. The work of this squadron is considered so vital that it continues in 1996, still equipped with three Nimrod R1s.

The only home-based photo-reconnaissance unit in 1968 equipped with Canberra PR 7s and PR 9s was 58 Squadron at Wyton. Detachments were in course of completing a number of surveys overseas before the squadron was disbanded in September 1970.

Coastal Command became part of Strike Command in November 1969, forming No 18 Group in the new organisation. It brought with it six squadrons equipped with the redoubtable Avro Shackleton. These included the earliest MR 1, which had first entered service in April 1951, the 'extended' version known as the MR 2 which was introduced almost two years later, and the MR 3, with a tricycle undercarriage and various other improvements, which was supplied to squadrons from August 1957 onwards. The search for a jet replacement for this venerable aircraft had been continuing for some time, however, and it was found in another

The Hawker Siddeley Buccaneer first entered service with the RAF in October 1970, primarily as a maritime strike aircraft, and eventually equipped five squadrons. Buccaneers also served in Germany and later in the Gulf War, where one of their tasks was to act as target designators for Tornados carrying Paveway laser-guided bombs. This photograph shows Buccaneer serial XN981 of 12 Squadron from Lossiemouth in Morayshire. It is armed with Martel anti-shipping missiles, AJ168 TV guided with the blunt nose and AS37 anti-radar with the pointed nose. Behind it is Buccaneer serial XZ432 of 237 Operational Conversion Unit from the same station. (Flight Lieutenant I. Gilchrist RAF)

Above, left: The F126 reconnaissance camera, size 25-inch by 16-inch, takes about 300 exposures of 9-inch by 9-inch. It is primarily designed for medium or high altitude in daylight, without flash facility, but is fitted with an automatic exposure control which enables photography at dusk. The movement of the camera over the ground is balanced by an 'image movement compensation' system, controlled remotely by input data of velocity and height, so that the aircraft can be flown at a wide range of altitudes and speeds. *Above, right*: The F135 camera was designed for low-altitude reconnaissance, both day and night. In size, it is about 12-inch by 8½-inch by 9-inch. It has a twin lens arrangement which allows photographs to be taken in alternate sequence, giving a good overlap of 50 per cent. The picture size is 2¼-inch by 2¼-inch, and 1,000 exposures can be taken (500 on each track). An automatic exposure control sets both the aperture and shutter to suit light conditions, both at day and night. The mechanism also incorporates 'image movement compensation', to correct the effect of speed of the aircraft. (Both photos: Flight Lieutenant G.H. Parry RAF (Ret'd))

Nine Avro Vulcan B2s were modified as Vulcan MM2s to carry out the role of long-range marine reconnaissance. They entered service with 27 Squadron at Waddington in Lincolnshire in November 1973 and continued in service until March 1982. This Vulcan B2 serial XM598 continued as a bomber at present on display at the RAF. (Squadron Leader P.J. Thompson RAF (Ret'd))

Lockheed Hercules C3 serial XV301 of 47 Squadron, fitted with a refuelling probe, at Lyneham in Wiltshire in 1991. These aircraft first entered RAF service in 1966 and, in their modified form, were the standard military transport in 1995. (R.C. Nesbit)

adaptation of the civilian Comet airliner. This entered RAF service in October 1970 as the Hawker Siddeley Nimrod MR I and, with its fin-mounted radome, integrated navigational system and digital computer, quickly replaced all the RAF's Shackletons apart from those supplied to 8 Squadron soon after it was re-formed at Kinloss in Morayshire on 1 January 1972. This new version was the Shackleton AEW which was converted from the MR 2 and carried a huge radome under the nose. Eleven of these Shackleton aircraft were converted and they remained the only Airborne Early Warning aircraft supplied to the RAF until Boeing E–3D Sentries were purchased from America and entered service with 8 Squadron in 1991. By this time, Shackletons had served for forty years.

Coastal Command also contributed five squadrons of helicopters, equipped with either the Westland Wessex HC 2 or the Westland Whirlwind HAR 10. Helicopters had proved their worth overseas in casualty evacuation and Army support and their development in this capacity continued apace in Britain. However, the Wessexes and Whirlwinds of No 18 Group were employed primarily in the search and rescue role around the coasts of Britain, although they could also be used for photo-reconnaissance. The transport of troops by helicopter was carried out by Air Support Command, as Transport Command had been renamed in 1967.

Conventional cameras continued in widespread use in the tactical role. This function was carried out by aircraft of the former Fighter Command, which had become No 11 Group of Strike Command. The cameras were fitted in fast and manoeuvrable interceptors adapted for the purpose, and many of these served in RAF Germany as a separate Command under Nato. The Canberra PR 7s in Germany were being phased out at this stage, in favour of these

newer jets. No 80 Squadron was disbanded at Brüggen in September 1969, followed by 17 Squadron at Wildenrath three months later. No 31 Squadron at Laarbruch soldiered on until March 1971 but was then disbanded.

By 1972 seven squadrons equipped with new tactical reconnaissance jet aircraft were based at Brüggen, Laarbruch and Wildenrath, from where they confronted the potential enemy, the Soviet Union. Four of the squadrons were equipped with the McDonnell Douglas Phantom FGR 2, which had first entered RAF service three years previously. This aircraft carried up to five day or night cameras in a reconnaissance pod made by the electronics group EMI. During the day, these usually consisted of four F95 cameras and one F135 camera. At night, four F135 cameras were carried, together with electronic sensors such as the new Sideways-Looking Reconnaissance Radar (SLRR), which could pick up fairly large objects at night, and a heat-seeking Infra-Red Linescan (IRLS), which recorded the relative temperatures of objects on the surface. In addition, the pod carried a Modulator Data Converter which recorded the position, speed and direction of the aircraft on the film strip.

The remaining three tactical squadrons in Germany employed the British Aerospace Harrier GR 1, which came into service in July 1969. Apart from its remarkable Short Take-Off and Vertical Landing (STO/VL) capabilities with a full load, this aircraft carried a single F95 camera facing obliquely to port. It could also carry a reconnaissance pod, often fitted with four F95 cameras facing alternately to port and starboard, a single F135 camera and a data unit. Of course, these cameras could be replaced with others or the combination altered as each sortie demanded.

Since these two types of tactical photo-reconnaissance aircraft flew at very low level and at high speed over their targets, blurring

An Air Transportable Reconnaissance Exploitation Laboratory (ATREL) at RAF Cosford in 1991. These laboratories can be flown to the area of operations, where several can be joined by vestibules to form a complete imagery exploitation laboratory. (J.K. Nesbit)

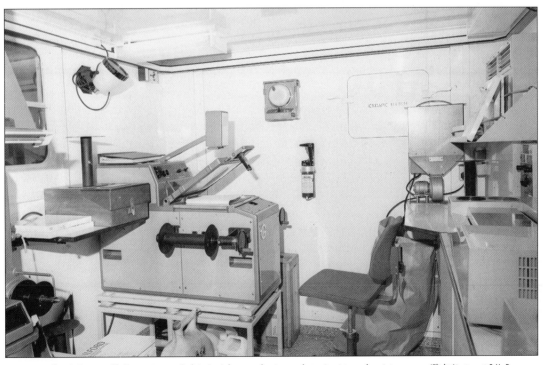

Interior view of an Air Transportable Reconnaissance Exploitation Laboratory showing an electronic printer and a print processor. (Flight Lieutenant G.H. Parry RAF (Ret'd))

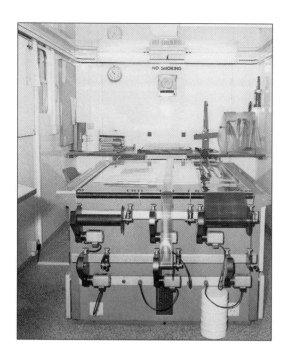

Interior view of an Air Transportable Reconnaissance Exploitation Laboratory showing a 'seven-strand viewing table'. (Flight Lieutenant G.H. Parry RAF (Ret'd))

Moveable Air Reconnaissance Exploitation Laboratories (MARELS), which can be transported to an area of operations on low-loader trucks. (Flight Lieutenant G.H. Parry RAF (Ret'd))

of the exposure would have ruined the result without the Image Movement Compensation (IMC) which had been introduced in the Second World War and thereafter steadily improved. This ensured that the film in the camera was set to move in such a way as to match the relative speed of the aircraft over the ground, by means of direct inputs giving speed and altitude.

The RAF's School of Photography at Cosford continued its work, but in 1972 became the Joint School of Photography (JSOP) when the Royal Navy's school at Lossiemouth, which had trained both Navy and Army students, closed down. From this time, JSOP at Cosford came under the joint control of the three services, and officers have been appointed from each to command the school.

Other improvements at this stage concentrated on reducing the time taken from the moment the reconnaissance aircraft landed to the provision of intelligence information about the enemy. Mobile Reconnaissance Intelligence Centres (RICs) were provided, on the lines of the mobile units which were employed with great success in the Second World War but with the addition of Air Transportable Reconnaissance Exploitation Laboratories (ATRELs) which could be flown at short notice to the area of operations, usually in the Lockheed Hercules of Air Support Command, formerly named Transport Command. This joined Strike Command in September 1972 to become No 46 Group. The structure of Strike Command thus became far simpler than the numerous Commands which had preceded it.

RAF photographic activities continued to concentrate on tactical work and in March 1974 the Sepecat Jaguar GR 1 was introduced, replacing the Phantom in Germany and at home. This could also carry a reconnaissance pod, containing an Infra-Red Linescan and four F95 cameras, two of which were sometimes replaced with F126 vertical cameras. Eight RAF squadrons were equipped with this machine, three in Strike Command and five in RAF Germany. In 1995, the Jaguar GR 1A was still in service with the RAF.

On 10 April 1975 the whole of the RAF's Strike Command was added to Nato, becoming known within this organisation as United Kingdom Air Forces. The area of Nato extended from the North Pole to the Tropic of Cancer and included much of Europe and the Atlantic within its sphere of operations. The role of this powerful organisation remained that of vigilance, providing a potent deterrent against any threat from the Soviet Bloc, fortunately without having to resort to hostilities.

When the home-based RAF squadrons were eventually drawn into conflict, it was in an unexpected part of the world, the South Atlantic, after the Falklands Islands were invaded by Argentine forces on 2 April 1982. The dependency of South Georgia was invaded the following day. British rule in the Falklands had prevailed for over two hundred years and its inhabitants looked to their home country for protection, even though they were about 8,000 miles distant from London. At this time, Britain's overseas commitments were largely concentrated in Germany but her response was remarkably swift. The first vessels of the South Atlantic Task Force left Portsmouth on 5 April, while intense but fruitless diplomatic efforts were made to persuade Argentina to withdraw.

The war was fought by British combined forces, with the majority of the soldiers and marines landed from ships, but of course aircraft of the Royal Navy, Army and the RAF also played a crucial role in the ultimate victory. Numerically, the Sea Harriers and helicopters of the Fleet Air Arm formed the greater part of the strike force, although some of its Sea Harriers were flown by RAF pilots.

The fighter and reconnaissance version of the McDonnell Douglas Phantom, the FGR, first entered service with the RAF in Germany in June 1970. This aircraft, serial XV406 of 43 Squadron at Leuchars in Fife, was photographed in November 1970 while carrying four Raytheon Sparrow air-to-air missiles and a reconnaissance pod. (Hawker Siddeley Aviation)

A camera pod being fitted on a Phantom FGR 2 of 2 Squadron in 1973, when the squadron was based at Laarbruch in Germany. (*Aeroplane Monthly*)

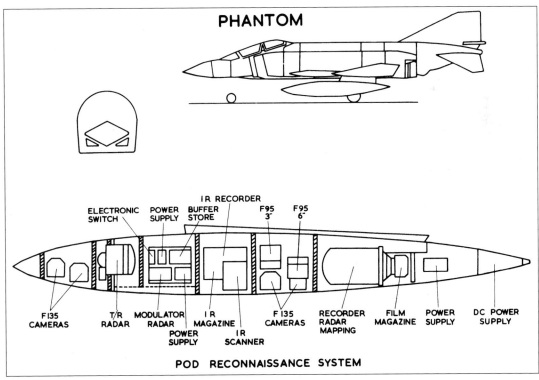

PHANTOM

IR RECORDER

ELECTRONIC SWITCH

POWER SUPPLY

BUFFER STORE

F95 3"

F95 6"

F 135 CAMERAS

T/R RADAR

MODULATOR RADAR

POWER SUPPLY

I R MAGAZINE

I R SCANNER

F 135 CAMERAS

RECORDER RADAR MAPPING

FILM MAGAZINE

POWER SUPPLY

DC POWER SUPPLY

POD RECONNAISSANCE SYSTEM

An example of the contents of the sensors on the pod carried by the Phantom FGR 2 when employed on night reconnaissance. In this instance the F95 cameras would be fitted but not used. (Flight Lieutenant G.H. Parry RAF (Ret'd))

They were backed by light helicopters of the Royal Marines and the Army Air Corps. The contribution of the RAF consisted of Vulcans, Hercules, Victors, Harriers, Nimrods and VC10s, with Sea King and Chinook helicopters. They were opposed by the Argentine Air Force, one of the strongest in Latin America, with some aircraft already installed on the short runway of 4,200 feet at Port Stanley airfield in the Falklands but with the majority of their modern fighters 400 miles distant in their home country.

The British could not have attempted to regain the Falklands without the facility provided by the Americans of their Wideawake staging airfield at Ascension, a British island in the Atlantic roughly equidistant between England and the war zone. Nevertheless the logistical problems were formidable, with supplies carried by RAF Hercules refuelled in flight by Victors. The first elements of the Task Force sailed from Ascension Island on 16 April for the Falklands, led by the carriers HMS *Hermes* and *Invincible*. At this stage its air component consisted of twenty Sea Harriers of the Fleet Air Arm, together with Westland Sea King, Wessex, Lynx and Wasp helicopters from the same service. The Army Air Corps and the Royal Marine Commandos of the Task Force were supported by their own Westland Scout and Aerospace/Westland Gazelle helicopters, employed mainly on reconnaissance.

The first maritime photo-reconnaissance sorties were carried out from Wideawake by Nimrod MR 1s of the RAF's 42 Squadron, which flew from their base at St Mawgan in Cornwall. The aircraft carried Harpoon anti-ship missiles and were additionally fitted with pylons which enabled them to carry four Sidewinder missiles, although these weapons were never used. This detachment from 42 Squadron was replaced on 12 April by Nimrod MR 2s of 120, 201 and 206

Squadrons from Kinloss in Morayshire, fitted with more effective Searchwater radar equipment.

Some of the Victors also carried out photo-reconnaissance sorties, after being converted from their tanker role with equipment taken from retired Vulcan SR 2s. The first sortie took place on 20 April from Wideawake over South Georgia, in a flight of over fourteen hours, and this was followed by two more flights. The dependency was retaken on 25 April by a small task force under the command of the Royal Navy which left Gibraltar in early April, headed by two destroyers and carrying Lynx and Wessex helicopters. The tasks of the Victors were to supply intelligence about the Argentine forces and the presence of any pack ice or icebergs in the vicinity of South Georgia. Each sortie required four refuelling tankers on both the outward and return flights. Meanwhile the Nimrod MR 2s from Kinloss were modified by installing in-flight refuelling probes which, from 9 May, enabled them to fly on maritime photo-reconnaissance sorties of up to nineteen hours.

There is little doubt, however, that the RAF felt the loss of Airborne Early Warning aircraft with sufficient range and modern equipment for the task in hand. A long-standing programme to convert Nimrods to this role was in progress but never came to fruition. It was eventually cancelled in December 1986, when the Boeing E–3D Sentry was ordered. Meanwhile, it was believed by some aviation observers that Sentries of the USAF may have supported the RAF in the Falklands campaign.

While these maritime reconnaissance flights were taking place, the Argentine forces on Aeroporto Malvinas, as they had confidently renamed Stanley airport, received a foretaste of their unpleasant future. At a very early hour on 1 May a stick of twenty-one 1,000-lb bombs was dropped across the

The Sepecat Jaguar was first introduced into the RAF in 1974 as a supersonic fighter which could also be employed on ground attack and tactical reconnaissance. This Jaguar GR 1A was painted in desert pink for the Gulf War and fitted with a reconnaissance pod, a Sidewinder missile and an electronic counter-measures fit. (Senior Aircraftman N. Green RAF)

The British Aerospace Harrier GR 3 was updated from the GR 1 which, in July 1969, was the first 'vertical take-off and landing' aircraft to enter any air force in the world. Although designed as a single-seat aircraft in the ground attack role, these early marks also had a photo-reconnaissance capability, with one F135 vertical and four F95 oblique cameras in a pod. This Harrier GR 3 of 1 (Fighter) Squadron at Wittering in Cambridgeshire participated in the Falklands campaign. (Flight Lieutenant R.D. Chalmers RAF (Ret'd))

The last version of the long-lived Avro Shackleton was the Advanced Early Warning adaptation, twelve of which were converted from MR 2s from 1971 onwards. The bulky radome under the nose carried the special equipment. All were supplied to 8 Squadron, at first based at Kinloss in Morayshire but moving to Lossiemouth in August 1973. Shackleton AEW 2s remained in service until 1991. They were named after characters in the children's BBC TV programme *Magic Roundabout*, serial WR963 in this programme being *Ermintrude*. (Flight Lieutenant R.D. Chalmers RAF (Ret'd))

runway by a Vulcan B2 of 44 Squadron from Wideawake, with a crew from 101 Squadron. This bomber arrived over the airfield after being refuelled on numerous occasions by Victors. The main purpose of this attack was to deny the airfield to the Mirages and Super Etendards of the Argentine Air Force on the mainland, which might have been able to use the short runway with the aid of arrester gear. It was followed at dawn by a low-level strike by Sea Harriers of the Task Force, against both the airport and a grass airfield at Goose Green. The counter-invasion had begun, and the Falkland Islanders knew that liberation would follow.

The first RAF tactical strike aircraft employed on the enterprise were nine Harrier GR 3s of 1 Squadron at Wittering, which had made record flights of over nine hours to Wideawake between 3 and 5 May, refuelled en route by Victors. Six of these embarked on 8 May for the Falklands in the container ship *Atlantic Conveyor*. The other three followed later, together with five more, after their defensive role at Wideawake had been taken over on 24 May by Phantom FGR 2s of 29 Squadron from Coningsby in Lincolnshire. The first six RAF Harriers together with Sea Harriers, were transferred between 18 and 19 May to the aircraft carrier HMS *Hermes*, joining other Sea Harriers and the Sea Kings of the Fleet Air Arm. Four Boeing Vertol Chinook HC 1 helicopters from the RAF's 18 Squadron based at Odiham in Hampshire were also carried by *Atlantic Conveyor*, but the Sea King HAR 3 helicopters provided by the RAF's 202 Squadron at Brawdy in Pembrokeshire remained at Ascension Island, where they were employed on search-and-rescue duties and on transporting stores.

The battle for the Falklands was bitter and bloody, fought by all arms of the British forces, although thick fog reduced flying activities for the first three weeks of May.

Operating from the mainland, the Argentine Air Force attacked the Task Force with great determination and courage. In spite of heavy losses, its pilots sank the destroyer HMS *Sheffield* on 4 May, the frigate HMS *Ardent* on 21 May, the frigate HMS *Antelope* on 23 May and the destroyer HMS *Coventry* on 25 May. They damaged the container ship *Atlantic Conveyor* so badly on 25 May that she sank three days later. Three of the RAF's four Chinook helicopters were destroyed when the latter vessel was hit by an Exocet missile, but the remaining aircraft carried out magnificent service until the end of the campaign. The Royal Fleet Auxiliary *Sir Galahad* was sunk by air attack on 8 June, while *Sir Tristram* was badly damaged.

Once the RAF Harriers arrived, the FAA Harriers were able to concentrate on defensive operations and air combat, in which they proved superior to the attacking aircraft. The RAF Harriers acquitted themselves extremely well in attacks against heavily defended ground targets, the first of which took place against fuel dumps on 20 May, the day before the main landings of troops began. By 9 June, they also operated from a short aluminium strip at San Carlos Bay. No records have yet been released of any photo-reconnaissance work, but of course the aircraft were capable of carrying out such duties.

Ten FAA or RAF Harriers were lost, of which five were in accidents. Much tactical reconnaissance was carried out by Scout and Gazelle helicopters. Twenty-three helicopters were lost, 19 of them accidentally or sunk in vessels. It was estimated that 117 Argentine aircraft were destroyed or probably destroyed, over half of which were helicopters, and about 30 more were captured. The campaign ended with a complete victory for the British forces on 14 June when the demoralised Argentine troops surrendered.

The Westland/Aérospatiale Puma was one of the products of a joint Anglo-French manufacturing arrangement, which first entered RAF squadron service in June 1971. It is used for casualty evacuation, troop carrying and as a gunship. (The Westland Group)

The Westland Wessex first entered RAF service in 1964, for tactical reconnaissance and ground assault. Some are still in use for search and rescue duties. This Wessex HC2 serial XT601 of A Flight 22 Squadron at Chivenor in Devon was photographed on 15 December 1986 when the photographer Jane Cowderoy, dressed in orange survival suit, was about to be winched up with the assistance of the navigator Flight Lieutenant Bob Lander. (R.C. Nesbit)

The winchman of Wessex HC2 serial XT601, Flight Sergeant Ken Tucker, being lowered on to a tiny rock off the steep cliffs of Lundy Island, 300 feet below, during a practice exercise. He reached it while the sea was foaming and spray blowing over him. (Jane Cowderoy)

Westland Sea King HAR 3 helicopters were delivered to the RAF from December 1977 onwards for long-range search and rescue work. They replaced the Whirlwinds and are also replacing the Wessexes. This Sea King serial ZE368 was on the strength of 202 Squadron, based at Finningley in Yorkshire. (The Westland Group)

The EH101 is a multi-role helicopter produced by EH Industries, a company formed by Westland Helicopters and Augusta. The Royal Navy variant, named 'Merlin' is fitted with the latest detection equipment and can carry four homing torpedos. The Military-Utility variant was under order for the RAF in 1995. The Westland Group)

The Panavia Tornado GR 1 arrived in RAF service slightly too late to participate in the Falklands War. The first operational unit to receive this formidable two-seater was 9 Squadron at Honington in Suffolk during January 1982, but eventually ten squadrons were equipped with the aircraft. The GR 1 was (and remains) a low-level, tactical aircraft fitted with radar which enabled it to find its target in all weathers and at night. It was followed in 1984 by the Tornado F2 interceptor version. In 1990 the Tornado GR 1A arrived, a low-level reconnaissance version which acts as a pathfinder for the GR 1 and other aircraft, or records the results of their attacks. It is fitted with the TIRRS (Tornado Infra-Red Reconnaissance System). Part of this equipment consists of an Infra-Red Line Scanner which sweeps from side to side along the track of the aircraft. However, since the aircraft flies at low level, the picture definition near either horizon is less well defined. To compensate for this defect, two Sideways Looking Infra-Red sensors are also fitted, providing high resolution near the horizons. Computers 'stretch' these distant recordings so that the results, combined with those of the Infra-Red Line Scanner, are similar to vertical photography at a high level. This system is positioned below the fuselage in place of two 27–mm cannons of the GR 1, with the recordings displayed on a TV-type screen in the navigator's position. The GR 1A was not designed to carry conventional cameras but the imagery of the system is of high quality and the results are video-taped for later analysis. Moreover, it is effective both by day and at night without the use of photo-flashes. In addition to its remarkable reconnaissance work, the machine has a secondary attack role.

The next major conflict in which the RAF participated was the Gulf War of 1991/2. This arose from Iraq's claim to Kuwait, a sheikdom which had been granted independence by the British in 1961. The Iraqis had never recognised this new state and, when their long war with Iran ended in the late 1980s, felt strong enough to invade the Sheikdom and acquire its oil resources. On 2 August 1990 troops of the Iraqi Republican Guard crossed the frontier, brushed aside isolated pockets of Kuwaiti resistance and soon occupied the whole country.

The government of Saudi Arabia invited foreign countries to send troops to protect its country from potential aggression, while the Security Council of the United Nations imposed strict sanctions on trade with Iraq. From 7 August strong contingents of the USAF flew to Saudi Arabia and two days later the British Government announced that its forces would also move to that country and the Gulf States, forming part of what became known as the Coalition Force. Strategic and radar reconnaissance of Iraq was provided by aircraft of the USAF, including the U–2R, while satellites were also employed.

By 16 January 1991, the day before Operation 'Desert Storm' began to retake Kuwait, about 600,000 troops, 4,000 tanks and 150 warships were available within Saudi Arabia, the Gulf States and Turkey, apart from the air forces. It was estimated by the Iraqis that the equivalent of the force designed to combat the entire Warsaw Pact countries was ranged against them.

By this time the RAF had contributed 18 Tornado F3 interceptors, 40 Tornado GR 1s for tactical bombing operations, 6 of the new Tornado GR 1As for reconnaissance, 12 Jaguar GR 1As for tactical attacks and photo-reconnaissance, 17 Victor K2 or VC10 K2 tankers, 3 Nimrod MR 2s, 12 Chinook HC 1 helicopters, 19 Puma helicopters, 7 Hercules transports and 1 BAe 125 communications aircraft. These aircraft were detached from various squadrons, none of

The Hawker Siddeley Nimrod was developed from the Comet airliner as a maritime reconnaissance aircraft, first entering RAF service in October 1969. This Nimrod MR 2 of 42 Squadron was photographed at RAF St Mawgan in Cornwall in November 1985, showing bomb doors open to receive McDonnell Douglas *Harpoon* anti-shipping missiles and Electronic Support Measures (ECM) on top of the fin. Magnetic Anomaly Detector (MAD) equipment, developed to pick up alterations in the Earth's magnetic field from a submarine or surface vessesl, was in the tail. (R.C. Nesbit)

The five screens of a Marconi AQS-901 digital processing and display system in a Nimrod MR 2. These are known as the 'wet' equipment, which deals with signals received from sonobuoys dropped from the aircraft. These detect the position of a submarine prior to launching torpedos from the bomb bay. (R.C. Nesbit)

The Electronics Support Measures (ESM), or Searchwater radar, are known as the 'dry' equipment. Signals returned from a surface vessel are processed by computer and displayed on the screen. (R.C. Nesbit)

The tactical position in the navigators' compartment of a Nimrod, with the input data from the 'wet' and 'dry' operators displayed on a 24-inch screen (switched off in this photograph). The weapons system for anti-submarine torpedos is on the right, with the author sitting in front of the equipment. (R.C. Nesbit)

which flew out in their entirety, and formed composite squadrons in the Gulf. However, the total strength of about 7,000 personnel included squadrons of the RAF Regiment. The aircraft were followed by other detachments, including twelve Hawker Siddeley Buccaneer S2Bs. This ageing aircraft had been introduced into the RAF in 1969. It had been employed initially in the maritime strike role but was also capable of operating over land and in the event was to give a good account of itself. The Royal Navy and the Army also contributed helicopters, both for strike and reconnaissance.

The air attack, once launched, was awe-inspiring in its ferocity and effectiveness. Among the first to participate were the Tornado GR 1s, whose crews were given the highly dangerous task of putting Iraqi runways out of action with JP233 cluster bombs, in night attacks. Four Tornados were lost in four days, but eight Iraqi airfields were closed. Then they operated against Iraqi supply lines, storage dumps and hardened shelters, often working in combination with Buccaneer S2Bs. The Tornados used thermal imaging and laser guided bombs while the Buccaneers were fitted with laser designator pods which further directed these bombs to their targets. Three more Tornados were lost, one in an accident, but all the Buccaneers returned.

The Tornado GR 1As carried out reconnaissance at night from 18/19 January, each bringing back up to one hour's material for analysis. The first task given to them was the hunt for Iraqi Scud missiles, which were mobile and elusive. They were causing damage and casualties with random attacks against population centres in Israel. Several of these missiles and launchers were located and destroyed, after photo-interpreters of the Reconnaissance Intelligence Centre at Dhahran had examined the expanded imagery on large TV screens. The GR 1As

also carried out other pre- and post-attack reconnaissance, including searches for suitable infiltration routes to be used by Special Forces. Although they formed only part of the reconnaissance units within the Coalition Air Forces, these six aircraft flew on 125 sorties, most of which were classed as successful.

The three Nimrods employed their Searchwater radar to good effect, not only supplementing the information provided by E-3 Sentries of the USAF but largely replacing it. They provided picture images for the US aircraft carrier *Midway* and tactical directions for Lynx helicopters armed with Sea Skua missiles.

The Jaguars flew by day, concentrating at first on naval targets by using high velocity rockets. After sinking or damaging fifteen such vessels, they turned to Iraqi missile sites and artillery batteries along the Kuwaiti coast. These were mobile but moved only at night. Thus pods were fitted to the Jaguars for oblique photography during daylight. The aircraft operated in pairs, one carrying cameras of long focal length and the other with cameras of short focal length. After photo-interpretation, the targets were attacked on the same day, when American clusters bombs were dropped with devastating results. No Jaguars were lost throughout the entire war.

By the time the Coalition ground forces attacked, on 24 February, most of the aircraft of the Iraqi Air Force had been destroyed while some of the remainder had fled the country. The Iraqi Army then suffered enormous casualties as they retreated from Kuwait and fled towards Baghdad. After Iraq surrendered on 28 February, it was estimated that some 3,400 of her tanks had been destroyed, as well as 2,400 armoured personnel carriers, 2,000 artillery pieces, 25 warships or auxiliary vessels, with probably over 100,000 lives lost. The RAF contributed

Stanley Airport in the Falklands, which the Argentines had optimistically renamed Aeroporto Malvinas, photographed on 16 June 1982, two days after the Argentines capitulated. Fake bomb craters made from dirt had been placed on the runway, close to the genuine bomb craters, to deceive British photo-interpreters into believing that attacks made by Vulcan bombers from Ascension Island had scored direct hits on the airport's only runway. (*Aeroplane Monthly*)

The Panavia Tornado GR 1A is a version of the supersonic tactical strike aircraft which first entered operational service in January 1981. It carries infra-red scanners and can operate at a very low level, sweeping large areas and recording the results on a TV-type screen in the navigator's compartment. (British Aerospace)

The Boeing E-3D Sentry began service during 1991 with 8 Squadron at Waddington in Lincolnshire, replacing the venerable Shackleton Airborne Early Warning aircraft. The enormous rotadome antenna mounted on the Boeing 707 airframe is the most distinctive feature of this remarkable aircraft, which is capable of maritime reconnaissance as well as acting as a command post and detecting aircraft at all altitudes. This photograph shows serial ZH101, one of seven Sentries with which 8 Squadron was equipped in 1995 (British Aerospace)

A Hawker Siddeley Buccaneer, painted in 'desert sand', at RAF Lyneham in Wiltshire shortly after the end of the Gulf War. The 'Hello Sailor' motif was particularly suitable for maritime strike and reconnaissance, but the main role of the robust Buccaneer in the Gulf War was laser designation for bombs dropped by Tornados. (R.C. Nesbit)

The Canberra PR 9, fitted with two Rolls-Royce engines of 11,250-lb thrust, first entered service with 58 Squadron in January 1958 as the RAF's high-altitude photo-reconnaissance aircraft, capable of flying above the enemy fighters of that time. Some were still in service in 1995 with 39 (No 1 PRU) Squadron at Marham in Norfolk, such as serial XH168 shown here. (39 (No 1 PRU) Squadron)

The Hycon Type B camera, originally designed for the U-2 project, was fitted with a smaller magazine for use in Canberra photo-reconnaissance aircraft. The camera was built by the Hycon Corporation of California to a specification written by Dr Edwin Land, the inventor of the Polaroid camera. The lens, which has a focal length of only 36 inches, was designed by Dr James Baker and manufactured by new computer-driven techniques of grinding and polishing. A thin plastic film was devised by Eastman Kodak, allowing the U-2 to carry two rolls, each over 5,000 feet in length. About 4,000 paired negatives could be obtained from a single mission, each covering an area 6 miles square from an altitude of about 52,000 feet, in which objects as small as 30 inches across could be distinguished. The camera weighed about 500 lb and only some twenty-five were built. Known as the System 111B, it is at present in use by 39 (No 1 PRU) Squadron at Marham in Norfolk, which is engaged on survey work with Canberra PR 9s and PR 7s. This example is on display with the Imperial War Museum at Duxford in Cambridgeshire. (Chris Pocock)

When the Eurofighter EF2000 enters RAF squadron service, it will be fitted with wingtip pods containing electronic surveillance measures and electronic counter-measures. This Eurofighter serial ZH588 is one of three prototypes in existence in 1995. (British Aerospace)

A corner of the museum in the Joint School of Photography at RAF Cosford. The long black exhibit behind the glass case is a German FK3M, an infra-red camera with a 3-metre focal length used for recording British shipping in the English Channel during the Second World War. The white exhibit on the right is a Cintel Electronic Printer, which was used by the RAF for printing negatives of 9-inch by 9-inch, with controllable density correction. Models for planning the D-Day invasion of June 1944 can be seen top left. (Sergeant D. Jenkins RAF (Ret'd), courtesy RAF Cosford Museum)

to this decisive and awesome victory by flying the second largest number of missions of all the air forces in the Coalition Forces.

Soon after the Gulf War ended, 8 Squadron at Waddington in Lincolnshire became operational with the Boeing E–3D Sentry, the crews having trained initially at the Nato air base of Geilenkirchen in Germany. At present, this complex Airborne Early Warning aircraft is the most modern version of a machine which entered service with the USAF in the late 1970s. Capable of undertaking flights of up to twelve hours without refuelling, it is fitted with an enormous rotodome which tracks both airborne and maritime targets from a distance of hundreds of miles. It acts as a flying headquarters for Command, Control, Communications and Intelligence, and the RAF squadron forms part of any Nato rapid reaction force.

Since the Gulf War, the Russian communist system has collapsed and the Cold War is at an end. The RAF is pulling out of Germany and in course of contracting yet again. Reconnaissance and policing duties are still required over Iraq and the fragmented countries of the former Yugoslavia, although fortunately actual conflict is a rarity. Another area which has been reconnoitred extensively by the RAF is Northern Ireland, although no information on this subject has yet been released.

In early 1995, the tactical reconnaissance strength of the RAF consisted of 6, 41 and 54 Squadrons, equipped with Jaguar GR 1As and based at Coltishall in Norfolk, and 2 and 13 Squadrons, equipped with Tornado GR 1As and based at Marham in Norfolk. For maritime patrol, there are 120, 201 and 206 Squadrons, equipped with Nimrod MR 1s and based at Kinloss in Morayshire. Electronic intelligence is provided by the Nimrod R1s of 51 Squadron at Waddington in Lincolnshire, while 8 Squadron at the same

station is equipped with E–3D Sentries for airborne early warning. The names of two famous photo-reconnaissance units of the past have now been combined, forming 39 (No 1 PRU) Squadron at Marham. This squadron is equipped with Canberra PR 9s and PR 7s, and is engaged primarily on reconnaissance duties with the System 111B camera and survey work with Zeiss RMK 15/23 and RMK 30/23 cameras.

In 1995, the Joint Air Reconnaissance Intelligence Centre (UK) – JARIC (UK) – still continued its work at RAF Brampton. The Joint School of Photographic Interpretation (JSPI) is now based at RAF Wyton where it is sponsored by the Ministry of Defence but under the operational control of the Commandant of the Intelligence Centre at Ashford in Kent. Also in 1995, the Joint School of Photography (JSOP) at RAF Cosford celebrated the 80th year since it began its existence as an RFC unit at Farnborough.

The Association of RAF Photography Officers (ARAFPO), which was formed in December 1965, is run from RAF Brampton. Another association is the Medmenham Club, which was formed in July 1946 from wartime photo-interpreters and later became available to officers who passed the Long Photographic Interpretation course at the JSPI. A more recent association is the Boy Entrant Photographers' Association (BEPA), which was formed in 1987 for boys who trained pre-war at the RAF School of Photography when it was located at Farnborough. BEBA has now been succeeded by the RAFBEPA which was inaugurated in 2000 for all Boy Entrants and Craft Apprentices who trained at the RAF Schools of Photography.

The pace of technological advance in reconnaissance increases steadily. The introduction of the video tape in the system fitted to the Tornado GR 1A has removed the

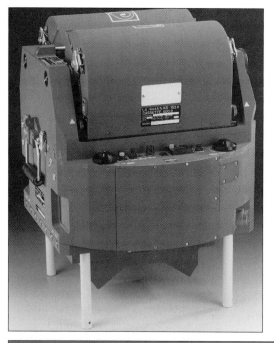

The Zeiss KS-153 camera is used by the RAF for low- to medium-altitude photo-reconnaissance at high speed. The Trilens version shown here has an assembly of three 80-mm lenses with an aperture range of f/2.56 to f/16 and a focal plane shutter giving speeds of up to 1/2,000th of a second. It utilises a single film of 240 mm width and up to 152 metres in length, giving a coverage of 143.5 degrees laterally and 48.5 degrees along the track, with three across-track images per frame. The camera has forward movement compensation and automatic exposure control, achieving results of remarkable clarity. (Carl Zeiss Ltd)

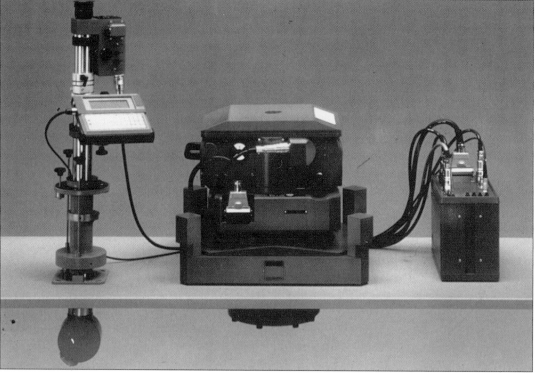

The Zeiss RMK A camera system and the newer RMK TOP camera system are similar in their application, being employed mainly for aerial survey. Both use interchangeable camera body/lens units which have lenses of different focal lengths and angular coverage. The cameras have rotating disc shutters giving a wide range of speeds and incorporate forward movement compensation and automatic exposure control. The film used is 240 mm wide and 150 metres long. This picture shows a typical camera with its magazine, peripheral control units and a navigation telescope. (Carl Zeiss Ltd)

processing which was required with 'wet' film. If circumstances permit, the navigator can pass back information on his screen by radio, as it appears. As a further refinement, the combination of a data-link with the system is now enabling interpreters on the ground to examine a copy of the tape as it appears, so that commanders can assess enemy territory and formations while the aircraft is in flight.

Another item of equipment which can be used for reconnaissance is TIALD (Thermal Imaging Airborne Laser Designator), although this pod was first fitted to Tornado GR1s in the Gulf War for the purpose of guiding bombs dropped at medium level by other aircraft. The pod contains an infra-red sensor, either for use at night or over targets with a strong thermal contrast against their backgrounds. It also includes a laser designator, a target tracker and a transceiver unit. When the target is acquired on the video display in the navigator's cockpit, the tracker

is locked on to it and guides the bomb. However, it has been found that the system is also admirable for the purpose of medium-level reconnaissance, giving the RAF a useful tool for surveillance over Iraq and other countries under the authority of Nato.

Yet another introduction takes the form of electro-optical sensors which replace film in conventional cameras, recording imagery on tape with a very high degree of resolution. Once again, these can be transmitted to the ground by data-link.

Technology is advancing to the point where enemy formations will be visible to RAF commanders in all weathers, by day and night, at all times. It is a far cry from the airsick observer in his spinning and buffeting balloon at the turn of the century, peering at the enemy through binoculars and dropping messages or reporting when back on the ground, but the essential principles and value of aerial reconnaissance remain the same.

BIBLIOGRAPHY

Place of publication given only if outside London.

Aart, Dick van der. *Aerial Espionage*. Shrewsbury, Airlife, 1984.

Ashworth, Chris. *RAF Coastal Command 1936–1969*. Sparkford, Patrick Stephens, 1992.

Association of Royal Air Force Photography Officers. *The History of Air Photography in the Royal Air Force* (5 Parts). Private printing, 1977–1982.

Barker, Ralph. *Aviator Extraordinary*. Chatto & Windus, 1969.

Brabazon of Tara, Lord. *The Brabazon Story*. Heinemann, 1956.

Braybrook, Roy. *Battle for the Falklands (3) Air Forces*. Osprey, 1982.

Brooks, Andrew J. *Photo Reconnaissance*. Ian Allan, 1975.

Burrows, William E. *Deep Black*. Bantam Press, 1988.

Campbell, Duncan. *The Unsinkable Aircraft Carrier*. Michael Joseph, 1984.

Cooke, Ronald C. and Nesbit, Roy Conyers. *Target: Hitler's Oil*. William Kimber, 1985.

Crickmore, Paul F. *Lockheed SR–71 Blackbird*. Osprey, 1986.

Deuel, Leo. *Flights into Yesterday*. MacDonald, 1969.

Falls, Cyril. *The First World War*. Longmans, 1960.

Foster, Peter R. *RAF Buccaneer*. Ian Allan, 1987.

Fox, Alan. *A Very Late Development*. University of Warwick, Industrial Relations Research Unit, 1990.

Halley, James J. *The Squadrons of the Royal Air Force & Commonwealth 1918–1988*. Tonbridge, Air Britain, 1988.

Hinsley, F.H. et al. *British Intelligence in the Second World War*. 6 volumes, HMSO, 1979–1990.

Jackson, Paul. *RAF Strike Command*. Ian Allan, 1984.

James, John. *The Paladins*. MacDonald, 1990.

Joint Air Reconnaissance Centre (UK). *A Short History*. RAF Brampton, private printing, 1971.

Jones, H.A. and Raleigh, Sir Walter. *The War in the Air*. 7 volumes, Oxford University Press, 1928.

Jones, R.V. *Most Secret War*. Hodder & Stoughton, 1978.

Kennedy, Colonel William V. *The Intelligence War*. Salamander, 1983.

Lee, Air Chief Marshal Sir David. *Eastward*. HMSO, 1984.

——. *Flight from the Middle East*. HMSO, 1980.

——. *Wings in the Sun*. HMSO, 1989.

Lewis, Peter. *British Aircraft 1809–1914*. Putnam, 1962.

Mead, Peter. *The Eye in the Air*. HMSO, 1983.

Middlebrook, Martin and Everitt, Chris. *The Bomber Command War Diaries*. Penguin, 1990.

Morse, Stan. *Gulf War Debrief*. Aerospace, 1991.

Pocock, Chris. *Dragon Lady*. Airlife, 1989.

Powys-Lybbe, Ursula. *The Eye of Intelligence*. William Kimber, 1983.

Price, Dr Alfred. *The Spitfire Story*. Jane's, 1982.

——. *Panavia Tornado*. Ian Allan, 1988.

Public Record Office (select references only):
AIR 14/4078 RAF Benson, Photo-Reconnaissance Convention 1950/1.
AIR 41/6 1945 Photo-Reconnaissance 1914–Apr 1941.
AIR 41/7 1948 Photo-Reconnaissance May 1941–May 1945.

Pyner, Alf. *Air Cameras RAF & USAAF, 1915–1945*. Burnham-on-Crouch, private printing, 1988.

Rawlings, John D.R. *Coastal Command and Special Squadrons of the RAF and their Aircraft*. Jane's, 1982.

——. *The History of the Royal Air Force*. Temple Press, 1984.

Richards, Denis and Saunders, Hilary St G. *Royal Air Force 1939–45*. 3 volumes, HMSO, 1954.

Ross, Tony, *75 Eventful Years*. Canterbury, Wingham Aviation Books, 1993.

Smith, Constance Babington. *Evidence in Camera*. Chatto & Windus, 1958.

Spooner, Tony. *Warburton's War*. William Kimber, 1987.

Stanley, Colonel Roy M. *World War II Photo Intelligence*. Sidgwick & Jackson, 1982.

Sturtivant, Ray. *The Squadrons of the Fleet Air Arm*. Tonbridge, Air-Britain, 1984.

Taylor, John W.R. *Combat Aircraft of the World*. Ebury Press and Michael Joseph, 1969.

Thetford, Owen. *Aircraft of the 1914–1918 War*. Harborough, 1954.

——. *Aircraft of the Royal Air Force since 1918*. Putnam, 1988.

Willis, Steve and Holliss, Barry. *Military Airfields in the British Isles 1939–1945*. Enthusiasts Publications, 1989.

APPENDIX I

SECOND WORLD WAR PHOTO-RECONNAISSANCE STRATEGIC UNITS AND SQUADRONS

NORTH-WEST EUROPE

HESTON FLIGHT
Heston   Sep 1939–Nov 1939

Lockheed 12A   Sep 1939–Nov 1939
Beechcraft   Sep 1939–Nov 1939
Blenheim IV   Sep 1939–Nov 1939
Spitfire PR I   Oct 1939–Nov 1939

Wg Cdr F.S. Cotton   Sep 1939–Nov 1939

On 1 November 1939 Heston Flight was renamed No 2 Camouflage Unit.

NO 2 CAMOUFLAGE UNIT
Heston   Nov 1939–Jan 1940

Lockheed 12A   Nov 1939–Jan 1940
Spitfire PR I   Nov 1939–Jan 1940
Blenheim IV   Nov 1939–Jan 1940

Wg Cdr F.S. Cotton   Nov 1939–Jan 1940

On 17 January 1940 No 2 Camouflage Unit was renamed the Photographic Development Unit.

SPECIAL SURVEY FLIGHT
 (DETACHED FROM NO 2 CAMOUFLAGE UNIT)
Lille/Seclin   Nov 1939–Nov 1939
Coulommiers   Nov 1939–Feb 1940

Spitfire PR I (various)   Nov 1939–Feb 1940

Wg Cdr F.S. Cotton   Nov 1939–Feb 1940

On 10 February 1940 the Special Survey Flight was renamed 212 Squadron.

212 SQUADRON
Coulommiers   Feb 1940–Jun 1940

Spitfire PRI (various)   Feb 1940–Jun 1940

Wg Cdr F.S. Cotton   Feb 1940–Jun 1940

On 18 June 1940, 212 Squadron was absorbed by the Photographic Development Unit.

PHOTOGRAPHIC DEVELOPMENT UNIT
Heston   Jan 1940–Jly 1940

Lockheed 12A   Jan 1940–Jun 1940
Spitfire PR I (various)   Jan 1940–Jly 1940
Hudson I   Feb 1940–Jly 1940
Blenheim IV   Jan 1940–Jly 1940

Wg Cdr F.S. Cotton   Jan 1940–Jun 1940
Wg Cdr G.W. Tuttle   Jun 1940–Jly 1940

On 8 July 1940 the Photographic Development Unit was renamed the Photographic Reconnaissance Unit.

PHOTOGRAPHIC RECONNAISSANCE UNIT
Heston   Jly 1940–Nov 1940

Spitfire PR I (various)   Jly 1940–Nov 1940
Blenheim IV   Jly 1940–Nov 1940
Hudson I   Jly 1940–Nov 1940

Wg Cdr G.W. Tuttle   Jly 1940–Nov 1940

On 16 November 1940 the Photographic Reconnaissance Unit was renamed No 1 Photographic Reconnaissance Unit.

NO 1 PHOTOGRAPHIC RECONNAISSANCE UNIT

Heston	Nov 1940–Dec 1940
Benson	Dec 1940–Oct 1942

Spitfire PR I (various)	Nov 1940–Oct 1942
Spitfire PR IV	Mar 1941–Oct 1942
Blenheim IV	Nov 1940–May 1941
Hudson I	Nov 1940–Dec 1940
Maryland I	Jun 1941–Oct 1942
Mosquito PR 1	Aug 1941–Oct 1942
Mosquito PR IV	Aug 1942–Oct 1942

Wg Cdr G.W. Tuttle	Jly 1940–Nov 1941
Wg Cdr J.A.C. Stratton	Nov 1941–Apl 1942
Wg Cdr S.L. Ring	Apl 1942–Oct 1942

On 19 October 1942 No 1 Photographic Reconnaissance Unit was disbanded and its parts formed into 540, 541, 542, 543 and 544 Squadrons.

540 SQUADRON

Leuchars	Oct 1942–Feb 1944
Benson	Feb 1944–Mar 1945
Coulommiers	Mar 1945–May 1945

Mosquito PR IV	Oct 1942–Sep 1943
Mosquito PR IX	Jun 1943–Dec 1944
Mosquito PR VI	Nov 1944–May 1945
Mosquito PR XVI	Jun 1944–May 1946

Wg Cdr M.J.B. Young	Oct 1942–May 1943
Wg Cdr Lord Douglas-Hamilton	May 1943–Mar 1944
Wg Cdr J.H.R. Merrifield	Mar 1944–Sep 1944
Wg Cdr A.H.W. Ball	Sep 1944–May 1945

541 SQUADRON

Benson	Oct 1942–May 1945

Spitfire PR IV/PR VII	Oct 1942–Nov 1943
Spitfire PR IX	Nov 1942–Dec 1943
Spitfire PR XI	Jan 1943–May 1945
Spitfire PR X	May 1944–Jan 1945
Mustang III	Jun 1944–May 1945
Spitfire PR XIX	Sep 1944–May 1945

Sqn Ldr D.W. Steventon	Oct 1942–Jly 1943
Sqn Ldr E.A. Fairhurst	Jly 1943–Nov 1943
Sqn Ldr J.H. Saffey	Nov 1943–Sep 1944
Sqn Ldr E.A. Fairhurst	Sep 1944–May 1945

542 SQUADRON

Benson	Oct 1942–May 1945

Spitfire PR IV/PR VI/PR VII	Oct 1942–Mar 1943
Spitfire PR IX	Feb 1943–Jly 1943
Spitfire PR XI	Feb 1943–May 1945
Spitfire PR X	Jun 1944–May 1945
Spitfire PR XIX	May 1944–May 1945

Sqn Ldr D. Salway	Oct 1942–Jun 1943
Sqn Ldr D.L. Lee	Jun 1943–Jly 1943
Sqn Ldr D.M. Furniss	Jly 1943–Dec 1943
Sqn Ldr D.B. Pearson	Dec 1943–Mar 1944
Sqn Ldr A.H.W. Ball	Mar 1944–Sep 1944
Sqn Ldr G.B. Singleton	Sep 1944–May 1945

543 SQUADRON

Benson	Oct 1942–Oct 1943

Spitfire PR IV/PR VII	Oct 1942–Oct 1943
Spitfire PR IX	Nov 1942–Oct 1943

Sqn Ldr A.E. Hill	Oct 1942–Oct 1942
Sqn Ldr G.E. Hughes	Oct 1942–Oct 1943

On 18 October 1943, 543 Squadron was disbanded.

544 SQUADRON

Benson	Oct 1942–May 1945

Wellington IV	Oct 1942–Apl 1943
Anson I	Oct 1942–Mar 1943
Spitfire PR IV	Oct 1942–Oct 1943
Maryland I	Dec 1942–Feb 1943
Mosquito PR IV	Mar 1943–Sep 1943
Spitfire PR XI	May 1943–Oct 1943
Mosquito PR IX	Sep 1943–Mar 1945
Mosquito PR XVI	Mar 1944–May 1945

Sqn Ldr W.R. Acott	Oct 1942–Jly 1943
Sqn Ldr J.P.H. Merrifield	Jly 1943–Oct 1943
Wg Cdr D.C.B. Walker	Oct 1943–Nov 1943
Wg Cdr D.W. Steventon	Nov 1943–May 1945

NO 3 PHOTOGRAPHIC RECONNAISSANCE UNIT

Oakington	Nov 1940–Aug 1941

Spitfire PR I	Nov 1940–Aug 1941
Wellington IC	Nov 1940–Aug 1941
Sqn Ldr P.B.B. Ogilvie	Nov 1940–May 1941
Sqn Ldr N.H.E. Messervy	May 1941–Aug 1941

On 21 August 1941 No 3 Photographic Reconnaissance Unit was disbanded.

MALTA, AFRICA AND ITALY

431 (GENERAL RECONNAISSANCE) FLIGHT

Luqa	Sep 1940–Jan 1941

Maryland I	Sep 1940–Jan 1941
Skua	Sep 1940–Dec 1940
Blenheim IV	Oct 1940–Nov 1940

Sqn Ldr E.A. Whiteley	Sep 1940–Jan 1941

On 10 January 1941, 431 (General Reconnaissance) Flight became 69 Squadron.

69 SQUADRON

Luqa	Jan 1941–Oct 1941
Takali	Oct 1941–Nov 1941
Luqa	Nov 1941–Feb 1944
Montecorvino	Feb 1944–Apl 1944

Maryland I/II	Jan 1941–Sep 1942
Hurricane I/II	Jan 1941–Feb 1942
Beaufort I	Aug 1941–Sep 1941
Blenheim IV	Sep 1941–Oct 1941
Mosquito PR I	Jan 1942–Mar 1943
Beaufighter IC	Jan 1941–Feb 1942
Spitfire PR IV	Mar 1942–Feb 1943
Baltimore I/II	Jun 1942–Apl 1943
Wellington VIII	Aug 1942–Feb 1943
Baltimore III/IV	Apl 1943–Apl 1944
Baltimore V	Jan 1944–Apl 1944

Sqn Ldr E.A. Whiteley	Jan 1941–Jun 1941
Sqn Ldr R.D. Welland	Jun 1941–Jly 1941
Sqn Ldr E. Tennant	Jly 1941–Sep 1941
Wg Cdr J.N. Dowland	Sep 1941–Jan 1942
Wg Cdr E. Tennant	Jan 1942–Jun 1942
Plt Off J. Foster	Jun 1942–Jly 1942
Plt Off R. Munro	Jly 1942–Aug 1942
Sqn Ldr/Wg Cdr A. Warburton	Aug 1942–Mar 1943
Wg Cdr R.C. Mackay	Mar 1943–May 1943
Wg Cdr T.M. Channon	May 1943–Apl 1944

On 8 February, B Flight 69 Squadron became 683 Squadron. On 2 April 1944 the remainder of 69 Squadron began moving to the UK.

683 SQUADRON

Luqa	Feb 1943–Nov 1943
El Aouina	Nov 1943–Dec 1943
San Severo	Dec 1943–Aug 1945

Spitfire PR IV	Feb 1943–Jly 1943
Spitfire PR XI	Apl 1943–Sep 1943
Mosquito PR IV/PR VI	May 1943–Jun 1943
Spitfire PR XIX	Sep 1944–Aug 1945

Wg Cdr A. Warburton	Feb 1943–Oct 1943
Sqn Ldr H.S. Smith	Oct 1943–Aug 1944
Sqn Ldr R.T. Turton	Aug 1944–Apl 1945
Sqn Ldr E.R. Pearson	Apl 1945–Aug 1945

INTELLIGENCE PHOTOGRAPHIC FLIGHT

Heliopolis	Jun 1940–Mar 1941

Hudson I	Jun 1940–Mar 1941
Hurricane I	Jan 1941–Mar 1941

Sqn Ldr H.C. Macphail	Jun 1940–Mar 1941

On 17 March 1941 the Intelligence Photographic Flight was renamed No 2 Photographic Reconnaissance Unit.

NO 2 PHOTOGRAPHIC RECONNAISSANCE UNIT

Heliopolis	Mar 1941–Nov 1942
LG 219	Nov 1942–Feb 1943

Hudson I	Mar 1941–Apl 1941
Hurricane I/II	Mar 1941–Feb 1943
Electra 10A	Apl 1941–Feb 1943
Beaufighter IC	Sep 1941–Feb 1943
Spitfire PR IV	Apl 1942–Feb 1943

Sqn Ldr H.C. Macphail	Mar 1941–Jun 1942
Sqn Ldr J.R. Whelan	Jun 1942–Feb 1943

On 1 February 1943 No 2 Photographic Reconnaissance Unit became 680 Squadron.

680 SQUADRON

LG 219	Feb 1943–Dec 1943
Matariva	Dec 1943–Aug 1944
San Severo	Aug 1944–Feb 1945
Deversoir	Feb 1945–May 1945
Beaufighter IC	Feb 1943–Feb 1943
Spitfire PR IV	Feb 1943–May 1944
Hurricane I/II	Feb 1943–May 1945
Spitfire PR IX	Feb 1943–May 1945
Spitfire PR XI	Aug 1943–May 1945
Baltimore IIIA/V	Feb 1944–May 1944
Blenheim IV	Feb 1944–Jly 1944
Mosquito IX/XVI	Feb 1944–May 1945
Wg Cdr J.R. Whelan	Feb 1943–Oct 1944
Wg Cdr J.C. Paish	Oct 1944–Mar 1945
Sqn Ldr P.A. Friend	Mar 1945–May 1945

NO 4 PHOTOGRAPHIC RECONNAISSANCE UNIT

Benson	Sep (1942–Sep 1942
(then en route to North Africa)	
Maison Blanche	Nov 1942–Feb 1943
Spitfire PR IV	Oct 1942–Feb 1943
Sqn Ldr A.H.W. Ball	Oct 1942–Feb 1943

On 1 February 1943 No 4 Photographic Reconnaissance Unit became 682 Squadron.

682 SQUADRON

Maison Blanche	Feb 1943–Jun 1943
La Marsa	Jun 1943–Dec 1943
San Severo	Dec 1943–Sep 1944
Peretola	Sep 1944–May 1945
Spitfire PR IV	Feb 1943–May 1944
Spitfire PR IX	Apl 1943–May 1945
Mosquito PR IV/PR VI	Apl 1943–Jly 1943
Spitfire PR XIX	Sep 1944–May 1945
Sqn Ldr A.H.W. Ball	Feb 1943–Jly 1943
Sqn Ldr J.T. Morgan	Jly 1943–Jly 1944
Sqn Ldr R.C. Buchanan	Jly 1944–Mar 1945
Sqn Ldr H.B. Oldfield	Mar 1945–May 1945

1437 (STRATEGIC RECONNAISSANCE) FLIGHT

Fuka	Nov 1941–Dec 1941
Tmimi	Dec 1941–Jan 1942
Wadi Natrun	Jan 1942–Apl 1942
Burg el Arab	Apl 1942–Nov 1942
Tmimi	Nov 1942–Dec 1942
Benina	Dec 1942–Dec 1942
Magrun	Dec 1942–Jan 1943
Marble Arch	Jan 1943–Jan 1943
Tamet	Jan 1943–Jan 1943
Darragh	Jan 1943–Feb 1943

1437 (STRATEGIC RECONNAISSANCE) FLIGHT (cont.)

Castel Verde	Feb 1943–Apl 1943
Senem	Apl 1943–May 1943
Monastir	May 1943–Jly 1943
Sorman West	Jly 1943–Jly 1943
Luqa	Jly 1943–Aug 1943
Francesco	Aug 1943–Oct 1943
Foggia	Oct 1943–Oct 1943
Maryland I	Nov 1941–Apl 1942
Baltimore I/II	Apl 1942–Jly 1943
Mustang A–36	Jly 1943–Oct 1943
Sqn Ldr S. Ault	Nov 1941–Jun 1943
Sqn Ldr S.G. Welshman	Jun 1943–Oct 1943

On 13 October 1943, 1437 (Strategic Reconnaissance) Flight was disbanded.

60 (SAAF) SQUADRON

Heliopolis	Jly 1941–Nov 1941
Fuka	Nov 1941–Dec 1941
Tmini	Dec 1941–Jan 1942
Heliopolis	Jan 1942–Jly 1942
Beirut	Jly 1942–Aug 1942
Abbassia	Aug 1942–Aug 1942
LG 100	Aug 1942–Sep 1942
LG 201	Sep 1942–Nov 1942
Tmini	Nov 1942–Dec 1942
Benina	Dec 1942–Jan 1943
Marble Arch	Jan 1943–Jan 1943
Darragh	Jan 1943–Feb 1943
Castel Benito	Feb 1943–Mar 1943
Senem	Mar 1943–Apl 1943
El Djem North	Apl 1943–Apl 1943
Monastir	Apl 1943–May 1943
Sorman	May 1943–Jly 1943
Sabratha	Jly 1943–Sep 1943
Ariana	Sep 1943–Nov 1943
El Aouina	Nov 1943–Dec 1943
San Severo	Dec 1943–May 1945
Maryland I/II	Aug 1941–Jun 1943
Baltimore II	Oct 1942–Jun 1943
Baltimore III	Oct 1942–Aug 1943
Mosquito PR IV	Feb 1943–Oct 1943
Mosquito PR VI	Jly 1943–Dec 1943
Mosquito PR IX	Jly 1943–Sep 1944
Mosquito PR XVI	Feb 1944–May 1945
Maj S.B.F. Scott	Jly 1941–Oct 1941
Maj E.U. Brierley	Oct 1941–Jun 1942
Maj O.G. Davis	Jun 1942–Jly 1943
Maj E.U. Brierley	Jly 1943–Apl 1944
Maj O.G. Davies	Apl 1944–Aug 1944
Maj D.W. Allan	Aug 1944–Jan 1945
Maj P.P. Daphne	Jan 1945–May 1945

200 SQUADRON (PR FLIGHT)
Jeswang (Gambia)   Dec 1941–Mar 1943

Hudson III   Dec 1941–Mar 1943
Maryland I   Jan 1942–Mar 1942

Wg Cdr B.O. Dias   Mar 1942–Sep 1942
Wg Cdr W.H. Ingle   Sep 1942–Mar 1943

128 SQUADRON (PR DETACHMENTS AT JESWANG)
Hastings (Sierra Leone)   Oct 1941–Mar 1943

Hurricane IIB   Oct 1941–Mar 1943
Spitfire PR IV   Oct 1942–Dec 1942

Sqn Ldr B. Drake   Oct 1941–Mar 1942
Sqn Ldr J.I. Kilmartin   Mar 1942–Aug 1942
Sqn Ldr H.A.B. Russell Aug 1942–Mar 1943

On 8 March 1943, 128 Squadron was disbanded.

INDIA AND SOUTH EAST ASIA

NO 4 PHOTOGRAPHIC RECONNAISSANCE UNIT
Seletar   Nov 1941–Feb 1942

Beaufort   Nov 1941–Nov 1941
Buffalo   Nov 1941–Feb 1942

Sqn Ldr C.G.R. Lewis   Nov 1941–Feb 1942

On 15 February 1942 No 4 Photographic Reconnaissance Unit was disbanded.

NO 3 PHOTOGRAPHIC RECONNAISSANCE UNIT
(AT FIRST NAMED NO 5 PRU)
Dum-Dum   Apl 1942–May 1942
Pandaveswar   May 1942–Jun 1942
Dum-Dum   Jun 1942–Jan 1943

B–25C Mitchell   Apl 1942–Jan 1943
Hurricane IIA/IIB/IIC May 1942–Jan 1943
Spitfire PR IV   Oct 1942–Jan 1943

Sqn Ldr A.C. Pearson Apl 1942–May 1942
Wg Cdr S.G. Wise   May 1942–Jan 1943

On 25 January 1943 No 3 Photographic Reconnaissance Unit was renamed 681 Squadron.

681 SQUADRON
Dum-Dum   Jan 1943–Dec 1943
Chandina   Dec 1943–Jan 1944
Dum-Dum   Jan 1944–May 1944
Alipore   May 1944–May 1945
Mingaladon   May 1945–Aug 1945

B–25C Mitchell   Jan 1943–Sep 1943
Hurricane IIB   Jan 1943–Nov 1943
Spitfire PR IV   Aug 1943–Dec 1944
Spitfire PR XI   Oct 1943–Aug 1945
Mosquito PR VI/PR IX Aug 1943–Sep 1943
Spitfire PR 19   Aug 1945–Aug 1945

681 SQUADRON (cont.)
Wg Cdr S.G. Wise   Jan 1943–Dec 1943
Wg Cdr F.D. Procter   Dec 1943–Apl 1945
Wg Cdr D.B. Pearson Apl 1945–Aug 1945

On 29 September 1943 the twin-engined aircraft of 681 Squadron were transferred to the newly formed 684 Squadron, together with their crews.

684 SQUADRON
Dum-Dum   Sep 1943–Dec 1943
Comilla   Dec 1943–Jan 1944
Dum-Dum   Jan 1944–Apl 1944
Alipore   Apl 1944–Aug 1945

Mitchell B–25C   Sep 1943–Aug 1945
Mosquito PR II   Sep 1943–May 1945
Mosquito PR VI   Sep 1943–May 1945
Mosquito PR IX   Sep 1943–May 1945
Mosquito PR XVI   Feb 1944–Aug 1945
Beaufighter VI/X   Aug 1945–Aug 1945
Mosquito PR 34   Jly 1945–Aug 1945

Sqn Ldr B.S. Jones   Sep 1943–Dec 1943
Wg Cdr W.B. Murray Dec 1943–Nov 1944
Wg Cdr W.E.M. Lowry Nov 1943–Aug 1945

160 SQUADRON (CEYLON)
Ratmalana   Feb 1943–Aug 1943
Sigiriya   Aug 1943–Aug 1944
Kankesanturai   Aug 1944–Feb 1945
Minneriya   Feb 1945–Aug 1945

Liberator III/IIIA   Feb 1943–Jun 1945
Liberator V   Jun 1943–Aug 1945
Liberator VI   Jun 1944–Nov 1944

Wg Cdr C.A. Butler   Feb 1943–Jan 1944
Wg Cdr G.R. Brady   Jan 1944–Nov 1944
Wg Cdr J.N. Stacey   Nov 1944–May 1945
Wg Cdr G. McKenzie May 1945–Aug 1945

APPENDIX II

ADRIAN WARBURTON

Since the first edition of this book was written, the mystery of Adrian Warburton's disappearance has been solved.

Although the targets he was scheduled to photograph on 12 April 1944 were not listed in American records, there was information about another pilot on the operation. He was Captain Carl Chapman, who was very experienced with Lockheed F-5s. His machine was F-5B serial 42–68205 and his mission over southern Germany was No. BB21, to photograph the airfields of Erding, Landau-Ganacker, Regensburg-Obertraubling (where the new Me262 jet fighter was being produced), Schwäbisch-Hall and Straubing. Both F-5s were to be escorted by eight P-51 Mustangs of the 357th Fighter Group, although in the event only two of these managed to make contact.

The two F-5s flew in company before splitting up for their separate targets. Chapman carried out his photography and headed for a position where he was scheduled to rendezvous with Warburton and then fly on to Alghero in Sardinia. He circled for a while, calling on the R/T, but when Warburton did not show up flew on to Sardinia. Later in the same day, he flew back to Mount Farm on mission No. BB23, photographing French airfields.

On 19 August 2002 a German archaeologist in the Landsberg district of southern Germany, Dr Anton Huber, began to excavate a site in a field south-east of Egling on the river Paar, where an Allied aircraft was known to have crashed at about 1145 hours local time on 12 April 1944. His action was based mainly on researches carried out by the German air historian Hans Grimminger, who had used a process of elimination to conclude that the aircraft in the crash site must be the machine flown by Adrian Warburton.

Witnesses, who were boys at the time, stated that the aircraft came from the direction of Lechfeld airfield, flying low and trailing smoke, while there were bursts of flak in the air. Lechfeld was where four Me262 jet fighters were being tested. The aircraft flipped over on its back and dived into soft earth, causing a fairly shallow crater. The Wehrmacht found the wreck but most of the parts on the surface were pushed into the crater. Some of this wreckage, including a wing and one of the engines, was cleared in 1951/1952 during land consolidation work.

Dr Huber located the exact site with the help of a field map and air photography provided by the US Army. He recovered an Allison V-1710 engine from the port wing; this was number AF 42–9475 and a plate indicated that it was installed in an F-5 Lightning. There was a propeller apparently grazed by two bullets. A length of film, burnt at both ends, was about 10 inches wide; the standard American K-17 camera had a 9 x 9 inch exposure format. There was also a fragment from a sleeveless pullover. It all seemed to fit the last flight of Adrian

Warburton, provided there was no confusion over dates. Lechfeld was attacked on 13 April 1944 by almost a hundred B-24 Liberators of the 2nd Bombardment Division, escorted by fighters, and there were losses on that occasion.

Human and other remains found by Dr Huber were handed to the police at Fürstenfeldbruck and examined by the US expert in the area, David Roath. His researches confirmed that the wreckage was indeed the F-5B flown by Adrian Warburton. The Personnel Management Agency at RAF Innsworth, which is the official body handling such matters in Britain, has confirmed to this author that the human remains are those of Adrian Warburton and that there will be a military funeral.

A distant photograph of Lockheed F-5B serial 42–68205 flown by Wing Commander Adrian Warburton from Mount Farm in Oxfordshire, still smouldering after crashing on 12 April 1944 in a field near Egling in Southern Germany, under guard by a soldier of the Wehrmacht. (Central News South)

A scrap of camera film, about 10 inches wide, which was found partially folded within the wreckage. (Richard Chapman)

Parts of the wreckage recovered at Egling – port propeller, crankshaft, pistons and other components. (Richard Chapman)

Press reporters and witnesses of the crash looking at the first components excavated from the crater in August 2002. (Richard Chapman)

INDEX

All page references are given in italic to avoid confusion with, for example, squadron numbers. Illustrations are not listed.

Aachen, *87*
Adadan, *58, 271*
'ABC', *188*
Aberdare Mnts, *272*
Abu Sueir, *271*
Acott, W.T., *146*
Aden, *66, 76, 127, 274, 276, 279*
Adenauer, K., *258*
Aerofilms Ltd, *93*
Aeronautical Research & Sales Corp., *72*
Afrikanda, *124, 182*
Airborne Early Warning, *298, 304, 319*
Aircraft
  Anson, *132, 146, 241, 271, 274, 288*
  Army No 1, *8*
  Auster, *272, 276, 285, 288, 291*
  Avro 504, *14*
  BAE 125, *311*
  Baltimore, *136, 142, 164*
  Barracuda, *182, 314*
  Battle, *97, 99*
  BE2, *10, 14, 18, 35, 48*
  BE8, *14*
  BE12, *48*
  Beaufighter, *135, 136, 221, 286*
  Beaufort, *114, 128, 142, 214*
  Beechcraft, *79, 84*
  Belvedere, *292*
  Blenheim, *63, 76, 79, 80, 84, 93, 96, 97, 135, 217, 218*
  Blériot Experimental, *30*
  Blériot XI, *16*
  Blériot XI–2, *13*
  Blériot XII, *14*
  Boeing KC–29, *254*
  Boeing RB47, *254*
  Bombay, *99*
  Boston, *135*
  Bristol Fighter, *58*
  Bristol Scout, *53*
  Buccaneer, *314*
  Buffalo, *214, 217, 218, 236*
  Canberra bomber, *263, 273*
  Canberra PR 3, *257*
  Canberra PR 7, *257, 263, 272, 273, 276, 292, 298, 319*
  Canberra PR 9, *279, 280, 281, 295, 319*
  Catalina, *118, 120, 126, 214*
  Chinook, *276*
  Chipmunk, *276*
  Comet, *263, 295, 298*
  Dakota, *221, 285, 286*

DH2, *35*
DH9, *58*
'Dinah', *214, 231*
Do17, *238*
Do18, *96*
Dragonfly, *291*
E-type, *30*
Fairey IIIF, *58*
Farman Experimental, *30*
Farman, Henri, *13*
Farman, Maurice, *18*
Farman 'Shorthorn', *13*
FE2, *35*
Fiat CR42, *132*
Flying Fortress, *140, 156, 164, 170, 188, 200*
Flyer, *8*
FW189, *238*
FW190, *166*
Gazelle, *304, 307*
Gladiator, *127*
Gotha, *43*
Halifax, *188, 200, 203*
Hampden, *126*
Harrier, *298, 307*
Harvard, *272*
Hastings, *263, 273*
He111, *197*
Henschel, *126, 238*
Hercules, *301, 304, 311*
Hudson, *94, 97, 99, 111, 120, 127, 132, 140, 142, 214, 217*
Hunter, *273*
Hurricane, *63, 94, 127, 132, 135, 136, 140, 142, 214, 217, 218, 221, 222, 226, 231, 236*
Jaguar, *301, 314, 319*
Ju86 P2, *111*
Ju87, *173*
Lancaster, *149, 188, 200, 203, 210, 241, 267, 268, 271*
Liberator, *153, 200, 226, 231*
Lincoln, *257, 272, 274*
Lockheed F–4, *145, 153*
Lockheed F–5, *153, 173, 174, 231*
Lockheed 10A, *132*
Lockheed 12A, *72, 76, 84, 87, 97, 127*
Lockheed U–2, *258, 263, 311*
Lovochkin LA–11, *249*
Lynx, *304, 314*
Lysander, *80, 97, 132, 218, 226*
Maryland, *96, 120, 127–9, 132, 135, 136, 140, 142*

Me109, *80, 96, 145*
Me163, *156*
Me262, *197*
Meteor, *249, 263, 271–4, 291*
MiG, *124*
MiG–15, *254, 274*
MiG–17, *258*
Mirage, *307*
Mitchell, *221, 222, 226, 227*
Mosquito PR 1, *118, 120, 122, 126, 135*
Mosquito PR IV, *114, 142, 146, 149, 164, 166, 170, 227*
Mosquito PR IX, *145, 166, 170, 174, 179, 186, 191, 227*
Mosquito PR XVI, *179, 186, 191, 227, 267*
Mosquito PR 34, *237, 241, 244, 249, 267, 268, 282, 285, 292*
Mustang, *153, 166, 186, 191, 195, 236*
Neptune, *263*
Nieuport Scout, *35*
Nieuport, *17, 66*
Nimrod, *263, 280, 281, 295, 298, 311, 314, 319*
Pembroke, *274*
Phantom, *298, 301, 307*
Pioneer, *276, 291*
Privateer, *249*
Puma, *311*
Puss Moth, *221*
RB–45C Tornado, *249, 254, 257*
Reconnaissance Experimental, *30*
Republic F–84F, *273*
Scapa, *66*
Scouting Experimental, *30*
SE5A, *35, 53*
Sea Harrier, *301, 307*
Sea King, *304, 307*
Sentry, *298, 304, 314, 319*
Shackleton, *263, 272, 274, 279, 280, 292, 294*
Spad, *53*
Spitfire I, *63, 79, 97*
Spitfire FR 18, *285*
Spitfire PR IA, *87, 93, 94, 108*
Spitfire PR IB, *93, 94, 108*
Spitfire PR IC, *97, 108, 118*
Spitfire PR ID, *114, 118, 122, 124, 126*
Spitfire PR IE, *108*
Spitfire PR IF, *108*

Spitfire PR IG, *111, 118*
Spitfire PR IV, *136, 140, 142, 145, 146, 149, 156, 164, 166, 182, 226*
Spitfire PR IX, *170, 174, 191*
Spitfire PR XI, *149, 164, 166, 176, 179, 186, 191, 227, 237*
Spitfire PR XIX, *179, 241, 244, 267, 282, 285*
Spitfire VB, *166*
Spitfire VC, *167*
Spitfire XVIIIE, *267, 268*
Stirling, *63, 188, 200, 203*
Stratojet, *254*
Sunderland, *128, 129, 132, 263, 291*
Super Electra, *14, 94*
Super Etendard, *307*
Superfortress, *249*
Swordfish, *118, 128, 129*
Sycamore, *263, 272, 273, 291*
Tabloid, *14*
Tempest, *268*
Thunderbolt, *156*
Tornado GR1, *295, 311, 314, 319, 321*
Typhoon, *186, 195*
Valetta, *273*
Valiant, *273, 295*
Vampire, *271, 291*
VC10, *311*
Venom, *273, 274, 291*
Victor, *295, 307, 311*
Vildebeest, *214, 217*
Vincent, *66*
Vulcan, *279, 280, 295, 304*
Warhawk, *218, 221, 231, 236*
Warwick, *268*
Washington, *249*
Wasp, *304*
Wellesley, *96*
Wellington, *142, 146, 191, 198, 203*
Wessex, *294, 298, 304*
Westland Scout, *304, 307*
Whirlwind, *274, 280, 292, 298*
Yak, *124*
Aircraft Operating Co., *93, 104*
Air Forces
ALLIED:
    Allied Central Interpretation Unit, *182, 238*
    Joint PR Committee, *182*
    Mediterranean Air Command, *145, 164, 170, 173*
    Mediterranean Allied Air Force, *173, 267*
    Mediterranean Allied PR Wing, *173, 174, 176*
    North African Central Interpretation Unit, *145, 164*
    North African PR Wing, *145, 164, 166, 167, 173*

North African Tactical Air Force, *166, 170*
Northwest African Air Force, *145*
Second Tactical Air Force, *153, 160, 191, 192, 195, 238, 241*
No 106 (PR) Group, *179*
No 171 (PR) Force, *231, 236, 237*
RAF:
    AI 1(H) Photo-Interpretation, *80*
    British Air Force of Occupation, *241, 244, 254*
    Central Gunnery School, *257*
    Central Photo Establishment, *238, 244*
    Central Reconnaissance Establishment, *263, 265*
    Coastal Area, *54*
    Eastern Air Command, *145, 164*
    Far East Air Force, *286, 291, 292*
    Independent Bombing Force, *43, 54*
    Joint Air Photo-Interpretation Centre, *238, 244, 263*
    Joint Air Reconnaissance Intelligence Centre, *263, 265, 319*
    Joint School of Photography, *90 footnote, 301, 319*
    Joint School of Photo-Interpretation, *263*
    Middle East Command, *276*
    Mobile Field Photo Section, *164, 167, 174, 176, 192, 195, 197*
    Mobile Reconnaissance Intelligence Centre, *301*
    Near East Command, *276*
    Northern Area, *54*
    RAF Germany, *263*
    RAF Mediterranean and Middle East, *267*
    Rhodesian Air Training Group, *272*
    School of Photography, *54, 63, 66, 84, 238, 244, 263*
    Second Tactical Air Force, *254, 263*
    Southern Area, *54*
    Western Air Command, *142, 145*
Groups:
    No 1, *265, 295*; No 3, *114, 145, 203, 244*; No 5, *213*; No 8, *206, 298, 319*; No 11, *84, 298*; No 16, *104*; No 18, *265, 295, 298*; No 46, *301*; No 83, *191, 193*; No 84, *58, 191, 192, 281*; No 90, *249, 265*; No 100, *249*;
    No 106, *179, 182, 238*; No 221, *221*
Wings:
    Construction, *191*; No 34, *153, 191, 192, 195, 197, 285*; No 35, *191, 192, 195, 197*; No 39 (RCAF), *191, 192, 195*; No 106, *153*; No 171, *227, 231*; No 285, *136, 164, 166, 167, 170, 176, 294*; No 336, *170,*

173, 174, 176; No 347, *237*; No 904, *285*
Squadrons:
    No 1, *307*; No 1 (India), *226, 231*; No 2, *191, 244, 249, 319*; No 4, *191*; No 6, *319*; No 6 (India), *231*; No 7 (India), *236*; No 8, *66, 319*; No 9, *311*; No 13, *267, 268, 271–4, 276, 280, 281, 292*; No 16, *153, 191*; No 17, *218, 263, 298*; No 18, *307*; No 20, *226*; No 22, *114, 128*; No 26, *292*;
    No 27, *295*; No 28, *226, 231*; No 29, *307*; No 31, *263, 298*; No 36, *214*;
    No 37, *267, 268, 271, 272, 274, 279, 280*; No 38, *267, 268, 271, 272, 276, 280*; No 39, *142, 276, 280, 319*; No 40 (SAAF), *136, 166, 167*; No 41, *319*;
    No 42, *304*; No 44, *307*; No 47, *58*; No 51, *263, 295, 319*; No 54, *319*; No 58, *241, 273, 274, 276, 279*; No 60, *58, 218*; No 60 (SAAF), *132, 136, 142, 145, 164, 166, 170, 173, 176*; No 67, *218*; No 69, *132, 142, 145, 169, 191, 263, 276*; No 72, *226*; No 80, *263, 298*; No 81, *285, 288, 291, 292, 294*; No 82, *241*; No 83, *191, 210*; No 84, *58*; No 88, *288, 291*; No 90, *188*; No 95, *128, 140*; No 100, *214*; No 101, *188, 254, 307*; No 103, *292*; No 110, *236, 292*; No 114, *276*; No 120, *304, 319*; No 128, *140*;
    No 138, *188*; No 139, *210*; No 140, *118, 146, 153, 186, 191*; No 144, *122, 124*; No 149, *188*; No 160, *226, 231*; No 168, *191*; No 192, *249, 263*;
    No 194, *291*; No 199, *188*; No 200, *140*; No 201, *304, 319*; No 202, *66, 127*; No 203, *280, 281*; No 204, *140*;
    No 205, *291, 292, 294*; No 206, *304, 319*; No 208, *58, 132, 136, 267, 268, 271–4*; No 209, *118, 288, 291*; No 210, *122, 124, 280*; No 212, *93, 94, 97*; No 213, *268*; No 214, *188*; No 218, *188*; No 223, *135*; No 224, *96*; No 225, *170, 292*; No 227, *142*; No 230, *276*; No 248, *221*; No 267, *291*; No 268, *191*; No 269, *120*; No 284, *274*; No 333 (Norwegian), *160*; No 400 (RCAF), *191*; No 414 (RCAF), *191*; No 430 (RCAF), *191*; No 455 (RAAF), *122, 124*; No 540, *146, 153, 156, 179, 241, 244, 257, 263*; No 541, *146, 149, 153, 156, 179, 241, 263*; No 542, *146, 149, 153, 179, 241, 257, 263*; No 543,*

146, 153, 156, 160, 179, 263, 295;
No 644, 146, 149, 153, 179, 197,
241; No 617, 149, 188, 197; No
621, 268; No 656, 285;
No 680, 145, 164, 170, 173; No
681, 226, 227, 236, 237, 282, 285;
No 682, 145, 164, 170, 173, 174,
176, 267; No 683, 145, 164, 170,
173, 176, 267, 268, 271; No 684,
227, 231, 236, 237, 282, 285
Flights:
Air Survey, 58; Heston, 84, 87, 94;
Intelligence Photographic, 127;
Special Survey, 87, 93; No 431, 128,
132;
No 1416, 118; No 1417, 271, 274;
No 1426, 274; No 1437, 136, 166,
167
Units:
Central Interpretation, 111, 120, 140,
153, 182, 186, 241; Far Eastern
Photo Intelligence, 221; Mobile Photo
Printing, 90, 97; Middle East Central
Interpretation, 136; Photo
Development, 93, 94, 99, 104; Photo
Interpretation, 104, 107, 111; Photo
Reconnaissance, 104; No 2
Camouflage, 87, 93; No 8
Operational Training, 146; No 1
Photo Reconnaissance, 114, 118,
120, 126, 129, 146, 156, 221; No 2
Photo Reconnaissance, 114, 127,
129, 132, 135, 136, 145, 221; No 3
Photo Reconnaissance, 114, 118,
221, 226; No 4 Photo
Reconnaissance, 145, 214; No 5
Photo Reconnaissance, 221
RFC:
Central Flying School, 10
School of Photography, 35, 40
Wings:
First, 22, 26; Second, 22; Third,
22; Fifth, 52
Squadrons:
No 1, 11; No 2, 14, 22, 26; No 3,
13, 14, 16, 18, 22, 26; No 4, 14,
22;
No 5, 14, 22; No 6, 22, 27; No 9,
18, 22; No 29, 66
FRENCH:
1ère Escadrille, 174
Groupe de Reconnaissance 2/33,
170, 174
USAAF/USAF:
Strategic Air Command, 244, 254
Western Air Command, 145
Wings:
90th, 170, 176; 325th, 173, 179
Groups:
3rd, 142, 164, 170, 174, 176; 5th,
170, 174, 176; 7th, 153, 179; 8th,

231; 10th 186; 25th, 179, 186;
67th, 186; 91st, 249
Squadrons:
1st Weather Reconnaissance, 258;
5th, 164; 12th, 164; 13th, 153;
14th, 153; 15th, 164; 23rd, 174;
72nd, 249; 111th, 166; 803rd,
188
Air India Survey & Transport Co., 218
Airships
Beta, 10
'Blimp', 10
Delta, 10
Gamma, 10
Nulli Secundus, 8
Zeppelin, 10
Air to Surface Vessel, 263
Air Transportable Recce Exploitation
Lab, 301
Akrotiri, 272, 273, 276, 280, 281
Akyab, 221, 226, 236
Aldershot, 8
Alexandria, 128, 136
Alghero, 174
Algiers, 145, 170
Alipore, 231, 236, 285
Altazimeter, 107
Altenfjord, 122, 124, 160, 182
American Volunteer Group, 218
American Armament Corp., 66, 72
Amiens, 195
Anacosta, 153
Andaman Islands, 222, 226
Anglo-Persian Oil Co., 58
Antwerp/Deurne, 195
Archangel, 122
Archbald, J.E., 140
Ariana, 170
Army Aircraft Factory, 10
Army units (British and American)
American 1st Army, 191
American 5th Army, 173, 176
British 1st Airborne Division, 120
British 2nd Army, 191, 192
British 8th Army, 136, 145, 167, 173,
176
British 14th Army, 231, 236
British Air Battalion, 10, 11
British Army Air Corps, 276
Canadian 1st Army, 192, 195, 197
Canadian 1st Division, 27
Coldstream Guards, 10
Grenadier Guards, 8
Hon Artillery Co., 1
King's African Rifles, 272
Lincolnshire Reg., 35
School of Ballooning, 4, 8
School of Military Eng., 4
Trucial Oman Levies, 271
Arras, 43, 90, 93
Ascension Island, 304, 307

Ashford, 319
Asmara, 76
Assab, 127
Assn of RAF Photo Officers, 319
Aswan High Dam, 273
Atbara, 76
Attlee, C., 254
Auderville, 120
Augsburg, 197
Augusta, 76

Baghdad, 53, 96
Baghdad Pact, 272, 276
Bahrein, 274, 279
Baines, C.E., 128
Baku, 96, 97, 111, 127
Ball, A.H.W., 145, 164, 170
Balloon Factory, 10
Balloons
Drachen, 30
Kite, 40
Le Géant, 4
Pioneer, 4
Ballykelly, 280
Bangkok, 218, 227, 291
Barber, B.K., 176
Barksdale, 254
Barrackpore, 222
Barratt, A.S., 93
Basingstoke, 11
Bastia-Borgo, 174
Bathurst, 140
Batum, 96, 97, 111, 127
Bayley, K.H., 122
BBC Timewatch, 249
Beamish, C.E. St J., 237
Beaumont, Capt, 4
Bear Island, 122
Beira, 280
Belleroy, 195
Benghazi, 128, 132
Bennett, D.C.T., 203, 208, 210
Benson, 111, 114, 118, 120, 122, 140,
142, 145, 146, 182, 186, 237,
241, 244, 249
Beny-sur-Mer, 192, 195
Bergen, 118, 120
Berlin, 76, 210, 213, 244, 254
Bernice, 76
Bissett, LAC, 96
Bizerta, 166
Black, J.W., 4
Black Forest, 72
Blackburn, R., 8
Blackpool, 238
Blake, G., 1
Blanchard, J-P., 1
Bleaaw, J.P., 166
Blériot, L., 8, 11
Bletchley Park, 107, 135
Bödö, 263

Boisney, *195*
Boothman, J.N., *182*
Bordeaux, *99, 120*
Boston, *4*
Boulogne, *97, 108, 188*
Boy Entrant Photographers' Assn, *319*
Braithwaite, J.D., *221*
Brampton, *263, 319*
Brawdy, *307*
Brest, *114, 122*
Briggs, D.A., *118*
Brindisi, *128*
British Bombing Survey Unit, *238*
Broome, C.G., *111*
Brown, A.M., *132*
Brown, F.D.C., *227*
Brown, H.C. Jr, *153*
Bruchsal, *72*
Brüggen, *298*
Bruneval, *120*
Brussels, *195*
Buraimi Oasis, *271*
Burke, C.J., *22*
Burma–Siam Rly, *222*
Burton, F.E., *96, 97, 111*
Butcher, LAC, *94*
Butt, D.M.B., *198*
Buxton, G.J., *127, 135*

Caen, *188*
Cairo, *76, 127, 136, 267*
Calais, *8, 156, 186*
Calcutta, *218, 222*
Calvados Bay, *186*
Cambrai, *43*
Cameras
  A-type, *26, 35*
  B-type, *35*
  C-type, *35*
  E-type, *35*
  Eyemo, *213*
  F8, *58, 114, 226*
  F24, *58, 66, 72, 80, 84, 87, 93, 97, 108, 111, 114, 120, 129, 132, 135, 140, 149, 153, 191, 198, 206, 208, 222*
  F49, *241*
  F52, *120, 136, 166, 186, 257*
  F89, *289*
  F95, *257*
  F96, *295*
  F97, *206*
  F117, *265*
  F126, *301*
  F135, *298*
  G45, *149, 195*
  Hycon-B, *258*
  Kodak Bantam, *213*
  K–17, *145, 153*
  K–19, *191*
  L-type, *42*
  LB-type, *42*

  Leica, *76, 210*
  'Master and Slave', *206, 208*
  Pan Ross, *11*
  P7, *58*
  System 111B, *319*
  Watson Air, *11, 13*
  WA-type, *35*
  Zeiss RMK, *319*
Camotint, *72, 79, 111*
Campbell, C.D.M., *22, 26, 35*
Campbell, K., *118*
Canary Islands, *140*
Cap d'Antifer, *120, 186*
Cap Fréhel, *186*
Cape Verde Islands, *140*
Carter, R.H., *140*
Casablanca, *145*
Caserta, *267*
Castel Benito, *72*
Catania, *76, 166*
Catcheside, B.R., *140*
Cavendish, H., *1*
Cayley, G., *4*
Cento, *276, 280*
Challerton, *87*
Chandina, *227*
Changi, *285, 286, 292, 294*
Channon, T.M., *164*
Cherbourg, *97, 120, 160, 186*
Cherwell, Lord, *198*
Chiengmai, *218, 222*
China Bay, *231*
Chittagong, *227*
Churchill, W., *93, 100, 114, 145, 164, 198, 244, 254, 257*
Coalition Force, *311*
Cochrane, R., *254*
Cockfosters, *111*
Cocos Islands, *237, 282, 285*
Cody, S.F., *8, 10*
Cologne, *200*
Colombo, *218*
Coltishall, *319*
Colvin, H., *135*
Comilla, *227*
Comiso, *76*
Compiègne, *16*
Coningsby, *307*
Convoy PQ17, *122*
Convoy PQ18, *122, 124, 126*
Copenhagen, *76*
Corbishley, P., *118*
Corfu, *164*
Cos, *76, 173*
Cosford, *90 footnote, 263*
Cottam, G.V., *124*
Cotton, F.S., *66, 72, 76, 79, 84, 87, 90, 97, 99, 100, 104, 114, 127, 146*
Cotton, L.J., *122*
Coulommiers, *87, 241*

Craig, G.J., *222, 226, 231*
Crampton, J., *254*
Crawford, O.G.S., *241*
Cunningham, A., *128*

Dakar, *129, 140*
Dakeyne, P.L., *108*
Dallmeyer Co., *58, 213*
Danesfield House, *111*
Daniels, G., *241*
Davies, J.M., *156, 182*
Davies, O., *164, 166*
Debden, *93*
Decca Navigator, *241*
de Gaulle, C., *129*
de Havilland, G., *10*
Den Helder, *186*
Denver, *153*
Derna, *76*
de Rozier, J-F-P., *1*
de Saint-Exupéry, A., *174*
de Thuisy, Lt, *129*
Deuxième Bureau, *66, 72*
Deversoir, *267*
Dhahran, *214*
Dhekelia, *276*
Dieppe, *122, 188*
Directorate of Scientific Research, *58*
'Discoverer' satellite, *263*
Dixon, A.J., *96, 111*
Dixon, J.H., *156, 160, 182*
Don Muang, *285*
Doolittle, J.H., *179*
Dortmund, *94*
Doula, *129*
Dover, *8, 11, 186, 188*
Dowding, H.C.T., *18, 87*
Drygalla, R., *114*
Dufaycolor Corp, *66, 76, 90*
Duisburg, *94*
Dulag Luft, *108*
Dum-Dum, *222, 227*
Dumeirah, *66*
Dunkirk, *14, 97, 108*
Düren, *210*

Eades, L., *90, 213*
Earhart, A., *72*
Earle, A., *84*
Eastleigh, *272*
Eastman Kodak, *258*
Eberbach, *72*
Eggleston, J., *84, 87, 90 footnote*
Ein Shemer, *267, 268*
Eisenhower, D.D., *257*
El Adem, *76*
El Alamein, *142*
'Elint', *249*
Elsdale, H., *8*
EMI Co., *298*
Enigma machine, *107, 120, 135*

Enschede, *195*
Eoka, *272, 274, 276*
Evidence in Camera, *100 footnote*
Exocet missile, *307*
Eyre, R.R., *160*
Fairford, *254*
Fairhurst, E.A., *124*
Falklands, *301, 304, 307, 311*
Farnborough, *10, 11, 35, 40, 54, 63, 80, 87, 90, 104, 238, 319*
Farouk, King, *271*
Fayid, *268, 271*
Fécamp, *188*
Feltwell, *208*
Fisher, Plt Off, *140*
Fitzpatrick, Fg Off, *140*
Flash-bomb, *203, 208*
Fleming, I., *84*
Fletcher, J.E., *11*
Flushing, *84*
Foggia, *167, 173, 174, 176*
Fokker, A., *30*
Folney, *195*
Fontenay-le-Comte, *97, 99*
Fort Rouge, *195*
Fourah Bay, *140*
Fox, A., *222*
Francesco, *166*
Frankfurt, *76, 108*
Fraserburgh, *146*
Freetown, *129, 136, 140, 142*
French, J., *14, 16, 18*
Fresnoy, *195*
Freya radar, *120*
Friedrichshafen, *210*
Frisian Islands, *76*
Fuka, *135*
Fuller, R.L., *136*
Furniss, D.R.M., *124, 182*

Gaddafi, Col, *281*
Gallipoli, *44*
Gan, *291*
Gaydon, *263*
Gdynia, *118*
Gee radar, *198, 200*
Geilenkirchen, *319*
Geneva, *257*
Genoa, *118*
GH radar, *200, 210*
Gibraltar, *129, 142, 145, 146, 182, 281*
Giebelstadt, *257*
Gilze Rizen, *195*
Goerz-Anschutz Co, *58*
Gold Beach, *191*
Goodall, Fg Off, *140*
Goose Green, *307*
Gordon, General, *8*
Gorrill, V.I., *182*
Gort, Lord, *94*

Government Code & Cypher School, *107, 135, 142*
Graber unit, *90*
Grasnaya, *160*
Grenoble-Annecy, *174*
Grimstadtfjord, *118*
Grover, Capt, *4*
Grozny, *96*
Gura, *127*
H$_2$S radar, *200, 210, 213, 249, 265*
H$_2$X radar, *200, 249*
Habbaniya, *96, 132, 271*
Hadden, R., *136*
Hafun, *76*
Haifa, *268*
Haig, D., *43*
Hal Far, *127, 132*
Half Die, *140*
Hall, J.G., *143*
Hamburg, *149, 200*
Hamm, *72*
Hamshaw-Thomas, H., *53, 104, 156*
Hardman, D.R.I., *124*
Harpoon missile, *304*
Harris, A.T., *200*
Harrisburg, *153*
Hastings, *140*
Heath, W.H.G., *80*
Heidelberg, *72*
Heliogoland, *76*
Heliopolis, *76, 127, 129, 135, 136, 145, 164, 170*
Helwan, *96*
Hemming, H., *93*
Henderson, D., *14, 18, 22, 30*
Hendon, *118, 213*
Heraklion, *132*
Herschel, R., *135*
Heston, *72, 76, 84, 90, 96, 97, 99, 100, 107, 111, 114, 129*
Hill, A.E., *120, 146*
Hinaidi, *63*
Hiroshima, *237*
Hitler, A., *63, 76, 108, 167*
Hodsman, M., *140, 160*
Hong Kong, *294*
Honington, *311*
Horsfall, S.E., *120*
Houges, *18*
Hubbard, T.O'B., *13*
Hughes, G.E., *160, 173, 176*

Image Movement Compensation, *186*
Immelmann, M., *30*
Imphal, *231*
Incirlik, *258*
Indonesian Communist Party, *294*
Indonesian Independence Movement, *285*
Infra-Red Linescan, *298, 301, 311*

Iraq, *54, 63, 96, 311, 314*
Iwakuni, *288*

'J'-type trailer, *90, 129, 166*
Jersey, *99*
Jeswang, *140*
Jones, B.S., *227*
Jones, R.I., *96, 97, 127, 128, 132, 136*
Jones, R.V., *120*
Joubert, F., *11*
JP233 bomb, *314*
Juilly, *16*
Jullien, P., *4*
Juno Beach, *191, 192*

Kai Tak, *282, 285*
Kalafrana, *66, 127, 135*
Kaldadarnes, *120*
Kalvanes Bay, *114*
Kamaran, *76*
Kandalaska, *124*
Kapustin Yar, *257*
Karachi, *221*
Karlsruhe, *72*
Kaye, M.W., *236*
Kemarojam, *285*
Kenwright, B.R., *156, 160*
Khartoum, *8, 127*
Khormaksar, *66, 274, 276, 279, 280, 292*
Khota Bharu, *214, 217*
Khrushchev, N., *258*
Kiel, *97, 108, 213*
King, S.A., *4*
Kinloss, *298, 304, 319*
Kitchener, Lord, *27*
Kitty Hawk, *8*
Knickebein, *111*
Kodak Co., *58, 222*
Kohat, *58*
Kohima, *213*
Koster, P., *66*
Krefeld, *72*
Kuala Lumpur, *282, 286, 291*
Kuching, *292*
Kusnetsov, General, *124, 126*
Kut, *53*
Kuwait, *276, 279, 311, 314*

Laarbruch, *276, 298*
Labuan, *286, 292, 294*
La Charité-sur-Loire, *97*
La Fère, *16*
Lake Constance, *210*
Lakenheath, *258*
La Marsa, *164, 166, 167, 170, 173*
Lamboit, P., *90, 129, 227, 231*
Langley, *254*
Larkhill, *10*
La Pallice, *120*
La Rochelle, *97*

Lashio, *221*
Laughlin, *258*
Laws, F.C.V., *10, 11, 13, 14, 16, 18, 22, 26, 35, 40, 42, 43, 58, 63, 90, 114, 120*
Le Cateau, *16*
Leconfield, *257*
Lees, H.W., *206, 208, 210, 249*
Lefebvre, B., *129*
Le Havre, *120, 186*
Leipzig, *210*
Le Luc, *97*
LeMay, C., *254*
Lentini, *166, 167*
Leopard Rock, *280 footnote*
Leros, *76, 173*
Les Boraques, *8*
Leuchars, *96, 126, 149*
Lewis, C.G.R., *214*
Lewis, S., *214, 217*
Le Verdon, *120*
LG219, *145, 164, 170*
Lille, *87*
Littlehampton, *186*
Liverpool, *129*
Lloyd, H.P., *136*
Loch Erne, *118*
Loch Ewe, *122*
Lockbourne, *254*
Longbottom, M.V., *72, 76, 79, 84, 87*
Longmore, A., *127*
Loos, *30*
Lossiemouth, *301*
Lowry, W.E.M., *236*
Lowry Field, *153*
Ludlow-Hewitt, E., *94*
Ludwigshafen, *72*
Luftwaffe Club, *66*
Lunardi, V., *1*
Lüneburg, *257*
Luqa, *132, 136, 164, 166, 167, 267, 268, 272, 274, 280*
Lydd, *8*

Macdonald, A., *140*
Macedonia, *48*
MacKay, R.C., *145*
Mackenzie-Wishart, *26*
Macphail, H.C., *84, 96, 97, 111, 127, 129, 136*
Maddox, R.L., *4*
Madras, *231*
Maginot Line, *94*
Magnetic Anomaly Detector, *265*
Magwe, *218, 221*
Maison Blanche, *145*
Majunga, *280*
Makarios, Archbishop, *272–4*
Malayan Communist Party, *288*
Malayan Races Liberation Army, *288*
Maldives, *291*

Malta, *66, 76, 79, 96, 118, 127, 128, 135, 136, 142, 145, 268, 271, 272, 274, 276, 292*
Mandalay, *221, 236*
'Mandrel', *188*
Manifould, K., *120*
Manila, *291*
Mannheim, *72, 76*
Mareth Line, *145*
Marham, *319*
Marne, *16*
Marseille, *96, 97*
Martin, H.B., *254*
Masirah, *274*
Massawa, *76*
Matthews, T.J., *167, 176*
Mau Mau, *272*
Mauberge, *16*
May, A., *167*
Maymyo, *221*
Medhurst, C.E.H., *146*
Medmenham, *111, 120, 136, 145, 153, 156, 186, 238, 241*
Medmenham Club, *319*
Melsbroek, *195*
Mélun, *16*
Messina, *128, 167*
MI6, *66*
Mill, *195*
Millen, S.J., *114*
Millington, E.G.L., *164*
Mindega, *127*
Mingaladon, *218, 221, 222, 236, 282, 285, 286*
'Minuteman' missile, *258*
Miranda, A.J., *66, 72*
Modulator Data Converter, *298*
Money, J., *1*
Monte Cassino, *173*
Moore-Brabazon, J.T.C., *18, 22, 35, 42, 43*
Moscow, *182, 254*
Moulmein, *218*
Mount Farm, *146, 153, 186*
Muharraq, *279, 280*
'Mulberry' harbour, *192*
Munich, *174, 197*
Munster, *72*
Murmansk, *122, 254*
Murray, W.B., *227*
Musgrave, H., *11, 18*
Mussolini, B., *63*
Mutton, R., *84, 94*
Myritkyrina, *222*

'Nadar', *4*
Nagasaki, *237*
Nairobi, *272*
Naples, *173, 174*
Narvik, *122, 126, 149*
Nasser, G.A., *271, 272*

Nato, *244, 254, 257, 272, 276, 280, 301, 319*
Nesbit, T.O., *27 footnote*
Netheravon, *13*
Neuve Chapelle, *26, 27, 40*
New Sarum, *279*
Newmark, T.V., *182*
Nieuport, *16*
Nicobar Islands, *236*
Nicosia, *273*
Niven, R.H., *72, 76, 79, 84, 94, 99*
North Coates, *128*
Novaya Zemlya, *257*
Nuneham Park, *238, 263*

Oakington, *114*
Oberursel, *108*
Oboe radar, *200, 203*
Odiham, *13, 129, 192, 292, 307*
Oflag IXA, *111*
Ogilvie, P.B.B., *114*
Omaha Beach, *191*
'One Niners', *319*
Operation 'Chowhound', *213*
Operation 'Desert Storm', *311*
Operation 'Dracula', *236*
Operation 'Firedog', *286*
Operation 'Husky', *166*
Operation 'Manna', *213*
Operation 'Musketeer', *273*
Operation 'Overlord', *188, 192*
Operation 'Robin', *257*
Operation 'Torch', *140, 142, 145*
Operation 'Zipper', *236, 282*
Oran, *142, 145*
Ordnance Survey, *58, 63, 241*
Osnabruck, *210*

Pachino, *166*
Palembang, *217*
Palermo, *12*
Pandeveswar, *221*
Panetellaria, *66, 164*
Parke, G.D., *222*
Pattani, *214*
Pauillac, *120*
Pearson, A.C., *132, 221, 236*
Peck, R., *84, 87*
Peenemünde, *156*
Peirse, R., *84*
Perck, *195*
Peretola, *267*
Perkin, K.A., *218*
Peshawar, *263*
Pezearches, *16*
Pirbright, *8*
Ploesti, *174*
Plumetot, *192*
Poitiers, *97*
Polifka, K., *171*
Porri, C., *40, 66*

Port Said, *273*
Port Stanley, *304*
Porter, F., *13*
Portsmouth, *301*
Powers, F.G., *263*
Procter, F.D., *218, 227, 236*
Pusey, H.K., *182*

Quackenbush, R.S. Jr, *153*

Ramree Island, *236*
Rangoon, *218, 221, 222, 236*
Ras el Tin, *136*
Rawlinson, W., *84*
Reeves, A.H., *200*
Reggio, *167*
Reims, *44*
Rhodes, *132, 173*
Rhodes, H., *114*
Rice, E.A.B., *140*
Riddell, P.J.A., *80, 104, 182*
Ring, S.L., *120*
Risalpur, *58*
Robinson, F.A., *156, 160*
Roe, A.V., *8*
Rolls, C.S., *8, 18*
Rolls-Royce, *18*
Rome, *173, 176*
Rommel, E., *136, 188, 195*
Roosevelt, E., *140, 145, 164, 170, 173, 179*
Roosevelt, F.D., *145*
Rosser, T.S., *226*
Rostock, *114*
Rouen, *188*
Royal Aero Club, *18*
Royal Aircraft Est., *58, 87, 90, 104, 120*
Royal Aircraft Factory, *10, 11, 30*
Royal Air Force Museum, *213*
Rufiji, R., *48*
Rumsey, A.A., *111*
Rushford, *208*

Sabratha, *166*
Saigon, *285, 294*
San Carlos Bay, *307*
St Denis-Vestram, *195*
St Eval, *107, 111, 114, 146*
St Mawgan, *304*
St Nazaire, *118, 122*
St Omer, *22*
St Quentin, *16*
Salisbury, *279*
Salmond, J., *43*
Salmond, W.G.H., *18*
Salonika, *48*
Salway, D., *146*
Samos, *173*
San Severo, *173, 174, 176, 267*
Sandys, D., *156*
Sassoon, P., *63*

Saunders, A.E., *236*
Scampton, *295*
Scapa Flow, *182*
Schweinfurt, *174*
Scud missile, *314*
Sculthorpe, *249, 254*
Sea Skua missile, *314*
Searchwater radar, *314*
Searle, E.G., *182*
Seclin, *87*
Secret Intelligence Service, *84, 156*
Seletar, *214, 285, 288, 291, 292*
Sembawang, *286*
Semplak, *217*
Senlis, *16*
Serrit, *16*
Seychelles, *273*
Shaibah, *58, 132*
Shandur, *135*
Sharjah, *271, 280*
Shaw, G.S., *58*
Ships
    Antelope, 307
    Ardent, 307
    Ark Royal, 118
    Atlantic Conveyor, 307
    Bismarck, 114
    Charybdis, 280 footnote
    Coventry, 307
    Ektian, 129
    Gneisenau, 114, 122
    Hermes, 304, 307
    Hipper, 122, 126
    Hood, 118
    Illustrious, 128
    Invincible, 304
    Köln, 126
    Königsberg, 48
    Kota Gede, 218
    Lützow, 122
    Midway, 314
    Pennland, 129
    Prinz Eugen, 114, 122
    Scharnhorst, 114, 122
    Sheer, 122, 126
    Sheffield, 307
    Sir Galahad, 307
    Sir Tristram, 307
    Tirpitz, 93, 122, 126, 160, 182, 197
    U–110, 120
    U–570, 120
    Westernland, 129
Shirley, N., *136*
Short, H., *8*
Short, O., *8*
Shulga, M., *257*
Sidcot, *66*
Sideways-Looking Reconnaissance Radar, *298, 311*
Sidewinder missile, *304*
Siegfried Line, *76*

Sigonella, *280*
Singapore, *214, 217, 221, 282, 286, 292*
Singora, *214*
Slee, C.E., *210*
Slocum, S.D., *84, 94, 96*
Smalley, J.R.T., *108*
Smith, C.B., *100, 156*
Smith, H.S., *170*
Soissons, *44*
Somme, *40*
Sommervieu, *192*
Sopwith School, *22*
Sopwith, T., *8*
Sorman West, *164*
South Atlantic Task Force, *301*
South East Asia Treaty Org., *291, 294*
South Georgia, *304*
Spender, M., *93, 104*
'Sputnik' satellite, *258*
Stafford, *213*
Stalin, *97*
Stalingrad, *257*
Stettin, *114, 244*
Steventon, D.W., *146, 156*
Stradishall, *94*
Stratton, J.A.C., *120*
Street, A., *99, 100*
Stringer, H.B., *58, 87, 120*
Sturgiss, F.C., *206*
Suckling, M.F., *118*
Suez Canal, *48, 66, 268, 273, 274, 280*
Sullom Voe, *160*
Sulva Bay, *48*
Sumburgh, *124, 156, 182*
Sverdlovsk, *263*
Swebo, *221*
Swinemünde, *156*
Sword Beach, *191*
Sykes, F.H., *22*
Sylt, *76*
Syracuse, *166*

Tagore Palace, *222*
Taiping, *286*
Takali, *132*
Takoradi, *129, 140, 241*
'Tallboy' bomb, *197*
Tan Son Nhut, *285*
Taranto, *128*
Target indicator, *203, 210*
Tavoy, *218*
Taylor, A.L., *108, 120*
'Tear-drop' window, *72, 87*
Tel Aviv, *268*
Telecommunications Research Est, *200*
Templehof, *76*
Templer, J.L., *4, 8*
Tenedos, *48*
Tengah, *285, 286, 292, 294*
Thermal Imaging Airborne Laser Designator, *321*

Thornton-Pickard, *26*
Tigeaux, *87*
Timini, *135*
Tobruk, *135*
Tornado Infra-Red
   Reconnaissance System,
   311
Toulon, *142*
Tournachon, G.F., *4*
Toussos-le-Noble, *72*
Trapp, B., *160*
Treaty of Versailles, *58*
Trenchard, H.M., *22, 26, 30, 43,
   54*
Trieste, *244*
Tripoli, *72, 128*
Trondheim, *120*
Troodos Mnts, *274*
Truman, H.S., *249, 254*
Tunis, *72*
Tuttle, G.W., *93, 99, 100, 104,
   107, 108, 111, 120*
Twining, General, *258*
Type 35 Control, *203*

Ulm, *176*
Unilateral Declaration of
   Independence, *279*
Utah Beach, *191*

Vaenga, *122, 124, 182*
Valletta, *132, 135*

von Fritsch, W.F., *79, 241*
von Rundstedt, G., *186*
von Zeppelin, F., *8*
V–1 rocket, *156, 191, 197*
V–2 rocket, *156, 197*

Waddington, *319*
Wager, L., *124*
Walker, G.W., *124, 126, 127,
   132, 135*
Walker, R.G.M., *127, 132, 135*
Walton, S.R., *84, 87, 176*
Warburton, A., *128, 129, 135,
   136, 142, 164, 170, 173,
   174*
Warsaw Pact, *257, 263*
Watten, *156*
Watton, *249, 263*
Wavell, C., *107*
Wellesbourne Mountford, *238,
   263*
Welshman, S.G., *166*
Wembley, *93, 104, 111*
Wheatley, C.M., *94*
Whelan, J.R., *132, 136, 145, 164*
White, B., *135*
White, Flt Lt, *174, 176*
Whiteley, E.A., *132*
Wick, 107, *114, 118, 120*
Wideawake, *304*
Wiesbaden, *258*
Wild A5, *93*

Wildenrath, *298*
Wilhelmshaven, *76, 79, 93*
Williamson Co., *90*
'Window', *188*
Wingate, O., *226, 231*
Winterbotham, F.W., *66, 72, 84,
   107*
Wise, S.G., *221, 222, 227, 231,
   236, 237*
Wittering, *307*
Woolwich Arsenal, *4*
Wright, O., *8*
Wright, W., *8*
Wright, W.W., *218*
Wurtemburg, *72*
Würzburg radar, *120*
Wyton, *206, 208, 210, 257, 263,
   272, 276, 279, 280, 295,
   319*

Y Service, *107*
Yelahanka, *231*
Yenangyaung, *218*
Ymuiden, *84*
Young, M.J.B., *146*
Ypres, *27, 43*
Yundum, *142*
Yvetot, *188*

Zeiss Tessar, *26*